W9-CLL-134

Issues for Debate in American Public Policy

NINTH EDITION

CQ PRESS

A Division of SAGE
Washington, D.C.

SELECTIONS FROM **CQ RESEARCHER**

CQ Press
2300 N Street, NW, Suite 800
Washington, DC 20037

Phone: 202-729-1900; toll-free, 1-866-4CQ-PRESS (1-866-427-7737)

Web: www.cqpress.com

Cover design: Kimberly Glyder
Cover photo: AP Images

⊗ The paper used in this publication exceeds the requirements of the American National Standard for Information Sciences—Permanence of Paper for Printed Library Materials, ANSI Z39.48-1992.

Printed and bound in the United States of America

12 11 10 09 08   1 2 3 4 5

A CQ Press College Division Publication

Director	Brenda Carter
Acquisitions editor	Charisse Kiino
Marketing manager	Christopher O'Brien
Composition	Olu Davis
Managing editor	Stephen Pazdan
Production editor	Anne Stewart
Electronic production manager	Paul Pressau

ISSN: 1543-3889
ISBN: 978-0-87289-609-3

Contents

Annotated Contents

The 16 *CQ Researcher* reports reprinted in this book have been reproduced essentially as they appeared when first published. In the few cases in which important developments have since occurred, updates are provided in the overviews highlighting the principal issues examined.

EDUCATION

No Child Left Behind

More than five years have passed since President George W. Bush signed the No Child Left Behind Act. The controversial legislation mandates "highly qualified" teachers in every classroom and holds schools that accept federal funds accountable for raising the achievement of all students, most notably those with disabilities, those from low-income families, racial and ethnic minorities and those with limited English proficiency. Supporters call the law an evolutionary change in education policy—critics call it a revolutionary federal incursion into the historic domain of local districts and declare that it makes too many unfunded demands. Eight school districts and the nation's largest teachers' union sued the Department of Education over the law's funding provisions, and legislators in several states have introduced bills seeking exemptions from the law. Supporters, meanwhile, worry that No Child Left Behind is not being enforced stringently enough and is in danger of being diluted as Congress contemplates its renewal.

Student Aid

With a record number of students hoping to attend college next year—and fees higher than ever—finding a way to pay the bills will be tough for many. Congress and the Bush administration made common cause in 2007 to increase federal Pell Grants for students and reduce some student-loan interest rates. Nevertheless, critics say the increases will not go far enough. To help middle-class families, states increasingly offer merit-based grants for college aid. But with merit scholarships replacing need-based aid, low-income and minority students—who often do not have the grades required for scholarships—are finding their college dreams harder to realize. Meanwhile, longtime concern that private lenders rake in excess profits from their high-interest student loans has reached new heights. Investigations of student lending are being conducted in several states, even as universities and lenders settle allegations of loan fraud with New York's attorney general.

HEALTH CARE

Universal Coverage

Some 44 million Americans lacked health insurance in 2006—a number that has been climbing for two decades. Every month, about 2 million Americans become uninsured, at least temporarily, as lower-paying service jobs with minimal benefits replace union-dominated manufacturing jobs with health benefits—undercutting the nation's employer-based coverage system. Health costs—rising faster than wages or inflation—also push employers to drop coverage. Past legislative proposals for universal coverage relied heavily on government management, drawing fatal opposition from physicians and insurance companies. But now consensus may be forming around proposals requiring most Americans to buy private insurance with public assistance. Republican governors in California and Massachusetts back such plans, as does Sen. Barack Obama, the likely Democratic presidential nominee in 2008.

Fighting Superbugs

Antibiotics, the wonder drugs of the 20th century, are gradually losing their clout. Bacteria naturally develop resistance to antimicrobial drugs. In recent years, however, overuse of antibiotics has caused a growing number of staphylococcus bacteria to evolve into disease-causing "superbugs" resistant to drugs like methicillin. Hospital patients with MRSA, a potent, antibiotic-resistant staph infection, are four times as likely to die as other patients. Moreover, while most superbugs once thrived only in hospitals, new strains outside health facilities are killing healthy people. Adding to the concerns of public-health officials, drug companies are developing few new antimicrobials. Some activists urge strong curbs on all antimicrobial use, including stricter limits of antibiotics to promote fast growth in farm animals. Others oppose legal requirements for animal or human antibiotics, arguing that voluntary efforts are better able to keep pace with the fast-evolving world of microbes.

SOCIAL POLICY

Domestic Poverty

Despite sweeping welfare reforms in the 1990s and generally healthy economic growth in recent years, domestic poverty remains intractable. Moreover, signs are emerging that so-called "deep poverty" is growing sharply, most significantly among children. U.S. poverty is fueled by a long list of problems, including Hurricane Katrina's devastation, immigration, the growing income gap between rich and poor, the subprime mortgage fallout and education disparities. Conservatives say solutions must emphasize personal responsibility, higher marriage rates and fewer out-of-wedlock births. Liberals focus on the negative effects of government budget cuts for anti-poverty programs, tax cuts benefiting the wealthy and the need for more early-childhood-development programs. The Democratic Congress is making poverty a priority issue, as are some of the presidential candidates. President Bush himself acknowledged the gap between rich and poor, raising hopes that a bipartisan effort would be found to reduce poverty in the United States.

Gun Violence

The shooting rampage at Virginia Tech on April 16, 2007, has raised new questions about safety on college campuses and renewed the nation's perennial debate on gun control. Virginia Tech officials face questions about whether the 32 deaths could have been prevented or limited by more effective police action at the time or by more proactive steps earlier to deal with shooter Seung-

Hui Cho's history of mental instability. Nationally, the incident has focused attention on how to reduce gun violence, which annually claims around 30,000 lives—82 each day, far more than twice the Virginia Tech toll. A bill to strengthen the federal background-check system for gun purchasers is gaining support on Capitol Hill, even from the powerful National Rifle Association. But some gun advocates want states to ease weapons laws. They argue that allowing more people to carry weapons will deter gun crimes and enable potential victims to protect themselves.

ENERGY AND THE ENVIRONMENT

Oil Jitters
Vastly increased demand for oil in rapidly modernizing China and India, warfare and instability in the Middle East and the weakening U.S. dollar have revived fears of a new energy crisis. Gasoline shortages—and the accompanying lines at gas stations—were thought to have ended with the Carter administration. But as 2008 began, American drivers were paying more than $3 a gallon, and crude oil hit a milestone—$100 a barrel. Some oil experts warn of even bigger price shocks to come as oil-producing nations use more and more of their own oil and energy demand jumps 50 percent by 2030. Some experts predict an oil "production crunch" within four to five years that will have severe geopolitical and economic impacts, and one expert says the energy supply-demand gap could create "social chaos and war" by 2020. In any event, the days of cheap, plentiful oil appear to be over, and motorists may have to learn how to conserve energy.

Buying Green
Americans will spend an estimated $500 billion this year on products and services that claim to be good for the environment because they contain nontoxic ingredients or produce little pollution and waste. While some shoppers "buy green" to help save the planet, others are concerned about personal health and safety. Whatever their motives, eco-consumers are reshaping U.S. markets. To attract socially conscious buyers, manufacturers are designing new, green products and packaging, altering production processes and using sustainable materials. But some of these products may be wastes of money. Federal regulators check whether green labeling claims mislead consumers, while some critics complain that government mandates promoting environmentally preferable products distort markets and raise prices. Even if green marketing delivers on its pledges, many environmentalists say that sustainability is not a matter of buying green but of buying less.

Mass Transit Boom
Pressed by rising gas prices, highway gridlock and global-warming concerns, cities are spending unprecedented amounts on public transit systems—from streetcars and other "light-rail" lines to commuter trains and rapid-transit buses. They also are experimenting with "congestion-pricing" plans that impose tolls on motorists to induce them to use transit or alter driving habits. While traffic congestion is partly behind the transit boom, it is not the only force driving it. Some light-rail projects are built hand-in-hand with "transit-oriented developments"—walkable, mixed-use projects designed to attract residents, shoppers and office workers to urban neighborhoods. Cities from Portland, Ore., to Charlotte, N.C., have embraced rail projects, but critics argue that such ventures are not boosting ridership or reducing traffic. Some worry, too, that they benefit the wealthy at the expense of low-income residents whose needs may not be well served by new rail lines.

CIVIL LIBERTIES, CIVIL RIGHTS AND JUSTICE

Torture Debate
Countries around the globe—including the United States—are using coercive interrogation techniques in the fight against terrorism that critics say amount to torture. Despite international laws banning the practice, authoritarian nations have long abused prisoners and dissidents, and a handful of democracies have used torture in recent decades against what they considered imminent threats. U.S. soldiers in Iraq say they would torture suspects to save the lives of their comrades. Human rights advocates worry that the use of torture by the United States is legitimizing its use globally and destroying America's moral authority to speak out against regimes that abuse prisoners in far worse ways. U.S. officials credit "enhanced interrogation" methods with averting terrorist attacks. But many experts say information gained by torture is unreliable.

Hate Speech in America

When Don Imus labeled the Rutgers University women's basketball team "nappy-headed hos" in April 2007, it first looked to be just one more insult hurled in his long career. Imus was penalized initially with a two-week suspension. But when the incident appeared on the Internet site youtube.com, organizations ranging from the National Association of Black Journalists to the liberal media watchdog group Media Matters for America urged a tougher stance against racial stereotyping on public airwaves. Advertisers began pulling their sponsorship from Imus' show, and both networks that carried it—CBS Radio and MSNBC TV—fired him. The outcome was hailed by some as a long-needed response to an increasingly uncivil culture in which shock jocks, comedians, rappers and other media figures traffic in name-calling, racism and misogyny. However, other analysts say silencing Imus was unfair and could begin a purge of outspoken conservative radio hosts, including political commentators like Rush Limbaugh.

BUSINESS AND THE ECONOMY

Mortgage Crisis

More than 2 million borrowers will lose their homes to foreclosure because of subprime mortgage lending in recent years. With the housing market booming, lenders enticed many lower-income people into buying homes they could not afford by offering adjustable-rate mortgages (ARMs) with temptingly low initial "teaser" interest rates. Many loans did not require down payments or documented proof of income. Moreover, with real-estate prices rising, many homeowners used the higher value of their homes to get second mortgages to pay for extras like remodeled kitchens. But this year the housing market crashed and the party ended: the low teaser loans reset at higher interest rates, and many borrowers defaulted on their new, higher mortgage payments. When the dust settles, investors who bought mortgage-based securities stand to lose $160 billion or more. Congress and the Bush administration are debating how to help borrowers keep their homes and whether tough, new lending standards are warranted.

Aging Infrastructure

The deadly collapse in August 2007 of Minneapolis' Interstate I-35 West bridge over the Mississippi River tragically underscored the condition of the nation's highways, dams, wastewater treatment systems, electrical transmission networks and other infrastructure. Many facilities and systems are 50 to 100 years old, and engineers say they have been woefully neglected. Decades ago taxpayers, lawmakers and private companies found it relatively easy to ante up the huge sums needed to build vital infrastructure, but money for repairs and maintenance has been far tougher to come by in recent years. Federal and state lawmakers today often prefer to spend public dollars on high-profile convention centers and sports arenas, and anti-tax groups often fight tax hikes or utility-rate increases to pay for maintenance. But now lawmakers are debating whether aging infrastructure merits higher taxes or other measures, such as turning more highways into privately run toll roads.

HOMELAND SECURITY AND FOREIGN POLICY

Immigration Debate

The number of illegal immigrants in the country has topped 12 million, making immigration once again a central topic of debate. Moreover, with undocumented workers spreading far beyond traditional "gatekeeper" states such as California and Texas, complaints about illegal immigrants have become a daily staple of talk radio. Enacting tougher enforcement policies has become a dominant theme in the 2008 presidential campaign, particularly on the Republican side. Just in the past year, states and localities have passed hundreds of bills to crack down on employers and illegal immigrants seeking public benefits. But Congress has been unable to act, despite a bipartisan deal brokered last year by the Bush administration. A new administration and the next Congress will likely face what has proved so far to be an impossible task—curbing the number of immigrants without causing labor shortages in key economic sectors such as agriculture and hospitality.

U.S. Policy on Iran

The Bush administration is turning up the heat on Iran. In October 2007 President Bush said Iran's nuclear program raised the specter of World War III. Then Vice President Dick Cheney warned of "serious consequences" if Iran stayed on course as a "terror-supporting state." The heated rhetoric is widely seen as calculated to raise the specter of military action against Iran. Indeed, President Mahmoud Ahmadinejad calls the United States an international bully that is keeping Iraq violent in order to justify its continued occupation. He also vows to maintain Iran's nuclear development program, which he claims is not for creating weapons. But many observers—Israelis particularly—see the effort as a grave threat, prompting some U.S. hawks to advocate a preemptive strike on Iran's nuclear facilities. Other Iran-watchers say military action could further endanger U.S. forces fighting next door in Iraq. They urge the administration to aid dissidents rather than counter Iran by military force.

Cost of the Iraq War

The fifth anniversary of the Iraq War hit just as the subprime mortgage crisis and rising unemployment in the United States were turning the economic situation bleak. Against this backdrop, a Nobel laureate economist and a federal budget expert linked the economic downturn to the war and calculated its eventual total financial cost at $3 trillion and possibly even more, not to mention the tens of thousands of Americans and Iraqis being killed or wounded. President Bush dismisses the linkage argument, contending the war creates job opportunities at home and that military spending in Iraq and Afghanistan amounts to only a "modest fraction" of the U.S. economy. But even Republican lawmakers have been asking why U.S. taxpayers are funding much of the rebuilding of oil-rich Iraq while that nation reaps billions in profits thanks to record-high oil prices. For its part, the administration says Iraq is now starting to bear more of the reconstruction costs.

Preface

A re war costs contributing to the current economic downturn? Should employers be penalized for hiring illegal immigrants? Is buying green better for the environment than buying less? These questions—and many more—are at the heart of American public policy. How can instructors best engage students with these crucial issues? We feel that students need objective, yet provocative examinations of these issues to understand how they affect citizens today and will for years to come. This annual collection aims to promote in-depth discussion, facilitate further research and help readers formulate their own positions on crucial issues. Get your students talking both inside and outside the classroom about *Issues for Debate in American Public Policy*.

This ninth edition includes sixteen up-to-date reports by *CQ Researcher*, an award-winning weekly policy brief that brings complicated issues down to earth. Each report chronicles and analyzes executive, legislative and judicial activities at all levels of government. This collection is divided into seven diverse policy areas: education; health care; social policy; energy and the environment; civil liberties, civil rights and justice; business and the economy; and homeland security and foreign policy—to cover a range of issues found in most American government and public policy courses.

CQ RESEARCHER

CQ Researcher was founded in 1923 as *Editorial Research Reports* and was sold primarily to newspapers as a research tool. The magazine was renamed and redesigned in 1991 as *CQ Researcher*. Today, students are its primary audience. While still used by hundreds of journalists and newspapers, many of which reprint portions of the reports, the *Researcher*'s main subscribers are now high school, college and public libraries. In 2002, *Researcher* won the American Bar Association's coveted Silver Gavel Award for magazine excellence for a series of nine reports on civil liberties and other legal issues.

Researcher staff writers—all highly experienced journalists—sometimes compare the experience of writing a *Researcher* report to drafting a college term paper. Indeed, there are many similarities. Each report is as long as many term papers—about 11,000 words—and is written by one person without any significant outside help. One of the key differences is that writers interview leading experts, scholars and government officials for each issue.

Like students, staff writers begin the creative process by choosing a topic. Working with the *Researcher*'s editors, the writer identifies a controversial subject that has important public policy implications. After a topic is selected, the writer embarks on one to two weeks of intense research. Newspaper and magazine articles are clipped or downloaded, books are ordered and information is gathered from a wide variety of sources, including interest groups, universities and the government. Once a writer is well informed, he or she develops a detailed outline and begins the interview process. Each report requires a minimum of 10 to 15 interviews with academics, officials, lobbyists and people working in the field. Only after all interviews are completed does the writing begin.

CHAPTER FORMAT

Each issue of *CQ Researcher*, and therefore each selection in this book, is structured in the same way. Each begins with an overview, which briefly summarizes the areas that will be explored in greater detail in the rest of the chapter. The next section chronicles important and current debates on the topic under discussion and is structured around a number of key questions, such as "Can America afford universal health coverage?" and "Should the government do more to restrain hate speech?" These questions are usually the subject of much debate among practitioners and scholars in the field. Hence, the answers presented are never conclusive but rather detail the range of opinion on the topic.

Next, the "Background" section provides a history of the issue being examined. This retrospective covers important legislative measures, executive actions and court decisions that illustrate how current policy has evolved. Then the "Current Situation" section examines contemporary policy issues, legislation under consideration and legal action being taken. Each selection concludes with an "Outlook" section, which addresses possible regulation, court rulings and initiatives from Capitol Hill and the White House over the next five to ten years.

Each report contains features that augment the main text: two to three sidebars that examine issues related to the topic at hand, a pro versus con debate between two experts, a chronology of key dates and events and an annotated bibliography detailing major sources used by the writer.

ACKNOWLEDGMENTS

We wish to thank many people for helping to make this collection a reality. Tom Colin, managing editor of *CQ Researcher*, gave us his enthusiastic support and cooperation as we developed this ninth edition. He and his talented staff of editors and writers have amassed a first-class library of *Researcher* reports, and we are fortunate to have access to that rich cache. We also thankfully acknowledge the advice and feedback from current readers and are gratified by their satisfaction with the book.

Some readers may be learning about *CQ Researcher* for the first time. We expect that many readers will want regular access to this excellent weekly research tool. For subscription information or a no-obligation free trial of *Researcher*, please contact CQ Press at www.cqpress.com or toll-free at 1-866-4CQ-PRESS (1-866-427-7737).

We hope that you will be pleased by the ninth edition of *Issues for Debate in American Public Policy*. We welcome your feedback and suggestions for future editions. Please direct comments to Charisse Kiino, Chief Acquisitions Editor, College Division, CQ Press, 2300 N Street, N.W., Suite 800, Washington, D.C. 20037, or *ckiino@cqpress.com*.

—The Editors of CQ Press

Contributors

Thomas J. Colin, managing editor of *CQ Researcher*, has been a magazine and newspaper journalist for more than 30 years. Before joining Congressional Quarterly in 1991, he was a reporter and editor at *The Miami Herald* and *National Geographic* and editor in chief of *Historic Preservation*. He holds a bachelor's degree in English from the College of William and Mary and in journalism from the University of Missouri.

Thomas J. Billitteri is a freelance journalist in Fairfield, Pa., who has more than 30 years' experience covering business, non-profit institutions and related topics for newspapers and other publications. He has written previously for *CQ Researcher* on teacher education, parental rights and mental-health policy. He holds a bachelor's degree in English and a master's degree in journalism from Indiana University.

Marcia Clemmitt is a veteran social-policy reporter who joined *CQ Researcher* after serving as editor in chief of *Medicine and Health*, a Washington-based industry newsletter, and staff writer for *The Scientist*. She also has been a high school math and physics teacher. She holds a bachelor's degree in arts and sciences from St. Johns College, Annapolis, and a master's degree in English from Georgetown University.

Alan Greenblatt is a staff writer for Congressional Quarterly's *Governing* magazine, and previously covered elections and military and agricultural policy for *CQ Weekly*. A recipient of the National Press Club's Sandy Hume Memorial Award for political reporting, he holds a bachelor's degree from San Francisco State University and a master's degree in English literature from the University of Virginia.

Kenneth Jost, associate editor of *CQ Researcher*, graduated from Harvard College and Georgetown University Law Center, where he is an adjunct professor. He is the author of *The Supreme Court Yearbook* and writer and editor of *The Supreme Court A to Z* (both published by CQ Press). He was a member of the *CQ Researcher* team that won the 2002 American Bar Association Silver Gavel Award.

Peter Katel is a veteran journalist who previously served as Latin America bureau chief for *Time* magazine in Mexico City, and as a Miami-based correspondent for *Newsweek* and *The Miami Herald*'s *El Nuevo Herald*. He also worked as a reporter in New Mexico for 11 years and wrote for several nongovernmental organizations, including International Social Service and the World Bank. His honors include the Interamerican Press Association's Bartolome Mitre Award. He is a graduate of the University of New Mexico with a degree in university studies.

Barbara Mantel is a freelance writer in New York City whose work has appeared in *The New York Times*, *Journal of Child and Adolescent Pyschopharmacology* and *Mamm Magazine*. She is a former correspondent and senior producer for National Public Radio and has received such journalistic honors as the National Press Club's Best Consumer Journalism Award and Lincoln University's Unity Award. She holds a bachelor's degree in history and economics from the University of Virginia and a master's degree in economics from Northwestern University.

Seth Stern is a legal affairs reporter at *CQ Weekly*. He has worked as a journalist since graduating from Harvard Law School in 2001, including as a reporter for *The Christian Science Monitor* in Boston. He holds a bachelor's degree from Cornell University's School of Industrial and Labor Relations and a master's degree in public administration from Harvard's Kennedy School of Government. He is coauthoring a biography of Supreme Court Justice William J. Brennan Jr.

Jennifer Weeks is a *CQ Researcher* contributing writer in Watertown, Mass., who specializes in energy and environmental issues. She has written for *The Washington Post*, *The Boston Globe Magazine* and other publications, and has 15 years' experience as a public-policy analyst, lobbyist and congressional staffer. She holds a bachelor's degree from Williams College and master's degrees from the University of North Carolina and Harvard College.

1

No Child Left Behind

Barbara Mantel and Alan Greenblatt

President Bush visits with students in St. Louis, Mo., on Jan. 5, 2004, the second anniversary of the No Child Left Behind Act. Bush has called the sweeping overhaul of federal education policy the start of "a new era, a new time in public education." But today the bipartisan legislation is under heavy criticism from Republicans and Democrats alike. Besides seeking exemptions from parts of the law, legislators are pressing Congress for more money to implement the act.

From *CQ Researcher,*
May 27, 2005. (Updated May 21, 2007)

P olitics indeed makes for strange bedfellows: There was President Bush standing on a Boston stage flanked by four jubilant legislators, two Republicans and two Democrats, including liberal lion Sen. Edward M. Kennedy of Massachusetts. The occasion was the signing on Jan. 8, 2002, of the No Child Left Behind Act — a sweeping, bipartisan overhaul of federal education policy.

Cheering crowds greeted Bush and the four lawmakers that day as they touted the new law on a whirlwind, 12-hour tour of three states, with the president calling the legislation the start of "a new era, a new time in public education."

Kennedy, who played a key role in negotiating the bill's passage, told Bush: "What a difference it has made this year with your leadership." [1]

The law is actually the most recent reauthorization of the Elementary and Secondary Education Act (ESEA), which since 1965 has tried to raise the academic performance of all students.

"This legislation holds out great promise for education," said G. Gage Kingsbury, director of research at the Northwest Evaluation Association, in Lake Oswego, Ore. "But it also has strong requirements and includes a host of provisions that have never been tried on this scale before." [2]

No Child Left Behind (NCLB) increases the reach of the federal government into the management of local schools and raises the stakes for schools, districts and states. It increases funding for schools serving poor students, mandates "highly qualified" teachers in every classroom and holds schools that accept federal funds accountable for raising the achievement of all students. Schools that don't meet state benchmarks two years in a row are labeled "in need of improvement" and suffer sanctions.

Few States Make the Grade on Teacher Quality

Only three states — Connecticut, Louisiana and South Carolina — received a grade of A for their efforts to improve teacher quality, according to a 2005 assessment by *Education Week*. In every state except New Mexico, more than 50 percent of secondary teachers majored in the core academic subject they teach. But only eight states had more than 75 percent of secondary school teachers who majored in their core subject.

Rating State Efforts to Improve Teacher Quality

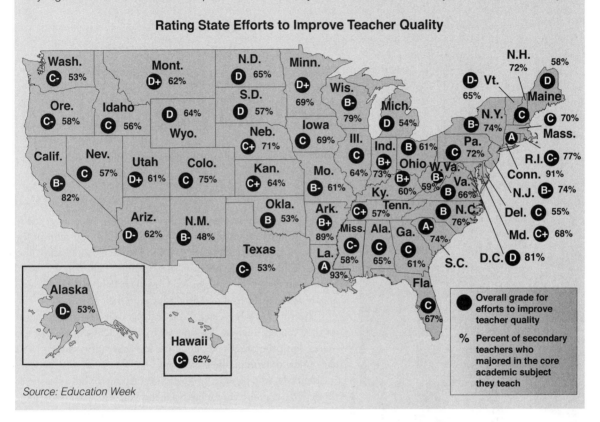

Source: *Education Week*

Most significantly, NCLB sets a deadline: By 2014 all students must be grade-level proficient in reading and math — as evidenced by their scores on annual tests in grades 3-8, and once in high school.

But more than five years after its passage, the bipartisan accord that produced the bill appears badly frayed. Kennedy now says No Child Left Behind "has been underfunded, mismanaged and poorly implemented and is becoming the most spectacular broken promise of this Republican administration and Congress. "America's children deserve better." [3]

In the states, politicians from both parties are equally unhappy, including GOP legislators from some "red states" that overwhelmingly supported Bush in last year's presidential election. "I wish they'd take the stinking money and go back to Washington," said state Rep. Steven Mascaro, R-Utah. [4]

"We have to fight back," Gov. John Baldacci, D-Maine, said. "We have to tell them we're not going to take it any more." [5]

It hasn't been just talk. In 2005, Utah's Republican governor signed legislation giving precedence to the state's education policies when they conflict with NCLB, and more than 30 states in all have introduced bills seeking release from some of the law's requirements.

Besides wanting exemptions from parts of the law, legislators are pressing Congress for more money to implement the act. Congress had appropriated $27 billion less

The ABCs of NCLB

Here are the basic provisions of the No Child Left Behind Act, which spells out its standards and requirements in more than 1,000 pages of regulations:

Standards and Testing — As in the previous version of the law, each state must adopt challenging standards for what its students should know and be able to do. Academic standards must contain coherent and rigorous content and encourage the teaching of advanced skills. States must also develop tests aligned to the standards and establish cutoff scores that classify student achievement as basic, proficient or advanced. What has changed is the amount of testing states must do. States must test children annually in grades 3-8 and once in high school. Previously, schoolchildren had to be tested only four times in grades K-12.

Public Reporting — For the first time, states must publicly report their test results, with student scores broken down into four subgroups: economically disadvantaged students; major racial and ethnic groups; students with disabilities and students with limited English proficiency. States must report each school's progress in raising student performance and the difference in teacher qualifications in high-poverty versus low-poverty schools.

Accountability — All students must reach proficiency in reading and math by 2014. States must establish annual benchmarks for their schools, with special emphasis on closing achievement gaps between different groups of students. Since 1994 states had been required to make "adequate yearly progress" (AYP) in raising achievement, but there was no firm timetable or deadline for students reaching proficiency. Now if a school does not make AYP, the state and district must develop a two-year plan to help the school improve.

Sanctions — If a school receiving Title I funds — designed to improve the performance of low-income students — does not make AYP in raising student performance for two years in a row, the state must designate it a school "in need of improvement." [1] Most states are applying this rule to all schools in a Title I district, even those that do not take Title I money. Students in these schools must be given the option of transferring out, and if a school fails to achieve its AYP for three consecutive years, it must pay for tutoring, after-school programs and summer school for those low-income students who remain. After four years, the state must restructure the school.

Teachers — For the first time, teachers must be "highly qualified," meaning they have a college degree and are licensed or certified by the state. Newly hired middle-school teachers must have a major or pass a test demonstrating their knowledge in the subjects they teach. Veteran teachers can do the same or demonstrate their competency through an alternative system developed by each state.

---

[1] About 55 percent of the schools in the nation's 100 largest districts were eligible for Title I funds in the 2001/2002 school year; http://nces.ed.gov/pubs2003/100_largest/table_05_1.asp.

---

than it authorized for the law's implementation by mid-2005. The following year, President Bush requested just $13.3 billion in funding for Title I programs — the heart of the law — out of $22.8 billion that had been authorized.

But the act's supporters say enough money is being provided, pointing out that federal funding for public education has increased by more than 30 percent since NCLB was enacted. "The education reforms contained in the No Child Left Behind Act are coupled with historic increases in K-12 funding," according to the Web site of Sen. Judd Gregg, R-N.H., who made the whirlwind trip with Bush and Kennedy three years ago. [6]

Nevertheless, in 2005 the National Education Association, the nation's largest teachers' union, sued the Department of Education on the grounds that the act is not properly funded. In addition, Connecticut also sued, estimating that NCLB will cost the state an extra $41.6 million dollars in the next few years. The atmosphere grew so disagreeable at times that Secretary of Education Margaret Spellings angrily called Connecticut officials "un-American."

Part of the states' resentment stems from the fact that Congress provides only 8 percent of total funding for public education — $536 billion in the 2004-05 school year — but since the 1960s has passed laws giving the Department of Education increasing powers over the nation's 96,000 schools. [7] The NCLB is the most far-reaching yet.

Supporters of the act say it represents an evolutionary change, while critics say it is a revolutionary incursion of the federal government into the historic domain of the states.

"I don't know any educator or parent who doesn't think our schools should be accountable," said Republican state Rep. Margaret Dayton. "The question is: To whom should they be accountable? Under No Child Left Behind our local schools are accountable to Washington, D.C., and here in Utah, we think our schools should be accountable to the parents and the communities where they are." [8]

Even supporters acknowledge that NCLB's provisions have been overwhelming for states without the administrative staff to implement the law.

In 2004, No Child Left Behind became "a significant force affecting the operations and decisions of states, school districts and schools," according to the Center on Education Policy, an independent advocate for public education. [9] For example, the law has compelled states and school districts to step up efforts to test students in more grades and put "highly qualified" teachers in every classroom. In addition, for the first time entire school districts have been labeled "in need of improvement."

However, as the law's requirements take hold, the debate about its fairness and efficacy has been escalating. Besides the debate over funding, critics argue that the law is too rigid and that too many schools — even good schools — are being told they need to improve. This has sparked widespread opposition to President's Bush's proposal to extend the law's annual testing requirements to high school students.

On the other side of the debate, many of NCLB's staunchest defenders worry that the Department of Education has become too flexible in implementing the law, citing a recent relaxation of requirements for testing disabled students and department approval of what some see as lax state plans to ensure that veteran teachers are "highly qualified."

And voices from all sides call for more guidance and technical support to localities from the Department of Education.

As the public discussion grows louder, leading up to the law's reauthorization fight in 2007, coalitions have begun to form. The American Association of School Administrators, the Children's Defense Fund, the Learning Disabilities Association of America, the National Education Association and several other groups joined together in 2004 to call for significant revisions in the law. Proponents — including the Citizens' Commission on Civil Rights, the National Alliance of Black School Educators, Just for Kids, the Education Trust and the Business Roundtable — formed their own coalition, called the Achievement Alliance, to vigorously defend the law.

As Congress begins its deliberations, the law is under attack from multiple directions. A group of 57 Republican legislators — including some of the bill's original cosponsors — introduced legislation early in 2007 that would allow any state that objects to the law's standards and testing requirements to excuse itself but continue to receive federal education aid. To answer their proposal, Kennedy several days later published an op-ed in *The Washington Post* headlined "No Retreat on School Reform." [10]

Bush, Kennedy and George Miller, the House education chairman, all vow to defend the law's main tenets during debate over its extension. But the widespread rancor NCLB has caused may mean its renewal will be delayed until the seating of the next Congress — and the election of a new president.

In the meantime, here are some of the questions parents, educators, children's advocates, lawmakers and researchers are asking:

Has No Child Left Behind raised student achievement?

The goal of the NCLB law is to ensure that by 2014 all children are at grade-level proficiency in reading and math. The law requires states to measure student achievement by testing children in grades 3-8 every year, and once in high school.

But each state determines its own academic standards, the courses taught, the standardized tests used and the cut-off scores that define a student as proficient. Thus, the rigor varies between the states, making it impossible to compare one state to another. Colorado may have reported 87 percent of its fourth-graders proficient in reading in 2003 and Massachusetts 56 percent, but no one knows what that says about the relative achievement of their students. [11]

It is possible, however, to look at student achievement within a state and ask, for example, how this year's fourth-graders compare to last year's.

With a growing number of states administering annual tests, researchers have conducted some preliminary studies. They all show that student achievement, for the most part, is improving.

Thousands of Schools Missed Progress Targets

Eleven thousand public schools — or nearly 12 percent of the nation's 96,000 public schools — failed in 2004 for the second year in a row to meet "adequate yearly progress" (AYP) targets set by the No Child Left Behind law. Such schools are labeled "in need of improvement" and must offer all students the right to transfer; after missing AYP for three consecutive years, they must offer low-income students supplemental services, like after-school tutoring. After four years, the state must restructure the school.

Number of Public Schools Needing Improvement
(based on failure to meet "adequate yearly progress" targets)

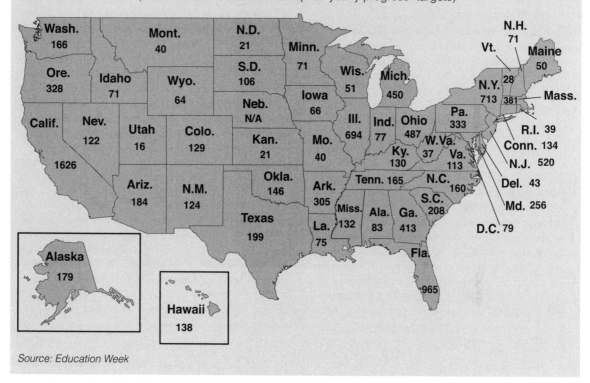

Source: Education Week

The Center on Education Policy surveyed states and a sampling of school districts and reported that 73 percent of states and 72 percent of districts said student achievement is improving. In addition, states and districts were more likely to say that achievement gaps between white and black students, white and Hispanic students, and English-language learners and other students were narrowing rather than widening or staying the same. [12]

Similarly, the Council of the Great City Schools, a coalition of 65 of the nation's largest urban school systems, reported that while math and reading scores in urban schools remain lower than national averages, they are rising and achievement gaps are narrowing. [13]

The Education Trust, a nonprofit advocate of school reform, also analyzed proficiency rates since No Child Left Behind took effect. It found that in most states it studied, achievement scores of elementary school students had risen, and achievement gaps had narrowed. But when the Trust looked at middle and high schools, the results were more mixed. While the majority of states in the study reported an increase in the percentage of proficient students, there was much less success in narrowing achievement gaps. [14]

Is Testing Crowding Out Art and Recess?

Testing required by the No Child Left Behind Act is taking a toll on education, says George Wood, an Ohio high school principal and director of The Forum for Education and Democracy. "School people are no fools," Wood wrote in the 2004 book *Many Children Left Behind*. "Tell them what they will be measured on, and they will try to measure up."

"Test preparation crowds out much else that parents have taken for granted in their schools," Wood said. Recess for elementary school students, nap time for kindergarteners and music and art for middle school students are some of the things being eliminated from the school day, he contends, along with reductions in class time for social studies and creative writing.

Diane Rentner, director of national programs at the Center on Education Policy, says the cutbacks haven't been too bad so far. "It's not huge, it's not a revolution yet," she says. In a March 2005 survey of school districts, the center found "a slight movement toward cutting down on other subjects to focus on reading and math," Rentner says.

More than two-thirds of districts reported that instructional time on subjects other than math and reading had been reduced minimally or not at all. However, 27 percent of the districts reported that social studies class time had been reduced somewhat or to a great extent, and close to 25 percent said instruction time in science, art and music had been reduced.

While the center's findings don't detail a revolutionary shift in class time, Rentner still calls the trend worrisome and expects that as state proficiency benchmarks rise, there may be additional pressure on schools to focus more time on reading and math. "It would be sad if there were no arts in the schools, and students didn't learn civic education," she says.

Rentner also points out another potentially troubling survey result: The poorer the school district, the more likely it was to require schools to allot a specific amount of time to math and reading. "You could jump to the next conclusion that low-income kids are receiving a less rich curriculum," Rentner says. While that might be necessary in the short term to bring kids closer to proficiency in math and reading, Rentner hopes that it doesn't have to continue.

It is this impact on low-income and minority schools that most concerns Wood. An opponent of NCLB, Wood calls for a moratorium on high-stakes testing until more research shows it to have some link to student success after leaving high school.

But Daria Hall, a policy analyst at the Education Trust, which generally supports the goals and methods of No Child Left Behind while criticizing the government's implementation of the law, says that's the wrong response. "We don't deny that focusing so much on math and reading means that other subjects might not receive the attention they deserve," says Hall. But that doesn't have to happen, she says, citing schools, many in poor districts, that have integrated math and reading instruction into their other subjects.

"So, for example, there is no need to give short shrift to social studies," she claims. "We can teach the content of social studies while at the same time covering state standards on reading." The same can be done, she says, with math and science.

But it's not something that one teacher or even one school can do alone, Hall adds. "There needs to be research from the U.S. Department of Education on how to effectively integrate standards across the curriculum," she says. "It needs to really be a systemic effort."

Delaware is a case in point. The state has made some of the largest strides in raising achievement and narrowing gaps among elementary students. For instance, the gap in Delaware between the percentage of reading-proficient white and Hispanic fifth-graders narrowed from 31 points in 2001 to less than five points in 2004, and for African-American students, the gap narrowed from 22 points to 16. [15] A 2006 study by the Education Trust found that the gap between whites and Hispanics had also narrowed. But in middle schools, achievement gaps have actually widened.

"It is a little harder to get a reform groundswell in middle schools and high schools," says Delaware's Secretary of Education Valerie Woodruff. "In math, for example, we don't have enough well-qualified teachers at the middle school level."

The fundamental question is how much of the documented improvement is a result of No Child Left Behind. Daria Hall, a policy analyst at the Education Trust, says it is a significant amount. Educators "are using the standards to develop a challenging curriculum for all students," she says. "They are using assessment results to inform their instruction in the classroom." NCLB, Hall says, gives administrators leverage to make needed changes.

Diane Stark Rentner, director of national programs at the Center on Education Policy, is hearing something different. The center did not specifically ask state and district officials if they thought the law was responsible for achievement gains. But Rentner says district officials later said they "were almost offended that No Child Left Behind would be viewed as this great catalyst of change because they felt like they had been working for years to improve student achievement."

"Our math curriculum has been completely reviewed from K-12 and in the majority of cases exceeds state standards," says Margo Sorrick, an assistant superintendent in Wheaton, Ill. For instance, the district now requires three years rather two years of math for high school graduation. "These changes have nothing to do with No Child Left Behind," says Sorrick.

But the law does shine a new light on those reforms. Now that states must report their progress in raising student achievement, the press routinely covers the release of so-called state report cards. Stiffening graduation requirements, revising the curriculum and replacing staff at the worst schools have taken on more urgency, Rentner says. "We jokingly say the news media have become the enforcer of the law," she adds.

But trying to figure out the law's exact impact is still all but impossible. Besides the difficulty of teasing out the roles of pre- and post-NCLB reforms, there are gaps in the data. Most states started testing students only about a decade ago, and many changed their tests, making before-and-after comparisons unreliable.

Several experts also warn that initial gains in achievement scores may be deceptive. Brian Stecher, a senior social scientist at the RAND Corporation, a nonprofit research organization, says that on new, high-stakes tests teachers often feel pressure to coach students in test-taking skills and to teach the material emphasized on the test. "That can allow you to get initially a relatively big gain in scores," Stecher says, "and then the increase tapers off."

That's of particular concern to states because the pace of recent improvement is not fast enough to ensure 100 percent student proficiency by 2014. "Progress needs to be accelerated," Hall says bluntly.

Are too many schools being labeled "in need of improvement?"

Holding states accountable for student achievement is central to No Child Left Behind. The law gives states a firm goal and a firm deadline, and to reach it each state must come up with annual benchmarks. In Wisconsin, for instance, 67.5 percent of a school's students had to be proficient in reading in 2005, 87 percent in 2011 and finally 100 percent in 2014. [16]

But it's not enough for a school to look at its students as a single, undifferentiated block. NCLB requires schools to divide students into subgroups — ethnic, racial, low-income, disabled and English-language learner — and each must meet the proficiency benchmarks as well.

Schools also must test at least 95 percent of students in a subgroup, meet state-determined attendance requirements and improve high school graduation rates.

Schools that meet all of these targets are deemed to have made "adequate yearly progress" (AYP). But if a school misses just one target it doesn't make AYP, and the district and state must create a two-year intervention plan. Options include reducing class size, providing extra help for disadvantaged students and increasing professional development for teachers. Local and state officials decide on the details, and the federal government provides extra funding.

Sanctions prescribed by the law, however, kick in when a school doesn't make AYP for two consecutive years. Such schools, if they take Title I funds, are labeled "in need of improvement" and must offer all students the right to transfer; after missing AYP for three consecutive years, they must offer low-income students supplemental services, like after-school tutoring. After four years, the state must restructure the school.

This system of accountability is among the most contentious elements of NCLB. While praising the overall goals of the law, the National Conference of State Legislatures called the system rigid and overly prescriptive. Too many schools, it said, are being labeled "in need of improvement," and the law, therefore, "spreads resources too thinly, over too many schools, and reduces the chances that schools that truly are in need can be helped." [17]

In 2004, 11,008 public schools — nearly 12 percent of the nation's total — were identified as needing improvement. [18] By 2006, about 1,750 schools nationwide had consistently failed to meet AYP and faced the law's ultimate sanctions, meaning they required dramatic overhauls. [19] "Essentially, all schools will fail to meet the unrealistic goal of 100 percent proficient or above," wrote testing expert Robert Linn, "and No Child Left Behind will have turned into No School Succeeding." [20]

But Kerri Briggs, acting Assistant Secretary for Elementary and Secondary Education, strongly disagrees. "We have identified schools that have beat expectations; there are several in many states," says Briggs. "We know it's possible."

Critics, however, say the accountability system has several flaws, such as not recognizing progress made by schools that start with large numbers of low-performing students. A school that significantly raises the percentage of students reading at proficiency, for example, would still not make AYP if that percentage remains below the state benchmark. Such schools "should be given credit," says Scott Young, a former senior policy specialist at the National Conference of State Legislatures.

But the law does provide a so-called safe harbor alternative for these schools: If a subgroup of students falls short of the benchmark, the school can still make AYP if the number below the proficiency level is decreased by 10 percent from the year before. But according to Linn, that's something even the best schools would have difficulty accomplishing. "Only a tiny fraction of schools meet AYP through the safe-harbor provision because it is so extreme," Linn wrote. [21]

After protests from both Republican and Democratic governors, Secretary Spellings announced in 2005 she would appoint a panel to consider allowing states to use a "growth model" to reward schools whose students make significant progress but that still miss AYP. Such a model would follow individual students as they move from grade to grade. By contrast, the current system compares the current fourth-grade class, for example, with last year's fourth-graders.

Kingsbury, at the Northwest Evaluation Association, likes the growth-model idea but says goals and timetables are needed. Otherwise, Kingsbury explains, "there is no guarantee students will end up at a high level of proficiency when they graduate."

Another frequent complaint is that the accountability system is too blunt an instrument. "The problem," says Patricia Sullivan, an education policy consultant and former director of the Center on Education Policy, "is the lack of distinction between the school that misses by a little and the school that misses by a lot." The school that misses the benchmark for one subgroup for two consecutive years is identified as needing improvement just like the school that misses the benchmark for several subgroups. Both face the same sanction: All students would have the option to transfer.

Since urban schools tend to be more diverse and have more subgroups, it is harder for them to make AYP. But the Education Trust's Hall says those who complain care more about the adults working in urban schools than the kids. "Is it fair to expect less of schools that are educating diverse student bodies?" Hall asks. "Is it fair to those students? Absolutely not."

The Department of Education has signaled its willingness to compromise, to a degree. Many districts have complained that requiring all students with disabilities to be grade-level proficient by 2014 is unfair and unrealistic. The law does allow 1 percent of all students — those with significant cognitive disabilities — to take alternative assessments. Secretary Spellings declared that another 2 percent — those with persistent academic disabilities — could take alternative tests, geared toward their abilities and not necessarily at grade level. States would have to apply to the Department of Education in order to use this option.

The reaction from educators was muted. Betty J. Sternberg, then Connecticut's education commissioner, said, "The percentages are fine. They help us. The problem may be in the details of what they are requiring us to do to have access to the flexibility." [22]

But advocates for disabled students worry that the department is backpedaling. Suzanne Fornaro, past president of the Learning Disability Association of America, is particularly concerned about students with learning disabilities: "If the changes result in lowering expectations, they might result in decreasing a student's access to the general curriculum and high-quality instruction."

Is No Child Left Behind improving the quality of teaching?

Teaching quality may be the single most important in-school factor in how well students learn. While it's difficult to know precisely what makes effective teachers, there are some common yardsticks, including mastery of their subject area. Yet government surveys show that, "One out of four secondary classes (24 percent) in core academic subjects are assigned to a teacher lacking even a college minor in the subject being taught." That figure rises to 29 percent in high-minority schools and 34 percent in high-poverty schools. [23]

NCLB required a "highly qualified" teacher in every classroom by the end of the 2005/2006 school year. Highly qualified teachers must have a bachelor's degree, be licensed or certified by the state and demonstrate that they know each subject they teach. New teachers can qualify by either passing a state test or having completed a college major in their subject area. Veteran teachers have a third option: an alternative evaluation created by each state, known by the acronym HOUSSE (high objective uniform state standard of evaluation).

Spellings pushed back that June 2006 deadline a few months before it was to take effect, giving states a one-year pass if they could demonstrate progress. A year later, only nine states had submitted plans that met all her requirements to demonstrate progress. [24]

In "Quality Counts 2005," a report by *Education Week*, researchers graded states on their efforts to improve teacher quality, looking at the amount of out-of-field teaching allowed, the quality of the state certification process and the amount and quality of professional development. Only three states got As, 14 got Bs and the rest received Cs and Ds. [25]

No Child Left Behind's ability to alter the picture may be limited, critics say. They point to the problems rural and urban schools are having recruiting and retaining skilled teachers and to many states' less-than-rigorous HOUSSE plans.

"I love my job. I know how kids learn," says Jon Runnalls, Montana's "Teacher of the Year" in 2003, "and for someone to come and say that now I'm not highly qualified, that's a slap in the face." Runnalls has taught middle school science for 31 years, but his college degree is in elementary education with an emphasis in science. According to NCLB, he'd have to go back to school, take a state test or pass the state's alternative evaluation. But Montana doesn't have a test, and its HOUSSE plan has not yet been approved by the Department of Education. It's really not a plan at all; it simply says that a veteran certified teacher is, by default, highly qualified.

Not surprisingly, Montana reports 98.8 percent of its classes are taught by highly qualified teachers.

Ten other states, like Montana, don't evaluate veteran teachers, arguing that the state certification process is a rigorous enough hurdle. But even many of the states that do have more elaborate HOUSSE plans have faced criticism.

Most states use a system in which veteran teachers accumulate points until they have enough to be considered highly qualified. "The most prevalent problem is that states offer too many options that veteran teachers can use to prove they are highly qualified — options that often have nothing to do with content knowledge," says Kate Walsh, president of the National Council on Teacher Quality. While states give points for university-level coursework, states also give them for sponsoring a school club, mentoring a new teacher and belonging to a national teacher organization. Teachers also get points for experience.

But according to Walsh, "The purpose of HOUSSE is to ensure that teachers know their content, not to count the number of years in the classroom." [26]

Even with the flexibility offered by the HOUSSE option, some schools in rural and urban areas are struggling to meet the law's requirements, although the Department of Education has given rural districts a three-year extension. After studying a rural district in Alabama that offered a $5,000 signing bonus to new teachers, researchers from the Southeast Center for Teaching Quality noted: "Central office staff told us that to ensure the bonus worked, they could only require recipients work two years. Most teachers take the bonus, serve their two years and leave." Urban districts the researchers studied struggled to find experienced teachers prepared to work with few resources and students with diverse learning and emotional needs. [27]

As a result, rural and urban schools are more likely to assign teachers to instruct in multiple subjects, often outside their field. These schools are also more reliant on teachers who have entered the profession through some alternative route, usually with little or no classroom experience. No Child Left Behind says such teachers are highly qualified if enrolled in an intensive induction and mentoring program and receiving high-quality professional development.

But Tom Blanford, an associate director for teacher quality at the National Education Association, says the quality of these programs is often poor. "We know what it takes to change classroom practice," Blanford says. "It has to do with knowledge, coaching, feedback and more knowledge, and it's a cyclical process. It's very rare that professional development meets those standards." Usually, he says, it's someone standing in front of a group of teachers lecturing them.

CHRONOLOGY

1950s-1960s *A legal challenge and federal legislation initiate an era of education reform.*

1954 In *Brown v. Board of Education*, the Supreme Court decides "separate educational facilities are inherently unequal."

1958 Congress passes National Defense Education Act in response to the Soviet launch of Sputnik.

1965 President Lyndon B. Johnson signs Elementary and Secondary Education Act (ESEA) providing funds to school districts to help disadvantaged students.

1966 Congress amends ESEA to add Title VI, establishing grants for the education of handicapped children.

1966 Sociologist James S. Coleman's "Equality of Educational Opportunity" report concludes that disadvantaged black children learn better in well-integrated classrooms, helping to launch an era of busing students to achieve racial balance in public schools. . . . Congress amends ESEA to add Title VII, called the Bilingual Education Act.

1970s-1980s *Studies criticize student achievement, and the standards movement gains momentum.*

1975 Coleman issues a new report concluding busing had failed, largely because it had prompted "white flight."

1980 U.S. Department of Education is established, ending education role of Department of Health, Education, and Welfare.

1983 National Commission on Excellence's "A Nation at Risk" report warns of a rising tide of mediocrity in education and recommends a common core curriculum nationwide.

1989 President George H.W. Bush convenes nation's governors in Charlottesville, Va., for first National Education Summit, which establishes six broad objectives to be reached by 2000. . . . National Council of Teachers of Mathematics publishes *Curriculum and Evaluation Standards for School Mathematics*.

1990s-2000s *Congress requires more standards, testing and accountability from the states.*

1994 President Bill Clinton signs the Goals 2000: Educate America Act, which adopts the goals of the first National Education Summit. The act creates the National Education Standards and Improvement Council, with the authority to approve or reject states' academic standards. The council, however, becomes ineffective after Republicans take control of Congress during midterm elections and object to the increasing federal role in education. . . . Clinton later signs Improving America's Schools Act of 1994, requiring significantly more testing and accountability than the original ESEA.

Jan. 8, 2002 President George W. Bush signs No Child Left Behind Act, increasing funding to states while also increasing federal mandates and sanctions to an unprecedented degree. States must increase student testing, place "highly qualified" teachers in every classroom and meet state-determined annual targets for student proficiency in reading and math. By 2014, all students must be 100 percent proficient. Title I schools not meeting annual targets must offer transfers to students and provide supplemental services, like tutoring.

April 7, 2005 Secretary of Education Margaret Spellings announces her willingness to provide some flexibility to states in meeting the requirements of No Child Left Behind.

April 19, 2005 Republican-dominated Utah legislature passes a bill giving priority to state educational goals when those conflict with NCLB and ordering officials to spend as little state money as possible to comply with the federal law.

April 20, 2005 The nation's largest teachers' union and eight school districts in Michigan, Texas and Vermont sue the Department of Education, accusing the government of violating a No Child Left Behind Act provision that states cannot be forced to spend their own money to meet the law's requirements. The suit is thrown out several months later, but Connecticut has pushed forward with a similar suit of its own. Forty-five of the nation's governors agree on a common means for determining graduation rates.

2006 The Bill and Melinda Gates Foundation releases a study calling poor graduation rates "The Silent Epidemic." The Bush administration allows Tennessee and North Carolina to track advancement of individual students from year to year in reading and math, a new way to measure progress under NCLB. The administration unveils a $100 million private voucher plan that the president wants added to NCLB.

2007 A commission headed by two former governors releases a report calling for an expansion of NCLB, proposing national standards and tests and sanctions for teachers with poorly performing students. Congressional committees begin hearings on NCLB reauthorization.

Are Schools' Graduation Rates Accurate?

The No Child Left Behind Act holds schools accountable not just for student achievement but also for graduation rates. High schools must raise their graduation rates if they are to make adequate yearly progress. Increasing the percentage of graduates is a worthy goal, but it serves another purpose as well. The requirement is designed to prevent schools from improving achievement scores by encouraging their lowest-performing students to leave.

The system depends, of course, on accurate reporting. But researchers say that high school graduation rates reported by most states are just not believable.

The problem: States don't really know how many kids are dropping out of school.

States "consistently underestimate the number of dropouts, thereby overstating the graduation rates, sometimes by very large amounts," says Jay P. Greene, a senior fellow at the Manhattan Institute for Policy Research. In a report, Greene called some states' rates "so improbably high they would be laughable if the issue were not so serious." [1]

Although a few school districts have been accused of falsifying dropout data, researchers don't believe deception is at the root of the problem. Rather, they say the cause is more benign: Most schools don't know what happens to students who leave. Did a student transfer to another school? Move to another state? Or really drop out? Trying to answer those questions may be a secretary or clerk who often has other responsibilities as well.

The National Governors Association has been working to convince its members to use the method of tracking all those who enter 9th grade and figure out how many of them actually graduate. A special issue of *Education Week* devoted to graduation rates in 2006 found that states tended to report graduation rates about 30 percent higher than would be the case under the individual-tracking method.

"You basically have to do detective work," says Christopher Swanson, a senior research associate at The Urban Institute's Education Policy Center. "That takes time, effort and resources that may not be available to the school." Swanson says schools don't have an incentive to distinguish dropouts from transfers if it means that the graduation rates they report will be lower as a result.

Even states with sophisticated systems to track individual students over time — and there are a handful — can still report inflated graduation numbers. Texas, which reported an 84.2 percent graduation rate for its Class of 2003, counts as graduates students who have left school and either received or are working toward a General Educational Development certificate (GED). [2] No Child Left Behind prohibits the practice.

Both Swanson and Greene have developed methods for estimating how many students are actually graduating that do not rely on dropout data. Instead, they use two pieces of basic information they say are less subject to manipulation: the number of students enrolled in high school and the number of graduates. Their formulas differ, but both researchers come up with similar graduation rates that are far lower than those published by the states.

For example, South Carolina reported a high school graduation rate of 77.5 percent for the class of 2002; [3] Greene calculated the rate as 53 percent. [4] California reported a 2002 graduation rate of 87 percent; Greene put it at 67 percent. Indiana reported a graduation rate of 91 percent; Greene says it was 72 percent.

To fix the problem, Greene would like to see all states assign each student a unique identifying number for tracking their school careers, with reasonable definitions of who is a dropout and who is a graduate and an auditing program to ensure the quality of the data.

"Starbucks knows exactly what it sells," Greene says. "Wal-Mart knows what inventory it has in every store. Schools have no idea."

Some states are developing such systems, but doing so will be time consuming and costly. In the meantime, some critics of the current reporting methods want the Department of Education to require states to estimate graduation rates using methods similar to Greene's or Swanson's. "The department's role does not end with the collection of data," the Education Trust says. "It must ensure that state calculations are accurate, complete and accessible to the public." [5]

However, federal education officials believe the responsibility lies elsewhere. While the Department of Education will provide technical assistance to states as they create more sophisticated systems for tracking students, it believes that the quality of the data is the states' responsibility. "Anytime there is a problem in the states, parties are always prone to point the finger," says Deputy Assistant Secretary for Policy Darla Marburger. "And folks point the finger at the U.S. Department of Education. But it is not really a problem in our house."

---

[1] Jay P. Greene, "Public High School Graduation and College Readiness Rates: 1991-2002," Education Working Paper No. 8, Manhattan Institute for Policy Research, February 2005, p. 2

[2] www.tea.state.tx.us/peims/standards/wedspre/index.html?r032.

[3] Education Trust, "Telling the Whole Truth (or Not) About High School Graduation," December 2003, p. 4.

[4] Greene, *op. cit.*, Table 1.

[5] Education Trust, *op. cit.*

Gov. Jon Huntsman, R-Utah, prepares to sign a state measure on May 2, 2005, defying the No Child Left Behind Act, aided by a Provo elementary school student. In the past year and a half, more than 30 states have introduced bills that would release them from some of the law's requirements.

What rural and urban schools need to do, according to Scott Emerick, a policy associate at the Southeast Center for Teaching Quality, is use federal funds more effectively to improve working conditions, design better professional-development programs and devise sophisticated financial incentives to attract and retain teachers. But Emerick says they often don't know how, and the federal government is not providing enough guidance.

"These districts need on-the-ground assistance beyond accessing a federal Web site that tells you what other people are doing," he says.

Is No Child Left Behind adequately funded?

The funding question is so contentious it has divided former congressional supporters of the law and prompted both Republican and Democratic state lawmakers to introduce bills exempting their states from portions of the law.

The issue also has generated nearly two-dozen studies from think tanks, lobbying groups, school districts and states. Their conclusions about the adequacy of funding range from modest surpluses to shortfalls of millions, and in a few cases, even billions of dollars.

Beneath the competing claims are radically different estimates of the costs of implementing the law. Researchers can't even agree on what costs should be included, let alone their size. Adding to the problem, said a study, "is the evolving nature of the regulations, guidance and other advisories issued by the U.S. Department of Education." [28]

After reviewing the studies, the National Conference of State Legislatures concluded a shortfall is more likely and released a report in 2005 calling for change. "We would ask Congress to do one of two things," says senior policy specialist Young. "Either increase funding to levels that would allow states to meet the goals of the law or provide states waivers from having to meet requirements where there is insufficient funding."

In response, the Education Department embraced the studies projecting plenty of funds. "The perpetual cry for more money . . . simply does not comport with the facts: Since taking office, President Bush has increased education funding by . . . 33 percent," said a department press release in 2005.

To understand the debate, it is helpful to break down the costs of implementing the law into two categories: complying with the letter of the law versus bringing students to grade-level proficiency by 2014, which several states claim may be much more costly.

To comply with the letter of the law, states must establish academic standards, create assessments, monitor schools' progress, help schools needing improvement, pay for students to transfer and receive tutoring and place a highly qualified teacher in every classroom. Connecticut recently called its estimate of these costs "sobering." The state said that through fiscal 2008 it would have to spend $41.6 million of its own money to comply with the law. [29] Minnesota said its cost would be $42 million. [30]

Other states go even further. They say doing what's explicitly called for in the law will not be enough to bring 100 percent of students to proficiency in reading and math by 2014. In order to reach that goal, several states say they'll have to do much more. "It might involve after-school services and making sure children are well nourished," Young says. "Early-childhood education is a big one, essential to preventing the achievement gap from occurring."

Ohio commissioned a study that adopted an expanded notion of costs and included summer school, an extended school day and intensive in-school student intervention. The study calculated the annual cost of fully implementing NCLB at $1.5 billion; the additional federal funding that Ohio receives through the law, however, is only $44 million. [31]

The authors of the Ohio study acknowledged, "the task of assigning costs to the requirements of No Child Left Behind presents a formidable challenge." [32] Their assumptions, and the assumptions of other state studies, have come under attack.

A report in *Education Next*, a journal devoted to education reform, last spring accused the state studies of gross exaggeration. The authors, including the chairman of the Massachusetts Board of Education, contended that while there may be a shortage of money to evaluate schools and help those that need intervention, the gap can be filled by giving states more flexibility to shift existing federal money around. And it concludes, "No one — neither critics nor supporters of NCLB — really has any idea what it would cost to bring all students to proficiency by 2014, or even if it can be done at all." [33]

Accountability Works, a nonprofit research and consulting firm, goes a step further, concluding there is "little solid evidence that NCLB is insufficiently funded." In fact, the firm concluded some states might even have surpluses.

Echoing *Education Next*, Accountability Works said the reports claiming NCLB provides insufficient funding contain significant flaws. "Often, expenditures that are not required by NCLB are included in the calculations," the report said. "In other cases, such studies included expenditures that were required by prior federal law." [34]

Given the huge range of estimates and the fact that some of the repercussions of the law are just beginning to be felt, it may take years for the true costs of implementation to become clear.

But one thing is clear: State education departments are often overwhelmed. Many don't have the staff or the expertise to effectively carry out No Child Left Behind's requirements: creating data systems to monitor each school's adequate yearly progress; putting teams together to help schools in need of improvement and, as more fail, to restructure schools; and evaluating outside suppliers of tutoring services. Many states have never had to do these things, on this scale, before, and the alarm has been sounded not only by the states but also by private researchers and even the Government Accountability Office.

The Department of Education's Briggs says the federal government is helping. "We have held conferences where we have tried to bring states together to learn together."

But many states say the problem is rooted in past state budget cuts and resulting staff reductions. The extra money provided by NCLB is being used to create assessment tests or reduce class size, with little left over to hire administrative staff. That's the case in Idaho, says Allison Westfall, public information officer at the state Department of Education. "We have a very small Title I staff — we're down to five people now — who are often on the road visiting schools," she says. "So we've had to bring in people from other departments, and we're stretched really thin." And there are no plans to hire.

"This lack of capacity — not a lack of will — on the part of most states is the single, most important impediment to achieving the gains of No Child Left Behind," said Marc Tucker, president of the National Center on Education and the Economy, a research group. On average, state education departments have lost 50 percent of their employees in the past 10 years, he says, calling it "the hidden issue." [35]

BACKGROUND

Federal Reforms

On April 11, 1965, President Lyndon B. Johnson returned to the Texas school he had attended as a child to sign the nation's first comprehensive education law, the Elementary and Secondary Education Act. "As president of the United States," he declared, "I believe deeply no law I have signed or will ever sign means more to the future of America." [36]

The primary assumption in ESEA — enacted as part of Johnson's War on Poverty — was that higher-quality education would move poor students out of poverty.

With ESEA, the federal government began to address the causes of the achievement gap. In the process, the federal role in education policy — until then a strictly local affair handled by the nation's 15,000 independent school districts — grew dramatically. ESEA's signature program, Title I, initially allocated more than $1 billion a year to school districts with high concentrations of low-income students. To administer the program, federal and state education bureaucracies grew, as did the federal and state roles in local school districts.

During the next decade, minority achievement improved marginally, but dissatisfaction with public education grew faster, as did resentment over federal infringement on local education affairs. In 1981, President Ronald Reagan took office vowing to abolish the U.S. Department of Education.

"These Are the Very Weakest Programs Offered"

Arthur E. Levine, president of Teachers College, Columbia University, led a four-year assessment of the 1,200 university programs that prepare most of the nation's school principals and administrators. Released in March 2005 by Levine's Education Schools Project, the study, "Educating School Leaders," says most university-based preparation programs for administrators range in quality from "inadequate to appalling." Levine recently discussed the report with writer Barbara Mantel.

CQ: Does No Child Left Behind make the issue of how we train school leaders more urgent?

AL: No Child Left Behind demands assessment; it demands effective curricula that will move students to achievement of standards and requires that all students achieve those standards. Principals and superintendents have to lead that transformation of the schools, which requires a very different set of skills and knowledge from their predecessors.

CQ: What is your overall characterization of university-based programs that train school administrators?

AL: The quality is very weak. These are the very weakest programs offered by America's education schools. While a relatively small proportion could be described as strong, the majority vary in quality from inadequate to appalling.

CQ: Do most principals and superintendents come through these programs?

AL: I can't give you numbers on superintendents. For principals, it is 89 percent.

CQ: In what areas do these programs fall short?

AL: First of all, the curriculum for the master's degree is irrelevant to the job of being a principal, appearing to be a random grab bag of survey courses, like Research Methods, Historical and Philosophical Foundations of Education and Educational Psychology.

CQ: Your report also talks about admission standards.

AL: The standardized test scores for students in leadership programs are among the lowest of all students at graduate schools of education, and they're among the lowest in all academe. But the larger problem is that the overwhelming majority of students in these programs are in them primarily for a bump in salaries. All 50 states give salary increases for educators who take master's degrees or graduate credits. So people want quickie programs and easy degrees. There is a race to the bottom among programs as they compete for students by dumbing down the curriculum, reducing the length of the program, cutting the number of credits required to graduate and lowering expectations of student performance.

CQ: Your report also says the degrees offered don't make sense.

AL: Generally the master's degree is considered prepa-

The next year, Reagan and Secretary of Education Terrell Bell appointed the National Commission on Excellence in Education to report on the quality of public education. Eighteen months later, the commission's explosive report, "A Nation at Risk," declared, "the educational foundations of our society are presently being eroded by a rising tide of mediocrity that threatens our very future as a Nation and a people." [37]

The report focused on how poorly American students compared with students from other countries; the steady decline in science scores; a drop in SAT scores; the functional illiteracy of too many minority students; and complaints from business and military leaders about the poor quality of U.S. high school graduates.

To overcome the problems, the report called for rigorous and measurable academic standards, establishment of a minimum core curriculum, lengthening of the time

spent learning that curriculum and better teacher preparation.

"A Nation at Risk" marked the beginning of a movement for national standards and testing. Over the next decade, seven groups received federal financing to develop standards for what students should know, including the National Council of Teachers of Mathematics, the National History Standards Project and the National Standards in Foreign Language. [38]

In September 1989, President George H.W. Bush — the self-described "education president" — convened an education summit in Charlottesville, Va. Ignoring traditional Republican reluctance to actively involve Washington in education policy, Bush teamed with the president of the National Governors' Association — Democratic Gov. Bill Clinton, who had been active in education reform in his home state of Arkansas.

ration for principalship and the doctorate for a superintendency. Why does anybody need a doctorate to be a superintendent? A doctorate is a research degree. What does that have to do with running a school system?

CQ: What are some of your key recommendations?

AL: States and school boards should eliminate salary increases based on taking degrees. Or they can give people raises based on master's degrees but require that the field be germane to their work. If you're a math teacher, I can understand giving an increase in salary for taking a degree in mathematics or advanced teaching skills. Number two: close down failing programs. States can clean this up if they want to. They are in charge of the authorization of university programs and the licensure of school administrators. But I would like to see universities try first before the states step in.

CQ: How much time would you give the universities to do this?

Arthur E. Levine, president, Teachers College, Columbia University

Columbia University

AL: I would give universities two years to clean up their house, and then the state has an obligation to step in if they fail to do that.

CQ: What other recommendations do you have for universities?

AL: Eliminate the current master's degree and put in its place something I've been calling a master's of educational administration, which would be a two-year degree combining education and management courses, theory and practical experience. The doctor of education degree (EdD) would be eliminated. It has no integrity and no value. The PhD in education leadership should be reserved for the very tiny group of people who wish to be scholars and researchers in the field.

CQ: And your last recommendation?

AL: There is a tendency of universities to use these programs as cash cows. They encourage these programs to produce as much revenue as possible by reducing admission standards, using adjuncts and lowering academic standards for graduation in order to get enough cash to distribute to other areas. Universities need to stop doing that.

"The movement gained momentum with the 1989 education summit," wrote Andrew Rudalevige, an associate professor of political science at Dickinson College, in Carlyle, Pa.[39] Bush and the governors set broad performance goals for American schools to reach by the year 2000. It was hoped that all children would attend preschool, that 90 percent of all high school students would graduate, that all students would be proficient in core subjects, that U.S. students would be first in the world in science and math, that every adult would be literate and every school free of drugs and violence.

In 1994, President Clinton signed the Goals 2000: Educate America Act, which adopted the summit's ambitious agenda and provided federal funds to help states develop standards. The real sea change came later that year, Rudalevige wrote, when reauthorization of ESEA "signaled a nationwide commitment to standards-based reform."[40]

The law required states to develop content and performance standards, tests aligned with those standards and a system to measure a school's "adequate yearly progress" in bringing all students to academic proficiency. But there was no deadline, and it took several years for the Education Department to develop the accompanying regulations and guidelines. By 1997, only 17 states were fully complying with the law, according to Krista Kafer, a Denver-based education consultant and former senior education policy analyst at the Heritage Foundation.[41]

In January 2001, former Texas Gov. George W. Bush became president, having made education a centerpiece of his campaign. Three days after his inauguration, he proposed what became the blueprint for No Child Left Behind. Its standards-and-testing strategy wasn't new, but accountability provisions were. They significantly raised the stakes for states, local districts and schools.

The proposal called for annual testing in grades 3-8, school and state report cards showing student performance by ethnic and economic subgroups, a highly qualified teacher in every classroom and sanctions for schools not showing progress in bringing students to proficiency.

Congress finally passed NCLB after nearly a year of intense debate and political horse-trading, which included the elimination of private school vouchers, increases in funding and, significantly, addition of a provision requiring that all students reach proficiency in math and reading in 12 years.

"The political compromises written into No Child Left Behind make the regulatory process crucial," said Rudalevige. [42] That's because the law grants the secretary of Education the power to grant waivers and interpret the rules and, until the bill is reauthorized, determine the flexibility states will have to meet their goals.

Achievement Gaps

Most educators say the best thing about No Child Left Behind is its focus on minorities and low-income students.

"When you say to a school that you expect every subgroup of kids to meet standards," says Delaware Education Secretary Woodruff, "that really makes schools pay closer attention to all kids." It is now possible, for instance, to track how minority and low-income students perform on state tests at each school and to calculate the achievement gaps between them and their peers. The fundamental goal of No Child Left Behind is to close these gaps while raising the achievement of all students, which has been the goal of education reforms for decades.

But to get a sense of how students have been performing historically, researchers must look to national data, because state testing is too new.

To get that information, the U.S. Department of Education has been measuring American students' achievement levels since 1969 through its National Assessment of Educational Progress (NAEP). NAEP periodically administers what it calls a "trend assessment" to a nationally representative sample of students at ages 9, 13 and 17 and breaks down the results for white, black and Hispanic students.

The data show that black and Hispanic students have made long-term gains, thus narrowing the achievement gap. From 1971 to 1999 for example, the difference between the average reading scores of 13-year-old white and black students shrank from 39 points to 29 points.

In math, the gap plummeted 14 points — from 46 points to 32 points. [43]

However, most of the reductions in the achievement gap occurred during the 1970s and 1980s, as minorities made notable gains while white students' average achievement increased slightly or not at all. Then, in the 1990s, the gap stopped shrinking; in fact, in many cases it grew. Black and Hispanic students continued making modest gains in math and Hispanic students in reading, but those improvements no longer exceeded those of whites. [44] By 2005, according to the National Center for Education Statistics, the gaps were still not measurably different from 1992.

"When achievement goes up for all groups," the Center on Education Policy noted, "African-American and Hispanic students must improve at a faster rate than others for the gap to close." [45]

While still smaller than decades ago, the achievement gap remains quite large. For instance, the 32-point difference in math scores for black 13-year-olds and their white peers in 1999 is the equivalent of roughly three grade levels. [46]

"What, then, are the most probable explanations for the achievement gap?" asked the Center on Education Policy in a report examining minority achievement. "A complex combination of school, community and home factors appear to underlie or contribute to the gap," it answered. [47]

Just as worrying to some observers is the gap in scores between NAEP and state-level assessments. States are allowed to determine measurements for proficiency among their own students, but their results seldom track NAEP scores within their borders, suggesting they have set their own bar too low. A University of California study released in 2007 found that the gap between national and state results has grown since NCLB's passage in 10 of the 12 states studied.

For instance, Texas reported that 82 percent of its fourth graders were proficient in reading in 2006, while the federal estimate was just 29 percent. In New Jersey, the state reported that 80 percent were proficient in reading in 2006, but federal data put the number at 38 percent.

"State leaders are under enormous pressure to show that students are making progress," said Bruce Fuller, a University of California professor of education and public policy. "So they are finding inventive ways of showing higher test scores." [48]

Of course, some states maintain that their assessment systems are superior to national ones. Florida has given "A" grades to hundreds of schools found deficient under

Should annual testing be extended to high school?

YES Bob Wise
President, Alliance for Excellent Education

Written for *CQ Researcher*, May 5, 2005

Achieving the national goal of building a better educated, more competitive work force for the 21st century requires effective tools. With two-thirds of high school students either dropping out or graduating unprepared for college, the majority of our nation's young people need more support than they are currently getting from their secondary schools and teachers. An increased number of required tests at the high school level could help to leverage the academic assistance many students require, if those tests are designed and implemented appropriately.

Last fall, President Bush set off a major debate when he proposed extending the reading and math tests required by the No Child Left Behind Act for third- through eighth-graders and in one year of high school to students in grades nine, ten and eleven. "We need to be sure that high school students are learning every year," he said.

At the Alliance for Excellent Education, we believe all children deserve an excellent education that prepares them for the economic and social challenges that follow high school. And we agree with the president that our schools must be held accountable for providing that high-quality education. Testing students during their high school years has the potential to provide needed data about their progress — as a whole, and by gender, race and ethnicity — and could allow us to better measure the effectiveness of the schools supposed to be preparing all of our young people to become productive members of American society.

But tests should help schools understand and address the needs of their students. If we are going to hold schools accountable for their students' ability to perform at high academic levels, we must also give them the resources necessary to provide the additional, targeted instruction that many teens need to become proficient in reading, writing, math and other subjects.

To be taken seriously by students, tests need to be relevant. High school tests should be aligned to the expectations of colleges and employers and provide both educators and students with a gauge to measure progress toward a successful transition to postsecondary education, technical training or rewarding jobs.

Finally, the federal government should fully cover the cost of designing and administering the exams, thus ensuring that states can adequately and effectively implement the tests they are required to give.

Tests alone won't make a difference. But as a part of a toolkit designed to improve the nation's graduation and college-readiness rates, they are worthy of our consideration.

NO Paul Houston
Executive Director, American Association of School Administrators

Written for *CQ Researcher*, April 27, 2005

High school reform should not focus on a test but rather on what is being learned. I recently visited the Olathe, Kan., school district to learn more about a series of programs called 21st Century Schools, which have been implemented in all the high schools. These are "vocational" schools. In other words, they are focused on the future work life of students, and the programs are very rigorous and produce great results. But more important, the programs are meaningful, engaging and hands on, using the students' motivation to create a vehicle for excellence.

As I walked through Olathe Northwest High School, I saw students and teachers engaged in hard work. In one classroom, they were constructing a "battlebot," a robot that is used in gaming to battle other robots — with the last one running being the winner. The students were looking forward to taking their creation to a national competition later this year. While this sounds fun (some may say "frivolous"), what is really happening is that students are experiencing deep learning about metallurgy, structures, engines, insulation and a hundred other things I didn't understand. They were excited and knowledgeable about what they were doing — and about how much fun they were having with the learning process.

There were about a dozen students who stayed after the bell to talk with me, and every one of them plans to attend college and study engineering. There is no shortage of engineering candidates in Olathe. I asked them why they liked what they were doing, and the answer was simple. One told me he got to use what he was learning in class. "Telling me that calculus is good for me isn't very meaningful," he said. "Now I see how I can use it."

I would suggest to those who want to reform high schools that the place to start is in places like Olathe, where the school district has figured out that the best way to get students to learn more is to give them engaging, imaginative work that creates meaning for them. And we must give schools adequate resources to provide state-of-the-art opportunities for students to receive hands-on learning.

Those who are interested in reform should focus on getting schools the resources they need to do the job and then challenging them to make schools interesting and engaging places. Reform will not be achieved by mandating more testing. Education has always been about the whole child, and unless we take that into consideration, the current effort to reform high schools will be just as unsuccessful as the others that preceded it.

NCLB. That fact drew national attention when Gov. Jeb Bush, the president's brother, held a news conference in 2006 to crow about an academic study that found Florida's system superior to the federal model. [49]

CURRENT SITUATION

States Push Back

Mounting state resistance to NCLB — including its level of funding and strict achievement timetables — has led to a mini-revolution in the states.

In 2004, legislatures in 31 states introduced bills challenging aspects of the law. [50] By mid-2005, 21 states had either introduced or reintroduced legislation. [51] In Colorado, Republican state Sen. Mark Hillman proposed allowing school districts to opt out of No Child Left Behind if they forgo Title I funds; he suggested a tax increase to replace the lost federal funds. In Idaho, two Republican state senators introduced legislation demanding that predominantly rural states be exempt from the law. In Maine, Democratic state Sen. Michael Brennan sponsored a bill directing the state's attorney general to sue the federal government if federal funding is insufficient to implement No Child Left Behind.

Despite the blizzard of proposals, however, only three states actually passed legislation. The Republican-dominated Utah legislature passed a bill on April 19, 2005 — and the governor signed it on May 2 — allowing schools to ignore NCLB provisions that conflict with state education laws or require extra state money to implement. Spellings warned that Utah could lose $76 million of the $107 million it receives in federal education funding.

"I don't like to be threatened," an angry state Rep. Mascaro told *The New York Times.* [52]

Raul Gonzalez, legislative senior director at the National Council of La Raza, which advocates for Hispanic-Americans, agrees that money is tight in states still suffering from a four-year-long budget crisis. [53] "States are trying to implement this law on the cheap," Gonzalez says, "because there isn't really enough money."

For example, under the law states are allowed to test English-language learners for up to three years in their native language, but most states don't have reading tests in native languages. "We're not accurately measuring what kids can do because we're using the wrong tests," he says.

Arizona and Virginia continue to battle the federal government over rules for testing children with limited English. Utah is still fighting about qualifications for its rural teachers. The Connecticut lawsuit continues to drag on past the two-year mark. But Perry Zirkel, a professor of education and law at Lehigh University, in Bethlehem, Pa., says the states' resistance to the law is still mostly "sparks, not fire." He points out that New Mexico, Virginia and Utah are the only states to pass legislation.

"Despite all the talk," Zirkel says, "I don't think there has been sufficient momentum to convince the majority of the public that No Child Left Behind is, on a net basis, a bad law."

Moreover, a coalition of Hispanic, African-American and other educators have voiced concerns that the Utah legislature's effort to sidestep provisions of the federal law might allow minority students to fall through the cracks. [54]

Teachers' Union Sues

One day after the Utah legislature made its move, the NEA and eight school districts in Michigan, Texas and Vermont sued the Department of Education, contending it is violating an NCLB provision that says states cannot be forced to use their own money to implement the law:

"Nothing in this Act shall be construed to authorize an officer or employee of the Federal Government to mandate, direct, or control a State, local education agency, or school's curriculum, program of instruction, or allocation of State or local resources, or mandate a State or any subdivision thereof to spend any funds or incur any costs not paid for under this Act."

"We don't disagree when the Department of Education says federal funding has increased," explained NEA spokesman Dan Kaufman. "We just don't believe that the funding has been enough for the types of really strict, comprehensive things that it requires states to do." The teachers' union wanted to see Congress appropriate the full amount it authorized when passing the bill. At that point, it was $27 billion short.

"We . . . look forward to the day when the NEA will join us in helping children who need our help the most in classrooms, instead of spending its time and members' money in courtrooms," the Department of Education said in response. [55]

The lawsuit was filed in the U.S. District Court for the Eastern District of Michigan, which has jurisdiction over one of the school districts joining the suit. The suit asks the court to declare that states and school districts do not have to spend their own funds to comply with NCLB and that failure to comply for that reason will not result in a cutoff of federal education funds.

A federal judge acted quickly to dismiss the suit, finding that Congress had not intended to pay for all of the costs imposed by NCLB. "If Congress meant to prohibit 'unfunded mandates' in the NCLB, it would have phrased [the law] to say so clearly and unambiguously," he wrote in his decision. [56]

"The courts' view is that if you have problems with this law, then go lobby Congress to change it," Lehigh's Zirkel says. In fact, the lawsuit may actually have been an indirect way to lobby Congress, he adds, and it may be effective because it's so public.

War of Words

Zirkel says Connecticut's decision to sue may also be an indirect attempt at lobbying Congress. In early April 2005, Connecticut Attorney General Richard Blumenthal announced he would sue the Department of Education on grounds that the federal government's approach to the law is "illegal and unconstitutional." [57] Connecticut's argument is essentially the same as the teachers' union's, but the state — which has a direct stake in the outcome — has better legal standing, Zirkel says. Blumenthal has estimated the annual testing required by the law would create an additional financial burden for the state, which now tests students every other year.

While a few school districts have sued the government over the law, Connecticut was the first state to do so. A federal judge in 2006 dismissed much of Connecticut's case but allowed the state to go forward with its claim that Washington treated it unfairly in negotiations over how to carry out the law. [58] As of mid-2007, that portion of the case had not been settled.

Meanwhile, the state's dispute with the Education Department had become very public. "We've got better things to spend our money on," former Connecticut Education Commissioner Sternberg said in explaining her opposition to annual testing. "We won't learn anything new about our schools by giving these extra tests." [59]

But Secretary Spellings clearly was not willing to compromise on annual testing, consistently calling it one of the "bright lines" of NCLB. She and Sternberg engaged in a war of words, with Spellings calling the law's opponents "un-American" and Sternberg demanding an apology.

Spellings also accused Connecticut of tolerating one of the nation's largest achievement gaps between white and black students. Sternberg has said the huge gap was due to the extraordinary performance of white students in Connecticut's affluent suburbs.

Reform Unlikely?

If the NEA's lawsuit and Connecticut's threat to sue are indirect ways of lobbying Congress, their timing may be off.

Jeffrey Henig, a professor of political science and education at Columbia University's Teachers College, says some constituents in prosperous suburban school districts are beginning to grumble as well-regarded schools fail to make "adequate yearly progress" because one or two subgroups of students miss proficiency targets.

"But I don't think it has really gelled into clear, focused pressure on Congress to reform the law," Henig says, adding that the situation could change if more schools fall into that category.

Moderate Democrats are committed to the law's focus on raising achievement levels for minority, low-income and disabled students, he says, and they fear that any reworking could result in easing the pressure on states to shrink the achievement gap. And a core group of Republicans is committed to the law's tough accountability provisions. Both groups, Henig says, would prefer "to hold to the legislation and to placate any dissatisfied groups through the regulatory process."

The Department of Education has already amended the law's regulations, guidelines and enforcement. For instance, in 2003 and 2004 it allowed English-language learners to be tested in native languages for their first three years, gave rural districts more time to place highly qualified teachers in classrooms and allowed some flexibility on testing participation rates.

In 2005, Spellings — then just three months into her new job as secretary — told states they could apply to test a greater portion of disabled students using alternative assessments. In addition, Spellings said she would grant states flexibility in other areas if they could show they were making real progress in closing achievement gaps and meeting proficiency targets.

But Young, formerly of the National Conference of State Legislatures, says states are trying to decipher what she means. "There is no indication of what that flexibility would include," he says, "and there is no indication of how states would be judged by these indicators."

So far, Spellings is holding firm on annual testing, but she did grant North Dakota a waiver temporarily allowing new elementary school teachers to be rated highly qualified without taking a state test. She also offered all states more time to meet the requirement for placing "highly qualified" teachers in all classrooms.

"The Department of Education is really feeling the heat and is trying to compromise," says educational consultant Scott Joftus, former policy director at the Alliance for Excellent Education.

The department also has allowed some states to lower the cutoff point for proficiency on their student assessment tests and to use averaging and other statistical methods to make it easier for schools to make adequate yearly progress. Young calls it gaming the system and expects it to continue unless Congress reforms No Child Left Behind.

OUTLOOK

As Congress prepares to extend the law, which it is scheduled to do in 2007, it will have to contend with critics from both the left and right. Prepared to engage in that battle is an unusual bipartisan coalition made up of President Bush, Secretary Spellings, Sen. Edward M. Kennedy and Sen. George Miller, the chairman of the House Education Committee. All have proposed various changes, but none will accept a retreat from the basic promise contained in the title of the law, that all children — even or especially those in populations that have traditionally been badly served — are entitled to a measurably decent education.

"When Republicans and Democrats take a look at this bill, I strongly urge them not to weaken the bill, not to backslide, not to say accountability isn't that important," Bush said at an April 2007 appearance at a Harlem charter school. [60]

The continuing controversy over the bill's approach and cost mean that the Bush administration's hopes of extending its tenets into high school or even college are probably dead letters for now. Kennedy and Miller support maintaining standards in lower grades and are focused on improving teacher quality and boosting spending.

Even the law's critics concede that it has focused attention and resources on groups of children who often had been neglected, including minority populations in urban districts and low-achieving students in the suburbs. But few students have been well served by the law's sanctions.

Only tiny fractions of eligible students have transferred out of so-called failing schools — less than 1 percent. Nationwide, only 18 percent of students have received free tutoring as they have become eligible for it. [61]

Meanwhile, the law's central goal — making sure that all students test as proficient by 2014 — is under increasing attack as being unrealistic and unobtainable. "There is a zero chance that we will ever reach a 100 percent target," said Robert L. Linn, codirector of the National Center for Research on Evaluation, Standards and Student Testing at UCLA. "But because the title of the law is so brilliant, politicians are afraid to change this completely unrealistic standard. They don't want to be accused of leaving some children behind." [62]

Under Spellings, the Bush Education Department has grown more flexible about allowing states leeway in meeting various goals under the law. But the underlying law remains something the administration wants to expand rather than from which to retreat. Spellings has joked that it's like Ivory soap: "It's 99.9 percent pure or something." [63]

Few lawmakers share that assessment. The National Conference of State Legislatures and the American Association of School Administrators have called for full federal funding to meet the law's requirements. The National Governors Association wants states to have much more authority in determining how to carry out the law's mandates.

Given the continuing controversy about the law and the criticism it generates among teachers unions, states, the education establishment and conservative lawmakers, most prognosticators say that the law's extension will be a tough sell. Many predict that Congress will fail to enact new legislation, leaving the job to a new Congress — and new president — in 2009.

But regardless of the short-term outcome, and despite its political problems, No Child Left Behind capped a fundamental shift in American education toward greater accountability and a move to place the blame for poor performance not on students themselves but on educators. That is a course that no new version of the law is likely to undo anytime soon.

NOTES

1. Dana Milbank, "With Fanfare, Bush Signs Education Bill," *The Washington Post*, Jan. 9, 2002.

2. Northwest Evaluation Association, "The Impact of the No Child Left Behind Act on Student Achievement and Growth: 2005 Edition," April 2005, p. 2.

3. http://kennedy.senate.gov/index_high.html.

4. Sam Dillon, "Utah Vote Rejects Parts of U.S. Education Law," *The New York Times*, April 20, 2005.

5. "Governor worried about costs of Bush education reform law," The Associated Press State & Local Wire, April 26, 2005.

6. http://gregg.senate.gov/forms/myths.pdf.

7. www.ed.gov/nclb/overview/intro/guide/guide_pg 11.html#spending.

8. National Public Radio, "Talk of the Nation," May 3, 2005.

9. Center on Education Policy, "From the Capital to the Classroom: Year 3 of the No Child Left Behind Act," March 2005, p. v.

10. Edward M. Kennedy, "No Retreat on School Reform," *The Washington Post*, March 26, 2007, p. A15.

11. *Ibid.*, p. 4.

12. *Ibid.*, p. 1.

13. Council of the Great City Schools, "Beating the Odds: A City-By-City Analysis of Student Performance and Achievement Gaps on State Assessments," March 2004, pp. iv-vi.

14. The Education Trust, "Stalled in Secondary: A Look at Student Achievement Since the No Child Left Behind Act," January 2005, p. 1.

15. University of Delaware Education Research and Development Center, "Awareness To Action Revisited: Tracking the Achievement Gap in Delaware Schools, State of Delaware Report," March 2005, p. 2.

16. www.dpi.state.wi.us/dpi/esea/pdf/wiaw.pdf.

17. National Conference of State Legislatures, "Task Force on No Child Left Behind: Final Report," February 2005, p. vii.

18. http://edcounts.edweek.org.

19. Stephanie Banchero, "Pupils Still Far Behind Despite Law," *Chicago Tribune*, Jan. 7, 2007, p. 1.

20. Center for the Study of Evaluation, "Test-based Educational Accountability in the Era of No Child Left Behind," April 2005, p. 19.

21. *Ibid.*, p. 14.

22. Susan Saulny, "U.S. Provides Rules to States for Testing Special Pupils," *The New York Times*, May 11, 2005, p. A17.

23. The data are from 2000, the most recent available. See The Education Trust, "All Talk, No Action: Putting an End to Out-of-Field Teaching," August 2002, p. 4.

24. Michael Alison Chandler, "For Teachers, Being 'Highly Qualified' Is a Subjective Matter," *The Washington Post*, Jan. 13, 2007, p. A1.

25. Education Week Research Center, "Quality Counts 2005," January 2005, p. 92. www.edweek.org/rc/index.html.

26. National Council on Teacher Quality, "Searching the Attic," December 2004, p. 12.

27. Southeast Center for Teaching Quality, "Unfulfilled Promise: Ensuring High Quality Teachers for Our Nation's Students," August 2004, pp. 8-9.

28. Augenblick, Palaich and Associates, Inc. "Costing Out No Child Left Behind: A Nationwide Survey of Costing Efforts," April 2004, p. 1.

29. Connecticut State Department of Education, "Cost of Implementing the Federal No Child Left Behind Act in Connecticut," March 2, 2005, p. iii.

30. Center on Education Policy, *op. cit.*

31. Ohio Department of Education, "Projected Costs of Implementing The Federal 'No Child Left Behind Act' in Ohio," December 2003, p. vi.

32. *Ibid.*

33. James Peyser and Robert Castrell, "Exploring the Costs of Accountability," *Education Next*, spring 2004, p. 24.

34. Accountability Works, "NCLB Under a Microscope," January 2004, p. 2.

35. Joetta L. Sack, "State Agencies Juggle NCLB Work, Staffing Woes," *Education Week*, May 11, 2005, p. 25.

36. www.lbjlib.utexas.edu/johnson/archives.hom/speeches.hom/650411.asp.

37. www.ed.gov/pubs/NatAtRisk/risk.html.

38. For background, see Kathy Koch, "National Education Standards," *CQ Researcher*, May 14, 1999, pp. 401-424, and Charles S. Clark, "Education Standards," *CQ Researcher*, March 11, 1994, pp. 217-240.

39. www.educationnext.org/20034/62.html.

40. *Ibid.*

41. Heritage Foundation, "No Child Left Behind: Where Do We Go From Here?" 2004, p. 2.

42. www.educationnext.org/20034/62.html.

43. National Center for Education Statistics, "Trends in Academic Progress: Three Decades of Student Performance," 2000, p. 39.

44. *Ibid.*, p. 33.

45. Center on Education Policy, "It takes more than testing: Closing the Achievement Gap," 2001, p. 2.

46. *Ibid.*, p. 1.

47. *Ibid.*, p. 3.

48. "Study Shows More Discrepancies between State, National Assessments of Student Proficiency," *The Washington Post*, April 16, 2007, p. B2.

49. Sam Dillon, "As 2 Bushes Try to Fix Schools, the Tools Differ," *The New York Times*, Sept. 28, 2006, p. A1.

50. National Conference of State Legislatures, "No Child Left Behind Quick Facts: 2005," April 2005.

51. www.nea.org/lawsuit/stateres.html.

52. Dillon, *op. cit.*

53. For background, see William Triplett, "State Budget Crisis," *CQ Researcher*, Oct. 3, 2003, pp. 821-844.

54. Dillon, *op. cit.*

55. U.S. Department of Education, "Statement by Press Secretary on NEA's Action Regarding NCLB," April 20, 2005, p. B1.

56. Kavan Peterson, "Schools Lose Round in NCLB Challenge," Stateline.org, Nov. 30, 2005.

57. Sam Dillon, "Connecticut to Sue U.S. Over Cost of School Testing Law," *The New York Times*, April 6, 2005.

58. Sam Dillon, "Connecticut Lawsuit Is Cut Back," *The New York Times*, Sept. 28, 2006, p. A18.

59. Michael Dobbs, "Conn. Stands in Defiance on Enforcing 'No Child,'" *The Washington Post*, May 8, 2005, p. A10.

60. Jim Rutenberg, "Bush Presses Schools Plan During Trip to New York," *The New York Times*, April 25, 2007, p. A20.

61. Banchero, *op. cit.*

62. Amit R. Paley, "'No Child' Target Is Called Out of Reach," *The Washington Post*, March 14, 2007, p. A1.

63. Paul Leavitt, "Education Chief Says Law Close to Perfect," *USA Today*, Aug. 31, 2006, p. 4A.

BIBLIOGRAPHY

Books

Meier, Deborah, and George Wood, eds., *Many Children Left Behind: How the No Child Left Behind Act Is Damaging Our Children and Our Schools*, Beacon Press, 2004.
Meier, the founder of several New York City public schools, and Wood, a high school principal and the founder of The Forum for Education and Democracy, and other authors argue that the law is harming the ability of schools to serve poor and minority children.

Peterson, Paul E., and Martin R. West, eds., *No Child Left Behind: The Politics and Practice of School Accountability*, Brookings Institution Press, 2003.
Peterson, director of the Program on Education Policy and Governance at Harvard, and West, a research fellow in the program, have collected essays that examine the forces that gave shape to the law and its likely consequences.

Rakoczy, Kenneth Leo, *No Child Left Behind: No Parent Left in the Dark*, Edu-Smart.com Publishing, 2003.
A veteran public school teacher offers this guide to parents for becoming involved in their children's education and making the most out of parent-teacher conferences in light of the new law.

Wright, Peter W. D., Pamela Darr Wright and Suzanne Whitney Heath, *Wrightslaw: No Child Left Behind*, Harbor House Law Press, 2003.
The authors, who run a Web site about educational law

and advocacy, explain the No Child Left Behind Act for parents and teachers.

Articles

Dillon, Sam, "New Secretary Showing Flexibility on 'No Child' Law," *The New York Times*, **Feb. 14, 2005, p. A18.**

Education Secretary Margaret Spellings has shown a willingness to work with state and local officials on No Child Left Behind, saying school districts need not always allow students in low-performing schools to transfer to better ones if it caused overcrowding.

Dillon, Sam, "Battle Over Renewing Landmark Education Law," *The New York Times*, **April 7, 2006, p. A10.**

Laying out the battlelines over reauthorization, with the law's original supporters remaining firm but opponents believing they have a chance to gut a law they have never liked.

Friel, Brian, "A Test for Tutoring," *The National Journal*, **April 16, 2005.**

Friel examines the controversy surrounding some of the outside tutoring firms providing supplemental services to students under provisions of No Child Left Behind.

Hendrie, Caroline, "NCLB Cases Face Hurdles in the Courts," *Education Week*, **May 4, 2005.**

Hendrie describes the hurdles facing the National Education Association's lawsuit against the Department of Education.

Ripley, Amanda, and Sonja Steptoe, "Inside the Revolt Over Bush's School Rules," *Time*, **May 9, 2005.**

The authors examine efforts by states to seek release from aspects of No Child Left Behind and the teachers' union's lawsuit against the federal government.

Thornburgh, Nathan, "Dropout Nation," *Time*, **April 17, 2006, p. 30.**

The high school dropout rate is higher than generally acknowledged, with researchers saying that one in three public high school students — and 50 percent of African-Americans and Hispanics — will fail to receive a diploma.

Tucker, Marc S., and Thomas Toch, "Hire Ed: the secret to making Bush's school reform law work? More bureaucrats," *Washington Monthly*, **March 1, 2004.**

The authors discuss staffing shortages at state departments of education that are slowing implementation of No Child Left Behind.

Weisman, Jonathan, and Amit R. Paley, "Dozens in GOP Turn Against Bush's Prized 'No Child' Act," *The Washington Post*, **March 15, 2007, p. A1.**

More than 50 Republican members of Congress support legislation that would severely undercut NCLB by allowing states to opt out of its testing mandates.

Reports and Studies

Center on Education Policy, *From the Capital to the Classroom: Year 3 of the No Child Left Behind Act*, **March 2005.**

The center examines the implementation of No Child Left Behind at the federal, state and local levels and points out positive and negative signs for the future.

Citizens' Commission on Civil Rights, *Choosing Better Schools: A Report on Student Transfers Under the No Child Left Behind Act*, **May 2004.**

The commission describes the early efforts to implement the school-choice provision of No Child Left Behind, calling compliance minimal.

National Conference of State Legislatures, *Task Force on No Child Left Behind: Final Report*, **February 2005.**

The panel questions the constitutionality of No Child Left Behind and calls it rigid, overly prescriptive and in need of serious revision.

Northwest Evaluation Association, *The Impact of No Child Left Behind Act on Student Achievement and Growth: 2005 Edition*, **April 2005.**

The association reports the percentage of proficient students is rising on state tests but also notes the disparity between the achievement growth of white and minority students.

Southeast Center for Teaching Quality, Unfulfilled Promise: Ensuring High Quality Teachers for Our Nation's Students, August 2004.

The center finds that rural and urban schools don't have the skills and training to recruit and retain highly qualified teachers and offers recommendations for change.

For More Information

Achieve, Inc., 1775 I St., N.W., Suite 410, Washington, DC 20006; (202) 419-1540; www.achieve.org. A bipartisan, non-profit organization created by the nation's governors and business leaders that helps states improve academic performance.

Alliance for Excellent Education, 1201 Connecticut Ave., N.W., Suite 901, Washington, DC; (202) 828-0828; www.all4ed.org. Works to assure that at-risk middle and high school students graduate prepared for college and success in life.

Center on Education Policy, 1001 Connecticut Ave., N.W., Suite 522, Washington, DC 20036; (202) 822-8065; www.cep-dc.org. Helps Americans understand the role of public education in a democracy and the need to improve academic quality.

Council of the Great City Schools, 1301 Pennsylvania Ave., N.W., Suite 702, Washington, DC 20004; (202) 393-2427; www.cgcs.org. A coalition of 65 of the nation's largest urban public school systems advocating improved K-12 education.

Editorial Projects in Education, 6935 Arlington Rd., Suite 100, Bethesda, MD 20814-5233; www.edweek.org. A nonprofit organization that publishes *Education Week*, *Teacher Magazine*, edweek.org and *Agent K-12*.

Education Commission of the States, 700 Broadway, Suite 1200, Denver, CO 80203-3460; (303) 299-3600; www.ecs.org. Studies current and emerging education issues.

The Education Trust, 1250 H St., N.W., Suite 700, Washington, DC 20005; (202) 293-1217; www2.edtrust. org/edtrust. An independent nonprofit organization working to improve the academic achievement of all students.

National Conference of State Legislatures, 7700 East First Pl., Denver, CO 80230; (303) 364-7700; www.ncsl.org. A bipartisan organization serving the states and territories.

Northwest Evaluation Association, 5885 Southwest Meadows Rd., Suite 200, Lake Oswego, OR 97035; (503) 624-1951; www.nwea.org. A national nonprofit organization dedicated to helping all children learn.

Southeast Center for Teaching Quality, 976 Airport Rd., Suite 250, Chapel Hill, NC 27514; (919) 951-0200; www.teachingquality.org. A regional association dedicated to assuring all children have access to high-quality education.

U.S. Department of Education, www.ed.gov/nclb/landing.jhtml?src=pb. Describes the provisions of the No Child Left Behind law.

Wrightslaw, www.wrightslaw.com. Provides information about effective advocacy for children with disabilities, including "Wrightslaw: No Child Left Behind."

2

Student Aid

Marcia Clemmitt

Harvard graduates celebrate at commencement on June 7, 2007. In December the university cut education costs by up to 50 percent for families that earn $120,000 to $180,000; tuition is waived for students from families earning under $60,000. Meanwhile, as merit-based scholarships replace need-based aid across the country, many low-income and minority students are finding it hard to finance their college dreams.

From *CQ Researcher*, January 25, 2008.

E ach month, Lucia DiPoi, a 24-year-old graduate of Tufts University in Boston, pays $900 toward her college debt — $65,000 in private loans, $19,000 in federal loans.

The first in her family to attend college, DiPoi blames some of her plight on her lack of financial knowledge. When grants and federal loans didn't cover enough of her fees, she took out private loans with interest rates of more than 13 percent. "How bad could it be?" she figured. [1]

Now she knows. DiPoi's loan burden is well above the average $20,000 in debt that American college graduates face, but it's not unusual. Many students from low-income families — and graduate students in particular — also face large burdens.

As the cost of higher education rises, grants for needy students have lagged behind, and more students are dependent on loans to finance their education. At the same time, worries about college costs have been reaching higher up the socioeconomic scale. In response, states and private colleges have launched new merit-based scholarships that shift some aid from the neediest students to middle- and even upper-income families. [2]

In-state tuition and fees (excluding room and board) for public, four-year schools average $6,185 for the 2007-2008 school year, up 6.6 percent from 2006-2007; out-of-state tuition averages $16,640. At private four-year schools, the average 2007-2008 tuition and fees is $23,712, up 6.3 percent from 2006-2007. [3] The cost of college has nearly doubled over the past 20 years, in inflation-adjusted dollars, and college tuition and fees have risen faster than inflation, personal income, consumer prices or even the cost of prescription drugs and health insurance. [4]

Student Debt Highest in New Mexico

College graduates in New Mexico in 2006 had an average of $28,770 in student debt, the highest of any state and almost 50 percent higher than the national average. Hawaii had the lowest average debt: $11,758 per student.

Average Student Debt by State, Class of 2006

Legend:
- Under $16,000
- $16,000-$18,999
- $19,000-$21,999
- $22,000-$24,999
- $25,000+

National Average: $19,646

* Nevada figures not available

Source: "Student Debt and the Class of 2006," The Project on Student Debt, September 2007

The increasing difficulty of paying for college and the importance of lending are bringing new attention to financial-aid issues. Congress recently passed legislation boosting the value of grants for low-income students and trimming subsidies for private education lenders. New York State Attorney General Andrew M. Cuomo reached legal settlements last year with more than two-dozen colleges where financial-aid officials had accepted kickbacks in exchange for steering students toward particular private lenders; similar investigations are ongoing in other states.

In December, pricey Harvard University — which had already waived tuition payments for students whose families earn less than $60,000 a year, announced a boon for middle-earners, cutting costs by as much as 50 percent for families that earn between $120,000 to $180,000. [5]

If the main job of financial aid is to make college education more accessible to lower-income and minority students, current financial-aid and cost trends aren't helping, some analysts say.

Three decades ago, there was a 30-percentage-point gap in college attendance between low-income students and other students, says Donald E. Heller, director of the Center for the Study of Higher Education at Pennsylvania State University. "And since that time they haven't gained any ground," he adds.

"Only 7 percent of high-school sophomores from the lowest quartile of socioeconomic status eventually earn a bachelor's degree, compared with 60 percent of those from the highest quartile," according to Associate Professor of Public Policy Susan M. Dynarski and doctoral candidate Judith Scott-Clayton, both at Harvard. "Only 12 percent of Hispanics and 16 percent of African-Americans eventually earn a B.A., compared with 33 percent of non-Hispanic whites." Moreover, the gaps persist "even among well-prepared students," so difficulties paying for college are at least partly to blame, the researchers say. [6]

Federal Pell Grants for low-income students — a big part of the money problem — have lagged behind rising costs for decades. "The purchasing power of the Pell Grant is less than half what it was in the 1970s," Heller says.

Need-based aid offered by states has been dropping in many places over the past decade, says Ross Rubenstein, associate professor of public administration at Syracuse University. While need-based grants are still the largest share overall, a growing proportion of state grants are merit-based scholarships, a "huge middle-class entitlement" that shifts the focus of aid programs away from expanding access for the neediest, he says.

Merit aid has virtues, though. Reserving some scholarship aid for top students might improve student achievement in high school, Rubenstein explains, noting it has been shown to have modest positive effects on student achievement in Georgia, for example, which launched the first state merit program, HOPE, in 1993. "I wouldn't want to see a merit-based system replace a need-based one, but it has its place," he says.

A certain level of merit aid might not be a problem, Heller says; he cites Indiana's program, which has been successful in promising aid to all students who graduate from high school with a C average. "But I would caution against" including additional criteria "such as SAT scores or requiring higher grade averages," he adds, because of racial gaps in SAT scores and the general discouraging effect such criteria have on low-income students who are hesitant about their college chances anyway.

Merit aid may create heavier loan burdens for low-income students. The University of Maryland recently discovered that low-income students were graduating with more debt than middle- and high-income students and concluded that its grant program — which had 60 percent merit-based awards — should be revamped to include more need-based grants. [7]

The biggest trend in college financing is the heavy reliance on loans, which make up about 70 percent of higher-education financing today. The loans include both federally guaranteed and subsidized loan programs and, increasingly, completely private, non-federally subsidized loans with much higher interest rates. (*See graphs, p. 29.*)

"Loans are ubiquitous as more and more students are borrowing," says Laura W. Perna, an associate professor at the University of Pennsylvania Graduate School of Education.

The federal government makes some loans directly and subsidizes private lenders to handle others. The private lenders came under fire last year, as reports surfaced of outsized bonuses paid even at many nonprofit lenders and sweetheart deals that some lenders gave college financial-aid officials who steered students toward their services.

"Ninety percent of students who receive loans choose their lender based on their schools' recommendation," according to the Center for American Progress, a liberal think tank. With education debt high and rising, "stu-

Costs Rose for State and Private Colleges

The average tuition and fees for private four-year colleges more than doubled in the past 30 years, to nearly $24,000 in the 2007-08 academic year.* During the same period, costs also doubled at public two-year schools and nearly tripled at public four-year institutions.

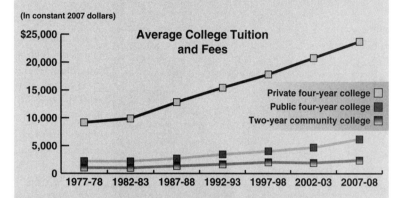

(In constant 2007 dollars)

Average College Tuition and Fees

Private four-year college □
Public four-year college ■
Two-year community college ▨

1977-78   1982-83   1987-88   1992-93   1997-98   2002-03   2007-08

* Tuition and fees constitute about two-thirds of the total budget for students at private four-year colleges but are just over one-third of the total budget for in-state students in public four-year colleges and less than 20 percent for public two-year college students.

Source: "Trends in College Pricing 2007," The College Board, 2007

dents should be able to count on their schools for impartial and helpful advice as they navigate a complicated and stressful process." Instead, "kickbacks" and "conflict of interest" put students at risk of doing business only with lenders who have offered the most blandishments to their colleges, the center said. [8]

But many college officials argue that students are getting excellent service from lenders and could suffer if they switched to direct government loans or if the number of private lenders was cut. "Private lenders tend to be more efficient, have better technology and are able to provide better services that aren't available from the government," said Seamus Harreys, dean of student financial services at Boston's Northeastern University. [9]

Disputes over private vs. public lending aside, however, mushrooming education debt is a trend that troubles many because of the financial burdens loans place on graduates.

Students don't understand the implications of the loans they apply for, according to the Federation of State PIRGs (public interest research groups). "The loan industry recommends that graduates . . . dedicate no more than 8 percent of their income to student-loan

AP Photo/Richard Drew

New York State Attorney General Andrew M. Cuomo, right, announces on May 31, 2007, an agreement between Columbia University and the National Association of Student Financial Aid Administrators to curtail improper student-aid practices. Investigations by Cuomo last year forced 10 private lenders to stop kickbacks to aid officials at two-dozen colleges in exchange for steering students to their firms. Similar investigations are ongoing in other states, including Missouri, Iowa and Pennsylvania.

repayment," according to PIRG analysts Tracey King and Ivan Frishberg, but students themselves "expected to contribute an average of 10.7 percent of future income." Furthermore, "students with larger debts more significantly overestimated the percentage of their income they could afford" for repayment. [10]

As students, college officials and political leaders wonder how future students will pay for higher education, here are some of the questions being asked:

Has the right balance been struck between merit-based and need-based aid?

Over the past decade and a half, public and private student-aid programs have increased the proportion of scholarships based on academic and athletic merit, many going to middle- and upper-class students. As a result, financially needy students have seen their share of the student-aid pie shrink.

Critics of the shift argue that achieving equity in education demands mostly need-based aid, since low-income and minority students still lag far behind in college attendance. But supporters of increased merit-based aid say merit scholarships spur students to work harder in high school and that, with college costs soaring, middle-class students deserve financial help, too.

Low-income students still get the most financial aid, but the share of aid claimed by students from wealthier families has increased in recent years. The Indianapolis-based Lumina Foundation for Education found that between 1995 and 2000 grants to students from families earning $40,000 or less increased by 22 percent, compared with a 45 percent boost for families making $100,000 or more. [11]

Many education analysts say merit-based grants, unlike need-based grants, don't increase low-income and minority access to higher education.

An adequate pool of need-based college aid actually improves high-school graduation rates, says Ed St. John, a professor of higher education at the University of Michigan. "Living in a state with more need-based aid increases the chances a low-income student will graduate," he says. "If a sophomore sees that there's aid, there's a bigger chance he'll finish."

"Poor kids don't think they can go to college, and their schools don't have the counselors" needed to explain how they can, St. John explains. A widely publicized need-based aid program can counter that perception. "Knowing you can afford to go allows people to do things they wouldn't do otherwise," he adds.

Merit-based aid does little to expand access for low-income students, says Rubenstein of Syracuse. "By targeting people with a B average, you're mostly targeting students who would go to college anyway," he says. State merit-based aid mainly helps the state keep its better students at in-state colleges, he says.

Often financed by lotteries, many state merit programs draw their funding from the mostly low-income people who play the games, while the aid flows mostly toward middle- and upper-income students, says Rubenstein. "There's no question that it's highly regressive."

Under a recent Massachusetts proposal, for example, more than 50 percent of students in the state's wealthiest school districts would qualify for scholarships compared to less than 10 percent in the poorest districts, according to Penn State's Heller. [12]

Similarly, private colleges' merit aid also boosts mainly the middle and upper classes. "If the private colleges don't refocus more dollars on students with high-level needs, they are going to become places that are totally closed to low-income students," said Sandy Baum, an economics professor at Skidmore College in Saratoga Springs, N.Y., and senior policy analyst for the New York-based College Board. [13]

Many low-income students are shut out from merit-based grants mainly because they attend very-low-performing schools, says Sara Goldrick-Rab, an assistant professor of education policy at the University of Wisconsin, Madison. "Essentially it's holding kids responsible for the poor K-12 program," she says.

Indeed, a recent analysis of a Michigan test that determines who gets state merit aid found that "schools with high numbers of minority students didn't even have the curriculum for the kids to take the whole test that would qualify them for the merit aid," says the University of Michigan's St. John.

Merit-based aid advocates contend that it exists for good reasons — to help deserving students get an education without plunging their families into debt. The high cost of college increasingly forces middle-class families to seek financial aid.

"The reality is even parents who work hard to save are coming up short" of college costs, said Mary Beth Moran, a financial adviser in Bloomingdale, Ill. [14]

"Middle-class families are being squeezed out," said Sharon Williams, college adviser at Elgin Academy in

Loans Are Now Biggest Source of Aid

In the past three decades federal education grants have been overtaken by federally guaranteed low-interest loans. Today, the ratio of loans to grants is seven to two, compared to just three to two in 1975-76 (top). Meanwhile, high-interest, wholly private loans have emerged in the past decade, largely in response to heavy marketing and the long, confusing federal loan applications. They represented 18 percent of all student loans in 2004-05, or double the percentage four years earlier (bottom).

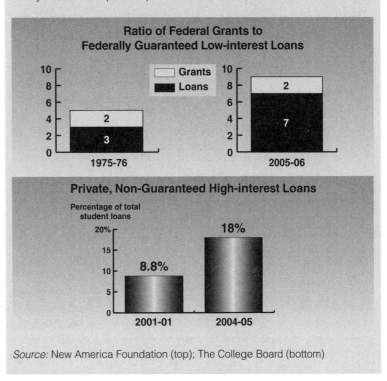

Source: New America Foundation (top); The College Board (bottom)

Elgin, Ill. "Need-based scholarships will not be there for them." [15]

Because of a growing perceived need among the middle class, but also because the public often doesn't like government programs that offer assistance without requiring something in return, merit-based aid is more politically popular, says William Doyle, an assistant professor of higher education at Vanderbilt University. That attitude shows up in public-opinion polls, he says. "People want reciprocity; they don't like entitlement-based grants."

"Mainly in response to middle-class demands, there was a huge surge in the 1990s and early 2000s of merit-based aid," says Rubenstein at Syracuse. The trend "has

States Providing More Grants

State grants to students have risen markedly over the past decade. Need-based grants totaled nearly $5 billion during the 2005-06 school year, more than a 50 percent increase over 1995-96. Merit based grants more than tripled, totaling about $1.9 billion in 2005-06.

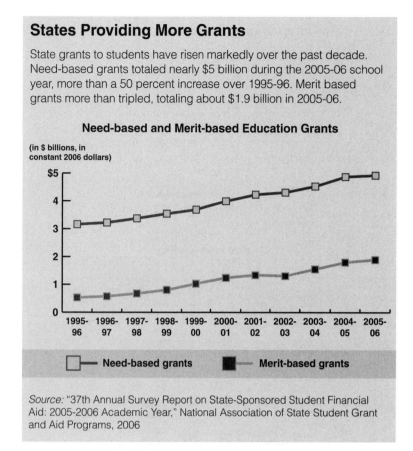

Need-based and Merit-based Education Grants

Source: "37th Annual Survey Report on State-Sponsored Student Financial Aid: 2005-2006 Academic Year," National Association of State Student Grant and Aid Programs, 2006

arships. Because their requirements are clear and simple, merit programs may encourage even low-income students to persist in preparing for college, explains the University of Pennsylvania's Perna. By comparison, the lengthy, complex applications of need-based programs "just leave a big question mark," as students remain in doubt for many months about whether they'll qualify for enough aid to allow them to afford their chosen school, she adds.

Georgia's HOPE Scholarships "provide an incentive for kids to work harder" in high school because they know for a fact they can claim the money if they attain the required grade average, says Rubenstein. High-school grades increased and not just because of grade inflation after the scholarship was launched, he says. In Georgia, many lower-income "kids really thought they couldn't go before the HOPE Scholarship established a simple rule: 'If I get that B, I can go,' " he says.

tapered off a bit, but I don't expect it to end. It's an extremely popular entitlement and hard to take away."

Some argue that merit-based aid ensures universities attract higher-quality students. "The incremental or marginal students that we have gained through [need-based] federal programs likely have extremely poor records with respect to college completion and probably shouldn't have been in college in the first place," said Richard Vedder, a former professor of economics at Ohio University and director of the Washington, D.C.-based Center on College Affordability and Productivity. [16]

While merit-based aid is skewed toward the middle class, it has helped students from poor families, Rubenstein points out. Georgia's merit-based HOPE Scholarship, for example, still increases aid to low-income students. With HOPE money in the system, all students receive substantially more aid than they did previously, he says. [17]

Merit-based programs have set criteria and specified award amounts, compared with most need-based schol-

Merit-based scholarships can be designed to be more equitable, says St. John. For example, Texas has a plan in which state colleges must accept the top 10 percent of the graduating class from any state high school, he says. Besides giving students from low-income and high-minority schools an equal shot, the program indirectly encourages the schools to improve, he says.

Has the right balance been struck between grants and loans?

Since the late 1970s, federal student aid has been shifting from grants toward loans, most provided by private lenders that the government guarantees against loss should students default. Furthermore, over the last decade limits on the amount of guaranteed-loan funding each student can claim have lagged behind college costs, and more lenders have sought out student customers. As a result, more students also have turned to fully private loans — offered at regular consumer interest rates, unsubsidized by the government — as part of their college-funding package.

Forty years ago, the belief that expanding college access resulted in substantial public benefit led to the establishment of most federal student-aid grant programs, says James C. Hearn, a professor of higher education at the University of Georgia. Educators and officials reasoned that students shouldn't have to bear all their college costs because education serves many other goals, such as creating smarter voters and a more civilized and cultured citizenry, he says.

Since then, however, the reigning political philosophy has shifted toward economic conservatism. Today, the financial-aid landscape is shaped by the idea that education delivers primarily personal, not public, benefits, and that idea favors loans, Hearn says.

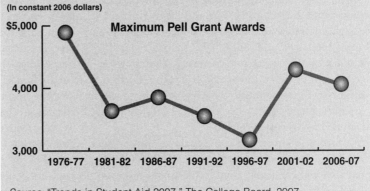

Size of Maximum Pell Grant Has Declined

The maximum Pell Grant award has declined nearly 20 percent in the past 30 years. The top grant today covers about 32 percent of average tuition, fees and room and board at public four-year colleges and 13 percent at private four-year schools. In 1986-87, maximum Pell Grants covered 52 percent of the costs at public four-year schools and 21 percent at private four-year institutions. Pell Grants are for low-income students and do not have to be repaid.

(In constant 2006 dollars)

Maximum Pell Grant Awards

$5,000 — 4,000 — 3,000

1976-77 1981-82 1986-87 1991-92 1996-97 2001-02 2006-07

Source: "Trends in Student Aid 2007," The College Board, 2007

Nevertheless, many analysts say that expanding college access to those who couldn't afford it on their own should remain the key goal of financial aid and that grants, not loans, are the best tool.

"The fact is that loans of any kind don't improve college access for low-income students," says Heller of Penn State. For one thing, lower-income families tend to be more loan-averse and often lack the experience and information to successfully navigate a loan-based system, he explains.

"Limits on borrowing also are among the factors that make the loan-heavy aid system not work for low-income kids," whose total college-funding needs are greater and often outstrip the slow-rising limit on federally guaranteed loans, says the University of Michigan's St. John.

Today's graduates carry an average of about $20,000 in education debt, says Amaury Nora, a professor of education leadership and cultural studies at the University of Houston. (*See map, p. 26.*) Add to that credit-card debt for books and meals, and "a lot of times students say, 'I can't keep this up,' " he adds. Debt often becomes a compelling additional reason students leave college, initially intending to return. But in a 10-to-15-year study of such "stop outs," only a handful of students who left

actually returned, contrary to conventional wisdom in education-policy circles, Nora says. "Once they're out, they're pretty much gone."

Nonetheless, loans really expand the reach of federal aid in dramatic ways simply by adding more money to the student-aid system than taxpayers would ever pony up in the form of grants, Hearn says. Because there are finite resources for grants, other funding must be found, he says.

Loans also "provide a better opportunity for choice of college for upper- and middle-income students," says Heller.

The current loan-grant balance "is still a pretty good system for middle-class kids," says St. John.

Graduates who complain that education debt is an unfair burden ignore the benefits they've reaped, argues Radley Balko, a senior editor at the libertarian Reason magazine, citing two medical students profiled on CBS News as burdened with a "mountain" of debt. The two were shown drinking Starbucks coffee and Vitaminwater, pricey habits, in Balko's opinion, for a couple so worried about expenses. He estimated their lifetime earnings would be $8.2 million, or "a tidy $7.7 million profit on the investment they made in their education. If only everyone had it so rough." [18]

Many analysts say a thoughtful balancing of loans and grants, plus greater flexibility on loan repayment, is the fairest way to distribute education funds. To make paybacks fairer, Congress passed the College Cost Reduction and Access Act in 2007, establishing new payback schedules for direct federal student loans that are "income-contingent," or based on graduates' earnings.

Basing the system mainly on income-contingent loans, instead of grants or non-income-contingent loans, could ultimately simplify applying for aid and perhaps do away with the complicated needs-analysis financial-aid application that scares off some students today, says Donald Hossler, a professor of educational leadership and policy studies at Indiana University, Bloomington. Need would be taken into account after graduation, instead of before enrollment, with high-earning graduates required to pay back their loans fully and low earners entitled to reduced payment.

An income-contingent payment scheme also might enable more students to select lower-paying, service-oriented careers like teaching, which some avoid because of worries about paying off their debts, Hossler says.

If money is tight, federal aid heavy on grants and income-contingent loans might be reserved for students in fields deemed to produce more public benefit — such as inner-city teaching — while students in fields that yield more individual benefit, like business, could rely more on traditional loans, says the University of Georgia's Hearn. "You can try to target your subsidies to public good" so taxpayers are on the hook only for educations that provide needed public services at a modest cost, he adds.

However, "some research shows we're not very good at playing the market" with targeted subsidies, Hearn says. In the 1960s and '70s, for example, the government used financial aid to lure people into nursing and engineering. But by the time the subsidies kicked in, market forces had erased the personnel shortages.

Do private lenders deliver good value for taxpayers and students?

Government-backed student loans come in two varieties: direct loans and loans offered by private lenders the government pays to participate in the program and guarantees against loss should students default. Debate has long raged over whether the government should remedy perceived shortcomings in the federally backed loan program by beefing up its own direct-loan programs and making it

tougher and less lucrative for private lenders to participate.

Supporters of retaining a large number of private lenders to students say the lenders aren't getting rich at the program's expense.

"No abnormal profits are being made in student loans," said Kevin Bruns, executive director of the industry group America's Student Loan Providers. Trimming federal subsidies to lenders could hurt students if banks respond by eliminating bonuses like discounted interest rates for payments that are made electronically or on time or waivers of some borrowers' fees, he said. [19]

Replacing loans made by private lenders with more direct government loans "would result in massive waste as well as burdensome red tape for students and parents," said John Berlau, a fellow in economic policy at the Competitive Enterprise Institute, a free-enterprise-oriented think tank. "The reason schools, with both programs to choose from, have stayed with the banks is that the banks offer the private sector's level of service," he said. "Some 600 schools have stopped participating in direct lending, and surveys of schools cite poor service as the primary reason." [20]

Some economic conservatives argue that all student aid should come in the form of private-sector loans or other private financial arrangements.

"The intellectual justification for expanded federal student-loan programs is extremely weak" because they've attracted only marginal students and encouraged colleges to be bigger spenders, said Vedder, at the Center on College Affordability and Productivity. "It is not clear that higher education has major positive spillover effects that justify government subsidies in the first place, and the private loan market that can handle anything from automobile loans to billion-dollar government bond sales can handle providing financial assistance to students." [21]

Late last year, lawmakers approved requiring lenders to bid for a limited number of spots in the loans-to-parents program, but private lenders generally oppose the move. Such an auction could backfire because unreliable lenders who give bad service might lowball the bidding and end up with all the business, said Bruns. "An auction creates that problem where everything is based on price," he said. [22]

But advocates of a strengthened government role argue that allowing large numbers of private lenders to offer federally backed loans costs a lot and is of questionable benefit.

The large number of lenders competing for student-loan business is evidence that private lenders have long received "excess subsidies," according to Michael Dannenberg, director of education policy at the liberal New America Foundation "There are reasons Sallie Mae's [Student Loan Marketing Association's] stock has increased by 2,000 percent in the last decade, and those reasons are a government guarantee against risk and very large government subsidies." [23]

Furthermore, the fact that the government guarantees private lenders 99 percent of a loan's value if a student defaults gives lenders "little reason to put resources into collecting payments from delinquent borrowers," he said. [24]

The idea that having more lenders in the program improves customer service through competition doesn't make sense, says Jason Delisle, research director for education policy at the New America Foundation. The loans are an identical commodity offered under government rules, so lenders have little room to customize loans or services, he says. In addition, lenders generally hold the loans on their own books for only a few months before selling them.

Because the subsidies are not market-based but negotiated by lenders and members of Congress, the private loan program has been plagued with "influence peddling" and "a dangerous amount of political influence," says Delisle, who sat in on discussions with lenders as a budget analyst for Sen. Judd Gregg, R-N.H.

"Without a market mechanism to set student-loan provider subsidy rates, banks will continue to inundate Congress and its staff with papers, meetings and phone calls pleading that a cut in that arbitrary subsidy rate would be 'catastrophic' to the lending business and that a lender-subsidy reduction means loans will no longer be made available to students," said Delisle. [25]

Education lenders complain to Congress that higher subsidies are necessary for their business to be profitable but often say the opposite to business associates, Delisle charges. "When Congress began considering this most recent round of subsidy cuts, Sallie Mae representatives told me and other congressional staffers that for the company to continue making federal student loans at the proposed lower subsidy rates, Sallie Mae would have to make the loans through its charity organization," he says.

"In other words, the proposed and now enacted subsidy cut" — in September 2007 Congress cut the subsidies by about half — "makes the federal student-loan business unprofitable, according to Sallie Mae," Delisle says. "But try to square that position" with recent Sallie Mae comments to a group that wanted to buy out the company. The potential buyers were worried that lower government subsidies would harm profitability, but "reports have those close to Sallie Mae" saying that the subsidy cuts' "effects on the company's earnings will be 'de minimis,'" Delisle says.

The buyout deal ultimately collapsed, however, and the company has recently reiterated to the U.S. Securities and Exchange Commission that Congress' 2007 subsidy cuts will substantially reduce profits from new loans and could potentially make the loans unprofitable. [26]

BACKGROUND

Gradual Beginnings

Financial aid to needy students dates back to 13th-century Europe. [27] But scholarship aid always has had mixed goals, which have complicated its development over the years. Some view student aid as mainly a boost for gifted but low-income individuals; others see it as a broad, public initiative for expanding access to education to the poor and to minorities. Many private and state universities have viewed it primarily as a means of boosting their own reputations by attracting higher-caliber students.

The first private colleges in America opened in the 17th century. Most then gave many grants to expand their enrollment and reputations. At Harvard in the 1700s endowed scholarships paid about half of school expenses for between a quarter and a third of students. New York University gave substantial grants to about half the students from the time it opened in 1831 through the mid-19th century; the grants enabled many to attend tuition-free.

But as private universities gathered students and solidified their reputations — and college education remained confined to the elite few — the days of generous grants waned.

Meanwhile, in the early days of state-funded colleges, financial aid as such was scarce, says Hearn of the University of Georgia. Instead, the states provided a virtually free education to all comers as a public good, he says.

While the picture varies from school to school, by the 1929-30 academic year, grant aid amounted to only 2.5 percent of U.S. college costs, including both tuition and living costs. Even after the Depression, when college charges fell and grant aid rose, grants amounted only to 3.6 percent of college costs by 1939-40.

CHRONOLOGY

1960s-1970s *As college prices rise, Congress creates loans and grants.*

1965 Federal Family Education Loan Program — then called the Guaranteed Student Loan Program — is launched.

1972 Congress creates Sallie Mae — the Student Loan Marketing Association — and establishes federal grants for low-income students, later named for Sen. Claiborne Pell, D-R.I.

1976 Congress allows states to issue tax-exempt bonds for education lending.

1977 College loans total $1.8 billion.

1978 Congress expands eligibility for Pell Grants to some middle-income students and makes federally guaranteed loans available to all income levels.

1979 Congress removes the cap on its subsidies to private education lenders, ensuring them good returns.

1980s *College costs rise, and pressure builds for aid to the middle class. With private lenders assured of high subsidies, loan volume explodes.*

1980 Parent Loans for Undergraduate Students — PLUS loans — allow parents at all income levels to borrow.

1986 Federal payments reimbursing lenders for education-loan defaults total more than $1 billion. . . . Private lenders barred from offering inducements to borrow, such as free appliances.

1989 College loans total $12 billion.

1990s *Private lenders begin marketing directly to students and parents. Merit-based scholarships proliferate in states.*

1990 A large guarantee organization, the Higher Education Assistance Foundation, collapses from loan defaults at for-profit colleges.

1992 Congress and the Clinton administration establish the federal Direct Lending Program to compete with private education lenders.

1993 Georgia uses lottery receipts to fund new merit-based HOPE scholarships for families with incomes below $66,000.

1994 College attendance peaks among welfare recipients.

1995 Georgia removes income restriction on HOPE Scholarships.

1996 Student loans total $30 billion. . . . Welfare-reform law directs low-income women toward jobs and away from college.

1997 Congress increases middle-class aid with tax credits, tax-free college savings accounts and tax deductions for student-loan interest.

2000s *More private lenders offer student loans at market rates without government guarantees, as rising tuitions see wealthier families seeking loans.*

2000 Private, non-government-backed loans total $4 billion. . . . Georgia allows HOPE Scholarship recipients to accept Pell Grants.

2002 Need-blind merit grants account for 24 percent of state education grants, up from 10 percent in 1992.

2005 Congress bars students from discharging most fully private education loans in bankruptcy.

2006 Non-federally guaranteed private loans for college education total over $16 billion. . . . Harvard waives tuition payments for families earning less than $60,000.

2007 New York Attorney General Andrew Cuomo investigates colleges that accept favors to steer students toward specific lenders. . . . Harvard expands tuition breaks to families earning up to $180,000. . . . Congress cuts subsidies to private lenders, ups Pell Grant funding and institutes income-dependent repayment for direct government loans. . . . Private investors back out of deal to buy student-lending giant Sallie Mae, which faces rising defaults after extending loans to risky borrowers.

2008 University Financial Services in Clearwater, Fla., settles charges it deceptively used Ohio University's logo and mascot to market loans.

Expanding Access

With the end of World War II, a new boom in financial aid began, along with new ideas about who would go to college. By the mid-20th century, large numbers of students became the first in their families to attend college.

In 1944, as the war was approaching its end, Congress enacted the Servicemen's Readjustment Act — the so-called G.I. Bill of Rights. As returning veterans signed up for classes, student aid quickly grew as a proportion of college costs, although the spurt was temporary. By 1949-50, student grants amounted to 55 percent of costs. That share fell to 14 percent by the 1959-60 school year, after G.I. benefits tailed off.

At the same time, colleges, especially state universities, were raising their fees — albeit gradually — after many decades of subsidizing all students by charging very low tuition.

"In the 1950s and 1960s, people began saying, 'We're subsidizing people who would go to college anyway. So why not charge something and aid students who can't afford it?' " says Hearn. Accordingly, at public colleges a new era of higher tuitions offset by financial aid for lower-income students replaced the old system under which states heavily subsidized lower tuition for all students in public universities.

With tuitions on the rise, the federal government as well as individual colleges launched new aid programs in the late 1950s. The new programs were influenced by the growing interest in seeing more students attend college, especially after the Soviet Union highlighted its national scientific prowess with the launch of the Sputnik satellite in 1957.

In 1954, a group of 95 private colleges and universities, mostly in the Northeast, formed the College Scholarship Service. Based on the philosophy that college aid should be largely based on need, the group set about developing standards and tools the schools could use to collect and assess a family's financial information and determine how much aid students required. [28]

In 1958, the National Defense Education Act financed low-interest college loans, with debt cancellation for students who became teachers after graduation. In 1965, Congress launched several aid programs, including a talent search to identify low-income students with academic ability and College Work-Study to subsidize schools' employment of needy students. [29]

By 1966-67, the poorest quarter of college students were getting 94 percent of their college costs paid for, 44 percent of it through grants, says Rupert Wilkinson, a former professor of history and American studies at England's University of Sussex. The aid dropped off steeply for the second-poorest quarter of students, however; only 38 percent of that group's needs were covered, 15 percent of it by grants, he says.

In 1972, Congress created Basic Grants, later renamed for Sen. Claiborne Pell, D-R.I. Initially proposed by the Nixon administration, the grants were designed to offer low-income students a basic subsidy large enough to ensure that they saw college as a possibility, but not so large that students wouldn't need to tap other sources.

Borrowers and Lenders

In addition to the various aid programs launched in 1965, Congress created the Federal Family Education Loan Program (FFELP) — then called the Guaranteed Student Loan Program — to offer federally backed loans through private lenders whom the government insured against default.

In the 1960s and early '70s student-lending programs didn't garner much attention, since college costs were still relatively low. Today, however, about 70 percent of federal student aid is in the form of government-guaranteed loans, while only about 20 percent is in the form of grants. Another 5 percent of aid is in the form of tax benefits, and the rest comes through various channels such as support for work-study programs. [30]

The growing importance of loans to students has become controversial over the last two decades. A "funding gap" between tuition and grant aid began in the early 1980s, "and that's where you begin to see students relying more on loans," says Karen Miksch, an assistant professor of higher education and law at the University of Minnesota. Since then, the funding gap has grown exponentially, she says.

Furthermore, with tuition rising and more students aspiring to college, middle-class families, which didn't qualify for public need-based grants, were clamoring for aid.

In 1979-80, Pell Grants covered 99 percent of costs. Today a Pell Grant covers only 36 percent of tuition and on-campus room and board at the average four-year public institution, By the 1990s the gap between a Pell Grant and tuition at a public school was $4,000; today, it's more than $6,000, Miksch says.

Low-Income Students Unaware of Aid

Clearer information is needed

College dreams for U.S. students — rich and poor — are at the highest levels ever. But when it comes to attendance and graduation, low-income students lag as far behind the middle class as they did 30 years ago.

More than 90 percent of students in all demographic groups now hope to attend college — the same expectation level for high-school graduation just a few years ago, says James C. Hearn, a professor of higher education at the University of Georgia. But while minority and low-income kids have quickly caught up to middle-class expectations, "big attainment gaps remain between what minority and low-income students aspire to do and what they actually do," he says.

For some of the students who hope to go to college but don't, the availability of aid is not the real problem, says Hearn. "Given the aid that's out there, there are still fewer low-income and minority students attending college than you'd expect," he says.

Some of the barriers between low-income students and college, such as bad schools and difficult family situations, are well-known and intractable. But many researchers are pointing to a hitherto unnoticed problem that's easier to fix:

Low-income students and their families are less likely to know that aid is available for them, possibly causing many to give up on their college dreams.

"It really relates to how people grow up and whether they think of themselves as being able to go or not," says Ed St. John, a professor of higher education at the University of Michigan.

While middle- and upper-class students and their families believe college is in the future and prepare for it, many lower-income students doubt they can make it. "And if you can't imagine being able to pay for college, why would you prepare for it?" asks Karen Miksch, an assistant professor of higher education and law at the University of Minnesota.

Research shows that "middle- and upper-class kids get information from a whole variety of sources," says Sara Goldrick-Rab, an assistant professor of education policy at the University of Wisconsin, Madison, including the Internet, high-school counselors and college-educated family friends. But lower-income students, most of whom attend schools lacking guidance counselors, rely mainly on friends and family with little college experience, she says.

"You're looking at two-thirds of the cost that now has to come from someplace else," Miksch adds.

For most, that "someplace else" is the private sector — specifically federally guaranteed private loans offered to both students and parents through several programs, such as federal Parent Loans for Undergraduate Students (PLUS), created in 1980.

Questions about how private lenders work in this arena stem mainly from the way the government pays them to participate, says the New America Foundation's Delisle. When the program started, no banks were willing to lend to college students, he says, so Congress guaranteed lenders against default and also provided generous subsidies to entice lenders into the game. Because the government isn't set up to do the work of a bank, it uses private lenders' infrastructure to make and manage the loans.

Driven by concerns that not all students would get access to loans, Congress allowed as many lenders as pos-

sible to participate in the program and set subsidies high enough to attract many lenders.

Beginning in the 1980s, however, concerns grew in Congress about whether private lenders manipulated the system to push students into inadvisable loans. In 1986, Congress barred banks and other lenders from offering students "inducements" to borrow — such as toasters or other appliances. [31]

Despite tighter rules, however, by the early 1990s Congress and President Bill Clinton remained convinced that lenders were unfairly getting rich off subsidies they received for offering federally guaranteed loans. In 1992, Congress created the Federal Direct Lending Program, which makes student loans without going through private middlemen, to compete with the private lenders in FFELP. In 1993, Congress called for direct government lending to make up 60 percent of federal student loans by 1998-99.

Informing students when they're in middle school that college aid will be available to them is crucial, because when students know they can go to college, they're more likely to stay in school and take courses that will prepare them for it, says Donald E. Heller, director of the Center for the Study of Higher Education at Pennsylvania State University.

He points to Indiana's successful Twenty-first Century Scholars Program targeting low-income eighth-graders. They are told that they can attend state colleges tuition-free or receive aid to attend a private college in Indiana if they graduate high school with a 2.0 average, use no illegal drugs or alcohol, commit no crimes and enroll in college within two years of graduation. [1]

Among 2,202 students enrolled in the program, 1,752 — nearly 80 percent — enrolled in a college in the state within a year of graduation, according to the Indianapolis-based Lumina Foundation for Education. [2]

Indiana also has a program to increase parental involvement, and it has worked, says Heller. It "creates a culture of college-going" and "gives the kids an incentive to prepare themselves," he says.

Congress could enact a similar early-commitment program, pledging federal Pell Grants to eligible middle-schoolers, says Heller. "By a conservative estimate, over 75 percent of students who get a free or reduced-price school lunch ultimately will be eligible for Pell," he says. "If they

knew about that and kept working in school because of it, they'd get a grant that's more than the average tuition at a community college," he says.

The current system of applying for aid is complicated for a good reason: to target aid to the neediest students. But the complexity itself puts low-income families at a disadvantage because they are more likely to be daunted by the form and less likely to find good help to prepare it, according to a study by Susan M. Dynarski and Judith E. Scott-Clayton of Harvard University's Kennedy School of Government. Dropping the federal-aid application form from 72 questions to a more manageable 14 would result in virtually no change in eligibility for Pell Grants, they found in a recent analysis. [3]

Furthermore, programs such as Georgia's HOPE Scholarship and Social Security student benefits provide plenty of evidence that simplified aid programs can increase college enrollments significantly, they found.

---

[1] For background, see "Meeting the Access Challenge: Indiana's Twenty-first Century Scholars Program," Lumina Foundation for Education, August 2002, www.luminafoundation.org.

[2] *Ibid.*

[3] Susan M. Dynarski and Judith E. Scott-Clayton, "College Grants on a Postcard," The Hamilton Project, The Brookings Institution, February 2007. Dynarski is an associate professor of public policy at Harvard; Scott-Clayton is a doctoral student.

These moves didn't eliminate the private sector's role in the student-aid business. In fact, critics see education lenders' hot competition for borrowers as evidence that the federal subsidies remain too high.

Furthermore, nonprofit student lenders have been set up in most states, says Delisle, and "members of Congress — including Republicans — say we have to keep the subsidy high because we have to keep the nonprofits in business," although there's little evidence that those organizations serve the program any better than the hordes of private lenders.

Lenders Fight Back

When Republicans took control of Congress in 1995, they expressed dismay at the burgeoning government-run Federal Direct Lending Program. By then, 1,300 colleges — about a third of the nation's total — had switched to direct lending, taking that market share away

from private lenders. Congressional leaders pressured Clinton to slow the program's growth.

They told him he would get no other legislation passed "if he continued to push direct lending," said Robert M. Shireman, a former top aide to Sen. Paul Simon, D-Ill., who sponsored the 1993 direct-lending expansion. [32]

Clinton agreed to back off, and private lenders stepped up their efforts to regain business. For example, private lenders such as Sallie Mae offered student borrowers discounted fees and interest rates that the federal government wasn't legally permitted to match.

To attract universities, private lenders launched incentives such as the "school-as-lender" programs. In these deals, universities agree to stop offering federal direct loans to their professional- and graduate-school students and lend the money themselves, backed by a private lender. Then the university sells the loans back to the private lender for a profit.

Non-Traditional Students Face Pitfalls

Many feel disconnected from campus life

As more Americans aspire to higher education, the number of non-traditional students — active military, older workers, immigrants — has skyrocketed, causing problems for the system and the students.

The earliest large-scale federal student-aid program was the G.I. Bill of 1944, which helped World War II vets attend college by providing money and new education programs to suit these non-traditional, often older students.

Today, the Pentagon still touts education funding as a benefit of military service, but today's system may not be working as planned. Of the veterans who entered four-year colleges in 1995, only 3 percent had graduated by 2001, compared with about 30 percent of students overall. Several reasons account for this low rate. Universities don't have to refund tuition for soldiers who are pulled out in mid-semester for overseas deployment, and the schools are allowed to terminate veterans' student status if they don't immediately re-enroll when they return from deployment. [1]

Military assurances that soldiers can attend college online from their bases also may be unrealistic for many. "I don't know how they expect us to take classes in Iraq," said Alejandro Rocha, 23, a Marine from Los Angeles. "I manned Humvees and rolled around in Humvees. . . . When we were back in the U.S., we were just training and training." Consistent study wasn't possible, Rocha said. [2]

Growing numbers of today's students are older and often work to support families, but financial-aid rules and practices sometimes make it difficult for them.

"A good 40 percent of Latino students are working off-campus," for example, says Amaury Nora, a professor of education leadership and cultural studies at the University of Houston. Working off-campus — which is often a side effect of inadequate aid — distances students from college life, with serious negative effects on their ability to persist in school, Nora says. "Students who work off-campus are 36 percent more likely to drop out."

Stress and disconnection are part of the reason, he adds. Emotional stress related to juggling off-campus jobs and classes and feeling strapped for money keeps students from fully participating in class and the other activities important to college life, he says. The less connected students feel, the more likely they are to drop out.

For most middle- and upper-income students, rising tuitions will only change which schools they attend, says William Doyle, an assistant professor of higher education at Vanderbilt University in Nashville, Tenn. "But for lower-income students, the price will cause them not to go to school, to work more or to go to school part time," all non-

In 2004, for example, the University of Nebraska made such a deal with the National Education Loan Network (Nelnet) and dropped direct federal loans. "The government could not match Nelnet's offer, which would provide the university with dollars it could apply to more-generous financial-aid packages for its students," said Stephen Burd, a fellow at the New America Foundation. [33]

Realizing that banks would pay for the right to be named a preferred lender, some universities actively sought out favorable deals from private lenders in return for abandoning the federal direct loan program. In 2003, for example, Michigan State University, the second-largest participant in the government-run program, asked private lenders to compete for its business.

The university openly asked lenders, "What will you do for us if we leave direct lending?" said Barmak Nassirian, associate executive director of the American Association of Collegiate Registrars and Admissions Officers. Other colleges soon followed suit, soliciting benefits from lenders such as staff support for financial-aid offices in return for dropping out of federal direct loans. "A giant sucking sound was inaugurated with this deal," Nassirian said. [34]

Lenders also offered discounts, university staff support and other benefits as inducements for colleges to name them "preferred lenders." Students aren't required to pick a lender on a college's preferred list, but with students and parents often overwhelmed by the complexity of college applications and financing, the vast majority do.

traditional paths that lower students' chance of graduating, he says.

"Once you see yourself as somebody who's working and also going to school, your chances of graduating decrease," says Doyle. Part-time study "pushes down your credit hours, and that robs you of momentum," partly because it makes graduation seem very far off indeed. Taking six credits per semester means it takes between eight and 10 years to finish college, a daunting prospect for most, he adds.

On-campus work-study jobs are an exception to the rule, says Karen Miksch, an assistant professor of higher education and law at the University of Minnesota. Work-study students tend to say, "My job, it was great. The people were so helpful," she says. Bosses on work-study jobs tend to be another voice helping students navigate the shoals of college, she adds.

Financial-aid rules sometimes trip up working students in unexpected ways, says Sara Goldrick-Rab, an assistant professor of education policy at the University of Wisconsin, Madison. Today, students' earnings count in

Military veteran Marc Edgerly, a sophomore at George Mason University, in Fairfax, Va., says he will have $50,000 in student loans when he graduates despite federal education assistance for vets.

AP Photo/Jacquelyn Martin

the income-qualification calculation for most aid, so that low-income students could literally work their way out of qualifying for aid, even though school would still be unaffordable, she says. "You can begin to work and find yourself without aid very quickly, and if you switch to part-time school, then your aid is cut."

The financial-aid system can work against non-traditional students in other ways, particularly if they are low-income students, Goldrick-Rab said. "We do not reward their choices. We penalize students who withdraw from school temporarily by stopping their financial aid and making it hard to restart. . . . We often fail to award full credit for courses our students take at other institutions, forcing them to repeat courses two or three times." College policies "are designed with traditional students, engaged in traditional attendance patterns, in mind." [3]

[1] Aaron Glantz, "Military Recruitment Lie: Pentagon's Education Pitch Is a Scam," *The Nation*, Nov. 29, 2007.

[2] Quoted in *ibid.*

[3] Sara Goldrick-Rab, "Connecting College Access With Success," *Wisconsin School Boards Magazine*, September 2005, p. 26.

"Lenders learned that it's much easier and more effective to market their goods and services to a couple of people at an institution than to thousands of customers," said Craig Munier, director of financial aid at the University of Nebraska, Lincoln, and chair of the National Direct Student Loan Coalition. [35]

With private lenders competing hard, direct government loan growth stalled, and private loans once again became the bulk of federal student lending. In 2005, $287 billion in guaranteed private loans were outstanding, compared with $95 billion in direct loans. [36]

Meanwhile, as college costs continued to rise, private lenders also began offering non-government-guaranteed, wholly private education loans.

In 2005-06, lenders issued $17.3 billion in such loans, whose terms reflect those in regular consumer lending, including much higher interest rates than federally guaranteed loans. [37] In the past few years, the number of these loans has skyrocketed, making up 18 percent of all education loans by 2005, compared with 8.8 percent four years earlier. [38] Also in 2005, lenders won a provision in a new federal bankruptcy law that makes it extremely difficult to discharge the loans through bankruptcy, leaving many students with huge outstanding debt that will dog them for decades.

The non-guaranteed private loans aren't subject to federal rules like the 1986 ban on offering "inducements" to borrow, and lenders have taken advantage of this to expand their markets. For example, Sallie Mae offered New York's Pace University a $4-million private-

Only 12 percent of Hispanics and 16 percent of African-Americans eventually earn a B.A. degree, compared with 33 percent of non-Hispanic whites, according to researchers, who say difficulty in paying for college is partly to blame. Above, Hispanic students at Hayes High School in Birmingham, Ala. Federal Pell Grants for low-income students have lagged behind rising costs for decades.

loan fund if it would agree to make Sallie Mae its exclusive lender. [39]

Analysts say two things are driving the growth of the private loan business: limits on the size of federally guaranteed loans that fall far short of covering annual college costs and the complexity of qualifying for federally backed loans.

"Borrowers have the private people coming to them" rather than having to seek them out, says Goldrick-Rab at the University of Wisconsin, Madison. Private lenders do direct mailings, and their application forms are faster and easier to complete than the Free Application for Federal Student Aid (FAFSA) forms, she says.

But she sees a big downside. "Financial-aid officers are seeing people getting private loans before they've maxed out" their eligibility for subsidized federal loans, and they could end up owing much more than they need to, she says.

Borrowers are "drawn to the '30 seconds and you'll be approved' type of approach we're seeing more and more of now," said Robert Shireman, director of the nonprofit advocacy group Project on Student Debt. [40]

Also in the last decade-and-a-half, states have increasingly created mainly merit-based grant programs. The proportion of state aid that is merit-based rather than

need-based had grown from 13 percent in 1994-95 to 27 percent by 2004-05. [41]

State merit-based aid wins political favor because it gives more support to the middle class.

The merit-based programs' main purpose may be state economic development, however. Such grants are pitched as economic development to attract good students to the state's schools and attract new residents, says Rubenstein of Syracuse. "We don't know if it's working," he says. "But now we have states competing against each other" to offer merit aid, which may reduce the grants' effectiveness in attracting upwardly mobile families to states.

Both state and private universities are currently in a merit arms race that may be cutting down what they're willing to spend on need-based aid, says Hossler of Indiana University. College rankings such as those published by *U.S. News & World Report* give big incentives for colleges to spend heavily on financial aid that could bring in students with higher SAT scores and a higher class rank, he says. Incoming freshmen with higher scores and grades mean "you automatically go up in the rankings," while with need-based scholarships or increased spending on faculty you don't, he says.

CURRENT SITUATION

In Congress

A full slate of financial-aid issues faces the new Democratic Congress and the Bush administration. Late in 2007, lawmakers modestly raised funding for Pell Grants, reduced interest rates on direct government loans, cut subsidies for private lenders and eased some students' loan burdens by making payments dependent on their incomes. [42]

The new law increases student financial aid by more than $20 billion over five years, paid for by cutting subsidies to lenders offering government-backed student loans.

The maximum annual Pell Grant for low-income students is slated to increase from $4,310 to $5,400 over five years. The reaction to the increase from college insiders was mixed.

"The increase in the Pell Grants is unprecedented in terms of its size," said Richard Doherty, president of the Association of Independent Colleges and Universities in Massachusetts. [43]

Should Congress do more to keep private lenders in the student-loan business?

YES
John Berlau
Director, Center for Entrepreneurship,
Competitive Enterprise Institute

From the CEI Web site.

Current federal student-loan programs are not perfect. They are a mishmash of subsidies and regulations that cause distortions, not the least of which is to raise the sticker price of tuition. That doesn't mean that it's not possible for the student-aid system to get worse. And that's what a bill from Massachusetts Sen. Ted Kennedy would likely do.

Under the plan, the government would basically bribe schools with extra federal aid to participate only in the Direct Lending program — rather than have subsidized dealings with private banks — a plan that would result in massive waste as well as burdensome red tape.

When signed into law by President Bill Clinton in 1993, "direct lending" was sold as a way to actually make money for the government by cutting out the "middleman." Since the 1960s, the government has subsidized banks and other firms that lend to students to make student loans more affordable. Advocates argued that the government would spend less money and could even profit if it made the loans and collected the interest itself.

As with many claims for government programs, direct lending hasn't yielded the benefits it promised. Not only is the program not making a profit, but over the decade it has been in existence the costs of direct lending have been coming in higher than the government's initial estimates, and these cost differences have been increasing.

At the same time, subsidized loans from banks have cost the government less than their estimated costs. The White House budget for fiscal year 2006 reported that direct lending has cost the government $7 billion more than initially predicted over the last decade, while subsidized loans have cost the government $5 billion less than they were estimated to cost. In the words of a report from the respected spending watchdog Citizens Against Government Waste, "the Direct Loan program flunks out."

Direct Lending has also failed in its promise to greatly reduce default rates. Department of Education statistics show a projected default rate above 15 percent for direct loans in 2005. The rate for subsidized loans was 13 percent.

In addition, some 600 schools have stopped participating in direct lending, and surveys of schools cite poor service as the primary reason.

If we were to make federal student loans totally government run, we would lose the innovation that private firms can show in servicing their customers, even in a situation that's not the free-market ideal.

NO
Sen. Edward M. Kennedy, D-Mass.
Chairman, Senate Health, Education, Labor and
Pensions Committee

Written for *CQ Researcher*, January 2008

Millions of students face staggering tuition bills, and recent graduates juggle an average of about $20,000 in student debt. Congress should do more — not to keep private lenders in the loan business but to help students afford college and deal with debt. We should reduce unnecessary subsidies to private lenders and use the savings to increase aid to the neediest students.

Last year, Congress passed a bipartisan law raising federal aid to college students by $20 billion — the largest increase since the G.I. Bill. That's significant progress, but far from enough. Each year, 400,000 qualified students are still unable to attend a four-year college because of cost.

We should redouble efforts to ensure that the loan program is run as efficiently as possible. I'm eager to see the results of a pilot program that requires private lenders to bid for the right to offer federally subsidized parent loans. This mechanism will ensure that lenders compete for subsidies. The Congressional Budget Office estimates it will save $2 billion. If it's successful, we should expand it to all federal student loans made by private lenders.

We should examine the role of loan-guaranty agencies, which too often focus on aggressively pursuing borrowers who have defaulted, rather than preventing borrowers from defaulting. Colleges should be encouraged to switch from the privately funded loan program to the Direct Loan program, which time and again has been shown to be cheaper to taxpayers, and is untainted by the recent student-loan scandals.

Predictably, lenders claim the new law cut subsidies too deeply and is causing some to leave the program. Recently, the industry issued a flawed analysis suggesting that the privately funded loan program is less expensive than the Direct Loan program. Lenders have made these arguments before. The reality is that today more than 3,000 lenders participate in the federal program. Lenders make millions of dollars in profits from higher-interest private loans, which have grown tenfold in a decade and now account for almost a quarter of education loans.

The new law has begun to restore balance to the grossly unfair system by directing funds to students, not to banks. This year, we'll continue reform by finalizing new ethics rules. We'll ensure that banks treat students who take out private loans fairly and give them good terms and service. Most important, we'll keep the focus on students, so more can afford college and have a genuine chance at the American dream.

Joy Mueller displays her sense of humor during graduation at New York University. Mueller, who earned a master's degree in digital design, says the computer and the piggy bank signify the money she is going to have to earn with her computer skills to pay off her student loan. The average American owes $20,000 after graduation. Many students from low-income families — and graduate students in particular — also face large debt burdens.

But Shelley Steinback, former general counsel of the American Council on Education, said that the increase would not have a really significant impact, given the likelihood of inflationary costs in everything that goes into providing higher education. [44]

Furthermore, whether the maximum authorized Pell Grant amounts are available each year will depend on whether funds are available in the federal budget. Already a budget squeeze has limited the funds for the first year of the expansion. For the 2008-09 school year, the new Pell maximum was set at $4,800, but in December

Congress approved an omnibus spending bill that trims it to $4,731. [45]

For student borrowers, the new law temporarily cuts interest rates on both direct and federally guaranteed subsidized undergraduate loans — so-called Stafford loans — from 6.8 percent to 3.4 percent over four years. After the four years are up, it reverts to a higher rate, because Congress could not find a way to pay for a longer-lasting cut. And that draws a skeptical response from many congressional Republicans.

"Reducing student-loan interest rates is a good sound bite," but the per-student savings will be small; it "may be one latte, it may be two lattes. It's kind of hard to tell with today's market for coffee," said Wyoming Sen. Michael Enzi, top-ranking Republican on the Senate Health, Education, Labor and Pensions Committee. [46]

The new law also establishes the income-contingent loan repayment advocated by groups such as the Project on Student Debt for direct federal loans to students — not parents — and offers loan forgiveness for some graduates in public-service-oriented jobs in schools, charities and some government service.

Under income-based repayment, set to begin in July 2009, student-loan repayments in the direct lending program will be capped at a percentage of income, and most remaining balances will be canceled after 25 years. No payments will be required for people earning less than 150 percent of the federal poverty level — about $31,000 for a family of four — and payments will increase on a sliding scale above that level, with the highest earners' payments capped at 15 percent of family income. The plan will be available to all students, including those already holding the loans.

Public-service workers in both government and non-government organizations can have their loan debt from the government direct-lending program canceled after 10 years if they've made all the payments and been consistently employed in public service.

Meanwhile, loan experts say that even loan programs with lower student burdens probably won't improve college access much for lower-income students. And that still remains the goal of many higher-education analysts and advocates.

Willingness to borrow varies across groups, with low-income and minority families and students worrying more about the risks of loans, says the University of Pennsylvania's Perna.

In addition to concerns about filling out complicated loan applications and being able to repay in the future, many low-income and minority students know neighbors and family members who didn't complete college and are saddled with hefty loans they must repay on a high-school graduate's wages.

"The biggest problem is this uncertainty about the return on investment," and "part of this concern is definitely justified," Perna says. "Low-income and minority students are less likely to finish," while those who graduate often leave their old neighborhoods, skewing perceptions among remaining families, who only see dropouts around them.

Loan Scandals

Law enforcement authorities as well as lawmakers continue to take a keen interest in education aid following reports of illegal activities by lenders. [47]

Beginning in late 2006 and accelerating last year, reports surfaced of financial-aid administrators accepting payoffs and luxury gifts — like hefty consulting fees and Caribbean trips — from education lenders, presumably in exchange for listing the lenders as "preferred" in college financial-aid material. The flurry of stories stemmed from a massive investigation conducted by New York Attorney General Cuomo into what he called "an unholy alliance" between college officials and lenders involving kickbacks and other inducements for colleges to steer students toward certain lenders.

Indeed, financial-aid directors at Columbia University and the University of Southern California reportedly sat on the governing board of a New Jersey company, Student Loan Xpress, while reaping profits from selling company stock. [48]

Ironically, some of the revelations came from student journalists at the University of Texas, Austin. They found evidence that their school's financial-aid office kept tabs on how many gifts, "lunches, breakfasts and extracurricular functions" loan companies offered the university staff and factored the gifts into its decisions about which lenders to recommend. The office's director was placed on leave in April 2007 when he was found to own at least 1,500 shares in the parent company of Student Loan Xpress, one of the lenders the university recommended. [49]

In April 2007 Cuomo announced the first settlements related to his investigation. More than two-dozen colleges and 10 lenders have signed pledges to abide by a new code of conduct that increases disclosure requirements on college-lending practices and bans gifts and compensation from lenders to college officials. [50] Colleges and lenders also have paid monetary settlements of more than $15 million as restitution to borrowers or as seed money for loan-education funds.

Investigations are ongoing in some other states.

Alarmed that Iowa students have a high debt burden — estimated at an average $22,926 for 2006 graduates, sixth-highest in the country — officials in 2007 investigated the nonprofit Iowa Student Loan Liquidity Corp., which the state created in 1979 to help make guaranteed loans available. [51] By 2007, the corporation was the state's dominant lender, with $3.3 billion in outstanding loans. Last fall, with the state attorney general investigating the agency's business practices, some Iowa lawmakers threatened to bar it from raising money for loans by issuing tax-free bonds. [52]

A similar nonprofit, the Pennsylvania Higher Education Assistance Agency, is also under scrutiny by state auditors after giving its senior employees $7 million in bonuses since 2004; the agency's chief executive resigned in October.

The Missouri Higher Education Agency also has paid millions of dollars in perks to senior executives. "They did not act like a state agency at all" but had "the mindset that they were a for-profit business," said state auditor Susan Montee. [53]

OUTLOOK

Generation Debt

As college costs soar, helping students pay for college will remain high on the agenda in the states and in Washington.

"We're at the intersection of two really important trends bumping against each other" that may change approaches to education finance, says Vanderbilt's Doyle. "One is the increasing importance of postsecondary education to attain a middle-class lifestyle." The other is a "bulge in the demographic pipeline," with the children of baby boomers — the baby-boom "echo" — set to create by 2009 the biggest generation ever with college aspirations.

Public pressure from all income groups for relief on college costs will only grow, and that likely means pressure on colleges to slow cost increases, says Doyle. "One thing we know is that states won't be doing a big tax increase" any time soon, he says. "So the question will be asked, 'Do the costs have to go up this fast?'"

"A couple of years of double-digit tuition increases and kids not getting the classes they need" will bring political pressure on the government and colleges to act, Doyle adds.

"Can institutions keep raising tuition without resistance? Probably not," says the University of Georgia's Hearn. "We may be hitting the point where public opposition" becomes a big factor in tuition decisions. "There may be some strong, strong resistance from students and families."

Already, the burden of education loans is heavy for many graduates in all income brackets, says Doyle. "I'm always surprised at the level of debt" even for "students from higher-income families," he says.

Most political trends point to a continuing evolution toward a system of loans and merit-based aid that helps the middle class, says Penn State's Heller. Political, not financial, imperatives are driving that shift, he emphasizes. "The merit-based aid that has cropped up in states in recent years could just as easily go to need-based aid, but political considerations work in the opposite direction."

The prospect of heavier reliance on loans and merit-based grants to help families with ever-rising college costs raises troubling questions about the future of college access for low-income, minority and immigrant students. The two fastest-growing parts of college aid — loans and merit-based grants — do little for those populations, as costs continue to rise.

Even colleges that currently make strong efforts to boost need-based grants and other assistance for low-income students probably won't do so indefinitely.

"Paying for 100 percent of need is expensive," said Yvonne Hubbard, director of student financial services at the University of Virginia. The school's need-based assistance program, AccessUVa, pays for everything for qualified students and costs the university about $20 million a year. [54]

The University of Illinois at Urbana-Champaign also has a strong program of need-based grants to improve access. Still, "What happens four years or 10 years down the road?" asked Daniel Mann, the school's director of financial aid, who doubts that future administrations will support the current ambitious aid program. [55]

The nation's burgeoning population of Hispanic immigrants also may mean that college attendance and graduation rates would decline, since Hispanics have "relatively low rates" of college attendance, says Penn's Perna.

"I'm a little skeptical of simple correspondences between college-graduation rates and money, but if nothing changes, we are going to see fewer college graduates" in years to come, says Indiana's Hossler.

NOTES

1. Quoted in Diana Jean Schemo, "Private Loans Deepen a Crisis in Student Debt," *The New York Times*, June 10, 2007.

2. For background, see Tom Price, "Rising College Costs," *CQ Researcher*, Dec. 5, 2003, pp. 1013-1044.

3. "Trends in College Pricing, 2007," The College Board, 2007, www.collegeboard.com/prod_downloads/about/news_info/trends/trends_pricing_07.pdf.

4. Jane V. Wellman, "Costs, Prices and Affordability," Commission on the Future of Higher Education, www.ed.gov/about/bdscomm/list/hiedfuture/reports/wellman.pdf.

5. Matthew Keenan and Brian Kladko, "Harvard Targets Middle Class With Student Cost Cuts," Bloomberg.com, Dec. 10, 2007.

6. Susan M. Dynarski and Judith E. Scott-Clayton, "College Grants on a Postcard: A Proposal for Simple and Predictable Federal Student Aid," The Hamilton Project, The Brookings Institution, February 2007.

7. Steven Pearlstein, "Cost-Conscious Colleges," *The Washington Post*, Nov. 16, 2007, p. D1.

8. Kate Sabatini and Pedro de la Torre III, "Federal Aid Fails Needy Students," Center for American Progress, May 16, 2007, www.americanprogress.org.

9. "What Financial Aid Officers Say," America's Student Loan Providers, www.aslp.us.

10. Tracey King and Ivan Frishberg, "Big Loans, Bigger Problems: A Report on the Sticker Shock of Student Loans," The State PIRGs, March 2001.

11. Quoted in Jay Mathews, "As Merit-Aid Race Escalates, Wealthy Often Win," *The Washington Post*, April 19, 2005, p. A8.

12. Donald Heller and Patricia Marin, "State Merit Scholarship Programs and Racial Inequality," The Civil Rights Project, 2004.

13. Quoted in Mathews, *op. cit.*

14. Quoted in Tara Malone, "Rising Tuition Hits Middle Class Hardest," [Chicago] *Daily Herald*, Nov. 21, 2004, www.collegeparents.org.

15. Quoted in *ibid.*

16. Richard Vedder, "The Real Costs of Federal Aid to Higher Education," *Heritage Lectures*, Jan. 12, 2007.

17. Ross Rubenstein, "Helping Outstanding Pupils Educationally," Education Finance and Accountability Project, 2003.

18. Radley Balko, "Government May Be Cause, Not Solution, to Gen Y Economic Woes," Cato Institute, July 12, 2006, www.cato.org.

19. Quoted in Larry Abramson, "Student Loan Industry Struggles Amid Controversy," "Morning Edition," National Public Radio, June 26, 2007.

20. John Berlau, "Ted Kennedy Says Eliminate Private Sector From Student Loans," Competitive Enterprise Institute Web site, April 4, 2007, www.cei.org/utils/printer.cfm?AID=5854.

21. Vedder, *op. cit.*

22. Quoted in Abramson, *op. cit.*

23. Michael Dannenberg, "A College Access Contract," New America Foundation Web site, www.newamerica.net.

24. Dannenberg, *op. cit.*

25. Jason Delisle, "The Business of Sallie Mae — Political Risk for Investors and Taxpayers," Higheredwatch.org, New America Foundation, Oct. 2, 2007, www.newamerica.net.

26. "Sallie Mae Decides To Be More Selective In Pursuing Loan Origination Activity," RTT News Global Financial Newswires, Jan. 8, 2008, www.rttnews.com/sp/breakingnews.asp?date=01/04/2008&item=103&vid=0.

27. For background, see Rupert Wilkinson, *Buying Students: Financial Aid in America* (2005), and Tom Price, "Rising College Costs," *CQ Researcher*, Dec. 5, 2003, pp. 1013-1044.

28. "History of Financial Aid," Center for Higher Education Support Services (Chess Inc.), www.chessconsulting.org/financialaid/history.htm.

29. Lawrence E. Gladieux, "Federal Student Aid Policy: A History and an Assessment," in *Financing Postsecondary Education: The Federal Role* (1995), U.S. Department of Education, www.ed.gov/offices/OPE/PPI/FinPostSecEd/gladieux.html.

30. "Higher Education," New America Foundation, www.newamerica.net/programs/educaiton_policy/fedearl_education_budget_project/higher_ed.

31. For background, see Kelly Field, "The Selling of Student Loans," *The Chronicle of Higher Education*, June 1, 2007.

32. Quoted in *ibid.*

33. Stephen Burd, "Direct Lending in Distress," *The Chronicle of Higher Education*, July 8, 2005.

34. Quoted in Field, *op. cit.*

35. Quoted in *ibid.*

36. Deborah Lucas and Damien Moore, "Guaranteed vs. Direct Lending: The Case of Student Loans," paper prepared for National Bureau of Economic Research conference, January 2007, www.newamerica.net/files/Guaranteed%20vs.%20Direct%20Lending.pdf.

37. "Private Loan Policy Agenda," Project on Student Debt, http://projectonstudentdebt.org/initiative_view.php?initiative_idx=7.

38. Aleksandra Todorova, "The Best Rates on Private Loans," *Smart Money*, June 20, 2006, www.smartmoney.com/college/finaid/index.cfm?story=private-loans.

39. Field, *op. cit.*

40. Quoted in Sandra Block, "Private Student Loans Pose Greater Risk," *USA Today*, Oct. 25, 2006.

41. "37th Annual Survey Report on State-Sponsored Student Financial Aid," National Association of State Student Aid and Grant Programs, July 2007, www.nassgap.org.

42. For background, see "Summary of The College Cost Reduction And Access Act (H.R. 2669)," News from NASFAA, National Association of Student Financial Aid Administrators, www.nasfaa.org/Publications/2007/G2669summary091007.html.

43. Alex Wirzbicki, "$20.2 Billion Boost in Student Aid Approved," *The Boston Globe*, Sept. 8, 2007, www.boston.com.111.

44. Quoted in *ibid.*

45. Jason Delisle, "Pell Grants Cut," Higheredwatch.com, New America Foundation, Dec. 18, 2007.

46. Quoted in Libby George, "Broad Student Aid Overhaul Clears," *CQ Weekly*, Sept. 10, 2007, p. 2620.

47. For background, see "Special Report: Student Loan Scandal," Education Policy Program, New America Foundation, www.newamerica.net.

48. John Hechinger, "Probe Into College-Lender Ties Widens," *The Wall Street Journal*, April 5, 2007.

49. Josh Keller, "University of Texas Financial-Aid Office Took Gifts From Lenders, Student Journalists Report," *The Chronicle of Higher Education*, May 11, 2007.

50. Meyer Eisenberg and Ann H. Franke, "Financial Scandals and Student Loans," *The Chronicle of Higher Education*, June 29, 2007.

51. "Student Debt and the Class of 2006," The Project on Student Debt, September 2007.

52. Jonathan D. Glater, "College Loans by States Face Fresh Scrutiny," *The New York Times*, Dec. 9, 2007.

53. *Ibid.*

54. Quoted in Karin Fischer, "Student-Aid Officials Say Efforts to Expand Access Need Widespread Backing," *The Chronicle of Higher Education*, Sept. 22, 2006.

55. Quoted in *ibid.*

BIBLIOGRAPHY

Books

Getz, Malcolm, *Investing in College: A Guide for the Perplexed*, Harvard University Press, 2007.
An associate professor of economics at Vanderbilt University outlines the questions parents and students should ask about colleges and their financial-aid programs.

Vedder, Richard, *Going Broke by Degree: Why College Costs So Much*, AEI Press, American Enterprise Institute, 2004.
A former Ohio University economics professor argues that for-profit universities can provide badly needed price competition for traditional colleges, where tuitions are skyrocketing because the schools are inefficient and spend too much subsidizing non-instructional programs like sports.

Wilkinson, Rupert, *Buying Students: Financial Aid in America*, Vanderbilt University Press, 2005.
A former professor of American studies and history at Britain's University of Sussex details the social and economic history of student financial aid.

Articles

Field, Kelly, "The Selling of Student Loans," *The Chronicle of Higher Education*, June 1, 2007.
Beginning with the creation of the direct federal-loan program in the early 1990s, which set up a government competitor to private student-loan firms, lenders competed to be colleges' "preferred" loan sources, offering discounts, gifts and other favors to woo financial-aid officers.

Fischer, Karin, "Student-Aid Officials Say Efforts to Expand Access Need Widespread Backing," *The Chronicle of Higher Education*, Sept. 22, 2006.
Officials at selective universities say need-based grants and personal support are needed to expand enrollment of low-income students in top schools.

Schemo, Diana Jean, "Private Loans Deepen a Crisis in Student Debt," *The New York Times*, June 10, 2007.
Non-government-guaranteed loans are becoming a bigger part of the college financing picture as costs climb, and, unlike guaranteed loans, interest rates can be as high as 20 percent.

Reports and Studies

"Course Corrections: Experts Offer Solutions to the College Cost Crisis," Lumina Foundation for Education, October 2005, www.collegecosts.info/ pdfs/solution_papers/Collegecosts_Oct2005.pdf.
Analysts assembled by a nonprofit group suggest technological and organizational changes to control rising costs.

***Recession, Retrenchment, and Recovery: State Higher Education Funding and Student Financial Aid*, Center for the Study of Education Policy, Illinois State University, October 2006, www.coe.ilstu.edu/ eafdept/centerforedpolicy/downloads/3R%20report1 0272006/3R_Final_Oct06_Updated%5B1%5D.pdf.**
Analysts explore the consequences for higher-education funding and student aid in an era where state governments face recurring severe budget shortfalls.

"Student Debt and the Class of 2006," The Project on Student Debt, September 2007, http://projectonstudent-debt.org/files/pub/State_by_State_report_FINAL.pdf.
An advocacy group finds District of Columbia students have the highest debt — an average of $27,757 — and Oklahoma grads the lowest: $17,680 on average.

Cook, Bryan J., and Jacqueline E. King, "2007 Status Report on the Pell Grant Program," American Council on Education, June 2007, www.acenet.edu/AM/Template.cfm?Section=Home&TEMPLATE=/CM/Cont entDisplay.cfm&CONTENTID=23271.
Analysts for a university membership alliance trace trends in the federal need-based grant program, finding that Pell grantees' median incomes are around $18,000, compared to $55,000 for other undergraduates.

Dynarski, Susan M., and Judith E. Scott-Clayton, "College Grants on a Postcard: A Proposal for Simple and Predictable Student Aid," The Hamilton Project, The Brookings Institution, February 2007, www.brook-ings.edu/~/media/Files/rc/papers/2007/02education_ dynarski/200702dynarski%20scott%20clayton.pdf.
Public-policy analysts at Harvard argue that a drastically simplified federal aid-application process would signifi-cantly increase college enrollment among low-income and minority students.

Haycock, Kati, "Promise Abandoned: How Policy Choices and Institutional Practices Restrict College Opportunities," The Education Trust, August 2006, www2.edtrust.org/NR/rdonlyres/B6772F1A-116D-4827-A326-F8CFAD33975A/0/PromiseAbandoned HigherEd.pdf.
A nonprofit group says higher-education and financial-aid policies aren't helping low-income and minority stu-dents catch up to their higher-income white peers.

Wolfram, Gary, "Making College More Expensive: The Unintended Consequences of Federal Tuition Aid," Policy Analysis No. 531, Cato Institute, January 2005, www.cato.org/pubs/pas/pa531.pdf.
An analysis prepared for a libertarian think tank argues that college costs would decrease if private aid, rather than government aid, helped students fund their studies.

For More Information

American Association of Collegiate Registrars and Admissions Officers, One Dupont Circle, N.W., Suite 520, Washington, DC 20036; (202) 293-9161; www.aacrao.org. Provides information and professional education on college-admissions issues and policies.

America's Student Loan Providers, www.studentloan-facts.org. Advocacy group of banks and other organizations that make federally guaranteed college loans.

Education Sector, 1201 Connecticut Ave., N.W., Suite 850, Washington, DC 20036; (202) 552-2840; www.educationsector.org. A think tank providing research and analysis on education issues, including financial aid.

Lumina Foundation for Education, P.O. Box 1806, Indianapolis, IN 46206-1806; (317) 951-5300; www.luminafoundation.org. Supports higher-education research and projects to improve college access.

National Association for College Admission Counseling, 1631 Prince St., Alexandria, VA 22314; (703) 836-2222; www.nacacnet.org. Provides information and news updates related to college admissions.

National Association of State Student Grant and Aid Programs, www.nassgap.org. Provides information on state financial-aid programs.

National Association of Student Financial Aid Administrators, 1101 Connecticut Ave., N.W., Suite 1100, Washington, DC 20036; (202) 785-0453; www.nasfaa.org. Sets voluntary standards and provides professional education on student financial aid.

New America Foundation, 1630 Connecticut Ave., N.W., 7th Floor; Washington, DC 20009; (202) 986-2700; www.newamerica.net. Liberal think tank provides research and analysis of higher-education issues, with a focus on financial aid.

Pell Institute for the Study of Opportunity in Higher Education, 1025 Vermont Ave., N.W., Suite 1020, Washington, DC 20005; (202) 638-2887; www.pellinstitute.org. Think tank that conducts research on college access and financial aid for low-income students.

Project on Student Debt, 1411 K St., N.W., Suite 1400, Washington, DC 20005; (202) 747-1959; http://projectonstudentdebt.org. Provides advocacy and information on the growing debt load carried by U.S. students.

U.S. PIRG, 218 D St., S.E., Washington, DC 20003; www.uspirg.org/higher-education. Consumer group advocating for more need-based financial aid and simplified aid-application processes.

3

Universal Coverage

Marcia Clemmitt

Many working Americans, like Daniel and Mindy Shea, of Cincinnati, are un- or under-insured. Young workers are hit especially hard: In 2004, a third of Americans ages 19-24 were uninsured. Only 61 percent of Americans under age 65 obtain health insurance through their employers. As health costs rise and incomes sag, more and more companies are dropping coverage, especially restaurants and small businesses.

AP Photo/David Kohl

From *CQ Researcher*,
March 30, 2007. (Updated May 7, 2008)

When Emily, a 24-year-old graduate student, discovered a lump on her thigh, her doctor told her to get an MRI to find out whether it was cancerous. But Emily's student-insurance policy didn't cover the $2,000 procedure, so she skipped it. [1]

Several weeks later, during outpatient surgery to remove the lump, Emily's surgeon found a rare, invasive cancer underneath the benign lump — a cancer with only a 20 to 40 percent survival rate. The skipped MRI could have detected the cancer much sooner, improving her chances for recovery.

Emily pieced together payment for her treatment from her school insurance, two state public-aid programs and a monthly payment plan that ate up more than 40 percent of her take-home income. But a year later she learned that annual health premiums for all students at her school would rise by 19 percent because a few, like her, had racked up high expenses. The price hike led many more students to skip purchasing the coverage altogether.

Advocates say such stories are a good reason why Congress should enact a universal health-insurance program. While Congress and the states have been expanding public health insurance programs covering the very poor — despite two vetoes by President Bush of congressional efforts to expand the State Children's Health Insurance Program in 2007 — students and lower-income workers increasingly are losing coverage or are finding, like Emily, that they can't afford adequate coverage.

Today, 44 million Americans — about 15 percent of the population — lack health insurance, usually due to job loss, student status, early retirement or because they have entry-level jobs or

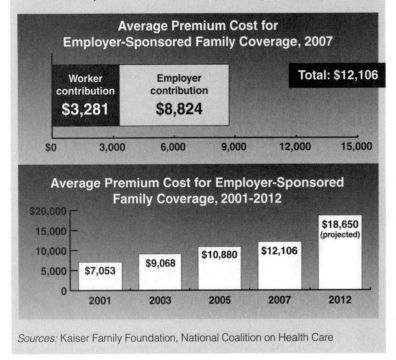

Cost of Premiums Rising Rapidly

The average annual cost of family health coverage has risen more than 50 percent since 2001, to $12,106, and is expected to exceed $18,000 in the next five years. Most of the cost is borne by the employer.

Average Premium Cost for Employer-Sponsored Family Coverage, 2007

Worker contribution	Employer contribution	Total: $12,106
$3,281	$8,824	

$0 3,000 6,000 9,000 12,000 15,000

Average Premium Cost for Employer-Sponsored Family Coverage, 2001-2012

2001	2003	2005	2007	2012
$7,053	$9,068	$10,880	$12,106	$18,650 (projected)

Sources: Kaiser Family Foundation, National Coalition on Health Care

premiums rose 40 percent faster than average wages and at a rate 75 percent above inflation. [6]

"Health insurance expenses are the fastest-growing cost component for employers," according to the National Coalition on Health Care. "Unless something changes dramatically, health insurance costs will overtake profits." [7]

All these issues have added renewed urgency to the question of universal health coverage. There is widespread agreement — among major employers, labor unions and leaders in both parties — that something has to be done to expand insurance to cover more Americans. But there is still plenty of debate about the best means of doing so — and how to pay for it all.

"If there's one thing that can bankrupt America, it's health care," warned U.S. Comptroller General David Walker, then chief of the Government Accountability Office, Congress' nonpartisan auditing arm, now president and CEO of the Peter G. Peterson Foundation. And in response to those who say the United States can "grow" its way out of uninsurance by creating more and better jobs with coverage benefits, Walker stated flatly: "Anybody that tells you we are going to grow our way out of this . . . probably isn't very proficient at math." [8]

The issue became central to the 2008 presidential race, with each of the major Democratic aspirants producing detailed universal coverage plan. These were big-ticket affairs. Sen. Barack Obama's plan would cost between $50 billion and $65 billion; one proposed by Sen. Hillary Clinton would cost roughly twice that.

Obama's proposal would maintain employer-based coverage for those who have it and, in fact, would require most employers to contribute toward workers' coverage. But unlike his opponents in the Democratic primary, Obama's plan would not require individuals to buy insurance, although parents would be required

work in a service industry or a small business. Only about 40 percent of businesses employing low-wage or part-time workers offer health benefits, and at $11,480 a year, the average family's health-insurance premium now costs more than a minimum-wage worker makes in a year. Young workers are hit especially hard: In 2005, 38 percent of Americans between the ages of 19 and 24 were uninsured. [2] And in the construction and service industries, only 80 percent of the managers have health coverage. [3]

And the situation is only expected to get worse. U.S. health spending is expected to double by 2015 — to more than $12,300 per person. [4] As health-care costs skyrocket, so does the cost of health insurance, whether purchased by individuals or by employers. Between 2000 and 2006, health premiums for employer-sponsored insurance jumped 87 percent, far outpacing inflation's 18 percent overall increase. [5] In 2007, health insurance

to buy insurance for their children. The government would more actively regulate insurance, in the hope that greater efficiency, particularly in the use of technology, would wring savings out of the present system.

The Republican candidates proposed tax credits and market-driven approaches. Sen. John McCain's plan stressed the need for cost containment over expanding coverage to all. He said of the Democrats, "They promise universal coverage, whatever its cost, and the massive tax increases, mandates and government regulation that it imposes." [9]

After securing the GOP nomination, McCain outlined his own strategy, which would call for a shift from people being insured through their employers toward paying for coverage more directly. He would encourage such a move by offering families a $5,000 tax credit to help pay their insurance bills.

Americans Without Health Insurance

In 24 states, between 14 percent and 19 percent of the adults ages 18-64 did not have health insurance in 2006. States with high levels of uninsured residents typically have minimal state and employer insurance coverage.

Percentage of People Ages 18-64 Without Insurance, 2006

■	23% and over
■	19-22.9%
■	14-18.9%
□	Under 14%

Source: Kaiser Family Foundation, statehealthfacts.org, 2006

The national debate took place in the wake of ambitious attempts — or talk — in many states about trying to create new sources of affordable coverage. Massachusetts launched a near-universal coverage plan in 2007 that has had bipartisan support, and Republican California Gov. Arnold Schwarzenegger entertained hopes of enacting a similar measure.

While the public often pictures the uninsured as being unemployed, the fact is that most un- and underinsured Americans have jobs. Only 60 percent of Americans under age 65 obtain health insurance through their employers — down from 69 percent in 2000. And as health costs rise and incomes sag, more and more companies are dropping coverage, especially very small businesses. Because insurers raise premium prices for high-cost groups — as happened with Emily's grad-school coverage — small companies whose employees get seriously ill or injured or pregnant often find themselves priced out of coverage altogether.

America's creeping lack of health coverage constitutes a crisis for the uninsured, even as the skyrocketing cost of

health care makes it inevitable that even more people will be uninsured in the future. If health premiums continue rising at their current rate, about 56 million Americans are predicted to be uninsured by 2013 — 11 million more than today, according to a University of California at San Diego study. [10] The increase will cause 4,500 additional unnecessary deaths per year and $16 billion to $32 billion in lost economic productivity and other "human capital," the study says. [11]

The leading public myth about the uninsured is that "people without health insurance get the medical care they need," said Arthur Kellerman, chairman of Emory University's Department of Emergency Medicine and co-chairman of an Institute of Medicine (IOM) panel that has called for universal coverage by 2010. [12]

In fact, the uninsured seldom receive appropriate care at the appropriate time, said Kellerman. "The uninsured are less likely to see a doctor or be able to identify a regular source of medical care and are less likely to receive preventive services," he said. [13] And uninsured children admitted to a hospital due to an injury are twice as likely

Universal Coverage Faces Financial Obstacles

Reducing health-care costs is the big challenge

Now that Americans appear to be reaching some consensus on the need for universal health coverage, major hidden obstacles — all involving money — must be overcome. Among those thorny financial issues are questions over who is going to pay for the coverage, how can affordable access be ensured for all and how can overall health-care costs be reduced.

Perhaps the most controversial issue is who will pay for the coverage. In 2005, employers paid 75 percent of workers' health-premium costs — about $500 billion compared to the approximately $170 billion that workers paid. [1] That's "most of the money outside the government that's spent on health care," says Stan Dorn, a senior research associate at the liberal Urban Institute. To work, any universal-coverage plan will have to either continue to use those employer contributions or come up with a suitable replacement for them.

That's why many universal-coverage proposals ask employers for financial contributions. But making those contributions both fair and adequate is difficult, mainly because businesses vary so widely in what they pay today: Many contribute nothing, but others pay hundreds of millions of dollars each year.

Dorn says policymakers may want to consider asking all employers to pay a set amount into a general pool but vary the amount by companies' line of business and their geographical location. That way, companies that compete with one another would share the same burden.

Lawmakers also must figure out how to ensure affordable access to all. Many Republican proposals for expanding coverage rely on tax subsidies to help more people buy individual health policies. Because such coverage wouldn't be tied to a job, it would be "portable," so employees who switch or lose jobs would not be without insurance.

But buying individual health insurance can be far more expensive than purchasing through an employer because insurers don't "pool" risks the way they do for workers under employer-based policies. So individual purchasers pay based on their family's health status and age, which makes it the most expensive way to buy health insurance. Moreover, insurers won't even sell coverage to some people because the companies themselves consider it unaffordable.

"The words 'kinda crummy' come to mind when I think of the individual market," said former Maryland Insurance Commissioner Steve Larsen, now a private attorney. For example, a case of mononucleosis and a chronic condition like hay fever is enough for some insurers to deem a potential buyer unaffordable. "And if you have any type of serious mental illness, forget it," he said. [2] A study by the Georgetown University Institute for Health Care Research and Policy found that a 62-year-old overweight moderate smoker with controlled high blood pressure was deemed an unaffordable risk 55 percent of the times he sought individual health coverage. [3]

to die and 46 percent less likely to receive rehabilitation after hospitalization, according to a 2007 study by the consumer advocacy group Families USA. [14]

The growing number of uninsured Americans also pushes up the cost of publicly subsidized health insurance like Medicare, the panel said. Working-age uninsured patients with uncontrolled diabetes or high blood pressure eventually enter the health system sicker than they would have been had they been insured. [15] And about 20 percent of those with schizophrenia and bipolar disorder are uninsured and end up in jail or prison when their untreated conditions trigger illegal behavior, said the panel. [16]

Adding to the problem, manufacturing and unionized jobs were the mainstay of job-based coverage, but their numbers have been dropping for more than 20 years. "I suspect you're going to see wholesale withdrawal of employer-sponsored health care" for anyone earning less than twice federal poverty-level wages, said National Governors Association Executive Director Ray Scheppach. [17]

"Economic security, jobs, health care and retirement security — those are all now one and the same issue," says Henry Simmons, president of the National Coalition on Health Care, which includes employers, unions and academic and other groups advocating universal coverage.

Buying an individual policy is more affordable for the young and healthy, says health-care consultant Robert Laszewski. His 20-something son found an individual health policy for $150 a month several years ago, but "if he was 58 years old, his premium would have been $1,500," he says. "If you're going to do universal health care, you can't age-rate premiums or bar people based on pre-existing conditions."

No matter how widely risk is shared, however, behind the high cost of insurance lurks the ever-rising cost of health care. "The 10,000-pound elephant in the room is cost," says Laszewski.

Health-care costs have been growing faster than the entire economy or any other sector in it for the past 45 years, says Gail Wilensky, a senior fellow at the nonprofit health-education foundation Project HOPE and former head of Medicaid and Medicare. "They can't go on doing it for the next 30 years" without crippling other parts of the economy, she says.

U.S. health-care costs are the world's highest because of insurers' high administrative and marketing costs and because American doctors and medical suppliers enjoy higher profits and salaries than their counterparts in other industrialized countries. [4]

In today's fragmented insurance system, insurers' efforts to attract the healthiest, cheapest customers add extra overall costs, point out Paul Menzel, a philosophy professor at Pacific Lutheran University in Tacoma, Wash., and Donald W. Light, professor of comparative health care at the University of Pennsylvania. [5] For example, they wrote, a Seattle survey found that 2,277 people were covered by 755 different policies linked to 189 different health-care plans.

"The $420 billion (31 percent!) paid [annually] for managing, marketing and profiting from the current fragmented system could be drastically cut" if insurers had to take all comers rather than carefully jiggering their policies, premiums and marketing strategies to attract only the healthiest, least expensive buyers, they said.

A key is to cut spending on care by "learning more about what works for whom," says Wilensky. But getting that information requires investment, she says.

In addition to cutting excess services, says Laszewski, making coverage affordable will ultimately mean sacrificing some of the health-care industry's high profits and salaries. International comparisons show that other countries spend less on health care while delivering the same amount or even more services to patients.

Americans don't understand that controlling cost is crucial to sustaining the health system, let alone expanding coverage, says Laszewski. "I'll bet you if you told consumers that if they lost their jobs, replacing their insurance would cost $15,000 or $16,000 a year, they'd understand that," he says.

---

[1] Aaron Catlin, Cathy Cowan, Stephen Heffler and Benjamin Washington, "National Health Spending in 2005: The Slowdown Continues," *Health Affairs*, January/February 2007, p. 148.

[2] Quoted in "Reinsurance for Individual Market Pricks Up Many Ears," *Medicine & Health*, "Perspectives," Oct. 28, 2002.

[3] "Hay Fever? Bum Knee? Buying Individual Coverage May Be Dicey," *Medicine & Health*, June 25, 2001.

[4] For background, see Marcia Clemmitt, "Rising Health Costs," *CQ Researcher*, April 7, 2006, pp. 289-312.

[5] Paul Menzel and Donald W. Light, "A Conservative Case for Universal Access to Health Care," *The Hastings Center Report*, July 1, 2006, p. 36.

Pension investment funds have recently realized that skyrocketing health-care costs could bankrupt Americans' future if they are not checked, says Simmons. Since Medicare covers only some of the health services needed by retirees, virtually all elderly people who can afford it also purchase private supplemental insurance to fill the gaps. But pension-fund investors are finding no investments that grow fast enough to allow retirees' savings income to keep up with the anticipated soaring cost of future Medicare and supplemental-coverage premiums.

While no one expects significant action from Congress until after the 2008 presidential election, federal policymakers increasingly acknowledge a need for action. Consensus appears to be growing for some type of hybrid universal coverage that combines public and private insurance.

"In the past the debate got bogged down because different groups wanted their first-priority proposal only," says Ron Pollack, founding executive director of Families USA. "One group would say, 'Coverage must be financed through public programs,' while another would say, 'There should be no government action in the marketplace,' And since everyone's second-favorite program was the status quo, nothing happened."

But that decades-old logjam may be breaking up, as advocates on all sides of the issue creep closer to one

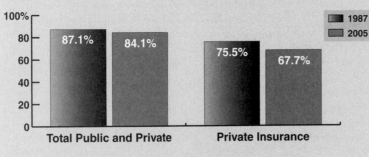

Private Insurance Coverage Dropped

The percentage of people with private health insurance dropped by 8 percentage points from 1987 to 2005 (right). At the same time, the percentage of people insured by either government or private insurance dropped 3 percentage points (left). As people lost private coverage, government picked up the slack to keep as many people insured as possible.

Percentage of Insured People by Type of Coverage

Source: U.S. Census Bureau, "Historical Health Insurance Tables"

another in their proposals. "The very grand visions on both sides" — a single-payer government system or relying on individuals saving money for their own care via Health Savings Accounts (HSAs) — "are both completely impossible in our political system," says Yale University Professor of Political Science Jacob Hacker.

Even President George W. Bush, a longtime proponent of individually purchased HSAs, softened that stance in his fiscal 2008 budget plan, which would have offered similar tax breaks to those buying all kinds of health insurance, not just HSAs, either as individuals or through employers. Bush continued to push the idea of empowering individuals through tax credits and market choice, rather than "government control," in his 2008 State of the Union address, but some critics said his vetoes of funding for children's health undermined his credibility on the question of health care expansion.

Paul Ginsburg, president of the nonpartisan research group Center for Studying Health System Change, says critics rightly point out that Bush's tax break doesn't target lower-income people who are most in danger of losing coverage. Nevertheless, "eventually, the Democrats may see that the president has given them something — a revenue source" to help pay for expanding coverage, he says.

All the major Democratic candidates for president in 2008 declared a commitment to universal or near-universal health coverage. "The U.S. auto industry is struggling, in part because of the rising cost of health care that this administration has done nothing to address," newly announced Democratic candidate Sen. Barack Obama, D-Ill., said in November 2006. "I have long proposed that the government make a deal with the Big Three automakers that will pay for a portion of their retiree health costs if they agree to invest those savings in fuel-efficient technologies." Health-care costs account for approximately $1,000 of the cost of each car produced by the America's largest automakers — more than they spend on steel. [18]

In 2006, as governor of Massachusetts, Mitt Romney backed legislation intended to achieve universal coverage — an idea he didn't talk up much during his bid for the GOP presidential nomination. Former House Speaker Newt Gingrich also has called for systemic reforms in the health-care system.

While a consensus may be developing on the need for some form of universal coverage, many contentious debates remain. For example, both the right and the left have criticized the California and Massachusetts plans for requiring individuals to buy health insurance, just as drivers are required to carry automobile insurance.

Nevertheless, many believe the country is on the verge of a focused, national debate on universal coverage. "In 2008, universal coverage will be up there with Iraq as top election issues," says Pollack.

As policymakers gear up for that debate, here are some of the questions being asked:

Can America afford universal health coverage?

Critics of universal-insurance proposals have long argued that while expanding coverage is desirable, covering everyone would simply cost too much. [19] Universal-coverage advocates, however, argue that current administrative expenses are high partly because the United States has a piecemeal system with many uninsured.

"It is impossible to get everybody covered," Bill Frist, R-Tenn., a transplant surgeon and then Senate majority leader, said in 2004. [20] State efforts have shown that universal coverage is not financially feasible, he said.

For example, his home state of Tennessee managed to cover about 93 percent of residents — a national high — by having Medicaid cover both the uninsured and the uninsurable. But "in attempting to do this the state is going bankrupt," he said, "and there is a major effort to backtrack." [21]

Universal-coverage plans generally are "unrealistic," said former Health and Human Services Secretary Tommy G. Thompson. "I just don't think it's in the cards. . . . "I don't think that administratively or legislatively it's feasible." [22]

While few politicians today will say America cannot afford universal coverage, both sides agree that the costs will be high. A study by the liberal Urban Institute says that in 2004 universal coverage would have added about $48 billion to the $125 billion the nation spent on health care for uninsured people — most of which was paid out of pocket by the uninsured or was delivered without compensation by doctors and hospitals. [23] A proposed universal-coverage plan for Maryland would raise that state's health spending by some $2.5 billion per year, while a Minnesota proposal to cover the state's 383,000 uninsured is projected to cost an estimated $663-$852 million in new annual funding. [24]

Most proposals for universal coverage call for increased government spending. And finding those dollars will be tough, given that the federal budget and many state budgets are facing substantial deficits. [25]

"The public sector has fewer resources" now compared to when the issue was debated previously, says Ginsburg, of the Center for Studying Health System Change. A lack of willingness or ability to commit new revenue has doomed at least one state plan, he adds. When Maine launched a universal-coverage initiative in 2003, the state "put almost no money in and got almost nothing out," he says.

The Democratic presidential hopefuls who have called for universal coverage "will be desperate for revenues when they put out their plans," says Robert Blendon, professor of health policy and management at the Harvard School of Public Health. "Money is going to be hard to come by. We've got defense costs that are very, very high."

Wages Lagged Behind Increases in Premiums

Workers' wages rose less than 3 percent from 2004 to 2005 while health-insurance premiums jumped 9 percent.

Comparing Increases in Health Insurance Premiums and Workers' Earnings, 2004-2005

Sources: Alliance for Health Reform; Kaiser Family Foundation and Health Research and Educational Trust, 2005

A 2006 Massachusetts law requiring every resident to purchase subsidized coverage — unless that coverage is "unaffordable" — is already running into an affordability crisis, said Jonathan Gruber, a professor of economics at the Massachusetts Institute of Technology. [26] The state has said it would subsidize only those who earn up to three times the federal poverty level (about $30,000 for an individual and $60,000 for a family of four), said Gruber. But "at three times poverty, health insurance is still expensive. . . . It's not feasible to have someone spend 20, 30 or 40 percent of income on health insurance." [27]

While some say universal coverage is too expensive for America, many economists point out that industrialized nations with universal coverage spend less per capita on health care than the United States. In 2005, for instance, the United States spent $6,401 per capita on health care while Australia spent $3,128; Denmark, $3,108; Germany, $3,287; Luxembourg, $5,352; Sweden, $2,918 and Switzerland, $4,177. [28]

Not only are Americans paying more for health care than those in any other industrialized country, but they are getting lower-quality care — by some measurements — than consumers in countries with universal coverage. While new drugs and technology have improved longevity and quality of life for many Americans, the United States is ranked 37th by the World Health Organization in overall quality of care, based on adult and infant mortality rates. The United States also ranks 42nd in life expectancy, according to international numbers from the Census Bureau and domestic numbers from the National Center for Health Statistics, compared with 11th two decades ago. [29]

Those stark realities, coupled with the fact that U.S. health-care costs are spiraling out of control, lead a growing number of analysts to argue that the United States can't afford not to have universal coverage.

"I've always believed universal coverage would carry significant costs and would bring daunting . . . economic challenges," said Harold Pollack, associate professor at the University of Chicago School of Social Service Administration. [30] But recently, he says, he has decided "there is no alternative" to pushing forward with universal insurance. "The current system is no longer able to accomplish important things we expect from our health care." [31]

Former Gov. John Kitzhaber, D-Ore. — an emergency-room physician who now heads the Oregon-based Archimedes Movement, a health-reform initiative — agrees. Economic growth depends on good health for all, he said. Good health "is the first rung on the ladder of opportunity . . . the cornerstone of a democratic society, allowing people to . . . be productive and to take advantage of the opportunities of upward mobility." [32]

Others argue that having more than 15 percent of the population uninsured means that all Americans pay more for health care. "The uninsured are one of the inefficiencies" driving health costs into the unaffordable range, says Robert Greenstein, executive director of the liberal Center on Budget and Policy Priorities.

"Reining in health-care cost growth" — which soared by 7 percent in 2006 alone — is a prerequisite for universal coverage, says Robert Laszewski, an independent health-care consultant and a former health-insurance executive. Health-insurance premiums grow even faster than costs, and neither government subsidies nor the incomes of lower-wage working people can keep up with the current growth rate for long, he says.

If coverage expansion were accompanied by efforts to rein in spending and improve care, "there's absolutely no doubt that you can have universal coverage without substantially raised costs," says Simmons, president of the National Coalition on Health Care. "Every other country does it" already, he says.

Universal coverage is needed to "get a [health-care] market that works," he adds. "You can't fix the issue of cost" — which affects everyone, insured and uninsured — "without universal coverage," he says. Absent a universal-coverage requirement, "what markets do is avoid risk," such as when insurance companies develop marketing and risk-assessment procedures to avoid selling policies to sick people. "It's an open-and-shut case that universal coverage is cheaper and better" than the status quo.

Getting everyone covered and specifying uniform benefit packages would create a huge, immediate, one-time financial saving, Simmons says. "Automatically, you're talking about hundreds of billions of dollars" in savings that "every other nation has already captured," partly accounting for lower costs abroad.

Should Americans depend on states to expand coverage?

In 2007, about 20 states made health-care expansion a top priority, with many considering universal coverage plans. That represented an important shift from earlier health policy debates, during which the problems of caring for the insured were driven by federal policy makers. "We can't wait for the federal government," said Linda Evans Parlette, deputy Republican leader in the Washington State Senate. "We better work with what we have at home." [33]

But ambitious plans in Washington State, as elsewhere, soon foundered due to their multi-billion dollar costs. With most states slipping into deficits in 2008, the debate about expanding health coverage quickly shifted back to the presidential campaign.

In California, Republican Gov. Arnold Schwarzenegger, Democratic legislators and top executives from the state's largest private insurer all proposed universal-coverage plans, but none were enacted. The California-based Kaiser Foundation Health Plan offered a plan to provide "near-universal coverage" within two years to California's 5 million uninsured — who represent a whopping 10 percent of all uninsured Americans. "Despite the greater dimensions of the problem in California, we believe that a state-based solution is possible," wrote Kaiser executives. [34]

Schwarzenegger did a great job selling the public on his universal-care plan, which would have required mandatory coverage by insurers, financing from employers and a mandate for all individuals to buy coverage (with the poor receiving a subsidy). A poll conducted a few months after his plan died in the state Senate showed that 72 percent of California voters approved of the idea. The fact that wasn't enacted, of course, hurt Schwarzenegger's approval ratings. [35]

In recent years, states have been far more active than the federal government in expanding health coverage. Massachusetts and Vermont passed universal-coverage laws in 2006, and Illinois created a program to cover all children.

States' uninsured populations vary widely around the country, so they are the natural venue for expanding coverage, say some analysts. "All states face different challenges in reducing the number of uninsured residents," so "imposing a one-size-fits-all program" at the federal level "will not work," said Arthur Garson, former dean of the University of Virginia School of Medicine. [36]

With no national consensus emerging on how to cover the uninsured, encouraging state action is the only way forward, said Stuart M. Butler, vice president for domestic and economic policy at the conservative Heritage Foundation. "Successful welfare reform started in the states," and coverage could be expanded by removing federal roadblocks and offering federal incentives to states "to try proposals currently bottled up in Congress." [37]

While federal laws restrict states' ability to expand Medicaid and set rules for employer-sponsored coverage, that hasn't stopped some states from expanding coverage, says Stan Dorn, a senior research associate at the liberal Urban Institute. In the early 1990s, for example, Minnesota and Washington state both "implemented coverage systems that succeeded brilliantly," he says.

Regardless of whether they succeed completely, state initiatives provide models and impetus for future national efforts, say many analysts. "The state action provides great momentum," says Dorn.

"States are hugely important," says Hacker at Yale University. "When two Republican governors" — Romney and Schwarzenegger — "break with the national party to propose universal coverage, that's a huge boost," he says.

Ginsburg, of the Center for Studying Health System Change, says the 2006 Massachusetts law has been a catalyst — "the answer to political gridlock." It is supported by both Republicans, who've traditionally been skeptical of universal coverage, and liberal Democrats who favor a single-payer system, he says.

The flurry of major state proposals shows the nation is ready for change, he says, even though "the federal government has been dysfunctional on domestic issues for many years." He predicts "a few more states" will expand coverage soon, but many states are limited in what they can accomplish.

All states can't emulate the Massachusetts model, said James J. Mongan, chief executive of the New England-based hospital and physician network Partners HealthCare, because Massachusetts is very different from most other states. [38]

"We started with half the problem solved," said Mongan, a former congressional health aide who also worked in the Carter administration. Only about 10 percent of Massachusetts residents were uninsured, compared to uninsurance rates in other states of 25 percent and higher. And the state was already spending more than $500 million annually to compensate hospitals for treating the uninsured. [39]

"Federal action ultimately [will] be essential," said Shoshanna Sofaer, professor of health policy at Baruch College in New York City and a member of the IOM insurance panel. States don't have the steady financing or the legal flexibility to expand coverage to all of their residents. One roadblock, she said, is the federal Employee Retirement Income Security Act (ERISA), which limits states' power to control insurance. [40]

"The best thing states can do is set up role models," says Brandeis University Professor of Health Policy Stuart Altman. "You can't design true national health insurance state by state, because you'd get past a few states, then stop."

While states' efforts are important, says the National Coalition on Health Care's Simmons, "we don't think that any single state, no matter how large," can accomplish universal coverage of its residents "without major federal policy changes." Many governors agree and acted on their own only because they're frustrated with a lack of federal action, he says.

Furthermore, even if all states achieved universal coverage, the result would be a cost-increasing nightmare — the last thing the health system needs, says Simmons. "If you think we have administrative complexity now, imagine 50 individual state programs."

CHRONOLOGY

1880s-1920s *Most European countries adopt compulsory health insurance.*

1895 German physicist William Roentgen discovers the X-ray, ushering in the age of modern medicine and rising health-care costs.

1920 Public commissions in California, New Jersey, Ohio and New York recommend universal state health coverage.

1926 The private Committee on the Cost of Medical Care (CCMC) endorses developing private health insurance; American Medical Association (AMA) opposes the idea.

1929 The first hospital prepayment insurance plan is launched for school teachers in Dallas, Texas.

1930s-1940s *Private hospital prepayment insurance spreads around the country, as hospitals worry they'll go under when poor patients don't pay. Congress and legislatures in at least eight states debate but don't enact compulsory health insurance.*

1935 Attempts to include health coverage in the new Social Security Act are unsuccessful.

1943 The first measure calling for compulsory national health insurance is introduced in Congress. . . . National War Labor Board declares employer contributions to insurance income-tax free, enabling companies to offer health insurance to attract workers.

1950s-1960s *Health spending and consumption rise rapidly, and workplace-based health insurance spreads. Medicare and Medicaid are enacted for the poor and elderly.*

1970s-1980s *Worries grow about health care becoming unaffordable. Presidents Nixon and Carter propose universal health coverage and health-care price controls. Cost controls reduce federal spending on Medicare, but doctors and hospitals shift their costs to employers.*

1990s *Federal government expands Medicaid and enacts a new children's health program, but employers begin dropping health benefits. Washington lawmakers shy away from large-scale coverage expansion after President Clinton's ambitious attempt to enact universal coverage fails.*

Sept. 22, 1993 Clinton unveils sweeping plan to reform U.S. health-care system.

Sept. 26, 1994 After a year of fierce debate, Senate leaders declare Clinton's bill dead.

1996 Congress enacts Health Insurance Portability and Accountability Act to make employer-provided coverage transferable between jobs and more accessible to the self-employed.

1997 Congress enacts State Children's Health Insurance Program (SCHIP) to help states cover children from low-income families.

2000s *As health costs and the ranks of the uninsured rise, Congress mulls new tax deductions and credits to help consumers buy coverage; interest grows in compulsory insurance.*

2002 Congress enacts Health Care Tax Credit, available to whose who lose their jobs due to foreign competition.

2006 Massachusetts enacts universal-coverage plan requiring all residents to buy health insurance. . . . Vermont enacts voluntary coverage plan with subsidized insurance and medical cost trimming. . . . Maryland plan to force large employers to supply coverage or pay into a state insurance pool is struck down in federal court.

2007 President Bush proposes replacing the tax break received by those with employer-based coverage with a tax deduction available to everyone. . . . Gov. Arnold Schwarzenegger, R-Calif., proposes universal, state-subsidized health insurance. . . . Bush twice vetoes congressional attempts to expand the State Children's Health Insurance Program.

2008 Schwarzenegger bill dies in California Senate. . . . San Francisco becomes the first city to attempt to provide universal coverage to its residents.

Should individuals be required to buy health insurance?

At the start of the new century, few people were advocating that all Americans be required to buy health insurance, but in recent years such voices have grown louder. With interest growing in a system that subsidizes the cost of private coverage, advocates say unless everyone participates no functioning insurance market can develop. Insurance is designed to even out annual health costs for everyone by having everyone pay similar amounts into an overall pool each year, whether they are healthy in that particular year or facing an unexpected sickness or injury.

But opponents on the left say mandating insurance is unfair to lower-income families who can't afford even heavily subsidized private insurance. And conservative critics say a requirement to purchase is undue government intrusion into private life.

"You can talk until you're blue in the face about risk pools and actuarial tables and all the green-eyeshade reasons that the health insurers need everyone to participate in order to write affordable policies. I understand all that, and I basically don't care," wrote lawyer and policy blogger David Kravitz about Massachusetts' new buying requirement. "It is fundamentally wrong to force people to buy an expensive product in the private market, simply as a condition of existing in this state," he wrote on the Blue Mass Group policy blog. [41]

Monitoring who is obeying the requirement and determining subsidy sizes creates "one more aspect of citizens' lives" that government would monitor, complains Michael D. Tanner, director of health and welfare studies at the libertarian Cato Institute. A mandate would also be extremely difficult to enforce, he says.

"An individual mandate crosses an important line: accepting the principle that it is the government's responsibility to ensure that every American has health insurance," said Tanner. "In doing so, it opens the door to widespread regulation of the health-care industry and political interference in personal health-care decisions. The result will be a slow but steady spiral downward toward a government-run national health-care system." [42]

The issue became heated during the Democratic presidential contest. Sen. Clinton's universal health proposal would have mandated that individuals buy insurance; Obama's plan only required that parents buy coverage for their children.

Clinton claimed that Obama's lack of an "individual mandate" would mean 15 million Americans would go without insurance. During a debate, she said to him, "We know it's politically controversial to say we're going to cover everyone, and you chose not to do that." [43]

Obama disputed Clinton's claim that 15 million would remain uninsured under his plan, which he argued would reduce costs enough so that more people could afford coverage. Robert Reich, who served as secretary of Labor under President Bill Clinton, claimed that more people would actually be covered under Obama's plan. It was unclear what sort of penalties Clinton would impose on individuals who failed to buy insurance.

Advocates of a mandate argue that if government can require automobile insurance to ensure that costs are paid when drivers cause accidents, then health insurance shouldn't be any different, notes Tanner. But economists say there are some key differences between the two kinds of coverage. For example, few people will drive more recklessly just because they have auto insurance. But the prevalence of generous health insurance has been shown to encourage patients to seek — and doctors to prescribe — more and sometimes unnecessary or unduly expensive treatments. [44]

Nevertheless, policymakers from both parties increasingly consider mandating health insurance "an essential accommodation to limited public resources," explains Ginsburg of the Center for Studying Health System Change. In 2004, for instance, then-Senate Majority Leader Frist said "higher-income Americans have a societal and a personal responsibility to cover in some way themselves and their children." [45] If those who can afford coverage don't enroll, the government should enroll them automatically in a high-deductible insurance plan that covers catastrophic expenses and obtain the payment for the premiums at tax time, Frist said. And the mandate should apply to the "very, very rich" initially, then expand over time, he said. [46]

Requiring everyone to buy coverage ensures that those with lower medical needs will pay premiums alongside those with expensive illnesses, analysts point out. "If the government says an insurance company must take whoever comes their way, they couldn't predict risk and might go broke" if only sicker people enrolled, says Marian R. Mulkey, senior program officer at the California Healthcare Foundation, which funds health-care research. A mandate like the one Schwarzenegger proposed "relieves this concern of insurers, who are businesses and must be on solid financial footing to offer benefits."

Looking Into the Future of Health Coverage

New proposals offer new approaches

With the number of uninsured Americans creeping inexorably upward, universal coverage became a hot political issue in the 2008 presidential campaign. Outside of the campaign, the state and federal plans being considered contain some new wrinkles that might help policymakers reach a compromise on how to expand coverage.

Massachusetts — A 2006 state law requires all residents to buy insurance or pay a penalty. Massachusetts will subsidize premiums for those earning under 300 percent of poverty level (about $60,000 for a family of four) and waive the coverage requirement if no "affordable" policies are available.

Coverage is sold through a state-operated market, the Massachusetts Health Insurance Connector, and the state has negotiated with insurers to get affordable premiums for comprehensive policies, something that proved to be more of an uphill struggle than lawmakers imagined.

"Massachusetts decided consciously not to grapple with rising health-care costs and decided to do it later," says Paul Ginsburg, president of the Center for Studying Health System Change, a nonpartisan research group. "Now they're having a problem with the bids coming in higher than expected."

That decision may doom the plan, says Robert Laszewski, a consultant and former insurance executive. Annual health-insurance premiums for the average Massachusetts family had already reached $15,000 a few years ago — higher than the current national family average of $12,000 — in part because of the state's high-cost academic medical centers and plethora of physicians, he points out. "Yet the Massachusetts legislature came up with $200 a month" — $2,400 a year — "as a reasonable premium for their plan," he laments.

Even though the state's poorest residents have now been exempted from the requirement that they buy insurance, the program has been successful enough to cause months-long waits for appointments with primary-care physicians in parts of the state. About 340,000 of the state's previously uninsured 600,000 residents had coverage by mid-2008. [1]

California — In 2007, Gov. Arnold Schwarzenegger unveiled a universal-coverage plan that also would have required all residents to buy a minimal level of coverage. Public programs would have been expanded to cover the lowest-income Californians, and subsidies would have helped others buy private insurance.

Insurers would have offered policies to all comers, at state-approved rates. Employers with 10 or more workers would have paid at least 4 percent of payroll for health insurance or pay that amount into a state pool. To trim costs, insurers would have been required to spend at least 85 percent of every premium dollar on patient care.

To entice more hospitals and doctors to participate in California's subsidized Medi-Cal program, the state would have increased payments to participating providers. This would also have eliminated what Schwarzenegger called the "hidden tax" — low public-program payments and uncompensated care for uninsured people that providers now pass along as higher prices to paying patients. The Medi-Cal pay boost would have been funded by a tax on non-participant doctors and hospitals.

Some employers were skeptical of the plan, which failed to be approved by the California legislature. The plan would have helped companies that already provide health benefits because it would have forced their competitors to ante up for health care also, said Scott Hauge, president of the advocacy group Small Business California. But that could be perceived as unfair by some companies with young workers, whose "invincibility-of-youth syndrome" means they'd prefer cash to health benefits they believe they don't need, he said. [2]

Insurers balked at being forced to spend 85 percent of premiums on patient care. "Wellpoint, California's biggest [for-profit] insurer, puts 80 cents on the dollar toward care, holding on to a full 20 cents for profits and administration,"

The Medicare drug benefit works similarly, says health-care consultant Laszewski. Medicare doesn't require seniors to enroll but strongly encourages it by imposing a financial penalty on those who wait to sign up, he says.

The drug benefit "created a huge pool of people from age 65 to 95," he explains. "And you allowed people in at the same rates no matter what their age or pre-existing condition, so long as they signed up as soon as they became eligible."

The proof of that approach is in the pudding, he says. Private insurers have "flooded the market with plans," and people are not faced with steeply escalating premiums as they age or their health worsens, he says.

Laszewski says. Nevertheless, "everybody knows that it can be done for less. In Medicare, 95 cents on every dollar goes to patient care."

President George W. Bush — The president wanted to replace the current unlimited government subsidy for employer-sponsored health coverage with a flat standard deduction available to everyone who buys at least catastrophic health coverage on their own or through an employer. Federal funds then would be available for states to improve their markets for individual health policies, where people would shop for non-workplace coverage.

Economists praised Bush for proposing to replace the government's current subsidy for health insurance — the exclusion from taxable wages of employer-sponsored coverage — with more widely available assistance. But some critics on both the left and right agreed the proposal didn't target the people most in need of subsidies and didn't help create enough affordable coverage for them to buy.

"Replacing the current tax treatment with a new standard deduction is a big step in the right direction," said Heritage Foundation Vice President Stuart M. Butler and Senior Policy Analyst Nina Owcharenko. Nevertheless, "an even better step would be to replace it with a tax credit," which would help lower-income families who are least likely to have insurance, they said. Unlike tax credits, which benefit everyone equally, Bush's proposed deduction had a much higher dollar value for higher-income people. [3]

Former Sen. John Edwards, D-N.C., is the first presidential candidate to propose a detailed universal health-care plan.

Getty Images/Ethan Miller

Arizona Sen. John McCain's plan is similar to what President Bush proposed. It would offer tax credits of $2,500 per individual and $5,000 for families to help them pay for their own insurance. The credits would be financed by eliminating the tax break employers receive for making contributions to employee health plans (although they could still deduct their insurance payments as a business expense). McCain expressed greater concern about controlling costs than expanding coverage, but he said he would create a "guaranteed access plan" to help provide coverage for certain high-risk individuals.

Illinois Sen. Barack Obama would require parents to buy insurance for their children and make all but the smallest employers either provide insurance or devote 6 percent of their payroll costs to helping the government insure those workers. He would expand eligibility for government programs offering coverage for the poor and let individuals buy coverage through a nationwide purchasing pool. He also claimed he could find billions in savings through stricter regulation of insurers and greater use of technology.

[1] Kevin Sack, "Universal Coverage Strains Massachusetts Care," *The New York Times*, April 5, 2008, p. A1.

[2] Renuka Rayasam, "Schwarzenegger Health Plan Raises Doubts." *U.S. News & World Report*, Jan. 10, 2007, www.usnews.com/usnews/biztech/smallbizscene/070110/schwarzenegger_health_plan_rai.htm.

[3] Stuart M. Butler and Nina Owcharenko, "Making Health Care Affordable: Bush's Bold Health Tax Reform Plan," *WebMemo No. 1316*, Heritage Foundation, Jan. 22, 2007.

BACKGROUND

America vs. Europe

From the beginning, America differed sharply from other industrialized nations in its approach to health insurance. While Europe turned to social insurance, in which all residents pay into a common fund that provides population-wide benefits, American physicians resisted, fearing such an approach would encourage government influence over the practice of medicine. [47]

The development of the American workplace-based insurance system echoed "themes that distinguish the

Stakeholder Groups May Balk at Changes

They fear paying more, losing coverage

As costs and the ranks of the uninsured soar, there's plenty not to like about the current health-care system. Nevertheless, many longtime stakeholders fear change. As has often happened in the past, insurance companies, health providers, employers and those with expansive work-based health coverage all may balk at the changes universal coverage may bring.

"You often see interest groups wearing a cloak of ideology," saying they oppose a reform plan on economic or philosophical grounds when they're really protecting their money, says Stanley Dorn, a senior research associate at the liberal Urban Institute.

For example, he says, during the bitter debate over President Bill Clinton's universal-coverage plan in the early 1990s, "you had companies that didn't provide insurance to their workers and knew they could lose money" if the proposal succeeded. "But they didn't talk about that. They talked about how evil it would be for the government to take over the health system."

Various employer groups are likely to weigh in on both sides of the debate. Those who offer health coverage as a benefit today are more likely to embrace the change, although they may still be hesitant to endorse all universal-coverage proposals, says Paul Ginsburg, president of the Center for Studying Health System Change, a nonpartisan research group. "They'd like to get out of the business of coverage long term, but the issue has always been whether they'd end up paying more in taxes" for a new universal coverage system than they spend now to provide benefits, he says.

Large, unionized employers like U.S. automakers initially supported the Clinton plan in 1993, said Walter Mahan, former vice president for public policy of DaimlerChrysler Corp.[1] Employers who didn't offer health benefits strongly opposed the Clinton plan, which, like many universal-coverage plans today, asked all businesses to chip in, including those that didn't offer health benefits before.

Caught somewhat off guard by ferocious opposition from businesses that didn't offer coverage — like restaurants and soda manufacturers — architects of the Clinton plan reduced the payments required from companies that had not previously offered coverage and hiked the amount asked from employers who offered coverage. Complaining of unfairness, unionized employers then pulled their support, said Mahan. The bad news for the new crop of

more general history of the United States," wrote Rosemary A. Stevens, University of Pennsylvania professor emeritus of the history of science. Social insurance was trumped by "the commitment to private solutions to public needs" and "the belief in local initiatives wherever possible."[48]

As the 19th century ended, Europeans leaned more toward "social democracy" — the belief the free market cannot supply certain human necessities, such as a minimum income to purchase food, clothing, housing and access to health services. Governments were seen as necessary to guarantee those needs, explains Thomas Bodenheimer, adjunct professor of family and community medicine at the University of California, San Francisco.[49]

In the late 1800s a conservative German government enacted the first social-insurance programs in hopes of heading off a wholesale movement toward more radical socialism with government ownership of industries. Supported by mandatory contributions from all citizens, the first programs paid out when people lost their livelihood through unemployment, disability or retirement. In 1883, Germany added health care to its social-insurance offerings, though with a twist. Unlike other programs, health insurance was run by privately operated "sickness funds." Social insurance, including for health care, soon became the European norm.

In the United States, lawmakers debated social insurance for decades and ultimately used it for a few programs. But health insurance remained a voluntary purchase, managed by private companies.

American liberals argued that social insurance for health would unite the entire population into a single risk pool and serve everyone's long-term interest, according to Bodenheimer. Though younger people would pay for older people, and healthy people for sick

reformers: More and more companies have been dropping coverage since then, so the constituency of businesses not offering coverage "is stronger now," he said. [2]

Insurers may have the biggest stake in the current system. Most analysts say proposals that would abolish private insurance in favor of a government-run universal plan modeled on Medicare are politically impossible today. However, most reform plans would force insurers to cover potentially sicker beneficiaries than most do today and would tighten rules for selling and marketing insurance policies.

Many insurers mistrust changes because the current employer-based system works well for them by weeding out the sickest populations, said former Rep. William Thomas, R-Calif., who chaired the House Ways and Means Committee. Employed people "have to get up every morning, go to work and carry out difficult and complex tasks." They're essentially prescreened to be, on average, healthier than the general population and thus easier to cover and still earn profits, he said. [3]

Insurers also distrust government-run "insurance exchanges" in many universal-coverage plans that would establish standard benefit packages, ensure affordability and replace insurers' marketing with government-scrutinized plan descriptions. Insurers have "traditionally hated" government limits on their marketing, says Dorn.

Virtually all economists say any health system reform must include cost cutting, including reining in salaries and profits of doctors, hospitals and drug manufacturers. Some proposals ask providers to put money in up front to support coverage proposals. Providers always push back against such steps.

For example, when Democratic Maine Gov. John Baldacci unveiled a universal-coverage program in 2003, he included a tax on insurance premiums along with both voluntary and mandatory price caps on many health services, without which the governor said the program could not survive. Maine's hospitals said they couldn't survive having prices capped.

"That cannot happen . . . without irreparably harming Maine's hospitals," said Warren Kessler, a consultant and former head of the Maine General Medical Center in Augusta. [4]

Finally, those who currently have good coverage are sensitive to any proposal that might make their own insurance worse or cost more. Interest groups like insurers and doctors who oppose any new plan "just have to play on the public's fear of losing what they now have," says Dorn.

---

[1] "Universal Coverage: It Can't Happen Here . . . Or Can It?" *Medicine & Health*, "Perspectives," March 31, 2003.

[2] Quoted in *ibid.*

[3] Quoted in "Thomas Takes Aim Again at Tax-Favored Employer Coverage," *Medicine & Health*, Feb. 16, 2004.

[4] Quoted in "Baldacci Says Everyone Must Give a Little to Fund Care," *Medicine & Health*, May 12, 2003.

people, this would even out in the end, progressives argued, since the young will one day be old and the healthy injured or sick. [50]

But conservatives answered that it's unfair to force young people to subsidize health care for older, sicker neighbors and that people will spend more prudently on medical care if they buy their own.

Sickness Insurance

The private market for what we call health insurance today — policies that pay medical bills — grew slowly, mainly because health costs were low, even in the early 20th century. Before 1920, there were virtually no antibiotics and few effective drugs, and X-rays had been discovered only in 1895. Most of the financial burden from illness was due to lost wages, so insurers sold income-protection "sickness" or "accident" insurance.

The first such policy was sold in 1850 by the Massachusetts-based Franklin Health Assurance Company. For a 15-cent premium, the policy paid $200 if its holder was injured in a railway or steamboat accident. [51]

Some employers offered sickness insurance as a worker benefit. In 1910, the catalog store Montgomery Ward and Co. established a group insurance plan to pay half of an ill or injured employee's salary. [52] In 1918, the Dallas, Texas, school system established sickness insurance to protect teachers against impoverishment during the great influenza epidemic. [53]

The mining, railway and lumber industries led the way in establishing insurance plans similar to modern HMOs (health maintenance organizations), paying medical costs. Their workers faced serious health risks and labored in remote locations where traditional care wasn't available. So companies established clinics that prepaid doctors fixed monthly fees to provide care.

Nevertheless, between 1910 and 1920, near the end of the so-called Progressive Era in American politics, "government-sponsored health insurance seemed a practical possibility in the United States," according to the University of Pennsylvania's Stevens. In 1920, expert panels in four large states — California, New Jersey, Ohio and New York — recommended universal state-sponsored health insurance. [54]

However, doctors, hospitals and insurance companies feared if universal coverage was adopted they would lose control and cash. The chairman of Ohio's commission complained about "the confusion into which the public mind had been thrown by the misleading, malicious and false statements emanating from an interested and active commercial insurance opposition." [55]

Soon, popular support for government-sponsored insurance dropped to a low level again, as financial worry receded in the 1920s economic boom. In the overall prosperity of that decade, the medical system flourished, and hospitals built new wings in the mood of general optimism.

By 1929, however, more than a third of hospital beds were empty, and many hospitals struggled to pay off the loans that had funded expansion. Baylor University Hospital in Dallas, for example, had $1.5 million in overdue loan payments for construction and was behind in other bills. "Baylor was just 30 days ahead of the sheriff," said one observer. [56] Baylor's crisis led to health insurance as we know it today.

In search of cash, Baylor made common cause with local employers. In late 1929, the Dallas school system set up a hospital-service prepayment plan that operated alongside its sick-benefit fund. For a monthly premium of 50 cents, teachers would get free hospitalization for 21 days and a one-third discount on additional days. Benefits became effective on Dec. 20, 1929, less than two months after the stock market crash. [57]

A few days later, elementary-school teacher Alma Dickson slipped on an icy sidewalk and broke her ankle. [58] Hospitalized with a cast, Dickson became the first patient in the first prepaid hospitalization plan, the forerunner of today's Blue Cross system. [59]

By 1935, 19 such plans had been created in 13 states, as hospitals struggled to stay afloat during the Great Depression. [60]

But many influential physicians argued that "prepayment" threatened professional independence. Recommendations that the nation adopt insurance to protect people against the rising cost of care amounted to "socialism and communism — inciting to revolution," wrote Morris Fishbein, editor of the *Journal of the American Medical Association.* [61]

Workplace Plans

During the 1930s, as businesses folded and millions sank into poverty, the United States made its largest-ever foray in social insurance.

Developed by Democratic President Franklin D. Roosevelt and enacted in 1935, Social Security is a mandatory, universal system that provides income support for retirees, severely disabled people, widows and under-age bereaved children. During the debate over passage, activists argued for including health insurance, but the administration declined, in part because it feared the contentious health issue might doom the whole plan. [62]

Later, members of Congress made unsuccessful attempts to extend social-insurance to health in 1943, 1945, 1947, 1949 and 1957. Nevertheless, by 1966, 81 percent of Americans had hospitalization insurance — mostly offered through their workplaces and often as a result of labor union demands — compared to only 9 percent in 1940. [63]

Unlike today, from 1940 to 1966 large unionized companies dominated the economy. Offered as a worker benefit, employer-sponsored health plans successfully pooled the risk and contributions of many employees in order to keep individuals' costs low and uniform, even in years when they had accidents or illness. And, since the sickest people are unlikely to be employed, relying on workplace-based plans allowed private insurers to more easily predict and control costs.

As the primary source of Americans' health insurance, the still union-dominated U.S. auto industry has evolved over the years into "a social-insurance system that sells cars to finance itself," said Princeton University economics Professor Uwe Reinhardt. [64]

But even in the early days, employer-provided insurance had limits. Many retired people, very low-income families and the disabled never had workplace-based insurance and were too poor to buy individual policies, for which they would be charged premiums based on health status.

After several years of debate, Congress in 1965 enacted a new compulsory, universal insurance plan — the Medicare program — to provide health coverage for elderly and some disabled people and Medicaid to

Should Congress enact President Bush's tax proposal for expanding health coverage?

YES
Stuart M. Butler, Vice President
Nina Owcharenko, Senior Policy Analyst
The Heritage Foundation

From the foundation's Web site, January 2007

President Bush's proposal to reform the tax treatment of health care takes a bold step toward fixing America's health system by widening the availability of affordable and "portable" health plans and by defusing some of the pressure that currently leads to higher health costs.

Although some Americans would have more of their compensation subject to taxes, this proposal is no more a tax increase than limiting or ending tax deductions to move toward a flatter tax system. It would remove distortions and inequities and make tax relief for health insurance more widely available.

While the proposal can be improved in ways that would further reduce uninsurance, it is a big step toward sound tax and health policy. It would treat all Americans equally by ending the tax discrimination against families who buy their own health insurance, either because they do not have insurance offered by employers or because they prefer other coverage.

Ending that discrimination would have the added advantage of stimulating wider choice and greater competition in health coverage, which will help moderate the growth in costs. It would also make it easier for families to keep their chosen plan from job to job, reducing the loss of coverage that often accompanies job changes.

The president's proposal could be improved. While replacing the tax treatment with a new standard deduction is a big step in the right direction, an even better step would be to replace it with a tax credit more like the current child tax credit — at least for those buying health coverage outside their place of work. A tax credit would especially help lower-income families. With a deduction, many families would still be unable to afford basic coverage, but a credit set at a flat dollar amount or a high percentage of premium costs would make coverage more affordable.

A tax credit could be grafted onto the president's current proposal and would strengthen it considerably.

By taking this step, Congress can help make the tax treatment of health care more equitable and efficient, help more Americans choose the coverage they want and retain it from job to job and begin to reduce the tax-break-induced pressure that is a factor in rising health costs.

NO
Karen Davis
President, The Commonwealth Fund

From the fund's Web site, January 2007

While it is encouraging that President Bush made health care a theme of the State of the Union address, his proposal to offer tax deductions to those who buy health insurance would do little to cover the nation's 45 million uninsured.

Under the president's proposal, Americans with employer-provided health insurance would have the employer contribution counted as taxable income. But anyone with health coverage — whether provided by an employer or purchased individually — would have the first $7,500 of income excluded from income and payroll taxes or, in the case of families, the first $15,000 of income.

Those purchasing coverage in the individual market would get a new tax break, as would those whose employer contribution currently is less than the new standard deduction for health insurance.

The proposal would increase taxes on workers whose employers contribute more to health insurance than the premium "cap" allows, such as those that serve a large number of older workers. The administration estimates this change would translate into a tax increase for about 20 percent of employees. However, this could rise to more than half of employees by 2013, if increases in health-insurance premiums continue to outpace general inflation. In addition, the president proposes diverting federal funds from public hospitals to state programs for the uninsured.

Although the plan would offer subsidies to people looking to buy insurance on the private market, it would fail to assist most of the uninsured. Insurance premiums would still be unaffordable for Americans with modest or low incomes. And the tax increase for employees would likely lead to the erosion of employer-sponsored health insurance over time.

The proposal wouldn't do anything to make individual coverage available or affordable for those with modest incomes or health problems. The Commonwealth Fund found that one-fifth of people who had sought coverage in the individual health-insurance market in the last three years were denied coverage because of health problems or were charged a higher premium. The proposal, unlike plans in California and Massachusetts, does not require insurers to cover everyone.

Nor would the proposal likely help the currently uninsured. More than 55 percent of the uninsured have such low incomes that they pay no taxes, while another 40 percent are in the 10-to-15-percent tax bracket and would not benefit substantially from the tax deductions.

provide health care for the poorest mothers with children, the elderly and the disabled.

Coverage Declines

With Medicare and Medicaid in place, most Americans had access to health care.

Nevertheless, health spending was rising sharply, and Presidents Richard M. Nixon and Jimmy Carter both proposed reforms to keep care affordable, including universal coverage. Neither plan gained traction, however.

Gradually, the higher costs and the changed nature of American business began to erode the work-based insurance system.

"Forty years ago, the largest private employer was AT&T, a regulated monopoly with guaranteed profits," wrote Stanford University Professor Emeritus Victor Fuchs and Ezekiel Emanuel, chairman of clinical bioethics at the National Institutes of Health. "If health-insurance premiums rose, they could easily be passed on to telephone subscribers." [65]

That changed, however, as union membership started declining in the 1980s, and manufacturing jobs began migrating overseas and U.S. companies began to compete with foreign competitors that don't offer health benefits. More and more Americans ended up working in the largely non-unionized service industry, which offered few benefits.

"Today, the largest private employer is Wal-Mart, which despite its size faces intense competition daily from a host of other retail outlets," Fuchs and Emanuel wrote. "When they offer health insurance, it must come out of their workers' wages; for minimum-wage employees, this is not possible." [66]

Over the past two decades, employer-sponsored coverage has gradually waned, along with the number of insured Americans. Government programs have grown and picked up some of the slack, however.

In 1987, fully 87.1 percent of Americans were insured, with 75.7 percent insured through private, mostly employer-sponsored, coverage. By 1999, the percentage of insured Americans had dropped to 85.5.percent, 71.8 percent through private coverage. In 2005, the overall percentage had dropped to 84.1 percent — 67.7 percent with private insurance. [67]

In the face of declining coverage, proposals to expand coverage have been advanced repeatedly by the White House, members of Congress, state and local governments and others. Only some small-scale efforts have gone anywhere, however.

In 1994, Tennessee used federal Medicaid dollars and state funding to create TennCare. State officials hoped money-saving HMOs could provide coverage to many lower-income people and sicker Tennesseans, who were ineligible for Medicaid and couldn't afford insurance on their own.

For a few years, the program saved money and enrolled 500,000 residents who would otherwise have been uninsured. But the federal government had agreed to contribute funding for only 1.5 million people, and when enrollment exceeded that cap, TennCare refused to accept new applicants and struggled financially. For the past several years, TennCare has fought to survive, plagued by charges of poor care at its HMOs and disputes with the federal government over funds.

Clinton Plan

The highest-profile recent effort to enact a universal health care plan was President Bill Clinton's ambitious proposal to restructure the nation's health care system, unveiled on Sept. 22, 1993. His Health Security Act was proposed at a time when the uninsured ranks had swelled to 40 million, and polls showed that up to two-thirds of Americans favored tax-financed national health insurance. [68] Yet, within a year Senate Democrats had pronounced the plan dead, the victim of bruising attacks by business, insurers and medical providers. [69]

Five days after his inauguration, Clinton announced that first lady Hillary Rodham Clinton would chair a health-care task force made up of Cabinet members and White House staffers. It held hearings for a year and produced a plan to attain universal coverage mainly through expanded private coverage. It aimed to offer people a choice of affordable coverage while maintaining the existing private insurance industry and holding down health-cost growth.

To do that, the Clinton panel proposed creating regional government-managed insurance markets to negotiate health-care and premium prices and insurance-benefit packages and to oversee insurance marketing. It also called for annual caps on health-coverage cost increases, and a requirement that all employers contribute to the cost of coverage.

But opposition soon grew from businesses that believed they had more to lose than to gain from change. Employers who didn't offer coverage balked at proposed fees to help finance the plan. Insurers objected to regulations aimed at keeping them from skimming off healthy customers. After 10 months of strenuous campaigns by opponents, public approval had dropped to a lukewarm 40 percent. [70]

Former first lady Clinton — now a Democratic senator from New York and a 2008 candidate president — has assured voters she still believes in universal health coverage.

Her plan would require large employers to provide workers with coverage or contribute to the cost of coverage. Those with 25 employees or fewer would receive tax credits to start or continue coverage. Individuals without employer coverage would also receive tax credits to buy policies.

The *Los Angeles Times* wrote after its 2007 unveiling, "Simple announcement of the plan represented something of a personal triumph for the New York senator, whose 1993-94 overhaul effort with her husband, then-President Clinton, went down to ignominious defeat. With the new plan, she could have a rare second chance to recast the nation's healthcare system." [71] Her plan may die if she does not win the Democratic presidential nomination, however.

For a decade after the dramatic failure of the first Clinton plan, lawmakers were frightened away from the issue, while conservative lawmakers said the booming 1990s economy would enable the United States to "grow its way" out of uninsurance by creating more and better jobs with coverage benefits.

But that did not turn out to be the case. From 1997 to 2001, the economy boomed and jobs were created, but rates of employer-sponsored health insurance did not rise. The late '90s experience "tells us that relying on economic growth alone to reduce the number of uninsured won't work," said Ginsburg at the Center for Studying Health System Change. [72]

Since Clinton's efforts, Congress has enacted two coverage expansions. The State Children's Health Insurance Program (SCHIP) was enacted in 1997. The Clinton administration and a bipartisan group of lawmakers led by Sens. Edward M. Kennedy, D-Mass., and Orrin G. Hatch, R-Utah, gave states federal matching funds to expand coverage for children in low-income families. Today, SCHIP operates in all states, making nearly all otherwise uninsured children with family incomes up to twice the poverty level eligible for public coverage.

With Republicans dominating the White House and, until recently, Congress, most recent debate over coverage focused on tax incentives to help Americans buy insurance. Criticized by lawmakers of both parties for offering too-small tax breaks in its early proposals, the Bush administration gradually expanded its plan each year but saw none enacted.

The only federal health-coverage expansion enacted in this decade was a tax credit to assist workers unemployed due to competition from international trade, enacted in 2002 after a long contentious delay. But the credit has reached only 10 to 20 percent of those eligible for it, says the Urban Institute's Dorn, which he calls a "tragic" outcome for states like North Carolina, where it was intended to help people facing "the largest layoff in the state's history — the closing of the textile mills."

The program failed to catch on because its premiums are too high, he says. "It's not realistic to ask people to pay 35 percent of premiums when they're not working" when working people pay only 15 to 25 percent of theirs, he says. In addition, the tax credit in most states could only be used for individual policies, whose premiums generally are based on age and health status. "Even with a 65 percent subsidy, people were facing an unaffordable $1,000 a month premium."

Over the past decade, some congressional Republicans also have proposed allowing business and professional groups to offer association health plans (AHPs), which would enable small businesses and the self-employed to band together to buy health insurance free from the state regulations that apply to individual and small-group insurance plans, which AHP advocates say unduly drive up coverage costs for small business.

In the 1970s Congress waived state insurance regulation for large employers to encourage them to provide coverage for workers. But today both Democratic and some Republican lawmakers staunchly oppose allowing AHPs the same freedom. AHP opponents argue that it is too easy for such loosely formed groups to skim off workers most likely to be healthy and low-cost, which would raise premium costs even higher for those left behind.

Meanwhile, outside of legislative chambers advocates increasingly have been calling for universal coverage. In 2004, a three-year-long Institute of Medicine study declared that eroding coverage poses such a threat that the federal government must launch a "firm and explicit" plan to achieve universal coverage by 2010. [73]

Many analysts agree that universal coverage has been stalled not because of a lack of knowledge of how to accomplish it but because lawmakers lack the will to demand sacrifices.

There are "at least four ways" to get universal coverage, says Simmons of the National Coalition on Health Care. "This problem is solvable. It does not require atomic science."

CURRENT SITUATION

Interest Grows

Nearly half the states considered universal coverage plans in 2007 and 2008, but none ultimately came to fruition. The problem was cost. Even the most ambitious states predicated their plans on more funding help from the federal government, which they knew would not be forthcoming until the end of the Bush presidency. But they hoped their actions might prod the presidential candidates and the ultimate victor to consider expanded health coverage an essential part of the national agenda.

Many Washington hands think the tide finally may be turning on the question of universal health. "One big difference between now and several years ago is that there is a loss of faith in employer-provided coverage as capable of covering everyone, including from unions and key business groups" who have been its strongest supporters, says Yale's Hacker.

Coalitions of interest groups came together in 2007 to announce support for universal coverage. The Health Coverage Coalition for the Uninsured (HCCU) advocated a phased-in approach to universal coverage, beginning with an expansion of SCHIP and creation of tax credits for families with incomes up to about $60,000, and then creating similar programs for childless adults. [74]

The coalition includes groups that have traditionally sparred over health care, including Families USA, the retiree organization AARP, the American Medical Association, the American Hospital Association and the health-insurance lobby America's Health Insurance Plans. "Organizations that have never spoken to one another in a friendly manner are now talking about this, and that has transformed the debate," says Pollack of Families USA.

Others aren't convinced. The HCCU's "rhetoric was wonderful," says Altman of Brandeis. "But the result shows how little they actually agree on."

Early in 2007, the Service Employees International Union joined with Wal-Mart, an employer whose limited health benefits have been sharply criticized by the union, to form the Better Health Care Together group, calling for "quality, affordable" universal health care by 2012. The group held a national summit to rally support but has not announced a proposal, saying only that it supports joint public and private-sector efforts. [75]

But Dana Rezaie, a Wal-Mart shelf stocker in Fridley, Minn., says, "Anybody can say they support something. They need to show they really do." After six years at the store, the widowed mother of three says she can't afford Wal-Mart's health plan. [76]

The biggest battle over health in Washington at the end of the Bush presidency was waged over the State Children's Health Insurance Program, or SCHIP. Congressional Democrats proposed expanding the program by $35 billion over five years, to $60 billion in all. This would have been financed by an increase in tobacco taxes. Democrats said the money would be enough to cover 10 million children.

There were Republicans who supported the effort, as SCHIP has been popular during the decade or so since its creation. But most opposed it, saying it was too costly, would have raised taxes too much and would have drawn too many middle-income families out of private insurance into the government coverage program.

Bush vetoed the package twice, and Democrats were unable to muster the two-thirds majority necessary to override him. Yet in his fiscal 2009 budget, Bush did propose a $19.3 billion expansion of SCHIP over five years — nearly four times the amount he had said he would accept the previous year.

In that same budget, however, Bush proposed reducing the expected increases in the two main government health programs. He sought to cut projected Medicare spending by $12.4 billion that year and by $178.2 billion over five years. He wanted to cut Medicaid by $1.8 billion and $17.4 billion over the same periods. This plan received a cold greeting in Congress.

State Steps

As health insurance gains momentum as a public issue, many states have flirted with expanding coverage, and three are struggling to get universal coverage off the ground.

Maine was first out of the gate, enacting the nations' first state-level universal coverage plan in 2003. Its Dirigo Health plan is complicated and remains a work in progress. An agency made up of public and private entities arranges for coverage through private insurers. Participating small businesses are required to pick up 60 percent of the cost of insuring their workers, with the state offering subsidies to qualifying workers. The Dirigo law also expanded coverage through Medicaid.

Maine's Dirigo Health program — named for the state motto, Latin for "I direct" or "I guide" — has extended coverage to 28,000 people since it was launched. There are plenty of people who contend that it is a failure and that it will surely fall far short of its original goal of providing universal coverage by 2009.

But it is still up and running and insuring more people at a time when coverage rates are shrinking, so it's continuing to inform efforts in other states.

Massachusetts followed in 2006 with its celebrated law requiring residents to buy health insurance, often with government assistance. A state-operated clearing-house — the Health Insurance Connector — helps consumers comparison-shop for affordable coverage. The state has struggled to define benefit packages that insurers can sell at "affordable" prices. Nonetheless, more than half the 600,000 Massachusetts residents who lacked insurance when the law was enacted now have it.

Vermont's new Catamount Health program focuses first on promoting information technology and other reforms to shave administrative costs and an evidence-based standard of care "community by community," says Emory University's Thorpe, who consulted on the program. Then the state will turn to expanding coverage.

Despite these mostly hopeful examples in the East, the California legislature rejected Gov. Schwarzenegger's proposal to require individuals to buy coverage. The plan would have been funded with contributions from multiple sources, including government, individuals, employers, insurers and health-care providers. The Assembly approved a version of the plan late in 2007, but it was killed in the Senate, largely due to concerns about cost.

In Texas, where more than 25 percent of the population is uninsured, Republican Gov. Rick Perry is looking for revenue sources to subsidize more coverage. In 2007 he proposed selling off the state lottery and putting part of the proceeds in an endowment fund to expand insurance coverage. [77]

A year earlier, Rhode Island began requiring insurers to develop "wellness benefit" policies to help individuals and small businesses afford at least basic coverage. [78] Other states, such as New Jersey, Pennsylvania and New York continue to float ideas for expanding coverage.

San Francisco in 2008 became the first city to attempt a universal health program, despite a federal judge's ruling just before it took effect that struck down a provision requiring employers with 20 or more workers to offer insurance or pay a fee to underwrite the city's program. Absent the mandate, city officials estimated that a third of San Francisco's 73,000 uninsured adults would be left without coverage. [79]

OUTLOOK

Health Politics

One of the surprising turns the health care debate took during the 2008 campaign was the shift away from the idea of imposing an individual mandate. After the idea was tried in Massachusetts, it seemed to gain great currency among both liberal and conservative policy makers. But neither the Republican nor the Democratic presidential nominee ultimately supported it.

For example, Obama's plan seeks to split costs among individuals, government and business. The plan would require parents to cover their children, expand eligibility for government programs for the poor and offer subsidies for individuals to buy coverage through a new nationwide pool similar to the federal employee plan. He would require nearly all employers to offer coverage to their workers or pay roughly 6 percent of their payroll to help government fund the cost of covering those workers.

McCain advocated a different approach. His plan would steer individuals toward buying their own coverage. It would also ease people away from relying on their employers for insurance by changing the nature of the tax incentives for employers offering insurance. Twenty-five hundred dollars worth of annual tax credits would be offered to individuals and $5,000 to families and great emphasis would be placed on trying to contain costs to make insurance more widely affordable, rather than expanding coverage through government programs.

The shape of the health care debate in Washington in 2009 and beyond clearly depends on which candidate ends up in the White House. But with the number of uninsured Americans remaining steadily high and employers and individuals finding health benefits increasingly unaffordable, it is clear that the health care debate will indeed be vigorous.

Some interest groups that helped bring down the Clinton plan have softened their stance, says Ginsburg at the Center for Studying Health System Change. In Massachusetts, he points out, insurers have accepted the new state-run insurance marketplace, even though in the past they would have preferred to send out their own people to market policies and avoid head-to-head consumer comparisons of plans. But insurers realize that their long-time bread and butter — employer-sponsored coverage — "has topped out," Ginsburg says, so they anticipate no growth unless they embrace government-sponsored expansions.

"There's [been] a dramatic change in national political attitudes," says Simmons of the National Coalition on Health Care.

But others say the country may still not be ready to make the concessions needed.

"It's not clear to me that life has changed very much," says Altman of Brandeis. Forces that have resisted change in the past "are stronger today," and "you have very weak leadership" from the White House and Congress.

Endorsement by Democratic presidential hopefuls doesn't necessarily mean much, says Harvard's Blendon. "Democratic primary voters disproportionately care about this," he says. But he suggests that different priorities, such as economic concerns and the war in Iraq, will prevail in the general election.

Furthermore, Americans generally "do not want an alternative health system," he continues. "They want to fix the one they have."

Unfortunately for politicians, the simplest, catchiest sound bite on health reform involves covering the uninsured, but that doesn't "play politically," says Blendon. While people do want everyone to have access to health care, "what they want most is cheaper premiums for themselves."

NOTES

1. Jay Himmelstein, "Bleeding-Edge Benefits," *Health Affairs*, November/December 2006, p. 1656.

2. "Total population and uninsured persons under age 65: Percent by selected population characteristics, United States, first half of 2005"; table available at www.meps.ahrq.gov/mepsweb/data_stats/summ_tables/hc/hlth_insr/2005/t4_d05.htm.

3. Diane Rowland, executive vice president, Henry J. Kaiser Foundation, "Health Care: Squeezing the Middle Class With More Costs and Less Coverage," testimony before House Ways and Means Committee, Jan. 31, 2007; for background, see Keith Epstein, "Covering the Uninsured," *CQ Researcher*, June 14, 2002, pp. 521-544.

4. Christine Borger, *et al.*, "Health Spending Projections Through 2015: Changes on the Horizon," *Health Affairs Web site*, Feb. 22, 2006.

5. Rowland testimony, *op. cit.*

6. "Employer Health Benefits: 2007 Summary of Findings," Kaiser Family Foundation, www.kff.org/insurance/7672/upload/Summary-of-Findings-EHBS-2007.pdf.

7. "Facts on Health Care Costs," National Coalition on Health Care, www.nchc.org.

8. Quoted in Steven Taub and David Cook, "Health Care Can Bankrupt America," CFO.com, March 6, 2007. For background, see Michael E. Chernew, Richard A. Hirth and David M. Cutler, "Increased Spending on Health Care: How Much Can the United States Afford?" *Health Affairs*, July/August 2003.

9. "McCain Says His Health Plan Cheaper, Better," *Chicago Tribune*, Oct. 12, 2007.

10. Todd Gilmer and Richard Kronick, "It's the Premiums, Stupid: Projections of the Uninsured Through 2013," *Health Affairs*, April 5, 2005, www.healthaffairs.org.

11. *Ibid.*

12. "Coverage Matters: Insurance and Health Care," statement of Arthur L. Kellerman, co-chairman, Consequences of Uninsurance Committee, Institute of Medicine, www7.nationalacademies.org/ocga/testimony/Uninsured_and_Affordable_Health_Care_Coverage.asp.

13. Quoted in "IOM Uninsured Report Cites Rising Costs, Attacks Myths." *Medicine & Health*, Oct. 15, 2001.

14. "The Great Divide: When Kids Get Sick, Insurance Matters," Families USA, March 1, 2007, www.familiesusa.org/assets/pdfs/the-great-divide.pdf.

15. "Expanding Coverage Is Worth It for All, IOM Panel Insists," *Medicine & Health*, June 30, 2003.

16. *Ibid.* For background, see Marcia Clemmitt, "Prison Health Care," *CQ Researcher*, Jan. 5, 2007, pp. 1-24.

17. Quoted in "States Scramble for Ways to Cover Working Uninsured," *Medicine & Health*, "Perspectives," Feb. 8, 2005.

18. Barack Obama, "Obama Statement on President's Meeting with Big Three Automakers," press release, Nov. 14, 2006, http://obama.senate.gov.

19. For background, see Marcia Clemmitt, "Rising Health Costs," *CQ Researcher*, April 7, 2006, pp. 289-312.

20. Quoted in "Frist: 100 Percent Coverage Impossible, 93 Percent Not Working So Well Either," *Medicine & Health*, Feb. 9, 2004.

21. Quoted in *ibid.*

22. Quoted in "Who Should Pay for Health Care?" PBS Newshour Extra online, Jan. 19, 2004, www.pbs .org/newshour/extra/features/jan-june04/uninsured _1-19.html.

23. Jack Hadley and John Holahan, "The Cost of Care for the Uninsured: What Do We Spend, Who Pays, and What Would Full Coverage Add to Medical Spending?" The Kaiser Commission on Medicaid and the Uninsured, May 10, 2004, p. 5.

24. "Maryland Universal Coverage Plan Estimated to Cost $2.5 Billion," *Healthcare News*, News-Medical.Net, Feb. 21, 2007, www.news-medical.net; also see "How Much Would It Cost to Cover the Uninsured In Minnesota? Preliminary Estimates," Minnesota Department of Health, Health Economics program, July 2006.

25. For background, see Marcia Clemmitt, "Budget Deficit," *CQ Researcher*, Dec. 9, 2005, p. 1029-1052.

26. "Universal Coverage Rx: Tax-Code Changes, Money, Insurance Pools and a Mandates," interview with Jonathan Gruber, "On My Mind: Conversations with Economists," University of Michigan Economic Research Initiative on the Uninsured, www.umich.edu.

27. *Ibid.*

28. "Health Expenditure Per Capita, Public and Private, 2005," www.oecd.org/dataoecd/1/44/39616601.pdf.

29. Stephen Ohlemacher, "U.S. Slipping in Life Expectancy Rankings," The Associated Press, Aug. 12, 2007.

30. "Pushed to the Edge: The Added Burdens Vulnerable Populations Face When Uninsured," interview with Harold Pollack, "On My Mind: Conversations With Economists," University of Michigan Economic Research Initiative on the Uninsured, www.umich.edu.

31. *Ibid.*

32. John Kitzhaber, "Why Start With the Health Care Crisis?" The Archimedes Movement, www.JoinAM .org.

33. Alan Greenblatt, "Gimme Coverage," *Governing*, June 2007, p. 40.

34. George C. Halvorson, Francis J. Crosson and Steve Zatkin, "A Proposal to Cover the Uninsured in California," *Health Affairs*, Dec. 12, 2006, www .healthaffairs.org.

35. Dan Walters, "Schwarzenegger's Failure on Health Care Sours Voters," *Sacramento Bee*, April 28, 2008.

36. Arthur Garson, "Help States Cover the Uninsured," *Roanoke Times*, May 26, 2006.

37. Stuart M. Butler, "The Voinovich-Bingaman Bill: Letting the States Take the Lead in Extending Health Insurance," *Web Memo No. 1128*, The Heritage Foundation, June 15, 2006.

38. Quoted in Christopher Rowland, "Mass. Health Plan Seems Unlikely to Be U.S. Model," *The Boston Globe*, April 14, 2006.

39. *Ibid.*

40. Quoted in "IOM Panel Demands Universal Coverage by 2010," *Medicine & Health*, "Perspectives," Jan. 19, 2004.

41. David Kravitz, "The Individual Mandate Still Sucks," Blue Mass Group, Jan. 30, 2007, www.bluemass-group.com.

42. Michael D. Tanner, "Individual Mandates for Health Insurance: Slippery Slope to National Health Care," *Policy Analysis No. 565*, Cato Institute, April 5, 2006, www.cato.org.

43. "Christopher Lee, "Simple Question Defines Complex Health Debate," *The Washington Post*, Feb. 24, 2008, p. A10.

44. "Problems of Risk and Uncertainty," The Economics of Health Care, Office of Health Economics, p. 26, www.oheschools.org/ohech3pg3.html.

45. Quoted in "Frist: Limit Tax Exclusion for Employer-Based Coverage," *Medicine & Health*, July 19, 2004.

46. *Ibid.*

47. For background, see Anne-Emmanuel Birn, Theodore M. Brown, Elizabeth Fee and Walter J. Lear, "Struggles for National Health Reform in the United States," *American Journal of Public Health*, January 2003, p. 86; Laura A. Scofea, "The Development and Growth of Employer-Provided Health Insurance," *Monthly Labor Review*, March 1994, p. 3; Thomas Bodenheimer, "The Political Divide in Health Care: A Liberal Perspective," *Health Affairs*, November/December 2005, p. 1426.

48. Rosemary Stevens, foreword to Robert Cunningham III and Robert M. Cunningham, Jr., *The Blues: A History of the Blue Cross and Blue Shield System* (1997), p. vii.

49. Bodenheimer, *op. cit.*, p. 1426.

50. *Ibid.*, p. 1432.

51. Scofea, *op. cit.*, p. 3.

52. *Ibid.*

53. Cunningham and Cunningham, *op. cit.*, p. 5.

54. Stevens, *op. cit.*, p. vii.

55. Quoted in Scofea, *op. cit.*

56. Quoted in Cunningham and Cunningham, *op. cit.*, p. 4.

57. *Ibid.*, p. 6.

58. "Dallas School Teachers, 1928," Rootsweb.com; http://freepages.history.rootsweb.com/~jwheat/teachersdal28.html.

59. Cunningham and Cunningham, *op. cit.*, p. 6. For background, see also "Sickness insurance and group hospitalization," *Editorial Research Reports*, July 9, 1934, from *CQ Researcher Plus Archive*, http://library.cqpress.com.

60. Scofea, *op. cit.*

61. Quoted in Cunningham and Cunningham, *op. cit.*, p. 18.

62. For background, see "Federal Assistance to the Aged," Nov. 12, 1934, in *Editorial Research Reports*, available from *CQ Researcher Plus Archive*, http://library.cqpress.com.

63. Cunningham and Cunningham, *op. cit.*

64. Quoted in Danny Hakim, 'Health Costs Soaring, Automakers Are to Begin Labor Talks," *The New York Times*, July 14, 2003, p. C1.

65. Victor R. Fuchs and Ezekiel J. Emanuel, "Health Care Reform: Why? What? When?" *Health Affairs*, November/December 2005, p. 1400.

66. *Ibid.* For background, see Brian Hansen, "Big-Box Stores," *CQ Researcher*, Sept. 10, 2004, pp. 733-756.

67. "Historical Health Insurance Tables," U.S. Census Bureau, www.census.gov.

68. Bridget Harrison, "A Historical Survey of National Health Movements and Public Opinion in the United States," *Journal of the American Medical Association*, March 5, 2003, p. 1163.

69. For background, see "Health-Care Debate Takes Off," *1993 CQ Almanac*, pp. 335-347, and "Clinton's Health Care Plan Laid to Rest," *1994 CQ Almanac*, pp. 319-353.

70. Harrison, *op. cit.*

71. Peter G. Gosselin and Peter Nicholas, "Clinton Lays Out New Healthcare Overhaul," *Los Angeles Times*, Sept. 18, 2007, p. A1.

72. "Rising Tide of Late '90s Lifted Few Uninsured Boats," *Medicine & Health*, Aug. 6, 2002.

73. "IOM Panel Demands Universal Coverage by 2010," *op. cit.*

74. "Unprecedented Alliance of Health Care Leaders Announces Historic Agreement," Health Coverage Coalition for the Uninsured, press release, Jan. 18, 2007, www.coalitionfortheuninsured.org.

75. Dan Caterinicchia, "Rivals Want Health Care for All," *Columbus Dispatch* [Ohio], Feb. 8, 2007.

76. Quoted in *ibid.*

77. Quoted in The Associated Press, "Texas Governor Has Funding Idea: Sell the Lottery," *The Washington Post*, Feb. 7, 2007, p. A7.

78. "Rhode Island: Making Affordable, Quality-Focused Health Coverage Available to Small Businesses," *States in Action: A Bimonthly Look at Innovations in Health Policy*, The Commonwealth Fund, January/February 2007.

79. Mary Engel, "S.F. to Go on With Healthcare Expansion," *Los Angeles Times*, Dec. 31, 2007, p. B1.

BIBLIOGRAPHY

Books

Derickson, Alan, *Health Security for All: Dreams of Universal Health Care in America*, Johns Hopkins University Press, 2005.
A professor of history at Pennsylvania State University examines the ideas and advocates behind the numerous 20th-century proposals for universal health care in the United States.

Funigello, Philip J., *Chronic Politics: Health Care Security from FDR to George W. Bush*, University Press of Kansas, 2005.
A professor emeritus of history at the College of William and Mary describes the politics behind a half-century of failed attempts at major health reform.

Gordon, Colin, *Dead on Arrival: The Politics of Health Care in Twentieth-Century America*, Princeton University Press, 2003.
A professor of history at the University of Iowa explains how numerous private interests — from physicians desiring autonomy to employers seeking to cement employer-employee relationships — have helped halt development of universal health coverage in America.

Mayes, Rick, *Universal Coverage: The Elusive Quest for National Health Insurance*, University of Michigan Press, 2005.
An assistant professor of public policy at Virginia's University of Richmond explains how politics and earlier policy choices regarding the U.S. health system shape the range of possibilities available for future reforms.

Richmond, Julius B., and Rashi Fein, *The Health Care Mess: How We Got Into It and What It Will Take to Get Out*, Harvard University Press, 2005.
Two Harvard Medical School professors recount the history of American medicine and trends in financing health care and conclude that the United States could afford universal health coverage.

Swartz, Katherine, *Reinsuring Health: Why More Middle-Class People Are Uninsured and What

Government Can Do, Russell Sage Foundation, 2006.
A professor of health policy and economics at the Harvard School of Public Health argues that more people could buy insurance and coverage would be cheaper if the federal government offered insurance companies financial protection for the highest-cost illnesses.

Articles

Appleby, Julie, "Health Coverage Reform Follows State-by-State Path," *USA Today*, April 5, 2006.
States take different approaches to expanding health coverage as worry over lack of insurance grows.

Gladwell, Malcolm, "The Moral Hazard Myth," *The New Yorker*, Aug. 29, 2005.
Some fear that large-scale expansion of health coverage would encourage patients to rack up higher amounts of useless health-care spending.

Holt, Matthew, "Policy: Why Is Fixing American Health Care So Difficult?" The Health Care Blog, Oct. 16, 2006; www.thehealthcareblog.com/the_health_care_blog/2006/10/abc_news_why_is.html#comment-2418315.
An independent health-care consultant — along with blog comments by analysts, businesspeople and members of the public — describes and discusses the interest-group politics that shape the universal-coverage debate.

Holt, Matthew, "Risky Business: Bush's Health Care Plan," Spot-On Blog, Jan. 25, 2007; www.spot-on.com/archives/holt/2007/01/bush_tax_deductions_and_the_lo.html.
An independent health-care consultant explains the concept of risk-pooling for insurance and the current tax break already enjoyed by workers with employer-sponsored coverage.

Reports and Studies

Burton, Alice, Isabel Friedenzoh and Enrique Martinez-Vidal, "State Strategies to Expand Health Insurance Coverage: Trends and Lessons for Policymakers," The Commonwealth Fund, January 2007.
Analysts summarize recent state initiatives to extend health coverage to more adults and children.

**"Covering America: Real Remedies for the Uninsured,"
Vols. 1 and 2, Economic and Social Research Institute,
June 2001 and November 2002.**
Economists assembled by a non-partisan think tank analyze multiple proposals for achieving universal coverage.

**Haase, Leif Wellington, *A New Deal for Health: How
to Cover Everyone and Get Medical Costs Under
Control*, The Century Foundation, April 2005.**
A health analyst for the nonprofit group outlines cost,
quality and coverage issues that the group says make it

necessary for the United States to switch to universal
coverage.

**"Insuring America's Health: Principles and
Recommendations," Institute of Medicine Committee on
the Consequences of Uninsurance, National Academies
Press, 2004.**
In its sixth and final report, an expert panel urges federal
lawmakers to create a plan for insuring the entire population by 2010.

For More Information

Alliance for Health Reform, 1444 I St., N.W., Suite 910,
Washington, DC 20005; (202) 789-2300; www.all-health.org. Nonpartisan, nonprofit group that disseminates
information about policy options for expanding coverage.

Economic Research Institute on the Uninsured,
www.umich.edu/~eriu. Researchers at the University of
Michigan who conduct economic analyses of the hows and
whys of uninsurance and coverage-expansion proposals.

Families USA, 1201 New York Ave., N.W., Suite 1100,
Washington, DC 20005; (202) 628-3030; www.familiesusa.org/contact-us.html. A nonprofit group that advocates for large-scale expansion of affordable health coverage.

The Health Care Blog, www.thehealthcareblog.com. Blog
published by health-care consultant Matthew Holt; analyzes coverage proposals and other insurance issues.

Heritage Foundation, 214 Massachusetts Ave., N.E.,
Washington, DC 20002-4999; (202) 546-4400;
www.heritage.org. Conservative think tank that supports
state-organized purchasing groups for health care.

Kaiser Family Foundation, 1330 G St., N.W.,
Washington, DC 20005; (202) 347-5270; www.kff.org.
Nonprofit private foundation that collects data and conducts research on the uninsured.

National Coalition on Health Care, 1200 G St., N.W.,
Suite 750, Washington, DC 20005; (202) 638-7151;
www.nchc.org. Nonprofit, nonpartisan group that supports
universal coverage; made up of labor, business and consumer groups, insurers and health providers' associations.

Physicians for a National Health Program, 29 E.
Madison, Suite 602, Chicago, IL 60602; (312) 782-6006;
www.pnhp.org. Nonprofit group that advocates for single-payer national health insurance.

4

Fighting Superbugs

Marcia Clemmitt

Doctors diagnosed pneumonia when 12-year-old Carlos Don, of Ramona, Calif., became ill in late January, but his flulike symptoms actually were caused by the antibiotic-resistant staph infection known as MRSA, and he died on Feb. 4. Once easily treated, staph infections have become drug resistant. A resistant pathogen that often afflicts wounded soldiers in Iraq has forced many infected limbs to be amputated.

From *CQ Researcher*,
August 24, 2007.

I n late January, 12-year-old Carlos Don — a sixth-grader in Ramona, Calif., who loved playing football and racing motorcycles — returned from several days at a school-sponsored trip with flulike symptoms. The local urgent-care center diagnosed pneumonia and assured his parents he'd be fine once antibiotics kicked in.

But within days Carlos was hospitalized and breathing with the aid of a ventilator. On Feb. 4, with his heart, lungs and other organs too damaged to function, he was taken off the ventilator. The cause of death was an often-fatal bacteria widely known as MRSA (methicillin-resistant staphylococcus aureus). [1]

Staph infections were once easily treatable with antibiotics. Over the past few decades, however, more staph bacteria and other pathogens — microbes that make us sick — have evolved into bacteria that are resistant to antibiotics like methicillin and cephalosporin — dubbed superbugs.

Until recently, MRSA mainly infected hospital patients. Today, however, many resistant bacteria are acquired outside hospitals, like the staph infection Carlos contracted. Known as CA-MRSA (community-acquired MRSA), it seems to be even more dangerous than its hospital-acquired cousin, HA-MRSA.

An antibiotic is designed to kill specific bacteria, but they can mutate and become resistant to the drug. Over time, such antibiotic-resistant bacteria can survive and multiply, producing an entire population of bugs that are difficult or impossible to kill with existing antibiotics, especially frequently used antibiotics. * (To reduce the chance that bacteria will become resistant, doctors urge patients to

---

* Antibiotics kill bacteria but not viruses, such as the common cold, flu and HIV/AIDS.

Few States Require Hospital Infection Reports

Only 17 states require hospitals to report infection rates or infection information. Twenty-seven states and Washington, D.C., have similar legislation pending. With the rise of "superbugs," patient-safety advocates say it's more important than ever for patients to pressure hospitals to control the spread of infections.

State Requirements for Reporting Hospital Infection Rates

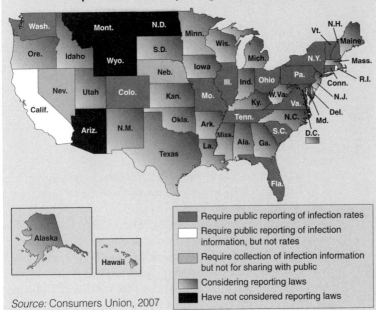

Require public reporting of infection rates

Require public reporting of infection information, but not rates

Require collection of infection information but not for sharing with public

Considering reporting laws

Have not considered reporting laws

Source: Consumers Union, 2007

Community-acquired MRSA may be the most frightening of the newly resistant pathogens, as Dee Dee Wallace, a 47-year-old mother of two in Mahotah, Wis., discovered late last year when she developed several skin infections. Her doctors thought they were minor, but after a "little red bump" on Wallace's knee "turned into white blisters," then "deep bone pain," doctors cultured her infection and discovered drug-resistant "flesh-eating" staph, she says.

Even the surgery that removed a chunk of her abscessed flesh — "down to where my husband could see the muscle lying on the bone" — didn't end Wallace's troubles. The bug lingered, eventually becoming resistant to vancomycin, the main antibiotic used to treat MRSA today, and it was months before she fully recovered.

A pediatrician's similar lack of awareness of CA-MRSA last year nearly claimed the life of a toddler from Santee, Calif., a San Diego suburb. The one-and-a-half-year-old, who'd never even had a cold, grew bloated and lethargic, his nostrils flaring as he struggled for breath, recalls his father, Scott Smith.

"We felt something was terribly wrong," but Bryce's pediatrician "said we were typical new parents" and repeatedly advised that they take the baby home and stop worrying, Smith says. Early on New Year's Day, with Bryce's condition worsening, his parents took him to the emergency room, where staff immediately suspected MRSA.

After a 55-day hospital stay — and surgery to remove part of his lung, through which the infection had eaten a hole — Bryce went home. He had to be given methadone to wean him from the narcotics he'd been sedated with during his long hospital stay, which included 49 days in intensive care.

The Smiths have switched doctors, and "our new pediatrician says she sees a case [of CA-MRSA] almost weekly," Smith says.

take all the antibiotics they are prescribed, even after an infection has been cleared up, because not using all the prescribed pills tends to kill off just the weaker bugs, leaving behind the stronger, more resistant bacteria.)

Shortly after antibiotics came into use in the 1940s, scientists and doctors observed that some bugs developed resistance, but only now are they beginning to understand the true scope of the danger from superbugs. Each antibiotic is "like a tank of gasoline," good for only so many uses, says John H. Powers, former lead medical officer for Antimicrobial Drug Development and Resistance Initiatives at the Food and Drug Administration (FDA).

"When it runs out, it runs out," says Powers, now senior medical scientist at Maryland-based SAIC Frederick, Inc., a research contractor for the National Institute of Allergy and Infectious Diseases.

Hospital-acquired MRSA is also on the rise. According to a 2007 study by the Association for Professionals in Infection Control and Epidemiology, 34 out of every 1,000 hospital patients (3.4 percent) have active HA-MRSA infections; another 12 patients are "colonized" with the bug, which means they could contract or spread the disease. That amounts to up to 1.2 million patients infected annually and between 48,000 and 119,000 deaths — far more than epidemiologists previously thought. A study released in 2005 by the U.S. Centers for Disease Control and Prevention (CDC) found that only 3.9 of every 1,000 patients (0.39 percent) had active MRSA infections. [2] At a minimum, treating HA-MRSA costs the United States between $3 billion and $4 billion annually. [3]

In fact, all bacteria — not just MRSA — and other microbes like viruses and fungi are becoming resistant to antimicrobial drugs. But antibiotic-resistant bacteria are causing the most concern, because most have been successfully treated with antibiotics for decades, while treating other kinds of microbes has been less successful.

Among other dangerous bacteria showing resistance, *klebsiella pneumoniae* can cause several kinds of urinary-tract and wound infections in hospitalized people, says Michael Feldgarden, research director of the Boston-based Alliance for the Prudent Use of Antibiotics. And if *klebsiella* develops resistance, Feldgarden explains, "a whole bunch of other organisms" will begin developing resistance as well.

Another hospital-based resistant pathogen, *acinetobacter*, has afflicted many soldiers wounded in the Iraq War, often forcing infected limbs to be amputated. [4] "It's totally resistant to all antibiotics but doesn't have

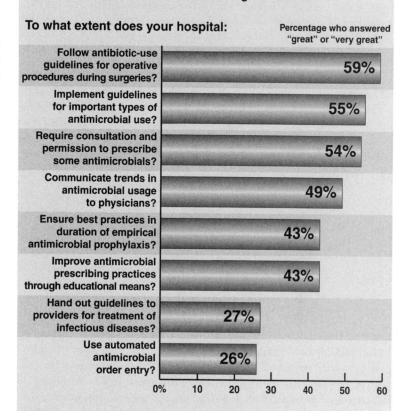

Fighting Drug Resistance in Hospitals

Fewer than 60 percent of U.S. hospitals follow recommended guidelines for antimicrobial use, according to a recent survey of infection-control personnel. And only 27 percent hand out guidelines for treatment of infectious diseases.

Control of Antimicrobial Use in U.S. Hospitals to Prevent or Control Drug Resistance

To what extent does your hospital:

Percentage who answered "great" or "very great"

Follow antibiotic-use guidelines for operative procedures during surgeries?	59%
Implement guidelines for important types of antimicrobial use?	55%
Require consultation and permission to prescribe some antimicrobials?	54%
Communicate trends in antimicrobial usage to physicians?	49%
Ensure best practices in duration of empirical antimicrobial prophylaxis?	43%
Improve antimicrobial prescribing practices through educational means?	43%
Hand out guidelines to providers for treatment of infectious diseases?	27%
Use automated antimicrobial order entry?	26%

Source: Alan J. Zillich, *et al.*, "Antimicrobial Use Control Measures to Prevent and Control Antimicrobial Resistance in US Hospitals," *Infection Control and Hospital Epidemiology*, October 2006; 448 infection-control practitioners

the virulence of MRSA," says Harold Standiford, medical director of infection control and antimicrobial effectiveness at the University of Maryland Medical Center in Baltimore.

And tuberculosis (TB) — which kills 2 million worldwide a year, more than any other infectious disease — is becoming increasingly resistant. In the five years from 2000 to 2005, multi-drug-resistant TB (MDR-TB)

How to Avoid Drug-Resistant Bugs

Hand washing is crucial

As antibiotics grow less effective, hygiene once again assumes a key role in protecting health.

Raised in an age before antibiotics, "Our grandparents told us, 'Wash your hands. Period. Wash before you eat. Wash after you go to the bathroom,'" says Stuart Levy, a professor of microbiology at Tufts University School of Medicine in Boston. Now, as the ability of antibiotics to treat infections wanes, those days are back, he says. "In developing countries, that means giving people clean water. For us, it means 'Wash.'"

Here are some other tips for staying healthy:

- Be especially careful about hygiene in moist, sweaty environments, like gyms. Athletic locker rooms, including in major-league professional sports, have become breeding grounds for dangerous bugs like methicillin-resistant staphylococcus aureus (MRSA). "You shouldn't be sharing clothes or towels or personal items like razors," says Jane D. Siegel, a pediatric infectious-disease specialist at the University of Texas' Southwestern Medical Center in Dallas.
- Avoid sharing personal objects like cell phones, too.

Alla Lulu, a sophomore biology major at the University of Arizona (UA), picked up a nasty face rash after borrowing a friend's phone, said Charles Gerba, a professor of environmental microbiology at UA and Lulu's uncle. The phone carried staph bacteria. [1]

- Avoid products like special soaps and detergents that contain antibacterials like the chemical triclosan. "There's no benefit to it over plain, old soap, and it drives resistance, so we need to be careful," says Allison Aiello, assistant professor of epidemiology at the University of Michigan School of Public Health. These antibacterials, which are hard to avoid, leave residues that continue killing at a low rate, thus driving bacteria to become resistant. In a recent survey 76 percent of liquid soaps contained triclosan, and 30 percent of bar soaps contained triclocarban, according to the Alliance for the Prudent Use of Antibiotics. [2] For tough cleanups, traditional antiseptics like alcohol, peroxide and bleach are the better choice. They kill quickly and leave no residue, so they're unlikely to increase resistance. Antibacterials like triclosan do have legitimate uses in health-care situations.

increased from 275,000 cases to at least 460,000, mostly in Russia, China and India. [5]

Inadequately treated MDR-TB may evolve further into "extensively drug-resistant" TB (XDR-TB), which is impervious to almost all drugs. It was the initial diagnosis given to Atlanta lawyer Andrew Speaker, who made headlines around the world in May for sneaking back into the United States after learning of his diagnosis — potentially exposing his fellow airline passengers to TB. Speaker claimed he feared he would die if he stayed in Europe, where he had honeymooned against doctors' advice.

Only 30 to 50 percent of patients with XDR-TB recover from the deadly illness. [6] Speaker was later found to have MDR-TB, not the lethal XDR variety. [7]

Not long ago, it was widely assumed that when a drug lost its potency, another would soon be available to replace it. But today "there are so few new drugs in the pipeline that if we don't act to prolong the effectiveness

of the drugs we've got, then we're in trouble," says Robert Guidos, director of policy and government relations at the Infectious Disease Society of America.

Although doctors know that overuse of antibiotics promotes resistance, controlling excessive antibiotic use has proven difficult. In many developing countries, for example, access to antibiotics is unregulated, says John McGowan, a professor of epidemiology at Emory University's Rollins School of Public Health in Atlanta. "You can walk into a pharmacy and get whatever you want" without a prescription.

Moreover, he says, countries like the United States promote resistance by creating "an artificial division" between individual care and the care given by public-health agencies. Private physicians often feel compelled to dose patients with the strongest, newest antibiotics, he explains, while public-health agencies want doctors to reserve such drugs for the toughest cases in order to

- Don't demand that your doctor give you an antibiotic, but if one is prescribed, take it for as long as directed. Otherwise, partly resistant bacteria still in your body can multiply and grow more resistant. [3]
- Don't take anyone else's antibiotic. It may not be appropriate for your illness and will kill off beneficial bacteria in your body. [4] "You've got hundreds of millions of bacteria in your intestines, and they ain't bothering you," says John H. Powers, former lead medical officer for the Food and Drug Administration's Antimicrobial Drug Development and Resistance Initiatives. In fact, many carry out important jobs, such as synthesizing vitamins like Vitamin K, used in blood clotting, he says. "Bugs get a bad rap. They're only bad if they get in the wrong place."
- If you're hospitalized, have someone there with you, especially on weekends and at night, says Lisa McGiffert, director of the Stop Hospital Infections project at Consumers Union. Hospital staff members might wash their hands and then touch the bed or a tray before touching you, but that shouldn't happen, says McGiffert. "You want them to go straight from the hand gel to you," she says. Health-care workers "know that and they mean to do it right, so they won't mind being reminded."
- When you have surgery scheduled, don't be afraid to ask the surgeon about the hospital's infection rate, says William Schaffner, chair of preventive medicine at the Vanderbilt University School of Medicine. Hospitals should also be able to tell you their hand-hygiene compliance rate, and you should ask, he says. "It is important to have a conversation with your surgeon," says McGiffert. "Just ask, 'Can you tell me what you do to prevent infections?' You should get a number of answers," including these: give antibiotics within 60 minutes of surgery; use the right antibiotic for the surgery; clip rather than shave the body pre-operation; keep the body warm during surgery and stop antibiotics within 24 hours of the surgery.

"You have to be your own advocate," says Dee Dee Wallace, a 47-year-old Wisconsin mom who had a life-threatening brush with a resistant skin infection this year that doctors responded to slowly. "You have to say, 'I don't think this is right.' You know your own body. Stick up for yourself. Don't let them say, 'Go home, you'll be fine.'"

---

[1] Quoted in Yusra Tekbali, *Arizona Daily Wildcat*, University of Arizona, "University Wire," Aug. 1, 2007.

[2] "Antibacterial Agents," APUA, www.tufts.edu/med/apua/Q&A_antibacterials.html.

[3] "When and How to Take Antibiotics," Alliance for the Prudent Use of Antibiotics, www.tufts.edu/med/apua/Patients/How2Take.html.

[4] *Ibid.*

prevent resistance from increasing.

Curbing the spread of infections through careful hygiene and isolation of the sick is crucial to slowing the spread of resistant microbes. But there is little consensus about what, if any, infection-control measures public-health agencies should impose.

"It's tough to make rules when everybody is not in agreement," says Standiford. For example, while he says it is important to screen at least some incoming hospital patients for MRSA — even if they show no signs of infection — he's unsure exactly who should be screened — surgical intensive-care patients, all intensive-care patients or some other group?

Antibiotics are also widely used on farms, not only to treat diseases that can spread to humans but also to increase animal growth rates, keep infection from breaking out in crowded barns and prevent crops from developing infections. [8]

But the amount of antibiotics used in agriculture is heavily disputed, primarily because no government agency collects the data. While most experts agree farms use many more antibiotics than humans do, debate rages over how seriously farm antibiotics affect human health. And while foodborne bacteria can grow resistant, few foodborne diseases are as virulent as MRSA. Moreover, benign resistant bacteria can transfer their resistance to pathogens, but there is no clear evidence that agricultural antibiotics have accelerated drug resistance among human pathogens like MRSA.

Several bills pending in Congress address resistance, as does at least one major bill in the works but not yet introduced. The proposals include incentives for drug companies to discover new antibiotics, stricter limits on farm use of antibiotics, a strengthened federal role in studying resistant infections and programs to combat them. Democratic leaders of the House and Senate

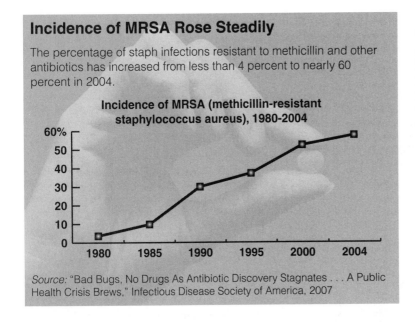

Incidence of MRSA Rose Steadily

The percentage of staph infections resistant to methicillin and other antibiotics has increased from less than 4 percent to nearly 60 percent in 2004.

Incidence of MRSA (methicillin-resistant staphylococcus aureus), 1980-2004

Source: "Bad Bugs, No Drugs As Antibiotic Discovery Stagnates . . . A Public Health Crisis Brews," Infectious Disease Society of America, 2007

health committees hope at least some of the provisions will be enacted this year, but action on the measures stalled during the summer while Congress debated other issues, including expansion of children's health insurance.

As lawmakers and infectious-disease specialists confront the rising tide of drug resistance, here are some of the questions being asked:

Should government agencies do more to combat superbugs?

With antibiotic-resistant bacteria on the rise — hospital-acquired MRSA, for example, soared from about 3 percent of hospital staph infections in 1980 to nearly 60 percent in 2004 — most experts agree the government should spend more on disease-surveillance and anti-resistance efforts. Moreover, they say hospitals, doctors and the drug industry aren't doing enough to stem the tide of resistance. But debate rages over whether they should be required to do more.

Ideally, Congress should establish an antibiotic-resistance coordinator who reports directly to the secretary of Health and Human Services (HHS), says Guidos of the infectious disease society. A direct line to the Cabinet is vital, he says, because other departments — including Defense, Veterans Affairs and Agriculture — also have roles to play.

Most other industrialized countries keep stricter tabs on how antibiotics are used — both for humans and agriculture — says Feldgarden of the Alliance for the Prudent Use of Antibiotics. Without knowing exactly what's being used and how, it's difficult to trace the cause and effect for microbes developing resistance or to issue accurate guidelines and alerts to hospitals and doctors, he says.

The U.S. data-gathering effort — the National Antibiotic Resistance Monitoring System (NARMS) — is "run on a shoestring" by three agencies, Feldgarden says, and data in some of their reports "are three years behind," so scientists can't get a real handle on how resistance is developing today. In addition, the agencies don't have authority to collect some of the data that would be most useful, he says.

"There are a lot of stakeholders with conflicting interests," he says, such as antibiotics manufacturers, who are unwilling to see their sales data made public.

But Neil Fishman, an associate professor of medicine at the University of Pennsylvania School of Medicine, says the government could gather much more information without compromising business secrets. "I don't care what Dr. Smith prescribes," he says. "I just need his state's use."

States also should be required to report incidents of MRSA, says Brian Currie, senior medical director of the Montefiore Medical Center at the Albert Einstein College of Medicine in Bronx, N.Y. "There's mandatory reporting for other communicable diseases in every state," he says, and MRSA should be on the list.

The private sector has not shown that it's able or willing to control infections or head off antibiotic resistance on its own, says Feldgarden. "We've got slightly more staph, and MRSA is going through the roof," he says, yet there has been no "forceful government intervention," such as shutting down hospitals. "The idea has been, 'Let doctors practice medicine.' But at some point, you have to say, 'You guys don't get to call the shots any more.' "

Yet, he warns, regulations would need to avoid unfairly scapegoating some hospitals. "If you're a hospital with an elderly population, you'll have a lot of MRSA even if you're doing a good job," he says. "So you can't just set a percentage level and tell people, 'Above that, and you're in trouble.' "

The Netherlands, for instance, has instituted "search and destroy" tactics in MRSA cases, says Feldgarden. Patients infected with MRSA are isolated, MRSA-colonized health-care employees are furloughed with pay and their families and pets are also checked and treated. The country's MRSA rate has dropped to 1 percent of its hospital-based staph infections, "while ours is 50 percent," he says.

However, the CDC doesn't have the authority to do what the Netherlands did, Feldgarden says.

Traditionally, states are the primary regulators of health care in the United States, but that approach can fail, says Feldgarden. "In the many tri-state areas, infections jump state lines," he says.

Whether or not they envision a stronger government role in fighting resistance, many analysts concede that private institutions aren't making much headway. For example, medical education has not focused much on resistance prevention, says Elaine Larson, associate dean of research at the Columbia University School of Nursing in New York City and director of the Center for Interdisciplinary Research on Antimicrobial Resistance.

Still, she and others remain skeptical of government efforts to force change.

Given Americans' predominantly private health system and their love affair with high-tech solutions, it's been difficult to develop a national policy that dissuades doctors from prescribing the most expensive, newest antibiotic first, says Larson. "I don't think a change is going to happen voluntarily," she says. Nevertheless, she's "not a big proponent" of legislating solutions because "it can take forever to change laws while microbes mutate very fast."

Even Fishman says the data do not yet support mandatory universal screening for MRSA. Universal screening "is the right strategy in some settings," he says, such as in academic medical centers that see the sickest

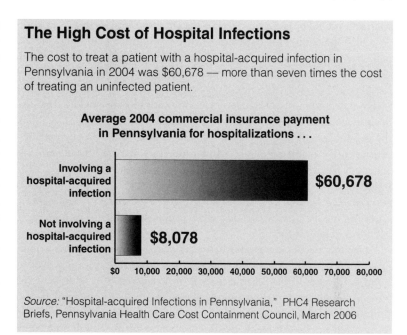

The High Cost of Hospital Infections

The cost to treat a patient with a hospital-acquired infection in Pennsylvania in 2004 was $60,678 — more than seven times the cost of treating an uninfected patient.

Average 2004 commercial insurance payment in Pennsylvania for hospitalizations ...

Involving a hospital-acquired infection: **$60,678**

Not involving a hospital-acquired infection: **$8,078**

$0 10,000 20,000 30,000 40,000 50,000 60,000 70,000 80,000

Source: "Hospital-acquired Infections in Pennsylvania," PHC4 Research Briefs, Pennsylvania Health Care Cost Containment Council, March 2006

patients. "But it might not be the correct strategy for a community hospital with low MRSA rates."

In addition, neither the Society for Healthcare Epidemiology of America nor the Association for Professionals in Infection Control and Epidemiology supports mandatory screening of patients showing no symptoms of active infection with MRSA or other antimicrobial-resistant pathogens. They fear any legislation would be written too narrowly and would not be flexible enough to apply to a newly developing resistance.

"Legislation in general is not sufficiently flexible to permit rapid response to local epidemiological trends," the groups maintain. [9]

Should the government make it easier for drug companies to bring new antibiotics to market?

With few if any new antibiotics being developed, some infectious-disease experts say the government should ease drug companies' path to creating new products. But other drug analysts argue that safety and public-health priorities must not be compromised.

"There are no drugs coming through the pipeline," says Guidos at the infectious disease society. With diseases like MRSA spreading, the government should consider major monetary incentives for companies to develop new antimicrobials, he says. For example, companies could be given a "wild card" patent extension — additional time to exclusively market some other lucrative drug they've developed — in exchange for developing the less profitable antibiotic. Drug patents run for 20 years from the date a patent application is filed.

From drug companies' standpoint, curbing antibiotic overuse makes drug development economically risky in the anti-infective field, says William Schaffner, chairman of preventive medicine at the Vanderbilt University School of Medicine in Nashville, Tenn. "As soon as one is developed, we immediately tell doctors, 'Don't use it, you dopes,' " he says. "We don't do that with Fords. I know of no other new product for which people say out in chorus, 'Don't use it.' "

Antibiotic development is further complicated by its heavy dependence on small producers, says Michael Bonney, CEO of Cubist Pharmaceuticals in Lexington, Mass. And unlike big pharmaceutical companies, smaller firms depend on the capital markets for borrowing funds for research and development, says Bonney, whose small company specializes in antibiotics for hospital-based infections.

"Lenders aren't devoted to antibacterials" and will put their dollars elsewhere if they don't see the promise of good returns, he says. "They pay a lot of attention to what's happening in Washington." Few small companies will be able to obtain cash to develop antibiotics if the law doesn't assure lenders they'll eventually make money, he says.

The federal government could buy and stockpile a new drug until resistance appears, Bonney says. But stockpiling "would have to work in concert with extending [the developer's] market exclusivity" for more years, so the company — not a generic competitor — would make money once the drug was in demand.

To offset the low profitability of so-called orphan drugs — which target serious diseases affecting fewer than 200,000 people — Congress in 1983 created development incentives for drugmakers. The law could be tweaked to help spur antibiotic development, says Michael Kurilla, director of the office of biodefense research affairs and associate director of biodefense product development at the National Institute of Allergy and Infectious Diseases.

Today, drugs for illnesses that affect populations just above the orphan-drug cutoff get no breaks, says Kurilla. "If you're at 250,000 patients or 10 million, it's all the

same." A "sliding scale" of incentives might support antibiotic development, he says.

Some pharmaceutical scientists argue the FDA is more concerned about safety today than in the 1950s and '60s — the golden age of antibiotic development — making the discovery of new drugs more challenging. The FDA should give more weight during the approval process to the potential benefits of new antibiotics instead of nixing those that show modest safety risks, says Jeffrey D. Alder, vice president of drug discovery and evaluation at Cubist.

"Some infectious diseases have a very high kill rate" — as high as 70 to 90 percent for staph aureus in the blood, for example — says Alder. "In those cases, almost everyone would say they'd want to be treated, even if it meant nausea" or some other side effect.

But some infectious-disease experts are wary of suggesting that companies don't have enough financial incentives, or that the FDA should make it easier to get antibiotics approved.

SAIC Fredericks' Powers, the former FDA infectious-disease officer, argues against offering financial carrots unless they're carefully targeted at companies developing antibiotics for virulent resistant infections like MRSA, not for self-resolving conditions like sinusitis. "The places where we need new antibiotics are very specific situations," he says.

He's skeptical of incentives because the FDA earlier had tried hard to make it easier for companies to develop antibiotics, but rather than stimulating development of drugs to treat more serious diseases, most companies focused on relatively minor problems like sinusitis, ear infections and bronchitis — most of which clear up on their own.

Some drug analysts also question the wisdom of further easing any FDA standards to help companies bring antibiotics to market.

For instance, in 2004 the agency approved the antibiotic Ketek — manufactured by the French firm Sanofi-Aventis — as a drug that might head off resistance in treating pneumonia, bronchitis and sinusitis. The company had tested the drug using FDA clinical-trial guidelines designed to speed approvals of new antibiotics.

The agency abandoned the guidelines as inadequate before Ketek received its final approval, but the drug was approved anyway because the agency felt it needed "to stand by prior agreements with industry," said David B.

Ross, a clinical assistant professor at George Washington University School of Medicine and Health Sciences in Washington and a former FDA physician who helped in reviewing Ketek. [10]

In 2006, the drug was linked to severe liver damage and failure in a small number of patients, but the agency was reluctant to react too strongly for fear of discouraging antibiotic development. For example, after a Ketek user died of liver failure, the FDA's only formal response was a few paragraphs in "an internal safety review written months later," said Ross. The FDA didn't re-label the drug to warn about liver damage until 16 months after the first report and didn't withdraw approval until Feb. 12, 2007 — a day before congressional hearings on Ketek's safety were to be held, he said.

The Ketek case suggests the agency, at least in some cases, has paid too little attention to antibiotics' downsides, said Ross. [11]

Powers says that rather than paying too much attention to the adverse effects of antibiotics — such as allergic reactions — the FDA and the medical community focus too much on the "inferred benefits" of antibiotics, which Powers says are often unproven. One pediatrician told Powers that he "will treat a million kids for ear infections to prevent one case of meningitis," Powers says. "I said, 'And you'll kill 10 with allergic reactions.'"

Powers also rejects drug company claims that testing is too costly. An antibiotic trial, he points out, only requires about 200 subjects, while a trial for a cardiac drug requires 10,000. "People say the FDA should lower the [testing] standards. But they already have."

Should Congress limit the use of antibiotics in farming?

Debate is fierce over antibiotic use in farming.

Because food animals like cows and chickens largely are raised today crammed into tight quarters rather than in open fields or pastures, antibiotics are used both to treat and to prevent communicable diseases. [12] Animals also get low doses of antibiotics to promote faster growth, and many crops are sprayed with antibiotics to kill bacteria. Consequently, most food — from milk to potatoes to beef — is likely to contain at least traces of the drugs. Food produced organically is prohibited from containing antibiotics. [13]

Advocates of stricter limits on farm use of antibiotics argue that, to slow development of antibiotic resistance among human pathogens, antibiotic use should be cut back. Farm animals can become reservoirs of resistant bacteria, they point out, and non-pathogenic bacteria can pass their resistance to bacteria that do make people sick.

But veterinary-drug manufacturers and farmers say there are few proven links between antibiotics used in farming and life-threatening drug-resistant infections in humans and that clamping down would lead to more foodborne illness. Epidemiological studies don't show that antibiotic-resistant bacteria in farm animals increase resistance in dangerous human diseases, says Michael Doyle, director of the Center for Food Safety at the University of Georgia.

Even if the illnesses humans sometimes pick up from food were to become antibiotic resistant, they are far less serious than other resistant pathogens like MRSA, he adds. "How many people have had untreatable foodborne illnesses? You can count them on two hands," he says. "You may have seen more hospitalizations, but you don't have deaths. I'm just not seeing the data to tell me that this is a public-health hazard like MRSA."

However, scientists at the National Institutes of Health's Fogarty International Center, which studies global health issues, say farm use of antibiotics can contribute significantly to drug-resistant disease in humans, even if the illness isn't life-threatening.

In a 2005 paper, infectious-disease ecologist David L. Smith and his colleagues compared the incidence of VRE — vancomycin-resistant *enterococci* — in humans in Europe and in the United States. They found that in the late 1990s in Europe — where vancomycin was used in hospitals and the related antibiotic avoparcin was used on farms — VRE rates outside the hospitals ranged from 2 to 12 percent of all enteroccus infections. Meanwhile, in the United States — where vancomycin was heavily used in hospitals but no avoparcin was used on farms — community VRE rates were below 1 percent. And community rates of VRE declined after the European Union banned avoparcin, demonstrating that agricultural antibiotics did contribute to VRE showing up in humans, said Smith. [14]

Europe has restricted use of agricultural antibiotics for the past decade. "We are never willing to accept that you first have to create a lot of dead people before you intervene," said Henrik C. Wegner, director of both the World Health Organization's Collaborating Centre for Antimicrobial Research and Foodborne Pathogens and the Danish Institute for Food and Veterinary Research.

CHRONOLOGY

1940s-1950s *Penicillin becomes the first widely available antibiotic, used to treat soldiers in World War II whose infected wounds would otherwise be deadly. By the mid-1940s, the first penicillin-resistant staph bacteria are found.*

1940 Oxford University pathologist Howard Florey isolates pure penicillin and demonstrates that it kills a wide range of pathogens, including strep and gonorrhea.

1943 Drug companies begin to mass-produce penicillin.

1958 American molecular geneticist Joshua Lederberg wins Nobel Prize in medicine for demonstrating bacteria's ability to exchange genetic material, which helps spread resistance.

1960s *Fast-developing resistance to antibiotics like tetracycline is spotted, but a large number of new antibiotics enter the market.*

1960 Methicillin is introduced in Great Britain.

1961 The first methicillin-resistant staph aureus infection (MRSA) turns up in a British hospital.

1963 MRSA appears in Denmark.

1967 Penicillin-resistant strep pneumonia is found in New Guinea.

1970s-1980s *Antibiotics are routinely prescribed for cold-like illnesses, even when they aren't bacterial. U.S. soldiers return from the Vietnam War with penicillin-resistant gonorrhea. People increasingly have weakened immune systems and need stronger antibiotics as more cancer patients are successfully treated, organ transplants increase and HIV/AIDS appears.*

1977 South African doctor Michael Jacobs finds a strep *pneumoniae* bacterium that resists every available drug.

1983 The first hospital-acquired intestinal infection becomes penicillin resistant.... Eighteen people in the Midwest are hospitalized with multi-drug-resistant salmonella food poisoning after eating beef from cows given antibiotics.

1986 Sweden bans use of antibiotics to make farm animals grow faster.

1990s *Big drug firms pull resources away from infectious-disease research. MRSA turns up outside hospitals.*

1992 Antibiotic-resistant bacterial infections kill record 13,000 hospital patients.

1998 Denmark taxes antibiotics used as animal-growth promoters.... European Union bans use of antibiotic used in humans for animal growth.

1999 Federal Interagency Task Force on Antimicrobial Resistance is launched.

2000s *More microbes become resistant, but public-health efforts to combat resistance lag.*

2000 Congress reauthorizes Public Health Services Act, enabling federal government to take stronger steps to combat resistance, but the measure is never funded.

2001 Terrorism-related anthrax scare leads some Americans to take the high-powered antibiotic Cipro "just in case" and stockpile it in their homes.

2003 Drug-resistant *acinetobacter* infects Iraq War wounded in military hospitals, leading to many amputations.

2005 France bans 12 sore-throat medications containing topical antibiotics.

2006 European Union bans using any antibiotic to promote animal growth.... Ketek, an antibiotic to treat bronchitis, pneumonia and sinusitis, is linked to severe liver damage.

2007 Cases of multiple-drug-resistant tuberculosis (TB) quadruple in South Africa's Western Cape Province.... World Health Organization launches plan to fight drug-resistant TB.... Scientists find avian-flu virus is naturally evolving resistance to anti-flu drugs.... Study finds 10 times as many MRSA cases in U.S. hospitals as previously thought.... Food and Drug Administration mulls approval of a new antibiotic for respiratory disease in cows, although infectious-disease experts argue the drug could create more resistant pathogens since similar antibiotics are used in human medicine.

"From our perspective, this is first and foremost a preventive action. It is not acceptable to sit and wait for the next MRSA." [15]

Moreover, he added, Denmark has had "fewer healthy people in the community who carry VRE in their guts since we stopped using growth promoters" on farms.

Many infectious-disease experts want the United States to follow Europe's lead in banning much antibiotic use on farms. "It's embarrassing that we're way behind Europe," says Columbia University's Larson.

Others complain the impact of agricultural antibiotics on resistance gets an undeserved pass in the United States. "Agribusiness is off the public radar screen," says Currie of Montefiore Medical Center. "We've had antibiotics developed where the resistance was high before the drug was [even] released," he says, because related drugs were already being used in agriculture.

At the very least, agricultural antibiotic users should release data on what drugs farms are using and how, says Guidos of the infectious disease society. "The animal-drug industry says [various] reported volume-of-use numbers are inflated," he says, "but we say, 'Prove it.' We want to see what is really going on."

Agriculture analysts say, however, that limiting antibiotics in farming would drive up the rate of foodborne illnesses, outweighing any so-far-undiscovered benefits for limiting their use. "When the European Union cut off some of the antibiotics used as growth promoters, more animals got sick," and the infected animals could pass the illnesses to consumers, says the University of Georgia's Doyle.

Indeed, some farm advocates and scientists say not enough attention is paid to the value of antibiotics on farms. "Antibiotics help farmers keep animals healthy with less strain on the environment," according to the Animal Health Institute, an association of animal-drug manufacturers. "More meat can be raised [on less land] with fewer animals because of the growth-promoting qualities of antibiotics." [16]

Ian Phillips, a professor of biological and chemical sciences at the University of London, says research suggests the added risk to human health caused by antibiotics being used as growth promoters "is small." But "the benefit to human health from their use, hitherto largely ignored, might more than counterbalance this." For instance, Phillips said, banning farm antibiotics except to treat sick animals has put more unhealthy animals into the human food chain in Europe. [17]

In another assessment, Phillips and other epidemiologists found the risk of increased antibiotic resistance related to antibiotic use in chickens "is small" compared to the increase in human foodborne illnesses that would result if the chickens' antibiotics were cut.

"Immediately following the removal of the antibiotic, animal illness levels might be expected to increase," they said, potentially making more people who ate the chicken sick. [18]

BACKGROUND

Bacterial World

Almost as soon as antibiotics came into use, microbes began developing resistance to them. [19]

In the 1940s and '50s, when penicillin was first used, it could kill most bacteria. But as early as 1945, the drug's discoverer, British bacteriologist Alexander Fleming, warned in a *New York Times* interview that misusing penicillin could quickly lead to the evolution of mutant bacterial strains not susceptible to the medicine, an outcome he'd already verified.

In the 1960s, when the antibiotic tetracycline was routinely prescribed for teenagers' acne, resistant bacteria turned up in patients "within a few weeks," says Columbia University's Larson.

That resistance develops quickly among microbes isn't surprising. The world is chock full of bacteria — and other microscopic organisms like fungi — "all fighting for their environmental niche," says SAIC Fredericks' Powers, the former lead infectious-disease officer at FDA. In fact, virtually all antibiotics today were derived from organisms that evolved to have bacteria-killing or bacteria-growth-inhibiting properties. "The bugs actually invented the antibiotics" in their evolutionary struggle for survival, Powers says.

Microbes abound in the environment, and they multiply quickly. "When we are born, 100 percent of our cells are mammalian," says Barry I. Eisenstein, senior vice president for medical affairs at Cubist Pharmaceuticals. "By the time we are 1 month old, only 10 percent [of our cells] are." That's because most of the cells in and on the body are bacterial — hundreds of trillions of them.

And, under optimal conditions, a single bacterium can produce a billion offspring in a single day. Furthermore, "out of a million bacteria, every one will

Doctors Turning to Ancient Remedies for Infections

Honey and copper doorknobs are said to work wonders

With superbugs developing resistance to many antibiotic drugs, doctors are trying out some old anti-infective remedies in hopes of finding additional tools to fight infection. Meanwhile, the search for new antibiotics goes on, with some scientists hoping to exploit the millions of microbial species — many in remote environments like hot springs or the sea bottom — for new kinds of antibiotic action.

Most future anti-infective drugs are likely to bypass killing bacteria, antibiotic-style, in favor of blocking their sickness-inducing properties. Microbes would be less likely to develop resistance to such drugs.

Honey was known to have anti-infective properties as far back as the ancient Mesopotamian kingdom of Sumer, 5,000 years ago. Today some doctors are using it again.

Jennifer Eddy, an assistant professor of family medicine at the University of Wisconsin School of Medicine, dressed an elderly diabetic man's ulcerated foot in honey-soaked gauze after the sore was attacked by drug-resistant bacteria, and amputation seemed the only option. In two weeks, the blackened foot began to heal, and a year later, the man was walking again. "I've used honey in a dozen cases since then," said Eddy. "I've yet to have one that didn't improve." [1] Some research suggests that bacteria are unlikely to become resistant to honey.

Another ancient antibacterial remedy — copper — is getting a trial in a British hospital. Healers in ancient Egypt, Greece and Rome all recognized copper's infection-killing

properties and used it to treat wounds. Despite its history of discouraging the growth of germs, however, little copper is found in modern hospitals, which gleam with stainless steel, even though germs can remain active on steel for days.

Now the Selly Oak Hospital in Birmingham, England, is testing whether replacing stainless steel fittings like door handles, bathtub faucets, toilet flush handles and grab bars with copper can help cut the spread of infections. The hospital was chosen for the trial in part because soldiers wounded in Iraq had become infected with MRSA while being treated in the facility. [2]

In the early 20th century, biologists discovered a way to treat infections using bacteriophages — viruses that invade certain species of bacterial cells and cause them to burst and die. The therapy was pioneered at Paris' Pasteur Institute and the Institute of Microbiology in Tbilisi, capital of the Soviet Republic of Georgia, home of George Eliava, one of the scientists who discovered bacteriophages. Eliava discovered the tiny killers when he returned after three days to look at a microscope slide of river water that had contained cholera bacteria and found the slide bacteria-free. [3]

In World War II, Soviet military medics used the viruses to treat infected wounds on the battlefield, and German Gen. Erwin Rommel's troops used phage therapy against infections in hot North Africa, where infection-causing bacteria thrive.

But as antibiotics came into wide use after the war, bacteriophage therapy was largely forgotten. Georgian scientists and doctors continued studying and even treating

have a mutation," any one of which might allow that cell and its offspring to survive exposure to an antibiotic, says N. Kent Peters, program officer for antibacterial resistance at the National Institute of Allergy and Infectious Diseases (NIAID).

Doctors' Orders

The good news is that, "everywhere you measure, there's been improvement in antibiotic use," says Schaffner, Vanderbilt's preventive medicine chairman. But while the message is getting through, and many doctors are becoming warier prescribers, "it's not enough," he says.

"We are not going to get a stream of antibiotics that will rescue us." [20]

New antibiotics aren't forthcoming, in part, because the easy-to-find ones were discovered long ago. Today's huge pharmaceutical companies increasingly are focused on high-profit drugs that patients take for chronic conditions, while small firms have trouble funding drug development at all and thus tend to seek more specialized niches.

"Why should we be investing in anti-infectives when people take them for seven to 10 days, while they'll take chronic-disease drugs" — such as antidepressants or cholesterol drugs — "for the rest of their lives?" an executive

patients with phages, but lack of money gradually crippled their research. Today, however, phage research is making a comeback, as superbugs strip traditional antibiotics of their power.

For example, researchers at the Massachusetts Institute of Technology and Boston University are using DNA technology to alter bacteriophages to produce enzymes that can kill specific infectious bacteria like *e. coli.* [4] The Food and Drug Administration also recently approved a bacteriophage product for food-processing companies to use to eliminate the dangerous foodborne microbe *listeria.* [5]

Meanwhile, new antibiotics still lurk in nature, waiting to be discovered, says Jeffrey D. Alder, vice president of drug discovery and evaluation at Cubist Pharmaceuticals in Lexington, Mass.

Only one in 100,000,000,000,000,000,000,000,000 (1 in 10 to the 25th power) of the world's microbes has been screened for antibiotic action, says Alder. Most of the vast number remaining grow in airless environments, in a narrow temperature range, or in difficult-to-access places. Earth's more remote and unusual environments could be the source for new antibiotic discoveries, some scientists believe.

The University of Hawaii, for example, hopes to set up a drug-discovery center "to take advantage of their unique isolated environment" that's home to hordes of unstudied microbes in hot springs, ocean thermal vents and the like, says Alder. DNA techniques make it possible to discover antibiotic and other microbial properties more easily than in the past, he says.

But most future anti-infective drugs will be developed according to a new paradigm, says Michael Kurilla, director of the office of biodefense research affairs at the National Institute of Allergy and Infectious Diseases. Lost in medi-

cine's long love affair with antibiotics is the fact that "you're really interested in curing a disease, not killing an organism," Kurilla says. Shifting the focus from killing bugs to blocking their sickness-causing toxins — as a tetanus shot or anthrax vaccine do — may be the best approach for future drug discovery.

"If we take care of the toxin," and your immune system is strong, "your body can clear" the bacteria on its own, says Kurilla.

Paratek Pharmaceuticals, a small Boston-based company started by Stuart B. Levy, a microbiology professor at Tufts University School of Medicine, takes such an approach. Paratek focuses on a protein that can inactivate the process by which bacteria cause illness. "The bacteria doesn't need it to live and grow, so because you aren't inhibiting the bacteria's survival, you're not selecting against it," and resistance is much less likely to develop, Levy says.

But so far, financial backers are hard to come by for novel approaches, Levy says. "Everybody loves the story. But when it comes to plunking the money down, they go to the guy next door who has an antibiotic."

[1] Quoted in Brandon Keim, "Honey Remedy Could Save Limbs," *Wired*, Nov. 11, 2006.

[2] Philippe Naughton, "Hospital Gets Copper Fittings in MRSA Trial," *The Times online*, March 13, 2007, www.timesonline.co.uk/tol/news/uk/article1509513.ece.

[3] For background, see Richard Martin, "How Ravenous Soviet Viruses Will Save the World," *Wired*, October 2003, www.wired.com/wired/archive/11.10/phages_pr.html.

[4] Brandon Klein, "Scientists Build Bacteria-Killing Organisms From Scratch," *Wired Science*, Wired Blog Network, July 10, 2007.

[5] "FDA Extends GRAS Approval LISTEX to All Food Products," *Food Ingredients First*, May 7, 2007, www.foodingredientsfirst.com.

at the large pharmaceutical company Eli Lilly once asked Cubist's Eisenstein, who directed infectious-disease research at Lilly in the early 1990s.

Ironically, systematic technical improvements in the drug-development process also act as a barrier to finding new antibiotics.

Chemists find new drugs by testing compounds from pharmaceutical companies' vast libraries of chemicals, explains Kurilla, the director of biodefense research affairs at NIAID. But as companies have refined their collections, "they've evolved a series of ideas about what makes a compound 'druggable' " — meaning that it is

absorbable and capable of penetrating human cells or entering the brain, he says.

"If you asked a chemist today if [the antibiotic chemicals] tetracycline or cephalosporin could be drugs, he'd say no," says Kurilla, because today's pharmaceutical chemists focus almost entirely on compounds that show potential for creating drugs that interact with human cells, such as the cholesterol-reducing drug Lipitor or the antihistamine Claritin. Chemicals with the potential to interact with bacteria — as antibiotics must — have been weeded out of the drug-discovery labs to make screening chemicals for drug potential more efficient, he says.

Simon Macario appeared to have a minor throat infection, but one morning he awoke screaming with pain. "By 10 that night he was dead" from MRSA, which was attacking his organs, says his mother. Until recently, MRSA mainly infected hospital patients. Today, however, many resistant bacteria are acquired outside hospitals and seem more dangerous than hospital-acquired infections.

The U.S. medical system also has built-in barriers to reducing the use of antibiotics. For instance, patients know antibiotics are wonder drugs and ask for them — even when their infections are viral, and antibiotics won't work. "It takes longer for a physician to explain why an antibiotic isn't a good idea" than to simply prescribe one, even if it's not indicated, says Larson, the associate dean of research at Columbia.

As a result, about 28 percent of doctors say they would order an antibiotic if a patient had a chest cold — a viral illness — says Feldgarden of the Alliance for the Prudent Use of Antibiotics, and the percentage doubles in the case of bronchitis. Furthermore, prescribing habits

inexplicably worsen as doctors-in-training advance through their medical education, he says.

Indeed, a study in the late 1990s showed that one of five U.S. prescriptions is for an antimicrobial drug, and 95 percent of them are unnecessary, Feldgarden says. Another study showed that doctors prescribe antibiotics for children's colds and earaches 65 percent of the time if they believe that parents expect them to, but only 12 percent if they don't. [21]

"Prescribing practices are difficult to change, so we need an array of interventions," says Vanderbilt's Schaffner.

Funds have been lacking for "social-marketing" campaigns to help change public attitudes. For instance, the Centers for Disease Control and Prevention (CDC) has developed a consumer-awareness program dubbed "Get Smart" but doesn't have enough money to launch it, says Ralph Gonzales, a professor of medicine, epidemiology and biostatistics at the University of California, San Francisco.

Gonzales tested a similar advertising campaign in Denver that raised public awareness by about 10 percent and cost about $150,000 to implement. The dent in attitudes is significant enough to lower antibiotic use, which would save money for insurance companies and Medicare and improve public health, says Gonzales. But only a few private insurers and cities have expressed interest.

The University of Pennsylvania's Fishman says the lack of quick, cheap diagnostic tests to identify what's making a patient sick is also a problem. "It's 2007, and we can only determine the cause of pneumonia 50 percent of the time, if we're lucky," he says. Thus, doctors often have to guess at the cause of an infection and use broad-spectrum antibiotics that kill multiple kinds of bacteria rather than an antibiotic narrowly targeting one bacteria. But broad-spectrum antibiotics should be reserved for resistant cases, Fishman says.

Technical hurdles have bedeviled development of quick, accurate diagnostics, such as the difficulty — or sometimes the impossibility — of growing some bacteria and viruses in the lab. The National Institute of Allergy and Infectious Diseases (NIAID) is pushing for development of diagnostics as fast as it can, "but cost is still an issue" in implementing them, says NIAID program officer Peters.

"Even when diagnostic tests work, though, many physicians are reluctant to narrow the therapy" once they get a diagnosis if they've already started treatment with another antibiotic, Fishman says. "In America, we tend not to stop the treatment."

"Education alone doesn't work" in changing prescribing behavior, says Donald Goldmann, a professor of infectious diseases at the Harvard School of Public Health and senior vice president of the Institute for Healthcare Improvement, which supports quality-improvement initiatives for health-care institutions. In fact, he says, physicians "will fudge" even when systems exist to warn doctors away from some drugs. One study found an "epidemic" of pneumonia at a hospital where doctors discovered they could prescribe a certain drug only if they "checked a box for pneumonia" on a prescription order form, he says.

The best intervention is "strong decision support" — good, specific information provided at the time and place of prescribing — and "tough feedback" showing doctors how they're doing compared to other physicians, Goldmann says.

U.S. doctors who treat patients outside of hospitals, however, are tied into few if any systems offering feedback, Schaffner says, making it even more difficult to mold non-hospital physician behavior. Some health-maintenance organizations and a few fledgling state Medicaid efforts, however, have made headway, he says. "Physicians really need to know what the standard of practice is and how they measure up to it," says Schaffner. "When they do, a light goes on."

Drug companies' "gross overpromotion" of the latest antibiotics exacerbates the problem, says Sidney Wolfe, director of the Health Research Group at the consumer organization Public Citizen. For example, after CDC guidelines declared that azithromycin (trade name Zithromax) should not be either a first- or a second-choice treatment for ear infections, the drug's manufacturer, Pfizer, "brought in academics to subvert the guideline," says Wolfe, who obtained and publicized an internal Pfizer memo about the policy.

The company's heavy promotion, including sponsoring the children's television program "Sesame Street" — "brought to you by the letter Z as in Zithromax" — made the drug the fifth most commonly prescribed in the United States by 2003. Nineteen states sued Pfizer to

Development of Antibacterials on the Decline

The number of antibiotic drugs approved in the United States has steadily declined in the past quarter-century, reflecting lack of interest by drug firms and the fact that many key drugs already have been developed.

Number of Approved Antibacterials in the U.S., 1983-2007

Source: "Bad Bugs, No Drugs As Antibiotic Discovery Stagnates . . . A Public Health Crisis Brews," Infectious Diseases Society of America, 2007

stop the promotion, but the $6 million in fines Pfizer paid was dwarfed by the $1.5 billion it earned in 2003 from Zithromax sales alone. [22]

At the federal level, the FDA has no authority to levy fines for overpromotion and can't regulate prescription-writing, but Wolfe says health-care payers, especially Medicare and Medicaid, should crack down on doctors' unjustified use of overhyped new antibiotics.

"I've been urging FDA to do more education" on prescribing, but not much has happened, says Wolfe. "CDC and the Centers for Medicare and Medicaid Services do some, but it is inadequate to counterbalance the vast amounts of advertising."

Ounce of Prevention

Since fewer antibiotics will be prescribed if fewer people get sick, curtailing the spread of infectious disease is key in fighting antibiotic resistance. [23]

In the past, resistant pathogens spread mainly in hospitals. But today an especially virulent strain of MRSA has emerged outside of hospitals, making infection control even tougher.

"Every hospital in the country has a policy for handling MRSA," but "we have failed dismally" in getting a handle on it, says Montefiore Medical Center's Currie. "A lot of the guidance on infection control is not data-based."

How Superbugs Develop Resistance Quickly

Speed and flexibility help them mutate

Bacteria can become resistant to antibiotics even if they have never come in contact with a human-made antibiotic. (Antibiotic drugs are derived from naturally occurring microbes that excrete substances that can kill bacteria or interfere with some of their vital natural processes.)

For example, wild animals in Australia have little or no exposure to antibiotics, but a study of *e. coli* bacteria from kangaroos and wombats found that 3 percent were resistant to the antibiotic amoxicillin. And hospital patients in India, Turkey and Poland were infected with methicillin-resistant *staphylococcus aureus* — MRSA — even before the antibiotic methicillin had been used in those countries. [1]

Large numbers of resistant bacteria usually don't evolve, however, until after the bacteria come in contact with the antibiotic. And over the years, scientists have discovered some traits that allow bacteria to evolve into a resistant population quickly, such as:

- **Speed.** Bacteria can evolve quickly partly because they reproduce so quickly. A human population can double about every 20 years. "For bacteria, it's every 20 minutes," says Barry I. Eisenstein senior vice president for medical affairs at Cubist Pharmaceuticals, in Lexington, Mass.

- **Exchangeability.** Many resistant bacteria can pass on their resistance genes to other bacteria, even if they're of different species. Humans' guts are filled with harmless bacteria that can block antibiotics. That's no problem unless a disease-causing bug enters the gut. Then the harmless but resistant bugs may pass their resistance to the dangerous bacteria, making them resistant, too. Often what's transferred is a "plasmid" — a hunk of DNA that isn't part of the bug's regular DNA — and some plasmids can carry resistance genes for several kinds of antibiotics. A bacterium that picks them up becomes a "superbug," resistant to more than one drug. A potential route to new antibiotic treatments would be drugs that block plasmid transfer, says N. Kent Peters, program officer for antibacterial resistance at the National Institute for Allergy and Infectious Diseases (NIAID).

- **Tendency to mutate.** In nature's ongoing war among microbes, mutant offspring with better ways to survive allow a species to evolve to overcome enemies. In recent years, scientists have found that something even more complicated occurs. When some bacteria are under pressure, such as from a dose of antibiotics, their offspring actually have more genetic mutations than usual, thus increasing the species' chance of evolving a means to survive, says Michael Kurilla, director of the office of biodefense research affairs at NIAID. A few researchers are exploring ways to block mutations, Kurilla says. When bacteria are under attack from an antibiotic that doesn't kill them, they "don't sit on their duffs," says Eisenstein. "They become more promiscuous," exchanging more genes with other nearby bacteria, which ups the chance they'll produce resistant offspring that can survive.

---

[1] Peter J. Collignon, "Antibiotic Resistance," *Medical Journal of Australia*, Sept. 16, 2002, p. 325, www.mja.com.au/public/issues/177_06_160902/col10836_fm.html.

The University of Maryland's medical center now screens everyone checking into its nine intensive-care units for MRSA, whether the patient shows signs of infection or not. "There's debate in the United States over whether [such] 'active surveillance' works," says medical director Standiford. "I believe it does and that it saves money in the long run" by identifying the "reservoirs of infection" — non-symptomatic patients who can spread the bug. "Every time you get MRSA in the blood-stream, it costs the hospital $20,000 at least" because the patient's stay is so much longer.

In hospitals, the confining of infected patients once halted the spread of contagion, but with the number of infections growing, many hospitals don't have enough separate areas to confine patients, says Allison Aiello, an assistant professor of epidemiology at the University of Michigan School of Public Health.

And with the new, highly virulent strain of MRSA

Should tighter restrictions be placed on antibiotics in animals?

YES Rep. Louise M. Slaughter, D-N.Y.
Chair, House Rules Committee

Written for *CQ Researcher*, August 2007

The overprescription and overuse of antibiotics has produced an increasingly widespread number of resistant microbes. Current global trends, including urbanization and global travel and trade, have increased the demand for antibiotics worldwide. That, in turn, has increased the opportunities for antibiotic misuse. Additionally, although more and more bacteria have become resistant to the limited availability of treatments, research and development of new antibiotics has been scarce.

Antibiotic resistance already has been labeled a top concern by the Centers for Disease Control and Prevention and a "crisis" by the World Health Organization. Bacterial infections resistant to existing treatments increase health-care costs by $4 billion to $5 billion each year. Two million Americans acquire a bacterial infection annually during stays at hospitals. Seventy percent of the infections they contract are resistant to the drugs prescribed for treatment, and 38 patients die every day as a result.

As a microbiologist, I have always been concerned that our nation's health policies have done little to deter microbial drug resistance. The question of how we can preserve the effectiveness of existing antibiotics is complex but demands an immediate response.

One area in which it is both feasible and logical to limit antibiotic overuse is in production of food animals. In North America and Europe, an estimated 50 percent of all antibiotics are used in food-producing animals and poultry. Much of this is not for treating sick animals but for preventing disease and promoting growth. As a result, huge numbers of animals are regularly exposed to subtherapeutic concentrations of antibiotics, with disastrous results.

To address this problem, I am the proud sponsor of the Preservation of Antibiotics for Medical Treatment Act, which would phase out antibiotics use in livestock for growth or preventative purposes unless manufacturers could prove such uses don't endanger public health. It would also provide federal funds to help farmers adopt other approaches to preventing illness among their herds, such as cleaner housing and natural supplements. This bill would not restrict the use of antibiotics to treat sick pets or other animals not used for food.

Options exist to combat the growing public-health threat from drug-resistant bacteria. We must reevaluate how we use antibiotics, beginning with situations we can control. Our ultimate goal should be the elimination of practices that threaten the health and well-being of our citizens. The lessons of the past are plain for all to see. If we ignore them, we will risk making antibiotic treatments a thing of the past.

NO Richard Carnevale
Vice President, Regulatory, Scientific and International Affairs, Animal Health Institute

Written for *CQ Researcher*, August 2007

Bans on antibiotics used to keep animals healthy have proven to be counterproductive. The United States should not risk animal health and human health by repeating these mistakes.

Following Denmark's ban on using antibiotics for growth promotion, the increase in animal illness and death in that country required veterinarians to nearly double their use of antibiotics to treat diseases.

The current U.S. regulatory system provides many layers of protection to ensure the safest possible use of antibiotics to keep animals healthy:

- The pre-market review process used by the Food and Drug Administration (FDA) to review antibiotics is arguably more stringent than the review of antibiotics for humans. Sponsors must demonstrate safety for both animals and the humans who consume the meat from treated animals. Also, measures imposed in 2003 require sponsors, prior to product approval, to assess the risk of resistant bacteria being transferred from animals to humans.
- Post-approval risk assessments that have been conducted and published by FDA, sponsors and researchers.
- Food-safety monitoring programs that have been established by government agencies and sponsors to track the development of antibiotic-resistant bacteria.
- Responsible-use programs that are specific to the different livestock species give veterinarians and producers specific guidelines to safely and properly use antibiotics in their health management systems.
- Pathogen-reduction programs that have successfully led to documented reductions in pathogens on meat, contributing to decreased foodborne illness.

Recent literature demonstrates the benefits of using antibiotics to keep animals healthy and the risks of letting politicians ban uses. These papers show that when antibiotics are removed without a careful assessment of the consequences, there is an increased risk of meat containing the kinds of pathogens that make people sick. Allowing producers to carefully use antibiotics to keep their animals healthy is important to our food safety system.

The FDA has in place a rigorous, science-based process for the approval of new animal drugs. This review process, combined with post-approval monitoring, risk assessments and adherence to proper-use principles, allows producers to use antibiotics to keep animals healthy, contribute to a safe food supply and minimize the risk of resistant bacteria transferring from animals to humans.

popping up in the community, infection control becomes even harder. More patients already have a resistant infection when they enter a hospital, and no one knows how the CA-MRSA strain spreads, says Robert Daum, a professor of pediatrics at the University of Chicago.

During the past decade, the federal government has taken stabs at attacking the antimicrobial-resistance problem but hasn't sustained its support. In 1999 the CDC established a Federal Interagency Task Force to Combat Microbial Resistance, which issued an action plan in 2001. [24] The inadequately funded panel, however, has the tools to do little "but issue an annual laundry list of uncoordinated activities," says Guidos of the Infectious Disease Society of America.

In 2000, Sen. Edward M. Kennedy, D-Mass., and former Sen. Majority Leader Bill Frist, R-Tenn., a cardiac surgeon, authorized $40 million in annual funding for resistance research and federal initiatives like the task force. But Congress never appropriated any funds, says Guidos. In 2001, for example, then-Rep. Sherrod Brown, D-Ohio — now a senator — and Sen. Orrin Hatch, R-Utah, sponsored legislation to fund the programs, "but no funding ever came," Guidos says.

Moreover, jurisdictional struggles between the CDC and the states makes surveillance of resistance difficult, says Feldgarden at the Alliance for the Prudent Use of Antibiotics. Too often, "there's a one-way highway for information. It goes up to the CDC and then doesn't get back to the states," he says. And states don't always hold up their end of the reporting bargain, he adds. "Unless they get money, states don't want to play nice with the CDC."

The CDC and state public-health agencies already issue many disease-surveillance reports, and "diseases don't go away. So if you want to add something" — such as resistance — "you need to add money," Feldgarden explains. But in recent years states haven't been adding money for public health.

"It's ridiculous that CVS [pharmacy] knows more about the [birthday] cards I send to my mother" than health agencies know about developing infectious outbreaks, says Feldgarden. "Real-time reporting is essential, because once you're beyond the anecdote stage, look out."

In any case, the states, the federal government and private organizations are unlikely to do much to institute anti-resistance measures until they get clear proof that they can save both lives and money, says Stuart B. Levy, a professor of microbiology at Tufts University School of Medicine in Boston. The Massachusetts Department of Public Health, for instance, is "very receptive" and is launching its own surveillance system, but doing it "on a shoestring," he says,

The Alliance for the Prudent Use of Antibiotics, which Levy founded, is mining hospital records for what it says will be the first solid statistics on the dollar cost of resistant infections. The CDC's current cost data "are all wrong" because the agency did not have access to the hospital cost information that tells the real story, says Christopher Spivey, the alliance's manager for business development and communications. The real costs are "quite breathtaking, much bigger than we thought," he says. He could not predict exactly when the data will be available.

CURRENT SITUATION

Under the Radar

Unlike in previous decades, MRSA is now invading facilities such as sports locker rooms, jails and day-care centers and threatens even healthy people, says University of Chicago pediatrics professor Daum, and it's more potent than hospital-acquired MRSA. After first turning up in a handful of cases, community-acquired (CA) MRSA has seen "an explosive increase over the past 10 years in city after city," he says, beginning in the Midwest and Texas, then spreading to the West Coast and finally in the East. "And when it comes, it doesn't leave."

Today "perfectly healthy people are coming in with MRSA infections," he says, whereas in the past they developed only in hospitalized patients.

And many times the victims have never heard of the disease. "When we got the cause of [our son's] death, I had never heard of MRSA," recalls Everly Macario, a public-health researcher and writer in Chicago whose year-and-a-half-old son Simon died of CA-MRSA in 2004. The child, who had appeared to have a minor throat infection, awoke screaming with pain one morning. Doctors later discovered that toxins from the bacteria were attacking his organs. "By 10 that night he was dead," Macario says.

While hospitals still have a tough time containing traditional, hospital-acquired MRSA in their facilities, containing the community-acquired version — which causes more severe illness and appears to be more contagious — presents a more daunting challenge, says Daum. And CA-MRSA is beginning to spread to hospitals.

State public-health agencies didn't immediately realize that the new MRSA was a public-health problem, because they thought it was hospital-related, says Daum. But the "CDC is now really on board with the idea that this is something new," he says.

And as Macario found, no one is safe. "My parents are scientists, so I'm anal about washing hands," she says. "In my own home I want everything to be immaculate. I had breast fed Simon for a year, and he was up to date on all his inoculations."

Scientists don't know how CA-MRSA is spread, says Daum. For example, "I don't know what the role of inanimate objects is," such as whether the bacteria can survive and spread to other people if a person with an abscess, for example, sits on a doctor's table, he says.

"Staph is an amazing foe," Daum says. Some bacteria are easy to fight because they have limited ways to carry out certain functions, such as adhering to human cells. If the immune system counters that method, it can neutralize the bug. But staph has multiple means of accomplishing some basic functions, making it much more formidable, he points out. And while vaccines usually stimulate the immune system to produce a key antibody that can stop a microbe, he says, "staph is not going to yield to an approach like that."

Legislation Uncertain

Efforts to shore up the federal response to drug resistance are moving forward in Congress, but it's not clear how much legislation — if any — will be enacted this year.

Both the House and the Senate have passed FDA-overhaul measures that also provide incentives for developing antibiotics. The bills would make orphan drugs eligible for special federal grants and contracts and offer longer periods for companies to retain exclusive rights to market their new antibiotics before they can be sold by generic-drug makers.

House and Senate lawmakers must still reconcile differences between the two versions, but a joint conference panel has yet to be appointed, partly because a bitter fight over children's health insurance has stalled progress of health legislation. [25]

Bills also are pending that would ban many uses of agricultural antibiotics, an especially contentious issue.

Finally, Rep. John Matheson, D-Utah, plans to introduce a measure establishing initiatives to jump-start federal efforts to combat resistance. Among other provisions, the bill would give the CDC task force greater authority; establish a surveillance network covering several geographic regions; provide incentives for development of new antimicrobials and require drug companies marketing new antibiotics to explain whether the drugs would increase resistance and if so, what steps would be taken to retard the spread of resistance.

Many infectious-disease experts — and especially the Infectious Disease Society of America (IDSA) — have pressed Congress to strengthen the federal government's anti-resistance efforts and offered suggestions to Matheson and others about what legislation should contain. "I have a lot of hope for the Matheson bill," says the University of Pennsylvania's Fishman, who chairs IDSA's Antibiotic Resistance Working Group. "There's a need to coordinate and oversee research, and a need for increased funding in all areas related to resistance, and it's critical to do it now."

To ease the bill's passage, Matheson probably will not make many specific demands on the private sector. Even so, the bill's introduction has been stalled for months.

The Democratic leaders of the two health committees hope to discuss both the farm-antibiotics measure and Matheson's bill, possibly in connection with the yet-to-be-held conference on the FDA bills. But the FDA bills' slow movement leaves the fate of the antibiotic legislation unclear.

Meanwhile, many states are moving to require hospitals to publicly report how many of their patients contract infections in hospitals.

Consumers Union has pushed for such laws over the past three-and-a-half years, and the effort is working, says Lisa McGiffert, director of the group's Stop Hospital Infections project. Hospital-related infections, including resistant ones, have been going on for decades "because there hasn't been a public outcry," she says.

To date, bills have been filed in 45 states, 17 of which require hospitals to report information about what infections their patients contract in their facilities, McGiffert says. Other states have voluntary reporting systems, but she prefers mandatory systems because they can be standardized so consumers can understand what the data mean. Four states — Pennsylvania, Missouri, Florida and Vermont — publish their reports online.

But most of the reporting requirements don't yet include antibiotic-resistant infections. "Data on resistant strains will come next," she says, as states perfect their systems.

OUTLOOK

Beyond Antibiotics

Without decisive action, drug resistance can only get worse, warn infectious-disease experts.

The drug-resistance issue "is at a tipping point right now, and I see it escalating dramatically and exponentially," says Associate Professor of Medicine Fishman at the University of Pennsylvania.

Despite her young son's death, public-health researcher Macario is optimistic but still wary about the future. "There are campaigns to urge prudent prescribing," she says, so "sometimes I think: 'There's hope. We can all rally together.' " But humans have a defense mechanism in which they say to themselves, " 'It won't happen to me.' "

"Without aggressive collaboration, we may be faced with a public-health crisis and return to the pre-antibiotic era," warns the Alliance for Prudent Use of Antibiotics in a paper laying out guidelines for medical practitioners. [26]

Nevertheless, a Chicken-Little-sky-is-falling attitude isn't warranted, since 20th- and 21st-century medicine has already developed many more tools besides antibiotics to combat infectious disease, says former FDA infectious-disease officer Powers. Despite headlines declaring the contrary, "we won't go back to the pre-antibiotic era," he says. Evidence for this comes from the fact that better public health and health care had already made many infectious diseases more tractable, even before the discovery of antibiotics, he says. For example, between 1935 and 1945 — before the public introduction of penicillin — mortality from pneumonia in industrialized countries had already dropped from 70 percent to 40 percent, and medical progress in non-antibiotic areas will continue, he says.

Meanwhile, researchers continue to seek new antibiotics, exploring for undiscovered, natural antimicrobial excretions from microbes in remote environments like the Amazon jungle, deserts and the ocean floor. They also are using genetic technology to screen for more "targets" within bacteria to attack with drugs. And some researchers are using DNA techniques to explore the antibiotic effects of microbes that can't be grown in the lab, by transferring genetic material from microbes that don't grow in the lab into other microbes that can be grown and studied there, says Kurilla, of the National Institute of Allergy and Infectious Diseases.

Future infectious-disease drugs may act on the human host rather than on the microbes, says Kurilla. Today's scientists hope someday to be able to identify host targets in human cells that will block the ability of a bacterium to complete its life cycle and produce an infection, he says.

Some small companies already are researching this area, while " 'big pharma' is watching from the sidelines," he says. If the research pans out, large pharmaceutical companies' chemical libraries — which primarily contain chemicals suitable for interacting with human cells — would become a richer resource for anti-infective drugs, he says.

Focusing on the host would "sidestep resistance," because bacteria would have a harder time producing the complex group of mutations needed to bypass a change in their human host, Kurilla says.

Up to now, infectious-disease medicine has focused too much on throwing antibiotics at infections, then depending on pharmaceutical companies to develop a new antibiotic when resistance and new infectious ills pop up, says Montefiore Medical Center's Currie. But with new antibiotics harder and harder to find, in the future that paradigm must change, he says.

"We should have a five- or 10-year goal of learning to pry ourselves" from the antibiotic-resistance treadmill, "kind of the equivalent of the Manhattan Project to build an atom bomb in five years," Currie says.

NOTES

1. For background, see "Severe Methicillin-Resistant Staphylococcus aureus Community-Acquired Pneumonia Associated with Influenza — Louisiana and Georgia, December 2006-January 2007," *Morbidity and Mortality Weekly Report*, Centers for Disease Control and Prevention, www.cdc.gov/mmwr/preview/mmwrhtml/mm5614a1.htm, April 13, 2007.

2. Judith Graham, "Hospital Infections on the Rise," *Chicago Tribune*, June 25, 2007, p. C1.

3. "Guide to the Elimination of Methicillin-Resistant Staphylococcus Aureus (MRSA) Transmission in Hospital Settings," Association for Professionals in Infection Control and Epidemiology, www.apic.org/

Content/NavigationMenu/GovernmentAdvocacy/
MethicillinResistantStaphylococcusAureusMRSA/
Resources/MRSAguide.pdf, March 2007.

4. For background, see Steve Silberman, "The Invisible Enemy," *Wired*, February 2007, www.wired.com/wired/archive/15.02/enemy.html?pg=2&topic=enemy&topic_set=.

5. Christopher J. Lettieri, "The Emergence and Impact of Extensively Drug-Resistant Tuberculosis," Medscape Pulmonary Medicine Web site, www.medscape.com/pulmonarymedicine, May 31, 2007.

6. Kathleen S. Swendiman and Nancy Lee Jones, "Extensively Drug-Resistant Tuberculosis (XDR-TB): Quarantine and Isolation, Congressional Research Service, June 5, 2007.

7. For background, see Lawrence K. Altman, "Traveler's TB Not as Severe as Officials Thought," *The New York Times*, July 4, 2007, p. A11.

8. For background, see Richard E. Isaacson and Mary E. Torrence, "The Role of Antibiotics in Agriculture," American Academy of Microbiology, www.asmusa.org, 2002; "Antimicrobial Resistance: Implications for the Food System," *Comprehensive Reviews in Food Science and Food Safety*, July 2006, pp. 71-137.

9. "SHEA/APIC: Talking Points on Legislative Mandates for Active Surveillance for MRSA and VRE in the United States," Society for Healthcare Epidemiology of America, www.shea-online.org/Assets/files/Active_SurveillanceTalking_Points.pdf.

10. *Ibid.*

11. David B. Ross, "The FDA and the Case of Ketek," *The New England Journal of Medicine*, April 19, 2007, p. 1601.

12. For background, see Jennifer Weeks, "Factory Farms," *CQ Researcher*, Jan. 12, 2007, pp. 25-48.

13. For background, see Kathy Koch, "Food Safety Battle: Organic vs. Biotech," *CQ Researcher*, Sept. 4, 1998, pp. 761-784.

14. David L. Smith, Jonathan Dushoff and J. Glenn Morris, Jr., "Agricultural Antibiotics and Human Health," in Public Library of Science, Medicine, www.pubmedcentral.nih.gov/articlerender.fcgi?artid=1167557, August 2005.

15. Quoted in Madeline Drexler, "APUA One-on-One: The Danish Experiment," *APUA Newsletter*, Alliance for the Prudent Use of Antibiotics, Issue No. 2, 2004, p. 1, www.tufts.edu/med/apua/Newsletter/APUA_v22n2.pdf.

16. "The Antibiotics Debate: Antibiotics and the Environment," Animal Health Institute, www.ahi.org.

17. Ian Phillips, "Withdrawal of Growth-Promoting Antibiotics in Europe and its Effects in Relation to Human Health," *International Journal of Antimicrobial Agents*, 2007 (in press).

18. Randall S. Singer, *et al.*, "Modeling the Relationship Between Food Animal Health and Human Foodborne Illness," *Preventive Veterinary Medicine*, 2007, p. 186.

19. For background, see Adriel Bettelheim, "Drug-resistant Bacteria," *CQ Researcher*, June 4, 1999, pp. 473-496; Stuart B. Levy, *The Antibiotic Paradox*, second edition (2002); Abigail A. Salyers and Dixie D. Whitt, *Revenge of the Microbes: How Bacterial Resistance Is Undermining the Antibiotic Miracle* (2005).

20. For background, see Donald E. Low, "Changing Trends in Antimicrobial-Resistant Pneumococci: It's Not All Bad News," *Clinical Infectious Diseases*, Supplement 4, 2005, pp. S228-233.

21. "Frequently Asked Questions: Get Smart: Know When Antibiotics Work," Centers for Disease Control and Prevention, www.cdc.gov/drugresistance/community/faqs.htm.

22. Barbara Mintzes, "Pharmaceutical Promotion and Prevention of Antibiotic Resistance," October 2005, www.pasteur.fr/applications/euroconf/antiinfectionstherapies/7_Mintzes_abstract_.pdf.

23. For background, see Betsy McCaughey, "Unnecessary Deaths: The Human and Financial Costs of Hospital Infections," Committee to Reduce Infection Deaths, www.hospitalinfection.org, 2006.

24. For background, see "The 2001 Federal Interagency Action Plan to Combat Antimicrobial Resistance," Union of Concerned Scientists, www.ucusa.org.

25. For background, see Alex Wayne, "Tough Negotiations Ahead on Children's Health Expansion, Medicare," *CQ Today*, Aug. 2, 2007.

26. "Antibiotic Resistance: Careful Antibiotic Use Can Help Control the Growing Problem," APUA, www.tufts.edu/med/apua/Practitioners/ABRcontrol.html.

BIBLIOGRAPHY

Books

Levy, Stuart B., *The Antibiotic Paradox,* **second edition, Perseus Publishing, 2002.**
A microbiology professor at the Tufts University School of Medicine explains the basic biology of bacteria and details the history of antibiotic use and misuse that is increasing the prevalence of drug resistance.

Salyers, Abigail A., and Dixie D. Whitt, *Revenge of the Microbes: How Bacterial Resistance Is Undermining the Antibiotic Miracle,* **American Society for Microbiology Press, 2005.**
Microbiology professors at the University of Illinois, Urbana-Champaign, chronicle the rise of resistance microorganisms and the hazards they pose to the health-care system.

Articles

Bryant, Howard, "Blitzing Microbial Infections," *The Washington Post,* **Aug. 3, 2006, p. E1.**
Five cases of drug-resistant staph infections turned up among members of the Washington Redskins in a two-year period, and drug-resistant infections are growing common in sports franchises. Steps the team has taken to combat infections include a new Jacuzzi with germ-killing ultraviolet light and locker-room benches with individual stools for each player.

Hester, Tom Jr., The Associated Press, "As Woman Marvels at Recovery, New Jersey Targets 'Superbug' Infections," *Newsday.com,* **Aug. 2, 2007.**
Gov. Jon Corzine, D-N.J., signs legislation requiring hospitals to screen patients for methicillin-resistant staph aureus (MRSA), implement new controls to prevent the spread of infections and report MRSA cases to the state.

Langreth, Robert, and Matthew Herper, "Biotech Engages in Germ Warfare," *Wired,* **June 9, 2006, www.wired.com/print/medtech/health/news/2006/06/71110.**
As antibiotic-resistance increases, small biotechnology companies are looking for new ways to combat bacterial infections.

Silberman, Steve, "The Invisible Enemy," *Wired,* **February 2007, www.wired.com/wired/archive/15.02/enemy.html.**
Soldiers wounded in Iraq encounter a severe drug-resistant infection — *acinetobacter baumannii* — during treatment in military medical facilities.

Von Bubnoff, Andreas, "Seeking New Antibiotics in Nature's Backyard," *Cell,* **Dec. 1, 2006, p. 867.**
Scientists are using DNA techniques and other new approaches to test the potential antibiotic effects of previously unstudied microbes from unusual environments.

Weiss, Rick, "FDA Rules Override Warnings About Drug," *The Washington Post,* **March 4, 2007, p. A1.**
A Food and Drug Administration advisory panel recommended rejecting a request to approve the antibiotic cefquinome for use in cattle because of the danger that more bacteria will become drug resistant, but the FDA argues that its drug-approval rules override those considerations.

Reports and Studies

Antibiotic Resistance: Federal Agencies Need to Better Focus Efforts to Address Risk to Humans From Antibiotic Use in Animals, **Government Accountability Office, April 2004.**
Congress' nonpartisan auditing office finds federal agencies aren't doing enough to pin down the precise health risks posed by antibiotic use on farms.

Bad Bugs, *No Drugs, Infectious Diseases Society of America,* **July 2004.**
Infectious-disease researchers argue that antimicrobial resistance is approaching a crisis and recommend that Congress provide incentives for companies to develop new antibiotics.

Impacts of Antibiotic-Resistant Bacteria, **Office of Technology Assessment, http://www.princeton.edu/~ota/disk1/1995/9503/9503.PDF.**
A nonpartisan federal agency reports on the history of antibiotic resistance and discusses federal policy options to combat it.

The Resistance Phenomenon in Microbes and Infectious Disease Vectors: Implications for Human Health and Strategies for Containment, **Forum on Emerging Infections, National Academy of Sciences, www.nap.ed/catalog/10651.html, 2003.**
A national expert panel discusses the science of developing resistance and strategies to control it, including economic approaches, health-care system changes and emerging technologies like bacteriophages.

Isaacson, Richard E., and Mary E. Torrence, *The Role of Antibiotics in Agriculture,* **American Academy of Microbiology, 2002.**

Microbiologists describe the long-running, contentious debate over how strictly governments should control antibiotic use on farms, concluding that science-based policy in the field is difficult to develop.

Laxminarayan, Ramanan, and Anup Malani, *Extending the Cure, Resources for the Future,* **www.extendingthe-cure.org/research_and_downloads.html, 2007.**
Economists who specialize in maximizing environmental resources analyze the human and scientific factors leading to increased antimicrobial resistance and discuss policy options.

For More Information

Acinetobacter Baumannii; www.acinetobacter.org. Web site run by individuals concerned about drug-resistant infections affecting U.S. soldiers.

Animal Health Institute, 1325 G St., N.W., #700, Washington, DC 20005-3104; (202) 637-2440; www.ahi.org. Organization of companies that manufacture veterinary drugs; advocates for farm use of antibiotics.

Alliance for the Prudent Use of Antibiotics, 75 Kneeland St., Boston, MA 02111-1901; (617) 636-0966; www.tufts.edu/med/apua/index.html. International group that supports research and projects to combat antimicrobial resistance.

Association for Professionals in Infection Control and Epidemiology, 1275 K St., N.W., Suite 1000, Washington, DC 20005-4006; (202) 789-1890; www.apic.org. Professional society that conducts research and education on resistance.

Centers for Disease Control and Prevention, Antimicrobial Resistance Program, 1600 Clifton Rd, Atlanta, GA 30333; (404) 639-3534; www.cdc.gov/drugresistance. Federal agency that coordinates the U.S. response to antimicrobial resistance.

DANMAP; www.danmap.org. A Danish agency that monitors antibiotic use in Denmark, the first country to enact strong government controls over all antibiotics.

Extending the Cure, Resources for the Future, 1616 P St., N.W., Washington, DC 20036; (202)-328-5000;

www.extendingthecure.org. Analyzes economic and other policy options for extending antibiotics' effectiveness.

Infectious Disease Society of America, 1300 Wilson Blvd., Suite 300, Arlington, VA 22209; (703) 299-0200; www.idsociety.org. Physicians' group that makes policy recommendations for combating resistance.

Institute of Food Technologists, 1025 Connecticut Ave., N.W., Suite 503, Washington, DC 20036-5422; (202) 466-5980; www.ift.org/cms/. Food scientists' group that studies antibiotic use from the point of view of food production.

Keep Antibiotics Working, P.O. Box 14590, Chicago, IL 60614; (773) 525-4952; www.keepantibioticsworking.com/new. Nonprofit group that combats drug resistance.

MRSA Notes; www.mrsanotes.com. Posts news updates and links about drug-resistant staph infections.

Society for Healthcare Epidemiology of America, 1300 Wilson Blvd., Suite 300, Arlington, VA 22209; (703) 684-1006; www.shea-online.org. Provides information and advocacy on antimicrobial resistance.

Stop Hospital Infections, Consumers Union; www.consumersunion.org/campaigns/stophospitalinfections/learn.html. Consumer group that advocates for state laws requiring hospitals to publicly report rates of infection.

5

Domestic Poverty

Thomas J. Billitteri

Hispanic day laborers negotiate with a potential employer in Homestead, Fla. As low-skilled immigrants, many living below the poverty line, move to the South and Midwest to work in meatpacking and other industries, debate intensifies over immigration's impact on native-born Americans at the bottom of the income scale. Newly released Census data for 2006 show that 36.5 million Americans — including nearly 13 million children — lived below the federal poverty line of $20,614 in income for a family of four.

From *CQ Researcher*,
September 7, 2007.

Marilem Bezear, a 52-year-old single parent in Harlem who lost her husband to cancer, was living in run-down public housing and working two jobs last winter, cleaning offices and doing clerical work for a temp agency.

"Together, after taxes, I bring home up to $300 a week," she told a congressional panel in February. "With this I pay my rent, food, telephone and payments for the loan that I took out for my daughter to go to college." When the temp agency has no work, Bezear scrambles for ways to meet expenses, like working the late shift at a bowling alley and "getting home at 4:30 in the morning."

Bezear added: "I am just one of many who live through these struggles. . . . Wages, education, training and health care are a necessity. I hope my testimony did not fall on deaf ears." [1]

It's a hope that many of America's poorest citizens would no doubt echo. Despite a relatively stable economy, an overhaul of the welfare system a decade ago and billions spent on programs for the needy, poverty remains pervasive and intractable across the nation.

Conservatives say solutions must emphasize personal responsibility, higher marriage rates and fewer out-of-wedlock births, while liberals blame the negative effects of budget cuts for anti-poverty programs, tax cuts benefiting the wealthy and the need for more early-childhood-development programs. The Democratic Congress has made poverty a priority issue. And a number of presidential candidates are focusing either squarely on poverty or more generally on ideas to narrow the growing gap between the rich and poor.

Newly released Census data for 2006 show that 36.5 million Americans — about one in eight — lived below the federal poverty line of $20,614 in income for a family of four. More than a third of

South Is Most Impoverished Region

Almost all the Southern states have poverty levels exceeding the national average of 12.3 percent of residents living in poverty. Mississippi leads the nation with a poverty rate of 20.6 percent. New Hampshire has the lowest rate, 5.4 percent.

Percentage of People in Poverty by State, 2006

Less than 10%
10.0-12.2%
12.3-14.9%
15.0% and over

U.S. Total: 12.3%

Source: "Historical Poverty Tables," U.S. Census Bureau, 2007

combined. Severe poverty hit a 32-year high in 2005, according to McClatchy Newspapers. [5]

• The gap between rich and poor is growing. In 2005, the average income of the top 1 percent of U.S. households rose $102,000 (adjusted for inflation), but the bottom 90 percent saw incomes rise $250, according to economists Thomas Piketty and Emmanuel Saez. [6] And the top 1 percent got the biggest share of national income since 1928. [7]

• The chance an average American family will see its income plummet at least 50 percent is roughly two-and-a-half times that of the 1970s. [8]

• At some time, most Americans will live at least one year below the poverty line, according to sociologists Mark R. Rank and Thomas A. Hirschl. [9]

Such trends have helped push poverty and broader issues of inequality and economic insecurity onto the national stage in ways not seen for decades. Two years ago, televised images of squalor in post-Katrina New Orleans refocused the nation's attention — at least temporarily — on poverty. More recently, the subprime mortgage debacle, higher gas prices and spiraling medical costs have edged millions of middle-class Americans closer to economic ruin. Meanwhile, Main Street angst is growing over globalization, which has contributed to the elimination of one-sixth of U.S. factory jobs in the past six years. [10]

Jacob S. Hacker, a political scientist at Yale University and author of the 2006 book *The Great Risk Shift: The Assault on American Jobs, Families, Health Care, and Retirement — And How You Can Fight Back*, says poverty is on the nation's radar for reasons that go beyond high-profile events like Katrina.

"Poverty is something the middle class cares about when it looks down and sees itself poised on the financial precipice," he says. The middle class is looking up, too, at those in the top income strata, and "there's a lot more discussion about [income] inequality." And finally, many middle-class Americans "have a deep concern about the fact that we're such a rich nation, and yet children and

them are children, and 3.4 million are 65 and older. And while the nation's poverty rate declined for the first time this decade, from 12.6 percent in 2005 to 12.3 percent last year, the number of children without health insurance rose to 11.7 percent in 2006. [2]

Indeed, among "rich" nations, the United States ranked second — behind Mexico — in poverty at the turn of the 21st century. [3]

"An astonishing number of people are working as hard as they possibly can but are still in poverty or have incomes that are not much above the poverty line," said Peter Edelman, a law professor at Georgetown University who was co-chairman of a poverty task force this year for the Center for American Progress, a Washington think tank. [4]

A number of indicators underscore the depth and breadth of American poverty:

• Those in "deep," or severe, poverty, with incomes of half or less of the official poverty threshold, number over 15 million — more than the populations of New York City, Los Angeles and Chicago

Gap Between Rich and Poor Widened

The top 1 percent of income households earned about 20 percent of the nation's total income in 2005, its highest share since 1929. From 2004 to 2005, the average income of such earners increased by $102,000, after adjusting for inflation. By contrast, the average income of the bottom 90 percent rose by $250.

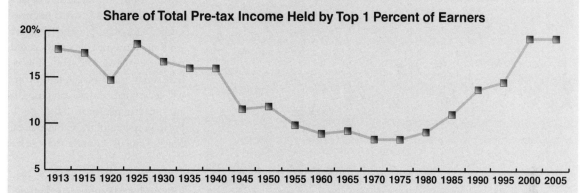

Share of Total Pre-tax Income Held by Top 1 Percent of Earners

Source: Thomas Picketty and Emmanuel Saez, based on IRS data; in Aviva Aron-Dine, "New Data Show Income Concentration Jumped Again in 2005: Income Share of Top 1% Returned to Its 2000 Level, the Highest Since 1929," Center on Budget and Policy Priorities, March 29, 2007

hardworking adults who moved into the labor market after welfare reform are struggling to get by."

While politicians in both major parties have spoken to concerns about middle-class vulnerability, Democrats have been focusing squarely on poverty and inequality, blending appeals for middle-class protections with rhetoric reminiscent of the 1960s "War on Poverty."

Since assuming control of Congress in January, Democrats have held several hearings on poverty, hunger and economic threats to the needy. Rep. Charles B. Rangel, D-N.Y., chairman of the powerful House Ways and Means Committee, declared this spring that "with the exception of getting the hell out of the Middle East, I can't think of anything more patriotic that we can do than eliminate poverty." [11]

In the 2008 presidential race, Sen. Hillary Clinton, D-N.Y., has accused the Bush administration of making the middle class and working families into "invisible Americans," [12] while Sen. Barack Obama, D-Ill., alluding to his work as a community organizer in Chicago, has said poverty "is the cause that led me to a life of public service." [13] Former Sen. John Edwards, D-N.C., has staked his campaign on the poverty issue, calling it "the great moral issue of our time." [14]

Among other contenders, Mayor Michael Bloomberg of New York — who dropped his affiliation with the Republican Party in June — has been among the most outspoken on poverty. On Aug. 28, the billionaire founder of Bloomberg News, who is thought to be considering a third-party presidential bid, proposed a sharp expansion in the Earned Income Tax Credit (EITC), which provides tax relief to the working poor, and called on politicians of both parties to move beyond ideology to overcome poverty. Bloomberg proposed roughly doubling the number of Americans eligible to benefit from the EITC to 19.7 million people. [15]

"We are beginning to hear a chorus of voices urging action on poverty," Rep. Jim McDermott, D-Wash., chairman of the House Ways and Means Subcommittee on Income Security and Family Support, said in April. [16]

Edelman, at the Center for American Progress, echoed the point. "There's a rising concern in the country about inequality," he said. "There's concern about giveaways to the really wealthy, and there's concern about economic insecurity. The poverty issue is embedded in that." [17]

Nevertheless, it remains unclear how far voters will go in supporting new programs for the poor. A mere 1 percent of respondents to a Gallup Poll in June ranked the

Democratic Candidates' Stands on Poverty

 Joseph Biden voted for the Fair Minimum Wage Act of 2007, which raised the minimum wage from $5.15 an hour to $7.25 an hour. Biden broke with his party to vote in favor of the Bankruptcy Abuse Prevention and Consumer Protection Act of 2005, which makes it harder for people to erase debt by declaring bankruptcy.

 Hillary Clinton accuses the Bush administration of turning the middle class into "invisible Americans," and says if she is elected president, "they will no longer be invisible." In 2002, Clinton was criticized by liberal groups for supporting an increase in the work requirement for welfare; she said that she supported the measure because it was tied to $8 billion in funding of day care for welfare recipients. She advocated for welfare reform under her husband's administration. As a senator, Clinton voted for an increase in the federal minimum wage.

 Christopher Dodd says that one of his policy priorities influenced by Catholic social teachings and the emphasis on the common good is "creating safety nets for the disadvantaged." As a senator, one of Dodd's priorities has been helping children, and he has authored numerous child care bills. Dodd has favored increases in the federal minimum wage.

 John Edwards has made reducing poverty the signature issue of his campaign, calling it "the great moral issue of our time." He has set a goal of ending poverty in 30 years by lifting one-third of the 37 million currently impoverished Americans above the poverty line each decade through a higher minimum wage, tax cuts for low-income workers, universal health care and housing vouchers for poor families.

 Mike Gravel says America's war on drugs must end because it "does nothing but savage our inner cities and put our children at risk." Gravel proposes to help end poverty by creating a progressive tax system in which consumers of new products would be taxed at a flat rate. This would encourage Americans to save, Gravel says. This proposed system would replace the income tax and Internal Revenue Service.

 Dennis Kucinich advocates ending the war in Iraq and using the money saved to fight domestic poverty, calling homelessness, joblessness and poverty "weapons of mass destruction." In July 2007, Kucinich said that he was in favor of reparations for slavery, saying, "The Bible says we shall and must be repairers of the breach. And a breach has occurred. . . . It's a breach that has resulted in inequality in opportunities for education, for health care, for housing, for employment."

 Barack Obama In the Illinois Senate, Obama helped author the state's earned income tax credit, which provided tax cuts for low-income families. Obama has supported bills to increase the minimum wage. In The Audacity of Hope, Obama describes what he calls America's "empathy deficit," writing that a "stronger sense of empathy would tilt the balance of our current politics in favor of those people who are struggling in this society."

 Bill Richardson As governor of New Mexico, Richardson took steps to combat poverty in the state, one of the nation's poorest. He eliminated the tax on food and offered tax breaks to companies paying above the prevailing wage. Richardson has backed a living wage in the state and created tax credits for the creation of new jobs.

Source: This information first appeared on www.pewforum.org. Reprinted with permission from the Pew Forum on Religion & Public Life and Pew Research Center.

The public's fickle interest in the poor has been evident in the two years following Hurricane Katrina, which produced some of the starkest and most widely disseminated images of urban poverty in American history.

"After Katrina, with its vivid images, a lot of people who have been working in the area of poverty reduction were excited. They said, 'now we have some visible images, now people will get excited, and we can push this anti-poverty platform," says Elsie L. Scott, president of the Congressional Black Caucus Foundation. "That lasted a month maybe, that excitement. Now that people in New Orleans have been dispersed around the country, people want to forget about it. They don't want to admit we have this kind of poverty in the United States."

Policy experts say it would be unfortunate if Middle America fails to recognize how much poverty undermines the nation's overall well-being. Childhood poverty alone saps the United States of $500 billion per year in crime and health costs and reduced productivity, according to Harry J. Holzer, a professor of public policy at Georgetown University. [20]

Rising poverty should be a concern even among those who don't see a moral obligation to aid the poor, experts warn. "The global competitiveness of the U.S. economy suffers if workers are too poor to obtain an education and modern job skills, the government loses tax revenue and spends more on public assistance because of poverty, and communities fall victim to urban decay, crime, and unrest," notes a recent study on severe poverty in the *American Journal of Preventive Medicine*. [21]

Yet, the American public has always had a tendency to blame the poor for their ills, some poverty experts lament. "There is a common perception that the problem with the poor folks in the United States is a problem

"gap between rich and poor" as the most important economic problem, and only 5 percent named "poverty, hunger and homelessness" as the most important "non-economic" problem. [18]

Likewise, Edwards has trailed his rivals for the Democratic nomination and even failed to capture much support from voters who are struggling financially. In a survey of independent voters, 40 percent of respondents in households earning less than $20,000 said they would not vote for Edwards if he were the Democratic nominee. [19]

with values," said Dalton Conley, chairman of the Department of Sociology at New York University. "It's not a values deficit at all; it's really a resource deficit." [22]

And that deficit can be steep. "Most Americans would be shocked to know that full-time male workers, at the median, earned no more in 2005 than they did in 1973" after taking inflation into account, says Sheldon H Danziger, a professor of public policy at the University of Michigan. And that wage stagnation came amid a boom in productivity in the 1990s, he adds.

"There's a tendency for people to blame the poor for their own circumstances," Danziger says. "And I don't think anybody would blame full-time male workers."

As Congress, policy experts and presidential candidates consider what to do about poverty, here are some of the questions they are asking:

Is extreme poverty growing?

In Savannah, Ga., not far from the lush parks and antebellum mansions of the city's fabled historic district, poverty runs wide and deep.

More than one-fifth of Savannah's residents live below the federal poverty line, and that's not the worst of it. * "We have six census tracts with over a 50-percent poverty rate," says Daniel Dodd, who directs a project that enlists Savannah's business community in helping the poor.

Republican Candidates' Stands on Poverty

 Sam Brownback voted for the 1996 welfare reform bill that required more work for recipients and placed limits on the amount of time they could receive benefits. He says poverty can best be addressed by encouraging people to get married, get a job and not have children out of wedlock. He has promoted a "marriage development account program" to help married couples get training, buy a car, get an education or purchase a house. Brownback has voted against increasing the minimum wage.

 Rudolph Giuliani advocates requiring welfare recipients to work or engage in job training to receive benefits. New York City's welfare rolls were cut by more than half while Giuliani was mayor, and he touts his overhaul of the city's welfare system as one of his major successes. During his 2000 senate campaign, Giuliani indicated that he would support an increase in the minimum wage if studies showed it would not reduce the number of available jobs.

 Mike Huckabee says one of his priorities is to address poverty because it's "consistent with me being pro-life." He calls his desire to fight poverty a "faith position" rather than a political position. He says it is impossible to address poverty without "prioritizing stable homes and families."

 Duncan Hunter says tax cuts are the best tool for reducing poverty because they enable the poor to save and support their families. He advocates what he calls a "Fair Tax," which would replace the national income tax with a national retail sales tax. As part of his anti-poverty agenda, he supports tariffs on Chinese imports to help preserve American manufacturing jobs.

 John McCain voted for a 1996 welfare reform bill that required more work for recipients and placed limits on the amount of time they could receive benefits. Although McCain voted for a bill to increase the federal minimum wage in February 2007, he has historically voted against minimum wage increases, arguing that they can hurt small businesses.

 Ron Paul In May 2007, Paul asserted that "subsidies and welfare" only provide poor people with "crumbs," while "the military-industrial complex and the big banks" receive "the real big welfare," further impoverishing the middle class and the poor. Paul opposes foreign aid, writing that "the redistribution of wealth from rich to poor nations has done little or nothing to alleviate suffering abroad."

 W. Mitt Romney As Massachusetts governor, Romney proposed a plan requiring more people to work in order to receive state welfare benefits, bringing Massachusetts policy in line with federal welfare reforms. He supports increasing the minimum wage to match inflation but vetoed a bill to raise it in Massachusetts, saying it called for increases that were too extreme and too abrupt.

 Tom Tancredo The Colorado Congressman advocates moving from an income-based tax to a consumption-based tax, which he says would create an "explosion of job opportunities and economic growth" that would benefit all sectors of society, particularly the poor. He also supports repealing the 16th Amendment and establishing a flat, national sales tax to alleviate the burden on American companies and "put billions back into the economy."

 Fred Thompson In May the actor and former U.S. senator criticized programs that would "redistribute the income among our citizens" as "defeatist." A policy of lowering taxes, he said, would stimulate economic growth and "make the pie bigger." In 1999 he voted against an increase in the minimum wage. He also voted to reduce taxes on married couples in 2000. He has yet to officially declare his candidacy.

Source: This information first appeared on www.pewforum.org. Reprinted with permission from the Pew Forum on Religion & Public Life and Pew Research Center.

---

* Many people who study domestic poverty criticize the way the government measures poverty, arguing the standard federal poverty index does not accurately count the poor. Presidential candidate John Edwards is among those who call for reform of the poverty measure. His Web site states that it "excludes necessities like taxes, health care, child care and transportation" and "fails to count some forms of aid including tax credits, food stamps, Medicaid and subsidized housing. The National Academy of Sciences has recommended improvements that would increase the count of people in poverty by more than 1 million." See also, for example, Reid Cramer, "The Misleading Way We Count the Poor: Alternatives to Our Antiquated Poverty Measure Should Consider Assets," New America Foundation, September 2003, and Douglas J. Besharov, senior scholar, American Enterprise Institute, testimony before House Subcommittee on Income Security and Family Support, "Measuring Poverty in America," Aug. 1, 2007.

TANF Assistance on the Decline

The number of households receiving financial support through the Temporary Assistance for Needy Families (TANF) program has declined every fiscal year since 1996. A monthly average of just over 4 million households received TANF assistance in 2006, less than a third of the number of recipients 10 years earlier.

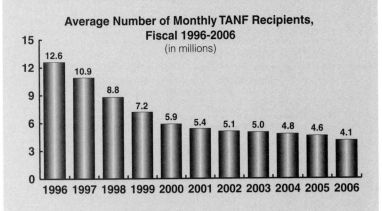

Average Number of Monthly TANF Recipients, Fiscal 1996-2006
(in millions)

Year	Value
1996	12.6
1997	10.9
1998	8.8
1999	7.2
2000	5.9
2001	5.4
2002	5.1
2003	5.0
2004	4.8
2005	4.6
2006	4.1

Source: "2008 Budget in Brief," Department of Health and Human Services, 2007

Savannah is hardly unique. At least one neighborhood of "concentrated" poverty — often defined as a place where at least 40 percent of residents live below the poverty line — exists in 46 of the nation's 50 biggest cities, according to Alan Berube, a fellow in the Metropolitan Policy Program of the Brookings Institution, a think tank in Washington. [23]

McClatchy Newspapers concluded this year that 43 percent of the nation's 37 million poor people live in severe poverty — sometimes called "extreme" or "deep" poverty. Severe poverty reflects those with incomes of less than half the federal poverty threshold — in other words, under $9,903 for a family of four and $5,080 for an individual in 2005.

"The number of severely poor Americans grew by 26 percent from 2000 to 2005," McClatchy reported. "That's 56 percent faster than the overall poverty population grew in the same period."

The rise in severe poverty extends beyond large urban counties to suburban and rural areas. "Severe poverty is worst near the Mexican border and in some areas of the South, where 6.5 million severely poor residents are struggling to find work as manufacturing jobs in the textile, apparel and furniture-making industries disappear,"

McClatchy noted. "The Midwestern Rust Belt and areas of the Northeast also have been hard hit as economic restructuring and foreign competition have forced numerous plant closings. At the same time, low-skilled immigrants with impoverished family members are increasingly drawn to the South and Midwest to work in meatpacking, food processing and agricultural industries." [24]

In Illinois, the rate of extreme poverty is the highest in the hard-hit Midwest, with more than 700,000 people in such straits, according to the Heartland Alliance for Human Needs & Human Rights, an advocacy group in Chicago. A family of four living in extreme poverty in Bellevue, Ill., would have monthly expenses of $2,394 but monthly income of only $833, the group says. [25]

But some researchers see little or no evidence that severe poverty is on the rise. Robert Rector, a senior policy analyst at the conservative Heritage Foundation, said "he's seen no data that suggest increasing deprivation among the very poor," according to the McClatchy report.

Rector "questioned the growth of severe poverty, saying that census data become less accurate farther down the income ladder. He said many poor people, particularly single mothers with boyfriends, underreport their income by not including cash gifts and loans." [26]

Such skeptical views extend beyond the severely poor. "While real material hardship certainly does occur, it is limited in scope and severity," Rector told a congressional panel this year. "Most of America's 'poor' live in material conditions that would be judged as comfortable or well-off just a few generations ago. Today, the expenditures per person of the lowest-income one-fifth . . . of households equal those of the median American household in the early 1970s, after adjusting for inflation." [27]

In fact, many more consumer items are within reach of a wider segment of the population — even the poor — than they were 30 or 40 years ago, thanks in part to globalization and the spread of discount retailers. But the cost of necessities such as health care and shelter have exploded, taking a much higher proportion of income than they once did.

Indeed, while the poor may have more material goods than in the past, many analysts say poverty is much more complicated than comparisons with earlier eras might suggest.

"On the one hand, the poor have vastly more consumer goods than a generation ago — TVs, cars, washing machines, dishwashers in many cases," says Hacker of Yale University. "But at the same time, if you think about where they are relative to middle-class Americans, to say nothing of those at the top, they're much further behind."

A major portion of the spending done by poor people is for basics, especially housing, transportation, child care and health care, and the poor have had a tough time keeping up with those costs, Hacker says. What's more, "the consumption of the poor is supported by higher levels of debt that can leave them extremely vulnerable."

And those most vulnerable are people who live in severe poverty. From 2000 to 2004, its prevalence rose sharply. The risk of extreme poverty is significantly higher for children than adults, and it is higher for African-Americans and Hispanics than for whites or Asian-Americans, according to the study in the *American Journal of Preventive Medicine*.

"Millions of Americans, overrepresented by children and minorities, have entered conditions of extreme poverty," the study said. "After 2000, Americans subsisting under these conditions grew as a class more than any other segment of the population." [28]

Reducing severe poverty is a daunting challenge that has spurred an outpouring of policy proposals from all sides of the political spectrum.

In Savannah, Dodd's project — called Step Up, Savannah's Poverty Reduction Initiative — represents one of the nation's most ambitious local anti-poverty efforts. Formed in 2004, it is a collaboration of more than 80 organizations representing business, local government, nonprofit organizations, neighborhood groups and others. It receives donations from several major foundations as well as other sources, including businesses.

Step Up's methods include asking employers and business executives to role play for a few hours what impoverished residents experience every day. "These things are quite eye-opening for a lot of people," Dodd says. The "poverty simulation" exercise reveals "how frustrating the

Step Up Savannah, one of the nation's most ambitious local anti-poverty efforts, is a collaboration of organizations from business, government, education and the nonprofit sector that helps residents of high-poverty neighborhoods become self-sufficient.

system is to navigate if you're making minimum wage, if you don't have the skills, and how hard it is to keep a job with what you're getting paid. There's transportation obstacles, crime," and other impediments. [29]

The exercise "provides a common frame of reference for the community and demystifies myths" about poverty, adds Dodd, who points out that welfare reform has led to a 70 percent reduction in government subsidies for the city's poor in the past seven years. [30]

Step Up's goals include expanding poor people's access to good jobs and quality health care, training them for career-level positions and expanding access to the EITC.

The effort grew from a realization that "we hadn't had a decline in poverty in 30 years," Dodd says. "People realized we'd thrown millions of dollars at this but hadn't had the impact we needed to have."

For all the project's earnestness, though, it remains unclear whether Step Up will succeed. "What I always tell people," says Dodd, "is we don't have it all figured out yet."

Has welfare reform reduced entrenched poverty?

In August 1996, President Bill Clinton's signature ended a six-decade practice of guaranteeing cash assistance to the poor. A new system required most people who get aid to work within two years of receiving it. The revised law also limited most aid to a total of five years. And it turned over to states and localities much of the control over how federal poverty money is dispensed. [31]

More then a decade later, experts are still debating whether the poor are better off.

Ron Haskins, a former Ways and Means Committee staff member who played a key role in the welfare overhaul, has written that "above all, welfare reform showed that work — even low-wage work — provides a more durable foundation for social policy than handouts." [32]

"Before welfare reform," Haskins, now a senior fellow at the Brookings Institution, said last year, "the main goal of state welfare programs was simply to give out money. But now the message families receive when they apply for welfare is that they need a job, that the 'welfare' program is there to help them find one and that they can receive cash benefits for a maximum of five years. As a result, welfare rolls plunged by over 60 percent, as many as 2 million mothers entered the labor force, earnings for females heading families increased while their income from welfare payments fell, and child poverty declined every year between 1993 and 2000. By the late 1990s, both black child poverty and poverty among children in female-headed families had reached their lowest levels ever."

Even after four years of increased child poverty following the 2001 recession, Haskins said, the rate of child poverty was still 20 percent lower than in 1993.

Haskins went on to say that "the success of welfare reform was created both by welfare reforms itself and by the work-support programs that provided tax credits, health insurance, nutrition supplements and child care to low-income working families." [33]

Yet, despite what many see as its positive effects, welfare reform remains a mixed bag. It is not clear, for example, to what degree welfare reform itself, along with its time limits on benefits, caused poverty rates to fall and work rates to rise.

"Welfare reform, and in particular the onset of time limits, arrived in the midst of an extremely tight labor market and a flourishing economy," says Katherine Newman, a professor of sociology and public affairs at Princeton University.

"So how much the shift toward work was attributable to the pull of a growing economy and [demand for] labor is very hard to sort out," she continues. "My sense is that welfare reform had something to do with it, but it's hardly the whole story. A lot had to do with favorable market conditions."

The Center on Budget and Policy Priorities, a Washington think tank, last year noted, among other negative trends, that while child poverty declined in the 1990s, as Haskins pointed out, it nonetheless rose sharply after 2000, as did the number of children living in severe poverty. [34] (*See sidebar, see p. 112.*)

Many anti-poverty advocates say even though welfare reform put more people to work, further steps are needed to ensure that families can climb out of poverty and stay there, and that poor children are protected.

Timothy M. Smeeding, director of the Center for Policy Research at Syracuse University, says welfare reform "turned the welfare poor into the working poor. You've got more self-respect, you're earning it, but the effect on kids is mixed." He calls for a system that will "make work pay," where "you go out and you work, you show the effort, you put in 1,000 hours, and we'll find a way to make sure you've got $15,000 or $20,000 and you're not poor."

In Wisconsin — where some of the earliest efforts at welfare reform took place — the rate of growth in the number of people living in poverty was higher in 2003-2004 than in any other state. [35] Richard Schlimm, executive director of the Wisconsin Community Action Program Association, a statewide association of community-action and anti-poverty groups, says welfare reform simply "has not worked," in reducing poverty in his state.

"Certainly it was the right thing to do, to get people working," Schlimm says. "But I've always believed poor people want to work, and they prefer work over welfare. . . . We successfully achieved the elimination of welfare, but I maintain that we had the wrong goal. The goal was to reduce poverty, and if we kept that in our sights we would have focused a whole lot [more] funding on that than we did."

Would more government spending on poverty help?

While welfare reform encouraged work and reduced government caseloads, many experts say the fight against poverty has only begun.

Some argue that reducing poverty depends in large measure on the poor exercising greater personal responsibility. "While it is often argued that the U.S. devotes far fewer resources to social welfare spending than other rich nations, the facts show otherwise," Rector of the Heritage Foundation said. "The good news is that remaining poverty can readily be reduced further, particularly among children. There are two main reasons that American children are poor: Their parents don't work much, and fathers are absent from the home." [36]

Others say more government spending on anti-poverty programs is the key, Schlimm, at the Wisconsin Community Action Program Association, says that to reduce poverty, the nation needs political leadership coupled with "a massive investment" in affordable housing, accessible health care, education and job creation for the poor. "Let's face it, we have committed massive investments in Iraq," he says, "and [with] half of that — even a fourth of that — focused on poverty in the United States, we could make remarkable strides."

Smeeding, the Syracuse University policy researcher, says U.S. poverty could be cut by a third to a half with an outlay of $45 billion to $60 billion a year, focused on three things: child care for working mothers; guaranteed child support for mothers who have established paternity with fathers who can't or won't pay because of disability or prison, and an expansion of the EITC.

Lawrence Mead, a professor of politics at New York University, advocates a stick-and-carrot approach with low-income men. "In 2005, there were more than 7 million poor men ages 16 to 50 in the United States, and only half of them worked at all," Mead wrote. "Among black men in poverty, nearly two-thirds were idle, and their employment has fallen steadily in recent decades."

Mead proposes using the child-support and criminal-justice systems to promote work among poor males. "Right now, these institutions depress male work levels by locking men up and by garnishing their wages if they do work," he wrote. "But they could be used to promote work. For example, men in arrears on their child support could be assigned to government-run work programs, as could parolees with employment problems. These men — about 1.5 million each year — would have to show up and work regularly — on penalty of going to jail. Both groups might also receive wage subsidies. The combination might instill more regular work habits."

Mandatory work for 1.5 million men would run $2 billion to $5 billion annually, according to Mead. "In return, governments could collect more in child support and spend less on incarceration." [37]

"Everyone recognizes that men are the frontier," Mead says. The ultimate goal, he says, should be to both reward and enforce work in ways the current system doesn't do now.

While spending on new programs is one approach to fighting poverty, some argue the solution isn't more outlays for anti-poverty programs but rather a mix of free-market capitalism and charity.

"Despite nearly $9 trillion in total welfare spending since Lyndon B. Johnson declared [the] War on Poverty in 1964, the poverty rate is perilously close to where it was when we began, more than 40 years ago," wrote Michael D. Tanner, director of health and welfare studies for the conservative Cato Institute think tank.

"Clearly we are doing something wrong. Throwing money at the problem has neither reduced poverty nor made the poor self-sufficient. . . . [I]f we have learned anything by now, it is that there are limits to what government programs — even reformed ones — can do to address the root causes of poverty.

"Observers have known for a long time that the surest ways to stay out of poverty are to finish school; not get pregnant outside marriage; and get a job, any job, and stick with it. That means that if we wish to fight poverty, we must end those government policies — high taxes and regulatory excess — that inhibit growth and job creation. We must protect capital investment and give people the opportunity to start new businesses. We must reform our failed government school system to encourage competition and choice. We must encourage the poor to save and invest.

"More importantly, the real work of fighting poverty must come not from the government, but from the engines of civil society. . . . [P]rivate charities are far more effective than government welfare programs." [38]

BACKGROUND

Warring on Poverty

Concerns about work, hardship and who deserves help go back to the roots of the Republic. The Virginia Assembly of 1619 decreed that a person found guilty of idleness would be forced to work under a master "til he shewe apparant signes of amendment." [39]

In the 19th century, poorhouses sprang up to accommodate a growing tide of desperate people flooding the cities from the countryside. Poverty flourished along with widespread indifference to the plight of the needy. After the Civil War the journalist and political economist Henry George called the United States a place where "amid the greatest accumulations of wealth, men die of starvation, and puny infants suckle dry breasts." [40]

Later came the first rudimentary efforts to measure poverty. In 1904 the social worker Robert Hunter set

1950s-1960s *Many Americans enjoy a post-war economic boom, but poverty persists. Poverty rate is 22.4 percent in 1959.*

1962 Michael Harrington's book *The Other America* helps spur President Lyndon B. Johnson's War on Poverty. . . . Welfare program is renamed Aid to Families with Dependent Children (AFDC).

1964 Congress establishes permanent food stamp program. . . . Federal government develops income thresholds to define poverty in American society.

1965 Congress enacts Medicaid to provide health care to low-income people.

1967 Congress establishes the Work Incentive Program, requiring states to establish job-training programs for adults receiving welfare.

1969 President Richard M. Nixon calls hunger in America an "embarrassing and intolerable" national shame.

1970s *The energy crisis, recessions and industrial restructuring put new strains on the poor.*

1975 Congress approves Earned Income Tax Credit (EITC), partly to offset the burden of Social Security taxes on low-income families and to provide an incentive to work.

1980s *Poverty programs of the 1960s and '70s come under scrutiny from the Reagan administration.*

1981 Congress cuts cash benefits for the working poor and lets states require welfare recipients to work.

1988 President Ronald Reagan signs Family Support Act, requiring states to implement education, job training and placement programs for welfare recipients.

1990s *Clinton administration pushes Congress to pass massive welfare reforms.*

1992 Democratic presidential candidate Bill Clinton pledges to "end welfare as we know it."

1993 Clinton expands EITC.

1996 Congress ends 60-year welfare entitlement program, passing a reform law that imposes work requirements and puts time limits on cash benefits.

1997 Federal minimum wage rises to $5.15 an hour.

1997 State Children's Health Insurance Program (SCHIP) is created.

1999 The government of British Prime Minister Tony Blair introduces a plan to end child poverty in Britain by 2020, spurring calls for a similar effort in the United States.

2000s *Hurricane Katrina devastates Gulf Coast, putting spotlight on poverty.*

2000 Federal poverty rate falls to 11.3 percent, lowest since 1974.

2004 Federal appeals court upholds the "living wage" law in Berkeley, Calif., rejecting the first major challenge to civic ordinances requiring contractors to pay above-poverty wages. . . . Poverty rate climbs to 12.7 percent

Aug. 29, 2005 Hurricane Katrina hits New Orleans.

2006 Congress reauthorizes Temporary Assistance for Needy Families (TANF) as part of Deficit Reduction Act.

2007 McClatchy Newspapers analysis finds that percentage of poor Americans living in severe poverty reached a 32-year high in 2005. . . . Congress spars with the Bush administration over expansion of SCHIP. . . . House Ways and Means Committee hearings focus on poverty and inequality. . . . Democratic presidential candidate John Edwards takes a three-day, 1,800-mile "Road to One America" poverty tour. . . . Federal minimum wage rises for the first time in a decade to $5.85 an hour; it goes to $6.55 in summer 2008 and $7.25 in summer 2009. . . . Poverty rate falls to 12.3 percent.

what might have been the first national poverty line — $460 per year for a five-member family in the Northern industrial states and $300 for a family in the South. [41]

In the post-World War I boom years, some Americans enjoyed unprecedented comfort and wealth, but poverty wracked much of the nation. Between 1918 and 1929, some 10 million families were poor. By 1933, in the depths of the Great Depression, a fourth of the labor force was without jobs, and an estimated 15 million families — half the American population — lived in poverty. [42]

World War II jump-started the U.S. economy, and in the 1950s and early '60s many Americans enjoyed middle-class prosperity. But not all saw their living standards rise. Poverty persisted and grew, much of it concentrated in the rural South, Appalachia and the gritty urban cores of the industrial North. Many Americans blamed the poor for their plight, dismissing racism, educational inequality and other entrenched societal ills as major factors in perpetuating poverty.

In 1962 Michael Harrington wrote in his groundbreaking book *The Other America: Poverty in the United States:*

"There are sociological and political reasons why poverty is not seen; and there are misconceptions and prejudices that literally blind the eyes. . . . Here is the most familiar version of social blindness: 'The poor are that way because they are afraid of work. And anyway they all have big cars. If they were like me (or my father or my grandfather), they could pay their own way. But they prefer to live on the dole and cheat the taxpayers.'

"This theory," Harrington went on, "usually thought of as a virtuous and moral statement, is one of the means of making it impossible for the poor ever to pay their way. . . . [T]he real explanation of why the poor are where they are is that they made the mistake of being born to the wrong parents, in the wrong section of the country, in the wrong industry or in the wrong racial or ethnic group. Once that mistake has been made, they could have been paragons of will and morality, but most of them would never even have had a chance to get out of the other America." [43]

By 1962, more than a fifth of Americans were living in poverty. Harrington's book helped spur Washington to act. [44]

A few months before his assassination, President John F. Kennedy directed his Council of Economic Advisers to study domestic poverty and recommend ways to fight it. [45]

Kennedy's successor, President Lyndon B. Johnson, followed through, declaring in his first State of the Union address, on Jan. 8, 1964, "unconditional war on poverty in America." Later that year Congress established the Office of Economic Opportunity, which attacked poverty through a phalanx of new programs, from Head Start — a school-readiness effort — to Job Corps, a training program for teens and young adults. [46] Johnson's fight against poverty also included a wide range of "Great Society" programs, from the 1964 Food Stamp Act to Medicare and Medicaid.

The War on Poverty persisted under the Nixon administration, which broadened the Food Stamp program and saw the passage of the Supplemental Security Income program for disabled people, among others. Even so, President Richard M. Nixon sought to dismantle the Office of Economic Opportunity, disbursing many of its programs among various federal agencies. The office was finally closed by President Gerald R. Ford in 1975.

Under Attack

By the 1980s and the start of the Reagan administration, poverty programs were under full-scale attack. The poverty rate, which dipped to just over 11 percent in the early 1970s, hit 15.2 percent in 1983. Conservatives, impatient with the Johnson-era philosophy of federally funded social aid for the poor, charged that the government's expensive programs were making poverty and dependence worse rather than better.

"[S]ome years ago, the federal government declared War on Poverty, and poverty won," Reagan famously said in his 1988 State of the Union address. "Today the federal government has 59 major welfare programs and spends more than $100 billion a year on them. What has all this money done? Well, too often it has only made poverty harder to escape. Federal welfare programs have created a massive social problem. With the best of intentions, government created a poverty trap that wreaks havoc on the very support system the poor need most to lift themselves out of poverty: the family."

The Reagan administration argued "that the social policies enacted in the 1960s and '70s had undermined the functioning of the nation's basic institutions and, by encouraging permissiveness, non-work and welfare dependence, had led to marital breakup, non-marital childbearing and the erosion of individual initiative," according to the University of Michigan's Danziger and

Military Families Face Financial Strain

"This spring our caseload doubled."

Meredith Leyva's work with military families recently as led her to a troubling conclusion: Poverty is growing among the ranks of deployed service members, especially those who have been seriously injured in Iraq or Afghanistan.

"This spring our caseload of both military families and wounded warriors doubled," says Leyva, who is the founder of Operation Homefront, a Santa Ana, Calif., charity that helps military families through 31 chapters nationwide. And, adds Leyva, whose husband is a Navy physician, "We saw a significant change in the types of cases. We're now seeing many more complicated and high-dollar crises that are compounded by deployment after deployment."

Meredith Leyva, founder of Operation Homefront.

Operation Homefront served approximately 1,700 families of wounded service members in 2006, Leyva says, and "over half and possibly more were living in poverty."

As for the 1.5-million-member military as a whole, however, little if any hard data exists on the extent of poverty in military families during the current conflict. Much of the government information on issues like food stamp use among military families predates the war.

Indeed, the financial health of military families can be a highly complicated and nuanced issue to analyze, even leaving aside the struggles of those dealing with catastrophic injury. "By any traditional measure of poverty . . . , military families are a lot better off than their civilian peers based on such things as age and education," says Joyce Raezer, chief operating officer of the National Military Family Association, a policy advocacy group in Alexandria, Va.

Still, she says some military families may be on the "financial edge," often because "they're young and financially inexperienced" and perhaps "prey for financial predators." Others may be strained by relocation demands that put them in temporary financial straits, she says

"My sense is that you don't have folks living in poverty so that day in and day out things are inadequate," says Raezer. "But it can be episodic, where they're strapped for cash because of the military lifestyle, financial inexperience and predators."

Most military families are ineligible for food stamps because the military housing allowance puts them over the eligibility threshold, Raezer notes.

Even so, in fiscal 2006 food-stamp redemptions at military commissaries rose about $2.3 million over the previous year, to $26.2 million. While it was not clear what caused the increase, three military stores affected by Hurricane Katrina and other storms accounted for more than 80 percent of the increase. [1]

Robert H. Haveman, a professor of economics and public affairs at the University of Wisconsin.

"The Reagan philosophy was that tax cuts and spending cuts would increase the rate of economic growth, and that the poor would ultimately benefit through the increased employment and earnings that would follow such growth," they wrote. "However, a deep recession in the early 1980s increased poverty, and the subsequent economic growth did not 'trickle down.' Although the economy expanded for many years in the 1980s, the wage rates of low- and medium-skilled male workers did not. On the other hand, the earnings of those in the upper part of the income distribution grew rapidly." [47]

Welfare Reform

The 1980s laid the groundwork for the radical shift in anti-poverty policy that was to come during the Clinton era. In 1993 Clinton pushed through a record expansion of the Earned Income Tax Credit. Then, Clinton signed the Personal Responsibility and Work Opportunity

In May, U.S. Reps. James McGovern, D-Mass., and Jo Ann Emerson, R-Mo., introduced a bill that would expand spending for federal nutrition programs, including a provision that would exclude combat-related military pay from income calculations for food-stamp eligibility. [2]

National Guard and active-duty families can feel financial strain differently. Lt. Col. Joseph Schweikert, state family program director for the Illinois National Guard, says "there are definitely families that go through financial hardships, sometimes due to deployments. But it varies from soldier to soldier, family to family. Some make more while deployed."

Nonetheless, at least 30 percent of Guard soldiers suffer a financial loss when deployed, he says.

Because the Guard offers a college-scholarship program, many young soldiers enlist, get a degree and then enter a well-paying career field. When they are mobilized, their pay may drop sharply. "It causes the family to go through a lot of hardships," Schweikert says, especially if the soldier doesn't have savings or a spouse's income to rely on.

Still, he suggests, many Guard members can be more stable financially than active-duty troops. Guard soldiers tend to be older and to have established civilian careers. Moreover, a working spouse will not have had to uproot periodically from a job, as often happens within the active-duty forces.

Wounded soldiers and their families attend a get-together sponsored by the Texas chapter of Operation Homefront at Brooke Army Medical Center at Fort Sam Houston.

"In active duty, a lot of time you have to transfer from base to base, and it's hard to establish a long-term career," Schweikert says.

Nonetheless, military families in both the Guard and regular forces may find it hard to avoid financial ruin, especially in cases of serious injury suffered in war.

When a soldier is deployed, a spouse may have to pay others to do jobs the soldier performed at home, such as mowing the lawn and maintaining the car, Leyva says. And if a soldier is wounded, she says, "his pay immediately drops while the expenses skyrocket." Often, a spouse takes leave from a job or quits altogether to be at the wounded soldier's bedside or to help the soldier through rehabilitation, spending long days or weeks away from home.

"Service members were never paid well," Leyva says, "but these extraordinary crises certainly overwhelm."

Leyva fears that poverty among veterans will skyrocket in the wake of the current war, as it did after the Vietnam conflict. "I think we're going to see a whole new generation of disabled veterans that are sort of the mirror images of the Vietnam veterans," she says. "It's as much about mental as physical wounds," she says, and it could lead to a new "generation of poverty."

---

[1] Karen Jowers, "Storms May Have Spurred Jump in Food-Stamp Use," *Air Force Times*, July 5, 2007, www.navytimes.com.

[2] The Feeding America's Family Act, HR 2129.

Reconciliation Act of 1996 — otherwise known as the Welfare Reform Act.

The move to overhaul welfare outraged some. Georgetown University's Edelman resigned from the Clinton administration in protest. In a blistering critique, Edelman wrote that the measure would lead to "more malnutrition and more crime, increased infant mortality and increased drug and alcohol abuse" and "increased family violence and abuse against children and women." [48]

But others have praised the reform measure. What the Clinton bill did, a *Boston Globe* columnist opined on the act's 10th anniversary, "was end the condescending attitude that the poor were incapable of improving their situation, and that 'compassion' consisted of supplying money indefinitely to women who had children, but no husbands or jobs." The bill "replaced deadly condescension with respect." [49]

Still, while welfare caseloads plummeted, poverty persisted, even among those who joined the labor force.

Did Recent Reforms Help Needy Families?

Bush administration tightened TANF work requirements

Mention welfare reform to a political observer, and it is Bill Clinton who typically comes to mind. It was candidate Clinton who pledged to "end welfare as we know it" and President Clinton who signed the landmark welfare reform act into law in 1996.

But the Bush era also has engineered significant reforms in the welfare system, changes that could have far-reaching effects on the nation's poor.

The most important came with last year's congressional reauthorization of Temporary Assistance for Needy Families (TANF), the federal block-grant program that replaced the old welfare system.

The reauthorization strengthened work requirements and closed a loophole so that separate state-funded TANF programs have to be included in work-participation calculations.

"In effect, the Bush administration and Congress put teeth back into TANF work requirements but set difficult benchmarks for state programs that are working with adult populations experiencing many barriers to employment," Scott W. Allard, an assistant professor of political science and public policy at Brown University, noted recently. [1]

Others looking back on more than a decade of welfare reform worry the recent changes in the welfare rules could make poverty trends worse. Two analysts at the Center on Budget and Policy Priorities, Sharon Parrott, director of the center's Welfare Reform and Income Support Division, and senior researcher Arloc Sherman, argue that even though changes in TANF a decade ago "played a role in reducing poverty and raising employment rates during the 1990s, our safety net for the poorest families with children has weakened dramatically." [2]

Among the trends they pointed to: child poverty fell in the 1990s, but began rising after 2000, and the number of children in "deep" poverty rose; the number of jobless single mothers receiving no government cash assistance has risen significantly, and TANF now helps a far smaller share of families that qualify for the program than it used to help.

Last year's reauthorization could weaken the safety net even more, the two analysts suggested. Welfare reauthorization requires states to place a much bigger portion of their TANF caseloads in work activities and restricts the kind of activities that can count toward state work-participation requirements, Parrott and Sherman noted. "In many cases,

"Basically, things are better than most people thought," Danziger says today. "On average, welfare recipients did much better moving from welfare to work, in part because the minimum wage was increased in 1997, the Earned Income Tax Credit expanded so much in the early '90s, states put so much into child-care subsidies, and the State Children's Health Insurance Program (SCHIP) came in. But the poverty rate among single mothers remains very high, and there's nothing new on the horizon."

Danziger noted in a 2006 paper that as many as 30 percent of single mothers who left welfare and took jobs are out of work in any given month. [50]

Advocates point out that it is possible to make real gains against poverty — and not just gains in cutting welfare caseloads. They point to big strides against child poverty in Britain, where in 1999 Prime Minister Tony Blair pledged to end child poverty by 2020.

'Elusive Dream'

But in cities and towns across America, President Johnson's 1964 pledge "not only to relieve the symptom of poverty but to cure it and, above all, to prevent it" remains an elusive dream. [51]

The loss of manufacturing jobs — and the stability and safety net they once provided — is a big reason the dream remains out of reach.

In Wisconsin, a state of 5.6 million people, the poverty rate shot from 8.2 percent to 11 percent over five years, says the Wisconsin Community Action Program Association's Schlimm. "I'm 58 and have lived in Wisconsin all my life, and it's very unusual to see those kinds of numbers," he says. It is the "loss of good jobs, manufacturing jobs" that is to blame.

"A lot of Wisconsin's good jobs support the auto industry," he continues. "And we're a paper-making state. Many of the papermakers moved. . . . When I got

state programs designed to address two of the biggest problems that have emerged over TANF's first decade — that parents who leave welfare for work often earn low wages and have unstable employment, and that many families with the greatest barriers to employment are being left behind — will no longer count toward states' work requirements," they wrote.

"In fact, the cheapest and easiest way for a state to meet the new work rules would simply be to assist fewer poor families, especially the families with barriers to employment who need the most help."

On top of that, the amount of basic federal block-grant funds for states has not been adjusted since 1996 and has lost 22 percent of its value to inflation, Parrott and Sherman wrote.

Some observers are more sanguine about the course of welfare reform. Writing in a "point-counterpoint" format with Parrott and Sherman, Lawrence Mead, a professor of politics at New York University and an architect of welfare reform, describes it as an "incomplete triumph." He says reform achieved its two main goals: Work levels rose sharply among poor mothers, the main beneficiaries of welfare. And caseloads plummeted.

Still, Mead says that the reform effort has had limitations. For one thing, he says, it did not create a system that promotes work on an ongoing basis through a combination of government incentives and emphasis on personal responsibility. He notes that 40 percent of those who have left welfare have not gone to work, and many welfare recipients have moved in and out of jobs.

Nor did welfare reform ensure that people leaving welfare for jobs will have enough income to live on, Mead says. "The situation has improved, but not enough."

And welfare reform did not adequately address the employment challenges among poor men, many of whom are fathers in welfare families, Mead says.

Nonetheless, Mead is hopeful the limitations of welfare reform can be addressed at least partly through engagement by the poor in the political process. Because more of the poor are working or moving toward work, they are in a stronger position to demand changes, such as payment of living wages, than they were under the old entitlement system of welfare, Mead says.

First, though, the poor must assert themselves both on the job and in the political sphere, he says.

"Finally," he writes, "what reform enforced was not work, but citizenship." [3]

---

[1] Scott W. Allard, "The Changing Face of Welfare During the Bush Administration," *Publius*, June 22, 2007.

[2] Sharon Parrott and Arloc Sherman, "Point-Counterpoint," in Richard P. Nathan, editor, "Welfare Reform After Ten Years: Strengths and Weaknesses," *Journal of Policy Analysis and Management*, Vol. 26, No. 2, 2007.

[3] Lawrence Mead, "Point-Counterpoint," in *ibid.*

---

out of college, you could go to a paper mill, and if it didn't work out, you could drive a couple of blocks down the street and find work with another company. In 1968 they paid $6 to $7 an hour. Now they pay $25. They're very coveted jobs. But there aren't as many of them. The economy hasn't been able to replace those very good jobs."

What matters most in the fight against poverty, many advocates contend, is leadership and political will.

The No. 1 problem is leadership, says David Bradley, executive director of the National Community Action Foundation. "We're not talking billions of dollars. We're talking receptivity to looking at ideas."

Bradley notes that the Johnson-era Office of Economic Opportunity was a laboratory for anti-poverty innovations. "For many years we've not had the federal government willing to fund and be experimental in partnering in new ideas on poverty. A lot of ideas start at the grass roots. I see incredible projects out there but no mechanism to duplicate them nationwide."

At the same time, Bradley laments that some in both political parties believe none of the ideas from the 1960s are worth keeping. "I find it frustrating that some candidates who are talking about poverty view anything that's gone on previously as not successful or not innovative or creative enough," he says. "If you're a program that started in 1964 or 1965, that doesn't mean by definition that you're still not innovative in your community."

Bradley is cautiously optimistic that a renewed commitment to fighting poverty is afoot in the nation. Political leaders in both parties are talking about the issue and the government's role in bringing about solutions, he points out.

But that will happen, Bradley says, only if solutions are not overpromised, the effort is bipartisan, innovation and creativity are part of the approach, sufficient government money is available and, "most important, if there is a general acceptance that the federal government wants to be a positive partner.

"It can be a partner that requires accountability," he says, "but a partner nevertheless."

CURRENT SITUATION

Presidential Race

It remains unclear how much traction the poverty theme will have in the 2008 presidential race. But as the campaign began moving into high gear this summer, poverty — and what to do about it — has been high on the list of priorities among several leading Democratic candidates, most notably Edwards and Obama.

Edwards has set the ambitious goal of cutting poverty by a third within a decade and ending it within 30 years. Echoing President Johnson's Great Society program, Edwards proposes a "Working Society" where "everyone who is able to work hard will be expected to work and, in turn, be rewarded for it."

To attack poverty, Edwards is pushing more than a dozen ideas, from raising the minimum wage, fighting predatory lending and reducing teen pregnancy to creating a million temporary "stepping stone" jobs for those having difficulty finding other work.

Obama has his own long list of proposals. He also backs a transitional jobs program and a minimum-wage increase, for example, along with such steps as improving transportation access for the working poor and helping ex-prisoners find jobs.

But deeper differences exist in the two candidates' approaches. "Edwards has focused on the malignant effects of the concentration of poverty in inner cities," *The Washington Post* noted. "He has argued for dispersing low-income families by replacing public housing with a greatly expanded rental voucher program to allow families to move where there are more jobs and better schools." Obama, on the other hand, has "presented a sharply different overall objective: fixing inner-city areas so they become places where families have a shot at prospering, without having to move." [52]

Part of what is noteworthy about the Edwards and Obama proposals is that they exist at all. Many Democratic candidates, including Sen. Clinton, have focused on the plight of the middle class rather than the poor. "Since the late 1980s," the columnist E. J. Dionne

Jr. noted, "Democrats have been obsessed with the middle class for reasons of simple math: no middle-class votes, no electoral victories." [53]

With the exception of recent comments by former Republican Bloomberg of New York, GOP rhetoric on poverty has not been nearly as prevalent as the Democrats'. In January, President Bush acknowledged that "income inequality is real," suggesting his administration might be poised to do more on poverty and perhaps get ahead of Democrats on the issue. [54] But more recently the administration has resisted congressional efforts to expand the SCHIP program, which benefits poor children.

Meanwhile, Republican presidential hopeful Mitt Romney echoed the longstanding conservative criticism of Democrat-backed social policies, declaring that Democrats are "thinking about big government, big welfare, big taxes, Big Brother." [55]

Anti-Poverty Proposals

In recent months several think tanks and advocacy groups have turned out policy proposals for reducing poverty. In April the liberal Center for American Progress advanced a dozen key steps to cut poverty in half in the next decade, including raising the minimum wage to half the average hourly wage, expanding the EITC and Child Tax Credit, promoting unionization, guaranteeing child-care assistance to low-income families and creating 2 million new housing vouchers "designed to help people live in opportunity-rich areas."

The center's main recommendations would cost roughly $90 billion annually — "a significant cost," it conceded, "but one that is necessary and could be readily funded through a fairer tax system." Spending $90 billion a year "would represent about 0.8 percent of the nation's gross domestic product, which is a fraction of the money spent on tax changes that benefited primarily the wealthy in recent years."

The Urban Institute estimated that four of the center's recommendations — on the minimum wage, EITC, child tax credit and child care — would cut poverty by about a fourth. Moreover, it said, both child poverty and extreme poverty would fall. [56]

A Brookings Institution proposal to "reinvigorate the fight for greater opportunity" includes seven recommendations for the next U.S. president, from strengthening work requirements in government-assistance programs, promoting marriage and funding teen pregnancy-

Should immigration be reduced to protect the jobs of native-born poor?

YES
Steven A. Camarota
Director of Research, Center for Immigration Studies

From testimony prepared for House Judiciary Committee, May 9, 2007

There is no evidence of a labor shortage, especially at the bottom end of the labor market where immigrants are most concentrated. . . . There is a good deal of research showing that immigration has contributed to the decline in employment and wages for less-educated natives. . . . All research indicates that less-educated immigrants consume much more in government services than they pay in taxes. Thus, not only does such immigration harm America's poor, it also burdens taxpayers. . . .

While the number of immigrants is very large . . . the impact on the overall economy or on the share of the population that is of working age is actually very small. And these effects are even smaller when one focuses only on illegal aliens, who comprise one-fourth to one-third of all immigrants. While the impact on the economy . . . may be tiny, the effect on some Americans, particular workers at the bottom of the labor market may be quite large. These workers are especially vulnerable to immigrant competition because wages for these jobs are already low, and immigrants are heavily concentrated in less-skilled and lower-paying jobs. . . .

It probably makes more sense for policymakers to focus on the winners and losers from immigration. The big losers are natives working in low-skilled, low-wage jobs. Of course, technological change and increased trade also have reduced the labor market opportunities for low-wage workers in the Untied States. But immigration is different because it is a discretionary policy that can be altered. On the other hand, immigrants are the big winners, as are owners of capital and skilled workers, but their gains are tiny relative to their income.

In the end, arguments for or against immigration are as much political and moral as they are economic. The latest research indicates that we can reduce immigration secure in the knowledge that it will not harm the economy. Doing so makes sense if we are very concerned about low-wage and less-skilled workers in the United States. On the other hand, if one places a high priority on helping unskilled workers in other countries, then allowing in a large number of such workers should continue.

Of course, only an infinitesimal proportion of the world's poor could ever come to this country even under the most open immigration policy one might imagine. Those who support the current high level of unskilled legal and illegal immigration should at least do so with an understanding that those American workers harmed by the policies they favor are already the poorest and most vulnerable.

NO
Gerald D. Jaynes
Professor of Economics and African-American Studies, Yale University

From testimony before House Subcommittee on Immigration, Citizenship, Refugees, Border Security, and International Law, May 3, 2007

We can acknowledge that immigration probably hurts the employment and wages of some less-educated citizens and still conclude immigration is a net benefit for the United States. The most methodologically sound estimates of the net effects of immigration on the nation conclude that the United States, as a whole, benefits from contemporary immigration. Properly measured, this conclusion means that during a period of time reasonably long enough to allow immigrants to adjust to their new situations, they produce more national income than they consume in government services.

Confusion about this issue is caused by some analysts' failure to make appropriate distinctions between immigration's impact on specific local governments and groups and its impact on the whole nation. Although benefits of immigration — such as lower prices for consumer and producer goods and services, greater profits and tax revenues — accrue to the nation as a whole, nearly all of the costs for public services consumed by immigrants are borne by localities and specific demographic groups. . . . Even so, inappropriate methods of analysis have led some analysts to overstate the costs of immigration even at the local level. . . .

On average, Americans receive positive economic benefits from immigration, but, at least in the short run, residents of particular localities and members of certain groups may lose. . . .

Democratic concepts of justice suggest the losses of a few should not override the gains of the many. Democratic concepts of justice also demand that society's least-advantaged members should not be paying for the immigration benefits enjoyed by the entire nation. A democratic society benefiting from immigration and debating how to reshape its immigration policies should also be discussing social policies to compensate less-skilled workers through combinations of better training, relocation and educational opportunities. . . .

[T]he evidence supports the conclusion that from an economic standpoint immigration's broader benefits to the nation outweigh its costs. An assessment of the effects of immigration on the employment prospects of less-educated native-born workers is that the effect is negative but modest, and probably is significant in some specific industries and geographic locations. . . . However, it is just as likely that the relative importance of less-educated young native [workers'] job losses due to the competition of immigrants is swamped by a constellation of other factors diminishing their economic status.

prevention efforts to subsidizing child care for low-wage workers, increasing the minimum wage and expanding the EITC.

"We need a new generation of anti-poverty policies that focus on requiring and rewarding work, reversing the breakdown of the family and improving educational outcomes," the proposal states. The $38.6 billion per year cost should not be incurred, the authors say, unless it "can be fully covered by eliminating spending or tax preferences in other areas." [57]

Many advocates emphasize the need to help poor people build their assets, such as savings accounts and home equity, as a way of propelling them out of poverty. Also key, they say, is the need to spend more on early-childhood programs to help keep youngsters from falling into poverty in the first place.

"Universal high-quality early childhood education is the single most powerful investment we could make in insuring poverty doesn't strike the next generation," says Newman of Princeton University.

Tax Policy

Proposals to adjust federal tax policy to help lift the poor into the economic mainstream are among those getting the most attention. Much of the discussion has focused on expansion of the child and earned income tax credits.

A letter sent to members of Congress last spring by hundreds of advocacy groups urged expansion of the child credit, which can reduce the tax liability of families with children. "The current income threshold — in 2007, it is $11,750 — excludes 10 million children whose families are too poor to claim the credit," the letter stated. "The threshold keeps rising with inflation, increasing the tax burden on the poor and dropping many families from the benefit altogether."

The letter added that according to the Tax Policy Center, operated by the Urban Institute and Brookings Institution, "half of all African-American children, 46 percent of Hispanic children and 18 percent of white children received either no Child Tax Credit or a reduced amount in 2005 because their families' earnings were too low." [58]

Along with the child credit, the EITC is widely cited as ripe for expansion.

Created in 1975 to protect low-wage workers from rising payroll taxes, the credit has been expanded several times, under both Republican and Democratic administrations. More than 20 million families benefit from more than $40 billion in credits today, according to Brookings' Berube. Most of those eligible for the credit have children under age 18 living at home and earn less than $35,000, according to Berube. In 2004 the average claimant received a credit of about $1,800. [59]

While claims of abuse have been leveled at the tax credit, it has generally been popular across the political spectrum because it encourages work, helps the needy and does not levy a cost on wealthier taxpayers. [60]

But anti-poverty advocates say the tax credit could be even more effective by making it easier for families with two earners to get the credit and extending it to single workers in their late teens and early 20s. [61]

"Childless adults are the only group of working tax filers who begin to owe federal income taxes before their incomes reach the poverty line," says the letter to members of Congress. Workers in that category got an average credit of only $230 last year, the letter said. "Increasing the amount of the credit for low-income workers not living with children would increase work incentives and economic security for millions of Americans working in low-wage jobs."

Making poor people aware of the tax credit is also an obstacle that must be overcome, advocates say. Many people who are eligible for the credit don't claim it, sometimes because of language or educational barriers.

Dodd, at Step Up in Savannah, says the Internal Revenue Service said $10 million to $12 million in credits go unclaimed in his city alone.

States and Localities

As federal policymakers wrestle with the poverty issue, states and localities are making inroads of their own. Mayor Bloomberg has been promoting a plan to pay poor families in New York up to $5,000 a year to meet such goals as attending parent-teacher meetings, getting medical checkups and holding full-time jobs. Patterned after a Mexican initiative, the plan aims to help poor families make better long-range decisions and break cycles of poverty and dependence that can last generations. [62]

Other efforts are afoot in the states. A proposed bill in the California Assembly, for example, would establish an advisory Childhood Poverty Council to develop a plan to reduce child poverty in the state by half by 2017 and eliminate it by 2027. [63]

Not all such steps pan out, though. In 2004, Connecticut passed legislation committing the state to a 50 percent reduction in child poverty by 2014, but child poverty has risen since then, an official of the Connecticut Association for Community Action complained this summer, blaming the failure to enact a state-funded EITC. [64]

As states seek ways to reduce the number of poor within their borders, they also are trying to adjust to the stiffer work requirements that Congress enacted last year when it reauthorized welfare reform. [65]

The new rules are forcing some states to adapt in creative ways. In California, for example, where less than a fourth of welfare recipients work enough hours to meet federal requirements, officials are moving some teenage parents, older parents and disabled people into separate programs paid entirely by state funds so they aren't counted in federal work-participation calculations.

Arkansas, on the other hand, has been sending monthly checks to the working poor. "Arkansas eventually aims to artificially swell its welfare population from 8,000 families to as many as 11,000 and raise the work-participation rate by at least 11 percent," according to a press report. "Officials hope the extra cash will also keep the workers employed." [66]

The tougher work rules have upset poverty advocates, who argue they damage efforts to help those most vulnerable or lacking in skills to prepare for the job market. "Some of the changes made it almost impossible in some ways for people to use the system to get out of poverty," said Rep. McDermott, the Washington Democrat. [67]

But others defend the approach. "The bottom line is that the only real way to get out of poverty is to find a job," said Rep. Wally Herger, a California Republican who chaired the House subcommittee that worked on last year's reauthorization. "There's always the line, 'Well, some people can't do it.' What that's really doing is selling those people short." [68]

OUTLOOK

Ominous Signs

The outlook for real progress against domestic poverty is mixed, especially in the near term.

On one hand, concerns about poverty, income inequality and declining mobility are playing a bigger role on the national scene than they have in years. The kind of political momentum that spurred the War on Poverty in the 1960s may be emerging again — albeit in a more muted fashion and with a different set of policy proposals.

But big obstacles remain, especially funding. Congress would face difficult fiscal choices if it sought to enact any major anti-poverty program, many analysts point out. Even the Democratic majority, which has long pushed for more spending for social programs, would face major barriers.

"The Democrats have committed to pay-as-you-go budgeting, so I don't think we'll have a major push on anti-poverty [programs] or on programs designed to help the poor and middle class" over the next four to eight years, says Yale's Hacker. "That's part of the reason for the public's frustration — we're hamstrung by the budgetary situation."

At the same time, a number of ominous developments have been occurring that suggest the poor will have an even rougher time financially than they have in recent years. The explosion in mortgage foreclosures, rising prices for basics like gasoline and milk and the ever-present threat of recession and layoffs all conspire most heavily against those with the fewest resources. Recently, job growth and expansion in the service sector have both been weaker than expected, indicating tougher times ahead for those on the economic margins.

Coupled with the uncertain economic outlook is the unresolved issue of immigration. Some analysts are less concerned about illegal immigrants taking low-paying jobs from native-born Americans as they are about the chance that immigrant groups will become mired in permanent poverty because of out-of-wedlock births and other social problems.

"In the long term," says Mead of New York University, "overcoming poverty probably does depend on restricting immigration" to 1970 levels. Curbing immigration, he says, not only would make more entry-level jobs available to native-born men — the group that Mead sees as a priority for anti-poverty action — but also help keep a new underclass from developing even as the nation struggles to reduce poverty in the established population.

As scholars and activists look ahead, some express optimism, as Lyndon Johnson once did, that poverty not only can be substantially reduced but actually eliminated. Others note that Johnson's vow to eliminate poverty raised expectations that were never satisfied.

"I think the poor are always going to be with us," says Bradley of the National Community Action Foundation. "Can we substantially reduce poverty? Yes. But the [idea] that somehow certain programs are going to eradicate poverty in America is just unrealistic."

NOTES

1. Testimony before House Ways and Means Subcommittee on Income Security and Family Support, "Hearing on Economic Opportunity and Poverty in America," Feb. 13, 2007.

2. Figures reflect U.S. Census Bureau data for 2006. For background, see Kathy Koch, "Child Poverty," *CQ Researcher*, April 7, 2000, pp. 281-304.

3. Timothy M. Smeeding, testimony before House Ways and Means Subcommittee on Income Security and Family Support, "Hearing on Economic Opportunity and Poverty in America," Feb. 13, 2007. The study is based on Smeeding's calculations from the Luxembourg Income Study.

4. Quoted in Bob Herbert, "The Millions Left Out," *The New York Times*, May 12, 2007, p. A25.

5. Tony Pugh, "U.S. Economy Leaving Record Numbers in Severe Poverty," McClatchy Newspapers, Feb. 22, 2007, updated May 25, 2007.

6. Aviva Aron-Dine, "New Data Show Income Concentration Jumped Again in 2005," Center on Budget and Policy Priorities, March 29, 2007, www.cbpp.org/3-29-07inc.htm.

7. David Cay Johnston, "Income Gap Is Widening, Data Shows," *The New York Times*, March 29, 2007, p. C1.

8. "Panel Study of Income Dynamics; Cross-National Equivalent File," Cornell University. Cited in John Edwards, Marion Crain and Arne L. Kalleberg, eds., *Ending Poverty in America: How to Restore the American Dream* (2007), The New Press, published in conjunction with the Center on Poverty, Work and Opportunity, University of North Carolina at Chapel Hill. Data are from Jacob S. Hacker, "The Risky Outlook for Middle-Class America," Chapter 5, p. 72.

9. Mark R. Rank, "Toward a New Understanding of American Poverty," *Journal of Law & Policy*, Vol. 20:17, p. 33, http://law.wustl.edu/Journal/20/p17 Rankbookpage.pdf.

10. Steven Greenhouse, "A Unified Voice Argues the Case for U.S. Manufacturing," *The New York Times*, April 26, 2007, p. C2.

11. Katrina vanden Heuvel, "Twelve Steps to Cutting Poverty in Half," Blog: Editor's Cut, *The Nation*, April 30, 2007, www.thenation.com/blogs/edcut? pid=190867.

12. Patrick Healy, "Clinton Vows Middle Class Will Not Be 'Invisible' to Her," *The New York Times*, March 11, 2007, www.nyt.com.

13. Quoted in Alec MacGillis, "Obama Says He, Too, Is a Poverty Fighter," *The Washington Post*, July 19, 2007, p. 4A.

14. Jackie Calmes, "Edwards's Theme: U.S. Poverty," *The Wall Street Journal Online*, Dec. 28, 2006.

15. Edward Luce, "Bloomberg urges US to extend anti-poverty scheme," FT.com (*Financial Times*), Aug. 29, 2007.

16. "McDermott Announces Hearing on Proposals for Reducing Poverty," press release, House Ways and Means Subcommittee on Income Security and Family Support, April 26, 2007.

17. Mike Dorning, "Will Poverty Make Political Comeback?" *Chicago Tribune*, June 3, 2007, p. 4.

18. Gallup Poll, June 11-14, 2007.

19. Jon Cohen, "Despite Focus on Poverty, Edwards Trails Among the Poor," *The Washington Post*, July 11, 2007, p. 7A.

20. Testimony before House Committee on Ways and Means, "Hearing on the Economic and Societal Costs of Poverty," Jan. 24, 2007.

21. Steven H. Woolf, Robert E. Johnson and H. Jack Geiger, "The Rising Prevalence of Severe Poverty in America: A Growing Threat to Public Health," *American Journal of Preventive Medicine*, Vol. 31, Issue 4, October 2006, p. 332.

22. Quoted in "Statement of Child Welfare League of America," House Ways and Means Subcommittee on Income Security and Family Support, "Hearing on Economic Opportunity and Poverty in America," Feb. 13, 2007. According to the statement, Conley's comment came in an ABC television profile of poverty in Camden, N.J., broadcast in January 2007.

23. Testimony before House Ways and Means Subcommittee on Income Security and Family Support, Feb. 13, 2007. Berube said concentrated poverty is defined by Paul Jargowsky of the University of Texas-Dallas as neighborhoods where at least 40 percent of individuals live below the poverty line.

24. Pugh, *op. cit.*

25. Nell McNamara and Doug Schenkelberg, *Extreme Poverty & Human Rights: A Primer* (2007), Mid-America Institute on Poverty of Heartland Alliance for Human Needs & Human Rights. For the Bellevue data, the report cites Pennsylvania State University, "Poverty in America (n.d.) Living Wage Calculator," retrieved Nov. 15, 2006, from www.livingwage.geog.psu.edu/.

26. Pugh, *op. cit.*

27. Testimony before House Ways and Means Subcommittee on Income Security and Family Support, Feb. 13, 2007.

28. Woolf, *et al.*, *op. cit.*

29. Peter Katel, "Minimum Wage," *CQ Researcher*, Dec. 16, 2005, pp. 1053-1076.

30. Sarah Glazer, "Welfare Reform," *CQ Researcher*, Aug. 3, 2001, pp. 601-632.

31. Dan Froomkin, "Welfare's Changing Face," www.Washingtonpost.com/wp-srv/politics/special/welfare/welfare.htm, updated July 23, 1998.

32. Ron Haskins, "Welfare Check," *The Wall Street Journal*, July 27, 2006, accessed at www.brookings.edu.

33. "Interview: Welfare Reform, 10 Years Later," *The Examiner*, Aug. 24, 2006, accessed at www.brookings.edu.

34. Sharon Parrott and Arloc Sherman, "TANF at 10: Program Results are More Mixed Than Often Understood," Center on Budget and Policy Priorities, Aug. 17, 2006.

35. Wisconsin Council on Children & Families, "Wisconsin Ranks First in Growth in Poverty: Census Bureau Reports," press release, Aug. 30, 2005. See also testimony of Richard Schlimm, House Ways and Means Committee, "Hearing on the Economic and Societal Costs of Poverty," Jan. 24, 2007.

36. Testimony before House Subcommittee on Income Security and Family Support, Feb. 13, 2007.

37. Lawrence Mead, "And Now, 'Welfare Reform' for Men," *The Washington Post*, March 20, 2007, p. 19A.

38. Michael D. Tanner, "More Welfare, More Poverty," *The Monitor* (McAllen, Texas), Sept. 8, 2006.

39. Proceedings of the Virginia Assembly, 1619.

40. Henry George, "Progress and Poverty," first printed in 1879. Quoted in H. B. Shaffer, "Persistence of Poverty," *Editorial Research Reports*, Feb. 5, 1964, available at *CQ Researcher Plus Archive*, www.cqpress.com.

41. Gordon M. Fisher, "From Hunter to Orshansky: An Overview of (Unofficial) Poverty Lines in the United States from 1904 to 1965-Summary, March 1994, retrieved at http://aspe.hhs.gov/poverty/papers/htrss-miv.htm.

42. *CQ Researcher, op. cit.*

43. Michael Harrington, *The Other America: Poverty in the United States* (1962), pp. 14-15.

44. U.S. Census data show the poverty rate for individuals was 22.2 percent in 1960; 21.9 percent in 1961; 21 percent in 1962; 19.5 percent in 1963; and 19 percent in 1964. For families the rate ranged from 20.7 percent to 17.4 percent in that period.

45. See H. B. Shaffer, "Status of War on Poverty," in *Editorial Research Reports*, Jan. 25, 1967, available at *CQ Researcher Plus Archive*, www.cqpress.com.

46. Marcia Clemmitt, "Evaluating Head Start," *CQ Researcher*, Aug. 26, 2005, pp. 685-708.

47. Sheldon H. Danziger and Robert H. Haveman, eds., *Understanding Poverty* (2001), Russell Sage Foundation and Harvard University Press, pp. 4 and 5.

48. Peter Edelman, "The Worst Thing Bill Clinton Has Done," The Atlantic Monthly, March 1997.

49. Jeff Jacoby, "Wefare Reform Success," The Boston Globe, Sept. 13, 2006, p. 9A.

50. Sheldon H. Danziger, "Fighting Poverty Revisited: What did researchers know 40 years ago? What do we know today?," Focus, University of Wisconsin-Madison, Institute for Research on Poverty, Spring-Summer 2007, p. 3.

51. Lyndon B. Johnson, "Annual Message to Congress on the State of the Union," Jan. 8, 1964.

52. MacGillis, *op. cit.*

53. E.J. Dionne Jr., "Making the Poor Visible," *The Washington Post*, July 20, 2007, p. A19.

54. Mary H. Cooper, "Income Inequality," *CQ Researcher*, April 17, 1998, pp. 337-360.

55. www.mittromney.com.

56. Mark Greenberg, Indivar Dutta-Gupta and Elisa Minoff, "From Poverty to Prosperity: A National Strategy to Cut Poverty in Half," Center for American Progress, April 2007, www.american-progress.org/issues/2007/04/poverty_report.html.

57. Ron Haskins and Isabel V. Sawhill, "Attacking Poverty and Inequality," Brookings Institution, Opportunity 08, in partnership with ABC News, February 2007, www.opportunity08.org/Issues/OurSociety/31/r1/Default.aspx.

58. Coalition on Human Needs, "Nearly 900 Organizations Sign Letter to Congress in Support of Expanding Tax Credits for the Poor," May 25, 2007, www.chn.org. The letter, dated May 24, 2007, was accessed at www.chn.org/pdf/2007/ctceitcletter.pdf.

59. Alan Berube, "Using the Earned Income Tax Credit to Stimulate Local Economies," Brookings Institution, www.brookings.org.

60. Adriel Bettelheim, "The Social Side of Tax Breaks," *CQ Weekly*, Feb. 5, 2007.

61. *Ibid.*

62. Diane Cardwell, "City to Reward Poor for Doing Right Thing," *The New York Times*, March 30, 2007, p. 1B.

63. The bill is AB 1118.

64. David MacDonald, communications director, Connecticut Association for Community Action, letter to the editor of the *Hartford Courant*, June 27, 2007, p. 8A.

65. Clea Benson, "States Scramble to Adapt To New Welfare Rules," *CQ Weekly*, June 25, 2007, p. 1907.

66. *Ibid.*

67. *Ibid.*

68. *Ibid.*

BIBLIOGRAPHY

Books

Danziger, Sheldon H., and Robert H. Haveman, eds., *Understanding Poverty*, Russell Sage Foundation and Harvard University Press, 2001.
Writings on domestic poverty range from the evolution of anti-poverty programs to health policy for the poor. Danziger is a professor of social work and public policy at the University of Michigan, Haveman, a professor of economics and public affairs at the University of Wisconsin, Madison.

DeParle, Jason, *American Dream: Three Women, Ten Kids, and a Nation's Drive to End Welfare*, Viking Adult, 2004.
A reporter looks at the effort to overhaul the American welfare system through the lives of three former welfare mothers.

Edwards, John, Marion Crain and Arne L. Kalleberg, eds., *Ending Poverty in America*, New Press, 2007.
Co-edited and with a conclusion by Democratic presidential candidate Edwards, this collection of articles reflects a progressive economic agenda.

Haskins, Ron, *Work Over Welfare: The Inside Story of the 1996 Welfare Reform Law*, Brookings Institution Press, 2006.
A former Republican committee staffer and a chief architect of welfare reform, Haskins tells the story of the political debates leading up to the historic welfare overhaul.

Articles

Bai, Matt, "The Poverty Platform," *New York Times Magazine*, June 10, 2007.
Taking a close look at presidential candidate John Edwards' focus on the poor, Bai says "the main economic debate in Democratic Washington" focuses on "the tools of economic policy — taxes, trade, welfare — and how to use them."

Dorning, Mike, "Will Poverty Make Political Comeback?" *Chicago Tribune*, June 3, 2007.
Since the 1960s, Dorning notes, "leading presidential candidates generally have not focused on the plight of the poor as a central issue.

Reports and Studies

Congressional Budget Office, "Changes in the Economic Resources of Low-Income Households with Children," May 2007.
This study charts income changes among the poor from the early 1990s.

Children's Defense Fund, "The State of America's Children 2005."
Marian Wright Edelman, founder and president of the Children's Defense Fund, writes, "Far less wealthy industrialized countries have committed to end child poverty, while the United States is sliding backwards."

Greenberg, Mark, Indivar Dutta-Gupta and Elisa Minoff, "From Poverty to Prosperity: A National Strategy to Cut Poverty in Half," Center for American Progress, April 2007.
The think tank's Task Force on Poverty says the United States should set a goal of halving poverty over the next decade.

Harrison, David, and Bob Watrus, "On Getting Out- and Staying Out-of Poverty: The Complex Causes of and Responses to Poverty in the Northwest," Northwest Area Foundation, 2004.
An estimated 2 million people live in poverty in the Northwest, more than 900,000 of them in severe poverty.

McNamara, Nell, and Doug Schenkelberg, "Extreme Poverty & Human Rights: A Primer," Heartland Alliance for Human Needs & Human Rights, 2007.
A guidebook explains how human rights advocacy can combat both global and domestic poverty.

Meyer, Bruce D., and James X. Sullivan, "Three Decades of Consumption and Income Poverty," National Poverty Center Working Paper Series, September 2006.
The study examines poverty measurement in the United States from 1972 through 2004 and how poverty rates have changed over the years.

Rector, Robert, "How Poor Are America's Poor? Examining the 'Plague' of Poverty in America," Heritage Foundation, Aug. 27, 2007.
A senior research fellow at the conservative think tank writes that " 'the plague' of American poverty might not be as 'terrible' or 'incredible' as candidate [John] Edwards contends."

Toldson, Ivory A., and Elsie L. Scott, "Poverty, Race and Policy," Congressional Black Caucus Foundation, 2006.
The four-part report explores affordable-housing policy, wealth-accumulation needs and strategies for reducing poverty and unemployment.

Woolf, Steven H., Robert E. Johnson and H. Jack Geiger, "The Rising Prevalence of Severe Poverty in America: A Growing Threat to Public Health," *American Journal of Preventive Medicine*, October 2006.
Woolf, a professor of family medicine, epidemiology and community health at Virginia Commonwealth University and lead author of this study, says the growth in severe poverty and other trends "have disturbing implications for society and public health."

For More Information

Center for American Progress, 1333 H St., N.W., 10th Floor, Washington, DC 20005; (202) 682-1611; www.americanprogress.org. A liberal think tank that issued a report and recommendations on poverty this year.

Coalition on Human Needs, 1120 Connecticut Ave., N.W., Suite 910, Washington, DC 20036; (202) 223-2532; www.chn.org. An alliance of organizations that promote policies to help low-income people and others in need.

Economic Policy Institute, 1333 H St., N.W., Suite 300, East Tower, Washington, DC 20005-4707; (202) 775-8810; www.epi.org. A think tank that studies policies related to the economy, work and the interests of low- and middle-income people.

Heritage Foundation, 214 Massachusetts Ave., N.E., Washington, DC 20002-4999; (202) 546-4400; www.heritage.org. A conservative think tank that studies poverty and other public-policy issues.

Institute for Research on Poverty, University of Wisconsin-Madison, 1180 Observatory Dr., 3412 Social Science Building, Madison, WI 53706-1393; (608) 262-6358; www.irp.wisc.edu. Studies the causes and consequences of poverty.

Mid-America Institute on Poverty, 208 South LaSalle St., Suite 1818, Chicago, Ill. 60604; (773) 336-6084; www.heartlandalliance.org. A research arm of Heartland Alliance, which provides services for low-income individuals.

National Community Action Foundation, 810 First St., N.E., Suite 530, Washington, DC 20002; (202) 842-2092; www.ncaf.org. Advocates for the nation's community-action agencies.

Step Up, Savannah's Poverty Reduction Initiative, 101 East Bay St., Savannah, GA 31401; (912) 644-6420; www.stepupsavannah.org. A coalition of more than 80 local business, government and nonprofit organizations seeking to reduce poverty.

U.S. Census Bureau, 4600 Silver Hill Road, Suitland, MD 20746; www.census.gov. Maintains extensive recent and historical data on poverty and demographics.

University of North Carolina Center on Poverty, Work and Opportunity, UNC School of Law, Van Heck-Wettach Hall, 100 Ridge Road, CB#3380, Chapel Hill, N.C. 27599-3380; (919) 962-5106; www.law.unc.edu/centers/poverty/default.aspx. A national forum for scholars, policymakers and others interested in poverty, established by presidential candidate John Edwards.

Urban Institute, 2100 M St., N.W., Washington, DC 20037; (202) 833-7200; www.urban.org. Studies welfare and low-income families among a range of issues.

6

Gun Violence

Kenneth Jost

The chilling video made by gunman Seung-Hui Cho is broadcast at a bar near the Virginia Tech campus on April 18. Cho mailed the profanity-laced tape to NBC News during a lull in his rampage — the worst mass shooting in U.S. history. The massacre renewed the perennial debate in the United States over gun control and raised new questions about safety on college campuses.

From *CQ Researcher*,
May 25, 2007.

S eung-Hui Cho was a faceless e-mail address when he ordered a .22-caliber Walther P-22 pistol for $267 from Wisconsin gun dealer Eric Thompson via the Internet on Feb. 2. The Virginia Tech senior drew no special attention when he picked the weapon up a week later from JND Pawnbrokers, near the spacious Blacksburg campus in southwest Virginia.

Cho was hardly more memorable a month later when he traveled in person to Roanoke Firearms about 35 miles away and made a $571 credit-card purchase of a 9 mm Glock 19 pistol and 50 rounds of ammunition. "A clean-cut college kid," said John Markell, the store's owner, quoting the after-the-fact description from the clerk who handled the March 13 transaction.

Twice, the Korean-born Cho presented the necessary identification — his Virginia driver's license, checkbook and immigration card — to complete the federal background check required for handgun purchasers. Twice, computers took only moments to display the needed authorization: PROCEED.

Nothing particularly distinguished Cho's transactions from any of the other estimated 2 million handgun purchases in the United States each year. Thompson in Wisconsin and the gun dealers in Virginia had no reason to know or even suspect that Cho was an extremely troubled young man whose bizarre and sometimes aggressive behavior had disturbed his parents, schoolmates and teachers for years.

Two years earlier, in fact, a state judge in Virginia had ordered Cho to receive outpatient psychiatric treatment after finding him to be "an imminent danger to himself" because of mental illness. Had they known that history, people at both stores said afterward, they would not have sold Cho the guns.

Most States Allow Concealed Weapons

Forty states have so-called right-to-carry laws allowing citizens to carry concealed firearms in public. In 36 of the states, "shall issue" laws require the issuance of permits for gun owners who meet standard criteria (top map). Only two states — Illinois and Wisconsin — and Washington, D.C., prohibit carrying altogether (bottom map).

Right-to-Carry Laws by State, 2006

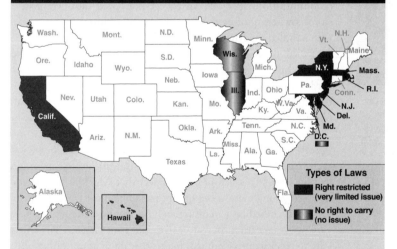

Source: Right to Carry Laws 2006, National Rifle Association Institute for Legislative Action, www.nraila.org

But they did. And so, on the morning of April 16, Cho used the weapons to kill 32 people on the Virginia Tech campus before taking his own life with a final shot to the head. The death toll — along with the 29 others wounded — marked Cho's intricately plotted, alienation-driven rampage as the worst mass school shooting in U.S. history. [1] (*See chart, p. 126.*) *

The massacre left the 26,000-student state university in a state of shock and brought forth outpourings of sympathy from officials and private citizens around the world. Hardly any time had passed, however, before the tragedy renewed the perennial debate in the United States over the rules for buying, selling and possessing firearms and the penalties for misusing them. [2]

The debate remains volatile in a country with what experts say is probably the highest rate of civilian gun ownership in the world and also the highest rate of gun-related injuries and deaths among major industrialized nations. Americans own what has been variously estimated as 200 million to 250 million firearms, around one-third of them handguns. Surveys indicate that more than 40 percent of all U.S. households own at least one firearm. [3]

Meanwhile, the number of gun-related deaths in the United States has been around 30,000 per year for

---

* The deadliest school attack ever in U.S. history appears to have been the dynamiting of a school in Bath, Mich., on May 18, 1927, by a school board member upset about a property tax increase. The death toll was put at around 40 children and several adults, including the bomber, Andrew Kehoe. (See Ryan Grim, "1927 School Attack More Deadly," *The Politico*, April 18, 2007, p. 6.)

more than two decades, according to the federal Centers for Disease Control and Prevention. For 2004 — the most recent year available — the number included 11,624 homicides and 16,750 suicides. [4] (*See chart, p. 128.*)

Gun advocates — including the powerful, 3-million-member National Rifle Association (NRA) — defend what they view as an individual constitutional right to use firearms in hunting, sport shooting and self-defense. They argue that gun owners and dealers are already subject to a web of federal, state and local firearm laws and regulations. The key to reducing gun violence, they say, lies with tougher penalties against criminals who use guns instead of more restrictions on gun owners.

"We have adequate gun laws on the books," says Andrew Arulanandam, the NRA's director of public affairs. "If a crime occurs, those criminals need to be prosecuted to the fullest extent of the law. The question becomes how do you make something that is already illegal more illegal."

Gun control advocates, including the influential Brady Campaign to Prevent Gun Violence, counter by depicting the widespread availability of handguns as a primary factor in the high rate of gun-related injuries and deaths. * They call for strengthening enforcement of existing federal laws barring possession of firearms by certain criminals, drug users and people with mental illness. They also favor restrictions on certain specific types of weapons or ammunition and generally oppose laws favored by gun groups easing the rules for the carrying of concealed weapons. (*See maps, p. 124.*)

---

* The Brady Campaign and the affiliated Brady Center to Prevent Gun Violence, formerly Handgun Control and the Center to Prevent Handgun Violence, were renamed in 2001 to honor former White House press secretary James Brady and his wife Sarah. James Brady was partially paralyzed in the 1981 assassination attempt on President Ronald Reagan; Sarah Brady heads the campaign and the center.

Background Checks Lack Mental Health Records

Out of 78 million background checks, only 2,608 people have been denied permission to purchase a gun on the basis of a mental health disqualification since the National Instant Criminal Background Check System began operation in December 1998. The pro-gun control group Third Way credits 22 states with providing records of mental health adjudications for use in gun background checks; the other 28 are said to provide few or no records for the purpose.

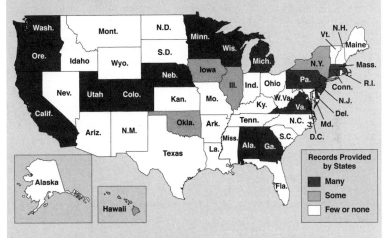

Source: Third Way, "Missing Records: Holes in Background Check System Allow Illegal Buyers to Get Guns," May 14, 2007; www.third-way.com

"We have weak, almost nonexistent gun laws in this country," says Paul Helmke, president of the Brady Campaign and its affiliated education arm, the Brady Center to Prevent Gun Violence. "And we're seeing almost the natural result of having weak, nonexistent gun laws with the Virginia Tech shootings and the 32 murders [in the United States] that happen every day."

The post-Virginia Tech debate features familiar arguments over the effectiveness of the landmark Gun Control Act of 1968 and the National Instant Criminal Background Check System, established in 1998 to enable gun dealers to enforce the act's prohibitions on gun ownership by criminals and others. But Cho's history of mental illness highlights an issue given less attention in the past: the conflicting federal and state definitions used to disqualify people with a history of mental illness from owning a gun.

Mental health groups, however, caution against viewing mental illness as an indicator of potential violence.

Virginia Tech Is Deadliest School Shooting

Last month's rampage by student Seung-Hui Cho at Virginia Tech is the deadliest school shooting in U.S. history. With 33 deaths, including Cho, the toll was more than twice the number killed at Columbine High School in 1999 or at the University of Texas in 1966.

Major Shootings at American Schools Since 1966

Date	Location	Dead and Wounded	Killer(s)
Aug. 1, 1966	University of Texas, Austin	14 dead (including gunman), 31 wounded	Student Charles J. Whitman
July 12, 1976	California State University, Fullerton, Calif.	7 dead, 2 wounded	University custodian Edward C. Allaway
Jan. 1, 1989	Cleveland Elementary School, Stockton, Calif.	6 dead (including gunman), 30 wounded	Stockton resident Patrick Purdy
Nov. 1, 1991	University of Iowa, Iowa City	6 dead (including gunman), 1 wounded	Physics graduate student Gang Lu
Feb. 2, 1996	Frontier Junior High School, Moses Lake, Wash.	3 dead	Student Barry Loukaitis
Aug. 15, 1996	San Diego State University, San Diego, Calif.	3 dead	Graduate student Frederick M. Davidson
Dec. 1, 1997	Heath High School, West Paducah, Ky.	3 dead, 5 wounded	Student Michael Carneal
March 24, 1998	Westside Middle School, Jonesboro, Ark.	4 dead, 11 wounded	Students Andrew Golden and Mitchell Johnson
April 20, 1999	Columbine High School, Littleton, Colo.	15 dead (including gunmen), 23 wounded	Students Eric Harris and Dylan Klebold
Aug. 10, 1999	North Valley Jewish Community Center Pre-School, Granada Hills, Calif.	5 dead	White supremacist Buford O. Furrow Jr.
Jan. 16, 2002	Appalachian School of Law, Grundy, Va.	3 dead, 3 wounded	Student Peter Odighizuwa
Oct. 28, 2002	University of Arizona College of Nursing, Tucson, Ariz.	4 dead (including gunman)	Student Robert Flores
March 21, 2005	Red Lake High School, Red Lake Indian Reservation, Minn.	10 killed (including gunman), 7 wounded	Student Jeffrey Weise
Sept. 2, 2006	Shepherd University, Shepherdstown, W.Va.	3 dead (including gunman)	Douglas Pennington, parent of two students
Oct. 2, 2006	West Nickel Mines School, Nickel Mines, Pa.	6 dead (including gunman), 6 wounded	Truck driver Charles Carl Roberts IV
April 16, 2007	Virginia Tech University, Blacksburg, Va.	33 dead (including gunman), 29 wounded	Student Seung-Hui Cho

Sources: "No Gun Left Behind: The Gun Lobby's Campaign to Push Guns Into Colleges and Schools," Brady Center to Prevent Gun Violence, May 2007; "The long history of deadly shootings at US schools," Agence France-Presse, April 16, 2007; Lauren Smith, "Major Shootings on American College Campuses," *The Chronicle of Higher Education*, April 27, 2007

Honberg, director of policy and legal affairs for the National Alliance on Mental Illness. "That's not borne out for the majority of people with mental illness."

The Blacksburg massacre is also giving new and urgent attention to questions of safety and security on the nation's college campuses. Some gun advocacy groups see Cho's ability to carry out the shootings, including the nine-minute rampage inside a classroom building, as an argument for lifting the ban on guns imposed by most schools, including Virginia Tech.

"The latest school shooting demands an immediate end to the gun-free-zone law, which leaves the nation's schools at the mercy of madmen," said Larry Pratt, executive director of Gun Owners of America, in a statement released on the day of the massacre. "It is irresponsibly dangerous to tell citizens that they may not have guns at schools."

Campus law enforcement officials, along with other police groups as well as gun control supporters, disagree. "The only folks who should have firearms on a campus are those people who are sworn and authorized to protect and are duly trained to do that," says Steven Healy, director of public safety at Princeton University and president of the International Association of Campus Law Enforcement Administrators.

Congress is considering legislation previously introduced to give states financial incentives to improve their reporting to the background-check system in hopes of plugging gaps in enforcement of the federal restrictions on gun possession. But the political climate is widely viewed as unfavorable for any broader measures. "In the

"It's very easy and very tempting when something as horrible as Virginia Tech occurs to assume that mental illness correlates with a propensity for violence," says Ron

very short run, I don't expect we'll do anything seriously," says David Hemenway, a professor at the Harvard School of Public Health and longtime gun control advocate.

Meanwhile, gun advocacy groups are hoping to preserve a major victory in the courts: a federal appeals court on March 9 struck down Washington's strict local law banning possession of handguns even in private homes. In a 2-1 decision, the U.S. Court of Appeals for the District of Columbia Circuit ruled that the 1976 measure violates the Second Amendment's guarantee of a right to bear arms.

The ruling contradicts the view long held but recently being reconsidered that the Bill of Rights provision protects state militias but does not establish an individual's right to own firearms. Washington Mayor Adrian Fenty is weighing whether to try rewriting the ordinance or to ask the Supreme Court to review the decision. (*See sidebar, p. 134.*)

With the Virginia Tech shootings still very much a scar on the national psyche, here are some of the major gun policy questions being considered:

Denver area high school students Rhianna Cheek (left), Mandi Annibel (center) and Rachel Roof (right) comfort one another during a candlelight vigil in Denver's Civic Center Park on April 21, 1999. The vigil honored the victims of the massacre at Columbine High School in Littleton, Colo., the previous day. Students Eric Harris and Dylan Klebold shot and killed 12 schoolmates and one teacher during a four-hour rampage and then turned their guns on themselves.

Should schools adopt additional security measures to try to prevent mass shootings?

Virginia Tech officials learned of a shooting in the West Ambler Johnston dormitory at around 7:15 a.m. on April 16, but postponed sending a campuswide e-mail about the incident for nearly two hours. University President Charles Steger later explained the initial suspect was wrongly thought to be a spurned boyfriend who had already left campus. But Steger also said a campuswide e-mail would have missed any students or faculty who were not online.

At Princeton University, administrators would have had other options, according to Healy of the campus law enforcement group. The emergency notification system for the New Jersey campus reaches students, faculty and staff up to eight different ways, using land lines, cell phones, e-mail and text messaging.

A "robust" notification system is needed, Healy explains, because e-mail is almost passé among Generation Next. "We've been slow to recognize that young people use text messaging" more than e-mail, he says. The system — useful in any emergency — is "not inexpensive," Healy says, "but it's not over-the-top expensive." And, yes, he adds, "It's definitely worth it."

"Redundant" emergency communication systems like Princeton's are among the recommendations the campus law enforcement group had listed for schools to consider before the Virginia Tech massacre. The agenda includes such common-sense steps as developing emergency-management plans not only for "active shooter" situations but also for various other potential hazards, coordinating with other local police agencies and actually practicing planned emergency responses.

"It's one thing to have a plan on paper," says Healy, who headed police departments at Syracuse University and Wellesley College before coming to Princeton in 2003. "It's another thing to play it out." [5]

Opposing groups in the gun policy debate agree campus security needs more attention, but they leave the particulars to others. "There's a universal agreement that we have a problem with gun violence in schools," says NRA spokesman Arulanandam. "If you look at the reality today, we protect our assets in our banks, we protect our airports, we protect special events more than we protect our children in our schools."

The NRA favors "a national dialogue" among experts and interested parties to figure out what needs to be

Annual U.S. Gun Deaths Near 30,000

Annually, there are roughly 30,000 U.S. gun deaths. The total number of firearm deaths in the United States decreased by around 12 percent from 1981 to 2004; a decrease in crime in the late 1990s may have been a factor.

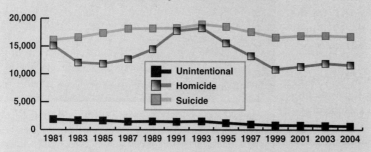

Gun Deaths by Intent, 1981-2004 *

Legend:
- Unintentional
- Homicide
- Suicide

* Does not include deaths by legal intervention or those with undetermined intent

Note: Comparisons over time are difficult because of a change in the reporting methodology.

Source: Web-Based Injury Statistics Query and Reporting System, Centers for Disease Control and Prevention

and effective, points to the use of alcohol as a more serious cause of campus violence. He finds no fault with steps such as improving emergency communication systems but cautions against looking for proof of their effectiveness. "If the problem it's intended to address is virtually nonexistent, it would be impossible to find out whether it is effective," he says.

Healy sees no overreaction in the post-Virginia Tech policy debates. "It's obviously heightened the sense of urgency," he says. But he cautions against expecting a guarantee against another Virginia Tech in the future.

"These types of situations can happen any time, anywhere," says Healy. "One hundred percent safety is a fallacy for all of us — not just colleges and universities, but for general society."

done, Arulanandam says. But he stops short of a step now called for by many gun advocates: allowing possession of guns on college campuses. "We're not advocating a policy change," he says.

For his part, the Brady Center's Helmke seconds the various suggestions for improving campus police training and planning. "Colleges try to do the right thing," he says. "We've learned from Virginia Tech there are things you can do better." But Helmke also points to what gun control supporters say is the need for stronger laws. "Colleges can't do it on their own," he says.

"The elephant in the room is the guns," says Harvard's Hemenway. "It's hard for any individual college to change that."

One gun policy expert, however, finds the rush to rethink campus security after Virginia Tech an overreaction. "Campuses are the safest places in America," says Gary Kleck, a professor at Florida State University's College of Criminology and Criminal Justice. "Serious violence on campus is the exception to the rule."

Kleck, a centrist on gun control issues best known for research depicting defensive gun use as generally safe

Should it be harder for someone with a history of mental illness to obtain a gun?

In December 2005, midway through his sophomore year, Seung-Hui Cho was referred to a mental health clinic by Virginia Tech police after he had threatened suicide following two female students' complaints he was harassing them. In a hearing held Dec. 14 after an overnight evaluation, special judge Paul Barnett found Cho to be "an imminent danger to himself" and ordered outpatient treatment. [6]

The judicial finding arguably disqualified Cho from buying a handgun under federal law. Virginia authorities, however, never fed that information into the federal background-check system. Why not? Unlike the federal law, Virginia's corresponding law specifically requires commitment to a mental hospital to block an applicant from purchasing a firearm. [7]

The information gap that might have blocked or at least delayed Cho from buying the guns he used in his rampage is not unique to Virginia. In fact, the pro-gun control group Third Way rates Virginia among the best in reporting mental health information to the FBI's instant-check system. Overall, the group reports, only 22 states provide mental health records to the system — "rendering this provision of the law useless in most states." [8]

Legislation to improve the background-check system — reintroduced in Congress after Virginia Tech — has the backing not only of gun control groups but also of the NRA, the most powerful of the gun advocacy groups. "Someone who's dangerous to himself or others because of mental illness shouldn't get a gun," says the Brady Center's Helmke. "That's what the law says."

"We've been on record for decades that records of those adjudicated as mentally defective and deemed to be a danger to others or to themselves should be part of the national instant-check system and not be allowed to own a firearm," says NRA spokesman Arulanandam. "The mental health lobby and the medical lobby are the impediments — they are against release of the records."

The rival Gun Owners of America, however, opposes any strengthening of a background-check system that it calls both ineffective and intrusive. "All the background checks in the world will not stop bad guys from getting firearms," the group's Web site declares.

Mental health groups are raising more specific concerns about the legislation. They warn that more extensive reporting of people with a history of mental illness will expose them to discrimination and prejudice and possibly deter some people from seeking treatment altogether. "We have real grave concerns about people with mental illness being a population that's singled out," says Honberg, at the National Alliance on Mental Illness.

"Even if someone was severely disabled 30 years ago, we have plenty of examples of people who have gone on to recover and are living independently and are working and are upstanding citizens," Honberg adds. "Do we want to include all those people in the database?"

The Gun Control Act of 1968 prohibits possession of a firearm by anyone "adjudicated as a mental defective" or who has been committed to any mental institution. The law defines a "mental defective" as a person who "is a danger to himself or others" or "lacks the mental capacity to contract or manage his own affairs" as a result of "marked subnormal intelligence" or "mental illness." The regulations broadly define adjudication to include "a determination by a court, board, commission or other lawful authority." [9]

The statutory phrase "mental defective" is both outmoded and stigmatizing, Honberg says. "It's a term no

AP Photo

Charles J. Whitman, 24, a student at the University of Texas, shot and killed 13 people and wounded 31 others on Aug. 1, 1966, from the school's 27-story tower using an arsenal of three pistols and four rifles. Two police officers eventually broke into the barricaded observation deck and shot the former Eagle Scout and Marine.

one has used for 30 to 40 years," he says. The regulatory provisions, he adds, are "vague and potentially overbroad."

The bills pending in Congress leave the definitions unchanged. Honberg suggests the mental health provisions should be amended to include "some durational limitation" as well as a process for someone to petition for removal from the list. More broadly, he worries about possible abuses from a more rigorously maintained list.

"We're concerned that the very agency charged with managing these records, the FBI, maintains a whole lot of other lists," Honberg says. "We're talking about a population that is oftentimes victimized by breaches of confidentiality and prejudice."

Gun Owners of America seconds those concerns. "What type of record are we talking about sucking in?" asks Mike Hammond, a legal and legislative adviser to the group.

The Brady Center's Helmke counters that states are being asked only for court records. "It's not checking hospital records or doctors' records," he says. "This shouldn't be something that discourages people from getting help for problems."

In Virginia, meanwhile, Democratic Gov. Tim Kaine has moved to tighten the state's law on access to guns for people with histories of mental illness. On April 30, he ordered state agencies "to consider any involuntary treatment order . . . whether inpatient or outpatient" as disqualifying an applicant from buying a gun. [10]

Should laws limiting the carrying of concealed weapons be relaxed?

When a disgruntled student at Appalachian School of Law in southwestern Virginia went on a deadly shooting rampage in January 2002, two students — one current and one former police officer — dashed to their cars to get their own guns. As gun advocates tell the story, former police officer Mikael Gross and sheriff's deputy Tracy Bridges brandished their weapons at the shooter, who dropped his gun and was then subdued with the help of two other, unarmed students. [*]

No one confronted Cho, however, during the shootings in the West Ambler Johnston dormitory or the nine-minute rampage inside Norris Hall. One reason, gun advocates say, is Virginia Tech's ban on private possession of firearms on campus — a proscription Gross and Bridges apparently disregarded at the Appalachian law school.

"If there were more responsible, armed people on campuses, mass murder would be harder," writes Glenn Reynolds, a law professor at the University of Tennessee and author of the conservative blog InstaPundit. [11]

Gun advocates point to the Appalachian law school incident as one among many examples showing "defensive gun use" is both more common and more effective in protecting lives and property than widely assumed or acknowledged by gun control supporters. They favor easing laws on carrying concealed weapons and repealing "gun-free zone" laws that prohibit carrying a weapon in specific places, such as campuses.

Police organizations and gun control advocates disagree. They depict defensive gun use as rare and risky and widespread carrying of weapons as an invitation to more gun violence. And they specifically dispute any suggestion that an armed student or teacher might have been able to prevent or limit Cho's rampage at Virginia Tech.

"Every time I play that out, I come up with worse results," says Healy of the campus police group. "When you have untrained people with obviously someone who was extremely mentally ill and several [police] agencies responding simultaneously, it's a recipe for disaster."

"What we're wishing for is that John Wayne or James Bond had been sitting in the classroom," says the Brady Center's Helmke, who as mayor of Ft. Wayne, Ind., directed the city's police department before his present position. "In the real world, it doesn't work that way."

The use of guns in self-defense has been an especially contentious piece of the gun policy debate since the early 1990s, when Florida State's Kleck produced research that is now used to estimate as many as 2.5 million defensive uses of guns per year in the United States. Seven years later, economist John Lott, then at the University of Chicago, coauthored a study claiming that states with laws making it easier to carry concealed handguns had lower overall crime rates than those without such laws.

Expanded later into books, both studies drew fire immediately from gun control organizations on policy grounds and from like-minded academics, who have exhaustively documented what they regard as patent flaws in the statistical methods used. [12] Whatever the validity of the studies, they both became useful ammunition for gun advocates in resisting additional gun measures and, in particular, in easing laws allowing qualified citizens to carry concealed weapons.

With eased carry laws on the books today in 40 states, gun advocates continue to endorse them and urge the rest of the states to follow suit. "Law-abiding people have the right to defend themselves," says the NRA's Arulanandam. "The sad reality is that just because you're

---

[*] Three people were killed and three others wounded in the incident. Gross' and Bridges' use of a weapon in subduing the shooter, Peter Odighizuwa, went unmentioned in most news stories. Odighizuwa pleaded guilty to capital murder and other counts in February 2004 and received six life prison sentences.

outside your home, you're not immune from crime. Crime can happen to anyone, anywhere."

Gun control supporters, on the other hand, oppose what they call the "radical liberalization" of concealed carry laws pushed by gun advocates. "An armed society is an at-risk society," a Brady Center position paper declares. The paper cautions that people "underestimate" the difficulty of successfully using a gun for self-defense and also warns that the availability of weapons allows minor arguments to escalate into "deadly gun play."

Lott, now a visiting professor at the State University of New York, Binghamton, and Kleck continue to defend their studies and their policy conclusions. Lott, for example, strongly argues against laws creating gun-free zones. "You unintentionally make it safer for the criminal because there's less for them to worry about," he says.

Kleck insists that despite contrary examples cited by gun control opponents, people using guns in self-defense rarely injure themselves and typically succeed in preventing injury or loss of property at the criminal's hands. Interestingly, Kleck rejects Lott's conclusion that concealed-carry laws lower overall crime rates and points to studies showing that only a small fraction of people ever actually carry weapons. But Kleck says he still favors those laws on self-defense grounds.

Harvard's Hemenway, however, insists that guns represent a greater risk than a potential benefit for public safety. "There's strong evidence that where there are more guns generally, there are lots, lots, lots more gun problems," he says.

As for guns on campus, Hemenway professes horror. "I would expect it would rarely do much good, and it has enormous potential for harm," he says. "The notion of allowing drunk frat boys to go around campus armed, that would be scary for me."

BACKGROUND

"Gun Culture"

Guns have been an important but controversial part of American life since Colonial times. The citizen soldier of the Revolutionary era and the rifle-carrying frontiersman of the Western expansion are mythic figures of U.S. history. But so too are the machine-gun-wielding gangsters of the early 20th century and the heat-packing street thugs of the urban underclass at the century's end.

Concern about gun crimes led to new, stricter gun control laws beginning in the early 20th century and culminated in the law that Congress passed in 1968 after the decade's wrenching assassinations of national leaders, including President John F. Kennedy. [13]

The historian Richard Hofstadter famously gave a name to Americans' attachment to firearms with an article in 1970 entitled "America as a Gun Culture." [14] Political scientist Robert Spitzer at the State University of New York, Cortland, notes in his overview of the gun debates that even gun control proponents acknowledge the special role of firearms in U.S. history. [15] Still, the exact extent of gun ownership and gun use through history is hotly disputed.

In the most dramatic dispute, historian Michael Bellesiles won wide attention and acclaim in 2000 for his book, *Arming America*, minimizing the role of private ownership of guns before the Civil War, but he had to resign from a professorship at Emory University amid accusations of questionable scholarship. After dropping a previous reference to Bellesiles' work in his most recent edition, Spitzer nevertheless reiterates two widely shared generalizations that citizen militias played a lesser role in the Revolutionary War and armed frontiersmen a lesser role in westward expansion than gun advocates contend or popular literature and media depict. [16]

Gun laws also date from Colonial times in America and from the early days of newly established frontier towns in the 19th century, according to historian Alexander DeConde. [17] The modern era, however, dates from the enactment of a strict New York law in 1911 that state Sen. Timothy Sullivan proposed after the heavily publicized shooting of New York City's mayor in 1910. The Sullivan law — still on the books — prohibits owning or carrying a concealable weapon except with a permit, issued for two years and only on a showing of "proper cause."

Two decades later — with the so-called gangster era still near its height — Congress passed the first major federal gun laws, but both laws emerged weaker than proposed because of opposition from, among others, the NRA. The National Firearms Act of 1934 required registration of and a prohibitive tax on sawed-off shotguns and machine guns, but handguns were dropped from the original version. The Federal Firearms Act of 1938 required federal licensing of firearms manufacturers and dealers and prohibited sales to criminals, but prosecutions were made virtually impossible by a requirement to prove a knowing violation.

CHRONOLOGY

Before 1960 *"Gun culture" is influential in the United States; first federal gun laws are passed.*

1911 New York's "Sullivan law" requires state-issued license to possess a handgun.

1934, 1938 National Firearms Act sets high tax on machine guns, sawed-off shotguns; handguns exempted. . . . Federal Firearms Act requires licenses for gun manufacturers, dealers; ban on gun sales to criminals proves unenforceable.

1939 Supreme Court upholds National Firearms Act; ruling appears to limit Second Amendment.

1960s-1970s *Violent crime, political assassinations trigger new gun law.*

1966 University of Texas student kills 13, wounds 31 others in sniper shootings from tower on Austin campus; police charge observation deck and shoot killer.

1968 After Martin Luther King, Robert F. Kennedy assassinations Congress enacts Gun Control Act, barring interstate firearms sales or sale of guns to criminals, "mental defectives" or others.

1970s National Rifle Association stiffens opposition as anti-gun groups form to get stricter gun laws.

1980s-1990s *Gun advocates, gun control supporters swap victories.*

1981 White House press secretary Jim Brady is left partially paralyzed during assassination attempt on President Ronald Reagan; Brady and wife Sarah become prominent gun control advocates.

1986 Reagan signs Firearm Owners Protection Act, legalizing interstate sale of rifles, shotguns; eases other 1968 restrictions.

1989 Drifter Patrick Purdy uses AK-47 to kill five, wound 30 in Stockton, Calif., schoolyard before killing himself; incident spurs President George H. W. Bush to ban some assault rifles.

1993 Democratic-controlled Congress passes Brady Handgun Violence Prevention Act, signed by President Bill Clinton; establishes five-day waiting period for buying guns to allow background checks; instant check system to be established within five years.

1994 Congress bans assault weapons for 10 years. Republicans win control of Congress in November, dooming further gun control measures.

1995, 1997 Supreme Court Justices Clarence Thomas, Antonin Scalia endorse individual rights view of Second Amendment.

1999 Columbine High School massacre spurs new school security and anti-bullying measures.

2000-Present *Gun debate dormant, renewed by Virginia Tech massacre.*

2000 Gun control viewed by some as a liability for Democrat Al Gore in presidential campaign; some in party de-emphasize issue.

2002 Disgruntled student Peter Odighizuwa kills three, wounds three at Appalachian School of Law in Grundy, Va.; two police officer-students use their guns to help subdue him. . . . Bush administration tells Supreme Court Second Amendment protects individual right to firearms.

2004 Republican-controlled Congress allows assault weapon ban to expire.

2005 High-school student Jeffrey Weise kills nine, wounds seven at school on Red Lake Indian Reservation in Minnesota.

2006 Democrats win control of House, Senate; muting of gun control issue viewed by some as factor.

2007 Federal appeals court strikes down District of Columbia handgun ban (March 9); gun control advocates leery of appealing. . . . Student Seung-Hui Cho kills 32 at Virginia Tech before killing himself; university officials' actions questioned, defended; Congress urged to tighten background check system; gun advocates want to lift campus gun bans, but administrators, law enforcement disagree.

Another two decades later, a public concerned with rising crime, especially among juveniles, began to voice support for stricter gun laws. [18] The calls for federal action intensified in the 1960s, driven in part by the rising crime rate but more significantly by the seeming epidemic of assassinations beginning with Lee Harvey Oswald's use of a mail-order rifle to kill President John F. Kennedy in 1963. As Kennedy's successor, President Lyndon B. Johnson capitalized on the shock over the killing and his own considerable legislative skills to gain congressional approval of a long list of domestic policy initiatives. But his support of a broad gun control bill failed to move lawmakers until two more assassinations in 1968: civil rights leader Martin Luther King Jr. on April 4 and Sen. Robert F. Kennedy, D-N.Y., on June 5 — the evening of his victory in California's Democratic presidential primary.

In successive messages to Congress in June 1968, Johnson called first for banning the out-of-state sale of rifles, shotguns and ammunition and then, more broadly, for national registration of all firearms and federal licensing of all gun owners. Polls registered strong public support for gun control. [19] Two weeks after Robert Kennedy's death, a Harris poll found 81 percent of Americans favored gun registration. But an effective grass-roots lobbying campaign by the NRA helped doom the licensing and registration provisions.

As enacted, the Gun Control Act of 1968 banned the interstate shipment of firearms or ammunition to individuals and prohibited the sale of guns to convicted felons, fugitives, drug addicts, the mentally ill or minors. It also strengthened licensing and record-keeping requirements for gun dealers and collectors. As Spitzer notes, the measure was "the most sweeping federal gun regulation" in U.S. history but also "very modest" in scope. As a result, he writes, the law's actual impact was "minimal." Nevertheless, gun advocates "immediately set to work to erode the act, if not overturn it entirely." [20]

Gun Debates

With the passage of the 1968 law, gun control debates became if anything more polarized and more volatile. Gun control proponents continued to call for stricter regulation, while pro-gun groups and individual gun owners intensified efforts to block new restrictions and relax existing laws. Over time, Republicans hardened their position against additional gun controls. Through the 1990s,

Democrats supported some gun control measures, but some in the party began downplaying the issue after 2000 as many strategists came to view it as a handicap in presidential campaigns and some congressional races.

In the early 1980s, the opposing lobbies swapped largely symbolic victories. Morton Grove, Ill., banned handguns in 1981. Kennesaw, Ga., responded a year later by requiring all households to own a gun. The Kennesaw ordinance was later amended to be discretionary, and Morton Grove's has been largely unenforced. After its ban was upheld in court, however, gun advocates responded by seeking and winning passage of laws in many states that pre-empted local firearms regulations — leaving the issue with state legislatures, where gun groups had greater clout. Gun control supporters countered with ballot measures that voters in some states approved.

At the federal level, gun control opponents achieved a signal victory in 1986 with passage of a law that neutralized some of the major provisions of the 1968 law. Culminating a six-year fight, the Firearms Owners Protection Act permitted the interstate sale of rifles and shotguns — but not handguns — if legal in the buyer's and seller's states. It also allowed gun dealers to sell at gun shows and made it easier for individuals to sell weapons on an occasional basis. It also specifically prohibited any comprehensive system of firearms registration or centralized record-keeping on gun dealers. Despite opposition from some Democrats — and from police groups — the bill was approved by lopsided margins in both the Senate and the House and signed into law by President Ronald Reagan on May 19, 1986.

Gun control supporters responded by focusing on two major proposals — a national waiting period for handgun purchases and a ban on so-called assault weapons — which both became law early in the Clinton administration. The Brady bill won passage by substantial margins in late 1993 in the House and then in the Senate; President Bill Clinton signed it into law on Nov. 30, 1993. The bill's major provisions — a five-day waiting period to be replaced by an instant background-check system within five years — were backed up by federal funding to help states improve the computerization of criminal records. The instant-check system went into effect in 1998 even though gun control groups called for extending the five-day waiting period because of uneven state reporting of information needed to make the instant-check effective.

The Case of the Overturned Gun Ban

Will Washington's mayor appeal or rewrite law?

Gun rights advocates won a major victory in March when a federal appeals court struck down the District of Columbia's strict handgun ban by recognizing an individual right to keep and bear arms under the Second Amendment.

Now, gun rights advocates are in the unusual position of urging Mayor Adrian Fenty to appeal the ruling to the Supreme Court. They hope the high court will definitively approve a broad view of the Second Amendment that the justices and most state and federal courts have rejected until now.

Meanwhile, gun control groups worry about the prospects of an appeal to the Supreme Court. And Fenty apparently plans to take his time in deciding whether to ask the justices to review the ruling or ask the D.C. City Council to rewrite the law in the light of the appeals court's decision.

"It's a little early to say which way we're going to go," Fenty told a May 8 news conference. "We will weigh everything." [1]

The meaning of the Second Amendment — part of the Bill of Rights adopted in 1791 two years after ratification of the Constitution — has been a major dispute between gun rights and gun control groups at least since the 1960s. The amendment states: "A well regulated militia, being necessary to the security of a free state, the right of the people to keep and bear arms, shall not be infringed." [2]

Through history, the amendment has generally been interpreted to protect a "collective right" for states to organize and control militias, but not to bestow an individual right to own or possess firearms. The Supreme Court appeared to uphold that view in a somewhat cryptic 1939 decision, *United States v. Miller.* [3]

In its 2-1 ruling rejecting the D.C. handgun ban, the U.S. Circuit Court of Appeals for the District of Columbia reasoned that the amendment could not effectively protect state militias unless it also guaranteed an individual right to keep and bear arms. "Preserving an individual right was the best way to ensure that the militia could serve when called," Judge Laurence H. Silberman wrote.

The appeals court's March 9 ruling in *Parker v. District of Columbia* marked the first time a federal court had used the Second Amendment to strike down a gun regulation. [4] In the only previous appellate decision endorsing the individual view of the amendment, the Fifth U.S. Circuit Court of Appeals in New Orleans agreed in 2001 that the Second Amendment protects the individual right to bear arms, but it nevertheless upheld a federal prosecution of a Texas physician for carrying a pistol — even though he was under a court protective order. [5] Ten other federal appeals courts and 10 state courts have ruled the amendment does not create an individual right to bear arms.

In his opinion, Silberman said the Second Amendment permits "reasonable regulations" of firearms. But the District's nearly total ban on registration of handguns went too far, he said, because pistols are "the most preferred firearm" for self-defense in the home. The ruling also struck down a requirement that any handguns in a home be kept disassembled and trigger-locked and an interpretation of the District's ban on carrying a weapon that prevents moving a gun within a home.

The District's lawyers asked the full appeals court to rehear the case, but the judges rejected the request by a 6-4 vote. With Fenty equivocating about the District's next

The push for an assault weapons ban moved to the forefront after an anger-venting drifter used an assault rifle in the Stockton, Calif., schoolyard massacre in 1989. President George H. W. Bush earned the enmity of gun groups by banning imports of certain assault rifles. Clinton expanded the scope of Bush's regulatory ban in 1993 and meanwhile pushed Congress for a broader, legislative prohibition. In its final form, the ban outlawed for 10 years

sale and possession of 19 specified types of weapons and others with some similar characteristics. The bill won strong approval in the House and cleared the Senate after half-a-dozen Republicans provided the needed margin to thwart a filibuster. Clinton signed it on Sept. 13, 1994.

The two measures represented the peak of gun control supporters' influence. Broader gun controls became politically impossible after Republicans gained control of

step, lawyers for the plaintiffs are urging him to appeal to the Supreme Court.

"We would like the entire nation to benefit from our efforts," says Alan Gura, an Alexandria, Va., lawyer representing the six D.C. residents challenging the handgun ban. "We believe that this is a wonderful case with which to redeem Second Amendment rights for all Americans."

Gun control advocates, however, openly worry that the broad D.C. ban will be hard to defend. "Why is this the one we're going to be taking up to the Supremes?" asks Paul Helmke, president of the Brady Campaign to Prevent Gun Violence. [6]

The District has until Aug. 7 to ask the Supreme Court to hear the case. Two justices — Antonin Scalia and Clarence Thomas — are on record as endorsing the individual rights view of the Second Amendment. In addition, Justice Samuel A. Alito Jr. voted in dissent in a 1996 case to strike down the federal ban on machine guns while he was a judge on the Third U.S. Circuit Court of Appeals. In addition, the Bush administration is on record since 2002 as endorsing the individual-rights view. [7]

Washington, D.C., Mayor Adrian Fenty (left) and Assistant Chief of Police Winston Robinson voice disappointment with federal appeals court ruling on March 9, 2007, striking down the District of Columbia's strictest-in-the-nation handgun ban. The ruling rejected previous doctrine that the Second Amendment only protects states' rights to organize and control militias.

AP Photo/Jacquelyn Martin

"There's certainly a risk at the Supreme Court" for gun control advocates, says Carl Bogus, a professor at Roger Williams University School of Law in Cranston, R.I.

[1] Quoted in Carol D. Leonnig, "Gun Ban Ruling Puts Fenty on the Spot," *The Washington Post*, May 17, 2007, p. B1. Some other background drawn from story. See also, by same reporter, "Full Court Will Not Review Ruling," *ibid.*, May 9, 2007, p. B4; Gary Emerling, "Court Denies D.C.'s Gun Appeal," *The Washington Times*, May 9, 2007, p. A1.

[2] For opposing views of the Second Amendment, see Stephen P. Halbrook, *That Every Man Be Armed: The Evolution of a Constitutional Right* (2d. ed.), 1994; Carl T. Bogus (ed.), *The Second Amendment in Law and History: Historians and Constitutional Scholars on the Right to Bear Arms* (2000).

[3] The citation is 307 U.S. 174 (1939).

[4] *Parker v. District of Columbia*, 04-7401 (CA-DC March 9, 2007)http://pacer. cadc.uscourts.gov/docs/common/opinions/ 200703/04-7041a.pdf. All documents in the case are on a site maintained by Alan Gura, lawyer for the plaintiffs: www.gura-possessky.com/ parker.htm.

[5] The Fifth Circuit's decision is *United States v. Emerson*, 270 F.3d 203 (CA 5 2001). For a compilation of other cases, see Robert J. Spitzer, *The Politics of Gun Control* (4th ed.), 2007, pp. 34-35 and accompanying notes.

[6] Quoted in Leonnig, *op. cit.*, May 17, 2007.

7 See *Printz v. United States*, 521 U.S. 898 (1995) (Thomas, J., concurring); Antonin Scalia, *A Matter of Interpretation: Federal Courts and the Law* (1997), pp. 136-137 n. 13; *United States v. Rybar*, 103 F.3d 273 (3d Cir. 1996) (Alito, J., dissenting). For the government's position, see Linda Greenhouse, "U.S., in a Shift, Tells Justices Citizens Have a Right to Guns," *The New York Times*, May 8, 2002, p. A1.

both houses of Congress in the 1994 election. The Columbine High School shooting in 1999 spurred Senate approval of a package of restrictions, but the measure failed in the House. Five years later, with Republicans still controlling both houses, Congress allowed the assault weapons ban to expire.

Some Democratic strategists, meanwhile, were blaming the gun control issue for President George W. Bush's narrow victories over gun control supporters Vice President Al Gore in 2000 and Sen. John F. Kerry in 2004. Many analysts disputed the argument, but it gained credence in 2006 when Democrats regained control of the Senate, thanks in part to the election of gun-owning Democrats in two Republican-leaning states: Jon Tester in Montana and Jim Webb in Virginia.

Mayor Bloomberg's Gun Control Tactics Draw Fire

NRA says he's harassing 'law-abiding Americans'

All New York City Mayor Michael Bloomberg wants to do is get illegal guns off the streets. Crime control, not gun control, Bloomberg declares.

But the National Rifle Association (NRA) says Bloomberg is harassing gun dealers and trying to disarm law-abiding Americans. "A national gun-control vigilante," the NRA magazine, *America's 1st Freedom*, calls him in its April 2007 issue. [1]

Bloomberg, a moderate Republican, is drawing fire from the NRA and other gun advocates for a variety of tactics he insists are aimed only at enforcing existing and largely non-controversial gun regulations.

The second-term chief executive of the nation's largest city is sending undercover agents to conduct sting operations against out-of-state gun dealers to detect illegal gun sales. He is winning court settlements against some of the dealers but also drawing scorn from the NRA and resentment from officials in some of the states.

Bloomberg is also spearheading Mayors Against Illegal Guns, a coalition of more than 200 city chief executives that he helped start — and personally bankrolled — in fall 2006. The coalition is concentrating now on urging Congress to repeal a law that prevents the federal Bureau of Alcohol, Tobacco, Firearms and Explosives (BATFE) from sharing gun-trace data with local police. [2]

NRA officials deride both Bloomberg and the mayors' coalition. "He's become the poster boy for gun bans in America," says Wayne LaPierre, the NRA's chief executive officer, explaining the article in the group's magazine. When the mayors' coalition was forming, NRA spokesman Andrew Arulanandam said, the effort was misdirected.

"If the mayors were serious about reducing crime," he declared, "they would work with city prosecutors to enforce gun laws as opposed to having press conferences." [3]

Bloomberg blames illegally sold guns for much of the crime in New York City. He had city lawyers sue a total of 27 out-of-state dealers in May and December 2006, charging them with violating federal law by selling guns to "straw purchasers." In a straw purchase, a qualified gun purchaser fills out the paperwork for the federal background check and buys the gun for someone who would not be qualified to buy a gun. [4]

By March, 12 of the sued dealers had agreed to settlements that include monitoring of their operations, videotaping of transactions and training of store personnel. But the use of out-of-state undercover teams raised the ire of the

Guns and Schools

Gun policy debates in the United States since the 1960s have played out against the backdrop of recurrent fatal shootings at schools. Although school shootings have claimed relatively few lives in comparison to the total number of gun-related deaths, several of the incidents produced a pervasive sense of shock that added urgency to the gun debates. The Virginia Tech massacre, however, shook the nation profoundly and put gun policy back at the top of the national agenda after a period of relatively little action.

At least 30 major school shootings and massacres have occurred since the first — and also one of the deadliest — of the modern-era episodes: Charles Whitman's sniper shooting from the 27-story tower at the University of Texas in Austin on Aug. 1, 1966. [21]

Whitman, a UT student, killed 13 people and wounded 31 others, using an arsenal of three pistols and four rifles.

The lunch-hour massacre extended over 96 minutes until two Austin police officers broke into the barricaded observation deck and shot the former Eagle Scout and Marine. President Johnson responded to the tragedy by calling for stricter gun policies, but Congress did not act until after Rev. King and Sen. Kennedy were assassinated two years later. The tower sniper episode is credited, however, with prompting police departments to form SWAT ("specialized weapons and tactics") teams to handle such high-risk situations.

Three decades later, a rash of smaller-scale incidents over a period of several years presented what was in some respects a more troubling phenomenon: fatal

Virginia General Assembly, which passed a law in summer 2006 aimed at prohibiting the practice. [5]

Arulanandam says gun dealers violating the law should be prosecuted, but enforcement should be handled by the BATFE and "not the private police force of a billionaire politician." (Bloomberg amassed a fortune as head of a financial-information service before his election as New York's mayor in 2001.)

The mayors' issue in Congress stems from an appropriations rider sponsored by Rep. Todd Tiahrt, R-Kan., that limits the BATFE from sharing gun-trace data with local law enforcement unless related to a specific criminal case or investigation. Tiahrt says the amendment safeguards sensitive information that, if released, could jeopardize a criminal case. Bloomberg, however, says the limitation hampers local enforcement. And gun control groups say the amendment is principally aimed at protecting gun dealers and manufacturers from lawsuits. [6]

Tiahrt first added his amendment, which is supported by the NRA, to the BATFE funding measure in 2003. The NRA has been one of Tiahrt's major contributors since his first election to Congress in 1994. Today, Arulanandam says the amendment ensures that gun-trace information is used only for law enforcement purposes. "Politicians, special-interest groups and the media shouldn't have access to that information," he says.

But Bloomberg says the restriction handcuffs police departments. "Right now, federal law prevents our police officers from looking at all the data on guns used in crimes in our region," Bloomberg wrote in an op-ed article in *Newsweek* the week after the Virginia Tech massacre. "That means we can't easily identify crooked dealers and illegal trafficking patterns." [7]

Ten police organizations, including the International Association of Chiefs of Police, support repealing Tiahrt's amendment. But the Fraternal Order of Police, the largest police group, says repealing the amendment "could compromise the safety of law enforcement officers and the integrity of law enforcement investigations." [8]

---

[1] See Michael Bloomberg, "The Changing Gun Debate," *Newsweek*, April 30, 2007, p. 47; James O. E. Norell, "Tentacles," *America's 1st Freedom*, April 2007.

[2] www.mayorsagainstillegalguns.org.

[3] LaPierre quoted in Diane Cardwell, "N.R.A. Covers Bloomberg, and Results Aren't Pretty," *The New York Times,* April 15, 2007, sec. 1., p. 31; Arulanandam quoted in F. N. D'Alessio, "Bloomberg, Daley Lead Mayors in Coalition Against Gun Violence," Associated Press, Oct. 26, 2006.

[4] See Damien Cave, "6 Gun Dealers Will Allow City New Oversight," *The New York Times*, Dec. 8, 2006, p. A1.

[5] Associated Press, "Virginia Warns Bloomberg on New Gun Law," May 11, 2007.

[6] See Sam Hananel, "Lawmakers Ask Feds to Share Data on Guns," Associated Press, May 2, 2007. Some other background drawn from story.

[7] Bloomberg, *op. cit.*

[8] From a memo to the FOP executive board and other leaders from National President Chuck Canterbury, May 17, 2007; www.fop.net/servlet/display/news_article?id=441&XSL=xsl_pages%2fpublic_news_individual.xsl&nocache=12192484.

---

shootings at public schools by teenage or even pre-teenage students. In the deadliest of those incidents, two students at Columbine High School, near Littleton, Colo., killed 12 students and wounded 23 others on April 20, 1999, before committing suicide. Eric Harris and Dylan Klebold had plotted the massacre for a year as retaliation for what they saw as bullying and harassment from classmates. They used two sawed-off shotguns, a rifle and a semiautomatic pistol in a rampage that extended over more than four hours before the shooting stopped — allowing police to enter the school and find the bodies of Harris and Klebold and their victims.

Combined with earlier school shootings, Columbine spurred school districts around the country to institute new safety measures, including the use of metal detectors and security guards, as well as zero-tolerance policies for any student behavior deemed as even potentially violent. Many experts also called for stronger action by principals and teachers to prevent bullying or harassment of students by other classmates. [22] In Congress, lawmakers fashioned a post-Columbine bill that, among other things, increased penalties for providing guns to juveniles and prohibited importation of high-capacity ammunition clips. The Senate narrowly approved the measure, but gun control opponents voted it down in the House.

Cho's actions in the Virginia Tech massacre combined features of the University of Texas and Columbine shootings. Estranged from and resentful of his classmates, Cho specifically referred to Harris and Klebold as "martyrs" in the chilling videotape he mailed to NBC

Columbine killers Eric Harris, left, and Dylan Klebold, are shown at Columbine High School in a video they made for a school project before their rampage. They had plotted the massacre for a year in retaliation for what they saw as bullying and harassment from classmates.

News between the dormitory shootings and the classroom rampage two hours later. Like them, Cho apparently plotted the shootings over a long period — at least since the purchase of his first weapon two months earlier. At Norris Hall, Cho mimicked Whitman by sealing the building from the inside using chains and padlocks. And like Whitman — but unlike Harris and Klebold — Cho appears to have fired randomly.

Virginia Tech officials came under criticism almost immediately for failing to take quicker action to notify students and teachers about the shootings or to order a campus-wide "lockdown" — as had been done eight months earlier during a hunt for an escaped jail inmate. As Cho's history of disturbed behavior emerged, administrators also faced questions about whether other steps could have been taken to direct him to mental health treatment.

The day after the shootings, Gov. Kaine said he would create an independent commission to study the incident and recommend any steps to take. But Kaine said any gun policy debate was premature. "I think for people who want to take this after just 24 hours and make it into their political hobbyhorse to ride, I've got nothing but loathing for them," Kaine said. "They can take that elsewhere." [23]

CURRENT SITUATION

Making Campuses Safer

College campuses are relatively safe places, according to higher-education officials, but the Virginia Tech massacre is driving stepped-up efforts to make them safer.

Administrators at campuses around the country are putting new security measures in place while continuing to work on professionalizing campus police forces. Meanwhile, mental health experts are emphasizing the need to identify and provide treatment for students under stress and to address the legal and ethical issues of breaching confidentiality if a patient poses a risk of dangerous or violent behavior.

Just one week after the Virginia Tech shootings, the head of a university presidents' group told the Senate Homeland Security and Government Affairs Committee of steps undertaken by half-a-dozen universities "to prepare for the unthinkable and the unforeseen." [24]

Several of the measures cited by David Ward, president of the American Council on Education, seemed to directly address issues raised by Cho's rampage and Virginia Tech's response. Rice University and the University of Iowa, for example, are both installing improved campus communication systems, Ward told the committee. Johns Hopkins University is installing "smart" surveillance cameras linked to computers that can alert campus and local police of any suspicious situations. And the University of Minnesota has electronic access devices at 101 of its 270 buildings that can selectively lock and unlock doors and send emergency e-mail and phone messages.

Along with Ward, other witnesses called for colleges to have plans for dealing with any emergency or disaster. Healy of the campus law enforcement group and Irwin Redlener, director of the National Center for Disaster Preparedness at Columbia University's School of Public Health, both outlined steps for the federal government, such as establishing preparedness standards and studying ways to better identify students who are potential threats. Healy called for federal, state or local funding for campus police forces.

Colleges face problematic issues in dealing with students with mental health problems in part because of legal and ethical requirements of patient confidentiality. Two federal laws in particular limit sharing of informa-

Should guns be allowed on college campuses?

YES
Larry Pratt
Executive Director, Gun Owners of America

Written for *CQ Researcher*, May 2007

Gun-free school zones have proven to be a dangerous delusion that has resulted in people being forced to be victims.

The only people guaranteed to be safe in gun-free zones are criminals. They can count on the law-abiding being disarmed. In reality, gun-free zones are nothing more than criminal safe zones.

Criminals have proven that they not only disrespect laws, they are willing and able to break them. The island nation of Great Britain has banned guns. In 1997 they confiscated virtually all legal guns. Yet today, the police there estimate that England has twice the number of guns in the country — illegally. The press in Manchester refer to their city as "Gunchester."

Stricter gun control laws than those in the United States have not protected Canada, Scotland and Germany from mass murderers striking schools.

The solution is to empower the most responsible people in America to be intermixed with potential victims so that they might have the opportunity to be the first responders to head off attacks such as the one at Virginia Tech. We have enough people licensed to carry concealed firearms that we can now say with certainty that these are the folks who commit the fewest crimes in our society.

Concealed-weapons carriers commit even fewer violent crimes than do police.

Yet our federal and state laws (with a few exceptions such as Utah and Arizona) prohibit these potential Good Samaritans from being armed on our college campuses. One concealed-carry permit holder is a graduate student at Virginia Tech. After a murder at the edge of the campus last August, he wrote a letter to the editor of the local paper, confessing that he had not been carrying his gun on campus because he did not want to jeopardize his graduate career should he get caught. But afterwards, he noted, he considered the fact that had he been killed, that also would have jeopardized his graduate career.

We have seen that armed civilians, students and staff alike have been able to get their guns and stop campus killers in the past — such as in Pearl, Miss., (1997) and Grundy, Va., (2002). But in those cases, the heroes had to run to their cars and get their guns and run back to the scene of the crime to stop the killer, losing valuable time.

Armed self-defense works. Disarmament kills.

NO
Paul Helmke
President, Brady Campaign to Prevent Gun Violence

Written for *CQ Researcher*, May 2007

College campuses will not be safer if we give everyone a gun and encourage the crossfire. Schools should be sanctuaries where students can grow and learn in an environment free from the risks of gunfire. The fact that such sanctuaries have been invaded by dangerous individuals with guns is a reason to strengthen state and federal laws designed to keep guns away from people like the shooter at Virginia Tech, not to weaken policies that tightly restrict firearms on campus. A thorough Brady background check would have stopped the purchase of the guns used in that massacre. This is a far more effective way to reduce the risks of gun violence on college campuses, and one that carries no downsides.

Despite the horrific massacre at Virginia Tech, college and university campuses are much safer than the communities that surround them. College students are almost 20 percent less likely than non-students of the same age to experience violence, and 93 percent of the violence against students occurs off campus.

If students and teachers start carrying guns on campus, we can anticipate the increased dangers and risks that will follow: greater potential for student-on-student and student-on-faculty violence, and more lethal results when such violence occurs; an increased risk of suicide attempts ending in fatalities; and gun thefts and subsequent harm to people on and off campus.

The college-age years — 18 to 24 — are the most volatile years in most people's lives. These are the peak years for binge drinking and drug use, mental health challenges and suicide risks — and commission of violent gun crimes, including homicides. Two studies have confirmed that college gun owners are more likely than the average student to engage in binge drinking, need an alcoholic drink first thing in the morning, use cocaine or crack, be arrested for a DUI, vandalize property, be injured in an alcohol-related fight and get in trouble with police. Binge-drinking, drug-using students are dangerous enough; let's not give them guns.

The Virginia Tech shooter was a 23-year-old college student who the Commonwealth of Virginia thought was a lawful firearms purchaser. Allowing guns on college campuses would not only have armed him more easily, but other potentially dangerous individuals as well.

Adding more guns to a home, a state or a country leads to more gun violence, not less. The same lesson holds true for schools, too.

President Bill Clinton and James Brady, former press secretary to President Ronald Reagan, attend a ceremony commemorating the seventh anniversary of the Brady law. After he was wounded in a 1981 assassination attempt on Reagan, Brady and his wife, Sarah, helped pass the landmark gun-control legislation, which Clinton signed into law on Nov. 30, 1993.

tion about students with mental health problems. The Family and Educational Rights and Privacy Act generally prevents universities from disclosing student records, including any mental health counseling or treatment, to anyone — including the student's family. Separately, the Health Insurance Portability and Accountability Act prevents a health-care facility from communicating with an educational institution about any treatment it may have provided to a student.

Cho's family has indicated they were aware of his emotional difficulties from an early age, but it is not clear what information his parents had regarding his behavioral problems at Virginia Tech or the mental health proceeding in December 2005 when he was ordered to get outpatient psychological treatment. Virginia Tech mental health officials have declined to discuss Cho's case because of privacy laws, but it appears unlikely that the school was informed of the order. In any event, *Washington Post* reporters concluded three weeks after the shootings, neither the court nor the school followed up on the order. [25]

Russ Federman, director of counseling and psychological services at the University of Virginia, told the Senate committee a survey of university counseling centers indicated that about 9 percent of enrolled students sought psychological help in 2006, but a separate survey indicated a much larger incidence of emotional prob-

lems. The survey by the American College Health Association indicated that nearly half of students surveyed — 44 out of 100 — reported feeling so depressed it was difficult to function, 18 out of 100 reported a serious depressive disorder and 9 out of 100 had seriously considered suicide within the previous year.

Most psychological problems pose no special risk of violence, Federman said. But he said universities "need to be able to communicate with one another, and sometimes with parents, when student threat of harm reaches a threshold where the university community is no longer safe."

Federman believes the educational privacy law does allow discretion to breach patient confidentiality when necessary. But Redlener and Ward both urged the senators to revise the law to provide more discretion. "I think we got a positive response from Congress . . . on putting some flexibility into the law," Ward says.

Meanwhile, elected state officials are responding to Virginia Tech in various ways, according to *The Chronicle of Higher Education.* [26] Maine lawmakers are studying whether the state's colleges have appropriate authority to regulate firearms on campuses. By contrast, Gov. Rick Perry, R-Texas, and some Republican legislators are considering a possible repeal of the state law banning possession of firearms on campus. In at least two states — Florida and Wisconsin — governors are following Virginia's example in creating special panels to examine campus-security issues.

Improving Gun Checks

Gun control supporters are renewing efforts to strengthen the federal background-check system for gun purchases in the wake of the Virginia Tech massacre, but they acknowledge they have little chance of winning congressional passage of any other measures.

The information gaps in the National Instant Criminal Background Check System have been recognized by the government and advocacy groups on both sides of the gun policy debate for years. But they are now a primary focus of the post-Virginia Tech debate because of Cho's ability to purchase two pistols after a favorable background check despite a disqualifying prior adjudication of dangerousness due to mental illness.

Testifying before a House subcommittee on May 10, Brady Campaign President Helmke said the background check cleared Cho to buy the weapons because of "lethal loopholes" in the system. Virginia law did not count Cho's earlier diagnosis as disqualifying even though federal law did. Effective background checks "would have stopped the sale," Helmke told the House Oversight and Reform Domestic Policy Subcommittee. [27]

A ranking Justice Department official told the panel that both the FBI and the Bureau of Alcohol, Tobacco and Firearms have made "continuing efforts" to encourage states to correct what she called "the limited submission . . . of disqualifying mental health records." But Rachel Brand, assistant attorney general for legal policy, said some states have privacy laws prohibiting the furnishing of the information, and others lack the resources to do a better job.

National Alliance for Mental Illness lobbyist Honberg, however, called for narrowing the definitions used in the law before addressing states' failure to comply with reporting requirements. Honberg said the term "mental defective" used in the law is "vague and outmoded" and the use of involuntary commitment as a disqualification too broad. In addition, he said, the law should be amended to give persons with mental illness a procedure to be removed from the disqualified list and to limit the information provided to a person's name and address without specifying the reason for being on the list.

The NRA supports improving the background-check system, but a second, smaller gun group opposes moves to tighten the screening process. "It wasn't a good idea in theory," says Gun Owners of America consultant Hammond. "It's been used by people who don't like firearms to try to do away with firearms."

Legislation introduced in Congress would provide up to $350 million to states to improve their reporting of mental health and other records to the federal background-check system. The bill is sponsored in the House by Rep. Carolyn McCarthy, a New York Democrat whose husband was killed in 1993 by a gunman on the Long Island Rail Road. The chief Senate sponsor is another New York Democrat, Sen. Charles E. Schumer.

The bills seek to close another major gap in the background-check system by requiring states to automate criminal-justice records. Brand told the subcommittee that about half the arrest records in the interstate database scanned by the background-check system are missing dispositions. The missing information causes background checks to be delayed, often for more than three days, she said. An application not acted on after three days is approved by default.

In a new report, the pro-gun control group Third Way also points to large gaps in the background-check system despite some improvements since a comparable report in 2002. The number of mental health disqualifications in the federal database has increased from about 90,000 then to 234,628 today, the report says. But that number accounts for less than 10 percent of the 2.6 million such records that the Government Accountability Office estimates should be in the system. [28]

The report estimates that one-fourth of felony convictions are not available in the database. But it credits states with improved reporting of domestic violence misdemeanor convictions and restraining orders since Congress amended the law in 1996 to add those to the list of disqualifications for possessing or buying a firearm.

Support for the McCarthy-Schumer legislation is seen as building on Capitol Hill, but Third Way's vice president for policy Jim Kessler says the bill could languish if Congress does not move quickly. "There's a will to do something," says Kessler, a former Schumer aide. "But you have to strike while the iron's hot because when momentum fades, complacency takes over."

In his testimony, Helmke also called for requiring background checks for gun sales by private individuals, not just by licensed gun dealers as under current law. That change would close what gun control groups called the "gun show loophole" that allows buyers at those events to circumvent the background check. Helmke also called for restoring a ban on assault weapons such as Uzis and AK-47s. Kessler says he doubts that Congress will act on either of those issues.

The Bush administration has not taken a position on the McCarthy-Schumer legislation. But the administration has proposed a measure to give the attorney general discretion to deny gun sales to suspected terrorists. Sen. Frank Lautenberg, D-N.J., is sponsoring the administration proposal in the Senate.

OUTLOOK

"Our Minds Still Reel"

Congratulations mixed with condolences, smiles with tears, as Virginia Tech prepared to graduate some 4,800 students on the weekend of May 11-12 — less than four weeks after one of the school's own carried out the deadliest shooting by an individual in U.S. history.

"Today is a special day, a time of celebration," university President Steger told the crowd of 30,000 assembled in the school's Lane Stadium. But the celebration was necessarily "subdued," he added, in recognition of the "great tragedy" of April 16. "Our minds still reel from the violence," he said. [29]

Even as the nation reeled from the news of the massacre, however, gun violence continued elsewhere across the country. The day after Cho's rampage, New York City police said a 20-year-old man with a history of mental disturbance shot and killed his mother, her companion and her companion's health-care aide in what *The New York Times* account described as "a quiet Queens neighborhood." Three days later, a NASA worker apparently fearful of being fired barricaded himself inside a Johnson Space Center building in Houston and shot one of two hostages before killing himself. [30]

In an ironic symmetry, the Brady Campaign's Helmke notes that the death toll in Blacksburg — 32 not counting Cho — equals the daily average of gun homicides in the United States. "That's a Virginia Tech massacre every day in our streets and in our homes," Helmke says.

To stem the violence, gun control supporters call for stronger laws — by which they mean more thoroughgoing enforcement of existing restrictions on owning or possessing firearms, prohibitions on specific types of weapons or ammunition and mandatory safety features on firearms, especially handguns. Virginia Tech "points out to people how poorly enforced our laws are," Helmke says. "It points out to people how easy it is to get a gun."

The NRA and other gun groups also call for stronger laws, but they want stiffer penalties for people who commit crimes using guns. "Any substantive measure aimed at decreasing crime ought to have the vital component of the criminal, and stiffer penalty for the criminal, as the major part of it," says NRA spokesman Arulanandam.

The Virginia Tech massacre may change the climate on college and university campuses in ways comparable to the heightened emphasis on security in the United States after the Sept. 11 terrorist attacks in 2001. College campuses are not like airports, but security precautions are likely to increase. Virginia Tech graduates, for example, were asked to wear their academic gowns open and to pass through metal detectors.

"There will be more meetings between police chiefs and the [campus] operating officer. There will be more meetings about dorm safety," says American Council on Education President Ward. "There will be greater consciousness of the need to be aware of this potentiality."

"It would be an absolute shame if we weren't better prepared a year from now," says Princeton's Healy. "If this situation does not prompt people to action, I don't know what will."

Mental health advocates hope that Virginia Tech will also bring about increased attention to — and increased funding for — mental health services. "For us, the thing that the Virginia Tech tragedy teaches us the most is that we have in most parts of the country, including that part of Virginia, no mental health system," says the National Alliance on Mental Illness' Honberg. "As a result, people who need treatment tend to fall between the cracks. And that's what happened to [Cho]."

Opposing advocates and experts, however, doubt that Virginia Tech will fundamentally change the broader debate over gun policy. "The gun rights/gun control debate has prevailed for decades," says Arulanandam, "and it will likely prevail for another year or three years or five years — and possibly longer."

"Congress has not shown the political will to do anything," says Helmke. "When the immediate incident fades, it's a lot easier for elected officials to do nothing, especially when they're concerned about the perceived power of the gun rights advocates."

Reminders of the massacre were all around on the Virginia Tech campus, however, during commencement weekend. [31] Stone markers on the drill field bore the names of Cho's victims; nearby, on Cho's unmarked memorial, a printed sheet bore the biblical injunction: "You shalt not kill." Cho's name went unmentioned during the ceremonies. But his 27 student victims were awarded posthumous degrees.

"It is our sacred duty to mourn those who lost their lives so suddenly and tragically and to help their friends and their families through these most difficult of times," keynote speaker Gen. John Abizaid, former commander of the U.S. Central Command, told the audience.

Many of the graduates had already adopted the message. Written on their mortarboards for all to see was the motto unofficially adopted on campus since April 16: "We will prevail."

NOTES

1. Accounts of Cho's gun purchases drawn from Brigid Schulte, "Kaine May Seek More Data for Gun Sales," *The Washington Post*, April 25, 2007, p. 1A; Laurence Hammack, "Gun Sale Policy in Va. Broke Down, Lawyer Says," *Roanoke Times*, April 21, 2007, p. 5; Thomas Frank and Chris Colston, "Despite questions about mental state, Cho could buy gun," *USA Today*, April 19, 2007, p. 10A. For an early comprehensive account of Cho's mental state, see N. R. Kleinfield, "Before Deadly Rage, a Lifetime Consumed by a Troubling Silence," *The New York Times*, April 22, 2007, sec. 1., p. 1.

2. For background, see these *CQ Researcher* reports: Bob Adams, "Gun Control Debate," Nov. 12, 2004, pp. 949-972; Kenneth Jost, "Gun Control Standoff," Dec. 19, 1997, pp. 1105-1128; Richard L. Worsnop, "Gun Control," June 10, 1994, pp. 505-528.

3. A study completed in 1997 estimated 192 million privately owned firearms, including 65 million handguns. See "Guns in America: National Survey on Private Ownership and Use of Firearms, National Institute of Justice, May 1997, cited in Robert J. Spitzer, *The Politics of Gun Control* (4th ed.), 2007, p. 6. Jim Kessler, vice president for policy of the progressive, pro-gun control group Third Way, estimates current ownership at 250 million based on approximately 8 million background checks for new purchases per year with some reduction for lost or destroyed weapons; he says other estimates are lower. As for household ownership, in one recent poll 50 percent of those responding said they or someone in their household owned a gun; the account noted that previous polls had indicated household ownership rates of 42 percent to 48 percent. See Dana Blanton, "FOX News Poll: Would Tougher Gun Laws Have Helped Stop Virginia Tech Rampage?" April 22, 2007; www.foxnews.com/story/0,2933, 267085,00.html.

4. See "Web-Based Injury Statistics Query and Reporting System," Centers for Disease Control and Prevention; www.cdc.gov/ncipc/wisqars.

5. The group's Campus Preparedness Resource Center can be found at www.iaclea.org/visitors/wmdcpt/cprc/aboutcprc.cfm.

6. See Brigid Schulte and Chris L. Jenkins, "Cho Didn't Get Court-Ordered Treatment," *The Washington Post*, May 7, 2007, p. A1.

7. See Schulte, April 25, 2007, *op. cit.*; Michael Luo, "U.S. Law Barred Sale of Weapons to Campus Killer," *The New York Times*, April 21, 2007, p. A1.

8. Third Way, "Missing Records: Holes in Background Check System Allow Illegal Buyers to Get Guns," May 14, 2007; www.third-way.com.

9. The statutory provision is 18 U.S.C. section 922(d)(4); the regulations can be found at 27 CFR 555.11.

10. Tim Craig, "Ban on Sale of Guns to Mentally Ill Expanded," *The Washington Post*, May 1, 2007, p. B1.

11. Glenn Reynolds, "Armed college students mean fewer victims," *Rocky Mountain News* (Denver, Colo.), April 21, 2007, p. 28.

12. See Gary Kleck, *Targeting Guns: Firearms and Their Control* (1997); John R. Lott Jr., *More Guns, Less Crime: Misunderstanding Crime and Gun Control Law* (1998). For a summary of the critiques, see Spitzer, *op. cit.*, pp. 57-68.

13. Background drawn in part from *ibid.*

14. Richard Hofstadter, "America as a Gun Culture," *American Heritage*, October 1970, pp. 85ff.

15. See Spitzer, *op. cit.*

16. *Ibid.*, pp. 7-12. Bellesiles' book, *Arming America: The Origins of a National Gun Culture*, originally published by Vintage, was reissued by Soft Skull Press after Vintage discontinued publication in 2003. Bellesiles resigned from the Emory professorship at the end of 2002 after an academic panel concluded he had been guilty of "unprofessional and misleading work" — an accusation that Bellesiles denied. See "Author of Gun Report Quits After Panel Faults Research," The Associated Press, Oct. 27, 2002.

17. See Alexander DeConde, *Gun Violence in America: The Struggle for Control* (2000). DeConde is professor of history emeritus, University of California-Santa Barbara.

18. See "Firearms Control," *Editorial Research Reports*, Nov. 11, 1959, at *CQ Researcher Plus Archive*, CQ Electronic Library, http://library.cqpress.com.

19. See *Congressional Quarterly, Congress and the Nation, Vol. II*, 1965-1968, pp. 328-330.

20. Spitzer, *op. cit.*, p. 125.

21. See Agence France-Presse, "The long history of deadly shootings at U.S. schools," April 16, 2007. For additional background, see Kathy Koch, "School Violence," *CQ Researcher*, Oct. 9, 1998, pp. 881-904; and Kathy Koch, "Zero Tolerance for School Violence," *CQ Researcher*, March 10, 2000, pp. 185-208.

22. For background, see John Greenya, "Bullying," *CQ Researcher*, Feb. 4, 2005, pp. 101-124, and Sarah Glazer, "Boys' Emotional Needs," *CQ Researcher*, June 18, 1999, pp. 521-544.

23. See Carlos Santos and Rex Bowman, "Independent Panel to Study Actions Taken at Va. Tech," *Richmond Times-Dispatch*, April 18, 2007.

24. For coverage, see Adam Schreck, "Senate Hearing Focuses on Campus Safety," *Los Angeles Times*, April 24, 2007, p. A16; Michael Luo, "Senators Discuss Preventing College Attacks," *The New York Times*, April 24, 2007, p. A17.

25. Schulte and Jenkins, *op. cit.*

26. See Sara Hebel, "States Review Campus-Safety Policies," *The Chronicle of Higher Education*, May 11, 2007.

27. For coverage, see Peter Hardin, "Closing Firearm Loopholes Explored," *Richmond Times Dispatch*, May 11, 2007, p. A7; Dale Eisman, "Gun-Control Group: Cho Exposed Loophole," *The Virginian-Pilot* (Norfolk), May 11, 2007, p. A15.

28. Third Way, "Missing Records: Holes in Background Check System Allow Illegal Buyers to Get Guns," May 2007; www.third-way.com.

29. Accounts drawn from Rex Bowman, "Mourning Continues on Graduation Day," *Richmond Times Dispatch*, May 12, 2007, p. A1.

30. Cara Buckley and Thomas J. Lueck, "Queens Man Kills Mother and 2 Others, Then Himself," *The New York Times*, April 18, 2007, p. B1; Peggy O'Hare, Paige Hewitt, Mark Carreau and Bill Murphy, "JCS Shooter Lived in Fear of Losing Job," *The Houston Chronicle*, April 22, 2007, p. A1.

31. Some details from Greg Esposito, Christina Rogers and Anna Mallory, "The Promise of Tomorrow," *Roanoke Times*, May 12, 2007, Virginia Tech Commencement: p. 1; Joe Kennedy, "Emotions Run Gamut on Day of Joy Sorrow," *ibid.*, p. 2.

BIBLIOGRAPHY

Books

Bogus, Carl T. (ed.), *The Second Amendment in Law and History: Historians and Constitutional Scholars on the Right to Bear Arms*, New Press, 2000.
Ten contributors carefully examine the history and current meaning of the Second Amendment from a variety of perspectives — all concluding that it affirms the states' rights to organize a militia but not an individual right to possession of firearms. Bogus, a professor at Roger Williams University School of Law, provides an insightful overview of "the history and politics of Second Amendment scholarship" to open the book. Includes detailed chapter notes.

Halbrook, Stephen P., *That Every Man Be Armed: The Evolution of a Constitutional Right* (2d ed.), Independent Institute, 1994.
The longtime gun rights advocate traces what he calls "the deep history" of "the right of the citizen to keep arms" from Greek and Roman times through the American Revolution and subsequent U.S. history. Includes case index, detailed notes.

Hemenway, David, *Private Guns, Public Health*, University of Michigan Press, 2004.
A professor of health policy at Harvard's School of Public Health — and a gun control advocate — argues that gun violence and gun-related injuries are a major public health problem that calls for gun safety measures and nationwide licensing and registration of guns. Includes tables, appendixes, 46-page bibliography; an afterword is included in a paperbound edition issued in 2006.

Kleck, Gary, and Don B. Kates, *Armed: New Perspective on Gun Control*, Prometheus, 2001.

Two longtime critics of restrictive gun measures argue in eight separate chapters that academic scholarship and news coverage are slanted in favor of gun control, that defensive gun use is more common and more effective than gun control proponents contend and that the Second Amendment protects a personal right to possess firearms. Includes detailed chapter notes. Kleck, a professor of criminology at Florida State University, is author of the earlier book, *Targeting Guns: Firearms and Gun Control* (Aldine de Gruyter, 1997). Kates, a retired professor of constitutional law, is affiliated with Pacific Research Institute, a free-market think tank in San Francisco.

Lott, John R. Jr., *The Bias Against Guns: Why Almost Everything You've Heard About Gun Control Is Wrong,* **Regnery, 2003.**

An economist reargues with updated statistics his earlier thesis that states with higher gun ownership have lower crime rates overall and contends that news organizations and the government minimize the benefits of defensive gun use because of a bias against firearms. Lott is now a visiting professor at the State University of New York, Binghamton. His earlier book is *More Guns, Less Crime: Understanding Crime and Gun Control Laws* (2d ed.), University of Chicago Press, 2000.

Spitzer, Robert J., *The Politics of Gun Control* **(4th ed.), CQ Press, 2007 (forthcoming).**

A professor of political science at the State University of New York, Cortland, discusses the history of gun use and gun controls in the United States and the current political environment on the issue, along with a proposed "new framework" for gun policy. Includes detailed chapter notes.

Virginia Tech Massacre: News Coverage

National, regional and local news media covered the Virginia Tech massacre intensively from the day of the shootings (April 16, 2007) through the university's graduation ceremonies four weeks later (May 11-12, 2007).

The Roanoke (Va.) *Times* has PDFs of the special print sections for the week after the tragedy on its Web site (www.roanoke.com); the site also includes subsequent stories and a four-page graduation section.

The Richmond (Va.) *Times-Dispatch* and two other Media General news organizations — the *Lynchburg* (Va.) *News & Advance* and NewsChannel 10 in Roanoke — have a comprehensive Web site "Tragedy in Blacksburg" that includes the *Times-Dispatch's* four-page, same-day extra edition along with photos, slide shows, audio and video and profiles of each of the 32 people killed (http://media.mgnetwork.com/imd/VT Shooting/index.htm).

The New York Times and *The Washington Post* provided comprehensive coverage, much of which was used in preparing this report. In addition to stories specifically footnoted in the text, one vivid reconstruction of the shootings is David Maraniss, "That Was the Desk I Chose to Die Under," *The Washington Post*, April 19, 2007.

Time and *Newsweek* both published comprehensive packages on April 30, 2007. In addition to stories recounting the shootings, each of the magazines had articles exploring the causes of mass killings: Sharon Begley, "The Anatomy of Violence," *Newsweek*, pp. 40-46; Jeffrey Kluger, "Why They Kill," *Time*, pp. 54-59.

For More Information

Brady Center to Prevent Gun Violence, 1225 I St., N.W., Suite 1100, Washington, DC 20005; (202) 289-7319; www.bradycenter.org. Nonpartisan, grass-roots organization dedicated to ending gun violence without banning all guns.

Coalition to Stop Gun Violence, 1023 15th St., N.W., Suite 301, Washington, DC 20005; (202) 408-0061; www.csgv.org. Coalition of 45 national organizations — including religious organizations, child welfare advocates and public health professionals — pushing a progressive agenda to reduce firearm death and injury.

Gun Owners of America, 8001 Forbes Place, Suite 102, Springfield, VA 22151; (703) 321-8585; www.gunowners.org. Nonprofit lobbying organization defending Second Amendment rights of gun owners.

International Association of Campus Law Enforcement Administrators, 342 N. Main St., West Hartford, CT 06117-2507; (860) 586-7517; www.iaclea.org. Advances public safety for educational institutions through educational resources, advocacy and professional development.

National Alliance on Mental Illness, Colonial Place Three, 2107 Wilson Blvd., Suite 300, Arlington, VA 22201-3042; (703) 524-7600; www.nami.org. Grass-roots organization seeking to eradicate mental illness and improve the lives of those affected.

National Center for Disaster Preparedness, Mailman School of Public Health, Columbia University, 722 W. 168th St., 10th Floor, New York, NY 10032; (212) 342-5161; www.ncdp.mailman.columbia.edu. Academically based, interdisciplinary program focusing on the nation's capacity to prevent and respond to terrorism and other major disasters.

National Rifle Association, 11250 Waples Mill Rd., Fairfax, VA 22030; (800) 672-3888; www.nra.org. Promotes the safety, education and responsibility of gun ownership.

Second Amendment Foundation, 12500 N.E. 10th Place, Bellevue, WA 98005; (425) 454-7012; www.saf.org. Educational and legal policy center dedicated to promoting a better understanding about our Constitutional heritage to privately own and possess firearms.

Third Way, 2000 L St., N.W., Suite 702, Washington, DC 20036-4915; (202) 775-3768; www.third-way.com. Nonprofit, nonpartisan policy center for progressives incorporating as one initiative the former organization Americans for Gun Safety.

7

Oil Jitters

Peter Katel

Heavy traffic in Beijing last August reflects the rising demand for energy in China and other developing nations. China had just 22 million cars and "light-duty vehicles" in 2005, with 10 times as many projected by 2030. By comparison, the United States, with a quarter of China's 1.3 billion population, had 250 million motor vehicles.

AFP/Getty Images/Teh Eng Koon

On a recent trip to Beijing, David Sandalow saw the world's energy future, and it wasn't pretty. "They tell me there are almost 1,000 new cars a day on the streets," says Sandalow, a senior fellow at the Brookings Institution think tank. "If those cars and trucks use oil in the same way the current fleet does, we're in trouble, for a lot of reasons."

Sandalow, author of the 2007 book *Freedom From Oil*, isn't alone. [1] The top economic researcher at the International Energy Agency (IEA) recently gave oil industry representatives in London a dire warning. "If we don't do something very quickly, and in a bold manner," said Fatih Birol, "our energy system's wheels may fall off." [2]

Demand for the key fuel of modern life is shooting up, especially in the developing world, but production isn't keeping pace, the IEA reports. Within the next seven years, Birol predicted, the gap will exceed 13 million barrels of oil a day — or 15 percent of the world's current output. [3]

"Rising global energy demand poses a real and growing threat to the world's energy security," said the IEA's 2007 annual report. "If governments around the world stick with current policies, the world's energy needs would be well over 50 percent higher in 2030 than today. China and India together account for 45 percent of the increase in demand in this scenario." [4]

The IEA delivered its message when intense oil jitters had pushed crude oil prices as high as they've ever been: close to $100 a barrel in December 2007 and more than $3 per gallon at U.S. gas pumps.*

From *CQ Researcher*, January 4, 2008.

---

* The IEA was founded in Paris in 1974 during the first post-World War II oil crisis to help ensure a steady supply of reasonably priced fuel for the world's industrialized nations.

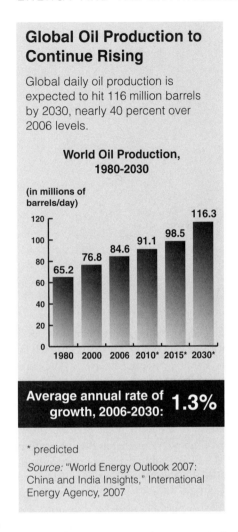

Global Oil Production to Continue Rising

Global daily oil production is expected to hit 116 million barrels by 2030, nearly 40 percent over 2006 levels.

World Oil Production, 1980-2030

(in millions of barrels/day)

Year	Production
1980	65.2
2000	76.8
2006	84.6
2010*	91.1
2015*	98.5
2030*	116.3

Average annual rate of growth, 2006-2030: 1.3%

* predicted

Source: "World Energy Outlook 2007: China and India Insights," International Energy Agency, 2007

The increases reflected a variety of concerns, including worries that supplies would be interrupted by possible U.S. or Israeli military strikes against Iran or a potential Turkish incursion into northern Iraq. "The latest run-up . . . has to do with fear," said Lawrence J. Goldstein, an economist at the Energy Policy Research Foundation. [5]

Fears of Middle East war choking off oil flow have hit several times since 1973, when Arab nations launched an oil embargo against the United States and other countries in retribution for their support for Israel in a war with its neighbors. Iraqi dictator Saddam Hussein prompted another scare when he invaded Kuwait in 1990.

This time, though, the headline-induced jitters have emerged along with deeper worries about a variety of developments: rising oil demand from rapidly industrializing China and India; depletion of oil reserves in the United States, Europe and possibly the Middle East and the fact that since the 1960s, most of the world's oil has switched from corporate to government ownership, as in Iran, Venezuela and Russia. [6]

"Nationally owned companies are less efficient, and the traditional international majors [big oil firms] don't control as much of the resource as they used to," says Kenneth B. Medlock III, an energy studies fellow at the James A. Baker III Institute for Public Policy at Rice University in Houston.

Meanwhile, the world's total production of about 84 million barrels a day is spoken for. There is virtually no spare oil — "excess capacity," in industry jargon. [7] The United States alone consumes nearly a quarter of today's world production — about 20 million barrels a day.

Concern about rising demand for oil by industrializing nations is compounded by the fact that oil is a non-renewable resource and plays such a major role in other parts of the global economy.

"Oil (and natural gas) are the essential components in the fertilizer on which world agriculture depends; oil makes it possible to transport food to the totally non-self-sufficient megacities of the world," writes Daniel Yergin, an oil historian and chairman of Cambridge Energy Research Associates, a consulting firm. "Oil also provides the plastics and chemicals that are the bricks and mortar of contemporary civilization — a civilization that would collapse if the world's oil wells suddenly went dry." [8]

Oil's central role in the world marketplace means that an economic slow-down can push down demand for oil, while an economic boom raises demand. With the sub-prime mortgage crisis slowing down the U.S. economy, oil prices are likely to fall somewhat, says J. Robinson West, chairman of PFC Energy, a Houston-based consulting firm. "Then the economy rebounds, and oil demand picks up again. That's when you're going to see prices go through the roof. There's going to be a crunch, where demand outstrips supply."

---

* On Jan. 2, 2008, crude oil prices hit the milestone $100-a-barrel mark for the first time. Violence in Nigeria's oil-producing region and speculative trading were blamed for the jump. In April 1980, during the turmoil that followed the 1979 Iranian revolution, prices were actually higher when adjusted for inflation: $102.81 a barrel.

West, who directed U.S. offshore oil policy during the Reagan administration, doesn't think the world is about to run out of oil altogether. He is a member of the chorus of oil-watchers who generally fault state-owned oil companies (except Saudi Arabia's and Brazil's) for not reinvesting at least some of their oil income in exploration and equipment maintenance — so they can keep the oil cash pouring in. "Politicians don't care about the oil industry, they care about the money."

Some other experts question how much of the run-up in oil prices is driven by doubts over supply capacity, and how much by financial speculators who benefit financially if prices move in the direction they have forecast. "The biggest thing that traders are now playing is the fear card," says Fadel Gheit, head energy analyst at Oppenheimer & Co., a Wall Street investment firm. "Commodity traders are spinning every piece of information that can embellish their position."

A 2006 report by the Senate's Permanent Subcommittee on Investigations of the Committee on Homeland Security and Governmental Affairs traced an energy futures trading boom to congressional action in 2000 that freed energy commodity trading on electronic exchanges from regulatory oversight. [9]

But traders make a convenient target, one economics writer argues. "They are speculating against real risks — the risk that oil from the Persian Gulf could be cut off; that hurricanes in the Gulf of Mexico could damage U.S. oil rigs and refineries; that political events elsewhere (in Russia, Nigeria, Venezuela) could curtail supplies," columnist Robert Samuelson wrote in *The Washington Post*. "High prices reflect genuine uncertainties." [10]

Further complicating the oil-supply picture, Saudi Arabia and other big producers are devoting an increasing percentage of their petroleum to expanding their own economies — effectively withholding oil from the market (*See p. 164*.) Advocates of the "peak oil" thesis argue that major global oil reserves — including those in Saudi Arabia — have hit the point

at which about half of the oil they can yield has already been produced.

"Over the years, we've just always assumed that over time we always find more oil — because over time we always found more oil," says Houston energy consultant Matthew R. Simmons, a leading proponent of the peak oil theory. But the world seems to have run out of mega-fields, he says.

In fact, Simmons says, major discoveries since the late 1960s can be counted on the fingers of one hand. In 1967 came Prudhoe Bay in Alaska; about 10 billion of its 13 billion barrels of recoverable oil already have been pumped, according to BP, which operates the field. [11]

Since then, exploration has yielded a 13-billion-barrel Caspian Sea reservoir owned by Kazakhstan, a 3-to-5-billion-barrel U.S. field 3,500 feet under the Gulf of Mexico and a 5-to-8-billion-barrel field off the Brazilian coast. [12]

Some experts say such recent discoveries suggest that new exploration and production technology will supply the world with oil into the indefinite future. "What's really happening is the opening up of a whole new horizon in the ultra-deep waters of the Gulf of Mexico, and it looks like the upside is very significant," said Yergin, a critic of peak oil theory. But, he added, "It will take time and billions of dollars to get there." [13]

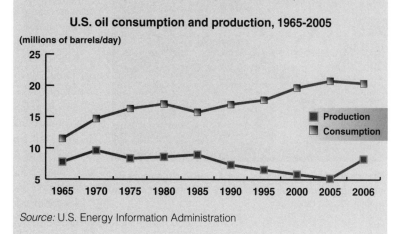

U.S. Oil Consumption Exceeds Production

The U.S. has continually consumed more oil than it has produced. The disparity between consumption and production exceeded 12 million barrels per day in 2006, forcing America to import more oil.

U.S. oil consumption and production, 1965-2005

(millions of barrels/day)

Production
Consumption

Source: U.S. Energy Information Administration

A gas station burns in Tehran on June, 27, 2007, during protests against efforts by the Iranian government to reduce consumption by imposing gas rationing.

Indeed, recent discoveries come nowhere near the spectacular discoveries that launched the oil age. The Middle East set the standard for mega-discoveries. Even after decades of production, its reserves were estimated at 266.8 billion barrels in 2006. Oil behemoth Saudi Arabia, for example, was producing 8.6 million barrels a day in August 2007. [14] U.S. production for 2006 was 5.1 million barrels a day.

But because Saudi Arabia doesn't release detailed figures on oilfield-by-oilfield production, Simmons questions the country's reserve estimates. "I don't think there's a shred of evidence" to back up Saudi reserve numbers, he says. More cautiously, the Government Accountability Office (GAO) notes the "potential unreliability" of reserve data from members of the Organization of Petroleum Exporting Countries (OPEC), among whom Saudi Arabia leads in reported reserves. That issue is "particularly problematic," the GAO reports, because OPEC countries together hold more than three-quarters of the world's known oil reserves. [15]

Cambridge Energy Research Associates estimates Middle Eastern reserves at 662 billion barrels as of November 2006 — or about 15 percent of the world's total reserves of 4.82 trillion barrels. "Key producing countries such as Saudi Arabia have a vast reserve and resource base," the firm reported. "There is no credible technical analysis that we are aware of that demon-

strates its productive capacity will suddenly fall in the near term." [16]

Other experts see production problems even if the peak oil theorists are wrong. Edward L. Morse, chief energy economist at Lehman Brothers, a New York investment bank, calculates that if Venezuela, Nigeria, Iraq and Iran were producing oil more efficiently, 6 million barrels a day more would be available to the world market. By contrast, the peak debate centers on technical issues, including the geology of oil reservoirs. Consequently, "Why should I believe in peak oil?" asks Morse, a deputy assistant secretary of State for energy policy during the Carter administration. The International Energy Agency guardedly shares Morse's skepticism about supply. "New capacity additions . . . are expected to increase over the next five years," the agency said. "But it is far from clear whether they will be sufficient to compensate for the decline in output at existing fields." [17]

To compensate, Birol said China, India and other big energy consumers need to step up energy efficiency efforts "right away and in a bold manner. We want more action, instead of more targets, more meetings and more talks." [18]

As oil-watchers monitor trends and conservation plans, here are some of the issues in debate:

Have global oil supplies peaked?

When a country's oil resources peak — or hit the point where half the oil is gone — it happens without warning, said a veteran energy company executive and researcher, Robert L. Hirsch, who conducted a peak-oil study in 2005 for the U.S. Department of Energy. That's what happened in North America, Britain, Norway, Argentina, Colombia and Egypt, Hirsch said. "In most cases, it was not obvious that production was about to peak a year ahead of the event. . . . In most cases the peaks were sharp, not gently varying or flat-topped, as some forecasters hope. In some cases, post-peak production declines were quite rapid." [19]

But Cambridge Energy Research Associates argues that a global peak — when it is reached many decades from now — will not mark the beginning of a precipitous drop-off. "Global production will eventually follow an "undulating plateau" for one or more decades before declining slowly," the firm said. [20]

A study by the nonpartisan GAO adds to the uncertainty over oil reserves. "The amount of oil remaining in the ground is highly uncertain," the agency concluded, "in part because the Organization of Petroleum Exporting Countries controls most of the estimated world oil reserves, but its estimates . . . are not verified by independent auditors." [21]

In part, debate turns on the extent to which oil producers can turn to so-called "unconventional" sources. Shale oil — a form of petroleum extracted by applying very high temperatures to certain types of rock formations abundant in parts of the American West — has been viewed for decades as an alternative to conventional crude oil. The GAO reported that one-half million to 1 million barrels a day could be extracted from U.S. shale within 10 years, though the process is expensive and energy-intensive. [22]

Oil can also be extracted from tar sands which have become one of Canada's major sources of petroleum. An oil-sands boom is under way in Canada, which is producing about 1.2 million barrels of oil from sands in Alberta Province, though the process requires burning so much natural gas that emissions have done considerable environmental damage. [23]

Cambridge Energy Research Associates said in its rebuttal of the "peak" thesis that oil sands and other unconventional sources may account for 6 percent of global production by 2030. [24]

Peak oil thesis advocates argue that unconventional sources won't suffice for the world's needs. They turn the argument back to the region still considered the globe's main petroleum reservoir, the Middle East. Houston investment banker Simmons says that a lack of verifiable information about Middle Eastern reserves lies at the heart of peak oil theory.

"These optimists — I'm happy they're so happy about things — but they have no data to base their case on," Simmons says. "We have passed peak oil, and demand is not going to slow down." Simmons' 2005 book, *Twilight in the Desert*, is a major text of the hypothesis. [25]

Simmons insists his projections and forecasts are more data-driven than those of peak oil critics. "That's one of the reasons I boldly predicted in 1995 that the North Sea was likely to peak by 1998-2000," Simmons says. "The major oil company people said I was nuts. All I did was look at the reports."

Experts agree the North Sea passed its high point and that the industry is doing its best to pump out the remaining crude. "Oil and gas production has peaked, [and] the industry is concentrating on managing the decline," said Trisha O'Reilly, communications director of Oil and Gas UK, the trade association of North Sea oil producers. "There's still a sizable prize out there." [26]

Some oil insiders accept parts of the peak oil argument, but others dismiss it as panic-mongering that only drives up prices for the benefit of price speculators. "Peak oil theory is a lot of baloney," says energy analyst Gheit, at Oppenheimer & Co. "We are consuming more, but we are finding more than we consume; reserves continue to bulge."

Vastly improved technology has facilitated the discovery of new reservoirs even in well-developed fields, Gheit and others argue. For example, he says, "In the old days, when they built the first platform in the North Sea, it was like a very big table made of concrete with hollow legs. Now there is something called sub-sea completion, where all the equipment is sitting on the ocean floor, and everything is robotically controlled."

West of PFC Energy agrees that while onshore U.S. fields and the North Sea have peaked and been squeezed "dry" thanks to technological advances, "there are parts of the Middle East and Russia that are virtually unexplored."

But peaking may be more widespread than some industry insiders say, another oil expert argues. "People are asking the right questions about peak oil, but they're asking about the wrong country," says David Pursell, managing director of Tudor Pickering, a Houston-based investment firm. "We know that Mexico has peaked. When does Russia peak?"

Will the rising energy needs of India, China and other developing countries keep oil prices high?

The newest twist in the volatile world of global oil economics is growing petroleum demand by Earth's two population giants — China (1.3 billion people) and India (1.1 billion people) — which together account for more than a third of the planet's 6.6 billion population. The two huge nations have been maintaining annual economic growth of about 10 percent a year, sparking intense demand among new members of their rising middle classes for cars and other energy-intensive consumer goods.

China had 22 million cars and "light-duty vehicles" on the road in 2005, with 10 times as many projected in 2030. In India, a tenfold increase is also expected — from 11 million to 115 million, according to the Paris-based International Energy Agency (IEA). [27] By comparison, there are about 250 million cars and other motor vehicles in the United States, or slightly more than one for each of the approximately 240 million adults in the population. [28]

Most Oil Belongs to OPEC Nations

Members of the Organization of Petroleum Exporting Countries (OPEC) held more than three-quarters of the world's 1.2 trillion barrels of crude oil reserves in 2006 (left). Most OPEC oil reserves are in the Middle East, with Saudi Arabia, Iran and Iraq holding 56 percent of the OPEC total (right).

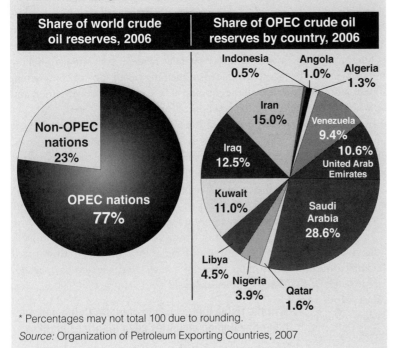

Share of world crude oil reserves, 2006

Non-OPEC nations 23%

OPEC nations 77%

Share of OPEC crude oil reserves by country, 2006

Indonesia 0.5%
Angola 1.0%
Algeria 1.3%
Iran 15.0%
Venezuela 9.4%
Iraq 12.5%
United Arab Emirates 10.6%
Kuwait 11.0%
Saudi Arabia 28.6%
Libya 4.5%
Nigeria 3.9%
Qatar 1.6%

* Percentages may not total 100 due to rounding.

Source: Organization of Petroleum Exporting Countries, 2007

If all countries maintain their present energy policies, the IEA says developing countries will account for 74 percent of the increase in worldwide energy use from all sources between 2005 and 2030, with China and Indian accounting for 45 percent of that boost. Developing countries now make up 41 percent of the global energy market. By 2030, if no policies change, those countries would account for 54 percent of world consumption. [29]

All in all, the IEA concludes, "The consequences for China, India, the OECD [Organization for Economic Cooperation and Development] and the rest of the world of unfettered growth in global energy demand are alarming . . . the world's energy needs would be well over 50 percent higher in 2030 than today."

The report goes on to recommend international efforts to reduce demand — for environmental reasons as well as to conserve oil and keep prices from skyrocket-ing. But some experts say the growing presence of China and India in the world energy market will keep prices high no matter what measures are taken.

"You're talking about economic development in two countries that comprise a little over one-third of the world population," says Medlock at the Baker Institute. "It's going to be difficult for the energy supply to expand production at a significant enough pace to drive down prices." Only an international economic slowdown could have that effect, he adds.

But Gheit of Oppenheimer & Co. argues that major price increases generated by continued growth in demand will force China and India to adapt, just as other nations do. "Energy conservation accelerates when prices go higher — even in China and India," he says. "That's the mitigating factor. Any developing economy becomes more energy-efficient with time."

Gheit adds that the Chinese and Indian governments have a highly efficient tool at their disposal if they want to curb demand: Both countries keep gasoline prices low through subsidies. "If gasoline subsidies were to cease, demand would crash," he says. "Roads will be half-empty."

But some oil experts say China's energy demands reflect far more than stepped-up car use. "The big thrust on Chinese demand is really on production of energy-intensive goods for their export industry," says Morse at Lehman Brothers. China's policy of keeping its currency undervalued to make exports cheaper is maintaining that effort — and causing the high energy demand that results.

Communist Party leaders in China oppose ending gasoline price subsidies, according to a Lehman Brothers analysis. And even if they were eliminated, "Chinese motorists might dip into their savings, and businesses might borrow more from banks to foot higher energy bills." In the long run, however, higher prices likely would force down demand, the analysis says. [30]

In the United States, meanwhile, high gasoline prices, perhaps combined with wider economic troubles, have reduced demand. Normally, lower demand would send prices down. But some experts say the high oil demand from China and India has changed the outlook. Long term, says Pursell of Tudor Pickering in Houston, prices are going to be higher in the next 10 years than in the past 10 years.

Nonetheless, the market system continues to function, some economists point out. "At these prices, an enormous incentive exists to develop new [oil] sources," says Robert Crandall, a senior fellow at the Brookings Institution and former director of the Council on Wage and Price Stability in the Ford and Carter administrations. "My guess is that after three-four-five years, new pools will be found."

But, Crandall cautions, new oil fields may sit in regions that are difficult to reach, for geographical or political reasons.

Can the federal government do anything to significantly reduce energy demand?

American worries about oil dependence and its effects on the global environment reached critical mass in December, when Congress passed, and President Bush signed, an energy bill designed to force major reductions in U.S. petroleum consumption. Bush, a former oilman, had previously acknowledged that the political climate now favors energy conservation. In his 2006 State of the Union address, he said, "America is addicted to oil." [31]

The new energy law includes tougher corporate average fuel efficiency (CAFE) requirement for cars and light trucks (including SUVs). They will have to meet a fleetwide average standard of 35 miles per gallon by 2020, compared with the present 27.5 miles per gallon for cars and 22.2 miles per gallon for light trucks. The bill also requires the production of 36 billion gallons of ethanol, the plant-based gasoline substitute, by 2022 — five times more than present production levels. [32]

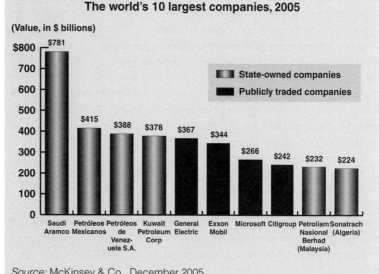

Top Oil Companies Are State-Owned

Six of the world's 10 biggest firms are state-owned oil companies from the Middle East or Asia. The largest is Saudi Arabia's Saudi Aramco, valued at $781 billion.

The world's 10 largest companies, 2005

(Value, in $ billions)

- State-owned companies
- Publicly traded companies

	Value
Saudi Aramco	$781
Petróleos Mexicanos	$415
Petróleos de Venezuela S.A.	$388
Kuwait Petroleum Corp	$378
General Electric	$367
Exxon Mobil	$344
Microsoft	$266
Citigroup	$242
Petroliam Nasional Berhad (Malaysia)	$232
Sonatrach (Algeria)	$224

Source: McKinsey & Co., December 2005

Due to the combined effects of the fuel efficiency standard and the ethanol production boost, "We will save as much oil as we would import from the Persian Gulf — 2.59 million barrels a day," says Brendan Bell, Washington representative of the Union of Concerned Scientists, citing projected oil demand if the law hadn't been enacted.

Some disappointment could be heard amid the cheers, however, because lawmakers balked at dealing with renewable electricity. "It's really unfortunate that we didn't have the renewable electricity standard or the incentives for wind and solar," Sen. Barbara Boxer, D-Calif., chairwoman of the Senate Environment and Public Works Committee, said. "But we'll fight for those another day." [33]

Still, opposition hasn't entirely died away. Rep. F. James Sensenbrenner Jr., R-Wis., who voted against the bill, had argued at a Nov. 14 hearing of the House Select Committee on Energy Independence and Global Warming that the new energy-use standards were unlikely to have much global effect on auto efficiency or on tailpipe emissions. "These regulations may work if everybody all over the world agreed to them and then actually complied with them," Sensenbrenner said. [34]

In addition to skepticism about the likely impact of a U.S. law on world energy use, critics are also asking whether markets can be relied on, without government involvement, to resolve supply-demand imbalances. That is, will prices rise in response to scarcity? In the classic supply-demand scenario, higher prices encourage companies to find and produce more oil, because they'll make more money — though if prices rise too much, demand drops.

Some experts who hold that world oil supplies are diminishing argue that the resulting problems are too big for the market alone to handle. "Intervention by governments will be required because the economic and social implications of oil peaking would otherwise be chaotic," said the report to the Energy Department directed by former energy executive Hirsch in 2005. [35]

But two years later, Hirsch warns that government action to reduce demand won't produce immediate results. "We have to do it, but we can't be unrealistic in our expectations," Hirsch says. "If you pass a dramatic increase in CAFE now, a significant number of new cars will not show up for about three years. It takes that long to get prepared with parts suppliers, assembly lines and so forth. And people may not buy the cars unless they're feeling pained or are required to by the government."

Government intervention would do far more harm than good, argues Jerry Taylor, a senior fellow at the Cato Institute, a libertarian think tank. "One thing markets are good at doing is allocating scarce resources among competing users, based on ability to pay," he says. "A peak in global oil production would send a very strong signal to consumers that oil is going to become scarce. If government decides to help steer the economy through a peak scenario, its main mission will be to dull that price signal to make sure consumers don't get it in the teeth."

But even some Wall Street energy experts argue that tougher fuel efficiency standards are long overdue. "If we'd had [the 35-miles-per-gallon] standard in place in 1990," says Morse of Lehman Brothers, "we'd be consuming 2 million barrels a day less now, and we'd be consuming 3 million barrels a day less if we had imposed the fuel efficiency standards on trucks that we have on cars."

No new standards or sudden consumer preference for fuel-efficient gasoline-electricity hybrid cars in the near future will have a dramatic effect on oil demand, another industry expert says. "It's a feel-good measure in the near term," says Pursell of Tudor Pickering in Houston. "In the long term, it probably makes sense. But we have roughly 150 million cars on the road." With so many cars, he says, requiring better fuel efficiency for new cars would take years to show results.

"So what can you do in the near term?" Pursell asks. "Drive less." He adds that his fellow Texans, who favor big vehicles on the long roads they travel, don't cotton to the idea of cutting back on time behind the wheel.

Another veteran oil analyst argues that market reaction to changing conditions is already well under way. "We have reached a saturation point on cars," says Gheit of Oppenheimer & Co., citing anecdotal but plentiful evidence of jam-packed streets and highways throughout the country. "Everywhere you go you're stuck in traffic. You go out and you can't find parking. These things are beginning to take a toll on the number of cars sold in North America."

And the cars that are sold are more fuel-efficient than earlier models, Gheit says. Hence the market is coming up with its own solutions. "You're seeing more and more advancement. Economic advancement comes with much more energy efficiency."

BACKGROUND

Energy Shock

In 1956, M. King Hubbert, a geologist for Shell Oil, told the American Petroleum Institute (API) that he had determined when U.S. oil production would hit its peak. After calculating the maximum reserves of U.S. oil fields (200 billion barrels) and the rates at which oil companies would keep pumping, he announced that the peak year would arrive in the 1970s. [36]

As it happened, U.S. production peaked in 1970, many experts say, when the United States was producing about 10 million barrels a day. Today, production has fallen by about half. [37] "We picked up again in the late '70s but still didn't go back to the previous high," says Ron Planting, an API economist.

But in 1956, Americans in general and the oil industry in particular believed American wells would be spouting oil and gas into the indefinite future. So when Hubbert announced his conclusion, "It was as if a physician had diagnosed virulent, metastasized cancer; denial was one of the responses," writes Kenneth S. Deffeyes, a retired professor of geology at Princeton University who was a protégé of Hubbert's at Shell. [38]

Some analysts take issue with the notion that Hubbert has been proved right. Technological advances have made it possible to probe oil and gas formations more accurately, leading to increased production in some cases, and recalculation — upwards — of reserves.

At the time of Hubbert's forecast, there was growing resentment among the oil-producing countries of the Middle East and Latin America of the power wielded by the "big eight" foreign oil companies, half of them American (the so-called "Seven Sisters," plus France's state-owned oil company). While the foreign companies controlled the price of a resource that the world depended on, the supplying countries had little say. [39] After a few years of quiet discussion, ministers from Saudi Arabia, Venezuela, Kuwait, Iraq and Iran convened in Baghdad in 1960 to form the Organization of Petroleum Exporting Countries. The objective was simple: to manage prices by controlling production.

In its early years, however, OPEC swung little weight, largely because the big oil companies were making major discoveries in countries that weren't — yet — members of the new organization. Over the years, the membership expanded to include Qatar, Indonesia, Libya, Nigeria and Angola. Two other countries — Ecuador and Gabon — joined in the 1970s but dropped out in the '90s.

As soon as the United States began depending on foreign oil, events showed that dependency had made the country vulnerable.

Following the 1973 Yom Kippur War, which pitted Israel against Egypt, Syria and Iraq, Arab OPEC nations retaliated against the United States and other Israeli allies by launching an oil embargo against them.

The embargo began on Oct. 17, 1973, and almost overnight 4 million barrels of oil a day were removed from world supplies. Demand rose 7 percent above supply, and international prices quadrupled from $3 a barrel to $12. Some saw the boycott as vindication of predictions that the energy foundation on which Western civilization depended would dry up. "The party is over," declared E. F. Schumacher, a British economist who had long prophesied an end to cheap oil. [40]

To prevent the high oil price from rippling through the economy, President Richard M. Nixon imposed price controls on oil. And his successor, Gerald R. Ford, established the Strategic Petroleum Reserve, an emergency stockpile that today has about 695 million barrels. [41]

But the boycott that gave rise to those measures ended in March 1974 — five months after it had begun. Egyptian President Anwar Sadat declared that the supply cutoff had served its purpose: to demonstrate to the West that it needed to push Israel to resolve its longstanding conflict with its Arab neighbors and with the Palestinians.

Even as the memories — and frustrations — of the Arab boycott faded, Ford's successor warned the country about potential future emergencies. "This is the greatest challenge our country will face during our lifetimes," President Jimmy Carter said in a nationally televised speech on April 18, 1977. [42] Some commentators said the speech paved the way for Ronald Reagan's 1980 election as president. Reagan portrayed himself as the optimistic alternative to gloomy Democrats.

Meanwhile, however, the 1979 Iranian revolution renewed America's sense of energy vulnerability after Shah Mohammed Reza Pahlavi — a close U.S. ally who ruled an oil superpower — was toppled by Muslim radicals who made anti-Americanism a tenet of their doctrine.

On Nov. 4, 1979, Iranian revolutionaries seized the U.S. Embassy and took 52 employees hostage — holding them for 444 days. Panic took hold of energy markets again, and prices shot up to the $45-per-barrel range, as high as they'd ever been. [43] During both the 1973 and 1979 crises American motorists sat in long lines at service stations, and some station owners who were short on supplies began rationing gasoline. During the second "oil shock," Congress funded research into alternative fuels and encouraged Americans to conserve fuel.

Then, even before the hostages were released in early 1981, Iraqi dictator Saddam Hussein attacked Iran. Oil exports by the two countries virtually ceased for a time, as production facilities were bombed during the first months of fighting in 1980. About 4 million barrels a day vanished from the market, setting off a new round of panic buying. The eight-year war eventually had little lasting effect on oil markets.

Consumers Go Wild

After the disruptions caused by war and revolution, market forces restored stability to oil trade. The law of supply and demand got a big assist from Saudi Arabia, the world's biggest oil producer. Worried that a prolonged period of high prices would cut oil demand by newly conservation-minded Western countries — and force

CHRONOLOGY

1950s-1970s *Oil imports ease concerns about decreasing U.S. oil supplies — until big oil-producing nations suspend their shipments.*

1956 Shell Oil geologist forecasts that the U.S. oil supply will plateau in the early 1970s.

1960 Saudi Arabia, Venezuela and other oil giants form Organization of Petroleum Exporting Countries (OPEC).

1970-1972 U.S. oil reserves peak, as predicted.

1973 Arab members of OPEC cut off oil exports to the United States and other allies of Israel, causing oil prices to skyrocket. The embargo ends in March 1974.

1975 President Gerald R. Ford signs the Energy Policy and Conservation Act, imposing fuel economy standards on carmakers.

1977 President Jimmy Carter calls energy conservation the country's biggest challenge.

1979 Revolution topples the U.S.-backed shah of Iran, prompting oil price spikes in the United States and other big oil-consuming nations.

1980s *New non-OPEC oil sources are discovered or come online, vastly expanding world oil supplies and causing prices to plummet.*

1980 Non-OPEC oil supply expands by about 6 million barrels a day after Mexico's daily production rises, new North Sea sources come online and drilling is stepped up in Alaska. . . . Iraq attacks Iran.

1983 OPEC cuts prices from $34 a barrel to $29.

1985 Oil falls to $10 a barrel; Saudi Arabia steps up output and abandons efforts to prop up prices.

1988 Iran-Iraq War ends, removing source of potential oil-market disruption.

1990s *Steady supply of cheap oil sparks popularity of gas-guzzling sport-utility vehicles (SUVs), but trouble looms by decade's end.*

1990 Automakers sell 750,000 SUVs; annual sales hit 3 million 10 years later. . . . Iraqi leader Saddam Hussein invades Kuwait, prompting fears about Saudi oil security.

1991 U.S.-led forces oust Iraq from Kuwait, maintain protective presence in Saudi Arabia.

1996 Russia begins developing oil production facilities in its Far East region. . . . Saudi Islamist Osama bin Laden releases manifesto attacking U.S. military presence in Saudi Arabia.

1998 Socialist Hugo Chávez is elected president of Venezuela.

2000s *Terrorism, war and fear of war disrupt oil prices in the Middle East.*

Sept. 11, 2001 Arab terrorists crash hijacked U.S. jetliners into the World Trade Center and Pentagon, killing nearly 3,000 people.

2002-2003 Venezuelan oil workers strike against the Chávez government's efforts to reduce production, pushing prices up.

2003 U.S.-led coalition invades Iraq, topples Saddam.

2004 Insurgents attack Iraqi oil facilities, prompting price fluctuations.

2005 Gas hits $3 a gallon in the U.S. . . . Author of a report on "peak oil" tells lawmakers government should prepare for possible oil shortage.

2006 Saudi Arabia's oil consumption rises by 2 million barrels a day in one year. . . . Chávez pledges to sell China 1 million barrels of oil a day by 2012.

2007 International Energy Agency warns of looming oil shortfall. . . . Crude oil price nears $100 per barrel. . . . President George W. Bush signs new energy bill including a fuel-efficiency standard of 35 miles per gallon for cars and light trucks by 2020. . . . Environmental Protection Agency denies California and 16 other states the right to set auto emission standards.

Jan. 2, 2008 Crude oil price hits $100.

prices lower — Saudi Arabia had been steadily increasing its production. Non-members of OPEC followed suit.

Other developments were at work as well. After the oil shocks of the 1970s, energy companies stepped up exploration outside the turbulent Middle East. By the early 1980s, the results began pouring in.

At least 6 million barrels a day were added to world oil supplies by Britain and Norway's production in the North Sea, a new pipeline from Alaska's rich North Slope to the port of Valdez and a major discovery in Mexican waters in the Gulf of Mexico. The new output, coming from outside the OPEC circle, was within striking distance of Saudi Arabia, which in 1981 reached a top daily production level of about 9.8 million barrels. [44]

Meanwhile, the effects of conservation measures adopted during the 1970s kicked in. The most significant was a 1975 law setting tough corporate average fuel efficiency (CAFE) standards for new cars of 27.5 miles per gallon by 1985. The measure would save about 2 million barrels of gasoline a day. [45]

Production from the new oil fields combined with new conservation efforts would have been enough by themselves to push oil prices down. But a third factor emerged as well: In a newly restabilized geopolitical environment, oil companies began selling off oil that they'd been holding in storage against the possibility of long-lasting shortages. Companies couldn't justify the considerable expense of warehousing the oil.

By March 1983, OPEC was feeling the pressure from an oil glut that it couldn't control by shutting down production, because much of the new supply came from outside the organization's control. So OPEC took the unprecedented step of cutting prices from about $34 per barrel to about $29. With the world oil supply still plentiful and with new CAFE standards reducing demand, prices kept falling even further. In 1985, with oil at $10 a barrel, Saudi Arabia gave up trying to limit OPEC output and stepped up its own shipments.

American automakers and consumers, meanwhile, reacted in their own ways. Unconcerned (for the moment) about oil prices and supplies, manufacturers began expanding their production of popular SUVs. Classified by the government as "light trucks," the gas-guzzling SUVs were subject to less rigorous fuel efficiency standards.

"Gasoline remained readily available, and its price stayed flat instead of soaring to the $20 a gallon level

once predicted by energy forecasters," a journalist specializing in the auto industry wrote in 1996. [46]

In 1990, carmakers sold 750,000 SUVs nationwide. By 2000, annual sales were approaching 3 million.

By the mid-1990s, however, there were warning signs that the latest cheap-oil era might be ending. The signs included a little-noticed 1996 anti-American manifesto by a Saudi Arabian millionaire and veteran of Afghanistan's U.S.-aided war against Soviet occupation in 1979-1989. By then, Osama bin Laden had developed a deep hatred for the United States, and he decried the presence in Saudi Arabia of American troops, which had been providing security for the oil giant ever since Saddam Hussein invaded Kuwait during the Persian Gulf War of 1990-1991. [47]

Tide Turns Again

The terrorist attacks of Sept. 11, 2001, for which bin Laden later claimed responsibility, might have been expected to cause a major disruption in the oil market. Indeed, only hours after the terrorists struck, prices on the International Oil Exchange in London rose by 13 percent, to $31.05 a barrel. And as rumors of major shortages swept through parts of the United States, some drivers in Oklahoma City saw prices at the pump surge to $5 a gallon. [48]

But the wholesale and pump price spikes proved momentary. No terrorists hit any oil facilities, and OPEC immediately issued a market-calming declaration that it would not use the oil weapon against the United States for whatever military action it took to answer the attacks. Overall, the average wholesale price paid by U.S. refineries in September was lower than they'd paid the previous month — a drop from $24.44 a barrel to $23.73. "By October 2001, the economy was having more effect on the price of oil — in terms of weakening oil demand and reducing oil prices — than the price of oil was having on the economy," the Congressional Research Service concluded in a report a year after the attacks. Demand weakened in part because airplane travel dropped in the immediate aftermath of the attacks. [49]

As the decade wore on, however, a series of developments began to push prices higher. By late 2004, oil was commanding about $50 a barrel. Analysts cited the effects of the war in Iraq in reducing that country's production and export capacity, as well as the economic booms already under way in China and India.

How Times Have Changed

Now petrostates are bailing out U.S. firms

Only a few decades ago, American oil companies stood among the petroleum giants that controlled most of the world's oil, and their profits largely were recycled back into the United States.

But times have changed. "For some time now," writes former Treasury Secretary Lawrence H. Summers, "the large flow of capital from the developing to the industrialized world has been the principal irony of the international financial system." [1]

In today's world, a tiny Persian Gulf state can rescue a major American bank from financial catastrophe using money earned from selling millions of barrels of oil. And politicians in Europe and the United States are nervous about their nations' companies being bought up by cash-swollen petrostates.

"Their wealth is a reminder to our politicians that the West is no longer the force it once was in the world," wrote Michael Gordon, fixed-income director at Fidelity International, a giant investment-management firm. "And just maybe, business leaders are ahead of the politicians in welcoming this infusion of new money into the global financial system." [2]

Last year, U.S. lawmakers of both parties scuttled a deal that would have allowed a company owned by the government of Dubai* to run six major U.S. ports. "This proposal may require additional congressional action in order to ensure that we are fully protecting Americans at home," wrote House Speaker J. Dennis Hastert, R-Ill. [3]

---

* Dubai is one of seven Arabian Peninsula city-states that constitute the United Arab Emirates.

Political jitters over the wide range of foreign government funds invested don't all center on the oil-rich countries. China, which has grown rich selling cheap goods to the rest of the world, has set alarm bells ringing on Wall Street over attempted investments in American and other Western companies. In 2005, a political firestorm forced China's state-owned oil company to abandon a bid to buy Unocal, a U.S. oil company. [4]

China's sheer size and strategic importance guarantee continuing interest in its investment projects. But high oil prices in 2007 have focused attention on efforts by oil-exporting countries to invest their profits — totaling a mind-boggling $3.4-$3.8 trillion — much of it in the West, according to the McKinsey Global Institute.

And the developing world's cash situation is expected to get even more dramatic in the future. "The most conservative assumptions you could think of, absent some catastrophic event, would have [these assets] double by 2012," Diana Farrell, the institute's director, said in December. [5]

In fact, even if the price of oil falls from current levels (now above $90 a barrel) to $50 a barrel, petrodollar assets would expand to $5.9 trillion by 2012, the institute says, fueling investment at a rate of about $1 billion a day. [6]

Political resistance to Middle Eastern oil profits buying up American companies surfaced even before oil prices skyrocketed in 2007. In 2006, Dubai PortsWorld bought a British firm that ran port operations in New York City, New Jersey, Philadelphia, Baltimore, Miami and New Orleans. Lawmakers of both parties lost no time in denouncing the deal with an Arab nation as a threat to

---

By 2005, gas prices nationwide had passed $3 a gallon. Oil and marketing experts had long contended that the $3 price was a critical threshold. Rebecca Lindland, an automotive industry analyst for Global Insight, a research firm in Waltham, Mass., had told *The New York Times* in 2004 that consumers would change their driving and car-buying behavior if prices at the pump exceeded $3 a gallon for at least six months. [50] The forecast proved accurate. As higher prices stayed steady, SUV lovers started shying away from sport-utility vehicles. "I

really want my Explorer back, but I'm thinking about not getting it because of gas prices," said Angie Motylinski, a bank teller in Sylvania, Ohio, whose lease was expiring. "If they gave me an awesome, awesome deal, I might consider it. But who's going to want it when gas is $3.19 a gallon?" [51]

Other Sylvanians were thinking similar thoughts. "If I had a dollar for every time that somebody said I'm looking for something with better gas mileage, I'd be a wealthy man," said Bill Roemer, the manager

national security, and the government of Dubai eventually sold its interest in the U.S. operations. [7]

But some international finance experts urge politicians and others to look at other implications, such as whether foreign-owned companies could end up unduly influencing domestic policy. "What about the day when a country joins some 'coalition of the willing' and asks the U.S. president to support a tax break for a company in which it has invested?" Summers asked, using Bush administration terminology for U.S. allies in the Iraq War. "Or when a decision has to be made about whether to bail out a company, much of whose debt is held by an ally's central bank?" [8]

In the 1950s, the oil-rich countries worried about foreign involvement in their economic and political affairs. For instance, the Iranians did not take kindly to the U.S.-organized 1953 coup in Iran that ousted Prime Minister Mohammed Mossadeq, who had nationalized a British-owned oil company. And oil-producing countries also resented foreign oil companies' control of petroleum pricing and marketing. Eventually, most countries nationalized their oil resources. [9]

Now the situation is almost reversed, with the industrialized countries coming to depend on the oil countries for oil as well as cash.

But that's not necessarily a bad thing, some experts note, because investments in the industrialized world give the oil

A firm owned by the government of Dubai backed out of a 2006 deal to run six U.S. ports after U.S. lawmakers protested.

countries a stake in maintaining stability and prosperity, not to mention a market for petroleum. "If the U.S. goes in the tank, the whole world goes in the tank," says Kenneth Medlock III, an energy research fellow at the James A. Baker III Institute for Public Policy at Rice University in Houston. "That would put a crimp in oil demand."

[1] See Lawrence Summers, "Sovereign funds shake the logic of capitalism," *Financial Times* (London), July 30, 2007, p. A11.

[2] See Michael Gordon, "Ignore the murk and myths on sovereign funds," *Financial Times* (London), Dec. 12, 2007, p. A13.

[3] Quoted in Jim VandeHei and Jonathan Weisman, "Bush Threatens Veto Against Bid to Stop Port Deal," *The Washington Post*, Feb. 22, 2006, p. A1.

[4] See Jad Mouwad, "Foiled Bid Stirs Worry for U.S. Oil," *The New York Times*, Aug. 11, 2005, www.nytimes.com/2005/08/11/business/worldbusiness/11unocal.html?_r=1&oref=slogin.

[5] See "Sovereign Wealth Fund Briefing," (transcript) Brookings Institution, Dec. 6, 2007, p. 16, www.brookings.edu/~/media/Files/events/2007/1206_sovereign_wealth_funds/1206_sovereign_wealth_funds.pdf.

[6] See "The New Power Brokers: How Oil, Asia, Hedge Funds, and Private Equity are Shaping Global Capital Markets," McKinsey Global Institute, October 2007, pp. 12-13, www.mckinsey.com/mgi/publications/The_New_Power_Brokers/index.asp.

[7] See Richard Simon and Peter Wallsten, "Bush to Fight for Port Deal," Los Angeles Times, Feb. 22, 2006, p. A1; "Dubai Firm Details Plans for U.S. Ports," *Los Angeles Times* (The Associated Press), March 16, 2006, p. C3.

[8] See Summers, *op. cit.*

[9] See Daniel Yergin, *The Prize: The Epic Quest for Oil, Money, and Power* (1992), pp. 511-512, 467-470.

of a local Chevrolet dealership. "With gas prices the way they are, people just aren't looking at minivans, SUVs, trucks." [52]

Petro-Nationalism

As prices spiraled upwards, a trend that had begun decades earlier suddenly took on new importance for oil-watchers. In the 1970s, publicly owned firms — all in the West — owned roughly three-quarters of global petroleum; today, state-owned oil companies own three-

quarters of the oil. [53] That poses a potential problem for the U.S because governments that control oil supplies may have economic and/or political reasons to limit their foreign sales. The 1973 OPEC oil embargo serves as a reminder of the potency of oil as a political weapon against the United States. And some producing countries may decide to increase the amount of oil they use at home. (*See p. 164.*) To be sure, the No. 1 international oil supplier, Saudi Arabia, still cooperates closely with the United States and other consuming countries. And

Plug-in Hybrids Offer Clean-Energy Future

New technology may enable motorists to burn less oil

I ts cities separated by hundreds of miles of windswept, open spaces, Texas may not be the place to start up a conversation about carpooling. "That's a very unpopular discussion to have here in Houston," says Kenneth B. Medlock III, speaking from his car.

"You look out on a freeway," says Medlock, an energy studies fellow at the James A. Baker III Institute for Public Policy at Houston's Rice University, "and all you see is car after car with a driver and no passengers."

Texans may be especially fond of their cars — but Lone Star State drivers aren't unique. Transportation (including airplanes and trucking) accounts for two-thirds of U.S. petroleum use, according to a July 2007 study by the National Petroleum Council. [1]

That's hardly a surprising statistic, given the size of the U.S. car and truck fleet: nearly 250 million vehicles in a nation of about 300 million. Relying on fuel efficiency standards alone to hold gasoline use in 2017 to what it was in 2005 would require improving average vehicle performance to 22 miles per gallon — a 25 percent improvement over today, researchers at the Baker Institute calculate. [2]

To reduce oil consumption to 2005 levels by conservation alone, every American would have to drive 45 miles a week less. "Basically, it's a lifestyle change," says Medlock, who worked on the study.

But some energy experts are arguing that new automotive technology will allow Americans to keep driving while burning less oil. They tout the plug-in hybrid electric vehicle (PHEV), a variant of the gasoline-electric hybrid car whose electric motor gets recharged from an ordinary wall socket. Limited-edition PHEVs — Toyota Priuses retrofitted by conversion companies or by enthusiasts — boast bigger batteries that allow drivers to cruise for about 20 miles on electric power alone, burning no gasoline. Unmodified Priuses can travel only about a half-mile on electricity alone, according to the Institute of Electrical and Electronics Engineers. PHEV advocates also say that recharging the cars at night uses surplus electricity that utilities hold in reserve for emergencies. [3]

The reliance on wall current, though, raises the question of whether the plug-ins wind up burning as much energy as the hybrid models now on sale. Alternative-energy advocates raise another objection. "If you start plugging in hundreds of cars all at once, you'll be finding out what the limits of the electricity grid are real quick," Paul Cass, a representative of Ballard Power Systems, a Canadian firm, told the *Los Angeles Times* at an alternative-vehicle convention. [4]

Nigeria and Brazil invite foreign companies to help develop national petroleum resources.

But Venezuela is headed by an anti-American president who has threatened more than once to cut off sales to the United States by its state-owned oil firm. President Hugo Chávez also plans to sell less oil to the United States and more to China. In fact, in 2006 the pugnacious Chávez vowed to sell 1 million barrels a day to China by 2012. [54]

And then there is Russia. A major buildup of production capacities in the country's Far East region has turned Russia into an oil behemoth. As such, it once again sees itself as a great power. And some of Russia's neighbors say it uses petroleum as a weapon. In winter 2006, vitally needed natural gas stopped flowing from Russia to the Republic of Georgia, headed by a president who tried to defy Russian supremacy in the region. Russia blamed a technical problem — an explanation Georgians rejected. [55]

But the major concern for private oil companies and oil-consuming countries such as the United States is not a cutoff in service by a state-owned oil firm. The big issues are access to oil fields and participation in production ventures. "Access really is a consideration," said oil historian and consultant Yergin. "Where can you go to invest money, apply technology and develop resources and bring them to market? Terms get very tough." [56]

In an ironic twist, some state-owned oil companies that have grown enormously wealthy recently have ridden to the rescue of some ailing U.S. companies. Notably, the Abu Dhabi Investment Authority spent $7.5 billion on a stake in Citigroup, bailing the big

Ballard makes hydrogen fuel cells for use in cars. Hydrogen technology, attractive to many because it uses no fossil fuels at all, is getting a big push from the government — $195.8 million in research and development money from the Department of Energy. Electric and hybrid-electric car research is getting $50.8 million. [5]

Technical arguments aside, the PHEV is far closer to dealer showrooms. "There are no truly viable hydrogen fuel cells on the market today," acknowledged Bud DeFlaviis, government-affairs director of the U.S. Fuel Cell Council, a trade group. [6]

The argument that plug-in hybrids don't reduce energy consumption overall has been persuasive, because non-nuclear power plants burn fossil fuels. That issue is especially important on the environmental-protection side of the alternative-energy debate.

But a July 2007 report gives ammunition to the PHEV advocates. After an 18-month study, the Electric Power Research Institute and the Natural Resources Defense Council (NRDC), an environmental group, concluded that widespread use of plug-in hybrids would, in 2050, reduce oil

Toyota and France's state-owned energy company plan to develop recharging stations for plug-in hybrid cars in major European cities.

consumption by 3-4 million barrels a day. It would also cut greenhouse gas emissions by 450 million metric tons a year — the equivalent of taking 82.5 million cars off the road. "Our results show that PHEVs recharged from low- and non-emitting electricity sources can decrease the carbon footprint in the nation's transportation sector," said David Hawkins, director of the NRDC Climate Center. [7]

Those numbers might be persuasive, even in Texas.

[1] "Hard Truths: Facing the Hard Truths About Energy," National Petroleum Council, July 2007, p. 46, www.npchardtruthsreport.org.

[2] See Kenneth B. Medlock III and Amy Myers Jaffe, "Gas FAQ: U.S. Gasoline Markets and U.S. Oil Import Dependence," James A. Baker III Institute for Public Policy, Rice University, July 27, 2007, pp. 3, 13, www.rice.edu/energy/publications/FAQs/WWT_FAQ_gas.pdf.

[3] See "Take This Car and Plug It," *IEEE Spectrum*, July 2005, http://iee-explore.ieee.org/iel5/6/31432/01460339.pdf?arnumber=1460339.

[4] Quoted in Ken Bensinger, "The Garage: Focus on autos; 2 'green' technologies race for driver's seat," *Los Angeles Times*, Dec. 8, 2007, p. C1.

[5] *Ibid.*

[6] *Ibid.*

[7] See "EPRI-NRDC Report Finds Environmental Benefits of Deploying PHEVs," July 19, 2007, www.nrdc.org/media/2007/070719.asp. Report accessible at www.calcars.org/calcars-news/797.html.

bank out of trouble. (A Saudi prince is also a major stockholder.) [57]

Abu Dhabi already owned shares in Advanced Micro Devices, a computer chip manufacturer, and bought a major American private-equity firm, the Carlyle Group. A "sovereign wealth fund" owned by Dubai, another Persian Gulf city-state, was forced to back out of a deal to manage some major U.S. ports. (*See sidebar, p. 158.*) The fund bought fashion retailer Barney's of New York in 2006, as well as a $1.2 billion stake in a U.S. hedge fund, the Och-Ziff Capital Management Group. These purchases are only the tip of the iceberg, and have prompted public worrying by Treasury Secretary Henry M. Paulson Jr. and finance ministers from the industrial countries about a lack of transparency in high-stakes global investing by petrostates. [58]

In fact, geopolitics experts including former Central Intelligence Director R. James Woolsey say profits from these investments could find their way into the coffers of terrorists, putting the United States in the ironic position of financing both sides in the war against terrorism.

CURRENT SITUATION

New Conservation Law

At year's end, environmentalists and the auto industry finally developed a fuel-efficiency standard they could agree on. The agreement opened the way for enactment on Dec. 18 of the first major petroleum-conservation law in decades. In addition to the new gasoline mileage requirements for cars and light trucks (including SUVs), the law

President George W. Bush celebrates with House Speaker Nancy Pelosi, D-Calif., Secretary of Energy Samuel Bodman, left, and other lawmakers after signing the 2007 Energy Act on Dec. 19. The legislation raises vehicle fuel economy standards for the first time in 32 years.

demands a major increase in production of ethanol, the alcohol substitute made from corn or other plants.

Environmentalists and automakers alike say the new mileage standard is a breakthrough that ends a long standoff over different requirements for cars and light trucks. The latter category includes SUVs — a favorite target of environmentalists who call them gas-guzzlers.

Under the new system, the 35-miles-per-gallon standard applies to the entire fleet of new cars and light trucks, by all makers, sold in the United States. Then, each manufacturer would have to meet an individual standard — one for each company — based on each of its models' "footprint," a size measurement based on a vehicle's wheel base and track width.

The legislation does demand that separate sets of standards be devised for cars and light trucks. "That wasn't our favorite provision," Hobson of the Union of Concerned Scientists says, "but since the overall target — the 35-miles-per-gallon standard — has to apply across both of those fleets, it was a compromise we accepted."

Industry leaders expressed support as well. "This tough, national fuel economy bill will be good for both consumers and energy security," Dave McCurdy, president of the Alliance of Automobile Manufacturers, said in a statement. "We support its passage." [59] McCurdy is a Democratic ex-House member from Oklahoma. The alliance is made up of the Big 3 U.S. automakers and some of the biggest foreign-owned firms, including Toyota, Volkswagen and Mitsubishi.

Another endorsement came from the Association of International Automobile Manufacturers. "It's not perfect, but I think we're going to be pleased," said Mike Stanton, president and CEO of that trade group, which represents Honda, Nissan, Hyundai and others, including Toyota. [60]

EPA Blocks States

The era of good feelings between environmentalists and the Bush administration that opened with the Dec. 18 passage of the energy bill proved short-lived. The very next day, the Environmental Protection Agency (EPA) prohibited California and 16 other states from setting their own carbon dioxide emission standards for cars and trucks. Tougher state standards were designed to step up action against global warming.

But the new energy bill makes such moves by states unnecessary because cars will be polluting less because they'll burn less fuel, EPA Administrator Stephen L. Johnson told reporters. "The Bush administration is moving forward with a clear national solution, not a confusing patchwork of state rules," he said. "I believe this is a better approach than if individual states were to act alone." [61]

California Gov. Arnold Schwarzenegger, a Republican sometimes out of step with the Bush administration, immediately vowed to challenge the decision in court. "It is disappointing that the federal government is standing in our way and ignoring the will of tens of millions of people across the nation," Schwarzenegger said. "We will continue to fight this battle." [62]

Twelve other states — New York, New Jersey, Connecticut, Maine, Maryland, Massachusetts, New Mexico, Oregon, Pennsylvania, Rhode Island, Vermont and Washington — had proposed the same standards as California. And the governors of Arizona, Colorado, Florida and Utah had pledged to follow suit. Had the EPA decision gone their way, an estimated one-half of the new vehicles sold in the United States would have had to meet the higher-than-federal air-pollution standards.

McCurdy saluted the EPA decision, tacitly referring to the potential widespread effect of the state-proposed standards. "We commend EPA for protecting a national, 50-state program," he said. "A patchwork quilt of inconsistent and competing . . . programs at the state level would only have created confusion, inefficiency and uncertainty for automakers and consumers." [63]

Environmentalists say they are confident the states will win out in the end. The EPA decision is a "short-

Are higher vehicle fuel-economy standards good energy policy?

YES Michelle Robinson
Director, Clean Vehicles Program, Union of Concerned Scientists

Written for *CQ Researcher*, December 2007

Requiring automakers to build more fuel-efficient cars and trucks is the patriotic, common-sense thing to do. Strengthened corporate average fuel economy (CAFE) standards will reduce our dependence on oil, save consumers billions of dollars, create hundreds of thousands of domestic jobs and dramatically cut global warming pollution. And it can be done using existing technology. How could anyone argue with that?

The fuel-economy standards instituted in 1975, albeit outdated, worked. If our cars and light trucks still had the same fuel economy they did in the early 1970s, we would have burned through an additional 80 billion gallons of gasoline on top of the 140 billion gallons we will consume this year. That would have amounted to an extra 5.2 million barrels of oil per day. At an average price for regular gasoline of about $2.50 per gallon, we would have forked over an extra $200 billion to the oil companies.

After decades of inaction, Congress has strengthened the standard. Cars, trucks and sport utility vehicles (SUVs) will be required to average at least 35 miles per gallon (mpg) by 2020, a 10-mpg increase over today's levels. A Union of Concerned Scientists (UCS) analysis found this would save 1.1 million barrels of oil per day in 2020, about half of what the United States currently imports from the Persian Gulf. Consumers would save $22 billion in 2020 — even after paying the cost of the improved fuel-economy technology. It would prevent more than 190 million metric tons of global warming emissions in 2020, the equivalent of taking 28 million of today's average cars and trucks off the road. And the new fuel-economy standard would create jobs. According to a UCS study, the standard would generate some 149,300 new domestic jobs in 2020.

Clearly, requiring cars and trucks to average at least 35 mpg by 2020 is smart energy policy. However, a better standard by itself would not ensure that we would avoid the worst consequences of global warming or conquer our national addiction to oil. To tackle these problems, the federal government also must require utilities to generate more of their electricity from clean, renewable energy sources; enact a low-carbon fuel standard to ensure that alternatives to oil are produced in an environmentally friendly way and adopt an economy-wide cap-and-trade program. That said, improving fuel-economy standards is a big step in the right direction.

NO Robert W. Crandall
Senior Fellow, The Brookings Institution

Written for *CQ Researcher*, December 2007

Proponents of increases in mandated corporate average fuel economy (CAFE) standards often claim that they would be good for consumers, promote job formation and solve various environmental and energy-security problems. It is important, therefore, to disentangle these claims and to ask if there are not better options available.

First, any claim that raising fuel economy would be good for consumers and create additional jobs is surely incorrect. A highly competitive new-vehicles market delivers cars and trucks that are responsive to consumer demand. Any attempt to mandate greater fuel economy will lead to smaller, less powerful vehicles with more expensive fuel-saving technology than demanded by consumers. Inevitably, this will lead some consumers to hold their vehicles a little longer before trading them in. The result: lower consumer satisfaction, lower vehicle output and fewer auto industry jobs. Is it any wonder that auto producers oppose these proposals?

Second, any proposal to raise CAFE standards must be based on offsetting, non-market "externalities" associated with new-vehicle use. The current proposals are motivated in part by the desire to reduce carbon emissions, the precursors to potential global warming. But new U.S. vehicles generate a very small share of these greenhouse gases. To reduce carbon emissions efficiently, everyone on the globe should face a similar marginal cost of emitting a gram of carbon into the atmosphere.

Surely, it makes little sense to legislate mandatory reductions in carbon emissions (through CAFE) for new U.S. passenger cars while letting older cars, buses and trucks off the hook and — indeed — even encouraging the continued use of these older cars. More important, it is sheer folly to try to reduce global warming by setting high fuel-economy standards in California, Massachusetts or Hawaii while ignoring the much-lower-cost opportunities available in constraining emissions from coal-fired power plants or coke ovens in China, India, Europe or the U.S. Raising U.S. fuel-economy standards is a very high-cost approach, even by Washington standards, to reducing the threat of global warming.

Third, if the goal is to reduce oil imports for national-security purposes, increased fuel-economy standards are still an inefficient, blunt instrument. We burn oil in power plants, home furnaces, industrial boilers and about 250 million cars, trucks and buses already on the road. Any attempt to reduce oil consumption and, therefore, imports, should impose equal per-gallon costs on all of these alternatives. Higher CAFE standards will not do this and will even exacerbate the problem by encouraging Americans to use older gas-guzzlers more intensively.

term roadblock," says Eli Hobson, Washington representative of the Union of Concerned Scientists, which is active in energy-conservation issues. "The states will move forward."

Meanwhile, some lawmakers launched their own response to the EPA decision. Rep. Henry A. Waxman, D-Calif., chairman of the House Committee on Oversight and Government Reform, as well as Sen. Boxer, announced they had begun investigating the action. Waxman warned the EPA staff to "preserve all documents" relating to the decision. [64]

New Paradigm

China and India aren't the only countries that have some oil-watchers worrying about global oil supplies. Traditional oil-exporting countries are now using more of their petroleum for their own needs, shipping less to foreign buyers.

Saudi Arabia, for example, consumed 2 million barrels a day more in 2006 than in 2005, a one-year increase of 6.2 percent. Some projections have Saudi Arabia burning more than one-third of its oil by 2020. [65]

The Middle East isn't alone in putting its own oil to work in newly expanded fleets of cars, as well as homes and factories. Even countries such as Mexico, whose oil fields are said to be nearly played out, are consuming more and shipping less. "Production is declining in Mexico," says West of PFC Energy, in part because the national oil company has been lax in exploration and maintenance.

"One country that's making a huge investment is Saudi Arabia," West says. "They're going to raise production capacity to about 12.5 million barrels a day, with surge capacity to 15 million barrels a day. My people are skeptical they can do more."

Saudi Arabia also has an aggressive and ambitious industrial expansion program on the drawing boards or already under way, including aluminum smelters, petrochemical plants, copper refineries and new power plants. But Saudi industrialist Abdallah Dabbagh, director of the Saudi Arabian Mining Co., which is building a smelter, confessed some doubt to The Wall Street Journal. "I think the Saudi government will have to stop and think at some point if this is the best utilization of Saudi's crude." [66]

At street level, new cars are clogging the streets and highways of most of the world's oil giants, in large part because government subsidies keep gasoline prices low.

Saudi Arabians, whose home electricity costs are also subsidized, typically leave their air conditioners running when they go on vacation. Air conditioning accounts for nearly two-thirds of Saudi Arabia's electricity production. [67]

In Venezuela, motorists pay 7 cents a gallon. As a result, Hummers — perhaps the ultimate in gas-guzzling SUVs — are much in demand. The seeming disconnect between Venezuela's growing fleet of massive vehicles and President Chávez' plans for a socialist society prompted an outburst from the president. "What kind of a revolution is this — one of Hummers?" Chávez asked on his television show in October. [68]

And in Iran, where gasoline costs only slightly more, a government attempt in 2007 to cut back on consumption by rationing — instead of cutting or lessening the subsidy — caused violent street protests. Venezuelans predict the same thing would happen if their gasoline subsidy disappeared or shrank. [69]

Concern about consumption is an issue that also applies to China and India — can they be persuaded to moderate their taste for the same amenities that people in developed countries have been enjoying for decades? The International Energy Agency says the issue isn't one of fairness but of numbers. "A level of per-capita income in China and India comparable with that of the industrialized countries would, on today's model, require a level of energy use beyond the world's energy resource endowment." [70]

By comparison, the question of whether Saudi Arabia should be building more power plants to fuel more air conditioners seems like an easier question — at least for non-Saudis.

OUTLOOK

Production Crunch?

Dire predictions invariably swirl around the question of Earth's energy resources. Oil historian and consultant Yergin counts present-day forecasts of imminent decline as the fifth set of such predictions since the petroleum industry began. "Cycles of shortage and surplus characterize the entire history of the oil industry," he wrote in 2005, dismissing the idea that this phase is inherently different. [71]

Still, even some oil-watchers who agree with Yergin on the fundamentals argue that the global panorama has changed enough to cause serious problems in the near term.

If world economic growth stays on track, says West of PFC Energy, "We believe in the likelihood of a production crunch coming between 2012 and 2014. The economic impact will be severe and the geopolitical impact will be severe."

The end result could be heightened competition for resources and "massive" transfer of wealth to oil-producing countries, West says.

To avoid such an outcome, research needs to focus — quickly — on finding technology that provides an alternative to petroleum as an energy source, West says.

"What energy research should do is prioritize limited numbers of areas, whether it's battery efficiency, or light materials with which to build automobiles." Up to now, he says, research has been unfocused.

The Brookings Institution's Sandalow argues that research has already developed a solution that's ready to go — "plug-in hybrids" — hybrid cars that are converted to recharge their electric motors on household current. Sandalow drives one himself. "In 10 years, all Americans will be aware of the option of buying a car that plugs into the power grid," he says. "We have a vast infrastructure for generating electricity in this country that does us almost no good for getting off oil. This is the breakthrough."

As he envisions it, the president could order all government vehicles to use plug-in technology. Overloads of the electricity system would be avoided by drivers plugging in at night, using reserve capacity that utilities build into their systems.

But some energy experts sound a note of caution. Hirsch, who directed the peak-oil study for the Department of Energy, supports plug-ins but says they can create as many problems as they solve. "Imagine you have a lot of plug-in hybrids, enough to make a difference in U.S. oil consumption. Recharging them in off-peak hours — you can do that for a while. But if you're going to have a big impact, then you're going to have to build a lot of power plants."

In general, Hirsch sees an unhappy energy future not very far down the road. Oil supplies will shrink, he says. "I think there's not much question we will be in serious, long-term recession, deepening recession," he says. "With oil shortages, you'll have much higher prices — and shortages meaning you just simply won't be able to get it."

The world economy will adjust, Hirsch says, but until then, "It's not a pretty picture. Companies will be cut-

Saudi Arabia, Canada Have Biggest Reserves

Saudi Arabia and Canada lead the world in oil reserves, with nearly 450 billion barrels — more than half as much as the next 10 nations combined.

Rank	Country	Barrels (in billions)
1.	Saudi Arabia	262.3
2.	Canada	179.2
3.	Iran	136.3
4.	Iraq	115.0
5.	Kuwait	101.5
6.	United Arab Emirates	97.8
7.	Venezuela	80.0
8.	Russia	60.0
9.	Libya	41.5
10.	Nigeria	36.2
11.	Kazakhstan	30.0
12.	United States	21.8

* As of Jan. 1, 2007

Source: "World Proved Reserves of Oil and Natural Gas, Most Recent Estimates," Energy Information Administration, Jan. 9, 2007

ting back on employment; a lot of people will lose their homes because they can't afford to meet mortgages. International trade will go down."

Energy analyst Medlock at the Baker Institute is far less pessimistic. "I see conservation forces coming to bear over the next decade, which will tend to trim the growth of demand. I do see new supplies coming on line, and a major interest in developing unconventional oil."

Such developments would avoid the continued price spikes that some predict. "I think it's well within the range of possibility to see oil prices in the range of $60 to $70 a barrel," Medlock says.

Simmons, widely seen as the leading voice of the peak oil thesis, sees no grounds for such optimism. Oil producers can indeed use natural gas liquids and other unconventional sources of energy to make up a shortfall in crude oil supplies, but that will only hasten the day when the real crunch begins, he says. "We are basically living on borrowed time," he says. The gap between demand and supply "creates social chaos and war" by 2020.

Or, in the best of all possible worlds, Simmons says, a government-directed effort will come up with alternatives to petroleum. "But if we spend three more years arguing if it's time to get into a program like that," he says, the future is grim.

Gheit, the veteran oilman now on Wall Street, dismisses all such talk.

Oil-exploration and production technology isn't standing still and will enable oil companies to keep producing petroleum, he says. "I can assure people we are not going to run out of oil any time soon."

NOTES

1. David Sandalow, *Freedom From Oil: How the next President can End the United States' Oil Addiction* (2007).

2. Quoted in "Transcript: Interview with IEA chief economist," FT.com, Nov. 7, 2007, www.ft.com/cms/s/0/3c8940ca-8d46-11dc-a398-0000779fd2ac.html?nclick_check=1.

3. *Ibid.*

4. "World Energy Outlook 2007 — China and India Insights," International Energy Association, p. 41, www.worldenergyoutlook.org (only executive summary available to public).

5. Quoted in Jad Mouawad, "Record Price of Oil Raises New Fears," *The New York Times*, Oct. 17, 2007, p. C1.

6. For background, see Peter Behr, "Energy Nationalism," *CQ Global Researcher*, July 2007, pp. 151-180.

7. For oil demand statistics, see "World Petroleum (Oil) Demand 2003-2007," Energy Information Administration, U.S. Department of Energy, updated Nov. 5, 2007, www.eia.doe.gov/ipm/demand.html.

8. Daniel Yergin, *The Prize: The Epic Quest for Oil, Money and Power* (1992), p. 15.

9. Gretchen Morgenson, "Dangers of a World Without Rules," *The New York Times*, Sept. 24, 2006, Sect. 3, p. 1.

10. Robert J. Samuelson, "Is There an Oil 'Bubble,' " *The Washington Post*, July 26, 2006, p. A17.

11. "Fact Sheet — Prudhoe Bay," BP, updated August 2006, www.bp.com/liveassets/bp_internet/us/bp_us_english/STAGING/local_assets/downloads/a/A03_prudhoe_bay_fact_sheet.pdf.

12. Heather Timmons, "Oil Majors Agree to Develop a Big Kazakh Field," *The New York Times*, Feb. 26, 2004, p. W1; "Chevron Reports Oil Find in Gulf of Mexico," *The New York Times* [Bloomberg News], Dec. 21, 2004, p. C5; Alexei Barrionuevo, "Brazil Discovers an Oil Field Can Be a Political Tool," *The New York Times*, Nov. 19, 2007, p. A3.

13. Quoted in Steven Mufson, "U.S. Oil Reserves Get a Big Boost," *The Washington Post*, Sept. 6, 2006, p. D1.

14. "Crude Oil Production by Selected Country," Energy Information Administration, U.S. Department of Energy, November 2007, www.eia.doe.gov/emeu/mer/pdf/pages/sec11_5.pdf. For historical reserves figure, see Yergin, *op. cit.*, pp. 499-500. For Saudi Arabia reserve estimate, see "Crude Oil — Uncertainty about Future Oil Supply Makes It Important to Develop a Strategy for Addressing a Peak and Decline in Oil Production," Government Accountability Office, February 2007, p. 62, www.gao.gov/new.items/d07283.pdf.

15. Government Accountability Office, *ibid.*, p. 20.

16. Peter Jackson, "Why the 'Peak Oil' Theory Falls Down," Cambridge Energy Resource Associates, November 2006, pp. 2, 10.

17. "World Energy Outlook 2007," *op. cit.*, p. 64.

18. Quoted in "Transcript: Interview with IEA chief economist," *op. cit.*

19. "Testimony on Peak Oil, Dr. Robert L. Hirsch, Senior Energy Program Advisor, SAIC," House Subcommittee on Energy and Air Quality, Dec. 7, 2005, http://energycommerce.house.gov/reparchives/108/Hearings/12072005hearing1733/Hirsch.pdf.

20. "Peak Oil Theory — 'World Running Out of Oil Soon' — Is Faulty; Could Distort Policy and Energy Debate," Cambridge Energy Research Associates, (press release), Nov. 14, 2006, www.cera.com/aspx/

cda/public1/news/pressReleases/pressReleaseDetails.aspx?CID=8444.

21. "Crude Oil — Uncertainty about Future Oil Supply . . .," *op. cit.*, p. 4.

22. *Ibid.*

23. See Tim Reiterman, "Canada's black gold glitters but tarnishes," *Los Angeles Times*, July 8, 2007, p. A1.

24. Jackson, *op. cit.*, p. 6.

25. Matthew R. Simmons, *Twilight in the Desert: The Coming Saudi Oil Shock and the World Economy* (2005).

26. Quoted in Thomas Catan, "UK prepares for the day the oil runs out," *Financial Times* (London), May 27, 2005, p. A20.

27. "World Energy Outlook," *op. cit.*, p. 122.

28. "USA Statistics in Brief — Population by Age, Sex, and Region," U.S. Census Bureau, updated Nov. 6, 2007, www.census.gov/compendia/statab/files/pop.html.

29. "World Energy Outlook," *op. cit.*, pp. 122, 77.

30. "Olympic Trials: China's bout with $90 oil," Lehman Brothers, Fixed Income Research, Nov. 16, 2007, p. 3 (not publicly available).

31. "President Bush Delivers State of the Union Address," The White House, Jan. 31, 2006, www.whitehouse.gov/news/releases/2006/01/20060131-10.html.

32. John M. Broder, "House, 314-100, Passes Broad Energy Bill," *The New York Times*, Sept. 19, 2007, p. A16; Steven Mufson, "House Sends President an Energy Bill to Sign," *The Washington Post*, Sept. 19, 2007, p. A1.

33. Quoted in Broder, *op. cit.*

34. "House Select Committee on Energy Independence and Global Warming Holds Hearing on State Efforts Towards Low-Carbon Energy," Congressional Transcripts, Nov. 14, 2007.

35. Robert L. Hirsch, *et al.*, "Peaking of World Oil Production: Impacts, Mitigation & Risk Management," Science Applications International Corp., February 2005, p. 5, www.projectcensored.org/newsflash/the_hirsch_report.pdf.

36. Kenneth S. Deffeyes, *Hubbert's Peak* (2001), pp. 1-5.

37. See "Crude Oil," *op. cit.*, Government Accountability Office.

38. Deffeyes, *op. cit.*, p. 134.

39. For background, see Behr, *op. cit.* Material in this sub-section is also drawn from Yergin, *op. cit.*

40. Quoted in *ibid.*, p. 615.

41. "Current SPR Inventory As Of Nov. 29, 2007," Strategic Petroleum Reserve, Department of Energy, www.spr.doe.gov/dir/dir.html.

42. "Speeches by President J. Carter Outlining the Critical Nature of the Energy Crisis and Recommendations for Legislation to Deal with Issue," April 18, 1977, *CQ Public Affairs Collection.*

43. Yergin, *op. cit.*, p. 702; "Imported Crude Oil Prices: Nominal and Real," Energy Information Administration, Department of Energy, undated, www.eia.doe.gov/emeu/steo/pub/fsheets/real_prices.html.

44. Yergin, *op. cit.*, pp. 699-703.

45. *Ibid.*, p. 718.

46. Doron P. Levin, "How Ford Finally Found the Road to Wellville," *Los Angeles Times Magazine*, March 10, 1996, p. 16.

47. See "The 9/11 Commission Report: Final Report of the National Commission on Terrroist Attacks Upon the United States," 2004, p. 48.

48. Neela Banerjee, "After the Attacks: The Energy Market," *The New York Times*, Sept. 13, 2001, p. A7; Brad Foss, "Gas Prices Shoot Up," *The Washington Post* (The Associated Press), Sept. 12, 2001, p. E4.

49. Gail Makinen, "The Economic Effects of 9/11: A Retrospective Assessment," Congressional Research Service, Sept. 27, 2002, p. 16, www.fas.org/irp/crs/RL31617.pdf.

50. Simon Romero, "Laissez-Faire My Gas-Guzzler, Already," *The New York Times*, Sept. 7, 2004, p. C1.

51. Quoted in Jeremy W. Peters, "On Auto-Dealer Lots, a Shift Away from Gas-Guzzling Vehicles," *The New York Times*, Sept. 1, 2006, p. C6.

52. *Ibid.*

53. Unless otherwise indicated, material in this sub-section is drawn from Behr, *op. cit.*

54. "China seals oil deal with China," BBC News, Aug. 25, 2006, http://news.bbc.co.uk/1/hi/business/5286766.stm.

55. "Millions in Georgia Without Heat," CNN, Jan. 24, 2006, www.cnn.com/2006/WORLD/europe/01/24/russia.gas/index.html. See also "Top World Oil Producers," Energy Information Administration, U.S. Department of Energy, www.eia.doe.gov/emeu/cabs/topworldtables1_2.htm.

56. Quoted in Behr, *op. cit.*

57. Steven R. Weisman, "Oil Producers See the World and Buy It Up," *The New York Times*, Nov. 28, 2007, www.nytimes.com/2007/11/28/business/worldbusiness/28petrodollars.html.

58. "Sovereign Wealth Funds: A Shopping List," DealBook, *The New York Times*, Nov. 27, 2007, http://dealbook.blogs.nytimes.com/2007/11/27/sovereign-wealth-funds-a-shopping-list/.

59. Quoted in John M. Broder and Felicity Barringer, "E.P.A. Says 17 States Can't Set Greenhouse Gas Rules for Cars," *The New York Times*, Dec. 20, 2007, p. A1.

60. *Ibid.*

61. *Ibid.*

62. Waxman letter to Johnson, Dec. 20, 2007, http://oversight.house.gov/documents/20071220111155.pdf; and Janet Wilson, "EPA chief is said to have ignored staff," *Los Angeles Times*, Dec. 21, 2007, p. A30.

63. See "Statement of President and CEO Dave McCurdy on National Fuel Economy Agreement," Alliance of American Automobile Manufacturers, Dec. 1, 2007, www.autoalliance.org/archives/archive.php?id=427&cat=Press%20Releases.

64. Quoted in Dave Shepardson, "Auto industry backs CAFE deal," *Detroit News*, www.detnews.com/apps/pbcs.dll/article?AID=2007712010414.

65. Neil King Jr., "Saudi Industrial Drive Strains Oil-Export Role," *The Wall Street Journal*, Dec. 12, 2007, p. A1.

66. Quoted in *ibid.*

67. *Ibid.*

68. Quoted in Simon Romero, "Venezuela's Gas Prices Remain Low, But the Political Costs May Be Rising," *The New York Times*, Oct. 30, 2007, www.nytimes.com/2007/10/30/world/americas/30venezuela.html?n=Top/Reference/Times%20Topics/People/C/Chavez,%20Hugo.

69. Ramin Mostaghim and Borzou Daragahi, "Gas rationing in Iran ignites anger, unrest," *Los Angeles Times*, June 28, 2007, p. A5; Najmeh Bozorgmehr, "Iran pushes on with fuel rationing in face of riots," *Financial Times* (London), June 28, 2007, p. A7. Also see Romero, *op. cit.*

70. "World Energy Outlook," *op. cit.*, p. 215.

71. Daniel Yergin, "It's Not the End of the Oil Age," *The Washington Post*, July 31, 2005, p. B7.

BIBLIOGRAPHY

Books

Huber, Peter W., and Mark P. Mills, *The Bottomless Well: The Twilight of Fuel, the Virtue of Waste, and Why We Will Never Run Out of Energy*, Basic Books, 2005.
A lawyer and a physicist argue that energy in all its forms is plentiful.

Sandalow, David, *Freedom From Oil: How the Next President Can End the United States' Oil Addiction*, McGraw-Hill, 2007.
A former Clinton administration official lays out a plan for reducing U.S. oil usage.

Simmons, Matthew R., *Twilight in the Desert: The Coming Saudi Oil Shock and the World Economy*, John Wiley & Sons, 2005.
A leading "peak oil" proponent cites evidence that Saudi Arabia has vastly exaggerated the amount of its oil reserves.

Yergin, Daniel, *The Prize: The Epic Quest for Oil, Money and Power*, Simon & Schuster, 1992.
An American oil expert provides a classic history of the global oil industry and its role in contemporary geopolitics.

Articles

Bradsher, Keith, "Trucks Propel China's Economy, and Foul Its Air," *The New York Times*, Dec. 8, 2007, p. A1.
China's reliance on trucking is growing by leaps and bounds, far ahead of the government's ability to regulate the industry.

Hagenbaugh, Barbara, "Gas pump gulps more of family pay," *USA Today*, May 17, 2007, p. A1.
Average American consumers suddenly are shelling out appreciably more to fill their tanks.

Hoyos, Carola, and Demetri Sevastopulo, "Saudi Aramco dismisses claims over problems meeting rising global demand for oil," *Financial Times* (London), Feb. 27, 2004.
The Saudi oil company responds to the first major stirrings of the "peak oil" movement.

King, Neil Jr., "Saudi Industrial Drive Strains Oil-Export Role," *The Wall Street Journal*, Dec. 12, 2007, p. A1.
Saudi Arabia's rapidly expanding consumption of its major product is making even some Saudi industrialists nervous.

Morse, Edward L., and James Richard, "The Battle for Energy Dominance," *Foreign Affairs*, March-April 2002, p. 16.
Two Wall Street energy specialists presciently examine the geopolitical effects of Russia's sudden emergence as a major player in world energy markets.

Murphy, Kim, et al., "Oil's Winners and Losers," *Los Angeles Times*, Nov. 24, 2007, p. A1.
High oil prices spell progress for some and disaster for others as new petroleum-market dynamics play out globally.

Rosenberg, Tina, "The Perils of Petrocracy," *The New York Times Magazine*, Nov. 4 2007, p. 42.
Focusing on Venezuela, a veteran writer reports that state-owned oil companies tend not to be models of efficient performance, nor reliable explorers for new energy deposits.

Weisman, Steven R., "Oil Producers See the World and Buy It Up," *The New York Times*, Nov. 28, 2007, p. A1.
Wall Street and Washington try to grasp the implications of oil-producing countries buying big chunks of major U.S. and European companies.

Reports and Studies

"Crude Oil: Uncertainty about Future Oil Supply Makes It Important to Develop a Strategy for Addressing a Peak and Decline in Oil Production," Government Accountability Office, February 2007, www.gao.gov/new.items/d07283.pdf.
The government should begin planning now for world oil supplies to peak, even if that moment is several decades away.

"Hard Truths: Facing the Hard Truths About Energy," National Petroleum Council, July 2007, http://downloadcenter.connectlive.com/events/npc07 1807/pdf-downloads/NPC_Facing_Hard_Truths.pdf.
The United States needs to rapidly prepare for a world in which oil is more difficult and more expensive to obtain, according to top energy experts and executives.

Medlock, Kenneth B. III, and Amy Myers Jaffe, "Gas FAQ: U.S. Gasoline Markets and U.S. Oil Import Dependence," James A. Baker III Institute for Public Policy, Rice University, http://bakerinstitute.org/ Pubs/WWT_FAQ_Gas2.pdf.
Two experts from a think tank in the U.S. oil capital explain the basics of energy use in the United States.

Rosen, Daniel H., and Trevor Houser, "China Energy: A Guide for the Perplexed," Center for International and Strategic Studies, Peterson Institute for International Economics, May 2007, www.iie.com/publications/papers/rosen0507.pdf.
China's manufacturing expansion, not automobile fleet growth, accounts for most of the country's rising oil demand.

For More Information

American Petroleum Institute, 1220 L St., N.W., Washington, DC 20005; (202) 682-8000; www.api.org. Lobbies for the U.S. oil industry; supports loosening restrictions on oil exploration on public lands.

Cambridge Energy Research Associates, 55 Cambridge Parkway, Cambridge, MA 02142; (617) 866 5000; http://cera.com. A widely cited consulting firm that provides public summaries of studies performed for clients.

Energy Information Administration, U.S. Department of Energy, 1000 Independence Ave., S.W., Washington, DC 20585; (202) 586-8800; http://eia.doe.gov. The government's energy statistics division provides access to a wide range of data on all aspects of oil and gas production and use.

International Energy Agency, 9, rue de la Fédération, 75739 Paris Cedex 15, France, (011-33 1) 40.57.65.00/01; www.iea.org. An organization of industrialized countries, almost all in Europe, that studies energy trends and recommends policies on conservation and related topics.

James A. Baker III Institute for Public Policy, Energy Forum, Rice University, 6100 Main St., Baker Hall, Suite 120, Houston, TX 77005; (713) 348-4683; www.rice.edu/energy/index.html. Nonpartisan think tank that sponsors research and forums on oil-related topics.

The Oil Drum; www.theoildrum.com. A collective blog (with separate editions for the United States, Canada, Europe and Australia/New Zealand). Part of the "peak oil" community; provides a discussion forum on issues of conservation and alternative energy sources.

Organization of Petroleum Exporting Countries, Obere Donaustrasse 93, A-1020, Vienna, Austria; (011-43-1) 21112-279; www.opec.org. The cartel publishes statistics, forecasts and policy documents on global oil supplies.

8

Buying Green

Jennifer Weeks

AP Photo/Alex Brandon

Actor Brad Pitt is spearheading the construction of 150 "affordable and sustainable" homes in hurricane-battered New Orleans. Activists say the key to protecting the environment is "buying green" — choosing products designed to reduce pollution and waste. Consumer spending accounts for about two-thirds of the $14 trillion U.S. gross domestic product, making eco-consumerism a potentially powerful influence on policy and the economy.

From *CQ Researcher*, February 29, 2008.

During Lent, many Christians commemorate the time that Jesus spent fasting and praying in the desert, according to the Bible, before taking up his ministry. Most churchgoers mark Lent by giving up alcohol, red meat or other luxuries. But this year two prominent British bishops called on the faithful to sacrifice something else: carbon emissions. Through steps such as insulating hot-water heaters, sealing drafts in their houses and changing to energy-efficient light bulbs, the church leaders urged observers to reduce their carbon footprints — the greenhouse gases (GHGs) emitted from human activities that contribute to global climate change. "We all have a pivotal role to play in tackling the stark reality of climate change," said Richard Chartres, Bishop of London. "Together we have a responsibility to God, to future generations and to our own well-being on this earth to take action." [1]

Although they may not cast the issue in religious terms, Americans are increasingly willing to take personal action to protect the environment. And while conservation has long been associated with sacrifices, such as driving smaller cars and turning down the heat, today some advocates argue that a comfortable lifestyle can be eco-friendly. The key, they say, is "buying green" — choosing products designed to reduce pollution, waste and other harmful impacts.

Activists have long recognized that consumer spending, which accounts for about two-thirds of the $14 trillion U.S. gross domestic product, can be a powerful influence on national policy. Consumer campaigns often stigmatize a product to highlight suppliers' unacceptable behavior. For example, civil rights activists in the 1950s and '60s boycotted segregated buses in Montgomery, Ala., and held sit-ins at lunch counters that refused to serve African-Americans. Both

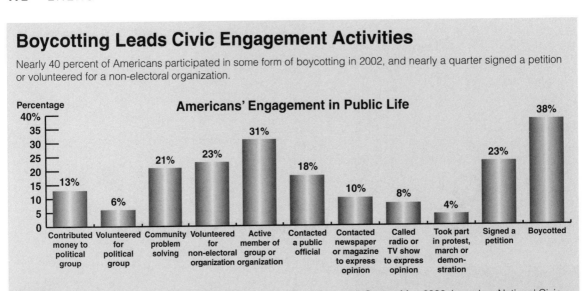

Boycotting Leads Civic Engagement Activities

Nearly 40 percent of Americans participated in some form of boycotting in 2002, and nearly a quarter signed a petition or volunteered for a non-electoral organization.

Americans' Engagement in Public Life

Percentage

Contributed money to political group	13%
Volunteered for political group	6%
Community problem solving	21%
Volunteered for non-electoral organization	23%
Active member of group or organization	31%
Contacted a public official	18%
Contacted newspaper or magazine to express opinion	10%
Called radio or TV show to express opinion	8%
Took part in protest, march or demonstration	4%
Signed a petition	23%
Boycotted	38%

Source: Scott Keeter, "Politics and the 'DotNet' Generation," Pew Research Center, May 2006, based on National Civic Engagement Survey 2002

strategies drew national attention to segregation in the South and built support for new civil rights laws.

Consumers can also reward positive behavior with their dollars. In the 1970s, the garment workers' union urged Americans to "Look for the union label" that identified clothing made in the United States instead of choosing products from low-wage foreign sources. Today eco-conscious shoppers are buying organically grown food, fuel-efficient cars and shares in socially responsible investment funds that target companies with strong environmental records.

According to the annual Green Brands Survey, U.S. consumers will spend about $500 billion on environmentally friendly products and services in 2008, double last year's amount. [2] A typical American family spends roughly $50,000 each year on food, clothing, shelter, transportation, health care, entertainment and other items. [3] (*See graph, p. 173.*) And consumers frequently use buying power to communicate their opinions: Boycotting or "buycotting" (deliberately choosing) products for political or ethical reasons are among the most common ways in which Americans express political views. [4] (*See graph, above.*)

"The consumer movement has quietly become part of the fabric of American society," says Caroline Heldman, an assistant professor of politics at Occidental College in Los Angeles and author of a forthcoming book on con-

sumer activism. "Environmental concerns are the most important motives that drive people to engage in consumer activism, and with concern about global warming so high, the public is primed to act if environmental groups can find tangible things for people to do."

However, not all green products deliver on their promises. Since it first issued guidelines for environmental marketing in 1990, the Federal Trade Commission (FTC) has acted against 37 companies for misleading consumers with green claims. [5] A recent survey by TerraChoice, an environmental marketing firm, suggests that "greenwashing" — making misleading environmental claims about a company or product — is becoming more pervasive as companies bring new green products to market. In a review of 1,108 consumer products that made environmental claims, TerraChoice found that all but one provided some form of false or misleading information. (*See sidebar, p. 180.*)

"Green labeling today is where auto-safety information was in the 1950s. Standards and certification programs are still emerging," says TerraChoice Vice President Scot Case. "This is unexplored territory, so marketers may be stretching the truth unintentionally. We think that the sudden interest in green just caught a lot of people off guard, and marketers were busy slapping buzzwords on packaging. But FTC's guidelines are clearly 15 to 20 years out of date."

Many issues are spurring interest in green products. In 2007 the Intergovernmental Panel on Climate Change, an international scientific association created to advise national governments, called global warming unequivocal and concluded with at least 90 percent certainty that human activities since 1750 had warmed the planet. [6] Repeated warnings about climate change are prompting many companies and individuals to shrink their carbon footprints. New products like renewable energy certificates and carbon offsets, which allow buyers to pay for green actions that happen elsewhere, make this task easier. (*See glossary, p. 174.*) But critics say that these commodities are feel-good gestures and do not always promote new, clean technologies.

Recent cases of contaminated food and toxic ingredients in common household products like pet food and toothpaste also are spurring consumers to seek out green alternatives. [7] Green consumption is a logical response to environmental threats, but Andrew Szasz, a sociologist at the University of California, Santa Cruz, believes that it could actually threaten environmental progress if consumers see it as a substitute for political action.

"A lot of people get environmentally conscious enough to get worried. Then they go buy everything green that they can afford and move on to something else," says Szasz, who calls the trend an example of "inverted quarantine" — citizens protecting themselves from danger by building barriers instead of organizing to reduce the threat. "Pressure from social movements to take toxic substances out of our water and air will create more progress than individual consumer actions," he argues.

Eco-consumption mirrors a similar trend in the business sector. Many U.S. companies are working to green their operations, both to appeal to the fast-growing market and because leaders are finding that environmental strategies can help cut costs and make their operations more efficient. [8] Many large corporations that have clashed with environmentalists in the past, such as DuPont, Monsanto and Waste Management, Inc., now highlight their commitments to environmental stewardship and sustainability. [9]

In a notable sign of corporate greening, the U.S. Climate Action Partnership (a coalition including Alcoa, General Electric, Shell and Xerox) called in early 2007 for prompt mandatory limits to slow and reverse the growth of GHG emissions. Many large companies have opposed mandatory GHG limits in the past, arguing that

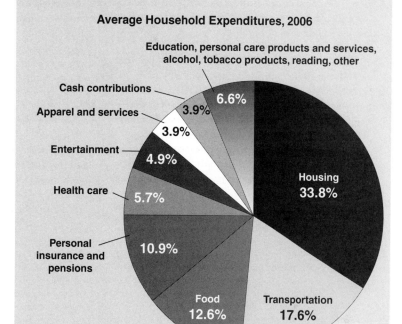

Average Household Spends Nearly $50,000

The average household spent $48,398 in 2006, including more than one-third on housing and 18 percent on transportation. According to a recent survey, U.S. consumers will spend about $500 billion on environmentally friendly products and services in 2008, double last year's amount.

Average Household Expenditures, 2006

- Education, personal care products and services, alcohol, tobacco products, reading, other: 6.6%
- Cash contributions: 3.9%
- Apparel and services: 3.9%
- Entertainment: 4.9%
- Health care: 5.7%
- Personal insurance and pensions: 10.9%
- Food: 12.6%
- Transportation: 17.6%
- Housing: 33.8%

Note: Percentages do not total 100 due to rounding.

Sources: Bureau of Labor Statistics; Green Brands Survey, 2008

A 21st-Century Carbon Glossary

The pollutant plays a key role in today's environmental efforts

Carbon footprint — The sum of all greenhouse gas (GHG) emissions caused during a specified time period by a person's activities, a company's operations or the production, use and disposal of a product.

Carbon neutral — Operating in a way that does not produce any net addition of GHGs to the atmosphere. For both businesses and individuals, becoming carbon neutral typically involves two steps: reducing GHG emissions that they generate directly, through steps such as conserving energy; and buying carbon offsets that equal whatever direct GHG emissions they cannot eliminate.

Carbon offset — An activity that reduces GHG emissions, such as planting trees to take up atmospheric carbon dioxide or producing energy from carbon-free fuels like wind and solar energy. Buying carbon offsets is a way of contracting out GHG emission reductions, typically because the offset project can reduce emissions more cheaply than the buyer can.

Carbon trading — Buying and selling GHG emission allowances (government permits to release a specific quantity of pollution) or emission-reduction credits, which may be issued by government under mandatory regulations or created by companies and individuals through voluntary trading schemes.

Greenhouse gases (GHGs) — Heat-trapping gases that absorb solar energy in the atmosphere and warm earth's surface. Six major GHGs are controlled under the Kyoto Protocol, but since carbon dioxide (CO_2) is the most abundant and causes the most warming, companies and governments convert their total emissions into CO_2 equivalents.

Renewable energy certificates (RECs) — Certificates that represent the environmental attributes of electricity produced from renewable sources and can be sold separately from the electricity itself. Investors can buy RECs to support green energy whether or not they are located close to the source. Some companies may market themselves as "powered by green energy," even though they use electricity from coal- or gas-fired power plants, because they buy RECs to equal their total electric power usage (thus helping to put that amount of carbon-free energy into the electric power grid).

putting a price on carbon emissions would drive up energy costs. [10] However, U.S.-CAP members contended that addressing climate change "will create more economic opportunities than risks for the U.S. economy." [11]

Corporate greening appears to be widespread but hard to measure because there is no authoritative definition of a green business. A recent report by Greener World Media found that green businesses are making progress toward some milestones, such as disclosing their carbon emissions and investing in new clean technologies. It also judged, however, that corporate America is treading water or falling behind on other targets, such as using more renewable energy and emitting fewer GHGs per unit of economic activity. "Green business has shifted from a movement to a market. But there is much, much more to do," the authors asserted. [12]

As environmentalists, business executives and consumers ponder what buying green can accomplish, here are some issues they are considering:

Do carbon offsets slow climate change?

Curbing climate change is difficult because greenhouse gases, especially carbon dioxide (CO_2), are produced from many routine activities like powering appliances and driving cars. Every year the average American generates roughly 10 to 20 metric tons of CO_2 through day-to-day activities, mainly through home energy use and transportation. [13]

Consumers can shrink their carbon footprints through steps such as adding insulation to their houses, buying more energy-efficient appliances and using public transit for some trips instead of cars. But if people want to do more, or have carbon-intensive lifestyles because they own large homes or travel frequently, they can buy carbon offsets from brokers, who use the money to fund projects elsewhere that reduce GHG emissions. Pollution offsets date back to the mid-1970s, when the Environmental Protection Agency (EPA) allowed industries to build new emission sources in regions with serious air pollution if they made larger reductions at existing sources nearby. This policy was written into the Clean Air Act in 1977 and later expanded to let companies earn and trade emission-reduction credits if they cut emissions below thresholds required by law.

"Offsets have an important role to play as we try to shrink our carbon footprint," says Mike Burnett, executive director of the Climate Trust, an Oregon nonprofit created to implement a 1997 state law that requires new power plants to offset some CO_2 emissions. The trust invests money from power plants, as well as businesses and individuals, in energy efficiency, renewable energy and other low-carbon projects to offset clients' emissions. "Oregon has pledged to reduce its GHG emissions 75 percent below 1990 levels by 2050. Investing in high-quality offsets can help us address climate change at the lowest overall cost, which will leave more money for other priorities," says Burnett.

The Climate Trust uses strict criteria to screen potential investments. Emission reductions must be rigorously quantified, and sponsors have to show that offset projects would not happen without funding from the trust — a concept called "additionality" to indicate that resulting GHG reductions must be additional to business as usual. For example, although installing underground systems at landfills to capture methane (a potent greenhouse gas produced when waste decomposes) is a popular type of offset, the trust would not invest in a methane-capture project if regulations already required the landfill operator to control methane emissions.

Not all providers are as strict. A 2006 study commissioned by Clean Air-Cool Planet (CACP), a New England nonprofit group, found that the market for voluntary carbon offsets was largely unregulated and had no

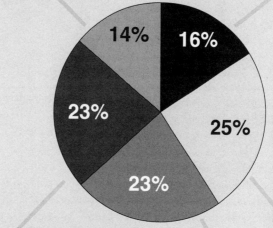

Some Buyers Are Greener Than Others

A 2006 study by the Natural Marketing Institute classified adult U.S. consumers into five categories based on their attitudes toward ethical consumption.

Unconcerneds — Do not consider social or environmental values in buying decisions.

LOHAS (Lifestyles of health and sustainability) — Make purchases based on belief systems and values, including environmental protection and social responsibility.

14% 16%

23% 25%

23%

Naturalites — Are interested in natural and healthy products, but their choices are driven more strongly by personal and family health concerns than by broader environmental

Conventionals — May recycle or give money to environmental groups, but do not shop based on a cohesive set of values; sometimes buy green products, especially items that offer economic savings.

Drifters — May believe in protecting the environment, but often think that measuring the impact of their consumer choices is too hard or don't know how to do it.

Note: Percentages add to more than 100 due to rounding.

Source: LOHAS Forum, "Understanding the LOHAS Consumer: The Rise of Ethical Consumerism," www.lohas.com

broadly accepted standards for defining or measuring offsets. Prices to offset a ton of carbon varied widely, as did the types of offsets available and the amount of information companies provided to customers. [14]

"There clearly are good offsets and not-so-good ones on the market, so the problem for buyers is finding the good ones," says CACP Chief Executive Officer Adam Markham. "If they don't buy good ones, they're not making a difference, and they're wasting their money."

A popular strategy that has raised questions is paying to plant trees. Growing plants absorb CO_2 from

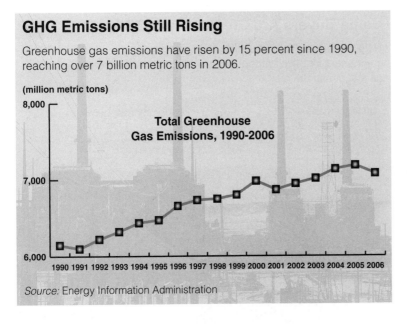

GHG Emissions Still Rising

Greenhouse gas emissions have risen by 15 percent since 1990, reaching over 7 billion metric tons in 2006.

Total Greenhouse Gas Emissions, 1990-2006

(million metric tons)

Source: Energy Information Administration

the atmosphere to make plant tissue, and trees also offer many other benefits, such as stabilizing soils and providing habitat for animals and birds. Movie stars Brad Pitt and Jake Gyllenhall, along with Home Depot, Delta Airlines and other corporations, have funded tree-planting projects from suburban Atlanta to Bhutan.

But trees don't always help the environment. Planting non-native species can soak up local water supplies and replace other valuable ecosystems such as prairie grassland. Moreover, calculating how much carbon various types of forests take up is an inexact science. And since trees eventually release carbon when they die and decompose (or are logged or burned down), they cycle carbon quickly and only remove it from the atmosphere for a matter of decades. In contrast, today's oil, coal and natural gas supplies represent much more permanent carbon reserves that formed when carbon-based plant materials were compressed in ancient, underground fossil beds. Burning these fossil fuels permanently releases carbon stores that have been sequestered for thousands of years and will not be recreated in the foreseeable future. [15]

"Forest offsets tend to be more risky because we know less about how much carbon they displace than we do for energy projects, and they're less likely to be permanent," says Markham. Instead, he prefers energy projects because it's easier to quantify the emissions that they displace and

demonstrate additionality. "Wind power and methane-capture projects tend to be pretty high-quality investments," Markham says.

But nothing is guaranteed. After the for-profit broker TerraPass provided offsets to help green the 2007 Academy Awards ceremony, an investigation by *Business Week* magazine found that six projects that generated TerraPass offsets would have taken place in any case. One, a methane-capture system installed by Waste Management, Inc. at an Arkansas landfill, was initiated in response to pressure from state regulators. TerraPass's investment was "just icing on the cake" for another project, a county official in North Carolina told *Business Week.* [16]

"There are a lot of new entrants into the market, so some offerings probably aren't as robust as others, and it's causing some confusion," says Burnett. "If this sector doesn't become more standardized within the next five years, government will have to step in. We don't necessarily need a single federal scheme, but it would be very useful to have a federally sanctioned panel of experts who could review offset products."

Beyond the characteristics of specific projects, some critics argue that carbon offsets don't reduce climate change because they let people keep doing high-carbon activities, which the offsets counterbalance at best. Worse, offsets may serve as cover for carbon-intensive activities. For example, a recent report from the Transnational Institute in Amsterdam, the Netherlands, points out that British Airways offers passengers an option to buy carbon offsets for their flights but is also pushing to expand British airports and short-haul flights, which will increase the company's total GHG emissions. [17]

"Offsets may be tarnished by revelations of practices that aren't credible. That would be a problem, because these tools can be quite useful if they're applied effectively," says Thomas Tietenberg, a professor of economics at Colby College in Waterville, Maine. "The consumer offset market is facing an important moment in terms of its credibility. It needs to get some agreement about what the standards are."

Should government require green purchases?

Government officials often want to boost demand for green products, even if they cost somewhat more, because these goods reduce pollution, conserve energy or keep waste out of landfills. One option is to mandate the use of green goods and services. But critics argue that government interference distorts markets and that setting environmental performance standards may deliver inferior products.

Renewable energy is perhaps the most widely mandated green commodity. As of January 2008, 26 states and the District of Columbia had adopted renewable portfolio standards (RPSs) requiring electricity suppliers to generate certain fractions of their power from renewable fuels like wind, solar energy and biomass. [18] Advocates would like to see a national renewable-energy requirement, but so far Congress has failed to enact one.

Most recently, in 2007 the House passed an energy bill that included a 15 percent RPS requirement by 2020, with utilities allowed to meet up to 4 percent of their targets through energy conservation. Supporters argued that the measure would reduce air pollutants and greenhouse gas emissions from fossil fuel combustion and spur the growth of a domestic renewable-energy industry. But the provision was dropped after critics charged that it would raise electricity prices and penalize regions with fewer renewable resources. (*See "At Issue," p. 187.*)

"The market should be allowed to work things out. We don't support having the government impose a mandate that says, "Thou shalt do this," says Keith McCoy, vice president for energy and resources policy at the National Association of Manufacturers. "Utilities and regulators in RPS states are looking at the right fuel mixes for their regions, but we need to take into account what's possible in different parts of the country."

RPS advocates want a national standard to push states that have been less aggressive in developing renewable energy. A national RPS "is absolutely achievable," said Rep. Tom Udall, D-N.M., a sponsor of the measure, during House debate. "[B]ut the full potential for renewable electricity will be left unrealized without the adoption of a federal program to enhance the efforts of these states." [19]

Governments can also ensure that products are at least somewhat green by establishing content or performance requirements. Measures such as building codes and energy-efficiency standards for appliances are one way to remedy a common problem: Many buyers don't know much about products, so it's hard to choose the

Growing numbers of eco-conscious shoppers are buying organically grown food today. Demand for organic and natural groceries has made Whole Foods the nation's largest natural food market chain.

best even if they want to. "If you're walking around a house looking at it, you have no idea what kind of insulation is in the walls or how efficient the heating system is, but building codes set some basic thresholds for performance," says Colby College economist Tietenberg.

Forcing manufacturers to comply with new standards may spur technical advances, but it can also challenge businesses to meet the new goals. When new energy-efficiency standards for top-loading washing machines went into effect in 2007, *Consumer Reports* gave low performance ratings to the first models that it tested. The Competitive Enterprise Institute (CEI), a think tank that opposes excessive regulation, accused the Energy Department of ruining a once-dependable home appliance. "Send your underwear to the undersecretary," CEI urged dissatisfied consumers. [20]

"If these technologies really are that good, we shouldn't need laws to force them down people's throats," says CEI General Counsel Sam Kazman. "We don't think that promoting energy efficiency is an appropriate role for government, but if that's the goal, the way to do it is with an energy tax, which would reduce energy use and create incentives to develop energy-saving technologies. One big attraction of regulations is that the public doesn't see them as tax increases — people perceive them as relatively cost-free."

Today, however, those energy-efficient washers look better. "What a difference a year makes," *Consumer Reports* commented in February 2008. The best high-efficiency top-loading washers were performing better, testers found, and *CR* pointed out that high-efficiency models could end up costing the same or less than standard machines over their lifetime when energy savings were factored in. [21]

Posing the issue as a choice between a free market or regulations is misleading, says Bill Prindle, deputy director of the American Council for an Energy-Efficient Economy (ACEEE). "The real issue is what the rules should be for market players. When you set boundaries and targets, manufacturers come up with very ingenious solutions that give customers great value," Prindle contends. He also notes that manufacturers and conservation advocates have negotiated some two dozen energy-efficiency standards since 2005 that subsequently were enacted into law. "These are largely consensus-based agreements. They wouldn't have passed otherwise," Prindle argues.

Another way to promote green technologies is through voluntary labeling programs that identify environmentally preferable products. The Energy Star program, administered by EPA and the Department of Energy, was launched in 1992 in response to a Clean Air Act provision directing EPA to find non-regulatory strategies for reducing air pollution. Energy Star defines superior energy efficiency standards for more than 50 types of residential, commercial and industrial equipment, including consumer electronics, heating and cooling systems and lighting. [22] EPA estimates that over 2 billion products with Energy Star labels were sold in 2006, saving 170 billion kilowatt-hours of electricity, or enough to power more than 15 million average American households for a year. [23]

Another program, Leadership in Energy and Environmental Design (LEED), was developed by the U.S. Green Building Council to identify highly energy-efficient buildings with extremely healthy indoor environments. [24] More than 800 buildings in the U.S. and worldwide have received LEED certification by scoring points on a fixed scale for features like energy and water conservation and indoor air quality. Many large corporations and universities have built LEED buildings to demonstrate environmental commitments.

Labeling programs complement requirements to use green products, says Tietenberg. "Mandates make sense as a floor, but you don't want to stop there. Labels like LEED provide something that performs above the minimum," he says. "They let buyers know that they are getting a certain value for their investment and communicate that fact to other people."

CEI's Kazman argues that green labeling programs can also be problematic. "Consumers don't get the full story if labels omit repair issues and the risk that very new technologies will have problems," he says. "And once items earn stars, there's a risk that the next step will be to mandate them. But we'd rather have government give advice and make recommendations than impose mandates."

Is buying green better for the environment than buying less?

Most observers agree that today's green consumption boom signals the mainstreaming of environmental values. In the 1980s eco-friendly products like soy milk and recycled paper were of uneven quality and were viewed as niche goods for a small subset of dedicated customers. Today megastores like Wal-Mart and Target offer green cleaning supplies, organic food and energy-efficient light bulbs.

"We've seen green waves before, but today there's better understanding of environmental issues, higher quality products and more consumer understanding," says Case at TerraChoice Environmental Marketing. "This issue has penetrated the heads of the average consumer and business executive."

With more consumers buying more earth-friendly products, some advocates say that environmental protection no longer has to mean scaling back affluent lifestyles. Instead, they assert, we can shop our way to sustainability. "We all need to be presented with better product choices that enable us to maintain the way of life to which we're accustomed without overtaxing the planet's ability to sustain it," said entrepreneur and satellite radio host Josh Dorfman, the self-styled "Lazy Environmentalist," in a 2007 interview. "As a nation, we don't really want to deal with [global warming]. We have neither the political leadership nor the political will, which is why I think that for now the environmental solutions presented have to be both effective and painless." [25]

This is a new perspective for the environmental movement, which has long argued that rampant economic growth and high consumption are root causes of environmental harm. Not all environmentalists agree that so-called checkbook environmentalism can save the planet. For one thing, critics argue, the green product boom has had little impact so far on U.S. greenhouse gas emissions. Since 1990 the emissions intensity of the U.S. economy (the amount of GHG emissions produced for every dollar of economic activity) has declined, but total GHG emissions have increased nearly every year due to overall economic growth. (*See graph, p. 176.*)

"True, as companies and countries get richer they can afford more efficient machinery that makes better use of fossil fuel, like the hybrid Honda Civic I drive," writes bestselling author Bill McKibben. "But if your appliances have gotten more efficient, there are also far more of them: The furnace is better than it used to be, but the average size of the house it heats has doubled since 1950. The 60-inch TV? The always-on cable modem? No need for you to do the math — the electric company does it for you, every month." [26]

Complicating the issue, many green living guides fail to distinguish between actions that have a major impact, like insulating your house, and those with smaller effects such as buying a natural-fiber shower curtain or dog leash. "People tend not to sort through which choices are important and which are insignificant. They view most actions as equally important," says Warren Leon, coauthor of *The Consumer's Guide to Effective Environmental Choices* and director of the Massachusetts Renewable Energy Trust. [27] (*See sidebar, p. 184.*) "I worry about products that are sold as green, often by promoters who sincerely believe in them, but that either don't work well or don't have a serious impact. Mediocre or trivial green products will turn consumers off in the long run," he warns.

"Greenwashing" further undercuts the impact of buying green by marketing products with vague claims like "All Natural," "Earth Smart" and other labels that are too general to document whether goods will help the environment or not. Some consumers analyze these slogans critically, but many are likely to take them at face value. According to a 2006 study by the Natural Marketing Institute, LOHAS (Lifestyles of Health and Sustainability) buyers, who make purchases based on belief systems and values, including environmental protection and social responsibility, account for only about 16 percent of U.S. consumers. (*See graph, p. 175.*)

Although LOHAS consumers are a relatively small segment of the market, green business experts say that they have significant influence. "LOHAS consumers push the envelope. They're always testing the boundaries, and they make decisions for the sake of the mission," says Ted Ning, who directs an annual business gathering in Colorado called the LOHAS Forum. "Once their items become mainstream, they move on to the next issue. For example,

instead of just buying organic food or locally grown food, now they're choosing food based on its carbon footprint."

LOHAS buyers also size up companies critically, says Ning. "They expect a lot of in-depth information to show whether products are authentic. Blogs and Web sites give people lots of ways to communicate, so if companies don't make that data available, there's an assumption that they have something to hide. And LOHAS consumers are evangelists, so they're proud to share their information. If you get on their wrong side, they'll bad-mouth you to death."

Businesses are keenly interested in LOHAS consumers, who represent an estimated $209 billion market for goods including organic food, personal and home care products, clean energy technologies, alternative transportation and ecotourism. [28] But it's not clear that this group's preferences can steer the entire U.S. economy toward sustainability.

"Consumers are most interested in high-quality, affordable products. That's still a larger driver than other environmental considerations, although green aspects often are tie-breakers," says TerraChoice's Case. Recent polls show that while Americans are increasingly willing to make lifestyle changes to protect the environment, they prefer easy actions like recycling over more demanding steps like reducing their carbon footprints. [29]

"Green labeling and marketing are market-based instruments that can be adopted quickly as our environmental knowledge grows, but in the long term they'll be seen as transitional steps," says Case. "Ultimately, we'll address these issues with other mechanisms like cap-and-trade systems and taxes."

BACKGROUND

Conservation Focus

Before the United States was a century old, early conservationists began to warn about threats to precious lands and resources. In his 1854 classic *Walden*, Henry David Thoreau decried loggers and railroads that encroached on his forest retreat. In 1876 naturalist John Muir wrote that California's forests, which he called "God's first temples," were "being burned and cut down and wasted like a field of unprotected grain, and once destroyed can never be wholly restored even by centuries of persistent and painstaking cultivation." [30]

CHRONOLOGY

1960-1980 *Environmentalists use lobbying, litigation and citizen action to curb pollution. . . . Congress imposes new regulations on businesses.*

1967 Congress enacts Clean Air Act.

1969 Congress passes National Environmental Policy Act, requiring environmental-impact studies for federal projects with potentially significant effects on the environment.

1970 Millions of Americans celebrate Earth Day on April 22. . . . Congress establishes Environmental Protection Agency and expands Clean Air Act.

1973 Endangered Species Act enacted.

1974 Safe Drinking Water Act enacted.

1978 Homeowners in New York's Love Canal neighborhood force federal government to pay for evacuating them from houses built atop toxic-waste dump.

1979 Three Mile Island nuclear power plant in Pennsylvania partially melts down, stalling the growth of nuclear energy.

1980 Superfund law assigns liability and fund cleanup at hazardous-waste sites. . . . Ronald Reagan is elected president on platform calling for reducing government's role.

1980-2000 *Global climate change emerges as major environmental issue.*

1987 Twenty-four nations initially sign Montreal Protocol, pledging to phase out chemicals that deplete Earth's ozone layer; dozens more sign in subsequent years.

1989 *Exxon Valdez* runs aground in Alaska, contaminating more than 5,000 kilometers of pristine coast with oil and killing thousands of animals and birds.

1990 Congress creates market-based allowance trading system to reduce emissions that cause acid rain. . . . Federal Trade Commission (FTC) brings first enforcement case against deceptive green marketing, challenging claims for "pesticide free" produce sold by Vons supermarkets.

1992 Delegates to the Earth Summit in Rio de Janeiro, Brazil, adopt first international pledge to cut greenhouse gas (GHG) emissions. . . . FTC issues marketing guides for green products and services.

1997 International conference approves Kyoto Protocol requiring GHG reductions but lets wealthy nations meet some of their obligations with offset projects in developing countries; U.S. signs but fails to ratify pact.

1998 U.S. Green Building Council launches Leadership in Energy and Environmental Design (LEED) program for rating energy-efficient, healthy buildings.

2000 British Petroleum re-brands itself BP and pledges to go "Beyond Petroleum" by investing in clean energy.

2001-2007 *As environmental concern grows, more companies offer eco-friendly products. Skeptics warn of "greenwashing."*

2000 Department of Agriculture issues final rule for certifying organic food.

2001 President George W. Bush rejects mandatory controls on GHG emissions. . . . Following the Sept. 11 terrorist attacks, Bush urges Americans to shop to help fend off economic recession.

2005 General Electric launches "Ecomagination" advertising campaign to demonstrate its environmental commitment. . . . Kyoto Protocol enters into force, including credits for carbon offset projects in developing countries. . . . European Union members begin trading carbon credits.

2006 Democrats recapture control of Congress, increasing support for policies to boost renewable energy and curb greenhouse gas emissions.

2007 FTC initiates review of green marketing guidelines and environmental products, including carbon offsets. . . . Toyota Prius hybrids surpass top-selling sport-utility vehicles.

Congress began putting lands under federal protection with the creation of Yellowstone National Park in 1872. It also established scientific agencies to manage natural resources, including the U.S. Fisheries Commission (later the Fish & Wildlife Service) in 1871 and the U.S. Geological Survey and Division of Forestry (later the Forest Service) in 1879.

But politicians mainly sought to develop and use resources, not to protect them in their natural states. To settle the West, Congress passed laws like the 1872 Mining Law, which allowed prospectors to buy mining rights on public lands for $5 per acre, and the 1878 Timber and Stone Act, which made land that was "unfit for farming" available for $2.50 per acre for timber and stone resources. These statutes often allowed speculators and large corporations to exploit public resources at far less than fair market value. [31]

Environmental advocates formed many important conservation groups before 1900, including the Appalachian Mountain Club, American Forests and the Sierra Club. Their members, mainly affluent outdoorsmen, focused on preserving land for hunting, fishing and expeditions. One notable exception, the Massachusetts Audubon Society, was founded in 1896 by two Boston society women who opposed killing exotic birds to provide feathers for fashionable ladies' hats. Within a year the group persuaded the state legislature to ban commerce in wild bird feathers. Its work later spurred Congress to pass national legislation and support a treaty protecting migratory birds. [32]

Although early groups won some notable victories, most conservation work was mandated by the federal government. Congress and Presidents Theodore Roosevelt (1901-1909) and William Howard Taft (1909-1913) set aside many important tracts of land as parks and monuments. Congress created the National Park Service in 1916 to manage these new preserves. But national policy also spurred harmful development, such as federally funded irrigation projects to help settlers farm in dry Western states. With government agencies urging them on, farmers plowed up the Great Plains, destroying their natural grass cover and helping to create the Dust Bowl when drought struck in the 1930s.

During the long tenure of President Franklin D. Roosevelt, (1933-1945) several important conservation programs were launched even as Western dam building accelerated. The Civilian Conservation Corps (CCC), also known as "Roosevelt's Tree Army," hired more than 3 million unemployed Americans to build fire towers, plant trees and improve parks across the nation. More than 8 million people worked for the Works Progress Administration on projects including roads, bridges and park lodges.

These were top-down programs, writes anthropologist Michael Johnson: "The federal government defined the problems, defined the solutions and then 'fixed' the problems by employing lots of people . . . the average citizen had an almost blind trust in the federal definition of problems and solutions." Moreover, while the CCC and other initiatives treated symptoms such as soil erosion, they failed to address human actions like plowing and over-grazing that caused the problems. [33]

Environmental Awakening

As the economy grew rapidly after World War II, human impacts on the environment became obvious. Pollutants from power plants, factories and passenger cars mixed in the atmosphere to create toxic smog. Offshore oil-drilling platforms appeared along California's scenic coastline. And Rachel Carson's 1962 book *Silent Spring* warned that widespread use of pesticides threatened ecosystems and human health.

Alarmed environmentalists began fighting back. In 1955 they rallied against a hydropower dam that would have flooded part of Dinosaur National Monument in Utah. A decade later, a coalition led by the Sierra Club helped to block a dam that would have inundated the Grand Canyon. Conservationists won a big victory in 1965 when a federal court allowed them to sue against a proposed electric power plant on Storm King Mountain in New York's Hudson Valley. [34] Courts previously had decided such siting issues on narrow technical grounds but in this case held that groups not directly involved in development projects could intervene to protect scenic resources. Litigation quickly became an important tool for environmental advocates.

Congress passed several key environmental laws in the 1960s, including the Wilderness Act (1964), which created a process for protecting land permanently from development, and the National Environmental Policy Act (1969), which subjected major federal actions such as building dams to environmental-impact studies. But new disasters spurred calls for further action. In 1969 an offshore oil well near Santa Barbara, Calif., ruptured and spilled oil along 30 miles of coastline. Five months later Ohio's

The Six Sins of 'Greenwashing'

Misleading environmental claims are common

A perfectly green product may not exist, but some certainly are much greener than others, according to a recent study by Pennsylvania-based TerraChoice Environmental Marketing. [1] It examined 1,018 consumer products that made a total of 1,753 environmental claims and found that every product but one offered false or misleading information. The firm identified six broad categories of misleading environmental claims, or "greenwashing":

- **The hidden trade-off:** Marketing a product as eco-friendly based on a single green attribute like recycled content, without addressing other issues such as where its materials come from or how much energy is required to produce it.
- **No proof:** Making environmental claims without providing information backing them up at the point of purchase or on the manufacturer's Web site.
- **Vagueness:** Touting products based on claims that are too vague to have any real meaning, such as "Non-Toxic," "All Natural" or "Earth-Friendly."
- **Irrelevance:** Offering a claim that is true but not important or helpful to consumers. For example, some products are labeled "CFC-Free," but ozone-destroying chlorofluorocarbons (CFCs) have been outlawed in the U.S. for several decades.
- **Lesser of two evils:** Selling a product with an environmental label even though it belongs to a class of goods that is generally bad for consumers' health or the environment, such as organic cigarettes.
- **Fibbing:** Providing false information or claiming a certification, such as USDA Organic, that the product has not actually earned.

Greenwashing matters for several reasons, the study contends. First, consumers will waste money and may conclude that environmentally friendly products do not work. Second, greenwashing takes business away from legitimate green products. This makes it harder for honest manufacturers to compete and slows the rate at which high-quality products penetrate the market.

Indeed, greenwashing was a factor in the demise of an early wave of green consumerism in the 1980s, says TerraChoice Vice President Scot Case, but more scrutiny this time may deter cheaters. "We'll know if things are improving when we repeat the study in a few months," says Case. "We're hopeful that attention from the media and the Federal Trade Commission [FTC] will help."

Consumers who want to ensure that they are getting green products have several options. First, they can look for seals of approval from organizations such as EcoLogo and Green Seal, both of which certify green products based on multiple criteria. [2] These eco-labeling programs are standardized under a set of principles developed by the International Organization for Standards.

Consumers also can check product labels and manufacturers' Web sites for information that supports green marketing claims. "Companies should be very careful not to claim that things are green, only that they are greener," says Case. "They shouldn't suggest that just because they've addressed one issue, it's a green product." The FTC has published guidance to help consumers sort through green advertising claims. [3]

Although greenwashing may be pervasive today, TerraChoice argues that green marketing can be a positive force. "[G]reen marketers and consumers are learning about the pitfalls of greenwashing together," the report states. "This is a shared problem and opportunity. When green marketing overcomes these challenges, consumers will be better able to trust green claims, and genuinely environmentally preferable products will penetrate their markets more rapidly and deeply. This will be great for consumers, great for business and great for the planet." [4]

---

[1] TerraChoice Environmental Marketing, "The 'Six Sins of Greenwashing," November 2007, www.terrachoice.com.

[2] For more information see www.ecologo.org and www.greenseal.org.

[3] U.S. Federal Trade Commission, "Sorting Out 'Green' Advertising Claims," www.ftc.gov/bcp/edu/pubs/consumer/general/gen02.pdf.

[4] TerraChoice, *op. cit.*, p. 8.

Cuyahoga River caught fire when flammable chemicals on its surface ignited.

On April 22, 1970, the first Earth Day, more than 20 million Americans attended rallies and teach-ins

designed to force environmental issues onto the national agenda. Activists followed up with lobbying and lawsuits. In response Congress passed a flurry of new laws, including an expanded Clean Air Act (1970), the Endangered

Species Act (1973), the Safe Drinking Water Act (1974), the Resources Conservation and Recovery Act (1976) and the Clean Water Act (1977).

"Citizens across the country became aware of what was happening to their physical surroundings," writes journalist Philip Shabecoff. "Equally important, they also acquired a faith — not always requited — that in the American democracy change was possible, that they could act as individuals and communities to obtain relief from the environmental dangers with which they were threatened." [35] Slogans like "Reduce, reuse, recycle" and "Think globally, act locally" underlined the importance of personal action.

While national groups pressured Congress and the new EPA, grassroots activists attacked local problems. In 1978 residents of the Love Canal neighborhood in upstate New York, led by housewife Lois Gibbs, forced the federal government to pay for moving them out of homes that had been built on top of an industrial-waste site. Groups with names like the Abalone Alliance sprang up to oppose new nuclear power plants, blocking some and delaying others.

Businesses and free-market advocates pushed back. President Ronald Reagan was elected in 1980 on a platform that called for reforming regulation and ensuring that benefits from environmental controls justified their costs. [36] During the campaign Reagan argued that air pollution had been "substantially controlled" in the United States and that laws like the Clean Air Act were forcing factories to shut down. [37] When he installed anti-regulation appointees like Interior Secretary James G. Watt and EPA Administrator Anne Gorsuch, many environmentalists worried that their recent victories would be reversed.

Working With Markets

As the Reagan administration learned, most Americans did not support a broad rollback of environmental laws. Public backlash against proposals such as selling off millions of acres of public lands drove Watt and Gorsuch from office. But environmentalists still faced a Republican administration and Senate majority that opposed new controls.

In response some groups began working with the private sector and developing market-based policies. Proponents of this environmental "third wave" contended that if regulations were more cost-effective and flexible, industries could be persuaded to cut pollution instead of having to be forced.

Their most visible success was promoting tradable permits to cut pollution. EPA had started experimenting in the 1970s with programs that allowed companies to earn and trade credits for reducing air pollutants such as carbon monoxide and particulates. Business leaders preferred this approach because instead of mandating specific control technologies, it let them decide how and where to make reductions. For example, instead of installing pollution controls a company might make its operations more efficient or switch to cleaner methods or products.

When Congress amended the Clean Air Act in 1990, some environmentalists supported a cap-and-trade system to reduce sulfur dioxide (SO_2) and nitrogen oxide emissions that caused acid rain. This approach set an overall cap on emissions and issued a fixed number of tradable emission permits to sources. Factories emitting less pollution than their allotments could sell extra permits to other sources — giving polluters an economic incentive to clean up, advocates asserted. [38]

The SO_2 trading program went into effect in 1995 and expanded in 2000. Many supporters praised it for cutting SO_2 releases sharply at a lower cost than industry had predicted. [39] However, acid rain remained a problem in areas located downwind from major pollution sources, such as the Adirondack Mountains, and emissions trading did not prove to be a panacea for other U.S. air pollution problems. [40]

During the 1990s some economic experts began to argue that going green made sound business sense. By reducing pollution, the theory held, companies would make their operations more efficient, which meant that they would use less energy and waste fewer raw materials. "Innovation to comply with environmental regulation often improves product performance or quality," business professors Michael Porter and Claas van der Linde asserted in 1995. [41]

As one step, some companies forged relationships with large environmental groups. [42] McDonald's worked with Environmental Defense to design a paperboard alternative to its polystyrene "clamshell" hamburger package, and the Rainforest Alliance helped Chiquita Brands develop social and environmental standards for its banana farms in Latin America. [43] However, critics argued that by accepting corporate donations and putting business executives on their boards of directors, environmentalists risked becoming too sympathetic to private interests. [44]

Guidelines for Eco-minded Consumers

Here's how to have the most impact

For many consumers, the biggest challenge of buying green is not finding earth-friendly goods but figuring out which choices have the biggest environmental impact. Green buying choices can be complicated, and green products often cost more than conventional alternatives.

Moreover, as journalist Samuel Fromartz observes in his history of the organic food business, few shoppers buy everything from premium suppliers like Whole Foods. Instead, regardless of income level, they buy organic in categories that matter to them, such as milk for their children, and choose other items of lower concern from conventional or discount stores. [1]

To help eco-minded consumers focus on purchases with the biggest environmental impact, *The Consumer's Guide to Effective Environmental Choices* identifies the biggest environmental problems related to household consumption: air and water pollution, global warming and habitat alteration. Then, by quantifying environmental impacts and linking these impacts to consumer products and services, authors Michael Brower and Warren Leon identify three household activity areas that account for most of these impacts: food, household operations and transportation.

To address these issues, Brower and Leon urge consumers to take steps such as driving fuel-efficient, low-polluting cars, eating less meat and making their homes energy-efficient. [2]

"A green purchase can have at least three results," says Leon. "First, it can favor a lower-impact product over conventional options. Second, it may allow you to consume fewer resources over the lifetime of the product. That's why energy choices are important — not only does energy use have significant environmental impacts, but you will use less energy every time you turn that appliance on."

As another example, consider a gardener who spends several hundred dollars on outdoor furniture. If she chooses items made from sustainably harvested wood, she may preserve several trees in a threatened forest. But if she uses the same money to buy a backyard composting bin, she can divert hundreds of pounds of food waste from landfills (which produce greenhouse gases as wastes break down and can leak and contaminate groundwater) during the years that she uses the bin.

Third, Leon argues, some green purchases can favor new environmentally friendly technologies or industries with big

Some smaller groups stuck to more aggressive tactics. San Francisco's Rainforest Action Network carried out scrappy direct-action campaigns that persuaded Burger King to stop using beef raised on former rainforest lands and Home Depot to sell only sustainably produced wood. The Earth Island Institute used negative publicity and a consumer boycott to make tuna companies adopt fishing practices that avoided killing dolphins in tuna nets. And major groups continue to vilify companies like oil giant Exxon/Mobil, whose opposition to action on global warming and support for oil drilling in the Arctic National Wildlife Refuge made it a prime environmental target. [45]

The 1997 Kyoto Protocol applied offsets to climate change in a provision called the Clean Development Mechanism (CDM), under which developed countries could meet part of their commitments by paying for projects that reduced GHG emissions in developing countries. This process was designed to reduce costs by letting industrialized nations cut GHG emissions in locations where environmental upgrades were cheaper. (GHGs dissipate widely throughout the atmosphere, so eliminating a ton of CO_2 emissions has the same impact on climate change wherever it occurs.)

Shopping for Change

National environmental policy became more contentious after George W. Bush was elected president in 2000 with strong support from energy- and resource-intensive industries. Many administration appointees pushed to loosen environmental regulations, and President Bush reversed a campaign pledge to limit greenhouse gas emissions that caused global warming, arguing that doing so would hurt the economy. [46]

growth potential. "By joining the early adapters who reinforce demand for a new product, you can help create a perception that it's a success," he says. However, it is important to note that some products will never become market phenomena because they have small niche markets. Only a small fraction of the Americans who drink wine will buy organic wine, but nearly everyone has to clean a bathroom at some point, so green cleaning supplies have a bigger prospective market.

The nonprofit Center for a New American Dream, which advocates for responsible consumption, offers a similar list of personal steps to "Turn the Tide":

- Drive less.
- Eat less feedlot beef.
- Eat eco-friendly seafood.

Installing compact fluorescent light bulbs is one of several tips for responsible consumption recommended by the Center for a New American Dream.

- Remove your address from bulk mailing lists.
- Install compact fluorescent light bulbs.
- Use less energy for home heating and cooling.
- Eliminate lawn pesticides.
- Reduce home water usage.
- Inspire your friends.

"None of Turn the Tide's nine actions involve drastic changes in your life, yet each packs an environmental punch," says the center. "In fact, every thousand participants prevent the emission of 4 million pounds of climate-warming carbon dioxide every year."[3]

[1] Samuel Fromartz, *Organic, Inc.: Natural Foods and How They Grew* (2006), pp. 248-53.

[2] Michael Brower and Warren Leon, *The Consumer's Guide to Effective Environmental Choices* (1999), pp. 43-85.

[3] Center for a New American Dream, "Turn the Tide," www.newdream.org/cnad/user/turn_the_tide.php.

Stymied at the federal level, environmentalists looked for other ways to leverage public support for green policies. Many advocacy groups deepened ties with businesses to influence corporate policies and earn political support from the private sector. They also urged members to target their buying power toward green goals. "People got tired of the gloom and doom approach. They wanted to hear about solutions," explained Bud Ris, executive director of the Union of Concerned Scientists from 1984 through 2003.[47]

Even as scientific consensus increased that human actions were causing global climate change, President George W. Bush opposed calls for mandatory controls on U.S. GHG emissions. Instead, in 2002 Bush pledged to reduce U.S. GHG emissions per dollar of economic activity by 18 percent by 2012. "This will set America on a path to slow the growth of our greenhouse gas emissions and, as science justifies, to stop and then reverse the growth of emissions," Bush said. However, many analysts noted, even if the American economy became 18 percent less carbon-intensive, its total GHG emissions would increase during that time as a result of normal economic growth.

Many corporations joined voluntary initiatives, however, like EPA's Climate Leaders program or the privately funded Pew Center on Global Climate Policy, both to show stockholders that they were paying attention to the environment and to discuss what kind of climate change policies would be most workable for businesses.[48] These partnerships required companies to measure their GHG emissions and develop strategies for reducing them. Companies also began exploring options like renewable energy certificates (RECs) and carbon offsets to reduce their carbon footprints.

Some companies turned growing concerns about pollution and climate change to their advantage with products that were both high-quality and green. Toyota's gas-electric hybrid Prius hatchback, which promised drivers 60 miles per gallon in city driving, debuted with limited sales in U.S. markets in 2000. By 2005 the Prius had become a symbol of green chic, and Toyota was selling 100,000 per year. And after the U.S. Department of Agriculture finalized standards for certifying organic food in 2000, Whole Foods rode growing demand for organic and natural groceries to become the largest natural food market chain in the nation.

CURRENT SITUATION

Keeping Standards High

As consumer interest in green products rises, regulators and environmentalists are taking a critical look at definitions and marketplace practices. Strong standards are needed, observers say, to prevent a new wave of greenwashing and help consumers avoid wasting money.

"The nature of marketing is to puff up products. That's why we have labeling laws, and there are struggles over who regulates what," says University of California sociologist Szasz. "The first struggle is over how regulated a product like organic food will be and who will do it. Then once the rules are written, debate over practices like greenwashing takes place within those boundaries."

In late 2007 the Federal Trade Commission (FTC) announced plans to review its green marketing guidelines and new green products such as carbon offsets. [49] FTC's guidelines offer advice for manufacturers on a variety of green products, but the commission may issue specific guidance on carbon offsets and RECs.

"We want to learn more about what these products are, how they work and how much activity is going on in the marketplace. We're also exploring how marketers are substantiating their claims and what consumers need to know about these products that we can provide," says FTC attorney Hampton Newsome.

The FTC is not an environmental agency, so it will not set specifications for individual products. Rather, it considers questions such as whether labels provide enough clear information for consumers to make judgments. For example, according to agency guidelines, a bottle labeled "50% more recycled content" would be ambiguous because the comparison could refer to a competing brand or to a prior version of the product. A label reading "50% more recycled content than our previous package" would be clearer. [50]

"Marketers have to substantiate express or implied marketing claims with competent and reliable evidence," says Newsome. "How consumers understand the claim is key, because that determines their purchasing decisions, not what the seller intended." Under the Federal Trade Commission Act, which outlaws unfair and deceptive trade practices, companies that make false or misleading claims could face penalties including injunctions or forfeiture of profits.

Many organizations are working to help standardize carbon offsets and define high-quality versions. There are a number of issues to consider, says Colby College's Tietenberg. "Quantification is important. The fact that something reduces greenhouse gases is useful, but you need to quantify how much it reduces them," he says. "You need to ensure that the initial reductions prevail through the life of the offset — for example, if you plant trees and the forest burns down, you don't get the offset. And you need a tracking system to keep people from selling the same offsets to multiple buyers."

Advocates also want to make green certification programs more rigorous. Some have criticized the LEED rating system for green buildings, saying that its checklists are simplistic and give too much weight to small steps, like installing bicycle racks, and not enough to bigger ones, such as renovating a historic building instead of razing it. [51] But the green building movement remains strong: By 2010, trade publications estimate that about 10 percent of commercial construction starts will be green projects (not all of which may seek LEED ratings). [52]

Watchdogs also see room for improvement in the Energy Star program. In 2007 EPA's inspector general reported that the agency was not doing enough to confirm that Energy Star products (which are tested by manufacturers, not EPA) performed at the promised level, or to prevent unqualified products from being labeled as Energy Star models. [53] The Government Accountability Office also criticized relying on manufacturers to test products and urged EPA and the Energy Department to look more closely at issues such as how many products are purchased because of Energy Star ratings. [54]

More Mandates?

Congressional supporters of a national renewable electricity portfolio standard have pledged to bring RPS legislation up again this year. Countering the argument that this policy would penalize some states, a study by the

Does the United States need a national renewable electricity portfolio standard?

YES Gov. Bill Ritter, Jr., D-Colo.

From testimony before House Select Committee on Energy Independence and Global Warming, Sept. 20, 2007

It has been our experience that [a renewable electricity portfolio standard] creates new jobs, spurs economic development and increases the tax base all while saving consumers and businesses money and protecting our environment. In 2004, following three years of failed legislative efforts, the people of Colorado placed the nation's first citizen-initiated renewable portfolio standard (RPS), Amendment 37, on the ballot. While the effort was opposed by virtually all Colorado utilities, including the state's largest utility — Xcel Energy — the effort passed by a wide margin. The Colorado RPS established a goal of 10 percent renewable resources by 2015 for Xcel Energy (along with the other Colorado Public Utilities Commission-regulated utility, Aquila).

In 2004, 10 percent was an ambitious goal: a little over 1 percent of Xcel's electricity was generated from renewable sources at that time. Today, it is the country's leading provider of wind energy. Xcel will meet the 10-percent-by-2015 goal at the end of 2007 — nearly eight years ahead of schedule.

Xcel has done what all successful businesses do — it adapted. While Xcel originally viewed the RPS as a burden, it soon recognized it as an opportunity, and the utility is now a great example of the successes that will come from our New Energy Economy. . . .

Renewable energy development of the future is not limited to wind. In Colorado, we are fortunate to have a broad mix of renewable resources, including wind on our Eastern Plains, solar in the San Luis Valley and southwest part of the state and geothermal all along our Western Slope. . . .

The committee has asked how a national renewable electricity standard will impact technologies in Colorado. Developments in wind technology have led the industry to be cost competitive with fossil fuel generation, but we need similar developments in both solar electric as well as concentrated solar technology. With the appropriate leadership from the federal government, these resources have the opportunity to join wind as a primary source of renewable power. . . .

As we saw with the RPS in Colorado — we encouraged the market through the RPS, and the market has responded. Investment, research and development are following the establishment of the RPS. A federal RPS provides more markets for renewable energy, prosperity for Americans in the heartland and a more responsible energy future for our nation.

NO Chris M. Hobson
Senior Vice President, Research and Environmental Affairs, Southern Company

From testimony before House Select Committee on Energy Independence and Global Warming, Sept. 20, 2007

Southern Company opposes a national renewable-energy mandate. We believe that mandates are an inefficient and potentially counterproductive means of increasing the production of cost-effective, reliable electric power from renewable sources. We prefer to seek cost-effective additions to our generation portfolio based on technological maturity, technical performance, reliability and economic cost. . . .

Our estimates show that a 15 percent federal renewable-energy mandate would far exceed the available renewable resources in the Southeastern region. To replace 15 percent of the nation's retail energy by 2020 would require approximately 80,000 wind turbines of 2 megawatt capacity each, or 2,200 square miles of land — an area larger than Delaware — for solar photovoltaic arrays, or 87,000 square miles of switch grass fields — an area the size of Minnesota. To replace 15 percent of just Southern Company's retail energy by 2020 would require approximately 6,900 wind turbines of 2 megawatt capacity each, or 200 square miles of land for solar photovoltaics, or 6,000 square miles of switchgrass fields — an area the size of Connecticut. . . .

Because the renewable resources that would be required to comply with a 15 percent mandate are not available in the Southeast, Southern Company would be required to comply largely by making alternative compliance payments to the federal government. . . . Because of the limited availability of renewable resources in our region and the fact that most of what is available will likely be more expensive than the 3 cents/kilowatt-hour price cap, the majority of the $19 billion cost to our customers will simply be payments to the federal government. Thus a nationwide [renewable portfolio standard] mandate could cost electricity consumers in the Southeast billions of dollars in higher electricity prices, with no guarantee that additional renewable generation will actually be developed. . . .

Not every technology will be well-suited to every region of the country. We do believe that the use of renewable energy to produce electricity can be increased, and we intend to play a key role in the research and development needed to reach such an objective. This is best reached by the enhancement of current strategies to provide incentives for the R&D as well as the use of renewable energy as compared to the adoption of a federal mandate for a single standard across the country.

Many grocery stores have begun selling reusable shopping bags as an alternative to environmentally unfriendly plastic bags.

American Council for an Energy-Efficient Economy (ACEEE) projects that electricity prices would be lower across the U.S. in 2020 and 2025 under a standard like that passed by the House in 2007 (combining renewable electricity and conservation) than without an RPS. A more aggressive standard that met 15 percent of electricity demand with renewable fuels and 15 percent through conservation would push prices even lower, ACEEE found. [55]

"Including energy efficiency brings down wholesale prices," explains ACEEE Deputy Director Prindle. Efficiency and renewables also complement each other, he says, because conservation projects can be put in place more quickly while new renewable energy projects are sited and built.

But opponents are likely to fight any new RPS proposals in 2008. Energy producers in the Southeast maintain that a national RPS will penalize their region, and the White House threatened to veto the 2007 energy bill over its RPS requirement. "A federal RPS that is unfair in its application, is overly prescriptive in its definition by excluding many low-carbon technologies and does not allow states to opt out would hurt consumers and undercut state decisions," National Economic Council Chair Allan Hubbard wrote to congressional leaders in late 2007. [56]

First Congress may have to revisit another controversial green mandate — the Renewable Fuels Standard (RFS), enacted in 2005 and expanded in 2007, which promotes bio-based transportation fuels like ethanol and biodiesel. [57] The original RFS, which was adopted to reduce U.S. dependence on imported oil and cut pollution from transportation, required refiners to use 5.4 billion gallons of renewable fuels (mostly blended with conventional gasoline) in 2008, rising to 7.5 billion gallons by 2012. The new law mandates 9 billion gallons in 2008, increasing to 36 billion gallons by 2022.

Most biofuel sold in the United States is ethanol made from corn, although researchers are starting to make ethanol from cellulosic sources (crop wastes and woody plants), which have a higher energy content and require fewer resources to produce. For the moment, however, much support for the RFS comes from farm-state lawmakers and agribusinesses invested in corn ethanol.

Many observers believe that the RFS is poorly designed and is producing unintended consequences. Two recent studies suggest that the push to expand biofuel crops may trigger such widespread land clearing that it increases climate change (by destroying forests that take up carbon) instead of reducing it. [58] And by driving up demand for corn, which also is used in animal feed and processed foods, critics say the mandate is increasing food prices. [59]

"The RFS has a narrow focus on a particular technology, and it doesn't strike a balance between demand and supply," says Prindle. "Also, it will take a lot of new capacity to meet the targets, including inputs like water and electricity as well as grain. You have to develop a massive new infrastructure across the middle of the country [where most corn is grown]." Colby College's Tietenberg seconds this perspective. "Mandates should be performance-based instead of requiring a specific input," he says. "You want to make sure the standard is clear but that there are flexible options for meeting it."

Green Is Red-Hot

Amid these debates, green marketing is spreading across much of the nation's economy. Today green labeling is most commonly found on office products, building materials, cleaning products and electronics. "In the 20 years between the last green bubble and this one, the only people who expressed strong interest in green products were large institutional purchasers like government agencies, colleges and hospitals, so green labeling had a very business-centric focus," explains TerraChoice's Case.

But now the message is penetrating into new sectors. Transportation, for example, accounts for about 27 percent of U.S. GHG emissions and is a major contributor to regional air pollution. A decade ago gas-guzzling sport utility vehicles (SUVs) and light trucks dominated the U.S. auto market, but in 2007 sales of gas-electric hybrid Toyota Prius hatchbacks surpassed the Ford Explorer, long the top-selling SUV. [60]

Now, with gas prices high and new fuel-efficiency standards signed into law, U.S. automakers are terminating some SUV lines, converting others to smaller "crossovers" and putting more money into alternative vehicles. In 2007 General Motors unveiled a concept model of the Chevrolet Volt, a plug-in electric car that uses a small gasoline engine as a generator to charge its batteries. GM is still designing the Volt but hopes to have it on the market by late 2010. [61] Other companies, including Toyota and Ford, are developing plug-in hybrids that can be recharged at standard 120-volt outlets.

Home and personal care products are also becoming increasingly green, in response to consumer alarm over recent reports describing toxic, hazardous and untested ingredients in common consumer goods. For example, laboratory testing carried out for the Campaign for Safe Cosmetics in 2007 found detectable levels of lead, a neurotoxic chemical, in many brand-name lipsticks. [62] Another recent study found increased levels of phthalates (chemical softeners that have been linked to reproductive problems and are banned from personal care products in the European Union) in infants who were treated with baby lotions, powders and shampoos. [63] Toys, food and beverage containers, upholstery, and other goods have also been found to contain compounds known or suspected to be hazardous to human health.

But this area is a major greenwashing zone, with marketers often relying on slogans that have no standard meaning. "While splashy terms and phrases such as 'earth-friendly,' 'organic,' 'nontoxic,' and 'no harmful fragrances' can occasionally be helpful, the ugly truth is in the ingredients list," the environmental magazine *Grist* advises in its green living guide. [64]

OUTLOOK

Focus on Carbon

Whichever party wins the White House in 2008, it appears likely that the United States will adopt binding GHG limits sometime after a new president takes office in 2009. All of the front-runners for president, including Democrats Hillary Rodham Clinton and Barack Obama

and Republican John McCain, support cap-and-trade legislation that would sharply reduce U.S. emissions by 2050 — a timetable that many scientists believe is needed to avert catastrophic global warming. [65]

Many companies can read the writing on the wall and are working to turn the issue to their advantage. "The business community sees tremendous opportunity in green products. It's a chance for companies to push technology and come up with innovative solutions," says the National Association of Manufacturers' McCoy. "We're on the cusp of some fascinating discoveries that could help solve our energy needs. We need to consider what research and development incentives government can offer to facilitate that, with manufacturers and the business community involved." Even Exxon/Mobil, long one of the strongest foes of binding GHG limits, has started to discuss what national controls should look like. [66]

With mandatory GHG limits in place, will green consumerism still have a role to play? Many observers see buying green as an important piece of the larger solution. "The reality is that we consume products every day. This is not going to change any time soon," says Dorfman, the "Lazy Environmentalist." "So we have to find more environmentally conscious ways to consume if we want to maintain our quality of lives and not see them degraded by climate change. . . . However, the solutions have to fit our lifestyles or the great majority of us won't even consider them." [67]

But green consumption and business/environment partnerships are not substitutes for political action, says Colby College's Tietenberg. "You need policies to level the playing field. If some firms are out there doing more and it costs more, they may have trouble competing and lose market share," he argues. "But if government sets rules that create a level playing field, business will take the ball and run with it. Many businesses are asking for national standards now."

Consumers who want to make a serious impact with their purchases need to learn which steps make the most difference. "People have a limited understanding of their carbon footprints," says Climate Trust Director Burnett. "They don't necessarily know what kind of fuel generates their electricity, or how significant airplane flights are." And comparing products' full life-cycle impacts can get complicated. For example, today many consumers are debating whether it is preferable to buy organically grown food that is shipped over long distances to market (generating GHG emissions in the process) or locally grown food that has been raised using less earth-friendly methods. [68]

"Wisdom is a curse — once you learn about these issues, you can't overlook them," says LOHAS Forum Director Ning. "But as we confront more problems like environmental toxins that stem from manufacturing processes, people are becoming more aware of design impacts. They're trying to understand more about how products work, and producers are trying to learn more about sustainability. Now that these ideas are becoming part of school curriculums, and people are talking about them more, our consciousness is only going to grow."

NOTES

1. Tearfund, "Senior Bishops Call For Carbon Fast This Lent," Feb. 5, 2008, www.tearfund.org.

2. Penn, Schoen, & Berland Associates, "Consumers Will Double Spending on Green," Sept. 27, 2007.

3. U.S. Bureau of Labor Statistics, Consumer Expenditure Survey, 2000-2006, www.bls.gov/cex/2006/standard/multiyr.pdf.

4. Karlo Barrios Marcelo and Mark Hugo Lopez, "How Young People Expressed Their Political Views in 2006," Center for Information & Research on Civic Learning & Engagement, University of Maryland, November 2007; Scott Keeger, "Politics and the 'DotNet' Generation," Pew Research Center, May 30, 2006; Lori J. Vogelgesang and Alexander W. Astin, "Post-College Civic Engagement Among Graduates," Higher Education Research Institute, University of California, Los Angeles, April 2005.

5. U.S. Federal Trade Commission, "The FTC's Environmental Cases," www.ftc.gov/bcp/conline/edcams/eande/contentframe_environment_cases.html.

6. Intergovernmental Panel on Climate Change, *Climate Change 2007: The Physical Science Basis, Summary for Policymakers* (2007), pp. 3, 5. For background, see Marcia Clemmitt, "Climate Change," *CQ Researcher*, Jan. 27, 2006, pp. 73-96, and Colin Woodard, "Curbing Climate Change," *CQ Global Researcher*, February 2007, pp. 27-50.

7. For background see Peter Katel, "Consumer Safety," *CQ Researcher*, Oct. 12, 2007, pp. 841-864, and Jennifer Weeks, "Factory Farms," *CQ Researcher*, Jan. 12, 2007, pp. 25-48.

8. For background see Tom Price, "The New Environmentalism," *CQ Researcher*, Dec. 1, 2006, pp. 985-1008, and Tom Price, "Corporate Social Responsibility," *CQ Researcher*, Aug. 3, 2007, pp. 649-672.

9. For details on these companies' pledges, see www.dupont.com/Sustainability/en_US/; www.monsanto.com/who_we_are/our_pledge.asp; and www.thinkgreen.com.

10. For background see Marcia Clemmitt, "Climate Change," *CQ Researcher*, Jan. 27, 2006, pp. 73-96.

11. U.S. Climate Action Partnership, *A Call for Action* (2007), p. 3, www.us-cap.org/USCAPCallForAction.pdf.

12. Joel Makower, *et al.*, *State of Green Business 2008* (2008), p. 3, www.stateofgreenbusiness.com/.

13. CarbonCounter.org, www.carboncounter.org/offset-your-emissions/personal-calculator.aspx; Union of Concerned Scientists, "What's Your Carbon Footprint?" www.ucsusa.org/publications/greentips/whats-your-carb.html.

14. *A Consumer's Guide to Retail Carbon Offset Providers* (2006), www.cleanair-coolplanet.org/ConsumersGuidetoCarbonOffsets.pdf.

15. Ted Williams, "As Ugly As a Tree," *Audubon*, September/October 2007.

16. Ben Elgin, "Another Inconvenient Truth," *Business Week*, March 26, 2007.

17. Kevin Smith, *The Carbon-Neutral Myth: Offset Indulgences for Your Climate Sins* (2007), pp. 10-11, www.carbontradewatch.org.

18. Federal Energy Regulatory Commission, "Electric Market Overview: Renewables," updated Jan. 15, 2008, www.ferc.gov/market-oversight/mkt-electric/overview/elec-ovr-rps.pdf.

19. *Congressional Record*, Aug. 4, 2007, p. H9847.

20. "Send Your Underwear to the Undersecretary," Competitive Enterprise Institute news release, May 16, 2007.

21. "Washers and Dryers: Performance For Less," *Consumer Reports*, February 2008.

22. For details see www.energystar.gov.

23. U.S. Environmental Protection Agency, "Energy Star and Other Climate Protection Partnerships 2006 Annual Report," September 2007, p. 15,

www.energystar.gov/ia/news/downloads/annual_report _2006.pdf. According to the Department of Energy, the average U.S. household uses about 11,000 kilowatt-hours of electricity annually; see www.eere.energy .gov/consumer/tips/appliances.htm.

24. For details see www.usgbc.org.

25. Jenny Shank, "An Interview With 'Lazy Environmentalist' Josh Dorfman," July 2, 2007, www.newwest.net/topic/article/an_interview_with_ lazy_environmentalist_josh_dorfman/C39/L39/.

26. Bill McKibben, "Reversal of Fortune," *Mother Jones*, March/April 2007.

27. Michael Brower and Warren Leon, *The Consumer's Guide To Effective Environmental Choices* (1999).

28. LOHAS Forum, "About LOHAS," www.lohas .com/about.htm.

29. Patrick O'Driscoll and Elizabeth Weise, "Green Living Takes Root But Habits Die Hard," *USA Today*, April 19, 2007; Anjali Athavaley, "A Serious Problem (But Not My Problem)," *Wall Street Journal Classroom Edition*, February 2008.

30. John Muir, "God's First Temples: How Shall We Preserve Our Forests?" reprinted in John Muir, *Nature Writings* (1997), p. 629.

31. For background see Tom Arrandale, "Public Land Policy," *CQ Researcher*, June 17, 1994, pp. 529-552.

32. Massachusetts Foundation for the Humanities, "Mass Moments," www.massmoments.org/moment .cfm?mid=262.

33. Michael D. Johnson, "A Sociocultural Perspective on the Development of U.S. Natural Resource Partnerships in the 20th Century," USDA Forest Service Proceedings (2000), p. 206.

34. *Scenic Hudson Preservation Conference v. Federal Power Commission*, 354 F. 2d 608 (1965).

35. Philip Shabecoff, *Earth Rising: American Environmentalism in the 21st Century* (2000), p. 7.

36. Republican Party Platform of 1980, adopted July 15, 1980, online at The American Presidency Project, www.presidency.ucsb.edu/showplatforms.php?platindex=R1980.

37. Joanne Omang, "Reagan Criticizes Clean Air Laws and EPA as Obstacles to Growth," *The Washington Post*, Oct. 9, 1980.

38. See "Acid Rain: New Approach to Old Problem," *CQ Researcher*, March 3, 1991.

39. Environmental Defense, *From Obstacle to Opportunity: How Acid Rain Emissions Trading Is Delivering Cleaner Air* (September 2000); Robert N. Stavins, "Experience with Market-Based Environmental Policy Instruments," Discussion Paper 01-58, Resources for the Future, November 2001, pp. 27-29.

40. See Charles T. Driscoll, *et al.*, *Acid Rain Revisited: Advances in Scientific Understanding Since the Passage of the 1970 and 1990 Clean Air Act Amendments* (2001); Mary H. Cooper, "Air Pollution Conflict," *CQ Researcher*, Nov. 14, 2003, pp. 965-988; and Jennifer Weeks, "Coal's Comeback," *CQ Researcher*, Oct. 5, 2007, pp. 817-840.

41. Michael E. Porter and Claas van der Linde, "Toward a New Concept of the Environmental-Competitiveness Issue," *Journal of Economic Perspectives*, Vol. 9, No. 4, fall 1995, p. 99.

42. For background see Tom Price, "The New Environmentalism," *CQ Researcher*, Dec. 1, 2006, pp. 985-1008.

43. Daniel C. Esty and Andrew S. Winston, *Green to Gold: How Smart Companies Use Environmental Strategy to Innovate, Create Value, and Build Competitive Advantage* (2006), pp. 70-71.

44. Mark Dowie, *Losing Ground: American Environmentalism at the Close of the Twentieth Century* (1995), pp. 114-124.

45. For details see "Exxpose Exxon," www.exxpose-exxon.com.

46. See Mary H. Cooper, "Energy Policy," *CQ Researcher*, May 25, 2001, pp. 441-464, and Mary H. Cooper, "Bush and the Environment," *CQ Researcher*, Oct. 25, 2002, pp. 865-896.

47. Steve Nadis, "Non-Government Organizations (NGOs) Mini-Reviews," New England BioLabs, www.neb.com.

48. For more information, see www.epa.gov/stateply/ index.html and www.pewclimate.org/companies_leading_the_way_belc.

49. For more information see www.ftc.gov/bcp/workshops/carbonoffsets/index.shtml.

50. U.S. Federal Trade Commission, "Complying With

the Environmental Marketing Guides," www.ftc .gov/bcp/conline/pubc/buspubs/greenguides.pdf.

51. Auden Schendler and Randy Udall, "LEED Is Broken; Let's Fix It," *Grist*, October 26, 2005; Stephen Del Percio, "What's Wrong With LEED?" *Green Building*, spring 2007.

52. McGraw Hill, *Green Building Smart Market Report 2006*, cited in "Green Building by the Numbers," U.S. Green Building Council, February 2008.

53. U.S. Environmental Protection Agency, Office of the Inspector General, "Energy Star Program Can Strengthen Controls Protecting the Integrity of the Label," Aug. 1, 2007, www.epa.gov/oig/reports/ 2007/20070801-2007-P-00028.pdf.

54. U.S. Government Accountability Office, "Energy Efficiency: Opportunities Exist for Federal Agencies to Better Inform Household Consumers," GAO-07-1162 (September 2007).

55. American Council for an Energy-Efficient Economy, "Assessment of the Renewable Electricity Standard and Expanded Clean Energy Scenarios," Dec. 5, 2007, http://aceee.org/pubs/e079.htm.

56. The full letter is posted online at http://gristmill .grist.org/images/user/8/White_House_letter_on_ CAFE.pdf.

57. For background see Peter Katel, "Oil Jitters," *CQ Researcher*, Jan. 4, 2008, pp. 1-24, and Adriel Bettelheim, "Biofuels Boom," *CQ Researcher*, Sept. 29, 2006, pp. 793-816.

58. Joseph Fargione, *et al.*, "Land Clearing and the Biofuel Carbon Debt," *Sciencexpress Report*, Feb. 7, 2008; Timothy Searchinger, *et al.*, "Use of U.S. Croplands for Biofuels Increases Greenhouse Gases Through Emissions from Land Use Change," *Sciencexpress Report*, Feb. 7, 2008.

59. Randy Schnepf, "Agriculture-Based Renewable Energy Production," Congressional Research Service, Oct. 16, 2007, pp. 16-20; Colin A. Carter and Henry I. Miller, "Hidden Costs of Corn-Based Ethanol," *The Christian Science Monitor*, May 21, 2007; "Food Prices: Cheap No More," *The Economist*, Dec. 6, 2007.

60. Bernard Simon, "Prius Overtakes Explorer in the U.S.," *Financial Times*, Jan. 11, 2008.

61. "Chevy Volt FAQs," www.gm-volt.com/chevy-volt-faqs.

62. Campaign for Safe Cosmetics, "A Poison Kiss: The Problem of Lead in Lipstick," October 2007, www .safecosmetics.org.

63. Sheela Sathyanarayana, *et al.*, "Baby Care Products: Possible Sources of Infant Phthalate Exposure," *Pediatrics*, February 2008.

64. Brangien Davis and Katharine Wroth, eds., *Wake Up and Smell the Planet: The Non-Pompous, Non-Preachy Grist Guide to Greening Your Day* (2007), p. 20.

65. "Compare the Candidates," *Grist*, www.grist.org/ candidate_chart_08.html.

66. Jeffrey Ball, "Exxon Mobil Softens Its Climate-Change Stance," *The Wall Street Journal*, Jan. 11, 2007.

67. Jenny Shank, *op. cit.*

68. For example, see Mindy Pennybacker, "Local or Organic? I'll Take Both," *The Green Guide*, September/October 2006, www.thegreenguide .com/doc/116/local, and John Cloud, "Eating Better Than Organic," *Time*, March 2, 2007.

BIBLIOGRAPHY

Books

Brower, Michael, and Warren Leon, *The Consumer's Guide to Effective Environmental Choices*, Three Rivers Press, 1999.
Although somewhat dated, this guide prioritizes consumer actions according to the scale of their environmental impacts based on extensive data and analysis. Brower and Leon, both senior environmental experts, draw on research by the Union of Concerned Scientists, a national environmental advocacy group.

Esty, Daniel C., and Andrew S. Winston, *Green To Gold: How Smart Companies Use Environmental Strategy to Innovate, Create Value, and Build Competitive Advantage*, Yale University Press, 2006.
Two Yale experts on business and the environment show how green strategies can help companies manage environmental challenges and gain an edge over competitors.

Szasz, Andrew, *Shopping Our Way to Safety: How We Changed from Protecting the Environment to Protecting Ourselves*, **University of Minnesota Press, 2007.**
Szasz, a sociologist, warns that the current green consumption boom could have negative impacts if it turns people away from broader political action.

Articles

"Climate Business/Business Climate," *Harvard Business Review*, **October 2007.**
A special report on the business challenges posed by climate change offers views from a dozen corporate and academic experts.

Davenport, Coral, "A Clean Break in Energy Policy," *CQ Weekly*, **Oct. 8, 2007.**
A national renewable electricity portfolio standard would trigger widespread changes in the ways that utilities produce power and state regulators oversee them.

Elgin, Ben, "Little Green Lies," *Business Week*, **Oct. 29, 2007.**
Auden Schendler, environmental director for Aspen Skiing Co., argues that many corporate greening actions are misleading and empty feel-good gestures.

Farenthold, David A., "Value of U.S. House's Carbon Offsets is Murky," *The Washington Post*, **Jan. 28, 2008.**
Critics say Congress wasted money by buying carbon offsets that funded activities already occurring.

Finz, Stacy, "Food Markets Getting Greener, More Sensual," *San Francisco Chronicle*, **Jan. 27, 2008.**
Consumers want healthier food raised using eco-friendly methods, and the grocery industry is responding.

Koerner, Brendan I., "Rise of the Green Machine," *Wired*, **April 2005.**
Koerner explains how Toyota made it cool to own a hybrid car.

Lynas, Mark, "Can Shopping Save the Planet?" *The Guardian* **(United Kingdom), Sept. 17, 2007.**
Numerous corporations are entering the green product market, but observers argue that at heart green marketing is all about sales, not sustainability.

Schultz, Abby, "How To 'Go Green' on a Budget," **MSN Money, June 29, 2007.**
Many green products are more expensive than conventional options, but consumers can make a difference if they choose their purchases carefully.

Underwood, Anne, "The Chemicals Within," *Newsweek*, **Feb. 4, 2008.**
Many common household products contain chemicals that could be harmful to humans. Concerns about health effects are driving many shoppers to seek alternatives.

Williams, Alex, "Don't Let the Green Grass Fool You," *The New York Times*, **Feb. 10, 2008.**
Many suburban Americans would like to shrink their carbon footprints, but skeptics argue that a lifestyle centered on big houses and multiple cars is inherently unsustainable.

Reports and Studies

A Consumer's Guide to Retail Carbon Offset Providers, **Clean Air-Cool Planet, 2006, www.cleanair-cool-planet.org/ConsumersGuidetoCarbonOffsets.pdf.**
An advocacy group that helps businesses, universities and cities and towns reduce greenhouse gas emissions describes key factors that contribute to the quality of carbon offsets and identifies some of the most credible offset providers.

Makower, Joel, *et al.*, *State of Green Business 2008*, **January 2008, www.stateofgreenbusiness.com.**
A report on the spread of green business practices finds that companies are gradually becoming more eco-friendly, but economic growth is offsetting many of the gains, and that the trend is very hard to quantify.

TerraChoice Environmental Marketing, "The Six Sins of Greenwashing," November 2007, www.terrachoice .com/Home/Six%20Sins%20of%20Greenwashing.
A study of environmental claims in North American consumer markets finds that virtually all purportedly eco-friendly products mislead consumers to some degree. More accurate green marketing, it asserts, will benefit consumers, businesses and the environment.

For More Information

American Council for an Energy-Efficient Economy, 1001 Connecticut Ave., N.W., Suite 801, Washington, DC 20036; (202) 429-8873; www.aceee.org. Supports energy-efficiency measures to promote economic prosperity and environmental protection.

Clean Air-Cool Planet, 100 Market St., Suite 204, Portsmouth, NH 03801; (603) 422-6464; www.cleanair-cool-planet.org. A nonprofit organization that partners with businesses, colleges and communities throughout the Northeast to reduce carbon emissions and educate the public and opinion leaders about global warming impacts and solutions.

Climate Trust, 65 SW Yamhill St., Suite 400, Portland, OR 97204; (503) 238-1915; www.climatetrust.org. Created to implement an Oregon law that requires new power plants to offset some of their carbon emissions, the Climate Trust produces greenhouse gas offset projects for energy companies, regulators, businesses, and individuals.

Competitive Enterprise Institute, 1001 Connecticut Ave., N.W., Suite 1250, Washington, DC 20036; (202) 331-1010; www.cei.org. A public policy research center dedicated to advancing the principles of free enterprise and limited government.

Consumers Union, 101 Truman Ave., Yonkers, NY 10703; (914) 378-2000; www.consumersunion.org. A nonprofit expert group that promotes a fair and safe market for all consumers; activities include testing and rating products and publishing Consumer Reports magazine, as well as GreenerChoices.org, a Web site focusing on green products.

Federal Trade Commission, 600 Pennsylvania Ave., N.W., Washington, DC 20580; (202) 326-2222; www.ftc.gov. Protects consumers' interests, promotes competition and advises businesses on eco-labeling; it is currently reviewing its green marketing guidelines.

LOHAS Forum, 360 Interlocken Blvd., Broomfield, CO 80021; (303) 822-2263; www.lohas.com. An annual business conference focused on the marketplace for goods and services related to health, the environment, social justice, personal development and sustainable living.

National Association of Manufacturers, 1331 Pennsylvania Ave., N.W., Washington, DC 20004; (202) 637-3000; www.nam.org. Promotes legislation and regulations conducive to economic growth and highlights manufacturers' contributions to innovation and productivity.

TerraChoice Environmental Marketing Inc., 1706 Friedensburg Road, Reading, PA 19606; (800) 478-0399; www.terrachoice.com. Conducts market research and advises on strategy, communication and policy issues.

9

Mass Transit Boom

Thomas J. Billitteri

To ease traffic congestion in Manhattan, Mayor Michael R. Bloomberg has proposed a "congestion-pricing" scheme to charge motorists to drive into the most crowded sections of the city on weekdays. The approach has been used in London and Stockholm, Sweden, and is getting close attention in the United States. Above, 42nd Street on Thursday, June 7, 2007.

From *CQ Researcher*, January 18, 2008.

Tampa officials think they might have the answer to a big headache for travelers: getting to and from the airport without getting tangled in traffic gridlock.

Last fall, Tampa officials showed a video animation of a six-car electric train whisking airport passengers along a 3.5-mile track to their terminal. If built, the train could link to a possible rail network connecting downtown Tampa to St. Petersburg 25 miles away.

Tampa Mayor Pam Iorio, a big supporter of building passenger rail service, urged people to compare the airport system's estimated cost — $190 million to $235 million — to the enormous sums spent to improve the region's Interstate highways.

"In the long run, this is cheaper," she said. Moreover, it would be "congestion-proof." [1]

Similar zeal for public transit is spreading nationwide. Pressed by population growth, rising gas prices, global warming and dizzying levels of traffic congestion, cities are pouring unprecedented amounts of money into "light-rail" systems, commuter trains, rapid-transit buses and other forms of public transportation.

Meanwhile, new ideas and technologies are helping to alleviate congestion in traffic-choked metropolitan areas. "Smart card" fare-collection systems allow electronic transfers among buses, subways and other transit modes. Online travel-planning tools, such as Google Transit and hopstop.com, enable commuters to navigate around cities. Car-sharing networks like Zipcar offer quick short-term access to vehicles when needed, reducing the need for car ownership. Planners are fashioning specially wired "e-burbs," such as La Plata, Md., in suburban Washington, D.C., to ease communication with remote headquarters and make it

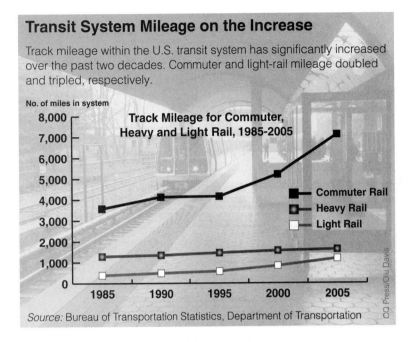

Transit System Mileage on the Increase

Track mileage within the U.S. transit system has significantly increased over the past two decades. Commuter and light-rail mileage doubled and tripled, respectively.

No. of miles in system

Track Mileage for Commuter, Heavy and Light Rail, 1985-2005

— Commuter Rail
— Heavy Rail
— Light Rail

Source: Bureau of Transportation Statistics, Department of Transportation

CQ Press/Oliu Davis

fleet between 1990 and 2000, and more than 13 million of those were in households that already had two or more vehicles. [7] In 2000, three of every four commuters got to work by driving alone. [8] Many of those drivers were immigrants of working age (25-45) — people who are on the roads, commuting to jobs.

Some light-rail systems are designed to help invigorate urban areas with "transit-oriented development" — upscale, walkable mixed-use neighborhoods built around transit stations. In 2001 a new streetcar system in Portland, Ore., spurred the transformation of a down-at-the-heels industrial zone, kicking off a surge of interest in streetcars that has spread from Albuquerque, N.M., and Sacramento, Calif., to Columbus, Ohio, and Kenosha, Wis. [9]

Today, 30 to 50 cities are planning, designing or building streetcar projects, according to Charles Hales, a former Portland city commissioner who led that city's streetcar revival. "It's not a fad," declares Hales, now a transit consultant for cities, "or if it is, it's going to be one that lasts a long time."

Advocates cite a recent rise in transit ridership as evidence drivers are ready to park their cars — at least occasionally — and take public transportation. After hitting bottom in the 1970s, trips on trains, trolleys, buses and other transit bounced up and down in a narrow range until the mid-1990s, then began to trend upward. (*See graph this page.*) So-called unlinked * passenger trips totaled 9.8 billion in 2005, the most recent year for which data are available, compared with 7.8 billion in 1995, according to the American Public Transportation Association. [10]

The association's president, William W. Millar, says transit's growth has important policy implications. "Public transit helps us meet the needs of people and solve problems that are important at all the levels — to

easier for workers to telecommute — a move that takes cars off the road. [2]

In addition, the Bush administration has been promoting toll lanes and other "congestion-pricing" tools as part of a broad "congestion initiative" aimed at mitigating gridlock in the nation's transportation systems. [3]

Perhaps the most notable trend, though, is an explosion in urban rail projects, including streetcars and other "light-rail" systems, typically electrically powered trains that share at least part of the right-of-way with cars. (*See "Glossary," p. 210.*) From 2002 through 2006, for instance, 921 new light-rail cars were delivered — up 75 percent from the previous five years. Deliveries of heavier commuter-rail cars rose by more than 200 percent. [4]

Growing traffic congestion is a major problem driving the transit boom. The Texas Transportation Institute estimates that congestion cost drivers 4.2 billion in lost hours and 2.9 billion gallons of wasted fuel in 2005 — the equivalent of 105 million weeks of vacation and 58 fully loaded supertankers. [5] Easing congestion not only relieves aggravated drivers and saves gas but also improves business. A study of the San Francisco Bay Area found that every 10 percent rise in commuting speed increased work output by 1 percent. [6]

Soaring vehicle ownership also fuels congestion. Roughly 30 million vehicles were added to the national

---

* "Unlinked" passenger trips denote the number of passengers who board public transportation vehicles. Passengers are counted each time they board vehicles no matter how many vehicles they use to travel to their destination.

meet national goals like reduction in greenhouse gases, reduce our reliance on foreign energy sources, you name it," he says. It also helps local communities support economic growth and deal with sprawl and a burgeoning elderly population, he adds.

But not all urban transportation experts are so enthusiastic. Critics argue that investing in expensive projects makes little sense outside of traditional urban megalopolises like the New York region, which alone accounts for about 35 percent of the nation's transit ridership. Despite the recent uptick in ridership, they point out, transit accounts for only a fraction of overall urban travel and ridership remains far below the World War II-era peak, when trips approached 25 billion per year.

The rush to build light rail comes in for especially harsh criticism. "There's a huge amount of money wasted on building rail," says Jonathan Richmond, an urban transportation consultant who has written widely on the subject. "It has pathetically low ridership and very little to show for it."

Buses Are Top Public Transportation Mode

More than 20 million so-called unlinked* bus rides were taken during the average weekday in 2005, constituting nearly 60 percent of all U.S. public-transportation trips. Heavy rail was a distant second with just under 10 million rides, about 29 percent.

Average Weekday Unlinked Passenger Trips, 2005

Mode	Average weekday unlinked trips	Percent of total
Bus	20.1 million	59.7%
Commuter rail	1.5 million	4.3%
Ferryboat	225,000	0.7%
Heavy rail	9,626,000	28.6%
Light rail	1,304,000	3.9%
Other rail	114,000	0.3%
Paratransit	427,000	1.3%
Trolleybus	367,000	1.1%
Vanpool	61,000	0.2%
Total	**33,641,000**	**100.1%**

Note: Percentages do not total 100 due to rounding; unlinked trips do not add to total due to rounding.

* Unlinked passenger trips are the number of passengers who board public transportation vehicles. Passengers are counted each time they board vehicles

Source: "Public Transportation Fact Book," 58th ed., American Public Transportation Association, May 2007

Some argue, too, that local leaders have created unrealistic expectations that transit systems will make urban life easier. "Transit has been sold as a way to solve congestion, air quality and other environmental problems and make places more livable," says Genevieve Giuliano, senior associate dean for research and technology at the University of Southern California's School of Policy, Planning and Development. Under most circumstances — notably, outside of very high-density corridors where demand exceeds the capacity of buses operating at the shortest possible intervals — rapid bus service is as effective as rail transit and far less expensive to build, she says.

The list of urban ills that transit is expected to solve is "very long," says Giuliano. "And, unfortunately, it could not possibly live up to that list. But you need the list to get the political support to fund it."

Transit projects also stir passionate debate between "smart growth" enthusiasts — who advocate reducing sprawl by encouraging high-density, close-in development along transit corridors — and those who call such efforts social engineering. "The notion that government agencies should be forcing people into situations because of a belief in how people ought to live in cities is crazy," says Robert Bruegmann, author of the controversial book *Sprawl: A Compact History*, which argues that mobility, choice and privacy are much easier for most people to find in sprawling areas than in densely populated ones.

With the population growing and with most people wedded to their cars, transit will remain an "insignificant factor" on the transportation scene, "short of some completely unforeseen turn of events," says Bruegmann, an expert on urban planning at the University of Illinois,

New streetcars in Kenosha, Wis., run on electricity on tracks alongside cars. Madison, Wis., is considering streetcars similar to those in Kenosha.

Chicago. "The only real way for transit to work is to completely change our cities," he says. "There's simply no evidence that will occur."

But developers in places like Charlotte, N.C., are betting on a growing demand for public transportation as well as places to live and work near transit lines. They are investing more than $1 billion in projects near stations planned for the region. "We always saw transit as a means, not an end," Planning Director Debra Campbell said. "The real impetus for transit was how it could help us grow in a way that was smart. This really isn't even about building a transit system. It's about place-making. It's about building a community." [11]

As cities continue to build and expand public-transit systems, here are some of the questions being asked by transit supporters and critics:

Will spending more on transit ease congestion?

Of all the benefits touted by public-transportation supporters, none resonates with the public as much as the idea that transit might reduce the mayhem on traffic-choked roads. "Congestion is a scourge on the United States," declares Millar of the American Public Transportation Association. He adds, "A comprehensive public transportation system . . . helps to reduce congestion and saves energy." [12]

It's an oft-repeated mantra among transit advocates.

"I never got caught in a traffic jam on I-96 15 years ago," U.S. Rep. Vernon J. Ehlers, a Michigan Republican from the Grand Rapids area, was quoted by the Michigan Land Use Institute, a "smart-growth" advocacy organiza-

tion. "Today, you drive in every morning and it's jammed up. . . . With the increase in traffic, what do you think is going to happen? We'll need light rail in 15 years. Public transit is very important for our future." [13]

But transportation specialists hotly debate the notion that public transit can curb traffic congestion. "Attempts to cope with rising traffic congestion by shifting more people to public transit are not going to work," argues Anthony Downs, a senior fellow at the Brookings Institution, a Washington think tank. "The automobile is and will remain a better form of movement for most people in spite of congestion." [14]

The author of the 1992 book *Stuck in Traffic* and the 2004 sequel *Still Stuck in Traffic*, Downs notes that only a fraction of commuting is done by public transit, a proportion that drops even more if New York is excluded. "In 2000 transit provided about 46.6 billion miles of movement while passenger miles traveled [in cars, small trucks and SUVs] . . . totaled about 4 trillion," Downs said. "In fact, transit's share of all passenger miles traveled in the U.S. from 1985 through 2000 averaged only 1.26 percent." [15]

Others also doubt the ability of transit — particularly expensive rail projects — to make a significant dent in congestion in a large urban region. While transit can reduce congestion on some high-density traffic corridors, says Michael D. Meyer, a professor of civil and environmental engineering at the Georgia Institute of Technology and former director of transportation planning and development for Massachusetts, most indicators show it can provide "an almost insignificant impact on congestion" across a metropolitan region.

"If you talk to the elected officials behind the scene," Meyer adds, they will often say they need to build transit systems "because . . . you can't be a world-class city unless you have a rail system, you need to be prepared for a future where gas may be God knows how many dollars per gallon and you need to be more sustainable." But "deep down," Meyer says, most realize that transit "isn't going to reduce congestion" significantly throughout a region.

But transit advocates see things differently. "How did we get into the problem of road congestion?" Millar says. "We spent . . . trillions of dollars building the 4 million miles of public road we have today. You simply cannot build your way out of congestion. Yes, there will be cases when roads need to be expanded or new roads need to be built, but it is a more balanced, multimodal approach that is ultimately going to give us the long-term solutions that we desire. For something like congestion, it's always easy to take a look at the short term and immediate cost and forget that you get a long-term benefit."

Todd Litman, executive director of the Victoria Transport Policy Institute, a research organization in British Columbia that studies international transportation and land use policies, says high-quality rail transit has several "congestion-reduction benefits." It tends to attract passengers who would otherwise drive, reducing congestion on roads running parallel to transit systems. It stimulates transit-oriented development, thereby reducing vehicle travel. And, it can lower "travel-time costs" incurred by people who shift to transit.

"Even if transit takes more minutes," according to Litman, "many travelers consider their cost per minute lower than driving if transit service is comfortable . . . allowing passengers to relax and work. . . ." [16]

Cities with high-quality transit systems benefit in other ways as well, Litman argues. Energy consumption, pollution and traffic fatalities drop substantially, as do parking-related costs, he says. "The research . . . shows very clearly that households save money by living in a city that has high-quality rail transit," Litman says.

Yet some urban transportation experts argue that even with congestion, cars can be faster and more flexible than rail transit, which operates on fixed routes and schedules.

"If you think in terms of the value of time as being one of the great factors in people's thinking, then public transit is going to have to compete to meet people's time needs, says Alan E. Pisarski, a transportation consultant and the author of a series of statistical reports on commuting trends published by the Transportation Research Board, part of the National Academy of Sciences. "Typically that's one of the weakest areas, in terms of getting people where they want to go when they want to go."

Randal O'Toole, a senior fellow at the Cato Institute, is blunter. "Light rail and streetcars may be cute, but they are S-L-O-W," wrote O'Toole, a longtime transit critic. "Portland's fastest light-rail line averages 22 miles per hour. Portland's streetcar goes about 7 miles per hour. I am waiting to see a developer advertise, 'If you lived here and rode transit home from work, you'd still be sitting on the train.' " [17]

But transit advocates say such analysis is misguided as it pertains to streetcars and congestion. Hales, the former Portland city commissioner, says that some transit pro-

jects — including Portland's streetcar line — are actually not meant to diminish congestion, but rather to increase it. The aim, he says, is to boost population density in downtown areas by attracting residents, shoppers and office workers to transit-oriented neighborhoods, making it easy for them to circulate among stops on the streetcar line.

Before Portland added the streetcars to its Pearl District in 2001, Hales says, the neighborhood had fewer than half a dozen businesses and only a couple of hundred residential units. Now the streetcar has helped transform the Pearl District into a trendy neighborhood with more than 250 commercial enterprises and 5,000 residences, he says. "So far, there's $3 billion of development within three blocks of the line. It's occurring at two to three times the density and pace that's happening in the rest of downtown."

It's that density and pace — not the lack of congestion — that city leaders wanted to generate with the streetcar line, says Hales, who now is helping to plan streetcars in Sacramento.

"In the United States, the streetcar has been about circulation in busy downtowns, or actually about making them busier," he says. "So I hope that they're causing congestion. That seems like an absurd thing to say, but what's absurd is that the only thing we're measuring when it comes to transit projects is their effect on road congestion. That's a very limited view."

Should government spend less on roads and more on transit?

Linked to the debate over congestion is the question of whether more government money should be flowing to transit projects.

Total government spending on transit grew about 80 percent in inflation-adjusted terms between 1980 and 2004, faster than the 12 percent growth in passenger trips and 24 percent growth in passenger miles traveled on transit, according to the Congressional Research Service. "It is often pointed out that while transit spending [amounted in 2004] to about 16 percent of all government highway and transit spending and about 14 percent of federal highway and transit capital expenditure . . . only about 2 percent of all trips are made by this mode.

"Even for commuting trips, for which transit is better suited, transit accounts for only 5 percent nationwide, a share that has changed little over the past two decades.

Solitary Commuting Is Most Popular

Nearly 100 million commuters drove alone to work in 2000 — more than a 50 percent increase over the previous 20 years. Carpooling and public transit have remained relatively constant.

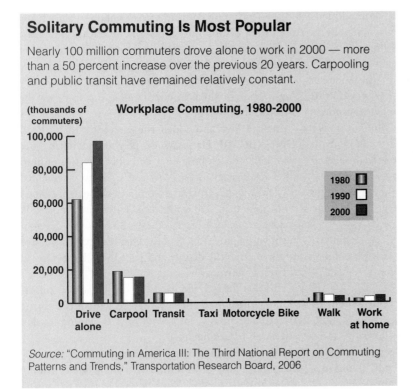

Workplace Commuting, 1980-2000

(thousands of commuters)

Legend: 1980, 1990, 2000

Source: "Commuting in America III: The Third National Report on Commuting Patterns and Trends," Transportation Research Board, 2006

Only in two cities, New York and Chicago, does the transit share rise above 10 percent. The effect, according to transit critics, is to shortchange highway spending, thereby causing highway conditions and performance, including highway congestion, to be worse than they would otherwise be." [18]

Many transit advocates argue, however, that the government's transportation funding priorities have been shortsighted. For decades, they say, the government's bias toward funding roads has encouraged sprawling development patterns that have limited Americans' mobility — a problem that is likely to grow more acute as the population ages and people look for alternatives to driving. [19]

"Why do we have [sprawling] development today? Because we followed for 80-some years a single-minded policy of subsidizing the automobile and the road system," says Millar of the American Public Transportation Association. "So you get what you pay for.

"This year we will spend close to $2 trillion on transportation — that's public and private spending," he adds. "Eighty percent of that will be spent on the highway network and private automobiles and things like

that. We are simply underinvested in public transit, so that in most communities in America public transit is not a viable option for most Americans."

Public-transportation advocates also cite what they see as a variety of economic benefits from funding transit systems. For instance, investing in transit creates new jobs and can raise real estate values, especially near stations, they say.

David Lewis, senior vice president of HDR/Decision Economics, a division of HDR Engineering, told a congressional subcommittee in 2007 that in Washington, D.C., for the average commercial property of about 30,500 square feet, "each 1,000-foot reduction in walking distance to a Metrorail station increases the value of a commercial property by more than $70,000."

"Transit creates statistically measurable economic value for communities, with benefits extending to both transit users and nonusers," he said." [20]

But critics of transit argue that far from being tilted too far toward highway spending, Washington bureaucrats have actually gone too far in promoting transit.

The Cato Institute's O'Toole argued that "the federal government has created a system that promotes wildly extravagant spending on mass transit and on rail lines in particular."

"[R]ail transit poses three major threats to regional transit service," he wrote. Overruns in construction costs "often force agencies to raise fares or cut service"; rail construction tends to put transit agencies "so heavily in debt that, during recessions and periods of low tax revenue, they are forced to make large cuts in service"; and "rail lines must be rebuilt about every 30 years, and reconstruction costs nearly as much as the original construction." [21]

O'Toole, who is director of the Thoreau Institute, a group in Oregon that says it "seeks ways to protect the environment without regulation, bureaucracy or central control," also argued that current laws give transit and labor unions power to veto federal grant projects. That, he contended, is a "bargain [that] favors high-cost transit systems over low-cost bus systems."

Transit agencies could contract out all their service to provide better service at lower cost, according to O'Toole, but "any plans by transit agencies to do so without a state mandate would be opposed by transit unions and thus would make the agencies ineligible for federal funds."

Worse, O'Toole argued, the Environmental Protection Agency (EPA) subsidizes "anti-highway activist groups to participate in transportation planning initiatives" and ties the funds to mandates for air-quality improvement projects. Both the anti-auto groups and the EPA guidelines, he contended, "favor rail transit over new roads. "Most cities would never consider building new rail systems without federal incentives to waste money. In fact, buses can provide the same level of service as trains for far less money." [22]

In a detailed rebuttal of O'Toole's analysis, Litman of the Victoria Transport Policy Institute calls it "outdated and biased, looking backward at the last century . . . rather than looking forward toward the changing transportation needs of the next century."

Although highways showed high annual return on investment during the 1960s when the Interstate Highway System was developed, Litman wrote, this has since declined significantly, a decline likely to continue because the most cost-effective projects have been implemented. Thus, he added, it "makes sense to invest less in roadways and more in public transit to maximize economic returns." [23]

Do toll lanes and other "congestion-pricing" schemes work?

In traffic-choked New York City, Mayor Michael R. Bloomberg last year proposed a controversial method for easing congestion and generating money for transit: Charge motorists to drive into the most crowded sections of Manhattan on weekdays. [24]

Bloomberg's proposal is a form of "congestion pricing," an approach that has been used in London and Stockholm and that is getting close attention in the United States — including strong support from the Bush administration.

Congestion pricing can take many forms, from high-occupancy toll (HOT) lanes to higher tolls during peak traffic hours to fees for driving into certain congested areas of cities. It is similar to the idea behind utility usage: consumers pay for what they use and sometimes pay more when demand is high. "I think there's perception roads are free, but we're paying one way or another," points out Paul Larrousse, director of the National Transit Institute at Rutgers University.

Congestion pricing can be used to manage traffic flows in order to relieve congestion, to encourage the use of mass transit and to generate revenue for transportation projects, including train or bus systems. Transportation experts say taxpayers and local politicians object to congestion pricing less when it is applied to new highways rather than being imposed on existing ones.

Supporters of congestion pricing say it eases bottlenecks on busy traffic corridors and speeds commutes for transit riders who share the road with autos. Grace Crunican, director of the Seattle Department of Transportation, calls congestion pricing "a good tool to manage and rationalize our system."

In Washington state, tolling operations began last summer on the Tacoma Narrows Bridge, using high-speed, nonstop electronic toll collection to help pay for bridge construction, maintenance and operation. This spring the state is expected to open nine miles of HOT lanes on busy State Road 167 using the same technology, with pricing varying with traffic demand. [25]

Elsewhere, congestion pricing has helped ease bottlenecks, encouraged people to shift to transit and raised money for transportation, according to a 2006 report by the U.S. Department of Transportation (DOT).

For example, it said the number of vehicles with more than three passengers rose 40 percent within the first three months of opening priced express lanes on California's SR-91, while ridership on buses and a nearby rail line remained steady. Along Interstate 15 HOT lanes in San Diego, revenues generated by toll-paying drivers helped pay for transportation improvements that contributed to a 25 percent increase in bus ridership, the DOT report said. [26]

"We're faced with increasing growth in population and employment, and there's nowhere near enough [money for roads] to handle the demand, says Meyer, the Georgia Tech professor. The only "clear option," he adds, is to adopt some form of congestion pricing, an approach being considered in his own city of Atlanta, where — despite a large rail system — traffic backups are among the worst in the nation.

Seattle's new streetcar begins its inaugural run from downtown on Dec. 12, 2007. The 1.3-mile line serves the developing area around the Fred Hutchinson Cancer Research Center. A streetcar passes one of the line's 11 stops every 15 minutes.

Transportation Secretary Mary E. Peters made similar arguments in a newspaper op-ed column last year, in which she criticized the notion of raising gasoline taxes to pay for building and maintaining roads, bridges and other transportation infrastructure.

"In addition to breeding wasteful spending, the gas tax does virtually nothing to reduce the explosion in highway congestion," she wrote, reflecting the Bush administration's long aversion to raising fuel taxes. "Gas taxes are levied regardless of when and where someone drives, creating a misperception that highways are 'free.' "

Peters continued, "[C]harging directly for road use holds enormous promise both to generate large amounts of revenue for reinvestment and to cut congestion. Ultimately, it will allow political leaders to reduce reliance on or even cut the inefficient array of fuel taxes, sales taxes and property taxes that are being funneled into transportation systems nationwide." [27]

But critics of congestion pricing argue that pricing schemes are no substitute for higher fuel taxes to finance crucial maintenance on America's aging roads and bridges. [28] Moreover, they say, congestion pricing hits poor and middle-class commuters the hardest.

"Proponents of congestion pricing say those who don't want to pay or cannot afford to pay increased commuting costs have other choices," Bill Graves, CEO of the American Trucking Associations and a former Republican governor of Kansas, wrote in a newspaper column last year. "But many low-income motorists can-

not change their work hours or child-care needs. Not everyone has access to public transit, which can take longer and is less reliable than traveling by car. The motorist's alternative to paying more at the toll booth is to find another route that is time-consuming and merely shifts congestion to other roads and neighborhoods." [29]

Rep. Anthony Weiner, D-N.Y., who represents sections of the boroughs of Queens and Brooklyn, called the Bloomberg congestion-pricing scheme a regressive tax on working middle-class families and small-business owners. "While I applaud the mayor for focusing on a long-term sustainability plan for the city, in this case the cure seems to be worse than the disease." [30]

BACKGROUND

Transit's Golden Age

Like a trolley running on hilly terrain, transit in America has had its steep ups and downs over the years.

The first horse-drawn street railways began service in New York in 1832, and the service had expanded to Cincinnati, Baltimore, Philadelphia and other cities well before the Civil War. [31] Cable cars came on the scene in 1873 in San Francisco and soon appeared elsewhere. [32]

Then in 1888 came a huge advance in public transit: the electric streetcar. [33]

"During the remainder of the golden age of mass transit" in the late 1800s and early 1900s, "the electric streetcar reigned supreme as the common man's magic carpet," wrote transportation expert George M. Smerk. "It was the shaper of cities. Electric lines were much cheaper to build than cable lines and much less costly to operate than animal-powered railways. They were also tokens of progress for most cities and, as such, many lines were built that were uneconomic, merely to show that a city was progressive." [34]

In the 1920s the nation's post-World War I economy boomed, and motorized vehicles began to take center stage. Buses became a popular mode of transit. At the same time, the car culture was becoming a central feature of U.S. society, fueling a rivalry between private mobility and public transit that grew more intense as time went on.

By 1929, more than 23 million private and commercial automobiles were registered in the United States — or roughly one car for every five Americans. [35] In prosperous cities such as Detroit and Los Angeles, automobiles were the most common means of transportation for most families. [36]

With more and more people traveling by car, transit's golden age was receding in the rear-view mirror. Then, as the Great Depression (1929-1939) battered the economy, transit ridership plunged. Suddenly tens of thousands of Americans had no jobs to travel to, and leisure trips were a luxury few could afford.

Meanwhile, transit hit another bend in the tracks. Electric utilities had for years provided money and management expertise to transit systems, but that trend faded after Congress passed the Public Utility Holding Company Act of 1935. The law forced the power companies to start shedding their transit subsidiaries and weakened transit's financial and management underpinnings. [37]

With the advent of World War II, transit ridership turned around. Suddenly, America was back on the job, with factory workers boarding streetcars, subways and buses to get to defense plants making bullets, ships and airplanes. The government rationed gasoline as well as rubber used in car tires, prompting the fortunate few who owned automobiles to keep them parked. Transit ridership soared to an all-time high of 23.4 billion trips in 1946. [38]

But the transit boom was short-lived. In the postwar economic revival, Americans abandoned transit in droves, choosing instead to get behind the wheel. By 1960, transit ridership had plunged to 9.3 billion trips — 40 percent of its wartime high — eventually falling to an all-time low in 1972 of 6.5 billion trips. [39]

Several trends accounted for the downturn — some of them subsidized by the federal government. During the 1950s and '60s, millions of families — often headed by veterans using low-interest government loans — bought homes and moved to the suburbs, places ill-served by transit systems. [40] Along with suburban sprawl came the nation's huge investment in roads, most notably the Interstate Highway System inaugurated during the Eisenhower administration. Automobile registrations doubled in less than a generation from about 40 million in 1950 to 80 million in 1967. In 1973, they broke the 100-million mark and kept climbing, despite an oil embargo, rocketing gas prices and recession. [41]

Meanwhile, other changes in American life discouraged transit ridership. The postwar workweek fell to five days, reducing work travel. While downtowns continued to be major employment hubs, many new jobs sprang up in outlying areas not easily accessible by transit. Retailing shifted from Main Street to suburban malls. Television's growing popularity kept people at home and reduced outings to the movies. And many inner-city neighborhoods, particularly in the Northeast, became blighted, accelerating flight to the suburbs and reducing transit use even more.

An Urban Problem

Not everyone liked the shift to an auto culture. Criticism of cars swelled in the 1950s. In his book on sprawl, Bruegmann of the University of Illinois at Chicago wrote: "Led by upper-middle-class residents of central cities in the Northeast . . . this group took a passionate dislike not just to the automobile but to an entire worldview that they believed supported it. For them the automobile was symptomatic of an individualistic, consumerist society run amuck." [42]

To some degree, these sentiments took hold. By the 1960s, many cities were starting to rethink the idea of autos as a solution to their transportation needs, William D. Middleton, a transportation historian and journalist, wrote in a history of rail transit in America. "While the development of expressways and freeways had encouraged and facilitated a massive shift of urban population to the suburbs, no amount of road building ever seemed to be enough to meet the growing demand that it created. More and more, too, cities began to recognize the destructive effects of massive highway construction on the urban community." [43]

Pressure also was growing for the federal government to subsidize the struggling urban transit systems. In 1961 President John F. Kennedy signed the Omnibus Housing Act, which provided limited funds for loans and grants for public transportation. In signing the act, Kennedy said mass transportation was "a distinctly urban problem and one of the key factors in shaping community development." [44]

The next year, Kennedy asked Congress to establish a program to help cities build and maintain public transportation systems. "To conserve and enhance values in existing urban areas is essential," Kennedy said in a message to Congress. "But at least as important are steps to promote economic efficiency and livability in areas of future development. Our national welfare therefore requires the provision of good urban transportation, with the properly balanced use of private vehicles and modern mass transport to help shape as well as serve urban growth." [45]

The year after Kennedy's assassination, President Lyndon B. Johnson signed into law the Urban Mass Transportation Act, establishing permanent federal support for transit. [46]

CHRONOLOGY

1800-1920 *Early transit services begin on the East Coast.*

1832 Horse-drawn street railways introduced in New York City.

1873 San Francisco starts cable car service.

1880s Electric streetcars introduced.

1892 First Chicago elevated line opens.

1904 New York begins subway service.

1920-1940s *After losing ground to the automobile, transit rebounds.*

1926 Peacetime ridership on public transportation hits 17.2 billion.

1939 General Motors' "Futurama" exhibit at New York World's Fair features automated superhighways.

1940s World War II industrialization and rationing of rubber and gas spur surge in transit ridership to record 23.4 billion passenger trips.

1950s-1960s *Growth of suburbs leads millions of Americans to buy cars and abandon public transportation.*

1961 President John F. Kennedy calls mass transportation a key factor "in shaping community development."

1964 Congress enacts Urban Mass Transportation Act.

1968 Federal government creates Urban Mass Transportation Administration.

1970s-1980s *Transit enters the modern age as big cities begin ambitious urban rail operations.*

1970s Recession and high inflation hit the nation; ridership on public transit reaches an historic low.

1970 National Environmental Policy Act requires environmental impact statements for transit and highway projects that receive federal money.

1972 San Francisco launches first computer-controlled heavy-rail transit agency.

1976 First segment of Metrorail system opens in Washington, D.C., area.

1979 Metropolitan Atlanta Rapid Transit Authority (MARTA) opens its first line.

1981 San Diego Trolley helps to start light-rail renaissance.

1984 Miami completes first part of Metrorail.

1990s *U.S. strengthens role of local planning organizations in charting future needs.*

1990 Americans with Disabilities Act requires transit agencies to serve people with disabilities.

1990 Los Angeles County opens initial light-rail segment.

1990 Clean Air Act imposes tough pollution standards on transit buses.

1991 Landmark Intermodal Surface Transportation Efficiency Act gives states new flexibility in use of transportation funds.

1995 Ridership in public transit begins to show a gradual increase

2000-Present *Policy makers put new focus on reducing congestion.*

2007 Gasoline prices exceed $3 per gallon. . . . Texas Transportation Institute study says traffic congestion creates a $78 billion annual drain on the economy. . . . Interstate 35 West bridge over Mississippi River in Minneapolis collapses, putting renewed focus on highway infrastructure. . . . Congressional Budget Office says highway account in Highway Trust Fund could run out of money by fiscal 2009.

2008 Washington's Metrorail imposes largest fare increase in its history.

In the 1970s, some of America's largest cities began building big "heavy-rail" systems that changed not only travel habits for tens of thousands of residents and visitors but also the urban landscape itself. San Francisco's Bay Area Rapid Transit District (BART) started passenger service on its regional metro system in 1972; the system now covers 104 miles. The first segment of Washington's Metrorail system opened in 1976, and Atlanta opened the first of its "MARTA" metro system lines in 1979. [47]

The Ronald Reagan administration did not share the Kennedy era's interest in the health and welfare of urban transit systems, however. Reagan sought to reduce federal spending through budget cuts and privatization of programs traditionally supported by government. "The Reagan administration made it clear that it wanted to do away with what it deemed to be the 'unseemly federal role in mass transportation,' " transportation expert Smerk wrote. [48]

Still, Congress ensured that money for rail project was available. "The reason for the interest of Congress is proof of the dictum of longtime Speaker of the House Thomas P. "Tip" O'Neill [D-Mass.] that all politics is local politics," Smerk wrote. ". . . [T]he simple and straightforward fact is that the federal mass-transit program touches virtually every congressional district and at least some of the constituents of every senator." [49]

Light Rails

Not all systems relied on federal money, though. In 1981, using only local money, San Diego became the first U.S. city to open a new light-rail system, using existing tracks. [50] Other cities also opened light-rail lines — Buffalo in 1984, Portland in 1986 (using money from a canceled freeway project) and then Sacramento and San Jose in California. [51] Seattle began a downtown trolleybus tunnel, and Los Angeles started building its subway system. [52]

Transit continued growing steadily in the 1990s, with new emphasis on "intermodalism" — combining various forms of transport, such as roads, rail, buses and ships.

The landmark Intermodal Surface Transportation Efficiency Act of 1991 gave states and localities flexibility to shift federal highway funds to transit projects. Seven years later the law's successor legislation, the Transportation Equity Act for the 21st Century, enabled states and local authorities to shift $8.5 billion from highways to transit — but only $40 million from transit to

highways, Rep. James Oberstar, D-Minn., chairman of the House Transportation and Infrastructure Committee, said in 2003. He added, "99.5 percent of the time, states and local authorities choose to flex funds from highways to transit." [53]

By the turn of the 21st century, cities were clamoring to build or upgrade big transit networks and create smaller systems, such as streetcar lines, to help revitalize urban neighborhoods. In 2005, as part of a Transportation Department reauthorization bill, Congress enacted a program to finance projects costing up to $250 million in which the federal portion is $75 million or less. Under that "Small Starts" program transit advocates saw a bright future for projects — such as streetcar systems — designed not just to move people but also to promote smart growth and spark economic development in urban neighborhoods.

Transit and urban planning proponents have complained, though, that the Federal Transit Administration has erected high hurdles for streetcar funding and is using Small Starts to emphasize rapid-transit bus routes over rail. The actions reflect the Bush administration's efforts to focus on easing highway gridlock rather than long-term urban planning.

The administration has "a very arduous and arcane process" for project evaluation with criteria that favor cost- and travel-time savings and congestion relief, says Hales, the former Portland city commissioner. But, he adds, "Does the federal government care about how Americans settle on the landscape and how they live? People are willing to pay handsomely to live in a more sustainable way. If the answer is 'yes,' then the transit issue is one place where the federal government can make a huge difference."

Hales says cities like Portland have come up with much of the money themselves for their streetcar projects, relying largely on local tax money.

"I don't see states and localities falling over themselves to come up with 50 percent of the cost of new highways," he says. "But here are cities waving wads of dollar bills [for streetcar projects], saying, 'We'll pay at least half of these things if [the federal government] will just say yes.' So in terms of leveraging federal dollars, transit projects in general and urban streetcar projects in particular, win hands down if the test is putting local money where the mouth is."

Yet, some analysts question the cost-effectiveness of light-rail projects. Researchers from the St. Louis Federal Reserve Bank wrote that "light rail is kept afloat by tax-

New Transit Projects Raise Questions

Do they ignore the needs of less-affluent riders?

As cities rush to embrace new transit projects and congestion-pricing ventures, some experts worry that the poor may be shortchanged.

Among the concerns:

- That tax-financed commuter-rail projects may benefit wealthier people, while bus services heavily used by poor people who don't own cars or have jobs near rail stops may suffer;
- That fare policies typically favor peak-hour long-distance commutes to downtowns and other white-collar destinations over shorter, off-peak trips common to low-income people juggling second- and third-shift jobs, child-care duties and other necessities;
- That light-rail systems are often intended to attract discretionary riders — an approach that may come at the expense of improving transportation services generally, including for the poor.

"Transit has two objectives," says Genevieve Giuliano, senior associate dean for research and technology at the University of Southern California's School of Policy, Planning, Policy and Development. "One is solving congestion and air-quality problems. The other is about basic mobility. By putting our eggs in the congestion and air-quality basket, we've made people who need mobility worse off. If we actually paid attention to the quality and availability of service, we'd be doing well toward both of those objectives. But we're going in the wrong direction."

In some localities, grass-roots advocates have taken up the call for greater equity in local transit.

In Los Angeles, the powerful Bus Riders Union gained a federal consent decree a little over a decade ago that forced the city to expand bus service.

In part, too, the equity issue has surfaced because of the way cities have developed. Central cities once were dominated by low-income and working-class residents, but rising urban real estate values and job creation in sprawling suburbs have pushed many of those people into the far reaches of metro areas. That makes their transit needs different from those who commute to downtown professional jobs.

"There's massive gentrification at the center of many cities, very often centered around these transit stops," says Robert Bruegmann, a professor at the University of Illinois, Chicago, who studies urban planning and sprawl. "If you're wealthy enough and you've got a job in the central business district, it provides a wonderful choice."

But, adds Bruegmann, "the lower middle class increasingly has moved out to the outer edge" of cities and relies on autos or buses to get to jobs that frequently are scattered throughout metro areas.

Even bus service, which Bruegmann says can be "long, arduous and uncomfortable," doesn't always meet the needs of the poor and can add to a city's traffic and pollution problems. One solution, he says, is to put more money into "on-demand transit" that allows patrons to summon vans or other transport vehicles exactly when and where they are needed.

payer-funded subsidies that amount to hundreds of millions of dollars each year."

"If light rail is not cost-efficient, nor an effective way to reduce pollution and traffic congestion, nor the least costly means of providing transportation to the poor, why do voters continue to approve new taxes for the construction and expansion of light-rail systems?" they wrote in 2004. Then they answered their own question: One reason is that although the benefits of light rail are highly concentrated, the costs are spread over the tax-paying population. They wrote: "The direct benefits of a light-rail project can be quite large for a relatively small group

of people, such as elected officials, environmental groups, labor organizations, engineering and architectural firms, developers and regional businesses, which often campaign vigorously for the passage of light-rail funding."

In St. Louis, they wrote, light rail ran about $6 per taxpayer annually — a sum modest enough to attract voter support even if a transit system is financially inefficient. "A large group of taxpayers facing relatively minimal costs can be persuaded to vote for light rail based on benefits shaped by the interested minority, such as helping the poor, reducing congestion and pollution and fostering development. Even if these bene-

The issue of transit equity can put local politicians in a difficult spot. On one hand, they have a responsibility to ease traffic and pollution problems, and they may also see new systems such as light rail as a way to project a modern, progressive image of their cities. But they also have a duty to serve the transportation needs of all citizens, including those who may never step foot in a trolley or train.

A few years ago, the *Los Angeles Times* noted the juggling act that faced Los Angeles Mayor Antonio Villaraigosa as he sought to deal with the city's massive transportation challenges. "The mayor wields considerable power over local transit decisions . . . but that power comes fraught with political peril," the newspaper editorialized.

Some transit experts worry that city transit buses in Los Angeles, above, and other cities will receive less funding than tax-financed commuter-rail projects.

Getty Images/David McNew

Villaraigosa promised to do both, but seeking transit equity hasn't been easy. Last year the *Times* noted that the Metropolitan Transportation Authority was building two rail projects, the Expo Line to Culver City and the Gold Line extension to East Los Angeles, at a $1.5 billion price tag. The MTA said that while rail accounted for only about 17 percent of the city's transit ridership, it was growing.

But critics weren't buying the rail projects. "You see how crowded the buses are, and yet . . . the Gold Line at 4 in the afternoon is practically empty," Joel Kotkin, a Los Angeles resident, told the newspaper. "Obviously, the buses are in demand much more than the more expensive stuff, so why aren't we putting more money into the buses?"

Added Kotkin, the author of *The City: A Global History,* "It seems to be unconscionable we could be raising fares so a few yuppies from Santa Monica can go downtown on the subway."[2]

"Invariably the [Metropolitan Transportation Authority board on which the mayor serves] has to choose between pleasing the powerful Bus Riders Union by maintaining and expanding bus service or pleasing business interests and wealthier constituents by expanding the rail system."[1]

[1] "The Politics of Power: Pumped-up public transit," *Los Angeles Times,* Aug. 13, 2005, p. 18B.

[2] Rong-Gong Lin II and Francisco Vara-Orta, "Transit fare hikes called unwise," *Los Angeles Times,* April 28, 2007, p. 1A.

fits are exaggerated and the taxpayer realizes the cost-ineffectiveness of light rail, it is probably not worth the $6 for that person to spend significant time lobbying against light rail."[54]

But transit supporters say rail transit does pay off. A 1999 study underwritten by private-sector business members of the American Public Transit Association found major economic benefits to transit investment. The study concluded, for instance, that in the year following each $10 million in transit capital funding, 314 jobs were created, business sales rose $32 million for each $10 million in transit operations spending, and more

than $15 million was saved in transportation costs to highway and transit users for every $10 million invested in transit in major metropolitan areas.[55]

And according to Litman, of the Victoria Transport Policy Institute, the St. Louis analysis ignored many benefits of rail transit and understated the costs of automobile travel on the same corridors.

"[It] would not be cost effective to provide light rail transit service everywhere," Litman wrote, but "when all costs and benefits are considered, rail transit is often the most cost-effective way to improve transportation on major urban travel corridors."[56]

Can a Daily Transit Pass Save the Planet?

Skeptics say claimed benefits are hyped

Among the many arguments that advocates make for transit, impact on the environment is at or near the top of the list.

"The most powerful weapon you can use to combat global climate change may be a daily transit pass," the American Public Transportation Association (APTA) declared last September in announcing a new study on reducing greenhouse gases.

But critics argue that transit's environmental benefits are vastly overstated. "No big deal," Wendell Cox, a prominent transit critic, wrote in response to transit's claimed role in cutting greenhouse gases. [1]

The study found that in comparison to other household actions that limit carbon dioxide, taking public transportation can be more than 10 times greater in reducing that greenhouse gas. [2]

"A solo commuter switching his or her commute to existing public transportation in a single day can reduce their CO_2 emissions by 20 pounds, or more than 4,800 pounds in a year," the study concluded.

It also said transit helps support higher-density land uses that reduce vehicle travel while helping cut household carbon dioxide emissions.

"The carbon footprint of a typical U.S. household is about 22 metric tonnes per year," the study concluded.

"Reducing the daily use of one low-occupancy vehicle and using public transit can reduce a household's carbon footprint between 25 [and] 30 percent."

In testimony to a congressional panel in spring 2007, APTA president William W. Millar said a separate study concluded that public transportation reduces petroleum consumption by 1.4 billion gallons of gasoline annually. [3] That savings results from the fact that transit carries multiple passengers per vehicle, reduces traffic congestion and does not rely exclusively on petroleum to power its fleets, Millar said.

"The transportation sector is the largest consumer of petroleum in the United States — accounting for 67 percent of America's petroleum consumption and 28 percent of our greenhouse gas . . . emissions," Millar stated. "If we are serious about reducing America's 'addiction to oil' and reducing [greenhouse-gas] emissions, then we must also reduce transportation-related petroleum consumption. This will require a multi-pronged approach that must include expanded public transportation use."

Millar told the panel that Congress should take a variety of legislative steps to promote public transportation use, including increasing federal support for transit agencies to buy buses that use new fuel- and pollution-reduction technology, and extending tax credits for alternative fuel vehicles past a scheduled 2009 expiration.

CURRENT SITUATION

Budget Woes

The current transit debates are occurring at a time when gasoline prices are rising, local and federal budgets are limited and policymakers increasingly are concerned about curbing climate change.

This past fall, for example, Congress debated a climate-change bill that would limit carbon emissions and auction the right to emit them, earmarking some of the revenues for transit projects. Others are calling for more of the burden for congestion and new infrastructure to be borne by automobile drivers, by using congestion-pricing and privatizing some roads and bridges — which essentially means charging tolls.

For instance, faced with a $1.8 billion financing gap for road improvements, Indiana negotiated a $3.85 billion deal with a foreign consortium to lease and operate the Indiana Toll Road for 75 years. [57] In Florida, more than 90 percent of new roads since the early 1990s have been toll roads, according to a state Transportation Department spokesman. [58]

Transit funds are limited because the Highway Trust Fund — which provides 80 percent of the federal portion of transit funding and is financed with gasoline taxes — is running out of money. The shortfall is blamed on a variety of causes, including a growing demand for infrastructure projects, an overcommitment of transportation spending by Congress, greater auto fuel efficiency (which reduces fuel-tax revenues) and spiraling infrastructure-construction costs.

But transit critics argue that public transportation's role in reducing pollution and saving energy is overblown.

Rail is not "the environmental panacea its advocates promise," contends Randal O'Toole, director of the Thoreau Institute and a senior fellow at the Cato Institute, a Washington think tank. "Light rail may seem to use less energy and emit less pollution than buses or cars. But rail lines must be supplemented by feeder buses that tend to run much emptier than the corridor buses the rail lines replaced. Empty buses mean high energy use and pollution per passenger, so the transit system as a whole ends up consuming more energy and producing more pollution, per passenger, than if it ran only buses."

O'Toole also criticized transit advocates who "brag that transit produces less carbon monoxide than autos. But carbon monoxide is no longer a serious environmental threat. Today's problems are nitrogen oxides, particulates and greenhouse gases. Diesel buses, and rail cars whose electric power comes from burning coal, produce far more of these pollutants than today's automobiles." [4]

Taking aim at the APTA study released in September, Cox said on the Thoreau Institute's Web site that "a full cost accounting of greenhouse gas emissions" would include "emissions from construction of transit and highway systems, construction of vehicles, extraction of fuel for electricity generation and refining, disposal of vehicles and other materials, vehicle maintenance and administrative support."

Cox conceded that without transit use, more congestion would occur near the cores of the largest downtown areas, such as Manhattan and Chicago's Loop. But, he wrote, "the impact would be slight" elsewhere, in "places like Portland, Phoenix and perhaps Paducah . . . where the great bulk of the nation's traffic-congestion delay occurs."

"[R]elatively tiny (and low-cost) improvements to automobiles will do far more to reduce [greenhouse gas] emissions without reducing people's mobility or forcing people to change their travel habits," Cox wrote. [5]

But Millar has a different view.

"While it is good public policy to require more fuel-efficient automobiles, increasing the use of transit can have a more immediate impact on our nation's transportation fuel consumption," he said. "It could take 20 to 30 years to see a complete turnover of the vehicle fleet. A household does not need to go to the expense of buying a new vehicle to make a difference. They can simply take advantage of the nation's existing bus or rail services to dramatically reduce their carbon footprint." [6]

[1] Wendell Cox, "Transit's Role in Reducing Greenhouse Gases: No Big Deal," accessed at http://ti.org/antiplanner/?p=257.

[2] American Public Transportation Association, "Public Transportation Use Substantially Reduces Greenhouse Gases, According to New Study," news release, Sept. 26, 2007. The study is Todd Davis and Monica Hale, "Public Transportation's Contribution to U.S. Greenhouse Gas Reduction," Science Applications International Corp., September 2007.

[3] The study is ICF International, "Public Transportation and Petroleum Savings in the U.S.: Reducing Dependence on Oil."

[4] Randal O'Toole, "Dispelling Transit Myths," *Charlotte Observer*, Oct. 12, 2007, p. 8A. The article is from remarks O'Toole prepared for a John Locke Foundation forum in Charlotte.

[5] Cox, *op. cit.*

[6] American Public Transportation Association, *op. cit.*

The Congressional Budget Office projected last fall that if annual spending continued at authorized levels, the transit account would have enough revenue to cover expenditures until 2012, but the highway account would be exhausted in fiscal 2009. [59] The Senate Finance Committee and the Transportation Department have been considering ways to shore up the fund. [60]

Federal money pays for about half of the $13 billion a year spent on transit construction and equipment, and about 5 percent of operating costs, with the rest of operating costs covered by state and local funds and fare-box revenue. Still, transit supporters are watching the fund carefully.

"We'll be OK until Congress gets around to the next [transportation] authorization bill" in 2009, says Jeffrey Boothe — a Washington lawyer who chairs the New Starts Working Group, a coalition that backs federal funding for transit projects — unless lawmakers move money from the transit account to the highway account as a stopgap measure.

In recent months policymakers and federal officials have been debating what to do about the nation's aging bridges and other infrastructure — prompted in part by last year's Interstate 35 West bridge collapse in Minneapolis. The gasoline tax is central to the debate.

House Transportation Committee Chairman Oberstar wants to raise the federal gasoline tax, which has remained at 18.4 cents per gallon since 1993. [61] He has proposed raising the tax by 5 cents and dedicating the revenue to a new bridge-maintenance fund. [62]

A Mass Transit Glossary

Aerial Tramway — Unpowered passenger vehicles suspended from a system of aerial cables and propelled by separate cables attached to the vehicle suspension system. The cable system is powered by engines or motors at a central location not on board the vehicle.

Automated Guideway Transit — Guided transit vehicles operating singly or multi-car trains with a fully automated system (no crew on transit units). Service may be on a fixed schedule or in response to a passenger-activated call button. Automated guideway transit includes personal rapid transit, group rapid transit and people-mover systems.

Bus — Rubber-tired vehicles operating on fixed routes and schedules on roadways, powered by diesel, gasoline, battery or alternative fuel engines.

Commuter Rail — Urban passenger train service for local short-distance travel operating between a central city and adjacent suburbs.

Monorail — Guided transit vehicles operating on or suspended from a single rail, beam, or tube. Monorail vehicles usually operate in trains.

Light Rail — Lightweight passenger rail cars operating singly (or in short, usually two-car, trains) on fixed rails in right-of-way that is not separated from other traffic for much of the way. Light-rail vehicles are driven electrically with power being drawn from an overhead electric line via a trolley or a pantograph.

Heavy Rail — High-speed, passenger rail cars operating singly or in trains of two or more cars on fixed rails in separate rights-of-way from which all other vehicular and foot traffic are excluded.

Source: Federal Transit Administration

But President Bush opposes any hike in gas taxes, as do fiscal conservatives. "The last thing we should do is raise the federal gas tax, which would give members of Congress a bigger slush fund for earmarks," said Rep. Jeff Flake, R-Ariz. [65]

Transportation Secretary Peters told the House Transportation and Infrastructure Committee that an increase in federal taxes and spending "would likely do little, if anything, without a more basic change in how we analyze competing spending options and manage existing systems more efficiently." She also cited a "disturbing evolution" in the federal transportation program, with more than 6,000 earmarks in the 2005 funding bill, which added up to a "truly staggering" $23 billion. [66]

The fate of the Highway Trust Fund remains unclear. Some observers think it is unlikely that whoever wins next year's presidential election will walk into the White House in early 2009 and raise the federal gasoline tax to shore up the fund. On the other hand, a funding crisis could spur Washington to pass a stopgap measure to keep the fund from running dry.

Rep. Peter DeFazio, D-Ore., who chairs the committee's Highways and Transit Subcommittee, also wants a gas-tax hike. "There is a tremendous cost to doing nothing," he said. "We have been treading water, and now we are beginning to sink." [63]

In January a divided National Surface Transportation Policy and Revenue Study Commission urged an increase of up to 40 cents per gallon in federal gas taxes over five years to help fix aging bridges and roads and expand transit, but dissenters — including Transportation Secretary Peters, the commission's chairwoman — disagreed, saying tolls and private investment are better options.

"A dramatic increase in the gas tax does not stand a snowball's chance in hell of passing Congress," said Rep. John Mica, R-Fla., the top Republican on the House Transportation and Infrastructure Committee. [64]

"There's nothing like a good crisis to get people's attention," says Meyer, the Georgia Institute of Technology professor. In any event, he adds, "something will have to happen. If nothing else, the construction industry is incredibly powerful. If they're not building those roads and transit systems and all those things they make money on, there will be pressure brought to bear on Congress."

Local Support

The shortfall in federal transportation funds is likely to push states and localities to come up with more money for transit systems, which would mean persuading voters to pay higher sales or gas taxes or tolls.

Boothe, the Washington lawyer, says voters have approved 70 percent of transit-related ballot initiatives in the past five years. "There's a fair amount of support at

Is "congestion pricing" a good strategy?

YES

Jeffrey N. Shane
Under Secretary for Policy, U.S. Department of Transportation

From testimony before Subcommittee on Highways and Transit, June 7, 2007

Taxing fuel consumption rather than road usage disconnects the price travelers pay for using the transportation system — and thus their decisions about when and how much to use it — from the true [cost] of travel. Today a U.S. automobile driver pays the equivalent of about 2-3 cents per mile in federal and state gas taxes.

Yet, when that driver uses a congested roadway during rush hour, he or she imposes between 10 and 50 cents per mile — and in some cases even more — in costs upon the other drivers stuck in traffic by taking space on the highway and exacerbating congestion.

Similarly, gas-tax charges for off-peak travel are not adjusted to reflect the lower costs of such travel. Moreover, the enormous cost savings potentially available from highway pricing are even closer than previously believed. Research in recent years confirms that very small reductions in the number of vehicles using a congested highway facility can produce significant increases in traffic speeds. . . .

By substantially increasing traffic speeds and preventing gridlock, pricing can substantially increase facility "throughput." Counterintuitively, this means that an initial diversion of drivers actually allows for *more* customers to be served in a given time period. . . .

The benefits of congestion pricing extend beyond simply enhancing the speed of travel and the efficiency of highways. Road pricing encourages the use of mass transit, and by reducing traffic delays it can enable the operation of high-speed, reliable, commuter transit services such as bus rapid transit. . . .

Pricing will improve fuel economy and reduce greenhouse gas emissions by cutting out stop-and-go movement and idling. Pricing will encourage more sustainable land-use patterns by providing transparent signals about the true costs of real estate development on the outskirts of major cities.

Finally, congestion-based user charges can dramatically improve project-planning processes by providing clear signals as to where and when the benefits of expanding capacity are likely to exceed the costs of providing that capacity.

As prices rise, the case for adding new lanes or roads becomes increasingly obvious, to say nothing of the new supply of revenues from pricing that can be used to finance the improvements. . . .

NO

James J. Baxter
President, National Motorists Association

From "Toll Roads: The Slippery Slope," www.motorists.org

Conservative and libertarian organizations have been on a campaign to convince the public that the solution to America's traffic problems, primarily congestion, is toll roads.

The arguments for toll roads are laced with references to "free-market principles," "proper pricing," "supply and demand" and "economic incentives." Most of these discussions have become so obfuscated with nonsensical ruminations that important realities are ignored.

A real market-based system has willing sellers, willing buyers and reasonably unfettered competition among sellers and among buyers. The limited role of government in this system is to make sure everyone operates under the same rules. . . .

Ultimately, sellers base their prices on their costs and the demand of buyers who want to buy their products or services. Competing sellers can drive the price down. Competing buyers can drive the price up. . . .

Any highway of any consequence falls flat . . . when it comes to market principles. First, highway corridors are not assembled by willing buyers in competition with other willing buyers who must negotiate with willing (and unwilling) sellers who are also in competition with one another. The "state" identifies the corridor it wants, establishes what it considers to be a politically and judicially acceptable price and condemns the land of those sellers who disagree. This is "market principles" figuratively at the end of a gun barrel.

In the case of so-called "private" toll roads, the state [exclusively] grants its eminent domain . . . authority to the toll road owner. Does this seem like an unfettered, private, market-based system? . . .

Toll road advocates argue that those who use the system the most will pay the most. . . . [B]ut who determines what the buyers should pay? Is it competing sellers of similar services? Do the buyers really have viable alternatives to buy highway services from other sources? . . .

[N]ew highways are not being delayed for lack of money. There are billions of gas-tax dollars being siphoned off for non-highway purposes, or covering the federal deficit. New highways aren't being built because there is significant political opposition to new highways. . . .

Toll roads are an inefficient, counterproductive component of our highway system. They foster corruption, political patronage and detract from needed improvements on the rest of the highway system. . . .

To reduce traffic congestion, certain lanes on I-394 in St. Louis Park, Minn., are restricted around-the-clock to toll-payers, bus riders, carpoolers and motorcyclists. Experts estimate that congestion cost U.S. drivers 2.9 billion gallons of wasted fuel in 2005 — the equivalent of 58 fully loaded supertankers.

the local level," he says. "We hope that doesn't cause a withdrawal of funds at the federal level."

Last fall's campaign season underscored the strong — but not always universal — support for transit-related ballot initiatives. In Charlotte, N.C., voters in Mecklenburg County overwhelmingly turned aside an effort to repeal a half-cent transit sales tax that generated $70 million in 2006, allowing the Charlotte Area Transit System to continue with an ambitious plan to expand rail and bus service. [67]

But in the Seattle area, voters in King, Snohomish and Pierce counties rejected the largest transportation tax proposal in Washington state's history. It would have raised the sales tax to 9.4 percent and boosted car-license fees in order to add 50 miles of light rail (at a cost of $30.8 billion), 186 miles of new highway lanes ($16.4 billion) and provide money for a new bridge. [68] Some observers blame the measure's defeat on its high cost and the fact that it combined highway and rail spending, which may have turned off transit supporters who chafe at seeing more highway lanes and cars.

Crunican, the Seattle transportation director, is optimistic about transit in her region. She notes that growth in average vehicle miles traveled in the Puget Sound region leveled off to zero in the past five years and that vehicle ownership statewide has fallen 20 percent in 20 years.

But in last fall's vote, some Seattle-area voters showed that they are carefully judging current transit projects and being cautious about further expansion. "I want to see how the [light-rail line linking downtown Seattle with the Seattle-Tacoma International Airport] goes before we put up 50 more miles of it," teacher Amy Larson said in explaining why she voted against the tax measure. [69] The 15.6-mile Sea-Tac line is scheduled to open in 2009.

Meanwhile, transit projects continue to spread. Dallas, Denver, Orlando, Phoenix, Salt Lake City and Sacramento are building or expanding transit systems, as are other cities. [70] "Everybody talks about smart growth now," said Robert Dunphy, senior resident fellow for transportation and infrastructure at the Urban Land Institute. "These cities understand that transit is a huge part of that." [71]

In Seattle, local leaders are working on several fronts to expand public transit, encourage development near stations and reduce car traffic. Besides the airport line, which is expected to carry 40,000 riders a day, a new streetcar line opened in December to serve a newly developed South Lake Union area, a former industrial zone that planners are making into a biotech hub for the region.

Last year the City Council voted to require Seattle, when building a new road or maintaining an existing one, to try to provide for as many travel modes as possible, including bike lanes, sidewalks and transit. Plus, Seattle-area voters recently passed a measure to boost funding for bus services, the city established a program to provide space for shared cars and it helped start a trip-planning service that seeks to reduce drive-alone commutes. Seattle also has eased the parking-space requirements for developments around light-rail stations and other urban centers.

"If you provide more parking, it just encourages people to drive," said John Rahaim, the city's planning director. [72]

As with many cities, Seattle sees transit as part and parcel of a larger plan that aims not only to bring sanity to the roadways but also to produce a healthier environment and a more economically vibrant economy.

"We're a metropolitan area, and we're trying to manage congestion," says Crunican. "If you're adding new jobs, which we're doing, and you're adding new housing units, which we're doing, you should expect more activity. And then the question is, can you leverage some of that activity onto greenhouse-friendly trips."

Besides, she says, "We're also an overweight society in general, and there's nothing wrong with healthier lifestyles."

OUTLOOK

Proactive Planning

With traffic congestion building, greenhouse gases growing and large numbers of Americans seeking sidewalk-friendly urban neighborhoods, public transit clearly seems to be on a roll. Even so, obstacles lie on the tracks.

For instance, transportation problems need regional solutions, but political and taxing jurisdictions typically stop at city or county borders. Tim Lomax, who heads the national congestion studies undertaken by the Texas Transportation Institute, warned in congressional testimony in 2007 against a "patchwork of solutions to large interregional problems with little to no continuity.

"We already recognize regional and in some cases national consequences flowing from any of a number of transportation problems." [73]

Within localities conflict among proponents of various transportation modes — such as buses, rail and highways — can lead to decision-making gridlock. Better financing techniques, stronger management and greater political courage are needed to bring down the "separate silos" that characterize metropolitan transportation networks and integrate them into smooth-running systems, says Joseph M. Giglio, a business professor at Northeastern University with extensive experience in transportation issues.

"Transit has its own operating mode, financing and engineering basis. And highways do. But the commonality is the customer," he says.

Transit will also have to move in lockstep with land-use planning, experts say. Otherwise, systems designed to reduce sprawl and ease congestion could have the perverse effect of making those problems worse.

And that risk doesn't exist only within cities. "In California, sprawl could increase several orders of magnitude if high-speed train services come to the Central Valley, connecting Bakersfield to [Los Angeles] and Fresno to San Francisco," warned Robert Cervero, chair of the Department of City and Regional Planning at the University of California, Berkeley.

Expanding rail services between metropolitan areas and even between states underscores the need for "proactive state land-use planning and management . . . if the unintended sprawl-inducing consequences of these investments are to be avoided," he wrote. [74]

Ultimately, the outlook for public transit seems mixed. On the one hand, population growth, global warming, traffic gridlock and the desire for new kinds of close-in development suggest significant demand for rail lines, rapid buses and other kinds of transit. On the other hand, tight financing, sprawl and Americans' reluctance to leave their cars present significant obstacles.

In the end, cities face difficult choices in how to allocate their precious transportation dollars.

As Pisarski, the author of the Transportation Research Board's exhaustive studies on commuting, says, "One question I always ask is, what percent of a problem am I solving with what percent of my resources?"

NOTES

1. Steve Huettel, "Airport board takes light rail for a virtual ride," *The St. Petersburg Times*, Nov. 2, 2007, wwww.sptimes.com.

2. For background see Kathy Koch, "Flexible Work Arrangements," *CQ Researcher*, Aug. 14, 1998, pp. 697-720.

3. In 2006, the U.S. Department of Transportation began a broad initiative, the "National Strategy to Reduce Congestion on America's Transportation Network," to help state and local governments develop strategies to deal with congestion. Approaches related to road congestion include "Urban Partnership Agreements" with metro areas that in part encompass plans for congestion-pricing demonstrations and expansion of rapid bus services. For background, see: http://transportation.house .gov/Media/File/Highways/20070607/SSM_HT_6-7-07.pdf.

4. American Public Transportation Association, "Public Transportation Fact Book," 58th Edition, May 2007, p. 19. Data are from *Railway Age*, 2006 totals are preliminary.

5. Press release, "Annual study shows traffic congestion worsening in cities large and small," Texas Transportation Institute. Data are from the institute's 2007 Urban Mobility Report, based on 2005 data, the latest available.

6. Robert Cervero, "Economic Growth in Urban Regions: Implications for Future Transportation," prepared for Forum on the Future of Urban Transportation, Eno Transportation Foundation, Washington, D.C., December 2006, p. 14.

7. Alan E. Pisarski, "Commuting in America III," Transportation Research Board, 2006, p. 38.

8. *Ibid.*, p. 62.

9. For background, see Alan Greenblatt, "Downtown Renaissance," *CQ Researcher*, June 23, 2006, pp. 553-576.

10. American Public Transportation Association, *op. cit.*, p. 12; 2005 data are preliminary.

11. Zach Patton, "Back on Track," *Governing*, June 2007.

12. "Statement on Texas Transportation Institute's Congestion Report by American Public Transportation Association President William W. Millar," www.apta.com, Sept. 17, 2007.

13. Andy Guy, "Looking for Modern Transit," Great Lakes Bulletin News Service, Michigan Land Use Institute, Jan. 27, 2006. For background, see Mary H. Cooper, "Smart Growth," *CQ Researcher*, May 28, 2004, pp. 469-492.

14. U.S. General Accounting Office, "Surface Transportation: Moving Into the 21st Century," May 1999, p. 24.

15. Anthony Downs, "How Real Are Transit Gains?" *Governing*, March 2002.

16. Todd Litman, "Smart Transportation Investments II: Reevaluating the Role of Public Transit for Improving Urban Transportation," Victoria Transport Policy Institute, Sept. 10, 2007.

17. Randal O'Toole, "Debunking Portland: The Public Transit Myth," TCSdaily.com, Aug. 15, 2007.

18. William J. Mallett, "Public Transit Program Issues in Surface Transportation Reauthorization," Congressional Research Service, Sept. 10, 2007.

19. By 2025, a fifth of Americans will be 65 or older, many of them unable to drive, the American Public Transportation Association states in its "Public Transportation Fact Book," May 2007. It cites an AARP/Surface Transportation Policy Project study that found that half of non-drivers age 65 and over stay home on any give day in part because they don't have transportation options. The study cited is Linda Bailey, Surface Transportation Policy Project, "Americans: Stranded without Options," April 2004.

20. Testimony before House Committee on Transportation and Infrastructure, Subcommittee on Highways and Transit Implementation of New Starts and Small Starts Program, May 10, 2007.

21. Randal O'Toole, "A Desire Named Streetcar: How Federal Subsidies Encourage Wasteful Local Transit Systems," Cato Institute, Jan. 5, 2006.

22. Cato Institute news release, "Federal Subsidies Derail Local Train Systems," Jan. 5, 2006.

23. Todd Litman, "Responses to 'A Desire Named Streetcar,' Victoria Transport Policy Institute, Feb. 1, 2006.

24. Michael M. Grynbaum, "New York Pitches 'Congestion Pricing' to Federal Officials,' *The New York Times*, June 26, 2007, p. 4B.

25. Testimony of Craig J. Stone, deputy administrator, Washington State Department of Transportation's Urban Corridors Office, U.S. House of Representatives Committee on Transportation and Infrastructure, Subcommittee on Highways and Transit, "Congestion and Mobility Hearing," June 7, 2007.

26. Federal Highway Administration, U.S. Department of Transportation, "Congestion Pricing: A Primer," December 2006.

27. Mary E. Peters, "The Folly of Higher Gas Taxes," *The Washington Post*, Aug. 25, 2007, p. A15.

28. For background, see Marcia Clemmitt, "Aging Infrastructure," *CQ Researcher*, Sept. 28, 2007, pp. 793-816.

29. Bill Graves, "Add roads, not tolls," *USA Today*, www.usatoday.com, Feb. 27, 2007.

30. Press release from office of Anthony D. Weiner, "Weiner Applauds Mayor for Thinking Big, But Says Put the Brakes on Regressive Congestion Tax," April 21, 2007.

31. William D. Middleton, *Metropolitan Railways: Rapid Transit in America* (2003), pp. 1-2.

32. Brian J. Cudahy, *Cash, Tokens and Transfers: A History of Urban Mass Transit in North America* (1990), p. 22.

33. George M. Smerk, *The Federal Role in Urban Mass Transportation* (1991), p. 35.

34. *Ibid.*

35. Federal Highway Administration, www.fhwa.dot.gov/ohim/summary95/mv200.pdf.

36. Robert Bruegmann, *Sprawl: A Compact History* (2005), p. 130.

37. Smerk, *op. cit.*, p. 43.

38. American Public Transportation, *Public Transportation Fact Book 2007*, p. 11.

39. American Public Transportation Association, *op. cit.*

40. The 1944 GI Bill of Rights provided low-interest home loans for veterans. For background, see Peter Katel, "Wounded Veterans," *CQ Researcher*, Aug. 31, 2007, pp. 697-720.

41. Federal Highway Administration, *op. cit.*

42. Bruegmann, *op. cit.*, p. 130.

43. Middleton, *op. cit.*, p. 107.

44. Federal Transit Administration, "The Beginnings of Federal Assistance for Public Transportation," accessed at www.fta.dot.gov.

45. *Ibid.*

46. Middleton, *op. cit.*, p. 107.

47. *Ibid.*, p. 243.

48. Smerk, *op. cit.*, pp. 6-7.

49. *Ibid.*, p. 241.

50. Cudahy, *op. cit.*, p. 202; and Middleton, *op. cit.*, p. 151.

51. *Ibid.*, p. 152.

52. Smerk, *op. cit.*, p. 241.

53. Remarks of James Oberstar, "Intermodal Transportation: The Potential and the Challenge," Center for Transportation Studies, University of Minnesota, March 16, 2003, accessed at www.cts.umn.edu/Events/ObserstarForum/203/Speech.html.

54. Molly D. Castelazo and Thomas A. Garrett, "Light Rail: Boon or Boondoggle?" Federal Reserve Bank of St. Louis, 2004.

55. Cambridge Systematics Inc. with Economic Development Research Group, "Public Transportation and the Nation's Economy," October 1999. The study was underwritten by the private sector business members of the American Public Transit Association, the predecessor of the American Public Transportation Association, Washington, D.C.

56. Todd Litman, "Evaluating Public Transit Benefits in St. Louis," Victoria Transport Policy Institute, July 27, 2004.

57. Jim Abrams, The Associated Press, "Frozen gas tax leads to toll roads," www.usatoday.com, May 20, 2007.

58. *Ibid.*

59. Statement of Robert A. Sunshine before the Committee on the Budget, U.S. House of Representatives, "Public Spending on Surface Transportation Infrastructure," Oct. 25, 2007.

60. Abrams, *op. cit.*

61. Humberto Sanchez and Lynn Hume, "Report on Traffic's Economic Drain Prompts Calls for Gas Tax Hike," *The Bond Buyer*, Sept. 19, 2007, p. 33.

62. Jim Snyder, "Democrats, White House diverge on gas tax," *The Hill*, Sept. 6, 2007.

63. Sanchez and Hume, *op. cit.*

64. The Associated Press, "Transit Panel Urges Gas Tax Increase," *The New York Times*, Jan. 15, 2008.

65. Kevin Bogardus, "Flake joins Bush administration in opposition to gas tax increase," *The Hill*, Sept. 7, 2007, p. 13. For background, see Marcia Clemmitt, "Pork Barrel Politics," *CQ Researcher*, June 16, 2006, pp. 529-552.

66. Statement of Mary E. Peters before House Committee on Transportation and Infrastructure, Sept. 5, 2007.

67. Steve Harrison, "Tax supporters, foes surprised by margin of victory," *Charlotte Observer*, Nov. 7, 2007, p. 1A.

68. Larry Lange, "Proposition 1: Voters hit the brakes," *Seattle Post Intelligencer*, Nov. 7, 2007, updated Nov. 9, 2007.

69. *Ibid.*

70. Patton, *op. cit.*

71. *Ibid.*

72. Keith Schneider, "Seattle and Other Cities' Mantra: Improve Transit, Reduce Traffic," *The New York Times*, Oct. 24, 2007.

73. Testimony before House Committee on Transportation and Infrastructure Subcommittee on Highways and Transit, "The Many Dimensions of America's Congestion Problem — And a Solution Framework," June 7, 2007.

74. Cervero, *op. cit.*, p. 17.

BIBLIOGRAPHY

Books

Bruegmann, Robert, *Sprawl: A Compact History*, University of Chicago Press, 2005.
An urban planning expert at the University of Illinois, Chicago, argues that many problems blamed on sprawl, such as traffic congestion, "are, if anything, the result of the slowing of sprawl and increasing density in urban areas."

Cudahy, Brian J., *Cash, Tokens, and Transfers: A History of Urban Mass Transit in North America*, Fordham University Press, 1990.
Cudahy spans American transit history from horse-drawn rail cars to automated transit systems.

Middleton, William D., *Metropolitan Railways: Rapid Transit in America*, Indiana University Press, 2003.
This oversize book by a noted authority traces the history of rapid transit and includes a useful appendix that maps metro and light-rail transit lines in major North American cities.

Smerk, George M., *The Federal Role in Urban Mass Transportation*, Indiana University Press, 1991.
The director of the Institute for Urban Transportation at Indiana University traces the long history of transit policy and explores both its successes and failures in intricate detail.

Articles

Bernstein, Sharon, and Francisco Vara-Orta, "Near the rails but still on the road," *Los Angeles Times*, June 30, 2007.
This article analyzes the results of the Los Angeles region's efforts to wean people away from autos through transit-oriented residential development.

Patton, Zach, "Back on Track: Sprawling Sun Belt cities discover a new way to grow," *Governing*, June 2007.
While focusing on Charlotte, N.C.,'s ambitious transit plans, Patton writes: "Sun Belt cities from Orlando to Phoenix are building out light-rail systems, in an historic break from the car-bound past."

Pucher, John, "Renaissance of Public Transport in the United States?," *Transportation Quarterly*, winter 2002.
A professor in the Department of Urban Planning at Rutgers University traces developments in public transit during the 1990s.

Reports and Studies

Davis, Todd, and Monica Hale, "Public Transportation's Contribution to U.S. Greenhouse Gas Reduction," Science Applications International Corp., September 2007.
This technical study examines the growth in pollution from vehicles and the potential role of public transportation in reducing it.

Heffernan, Kara, ed., "Preserving and Promoting Diverse Transit-Oriented Neighborhoods," Center for Transit Oriented Development: A collaboration of the Center for Neighborhood Technology, Reconnecting America, and Strategic Economics, October 2006.
A study sponsored by the Ford Foundation offers recommendations for creating more mixed-income, mixed-race housing near transit stations.

Hennessey, Bridget, Jason Jordan, Mary Karstens and Stephanie Vance, "Transportation Finance at the Ballot Box," Center for Transportation Excellence, 2006.
The report provides details on transportation ballot measures since 2000, plus five local case studies.

Maguire, Meg, Kevin McCarty and Anne Canby, "From the Margins to the Mainstream: A Guide to Transportation Opportunities in Your Community," Surface Transportation Policy Partnership, Final Edition, 2006.
Planning, community design and transportation options for communities are among the topics covered.

"Mobility 2030: Meeting the Challenges to Sustainability," World Business Council for Sustainable Development, 2004.
A report based on the work of a dozen international automotive and energy companies concludes "that the way people and goods are transported today will not be sustainable if present trends continue."

"National Strategy to Reduce Congestion on America's Transportation Network," U.S. Department of Transportation, May 2006.
The plan calls for more-efficient bus systems, new private-investment opportunities in transportation infrastructure, a reduction in freight bottlenecks and other steps to relieve congestion.

Pisarski, Alan E., "Commuting in America III," Transportation Research Board, The National Academies, 2006.
The third report in a series going back 20 years gives a detailed snapshot of commuting patterns and trends.

"Public Transportation: Benefits for the 21st Century," American Public Transportation Association, 2007.
The report surveys in great detail what it calls "the benefits that public transportation brings to individuals, communities and our nation as a whole."

"Public Transportation Fact Book," 58th Edition, American Public Transportation Association, May 2007.
This thick compendium of transit data covers modes ranging from trolleys to ferryboats and vanpools.

For More Information

American Public Transportation Association, 1666 K St., N.W., Suite 1100, Washington, DC 20006; (202) 496-4800; www.apta.com. Represents public bus and commuter rail systems and others involved in transit.

Center for Transportation Excellence, 1640 19th St., N.W., #2, Washington, DC 20009; (202) 234-7562; www.cfte.org. Policy research center on public transportation.

Community Transportation Association of America, 1341 G St., N.W., 10th Floor, Washington, DC 20005; (800) 891-0590; www.ctaa.org. Advocates for effective public and community transportation and improved mobility.

Federal Transit Administration, 1200 New Jersey Ave., S.E., 4th & 5th Floors - East Building, Washington, DC 20590; (202) 366-4007. Administers federal funding for public transit systems.

Reason Foundation, 3415 S. Sepulveda Blvd., #400, Los Angeles, CA 90034; (310) 391-2245. www.rppi.org. Research organization that studies market-oriented transportation policies.

Reconnecting America, 436 14th St., Suite 1005, Oakland, CA 94612; (510) 268-8602; www.reconnectingamerica.org. Advocates integrating transit into communities and hosts the Center for Transit-Oriented Development.

Surface Transportation Policy Partnership, 1100 17th St., N.W., 10th Floor, Washington, DC 20036; (202) 466-2636; www.transact.org. Nonprofit coalition that advocates transportation options that improve public health, the economy, the environment and social equity.

Taxicab, Limousine & Paratransit Association, 3849 Farragut Ave., Kensington, MD 20895; (301) 946-5701; www.tlpa.org. Trade association for taxi companies, airport shuttles and other passenger transporters.

University Transportation Center for Mobility, Texas Transportation Institute, Texas A&M University System, 3135 TAMU, College Station, TX 77843-3135; (979) 845-2538; http://utcm.tamu.edu. Studies congestion management and other transportation issues.

Victoria Transport Policy Institute, 1250 Rudlin St., Victoria, BC V8V 3R7 (Canada); (250) 360-1560; www.vtpi.org. Independent research organization that produces useful background on transportation issues.

10

Torture Debate

Seth Stern

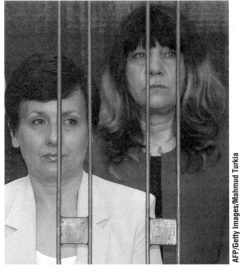

Nurses Valentina Siropoulu, left, and Valia
Cherveniashlka are among six Bulgarian medical
workers who were tortured while imprisoned for
eight years in Libya on charges they infected
hundreds of Libyan children with HIV-AIDS. They
were released in August. About 160 countries
torture prisoners, despite six international treaties
banning the practice.

From *CQ Researcher*,
September 1, 2007.

I t is called, simply, waterboarding. A prisoner is strapped to a
board with his feet above his head, his mouth and nose covered,
usually with cloth or cellophane. Water is then poured over his
face, inducing gagging and a terrifying sense of drowning.

The U.S. government — which has been accused of using waterboarding on detainees it suspects are terrorists — denies that it practices torture or cruel, inhuman or degrading treatment. The Central
Intelligence Agency (CIA) says it must use what it calls "enhanced
interrogation techniques" — to obtain critical information from
"enemy combatants" in the war on terrorism. [1] But human rights
advocates say waterboarding and other abusive interrogation tactics
are prohibited by international law.

To be sure, the United States is far from the worst offender when
it comes to mistreating prisoners. Even human rights advocates who
complain the most bitterly about the tactics used in America's war
on terror say they don't compare to those utilized by the world's
worst human rights abusers.

"Nothing the administration has done can compare in its scale to
what happens every day to victims of cruel dictatorships around the
world," Tom Malinowski, Human Rights Watch's Washington advocacy director, told the U.S. Senate Foreign Relations Committee on
July 26. "The United States is not Sudan or Cuba or North Korea." [2]

Indeed, about 160 countries practice torture today, according to
human rights groups and the U.S. State Department. [3] In July, for
example, six Bulgarian medical workers freed after eight years in a
Libyan prison said they had been tortured. "We were treated like
animals," said Ashraf al-Hazouz, one of the prisoners, who had been
accused of deliberately infecting Libyan children with the HIV-

Torture Still in Use Throughout the World

Some 160 countries practice torture, according to a 2005 survey of incidents reported by the U.S. Department of State and Amnesty International. Besides using torture to solicit information, some countries use it to punish or intimidate dissidents, separatists, insurgents and religious minorities. The Council of Europe accuses the U.S. Central Intelligence Agency (CIA) of using its rendition program to send kidnapped terror suspects to be interrogated in 11 cities — all in countries that practice torture.

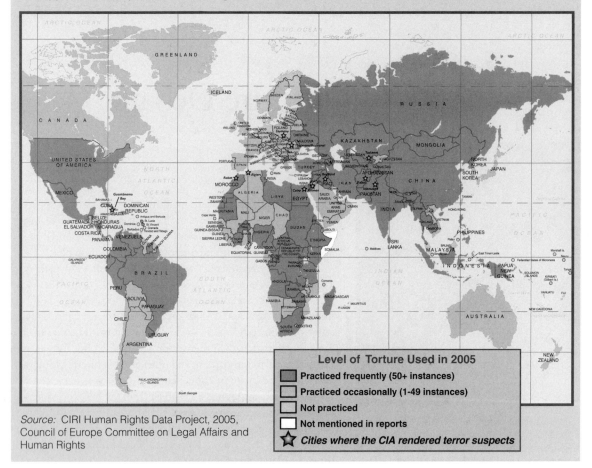

Level of Torture Used in 2005

- ▨ Practiced frequently (50+ instances)
- ▥ Practiced occasionally (1-49 instances)
- ☐ Not practiced
- ☐ Not mentioned in reports
- ☆ *Cities where the CIA rendered terror suspects*

Source: CIRI Human Rights Data Project, 2005, Council of Europe Committee on Legal Affairs and Human Rights

AIDS virus. Hazouz said the Libyans attached electrodes to his genitals and feet, unleashed attack dogs on him and tied his hands and legs to a metal bar, spinning him "like a chicken on a rotisserie." [4]

While other countries' abuse methods may seem more abhorrent, human rights advocates worldwide complain angrily that America's detention and interrogation practices in the post-9/11 war on terror have lowered the bar for torturers worldwide, giving habitual abusers a new justification for their behavior.

America's detention policies since Sept. 11, 2001, "are a gift to dictators everywhere" who "use America's poor example to shield themselves from international criticism and pressure," Malinowski said. Abusive governments now routinely "justify their own, longstanding practices of systematically violating basic human rights norms" by arguing that they — like the United States — must use torture to deal with the threat of international terrorism. [5]

U.S. counterterrorism policies that anger allies and human rights activists include the indefinite detentions

— without a guaranteed trial or right to counsel — of hundreds of alleged terrorists at Guantánamo Bay, Cuba, beginning shortly after 9/11. Then in April 2004 CBS' "60 Minutes II" televised explosive photographs that circulated around the world portraying harsh interrogation methods that reportedly had migrated from Guantánamo to the U.S.-run Abu Ghraib military prison near Baghdad. A year later *The Washington Post* revealed that the CIA was operating so-called "black sites" — secret prisons in Eastern Europe and Southeast Asia where detainees were subjected to extreme interrogation methods, allegedly including waterboarding. [6] Finally, news that the United States was kidnapping terror suspects from foreign locations and transporting them to interrogation sites in third countries with reputations for practicing torture — a tactic known as extraordinary rendition — triggered further global outrage. [7]

By adopting such measures, the United States has lost its moral authority to condemn torture and human rights abuses in other countries, say critics. "It's a very bad precedent for people to be able to say 'the U.S. — the biggest democracy promoter in the world — has to use it, why can't we?' " says physician Bhogendra Sharma, president of the Center for Victims of Torture in Nepal, which treats victims tortured by both the Nepalese government and Maoist guerrillas.

Few American ambassadors today "dare to protest another government's harsh interrogations, detentions without trial, or even 'disappearances,' knowing how easily an interlocutor could turn the

Severe Torture Still Used by Many Nations

According to the U.S. State Department and Human Rights Watch, the following nations are among those condoning widespread and particularly severe forms of torture:

 China: Prison guards are forbidden from using torture, but former detainees report the use of electric shock, beatings and shackles. Among those targeted for abuse are adherents of the outlawed Falun Gong spiritual movement, Tibetans and Muslim Uighur prisoners.

 Egypt: Government interrogators from the State Security Investigations arm of the Ministry of the Interior regularly torture suspected Islamic militants, including prisoners transferred to Egypt by the United States. Victims were kicked, burned with cigarettes, shackled, forcibly stripped, beaten with water hoses and dragged on the floor.

 Indonesia: Security officers in Aceh Province systematically torture suspected supporters of the armed Free Aceh movement, using beatings, cigarette burning and electric shock.

 Iran: Political prisoners are subjected to sensory deprivation known as "white torture" — they are held in all-white cells with no windows, with prison clothes and even meals all in white.

 Morocco: Terrorism suspects detained after a May 2003 attack in Casablanca were subjected to torture and mistreatment, including severe beatings.

 Nepal: Both government security personnel and Maoist rebels employ torture, including beating the soles of victims' feet, submersion in water and sexual humiliation.

 Nigeria: Armed robbery and murder suspects are subjected to beatings with batons, horse whips, iron bars and cables.

 North Korea: Captors routinely tortured and mistreated prisoners using electric shock, prolonged periods of exposure, humiliations such as public nakedness, being hung by the wrists and forcing mothers recently repatriated from China to watch the infanticide of their newborn infants.

 Russia: Russian security forces conducting so-called anti-terror operations in Chechnya mutilate victims and dump their bodies on the sides of roads.

 Uganda: Government security forces in unregistered detention facilities torture prisoners with caning and severe beatings and by inflicting pain to the genitals.

 Uzbekistan: Police, prison guards and members of the National Security Service routinely employ suffocation, electric shock, deprivation of food and water and sexual abuse. Prison regulations in 2005 permitted beatings under medical supervision.

Sources: "Human Rights Watch's 2007 World Report;" U.S. State Department "2006 Country Reports on Human Rights Practices"

Views Differ on U.S. Interrogation Tactics

A wide gulf exists between Americans' and Europeans' views of how the United States treats terrorism suspects. Americans are almost evenly split on whether the United States uses torture, but three-quarters of Germans and nearly two-thirds of Britons believe it does. And while just over half of Americans think U.S. detention policies are legal, 85 percent of Germans and 65 percent of Britons think they are illegal.

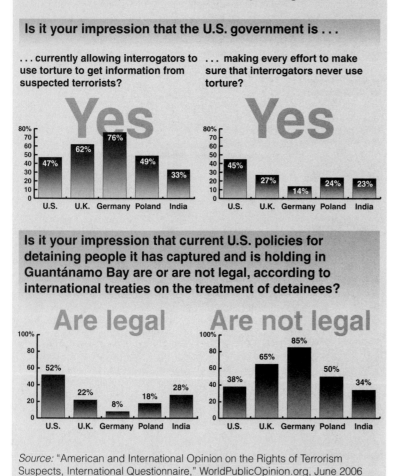

Is it your impression that the U.S. government is . . .

. . . currently allowing interrogators to use torture to get information from suspected terrorists?

. . . making every effort to make sure that interrogators never use torture?

Is it your impression that current U.S. policies for detaining people it has captured and is holding in Guantánamo Bay are or are not legal, according to international treaties on the treatment of detainees?

Source: "American and International Opinion on the Rights of Terrorism Suspects, International Questionnaire," WorldPublicOpinion.org, June 2006

The worldwide anger triggered by America's post-9/11 detention and interrogation policies stems not only from the perception that notorious governments now feel free to continue torturing prisoners. It also stems from widespread perceptions that:

• The United States' overwhelming military and technological superiority have made it arrogant, immune from having to abide by international norms.

• America's pervasive cultural influence has, since 9/11, "normalized" torture by spreading the concept across the globe that torture works and can be legally or morally justified.

• The United States has squandered its historic position as the world's leader in the fight against human rights abuses, opening itself to charges of being a hypocrite.

When the U.S. State Department released its annual report on human rights violators in 2005, both China and Russia said the United States has its own abuses to explain. "Unfortunately, [the report] once again gives us reason to say that double standards are a characteristic of the American approach to such an important theme," said a statement issued by the Russian foreign ministry. "Characteristically off-screen is the ambiguous record of the United States itself." [9]

Disappointment over U.S. tactics has been widespread. *El Tiempo*, a leading newspaper in Bogotá, Colombia, editorialized in 2005: "It seems incredible that these kind of un-civilizing backward steps are coming from a country which declares itself a defender of Western values and which has been so on more than one occasion." [10]

A 2006 survey of 26,000 people in 25 countries found that 67 percent disapproved of U.S. treatment of detainees in Guantánamo and other prisons. Some of the

tables and cite U.S. misconduct as an excuse for his government's own abuses," said a 2007 Human Rights Watch (HRW) report. [8]

Sarah Leah Whitson, HRW's director for the Middle East and North Africa, says when she visits officials in those regions to discuss their use of torture, their first reply now is often, "What about the United States? Go talk to the U.S. government."

highest disapproval rates were among America's closest allies in Europe — which have suffered their own terrorist attacks since 9/11 — and Middle Eastern allies such as Lebanon and Egypt, who fear the growing influence of Islamic extremists. [11]

But the 9/11 attacks did more than raise the profile of the torture debate in the United States. An Australian law professor has become one of the world's most vocal advocates for "life-saving compassionate torture," which he says is justified if it elicits crucial information needed to prevent future terrorist attacks and save innocent lives. (*See "At Issue," p. 235.*)

But critics of that argument point out that torture is not only used to extract life-saving information from terrorists but also to punish political dissidents, suspected criminals — who sometimes are innocent — and religious minorities. China, for instance, tortures members of the Falun Gong spiritual movement, Tibetan dissidents and Muslims from the Uighur region, according to Human Rights Watch.

In Iraq — where former leader Saddam Hussein was notorious for torturing political enemies — the U.S. occupation has not curbed the prevalence of torture by government agents or insurgents. In fact, say human rights advocates, the level of torture perpetrated by the Shiite-dominated Iraqi government and affiliated militias reportedly has escalated as the country has descended into civil strife. (*See sidebar, p. 224.*)

Despite the damage done to America's reputation by its counterterrorism tactics, President Bush in July said he was authorizing the CIA to reopen its overseas black sites. Bush had announced last September that the use of secret prisons had been suspended and that the prisoners were being transferred to Guantánamo. That decision was prompted by the U.S. Supreme Court's ruling that all U.S. detainees, including those held by the CIA, were covered by the Geneva Conventions' guidelines for the treatment of wartime detainees.

The administration said in July 2007 the CIA would comply with the conventions in its treatment of prisoners at the sites. But Bush's new order did not ban waterboarding or any other controversial interrogation techniques and gave interrogators wide latitude if their purpose is to gather intelligence needed to prevent terrorist attacks. [12]

The Bush administration and its supporters argue the United States is operating within the confines of U.S.

Vann Nath, one of only seven people to survive the Khmer Rouge's infamous Tuol Sleng prison, looks at a photo of Kaing Guek Eav, who ran the murderous regime's security service. Eav was recently found living in Cambodia as a born-again Christian. He was indicted by a U.N.-backed tribunal in July for his role in the torture and deaths of 14,000 men, women and children at the facility. His trial is expected to begin in 2008.

and international law and that aggressive interrogation methods are needed to protect against future terrorist attacks. "These are dangerous men with unparalleled knowledge about terrorist networks and their plans for new attacks," President Bush said in 2006. "The security of our nation and the lives of our citizens depend on our ability to learn what these terrorists know." [13]

With America seen as abandoning its role as the world's ethical standard-bearer, human rights groups complain that the European Union (EU) has not stepped up to fill the void. The EU has dragged its feet in questioning U.S. interrogation policies, say critics, and some EU countries have secretly allowed U.S. aircraft to use their airports for rendition flights. Some renditions involved innocent citizens who were tortured in countries long known to abuse prisoners, such as Egypt and

Torture Has Escalated in Iraq

Saddam's brutal legacy survives

The fall of Saddam Hussein and more than four years of U.S. occupation have done little to curb torture in Iraq. In fact, the level of torture perpetrated by government personnel and militias reportedly has escalated as the country has descended into what many consider a civil war.

The use of torture in Iraq is "totally out of hand," said Manfred Nowak, a U.N. official appointed to study torture around the world, and "many people say it is worse than it had been in the times of Saddam Hussein." [1]

Bodies brought to the Baghdad morgue often bear signs of acid-induced injuries, broken limbs and wounds caused by power drills and nails, said U.N. investigators. [2] The torture is mostly being perpetrated by the largely Shiite ministries of the Interior and Defense as well as by private Shiite militias, according to Sarah Leah Whitson, Human Rights Watch's program director for the Middle East and North Africa.

"The torture committed in the Ministry of Interior facilities we documented is certainly comparable to torture and abuse that's been recorded in the Baath prisons prior to the war," says Whitson.

In 2006 U.S. and Iraqi troops discovered a secret Baghdad prison run by the Interior Ministry, known as Site 4, where some of the more than 1,400 prisoners were found to have been subjected to systematic abuse.

Human rights advocates say the widespread use of torture is being fueled by the breakdown of law and order and the continued employment of officials who previously used torture during Saddam's regime. The weakened Iraqi central government has been unable to rein in the abuse of prisoners in these facilities, despite promises to do so. There has been less documented evidence of torture by Sunni insurgents, Whitson points out. Sunnis usually execute their victims, often by beheading.

A January 2005 report by Human Rights Watch found that police, jailers and intelligence agents — many of whom had similar jobs under Saddam — were "committing systematic torture and other abuses." Despite being "in the throes of a significant insurgency" in which thousands of police officers and civilians are being killed, the report said, "no government — not Saddam Hussein's, not the occupying powers and not

Syria. Besides generating outrage among close U.S. allies such as Canada, the incidents have led to prosecutions in Germany and Italy of Americans allegedly involved in the renditions.

As the Bush administration continues to defend itself against global criticism of its counterterrorism policies, these are some of the questions being asked:

Is torture effective?

Advocates and opponents of torture and other coercive techniques can look at the same evidence about their effectiveness and come to very different conclusions.

Take the case of Khalid Shaikh Mohammed, a senior al Qaeda operative and the alleged principal architect of the 9/11 attacks. He was captured in Pakistan in 2003 and interrogated by U.S. intelligence agents — reportedly using waterboarding — before being transferred to military custody at Guantánamo. [14] In a military hearing in March 2007 the Defense Department released a tran-

script of his confession in which he took credit for 31 different terrorist operations, including planning the 9/11 attacks in the United States and the beheading of *Wall Street Journal* reporter Daniel Pearl.

CIA Director Michael Hayden cited coercive interrogation techniques employed against detainees such as Mohammed (dubbed K.S.M. by intelligence agents) as an "irreplaceable" tool that helped yield information that has helped disrupt several terrorist plots since 9/11. "K.S.M. is the poster boy for using tough but legal tactics," said Michael Sheehan, a former State Department counterterrorism official. "He's the reason these techniques exist." [15]

But opponents of aggressive interrogation techniques, like Col. Dwight Sullivan, head defense lawyer at the Office of Military Commissions, cite Mohammed's serial confessions as "a textbook example of why we shouldn't allow coercive methods." [16]

Some intelligence experts doubt the veracity of portions of Mohammed's information. For one thing they

the Iraqi interim government — can justify ill-treatment of persons in custody in the name of security." [3]

The government of Iraqi Prime Minister Nuri Kamal al-Maliki has been slow to respond to reports of torture by governmental personnel, say human rights advocates. The Iraqi government "made all kinds of promises and commitments to investigate and review" allegations of torture in 2005, Whitson says, but since then the Interior Ministry "has only gone further outside control of the government," as war and sectarian violence have escalated. "There's not a commitment to making this issue a priority."

When British and Iraqi special forces raided the office of an Iraqi government intelligence agency in the southern city of Basra in March 2007, they found prisoners exhibiting signs of torture. Al-Maliki condemned the raid, but not the abuse it uncovered. [4]

Torture has continued since the start of the U.S. military occupation in Iraq. A 2004 report by the International Committee of the Red Cross found that after Saddam's fall Iraqi authorities beat detainees with cables, kicked them in the genitals and hung them by handcuffs from iron bars of cell windows for several hours at a time. [5]

Torture is also being employed in Kurdistan, a semi-autonomous region in northern Iraq that is the most stable part of the country. Human Rights Watch reported in July 2007 that detainees accused of anti-government activities were subjected to torture and other mistreatment. [6]

The torturers are security forces and personnel at detention facilities operated by the two major Kurdish political parties — the Kurdistan Democratic Party and the Patriotic Union of Kurdistan — which operate outside control of the region's government, the report said. Detainees have been beaten, put in stress positions and handcuffed for several days at a time.

Nonetheless, the abuses in Kurdistan do not equal those occurring elsewhere in Iraq. "Certainly the situation in mainland Iraq is much worse," says Whitson.

---

[1] BBC News, "Iraq Torture 'worse than Saddam,' " Sept. 21, 2006.

[2] *Ibid.*

[3] Doug Struck, "Torture in Iraq Still Routine, Report Says," *The Washington Post*, Jan. 25, 2005, p. A10.

[4] Kirk Semple, "Basra Raid Finds Dozens Detained by Iraqi Unit," *The New York Times*, March 5, 2007.

[5] "Report of the International Committee of the Red Cross on the Treatment by the Coalition Forces of Prisoners of War and Other Protected Persons by the Geneva Conventions in Iraq During Arrest, Internment and Interrogation," February 2004, www.globalsecurity. org/military/library/report/2004/icrc_report_iraq_feb2004.pdf.

[6] "Caught in the Whirlwind: Torture and Denial of Due Process by the Kurdistan Security Forces," Human Rights Watch, July 3, 2007, http://hrw.org/reports/2007/kurdistan0707/.

---

don't think a single operative — even one as high ranking as he — could have been involved in 31 separate terrorist plots. And those intimately associated with the Pearl case are highly skeptical that Mohammed himself murdered Pearl, as he claimed.

"My old colleagues say with 100-percent certainty that it was not K.S.M. who killed Pearl," former CIA officer Robert Baer told *New Yorker* writer Jane Mayer. And Special Agent Randall Bennett, who oversaw security at the U.S. consulate in Karachi when Pearl was killed, said "K.S.M.'s name never came up" during his interviews with those convicted in 2002 of the murder. [17]

Skeptics of torture's effectiveness say most people — to end their suffering — will provide false information. For instance, a torture victim deprived of his clothes will feel so "ashamed and humiliated and cold," said retired FBI counterterrorism agent Dan Coleman, "he'll tell you anything you want to hear to get his clothing back. There's no value in it." [18]

Others say torture doesn't work against zealots. "People who are committed to their ideology or religion . . . would rather die than speak up," says Sharma at the Center for Victims of Torture in Nepal.

Both opponents and supporters of coercive interrogation methods, however, agree torture is useful for other purposes. Many countries use torture to punish dissidents, separatists or guerrillas and to intimidate others from joining such groups. "The real purpose of torture is oppression of one or the other kind, to send a signal to anyone who is an opponent that there is a very, very grave risk," says Sune Segal, head of communications for the Copenhagen-based International Rehabilitation Council for Torture Victims, which collaborates with 131 treatment centers around the world. "It's not about soliciting information."

Underlying the debate is the fact that little scientific evidence exists about whether torture works. A recent Intelligence Science Board study concluded that "virtually none" of the limited number of techniques used by

U.S. personnel in recent decades "are based on scientific research or have even been subjected to scientific or systematic inquiry or evaluation." [19]

Darius Rejali, a political science professor at Reed College in Portland, Ore., says regimes that employ torture aren't likely to divulge their findings, and torturers themselves have very little incentive to boast about their work, which is punishable under international law. "Torture travels by back routes," Rejali says. "There's rarely training, so there is no particular mechanism for determining whether it works."

Experienced interrogators who have talked about their work say pain and coercion are often counterproductive. John Rothrock, who as a U.S. Air Force captain in Vietnam headed a combat interrogation team, said he didn't know "any professional intelligence officers of my generation who would think this is a good idea." [20]

Experts say the most effective interrogations require a trained interrogator. Coleman says he learned to build a rapport with even the worst suspects rather than trying to intimidate them. He would patiently work to build a relationship in which the target of his interrogation would begin to trust him and ultimately share information.

You try to "get them to the point, in the intelligence world, where they commit treason," he said. [21]

Is torture ever justified?

Australian law Professor Mirko Bagaric at Deakin University in Melbourne prompted a vigorous public debate in May 2005 when he suggested that torture is sometimes morally justified.

"Given the choice between inflicting a relatively small level of harm on a wrongdoer and saving an innocent person, it is verging on moral indecency to prefer the interests of the wrongdoer," Bagaric wrote in *The Age*, a leading daily paper in Melbourne. Such cases are analogous to a situation in which a wrongdoer threatens to kill a hostage unless his demands are met, he said. "In such a case, it is not only permissible but desirable for police to shoot (and kill) the wrongdoer if they get a 'clear shot.' " [22]

In the United States, Harvard Law Professor Alan Dershowitz has argued that the legal system should adjust to the reality that if it could prevent a catastrophic terrorist attack that could kill millions, interrogators will probably torture a suspect whether or not it's legal. In emergencies, he contends, courts should issue "torture warrants" to interrogators trying to prevent such attacks.

"A formal, visible, accountable and centralized system is somewhat easier to control than an ad hoc, off-the-books and under-the-radar-screen non-system," Dershowitz wrote. [23]

Those who justify torture in certain situations usually invoke a hypothetical "ticking time bomb" scenario in which interrogators torture a suspect to obtain information that can help prevent an imminent attack. Twenty-five years ago, long before the rise of Islamist terrorists, philosophy Professor Michael Levin of the City University of New York hypothesized a similar scenario in *Newsweek*.

"Suppose a terrorist has hidden a bomb on Manhattan Island, which will detonate at noon on 4 July. . . . Suppose, further, that he is caught at 10 a.m. that fateful day, but — preferring death to failure — won't disclose where the bomb is. . . . If the only way to save those lives is to subject the terrorist to the most excruciating possible pain, what grounds can there be for not doing so?" [24]

But opponents of torture say such perfect "ticking time bomb" scenarios occur in the movies, but rarely in real life. Interrogators usually aren't positive they have captured the one person with knowledge of a real plot. And even if they torture such a suspect, it usually won't prevent the attack because his accomplices will proceed without him, critics say.

"I was in the Army for 25 years, and I talked to lots of military people who had been in lots of wars. I talked to lots of people in law enforcement," says James Jay Carafano, a fellow at the conservative Heritage Foundation. "I've never yet ever found anyone that's ever confronted the ticking time bomb scenario. That's not the moral dilemma that people normally face." [25]

"The United States is a nation of laws," says Sen. Patrick J. Leahy, a Vermont Democrat who chairs the Senate Judiciary Committee, "and I categorically reject the view that torture, even in such compelling circumstances, can be justified." Even if harsh interrogation techniques do not rise to the level of torture, he said, they are probably illegal under international laws that prohibit cruel, inhumane or degrading treatment of prisoners.

Law professors and philosophers widely agree that torture is always immoral and should not be legalized. Once torture is allowed in extreme circumstances, they point out, it quickly spreads to less urgent situations. "It has a tendency to just proliferate," says Raimond Gaita, a professor of moral philosophy at King's College in London.

He cites the experience of Israel, which authorized coercive interrogation techniques in 1987 in limited circumstances. But interrogators in the field used more aggressive techniques with more suspects than intended.

Eitan Felner, former director of the Israeli Information Center for Human Rights in the Occupied Territories, writes the lesson of Israel's experience is "the fallacy of believing — as some influential American opinion-makers do today — that it is possible to legitimize the use of torture to thwart terrorist attacks and at the same time restrict its use to exceptional cases." [26]

Instead, torture should remain illegal and interrogators faced with the time-bomb scenario should be in the same legal position as someone who commits civil disobedience, say opponents. "Anyone who thinks an act of torture is justified should have . . . to convince a group of peers in a public trial that all necessary conditions for a morally permissible act were indeed satisfied," writes Henry Shue, a professor of politics and international relations at the University of Oxford. [27]

Human Rights advocates say that — while not explicitly endorsing torture — U.S. policies have changed the dialogue about torture around world. "It used to be these things were automatically bad," says Jumana Musa, advocacy director for Amnesty USA. "Now, there's a cost-benefit analysis and the notion that this isn't really that bad."

Have U.S. attitudes toward torture changed?

Some prominent American politicians and some soldiers, albeit anonymously, have recently endorsed torture as a way to prevent terrorist attacks or save lives.

At a May 2007 GOP presidential debate, Rudolph W. Giuliani, the mayor of New York during the Sept. 11 terror attacks, said if elected president he would advise interrogators "to use every method they could think of" to prevent an imminent catastrophic terror attack. Other candidates were even more explicit, embracing torture with an openness that would have been unheard of before 9/11. California Rep. Duncan Hunter said he would tell the Defense secretary: "Get the information," while Colorado Rep. Tom Tancredo endorsed waterboarding. [28]

Some U.S. military personnel who have served in Iraq express similar attitudes. More than a third of the 1,700 American soldiers and Marines who responded to a 2006 survey said torture would be acceptable if it helped save the life of a fellow soldier or helped get information, and

Getty Images/*The Washington Post*

An American soldier threatens an Iraqi detainee with an attack dog in one of the graphic Abu Ghraib prison abuse photos that shocked the world in 2004. Human rights advocates worldwide say America's harsh post-9/11 detention and interrogation practices lowered the bar for torturers worldwide. Twelve low-level U.S. military personnel have since been convicted for their roles in the abuse, which an Army investigation described as "sadistic, blatant and wanton criminal" abuse.

10 percent admitted to using force against Iraqi civilians or damaging their property when it wasn't necessary. [29]

But many top U.S. military leaders, interrogators and veterans denounce torture as ineffective and say it will only make it more likely that American captives will be tortured in the future. Sen. John McCain, R-Ariz., who was tortured while a prisoner of war in Vietnam, has spoken out forcefully against torture and led the 2005 effort in Congress to limit the kinds of interrogation methods U.S. military personnel can use.

"We've sent a message to the world that the United States is not like the terrorists. [W]e are a nation that upholds values and standards of behavior and treatment of all people, no matter how evil or bad they are," McCain said. Furthermore, he added, disavowing torture will "help us enormously in winning the war for the hearts and minds of people throughout the world in the war on terror." [30]

A 2006 public opinion survey by the University of Maryland's Program on International Policy Attitudes (PIPA) suggests that most Americans reject the use of torture. The PIPA poll found that 75 percent of Americans agreed that terror detainees had "the right not to be tortured." Fifty-seven percent said the United States should

CHRONOLOGY

1700s *Torture is banned in Europe.*

1754 Prussia becomes first European state to abolish torture; other European countries soon follow suit.

1900-1950 *Torture re-emerges, then is prohibited.*

1917 Russian Revolution gives birth to communism, which will foster totalitarian regimes that will torture perceived enemies of the state.

1933 Nazis take over Germany and soon begin torturing civilian prisoners.

1948 U.N. adopts Universal Declaration of Human Rights banning torture.

1949 Geneva Conventions ban all use of "mutilation, cruel treatment and torture" of prisoners of war.

1950s-1960s *Torture continues, despite international ban.*

1954 France tortures thousands of Algerians during Algeria's war for independence.

1961 Amnesty International is founded after two Portuguese students are jailed for seven years for toasting freedom.

1970s-1990s *Democracies — as well as authoritarian regimes — continue to torture.*

1971 British interrogators use the "five techniques" against Irish Republican Army suspects. European Court of Human Rights calls the methods illegal.

1975 Khmer Rouge takes over Cambodia and soon begins torturing and murdering thousands of detainees.

1978 Human Rights Watch is founded.

1987 Israel authorizes use of aggressive interrogation techniques during widespread Palestinian unrest.

1999 Israel's Supreme Court bans torture and abusive interrogation methods.

2000s-Present *Rise of Islamic terrorist attacks sparks increasing use of torture.*

2001 Muslim terrorists kill 3,000 in Sept. 11 attacks. . . . Hundreds of Muslims are detained in the United States and Afghanistan. . . . Fox Television's "24" begins showing U.S. agents using torture.

2002 First "enemy combatants" captured in Afghanistan arrive at Guantánamo naval base in Cuba. President Bush says they will be treated humanely, but that they are not protected by Geneva Conventions. . . . In September Syrian-born Canadian Maher Arar is detained during a stopover in New York and is sent to Syria for interrogation, where he is tortured.

March 30, 2004 U.S. Supreme Court rules Alien Tort Claims Act can be used to sue human rights abusers.

April 27, 2004 CBS News' "60 Minutes II" airs photographs of U.S. troops abusing prisoners at Abu Ghraib prison in Iraq.

November 2005 *Washington Post* reports the CIA detains terror suspects in secret prisons where detainees allegedly are subjected to coercive interrogation techniques. . . . U.S. government insists it does not torture. Congress passes Detainee Treatment Act, prohibiting torture and mistreatment of prisoners but limiting detainees' rights to challenge their detentions.

2006 On June 29, Supreme Court rules U.S. detainees are subject to the Geneva Conventions. . . . Military Commissions Act authorizes new courtroom procedures for enemy combatants but allows greater flexibility for CIA interrogations.

2007 A German court orders 13 U.S. intelligence agents arrested for their alleged role in rendering a German citizen to Afghanistan. . . . Canada apologizes to Arar for allowing him to be taken to Syria. . . . In July, President Bush authorizes the CIA to reopen secret overseas prisons. . . . International war crimes tribunal in Cambodia indicts former Khmer Rouge leader Kaing Geuk Eav for the torture and murder of thousands of prisoners. . . . Libya admits it tortured Bulgarian medical personnel imprisoned for eight years.

not be permitted to send terror suspects to countries known to torture, and 73 percent said government officials who engage in or order torture should be punished. Fifty-eight percent of Americans said torture was impermissible under any circumstances — about the same percentage as those in countries like Ukraine, Turkey and Kenya — but lower than the percentages in Australia, Canada and France. [31]

Some critics fear that since 9/11 U.S. television shows and movies have changed the way torture is portrayed, making torture more palatable to Americans and the rest of the world.

"It used to be the bad guys who used these techniques," says David Danzig of Human Rights First, a New York-based advocacy group that works to combat genocide, torture and human rights abuses. "You saw it infrequently — an average of four or five times a year — and when you did see it, it was space aliens or Nazis doing it, and it almost never worked. Now it's often the heroes who are using these techniques."

The number of instances of torture portrayed on television jumped from almost none in 1996 to 228 in 2003, according to the Parents Television Council. [32]

Fox Television's "24" has come to symbolize that almost tectonic shift in TV's treatment of torture. The hero of the show — which debuted two months after 9/11 — is Jack Bauer, a member of a unit charged with preventing catastrophic terrorist attacks, including nuclear and poison gas attacks on American cities such as Los Angeles. Bauer and his comrades have been shown using electrical wires, heart defibrillators, physical assaults and chemical injections to obtain information vital to preventing the attacks. [33]

The show's creator has insisted he is not trying to present a realistic — or glamorized — view of torture and that Bauer is portrayed as paying a high psychological price for using torture. [34]

But critics say the show — enormously popular in the United States and throughout the world — is changing how American citizens and soldiers view torture. "The biggest lie that has gained currency through television is that torture is an acceptable weapon for the 'good guys' to use if the stakes are high enough. . . . It is a lie," wrote John McCarthy, a journalist who was held hostage in Lebanon in the late 1980s. He accused the entertainment industry of "minimizing the true horrors of torture by failing to show the very profound impact it has on victims' lives." [35]

THE RACK.

AFP/Getty Images/Hulton Archive

Cuthbert Simpson, a Protestant martyr, suffers on the rack in the Tower of London in 1563. Torture has been used over the centuries to solicit information and to punish political and religious dissenters.

The show "leaves a message with junior soldiers that it's OK to cross the line in order to gather intelligence and save lives," said Danzig.

Senior American military officials were so worried about the show's impact that Brig. Gen. Patrick Finnegan, dean of the United States Military Academy, and top FBI and military interrogators visited the set in 2006. Finnegan told the show's creators it gives U.S. military personnel the wrong idea and has hurt America's image abroad by suggesting the United States condones torture. [36]

The show's impact on world opinion of Americans has been the subject of numerous debates — both in the United States and abroad — including a 2006 panel discussion at the Heritage Foundation. The show reinforces a world view of Americans as people who succeed by "breaking the law, by torturing people, by circumventing the chain of command," said David Heyman, director of Homeland Security at the nonpartisan Center for Strategic and International Studies, which focuses on security issues. [37]

Carafano, the Heritage fellow, said the program "just sort of confirms [the] prejudice" of those "who think ill of us" already. [38]

The show was also debated in June at a conference of North American and European judges in Ottawa, Canada. U.S. Supreme Court Justice Antonin Scalia argued that government agents should have more latitude

Careful Training Creates Soldiers Who Torture

Most defy sadistic stereotype

Torturers are made, not born. That was the finding of a Greek psychology professor who studied the military regime that came to power in Greece after a 1967 coup.

Until it fell in 1974, the dictatorship carefully trained soldiers to gather information and squelch dissent through torture. That's when Professor Mika Haritos-Fatouros tried to understand how the soldiers had been turned into torturers. In one of the most in-depth studies of torturers ever conducted, she interviewed 16 former soldiers and reviewed the testimony of 21 others and their victims. [1]

Many of her interviewees defy the stereotype of sadistic men who take pleasure in abuse. Haritos-Fatouros found that the torturers were simply plucked from the ranks of ordinary soldiers and trained. One, from a farm family, was a 33-year-old high school teacher married with two children by the time Haritos-Fatouros interviewed him. But for 18 months he had tortured prisoners and ordered others to do so.

The army sought young recruits from rural, conservative families who were physically healthy, of normal intelligence, conformist in nature and compliant. They underwent three months of intensive "training," during which they were broken down physically and mentally — a process that began almost before they arrived at the training facility. The abuse of the torturers-in-training intensified during the subsequent weeks as they were allowed little sleep and ordered to run or hop everywhere they went.

The aim "was to minimize all resistance by instilling in the cadets the habit of obeying without question an order without logic," Haritos-Fatouros wrote. [2] In short, they were programmed to blindly obey authority and dehumanize their victims.

Gradually, they were desensitized to torture. First, they participated in group beatings. One of the torturers said the first time he participated in a group beating he went to his cousin's house and cried. But it got easier each time, he said. Later, they ratcheted up to inflicting electric shocks and other serious abuse.

The underlying goal, Haritos-Fatouros concluded, was making the torturers believe they were "not, in fact, inflicting a savage and horrifying violation upon another human being."

"They brainwashed us," one torturer said. "It was only later we realized that what we did was inhuman. It was only after I finished my military service that it occurred to me that most of us beat up prisoners because we'd been beaten up ourselves." [3]

Another torturer told her, "When I tortured, basically, I felt it was my duty. A lot of the time I found myself repeating the phrases I'd heard in the lessons, like 'bloody communists' and so on. I think I became worse as time went on. I became more a part of the system. I believed in the whole system." [4]

Haritos-Fatouros' chilling conclusion: "We are all, under the right conditions, capable of becoming torturers." [5]

---

[1] Mika Haritos-Fatouros, *The Psychological Origins of Institutionalized Torture* (2003).

[2] *Ibid.*, p. 46.

[3] *Ibid.*, p. 95.

[4] *Ibid.*, p. 82.

[5] *Ibid.*, p. 229.

---

in times of crisis. "Jack Bauer saved Los Angeles," said Scalia. "He saved hundreds of thousands of lives." [39]

Scalia's comments sparked heated retorts from the other judges and a subsequent *Globe and Mail* editorial. "Jack Bauer is a creation of wishful thinking. . . . He personifies the wish to be free of moral and legal constraints. . . . That's why constitutions exist; it's so tempting when fighting perceived evil to call for Jack Bauer." But, left unchecked, the commentary concluded, "Jack Bauer will poison liberty's fount." [40]

The popular TV program, however, doesn't seem to have clouded the vision of a group of American high school students invited to the White House in June to receive the prestigious Presidential Scholar award. They handed President Bush a handwritten letter urging him to halt "violations of the human rights" of terror suspects. "We do not want America to represent torture," said the letter. [41]

BACKGROUND

Ancient Practice

Torture has been embraced by some of the world's most enlightened civilizations. Egyptian wall paintings and friezes depict scenes of horrific treatment of enemies. [42] In ancient Greece, slaves and foreigners could be tortured lawfully but free citizens could not. The same held true in ancient Rome, where free citizens could only be tortured in cases of treason. Slaves could be beaten, whipped, stretched on the rack or burned with hot irons — as long they were not permanently injured or killed. [43]

The use of torture in Europe expanded in the 13th century after Italian city-states began to require stricter proof of guilt in criminal trials. Before that, guilt or innocence was proven by combat or endurance trials in which God was expected to favor the innocent. [44] Under the reforms, defendants could only be found guilty if two witnesses testified against them or the accused confessed to the crime. When there were no witnesses, torture was used to produce confessions, a practice that would persist for the next 500 years in Europe.

Torture was also used to punish prisoners in public spectacles, often attended by cheering crowds. In the technique known as "pressing to plead" weights were piled on the prisoner's body, crushing him until he confessed — or died. Victims were also stretched on a device called the rack — sometimes until their bones were pulled out of their sockets. Britain's King Henry VIII used torture against those who challenged his position as head of the Church of England. Queen Elizabeth I employed torture against those suspected of treason.

Particularly brutal torture methods gained religious sanction during the inquisitions conducted by the Roman Catholic Church to stamp out heresy. In 1252, Pope Innocent IV formally authorized the use of torture against heretics. In Spain for instance, victims were bound to a turning wheel as various body parts — the soles of their feet or the eyes — were brought closer and closer to a fire. In Italy, victims were suspended by their arms — tied behind their backs — from a pulley attached to a beam. The "strappado," as it was called, was then repeatedly jerked to increase the pain. Weights sometimes were attached to the victim's feet to increase the agony, often fracturing bones and tearing limbs from the body. [45]

In the early 17th century, some Europeans tried to regulate torture. Dutch legal scholar Johannes Voet, for instance, argued that torture should only be used when there are "grave presumptions" against the accused. He also suggested that the youngest member of any group of defendants be tortured first, because the youngest was thought most likely to talk. [46]

In 1754 Prussia became the first modern European state to abolish torture. Ten years later, in his seminal book *On Crimes and Punishments*, Italian philosopher and penal reformer Cesare Beccaria denounced torture as "a sure route for the acquittal of robust ruffians and the conviction of weak innocents." The book reflected emerging Enlightenment-era ideals about individual rights and the proper limits on punishment. [47] Within a century, most of Europe had banned torture, in part because convictions without eyewitness testimony or confessions were increasingly allowed, reducing the need for torture. But torture continued to thrive in Africa, Asia and the Middle East. In 1852, for example, leaders of an outlawed religious group in Persia — modern-day Iran — were "made into candlesticks" — with holes dug into their flesh into which lighted candles were inserted. [48]

By 1874, French author Victor Hugo naively declared "torture has ceased to exist." But torture continued to be used against insurgents in Austria and Italy and against opponents of the Tsarist government in Russia.

Changing Norms

By the 20th century, social norms about punishment had changed; the upper classes no longer wanted to watch gruesome public spectacles. Torture sessions became secretive affairs, conducted in prison basements and detention centers. [49]

In the first half of the 20th century, torture was employed by totalitarian governments in countries such as Germany, Russia, Italy and Japan. [50] The Nazis tortured prisoners of war to get information and conducted horrific medical experiments on Jewish and Gypsy civilians in concentration camps. Japanese soldiers severely abused and tortured Allied prisoners.

After the horrors of World War II, torture and lesser forms of abuse known as cruel, inhumane and degrading treatment were outlawed by a series of treaties: the 1948 Universal Declaration of Human Rights, the Geneva Conventions of 1949 and the 1984 Convention Against Torture. (*See box, p. 232.*)

Five International Treaties Ban Torture

Torture has been banned by international treaties since 1948. Key provisions include:

Universal Declaration of Human Rights (1948)

No one shall be subjected to torture or to cruel, inhuman or degrading treatment or punishment.

Adopted by U.N. General Assembly on Dec. 10, 1948, www.un.org/Overview/rights.html.

Third Geneva Convention, Common Article 3 (1949)

Regarding the treatment of civilians and prisoners of war, "the following acts are and shall remain prohibited at any time:

   (a) violence to life and person, in particular murder of all kinds, mutilation, cruel treatment and torture;

   (b) taking of hostages;

   (c) outrages upon personal dignity, in particular humiliating and degrading treatment . . ."

Adopted on Aug. 12, 1949, by the Diplomatic Conference for the Establishment of International Conventions for the Protection of Victims of War, held in Geneva, Switzerland; effective Oct. 21, 1950, www.icrc.org/ihl.nsf/0/e160550475c4b133c12563cd0051aa66?OpenDocument.

International Covenant on Civil and Political Rights (1966)

Article 7
No one shall be subjected to torture or to cruel, inhuman or degrading treatment or punishment. In particular, no one shall be subjected without his free consent to medical or scientific experimentation.

Article 10
All persons deprived of their liberty shall be treated with humanity and with respect for the inherent dignity of the human person.

Adopted the U.N. General Assembly on Dec. 16, 1966, and opened for signature and ratification; became effective on March 23, 1976, www.unhchr.ch/html/menu3/b/a_ccpr.htm.

Torture persisted during the second half of the century, however, particularly in authoritarian countries. For instance, Soviet and Chinese communist regimes tortured political and religious dissidents. Cambodia's murderous Khmer Rouge military regime had a 42-page interrogation manual for use at its Tuol Sleng torture center during the 1970s.

Many repressive regimes were supported by the United States, which was fighting a proxy Cold War with the Soviet Union in developing countries like Vietnam, El Salvador and Guatemala. Because such governments were resisting socialist or communist insurgencies, the United States often provided them with guns, military aid and training, even though they were known to use torture.

In the 1970s, President Jimmy Carter broke with the past by announcing that the nation's foreign policy henceforth would be based on advancing human rights. Congress passed a law requiring the State Department to issue annual reports on the human rights records of any country that received U.S. economic or military aid. [51] Although the law remains on the books and the State Department continues to issue its annual human rights "country reports," the foreign policy focus on human rights faded under Carter's successor, Ronald Reagan, who placed fighting communism above protecting human rights.

Since the 1970s, however, greater scrutiny by Western governments, the U.N., the EU and human rights groups has prompted changes in how countries torture. Increasingly, methods were adopted that don't leave visible scars, such as beating the soles of feet, sleep deprivation, sexual humiliation and electric shock.

Democracies' Experience

It wasn't only communists and dictators who tortured captives after World War II. Democratic countries — including Great Britain, France and Israel — all used torture or other forms of abuse during the last half of the century, usually in response to what they viewed as imminent threats from religious or political dissidents.

But the democracies ended up alienating their own citizens as well as the occupied populations, according to

Protocol Additional to the Geneva Conventions of Aug. 12, 1949, relating to the Protection of Victims of International Armed Conflicts (1977)

Article 75: Fundamental guarantees

1. . . . persons who are in the power of a Party to the conflict . . . shall be treated humanely in all circumstances and shall enjoy, as a minimum, the protection provided by this Article without any adverse distinction based upon race, colour, sex, language, religion or belief, political or other opinion, national or social origin, wealth, birth or other status, or on any other similar criteria. Each Party shall respect the person, honour, convictions and religious practices of all such persons.

2. The following acts are and shall remain prohibited at any time and in any place whatsoever, whether committed by civilian or by military agents:

   (a) Violence to the life, health, or physical or mental well-being of persons, in particular:
   - (i) Murder;
   - (ii) Torture of all kinds, whether physical or mental;
   - (iii) Corporal punishment; and
   - (iv) Mutilation;

   (b) Outrages upon personal dignity, in particular humiliating and degrading treatment, enforced prostitution and any form of indecent assault;
   (c) The taking of hostages;
   (d) Collective punishments; and
   (e) Threats to commit any of the foregoing acts.

Adopted by the Diplomatic Conference on the Reaffirmation and Development of International Humanitarian Law applicable in Armed Conflicts on June 8, 1977; became effective on Dec. 7, 1979, www.unhchr.ch/html/menu3/b/93.htm.

Convention Against Torture and Other Cruel, Inhuman or Degrading Treatment or Punishment (1984)

Article 1

. . . the term 'torture' means any act by which severe pain or suffering, whether physical or mental, is intentionally inflicted on a person for such purposes as obtaining from him or a third person information or a confession, punishing him for an act he or a third person has committed or is suspected of having committed, or intimidating or coercing him or a third person, or for any reason based on discrimination of any kind, . . .

Article 2

1. Each State Party shall take effective legislative, administrative, judicial or other measures to prevent acts of torture in any territory under its jurisdiction.
2. No exceptional circumstances whatsoever, whether a state of war or a threat of war, internal political instability or any other public emergency, may be invoked as a justification of torture.
3. An order from a superior officer or a public authority may not be invoked as a justification of torture.

Article 3

1. No State Party shall expel, return ("refouler") or extradite a person to another State where there are substantial grounds for believing that he would be in danger of being subjected to torture.
2. For the purpose of determining whether there are such grounds, the competent authorities shall take into account all relevant considerations including, where applicable, the existence in the State concerned of a consistent pattern of gross, flagrant or mass violations of human rights.

Adopted by the U.N. General Assembly on Dec. 10, 1984, and opened for signature and ratification; became effective on June 26, 1987, www.unhchr.ch/html/menu3/b/h_cat39.htm.

Christopher Einolf, a University of Richmond sociologist who has studied the history of torture. Torture also proved difficult to control once it was authorized.

For instance, France initiated an intensive counterinsurgency strategy — which included torture — in Algeria after the Algerian National Liberation Front began a terrorist bombing campaign in 1956 to force France to cede control of the colony. France's strategy sometimes is cited as evidence that torture works. [52]

But Rejali at Reed College says France succeeded in gathering information because informants voluntarily cooperated — not as a result of torture. And tortured suspects often gave their interrogators the names of rival insurgents, dead militants or old hiding places rather than good information, he says.

Lou DiMarco, a retired U.S. Army lieutenant colonel who teaches at the Command and General Staff College, Fort Leavenworth, Kan., contends the French experience

Syrian-born Canadian citizen Maher Arar was picked up by the CIA in 2002 at John F. Kennedy International Airport in New York and taken to Syria, where he was imprisoned for a year and tortured with electric cables. He was later cleared of any links to terrorism. Human rights advocates say the CIA's so-called extraordinary rendition program "outsources" torture to countries known to abuse prisoners. The U.S. Justice Department said Syria had assured the United States it would not torture Arar.

in Algeria also proves the difficulty of controlling torture. "In Algeria, officially condoned torture quickly escalated to prolonged abuse, which resulted in permanent physical and psychological damage as well as death," he wrote. [53]

Similarly, the British, facing a spike in Irish Republican Army (IRA) violence in Northern Ireland in 1971, turned to aggressive interrogation techniques, including the "five techniques" — a combination of hooding, noise bombardment, food and sleep deprivation and forced standing. Individually, any one of these techniques could be painful, but taken together, "they induced a state of psychosis, a temporary madness with long-lasting after-effects," wrote John Conroy in his book, *Unspeakable Acts, Ordinary People: The Dynamics of Torture.* [54]

Tom Parker, a former British counterterrorism agent, says extreme interrogation methods had "huge" adverse consequences for Britain: They alienated Ireland — not a natural ally of the IRA — and enabled Ireland to successfully challenge British interrogation methods in the European Court of Human Rights.

Israel approved similar methods in 1987 after its security services were found to be using illegal interrogation techniques on Palestinian detainees in the occupied territories. Officials felt it would be better to allow a few psychological methods and "moderate physical pressure." But coercive methods proved hard to regulate and keep under control. [55]

In 1999, Israel's Supreme Court outlawed such techniques as cruel and inhuman treatment.

Post-9/11 Crackdown

After the 9/11 attacks, aggressive interrogation of suspects became a key — and highly controversial — part of U.S. antiterrorism strategy. On Nov. 13, 2001, President Bush signed an executive order allowing the military to detain and try "enemy combatants" outside the United States.

Defense Secretary Donald H. Rumsfeld announced the next month that enemy combatants detained in Afghanistan would be transferred to Guantánamo. In February 2002 Bush said the United States would treat the detainees humanely but did not consider them legitimate prisoners of war protected by the Geneva Conventions, which ban torture and "cruel, inhuman and degrading treatment."

U.S. interrogators used the same harsh methods designed to train American personnel to resist torture if captured. The so-called "Survival, Evasion, Resistance and Escape" (SERE) techniques included physical and mental pressure ("stress and duress") and sleep deprivation.

Rumsfeld formally approved many of these techniques in December 2002, including prolonged standing, use of dogs and the removal of clothing; he later rescinded approval for some of the methods. [56] Mohammed al-Qhatani — the alleged 20th 9/11 hijacker who had been captured along the Pakistani-Afghan border — says he was interrogated for 20-hour stretches, forced to stand naked while being menaced by dogs and barred from praying during Ramadan unless he drank water, which Islam forbids during Ramadan's fasting periods. The Pentagon said such techniques were designed to "prevent future attacks on America." [57]

Is torture ever justified?

YES
Mirko Bagaric
Professor of Law, Deakin University
Melbourne, Australia

Written for *CQ Researcher*, August 2007

Despite its pejorative overtone, we should never say never to torture. Torture is bad. Killing innocent people is worse. Some people are so depraved they combine these evils and torture innocent people to death. Khalid Shaikh Mohammed, who is still gloating about personally beheading American journalist Daniel Pearl with his "blessed right hand," is but just one exhibit.

Torture opponents must take responsibility for the murder of innocent people if they reject torture if it is the only way to save innocent lives. We are responsible not only for what we do but also for the things we can, but fail, to prevent.

Life-saving torture is not cruel. It is morally justifiable because the right to life of innocent people trumps the physical integrity of wrongdoers. Thus, torture has the same moral justification as other practices in which we sacrifice the interests of one person for the greater good. A close analogy is life-saving organ and tissue transplants. Kidney and bone marrow transplants inflict high levels of pain and discomfort on donors, but their pain is normally outweighed by the benefit to the recipient.

Such is the case with life-saving compassionate torture. The pain inflicted on the wrongdoer is manifestly outweighed by the benefit from the lives saved. The fact that wrongdoers don't consent to their mistreatment is irrelevant. Prisoners and enemy soldiers don't consent to being incarcerated or shot at, yet we're not about to empty our prisons or stop trying to kill enemy soldiers.

Most proponents of banning torture say it does not produce reliable information. Yet there are countless counter-examples. Israeli authorities claim to have foiled 90 terrorist attacks by using coercive interrogation. In more mundane situations, courts across the world routinely throw out confessions that are corroborated by objective evidence because they were only made because the criminals were beaten up.

It is also contended that life-saving torture will lead down the slippery slope of other cruel practices. This is an intellectually defeatist argument. It tries to move the debate from what is on the table (life-saving torture) to situations where torture is used for reasons of domination and punishment — which is never justifiable.

Fanatics who oppose torture in all cases are adopting their own form of extremism. It is well-intentioned, but extremism in all its manifestations can lead to catastrophic consequences. Cruelty that is motivated by misguided kindness hurts no less.

NO
Sune Segal
Head of Communications Unit International Rehabilitation Council for Torture Victims Copenhagen, Denmark

Written for *CQ Researcher*, August 2007

Taking a utilitarian "greater good" approach in the wake of 9/11/2001, some scholars argue that torture is justified if used to prevent large-scale terror attacks. That argument rests on several flawed assumptions.

The claim that torture — or what is now euphemistically referred to as "enhanced interrogation techniques" — extracts reliable information is unfounded. The 2006 *U.S. Army Field Manual* states that "the use of force . . . yields unreliable results [and] may damage subsequent collection efforts." As laid out in a recent *Vanity Fair* article, it was humane treatment — not torture — of a detainee that led to the arrest of alleged 9/11 mastermind Khalid Shaikh Mohammed. In the same article, a U.S. Air Force Reserve colonel and expert in human-intelligence operations, drives home the point: "When [CIA psychologists argue that coercive interrogation] can make people talk, I have one question: 'About what?' "

But even if torture did "work," is it justified when a suspect is in custody and presumed to possess information about an imminent attack likely to kill thousands of people?

No, for several reasons. First, the above scenario assumes the person in custody has the pertinent information — a presumption that is never foolproof. Thus, by allowing torture there would be cases in which innocent detainees would be at risk of prolonged torture because they would not possess the desired information.

Second, it might be argued that mere circumstantial evidence suggesting the detainee is the right suspect is enough to justify torture or that torturing a relative into revealing the suspect's whereabouts is acceptable.

Third, if one form of torture — such as "waterboarding" — is allowed to preserve the "greater good," where do we go if it doesn't work? To breaking bones? Ripping out nails? Torturing the suspect's 5-year-old daughter?

Fourth, torture is not a momentary infliction of pain. In most cases the victim — innocent or guilty — is marked for life, as is the torturer. As a former CIA officer and friend of one of Mohammed's interrogators told *The New Yorker* in an Aug. 13, 2007, article: "[My friend] has horrible nightmares. . . . When you cross over that line, it's hard to come back. You lose your soul."

That's why we refrain from torture: to keep our souls intact. Torture is the hallmark of history's most abhorrent regimes and a violation of civilized values. Taking the "greater good" approach to torture is intellectually and morally bankrupt.

But some within the administration disapproved. In July 2004 Alberto J. Mora, the Navy's general counsel, warned in a 22-page memo that circumventing the Geneva Conventions was an invitation for U.S. interrogators to abuse prisoners. [58]

His prediction was prescient. SERE techniques apparently migrated to U.S. facilities in Afghanistan and Iraq, where they were reportedly employed by inadequately trained and unsupervised personnel. What began as "a set of special treatments" had become routine, wrote Tony Lagouranis, a former Army interrogator in Iraq. [59]

In late 2003 American military personnel at Abu Ghraib prison committed the abuses that generated the most public outrage, thanks to graphic photographs taken by the soldiers involved that eventually were circulated by news media around the world. An Army investigation later detailed "sadistic, blatant and wanton criminal" abuse that included beating detainees with a broom handle, threatening male detainees with rape, sodomizing another with a chemical light stick and frightening them with dogs. [60] Twelve U.S. military personnel have since been convicted for their roles in the abuse.

Mistreatment of Iraqi detainees was not just limited to Abu Ghraib. A military jury convicted Chief Warrant Officer Lewis Welshofer of negligent homicide after an interrogation in a facility in western Iraq in which he put a sleeping bag over the head of Iraqi Gen. Abed Hamed Mowhoush, sat on his chest and covered the general's mouth while asking him questions. American civilian contractors working alongside CIA and military interrogators in Iraq have also been accused of mistreating detainees.

Ever since the 9/11 attacks, a furious legal debate, both inside and outside the Bush administration, has examined the kinds of coercive interrogation methods the military and CIA can employ and the extent to which the United States must abide by international law. In 2005 Congress sought to limit the use by U.S. personnel of cruel, inhumane and degrading treatment in the Detainee Treatment Act. [61]

Then in 2006 the Supreme Court ruled that all prisoners held by the United States — including those in CIA custody — were subject to Common Article 3 of the Geneva Conventions, which outlaws torture or cruel and inhuman treatment of wartime detainees. (*See box, p. 232.*) [62] Later that year Congress passed another bill, the Military Commissions Act, endorsed by the Bush

administration. It limited military interrogators to techniques that would be detailed in an updated *Army Field Manual.* The law did not specify, however, which interrogation methods CIA personnel can use — an omission designed to provide flexibility for interrogators at secret CIA facilities where "high value" prisoners are interrogated.

When *The Washington Post* revealed in 2005 that the CIA was operating secret prisons in eight countries in Eastern Europe, Thailand and Afghanistan, the administration had at first refused to confirm the story. [63] In 2006 Bush finally acknowledged the facilities existed, pointing out that, "Questioning the detainees in this program has given us information that has saved innocent lives by helping us stop new attacks — here in the United States and across the world." [64]

In 2007, Human Rights Watch and *The Post* detailed the experience of one former CIA detainee — Marwan Jabour, a Palestinian accused of being an al-Qaeda paymaster — who spent two years in a CIA-operated prison.

Jabour says he was kept naked for the first three months of his detention in Afghanistan. The lights were kept on 24 hours a day, and when loud music wasn't blasted through speakers into his cell, white noise buzzed in the background. And while he was frequently threatened with physical abuse, he says he was never beaten during 45 interrogations. He was also deprived of sleep and left for hours in painful positions. He was ultimately transferred to Jordanian and then Israeli custody, where a judge ordered his release in September 2006. [65]

CIA detainees also reportedly have been subjected to waterboarding and had their food spiked with drugs to loosen their inhibitions about speaking. [66]

The United States did not allow the International Committee of the Red Cross (ICRC) to visit the CIA's detainees until 2006. A subsequent ICRC report based on interviews with 15 former CIA detainees concluded that the detention and interrogation methods used at the "black sites" were tantamount to torture, according to confidential sources quoted in *The New Yorker.* [67]

The United States has strongly denied the ICRC's conclusions and claims the program is closely monitored by agency lawyers. "The CIA's interrogations were nothing like Abu Ghraib or Guantánamo," said Robert Grenier, a former head of the CIA's Counterterrorism Center. "They were very, very regimented. Very meticulous." The program is "completely legal." [68]

Unlike the CIA's secret prisons, the agency's use of so-called "extraordinary renditions" predated the 9/11 attacks. The first terror suspects were rendered to Egypt in the mid-1990s. [69] But the practice expanded greatly after 9/11, with up to 150 people sent to countries such as Morocco, Syria and Egypt between 2001 and 2005. Many, like Abu Omar — an imam with alleged links to terrorist groups — were snatched off the street. Omar, an Egyptian refugee, was kidnapped from Milan in February 2003 and sent to Egypt where he says he was tortured for four years before being released in 2007. [70]

U.S. officials have repeatedly insisted the United States does not send detainees to countries where they believe or know they'll be tortured. [71] But such declarations ring hollow for human rights advocates like Malinowski. "The administration says that it does not render people to torture," he told the Senate Foreign Relations Committee. "But the only safeguard it appears to have obtained in these cases was a promise from the receiving state that it would not mistreat the rendered prisoners. Such promises, coming from countries like Egypt and Syria and Uzbekistan where torture is routine, are unverifiable and utterly untrustworthy. I seriously doubt that anyone in the administration actually believed them." [72]

Renditions usually require the complicity of the countries where the suspects are grabbed. A 2006 report by the Council of Europe's Parliamentary Assembly tried to identify all the member countries that have allowed rendition flights to cross their airspace or land at their airports. [73]

One was the Czech Republic, which reportedly allowed three different jets to land at Prague's Ruzyne Airport during at least 20 different rendition flights, triggering anger from some Czechs. "No 'law enforcement,' 'intelligence,' or 'security' argument in support of torture can ever be anything but inhumane," wrote Gwendolyn Albert, director of the Czech League of Human Rights, in 2006 in *The Prague Post.* [74]

Former CIA operative Melissa Boyle Mahle condemns torture but has defended renditions and the need for absolute secrecy. "Renditions should be conducted in the shadows for optimal impact and should not, I must add, leave elephant-sized footprints so as to not embarrass our allies in Europe," she wrote in a 2005 blog entry. "During my career at the CIA, I was involved in these types of operations and know firsthand that they can save American lives." [75]

CURRENT SITUATION

Rendition Fallout

Kidnapping and shipping off allies' citizens to be harshly interrogated in foreign countries has strained relations with America's friends. Prosecutors in Germany and Italy are attempting to prosecute U.S. personnel for their role in renditions, and the rendition of Canadian citizen Maher Arar to Syria has chilled relations between Canada and the United States.

In Italy, the former chief of Italy's intelligence service is on trial for Omar's 2003 abduction in a case that threatens to ensnare top officials of the current and past Italian governments. A U.S. Air Force colonel and 25 CIA operatives also were indicted but are being tried in absentia because the United States has blocked their extradition. [76]

Similarly, a court in Munich ordered the arrest of 13 American intelligence operatives in January 2007 for their role in the kidnapping of a German citizen interrogated for five months at a secret prison in Afghanistan. But Germany, unlike Italy, does not allow trials in absentia, so an actual trial is unlikely because the United States will not extradite the defendants. [77]

Other European governments may be called to task for their role in U.S. renditions. Investigations have been initiated by Spain, and the Most Rev. John Neill — archbishop of Dublin — said the Irish government compromised itself by allowing rendition flights to land at Shannon Airport.

Meanwhile, on this side of the Atlantic, Canadian-U.S. relations are strained by the case of Syrian-born Canadian citizen Maher Arar. The McGill University graduate was returning to Canada from Tunisia in September 2002 when he landed at John F. Kennedy International Airport in New York during a stopover. U.S. immigration authorities detained him after seeing his name on a terrorist "watch" list.

After two weeks of questioning, he was flown to Jordan and then driven to Syria. During a yearlong detention by Syrian military intelligence, Arar says he was beaten with two-inch-thick electric cables. "Not even animals could withstand it," he said later. [78]

He was released in October 2003. A Canadian inquiry cleared Arar of any links to terrorism and said the Royal Canadian Mounted Police had given U.S. authorities erroneous information about him. Canada's prime minister apologized to Arar in January 2007 and announced an $8.9 million compensation package. Canada has also demanded an apology from the U.S. government and asked that Arar's name be removed from terrorist watch lists. [79]

U.S. federal courts have dismissed a lawsuit by Arar, and Attorney General Alberto R. Gonzales said Syria had assured the United States it would not torture Arar before he was sent there.

But Paul Cavalluzzo, a Toronto lawyer who led the government investigation of Arar's case, calls Gonzales' claim "graphic hypocrisy," pointing out that the U.S. State Department's own Web site lists Syria as one of the "worst offenders of torture."

"At one time, the United States was a beacon for the protection of human rights, whether internationally or domestically. Certainly, the Arar case was one example that lessened [that] view [among] Canadians."

Suing Torturers

Criminal prosecutions and civil lawsuits are pending against alleged torturers in several courts around the world.

In the United States, Iraqis claiming they were mistreated by American military personnel and private contractors are seeking redress under a little-used 18th-century law. The Alien Tort Claims Act, which originally targeted piracy, allows federal courts to hear claims by foreigners injured "in violation of the law of nations or a treaty of the United States."

In May 2007, the American Civil Liberties Union used the law to sue Jeppesen Dataplan Inc., a subsidiary of the Boeing Co., on behalf of three plaintiffs subjected to renditions. The company is accused of providing rendition flight services to the CIA. Two additional plaintiffs joined the suit in August. [80]

The law also was used in a class-action suit against Titan Corp. and CACI International Inc., military contractors that provided translators and interrogation services at Abu Ghraib. The suit asserts the two companies participated in a "scheme to torture, rape and in some instances, summarily execute plaintiffs." CACI called it a "malicious recitation of false statements and intentional distortions." [81]

The law was rarely used until the late 1970s, when human rights groups began suing abusive foreign officials. Since then it has been used to sue a Paraguayan police chief living in Brooklyn accused of torturing and killing a young man in Paraguay, an Ethiopian official, a Guatemalan defense minister and the self-proclaimed president of the Bosnian Serbs.

Advocates of such suits say they are important tools in holding abusers accountable. "It is truly a mechanism that provides for policing international human rights abuses where a criminal prosecution may not necessarily be feasible," says John M. Eubanks, a South Carolina lawyer involved in a suit that relies on the statute. The home countries of human rights abusers often lack legal systems that enable perpetrators to be held accountable.

"America is the only venue where they're going to be able to get their case heard," says Rachel Chambers, a British lawyer who has studied the statute.

Although the U.S. Supreme Court affirmed the use of the statute in 2004, legal experts disagree about just how much leeway the court left for future plaintiffs. [82]

Moreover, the statute can't provide redress in lawsuits against the U.S. government for the mistreatment of prisoners. The United States has successfully challenged such lawsuits by claiming sovereign immunity, a doctrine that protects governments against suits. The same defense has protected individuals sued in their official government capacity, according to Beth Stephens, a professor at Rutgers School of Law, in Camden, N.J. It is unclear how much protection private contractors such as CACI can claim for providing support services for interrogations.

Meanwhile, in Cambodia a U.N.-backed tribunal in July accused former Khmer Rouge leader Kaing Guek Eav of crimes against humanity for his role in the torture and deaths of 14,000 prisoners at Tuol Sleng. Only seven people who entered the prison emerged alive. The trial is expected to begin in 2008. [83]

And in Sierra Leone former Liberian President Charles Taylor is facing a U.N.-backed war-crimes tribunal for his role in financing and encouraging atrocities — including torture — committed during the civil war in neighboring Sierra Leone. The trial has been delayed until January 2008. [84]

The "Black Sites"

In July, when President Bush authorized the CIA's secret prisons to be reopened, the executive order laid out the administration's position on how the "enhanced interrogation" program will fully comply "with the obligations of the United States under Common Article 3" of the Geneva Conventions, which bans "outrages upon personal dignity, in particular humiliating and degrading treatment."

The president's order said the United States would satisfy the conventions if the CIA's interrogation methods don't violate federal law or constitute "willful and outrageous acts of personal abuse done for the purpose of humiliating the individual in a manner so serious that any reasonable person, considering the circumstances would deem the acts to be beyond the bounds of human decency."

The language appears to allow abusive techniques if the purpose is to gather intelligence or prevent attacks, say critics. "The president has given the CIA carte blanche to engage in 'willful and outrageous acts of personal abuse,' " wrote former Marine Corps Commandant P. X. Kelley and Robert Turner, a former Reagan administration lawyer. [85]

Human rights advocates are troubled by the executive order's lack of an explicit ban on coercive interrogation techniques such as stress positions or extreme sleep deprivation, which military interrogators are explicitly barred from using in the latest *Army Field Manual*, issued in 2006.

Media reports suggested the Bush administration also has sought to maintain other methods, such as inducing hypothermia, forced standing and manipulating sound and light. [86]

"What we're left with is a history of these kinds of techniques having been authorized, no explicit prohibition and we don't know what the CIA is authorized to do," says Devon Chaffee, an attorney with Human Rights First. "This creates a real problematic precedent."

Human rights advocates worry that foreign governments may cite Bush's executive order to justify their own coercive interrogations. "What they did is lower the bar for anybody," says Musa, the advocacy director for Amnesty USA.

In August, the American Bar Association passed a resolution urging Congress to override the executive order. [87] Also that month, Democratic Sen. Ron Wyden of Oregon vowed to block President Bush's nominee to become the CIA's top lawyer. Wyden said he was concerned that the agency's senior deputy general counsel, John Rizzo, had not objected to a 2002 CIA memo authorizing interrogation techniques that stopped just short of inflicting enough pain to cause organ failure or death.

"I'm going to keep the hold [on Rizzo] until the detention and interrogation program is on firm footing, both in terms of effectiveness and legality," Wyden said. [88]

OUTLOOK

No Panaceas

Human rights advocates worry countries that have tortured in the past will feel more emboldened to do so in the future as a result of U.S. government policies.

"This is just empowering the dictators and torturing governments around the world," said Whitson of Human Rights Watch.

They also worry that China, a rising superpower, is an abuser itself and has proven willing to do business with countries with histories of abuse in Central Asia and Africa.

HRW Executive Director Kenneth Roth also complains that — as its membership swells and the difficulty of reaching consensus grows — the European Union appears unable or unwilling to act. "Its efforts to achieve consensus among its diverse membership have become so laborious that it yields a faint shadow of its potential," he says.

The future direction of U.S. interrogation policies could depend heavily on the outcome of the 2008 American presidential election, which will likely determine the fate of what has become the most important symbol of U.S. detention policies: the prison for enemy combatants at Guantánamo. All the Democratic presidential candidates say they would close the facility, according to a study of candidate positions by the Council on Foreign Relations. [89]

On the Republican side, only two candidates — Rep. Ron Paul, R-Texas, and Sen. McCain — have advocated shutting the facility, and neither has been among the leaders in the polls. Mitt Romney, the former Massachusetts governor who has been among the front-runners this summer, suggested doubling the size of Guantánamo if he became president.

But regardless of who wins the election, human rights advocates do not look to a new occupant of the White House as a panacea. Amnesty USA's Musa says new administrations are often skittish about radically changing course from predecessors' foreign policies.

"It's not the absolute cure for all ills," she says.

NOTES

1. See Jonathan S. Landay, "VP confirms use of waterboarding," *Chicago Tribune*, Oct. 27, 2006, p. C5; and "Interview of the Vice President by Scott

Hennen, WDAY at Radio Day at the White House," www.whitehouse.gov/news/releases/2006/10/20061024-7.html. Also see John Crewdson, "Spilling Al Qaeda's secrets; 'Waterboarding' used on 9/11 mastermind, who eventually talked," *Chicago Tribune*, Dec. 28, 2005, p. C15. Also see Brian Ross and Richard Esposito, "CIA's Harsh Interrogation Techniques Described," ABC News, Nov. 18, 2005, www.abcnews.com.

2. Testimony by Tom Malinowski before Senate Committee on Foreign Relations, July 26, 2007.

3. David Cingranelli and David L. Richards, CIRI Human Rights Data Project, 2005, http://ciri.binghamton.edu/about.asp.

4. Quoted in Molly Moore, "Gaddafi's Son: Bulgarians Were Tortured," *The Washington Post*, Aug. 10, 2007, p. A8.

5. "In the Name of Security: Counterterrorism and Human Rights Abuses Under Malaysia's Internal Security Act," Human Rights Watch, http://hrw.org/reports/2004/malaysia0504/.

6. Dana Priest, "CIA Holds Terror Suspects in Secret Prisons," *The Washington Post*, Nov. 2, 2005, p. A1; also see Rosa Brooks, "The GOP's Torture Enthusiasts," *Los Angeles Times*, May 18, 2007, www.latimes.com/news/opinion/commentary/la-oe-brooks18may18,0,732795.column?coll=la-news-comment-opinions.

7. For background see Peter Katel and Kenneth Jost, "Treatment of Detainees," *CQ Researcher*, Aug. 25, 2006, pp. 673-696.

8. Kenneth Roth, "Filling the Leadership Void: Where is the European Union?" *World Report 2007*, Human Rights Watch.

9. Edward Cody, "China, Others Criticize U.S. Report on Rights: Double Standard at State Department Alleged" *The Washington Post*, March 4, 2005, p A14.

10. Lisa Haugaard, "Tarnished Image: Latin America Perceives the United States," Latin American Working Group, March 2006.

11. "World View of U.S. Role Goes from Bad to Worse," Program on International Policy Attitudes, January 2007, www.worldpublicopinion.org/pipa/pdf/jan07/BBC_USRole_Jan07_quaire.pdf.

12. See Karen DeYoung, "Bush Approves New CIA Methods," *The Washington Post*, July 21, 2007, p. A1.

13. See "President Discusses Creation of Military Commissions to Try Suspected Terrorists," Sept. 6, 2006, www.whitehouse.gov/news/releases/2006/09/20060906-3.html.

14. Crewdson, *op. cit.*

15. Jane Mayer, "The Black Sites," *The New Yorker*, Aug. 13, 2007, pp. 46-57.

16. *Ibid.*

17. *Ibid.*

18. Jane Mayer, "Outsourcing Torture," *The New Yorker*, Feb. 14, 2005, p. 106.

19. Intelligence Science Board, "Educing Information, Interrogation: Science and Art," Center for Strategic Intelligence Research, National Defense Intelligence College, December 2006, www.fas.org/irp/dni/educing.pdf.

20. Anne Applebaum, "The Torture Myth," *The Washington Post*, Jan. 12, 2005, p. A21.

21. Henry Schuster, "The Al Qaeda Hunter," CNN, http://edition.cnn.com/2005/US/03/02/schuster.column/index.html.

22. Mirko Bagaric, "A Case for Torture," *The Age*, May 17, 2005, www.theage.com.au/news/ Opinion/A-case-for-torture/2005/05/16/1116095904947.html.

23. Alan Dershowitz, *Why Terrorism Works: Understanding the Threat, Responding to the Challenge*, Yale University Press, 2003, pp. 158-159.

24. Michael Levin, "The Case for Torture," *Newsweek*, June 7, 1982.

25. " '24' and America's Image in Fighting Terrorism," Heritage Foundation Symposium, June 30, 2006.

26. Eitan Felner, "Torture and Terrorism: Painful Lessons from Israel," in Kenneth Roth, *et al.*, eds., *Torture: Does it Make Us Safer? Is It Ever OK? A Human Rights Perspective* (2005).

27. Henry Shue, "Torture," in Sanford Levinson, ed., *Torture: A Collection* (2006), p. 58.

28. See Brooks, *op. cit.*

29. Humphrey Hawksley, "US Iraq Troops 'condone torture,' " BBC News, May 4, 2007, http://news.bbc.co.uk/2/hi/middle_east/6627055.stm.

30. "Bush, McCain Agree on Torture Ban," CNN, Dec. 15, 2005, www.cnn.com/2005/POLITICS/12/15/torture.bill/index.html.

31. "American and International Opinion on the Rights of Terrorism Suspects," Program on International Policy Attitudes, July 17, 2006, www.worldpublicopinion.org/pipa/pdf/jul06/TerrSuspect_Jul06_rpt.pdf.

32. Allison Hanes, "Prime time torture: A U.S. Brigadier-General voices concern about the message the show '24' might be sending to the public and impressionable recruits," *National Post*, March 19, 2007.

33. Evan Thomas, " '24' Versus the Real World," *Newsweek Online*, Sept. 22, 2006, www.msnbc.msn.com/id/14924664/site/newsweek/.

34. Jane Mayer, "Whatever It Takes," *The New Yorker*, Feb. 19, 2007, www.newyorker.com/reporting/2007/02/19/070219fa-fact_mayer?printable=true.

35. John McCarthy, "Television is making torture acceptable," *The Independent*, May 24, 2007, http://comment.independent.co.uk/commentators/article2578453.ece.

36. Mayer, Feb. 19, 2007, *ibid.*

37. Heritage symposium, *op. cit.*

38. *Ibid.*

39. Colin Freeze, "What would Jack Bauer do?," *Globe and Mail*, June 16, 2007, www.theglobeandmail.com/servlet/story/LAC.20070616.BAUER16/TPStory/TPNational/Television/.

40. "Don't Go to Bat for Jack Bauer," *Globe and Mail*, July 9, 2007, www.theglobeandmail.com/servlet/story/RTGAM.20070709.wxetorture09/BNStory/specialComment/home.

41. The Associated Press, "Scholars Urge Bush to Ban Use of Torture," *The Washington Post*, June 25, 2007, www.washingtonpost.com/wp-dyn/content/article/2007/06/25/AR2007062501437.html.

42. See David Masci, "Torture," *CQ Researcher*, April 18, 2003, pp. 345-368.

43. James Ross, "A History of Torture," in Roth, *op. cit.*

44. John Langbein, "The Legal History of Torture," in Levinson, *op. cit.*

45. Brian Innes, *The History of Torture* (1998), pp. 13, 43.

46. Roth, p. 8.

47. Ross, p. 12.

48. Darius M. Rejali, *Torture & Modernity: Self, Society, and State in Modern Iran* (1994), p. 11.

49. *Ibid.*, p. 13.

50. Christopher J. Einolf, "The Fall and Rise of Torture: A Comparative and Historical Analysis," *Sociological Theory 25:2*, June 2007.

51. For background, see R. C. Schroeder, "Human Rights Policy," in *Editorial Research Reports 1979* (Vol. I), available in *CQ Researcher Plus Archive*, http://library.cqpress.com. Also see "Foreign Aid: Human Rights Compromise," in *CQ Almanac*, 1977.

52. Darius Rejali, "Does Torture Work?" *Salon*, June 21, 2004, http://archive.salon.com/opinion/feature/2004/06/21/torture_algiers/index_np.html.

53. Lou DiMarco, "Losing the Moral Compass: Torture & Guerre Revolutionnaire in the Algerian War," *Parameters*, Summer 2006.

54. John Conroy, *Unspeakable Acts, Ordinary People: The Dynamics of Torture* (2001).

55. Miriam Gur-Arye, "Can the War against Terror Justify the Use of Force in Interrogations? Reflections in Light of the Israeli Experience," in Levinson, *op. cit.*, p. 185.

56. Jess Bravin and Greg Jaffe, "Rumsfeld Approved Methods for Guantánamo Interrogation," *The Wall Street Journal*, June 10, 2004.

57. Department of Defense press release, June 12, 2005, www.defenselink.mil/Releases/Release.aspx?ReleaseID=8583.

58. Jane Mayer, "The Memo," *The New Yorker*, Feb. 27, 2006, pp. 32-41.

59. Tony Lagouranis, *Fear Up Harsh: An Army Interrogator's Dark Journey Through Iraq* (2007), p. 93.

60. A summary of the Taguba report can be found at www.fas.org/irp/agency/dod/taguba.pdf.

61. "Bush Signs Defense Authorization Measure With Detainee Provision," *CQ Almanac 2005 Online Edition*, available at http://library.cqpress.com.

62. The case is *Hamdan v. Rumsfeld*, 126 S. Ct. 2749 (2006).

63. Priest, *op. cit.*

64. "President Discusses Creation of Military Commissions to Try Suspected Terrorists," *op. cit.*

65. Dafna Linzer and Julie Tate, "New Light Shed on CIA's 'Black Site' Prisons," *The Washington Post*, Feb. 28, 2007, p. A1.

66. Mark Bowden, "The Dark Art of Interrogation," *The Atlantic*, October 2003.

67. Mayer, Aug. 13, 2007, *op. cit.*

68. *Ibid.*

69. Mayer, Feb. 14, 2005, *op. cit.*

70. Ian Fisher and Elisabetta Povoledo, "Italy Braces for Legal Fight Over Secret CIA Program," *The New York Times*, June 8, 2007.

71. Jeffrey R. Smith, "Gonzales Defends Transfer of Detainees," *The Washington Post*, March 8, 2005, p. A3.

72. Malinowski testimony, *op. cit.*

73. Council of Europe Parliamentary Assembly, "Alleged secret detentions in Council of Europe member states, 2006," http://assembly.coe.int/CommitteeDocs/2006/20060606_Ejdoc162006PartII-FINAL.pdf.

74. Gwendolyn Albert, "With Impunity," *Prague Post*, April 12, 2006, www.praguepost.com/articles/2006/04/12/with-impunity.php.

75. http://melissamahlecommentary.blogspot.com/2005/12/cia-and-torture.html.

76. Elisabetta Povoledo, "Trial of CIA Operatives is delayed in Italy," *The International Herald Tribune*, June 18, 2007.

77. Jeffrey Fleishman, "Germany Orders Arrest of 13 CIA Operatives in Kidnapping of Khaled el-Masri" *Los Angeles Times*, Jan. 31, 2007.

78. Mayer, Feb. 14, 2005, *op. cit.*

79. "Arar Case Timeline," Canadian Broadcasting Company, www.cbc.ca/news/background/arar.

80. Christine Kearney, "Iraqi, Yemeni men join lawsuit over CIA flights," Reuters, Aug. 1, 2007.

81. Marie Beaudette, "Standing at the Floodgates," *Legal Times*, June 28, 2004.

82. The case is *Sosa v. Alvarez-Machain*, 2004, 542 U.S. 692 (2004).

83. Ian MacKinnon, "War crimes panel charges Khmer Rouge chief," *The Guardian*, Aug. 1, 2007.

84. "Taylor Trial Delayed until 2008," BBC News, Aug. 20, 2007, http://news.bbc.co.uk/2/hi/africa/6954627.stm.

85. P. X. Kelley and Robert F. Turner, "War Crimes and the White House," *The Washington Post*, July 26, 2007.

86. Thomas, *op. cit.*

87. Henry Weinstein, "ABA targets CIA methods, secret law," *Los Angeles Times*, Aug. 14, 2007.

88. The Associated Press, "Dem blocking Bush pick for CIA lawyer," MSNBC, Aug. 16, 2007, www.msnbc.msn.com/id/20294826.

89. "The Candidates on Military Tribunals and Guantánamo Bay," Council on Foreign Relations, July 17, 2007, www.cfr.org/publication/13816/.

BIBLIOGRAPHY

Books

Bagaric, Mirko, and Julie Clarke, *Torture: When the Unthinkable Is Morally Permissible*, State University of New York Press, 2007.
Bagaric, an Australian law professor, argues torture is sometimes morally justified and should be legally excusable.

Conroy, John, *Unspeakable Acts, Ordinary People: The Dynamics of Torture*, Random House, 2000.
A reporter examines the history of torture.

Dershowitz, Alan M., *Why Torture Works: Understanding the Threat, Responding to the Challenge*, Yale University Press, 2003.
A Harvard law professor argues that torture will be employed by interrogators, so courts should issue "torture warrants" to bring some legal oversight to the process.

Haritos-Fatouros, Mika, *The Psychological Origins of Institutionalized Torture*, Routledge, 2003.
A sociologist explores the indoctrination of Greek torturers during military rule of the country during the 1970s.

Lagouranis, Tony, *Fear Up Harsh: An Army Interrogator's Dark Journey Through Iraq*, NAL Hardcover, 2007.
A former U.S. Army interrogator describes the use of coercive techniques by American soldiers.

Levinson, Sanford, ed., *Torture: A Collection*, **Oxford University Press, 2004.**

Essays by academics and human rights advocates examine the historical, moral and political implications of torture.

Rejali, Darius, *Torture and Democracy*, **Princeton University Press, 2007.**

A Reed College professor and expert on torture traces its history from the 19th century through the U.S. occupation of Iraq.

Articles

"Torture in the Name of Freedom," *Der Spiegel*, **Feb. 20, 2006, www.spiegel.de/international/spiegel/ 0,1518,401899,00.html.**

The German news magazine concludes the United States is ceding its moral authority on the issue of torture.

Bowden, Mark, "The Dark Art of Interrogation," *The Atlantic Monthly*, **October 2003, www.theatlantic .com/doc/200310/bowden.**

An American journalist examines interrogation methods employed by U.S. personnel since the 9/11 terrorist attacks.

Einolf, Christopher J., "The Fall and Rise of Torture: A Comparative and Historical Analysis," *Sociological Theory*, **June 2007, www.asanet.org/galleries/default-file/June07STFeature.pdf.**

A University of Richmond sociology professor explains the continued prevalence of torture during the 20th century.

Mayer, Jane, "Outsourcing Torture," *The New Yorker*, **Feb. 14, 2005, www.newyorker.com/archive/ 2005/02/14/050214fa_fact6.**

The reporter traces the history of the U.S.'s "extraordinary rendition" policy.

Mayer, Jane, "Whatever It Takes," *The New Yorker*, **Feb. 19, 2007, www.newyorker.com/reporting/2007/ 02/19/070219fa_fact_mayer.**

The article examines the popular television show "24" and its role in "normalizing" perceptions of torture.

Mayer, Jane, "The Black Sites," *The New Yorker*, **Aug. 13, 2007, p. 46, www.newyorker.com/reporting/ 2007/08/13/070813fa_fact_mayer.**

A journalist examines the history of the CIA's secret "black site" prisons for high-value terror suspects.

Ozdemir, Cem, "Beyond the Valley of the Wolves," *Der Spiegel*, **Feb. 22, 2006, www.spiegel.de/interna-tional/0,1518,401565,00.html.**

A Turkish member of parliament discusses a popular Turkish movie that depicts American soldiers mistreating Iraqi civilians.

Reports and Studies

"Alleged secret detentions and unlawful inter-state transfers involving Council of Europe member states," Committee on Legal Affairs and Human Rights Council of Europe Parliamentary Assembly, June 7, 2006, http://assembly.coe.int/CommitteeDocs/2006/2006060 6_Ejdoc162006PartII-FINAL.pdf.

An organization of European lawmakers examines the role of European governments in U.S. renditions.

"Educing Information, Interrogation: Science and Art," Foundations for the Future Phase 1 Report, Intelligence Science Board, December 2006, www.fas. org/irp/dni/educing.pdf.

Too little is known about which interrogation methods are effective.

"Tarnished Image: Latin America Perceives the United States," Latin American Working Group, www.lawg.org/docs/tarnishedimage.pdf.

A nonprofit group examines Latin American press coverage of U.S. policies, including its interrogation of detainees.

For More Information

Amnesty International USA, 5 Penn Plaza, New York, NY 10001; (212) 807-8400; www.amnestyusa.org. U.S.-affiliate of London-based international human rights organization.

Center for Victims of Torture, 717 East River Rd., Minneapolis, MN 55455; (612) 436-4800; www.cvt.org. Operates healing centers in Minneapolis-St. Paul and Liberia and Sierra Leone. Also trains religious leaders, teachers, caregivers and staff from other NGOs about the effects of torture and trauma.

Human Rights First, 333 Seventh Ave., 13th Floor, New York, NY 10001-5108; (212) 845-5200; www.humanrightsfirst.org. A New York-based advocacy group that combats genocide, torture and other human rights abuses; founded in 1978 as the Lawyers Committee for Human Rights.

Human Rights Watch, 350 Fifth Ave., 34th floor, New York, NY 10118-3299; (212) 290-4700; www.hrw.org. Advocates for human rights around the world.

International Rehabilitation Council for Torture Victims, Borgergade 13, P.O. Box 9049 DK-1022; Copenhagen K, Denmark; +45 33 76 06 00; www.irct.org. Umbrella organization for worldwide network of centers that treat torture victims.

Medical Foundation for the Care of Victims of Torture, 111 Isledon Rd., Islington, London N7 7JW; (020) 7697 7777; www.torturecare.org.uk. Trains and provides medical personnel to aid victims of torture.

Office of the High Commissioner for Human Rights, 8-14 Ave. de la Paix, 1211 Geneva 10, Switzerland; (41-22) 917-9000; www.unhchr.ch. United Nations agency that opposes human rights violations.

VOICES FROM ABROAD

Tony Blair

Then-Prime Minister, United Kingdom

What's the actual threat?

"People devote the most extraordinary amount of time in trying to say that the Americans, on rendition, are basically deporting people . . . and people spend very little time in actually looking at what the threat is that we face and America faces, from terrorism and how we have to deal with it."

— The Independent *(United Kingdom), February 2006*

Michael Ignatieff

Member of Parliament, Canada

Taking the high ground

"The moral imperative, 'Do not torture, any time, anywhere, in any circumstances,' is mandated by the United Nations convention against torture and other cruel, inhuman or degrading treatment or punishment. The fact that terrorists torture does not change these imperatives. Compliance does not depend on reciprocity."

— Business Day *(South Africa), April 2006*

Basil Fernando

Executive Director, Asian Human Rights Council

A benefit to the elite

"There is still reluctance on the part of Thai elite to eliminate torture. . . . [Those in power fear] police will no longer be an instrument in their hand. They have to accept that police can investigate everyone and that the police will become a friend of the ordinary man."

— Bangkok Post, *July 2006*

Editorial

The Indian Express

We are all capable of torture

"Living in a country where torture has become banal, we know it is just as likely to emanate from disgruntled and disaffected fellow citizens as it is from the institutions mandated to protect us — the army, the police, the paramilitary. When authoritarianism and violence become common currency across classes . . . then nobody has qualms disrespecting the basic tenets of civilised political discourse, behaviour, and transaction."

— *November 2005*

Manfred Nowak

Anti-Torture Investigator, United Nations

Torturers should pay the costs

"Countries where torture is widespread or even systematic should be held accountable to pay. . . . If individual torturers would have to pay all the long-term rehabilitation costs, this would have a much stronger deterrent effect on torture than some kind of disciplinary or lenient criminal punishment."

— *Address before U.N. Human Rights Council, Geneva, April 2007*

Narmin Uthman

Minister of Human Rights, Iraq

No torture in Abu Ghraib

"Abu Ghraib prison is currently under the supervision of the Human Rights Ministry, and our [inspection] committees have not found evidence of any use of torture. . . . The change in the treatment of [prisoners by] the jail guards in Abu Ghraib prison has had a great impact on changing the Americans' policy towards Iraqi prisoners in general."

— Al-Arabiya TV *(Dubai), February 2006*

Larry Cox

Executive Director, Amnesty International

EU needs better policies

"By the EU adopting anemic rules for the commerce of torture instruments, it essentially allows the practice to continue, now with an official wink and nod. These directives fail to provide broad and tough policies to guarantee that businesses do not profit by the sale of these repulsive tools."

— U.S. Newswire, *February 2007*

Kofi Annan

Then-Secretary-General, United Nations

Torture is torture, by any name

"Fifty-seven years after the Universal Declaration of Human Rights prohibited all forms of torture and cruel, inhuman or degrading treatment or punishment, torture remains an unacceptable vice. . . . Nor is torture permissible when it is called something else. . . . Humanity faces grave challenges today. The threat of terror is real and immediate. Fear of terrorists can never justify adopting their methods."

— *Speech during International Human Rights Day, December 2005*

11

Hate Speech

Marcia Clemmitt

The Rutgers University women's basketball team answers media questions about the derogatory remark made by popular shock jock Don Imus. The team later met with Imus and accepted his apology, but he was fired after public outrage led advertisers to abandon his program.

From *CQ Researcher*, June 1, 2007.

W hen radio host Don Imus offhandedly referred to the Rutgers University women's basketball team as "nappy-headed hos" on April 4, it was far from the first time that radio's original shock jock had used racist and sexist jokes on his program. Insults were long a stock in trade of "Imus in the Morning," the 10th-highest-rated radio talk show in the nation last April and also a staple on MSNBC's cable TV lineup, where ratings were rising.

To name just a few examples, in the early 1990s, Imus referred to then-*New York Times* White House correspondent Gwen Ifill, an African-American, as "the cleaning lady." [1] In December 2006, he used an anti-Semitic stereotype, calling the "Jewish management" of his employer, CBS Radio, "money-grubbing bastards." [2]

In 2001, *Chicago Tribune* columnist Clarence Page, then a regular guest on the program, asked Imus to promise to stop using phrases like "knuckle-dragging apes" to refer to black athletes and words like "thugs, pimps and muggers" to refer to non-criminal African-Americans. Imus agreed but quickly broke his pledge. [3]

The incident with the Rutgers team had a different outcome, however.

A liberal media-criticism group, Media Matters for America, noted the April 4 remark on its Web site. By April 6 the National Association of Black Journalists called for the 66-year-old Imus to be fired, and the Rev. Al Sharpton and other individuals and groups soon followed suit.

"Imus has a pathetic yet well-documented history of resorting to racist, sexist and homophobic commentary" and should resign or be fired, said National Association of Hispanic Journalists President Rafael Olmeda in a statement. [4]

Conservatives Are Top Talk Hosts

With at least 13.5 million weekly listeners, political commentator Rush Limbaugh drew the largest talk radio audience in fall 2006, followed by fellow conservatives Sean Hannity and Michael Savage. Don Imus, whose show was later canceled, was tied for 10th place.

Top Talk Radio Hosts, fall 2006

Host	Minimum Weekly Listeners	Host	Minimum Weekly Listeners
1. Rush Limbaugh	13.5 million	10. Dr. Joy Browne	2.25 million
2. Sean Hannity	12.5 million	Don Imus	
3. Michael Savage	8.25 million	Kim Komando	
4. Dr. Laura Schlessinger	8 million	Jim Rome	
5. Laura Ingraham	5 million	11. Bob Brinker	1.75 million
6. Glenn Beck	3.75 million	Tom Leykis	
Neal Boortz		12. Rusty Humphries	1.5 million
Mike Gallagher		Lars Larson	
7. Jim Bohannon	3.25 million	G. Gordon Liddy	
Clark Howard		Mancow	
Mark Levin		13. Alan Colmes	1.25 million
Bill O'Reilly		Al Franken	
8. Bill Bennett	3 million	Bill Handel	
Jerry Doyle		Hugh Hewitt	
Dave Ramsey		Lionel	
Ed Schultz		Stephanie Miller	
Doug Stephan		Randi Rhodes	
9. Michael Medved	2.75 million	14. Dr. Dean Edell	1 million
George Noory		Opie & Anthony	
		Michael Reagan	

Source: Talkers magazine, 2007

Beyond derailing Imus' nearly four-decade run as a radio host, the incident triggered a widespread debate about the public use of racist and sexist language, especially by shock jocks and some commentators, and in the lyrics of gangsta-rap music, which often refer to women as "bitches" and "hos," as Imus did.

Racist and sexist insults are common currency among radio shock talkers, who delight in "bringing private behavior out into public," giving the audience "the thrill of crossing that line," according to John Baugh, a professor of linguistics at Washington University in St. Louis. But when private language goes public, "a tremendous amount of bigotry can be exposed that's beneath the veneer" of polite society, Baugh says.

In the weeks since the Imus incident, radio networks have responded more firmly than usual to shock-jock forays into racist and sexist clowning, firing or suspending several hosts for comments not strikingly different from their usual fare.

Imus' former employer CBS Radio indefinitely suspended two New York shock jocks, JV and Elvis, for airing prank calls to Chinese restaurants that included terms like "shrimp flied lice." On May 15 XM Satellite Radio, a subscriber-only service not even carried over public airwaves, suspended shock jocks Gregg "Opie" Hughes and Anthony Cumia for 30 days for on-air comments surrounding a segment about a homeless man who declared he wanted to rape Secretary of State Condoleeza Rice and other women.

Some media analysts, noting that edgy content sells, predict the shock-jock crackdown is probably temporary.

Unlike some activists, the advertisers who abandoned "Imus in the Morning" "never intended to kill the show" and generally don't rule out sponsoring Imus again in the future, wrote Steve McClellan of AdWeek magazine.

Imus' show has long been a popular stop for politicians such as Sens. John McCain, R-Ariz., and John Kerry, D-Mass., as well as powerful Washington journalists like "Meet the Press" host Tim Russert. Though some long-time guests like former Boston Globe columnist Tom Oliphant defended their friend and depicted his remark as a joke that misfired, advertisers including General Motors and American Express became concerned about the burgeoning public scrutiny and intensifying coverage of the flap in the press and pulled ads from the show. On April 11, MSNBC canceled "Imus in the Morning"; CBS followed suit the next day. [5]

The program "helped sell marketers' products to more than 2 million mostly affluent viewers and listeners each week," garnering $33 million in ads annually for MSNBC and another $11 million for WFAN, the New York radio station where it originated. [6]

But some conservative commentators warn that those liberal activist groups that pushed for Imus' firing are carrying on with their agendas in the hope of ending the dominance of conservative talk on radio and television. One possible way of doing this would be advocating for the restoration of the Federal Communications Commission's Fairness Doctrine, a rule requiring broadcasters who air programs on controversial subjects to give significant time to all sides of an issue. The agency repealed it in 1987.

"It wasn't exactly clear to me how [liberals] intended to bring back the Fairness Doctrine," Cliff Kincaid, chief writer and editor at the conservative media-criticism group Accuracy in Media, said at an April 13 forum at the conservative Washington-based think tank Free Congress Foundation. "But I think now with the Imus affair, we know." It's a "short leap from firing Imus to going after [conservative commentator] Rush Limbaugh." [7]

Some of the loudest criticisms that followed the Imus affair were aimed not at racist and sexist language used by whites like Imus and Limbaugh but by black musicians — mainly in gangsta-rap lyrics.

"Now that we've gotten Imus taken care of, can we finally address what's going on with the misogyny among rappers?" asked columnist Sue Hutchison in the April 13 *San Jose Mercury News.* [8]

"Hypocrisy abounds" around the Imus firing because the same terms Imus used "go on in rap music on hundreds of radio stations around the country" without any protest from the same African-Americans who protested Imus' language, said Dick Kernan, vice president of the Specs Howard School of Broadcasting in Southfield, Mich. [9]

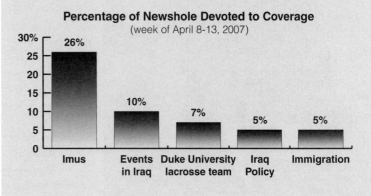

Imus Controversy Ignited Media Flood

In early April 2007, newspapers devoted more than a quarter of their "newshole" — the space devoted to news — to the controversy over Don Imus' racist remark about the Rutgers University women's basketball team. The next biggest topic was the Iraq War, which garnered just 10 percent of the newshole. Of all news stories so far in 2007 (not shown on graphic), only coverage of President Bush's troop "surge" in Iraq, in early January received more coverage (34 percent of the newshole). Total coverage of the Imus controversy received 26 percent of the coverage. Much of the Imus coverage revolved around the Rev. Al Sharpton, who skewered Imus on his talk show on April 9 and helped lead the campaign for Imus' firing.

Percentage of Newshole Devoted to Coverage
(week of April 8-13, 2007)

Imus	Events in Iraq	Duke University lacrosse team	Iraq Policy	Immigration
26%	10%	7%	5%	5%

Source: Project for Excellence in Journalism

Others argue that gangsta-rap lyrics and a radio broadcast aren't necessarily comparable forms of media. Hip-hop "was a quick and easy scapegoat," says Tony N. Brown, a sociologist at Vanderbilt University. But the offensive lyrics generally aren't on display to the general public, he says. "To get these particular lyrics that people are talking about, you have to buy them," and radio bleeps or deletes them, he says.

Anger about sexist lyrics and use of other derogatory language like "nigger" in some rap music has been protested in African-American communities for years, although that fact hasn't been much noticed by the mainstream media, wrote journalist Richard Prince of the Maynard Institute for Journalism Education in Oakland, Calif. At soul singer James Brown's funeral last December, the Rev. Sharpton recalled that Brown had asked him, "What happened that we went from saying, 'I'm black and I'm proud' to calling us niggers and hos and bitches?"

Getty Images/Ray Tamarra

Civil rights activist and radio host the Rev. Al Sharpton became one of the first voices to call for the firing of Don Imus after he made a racial and gender slur against the Rutgers University women's basketball team. Some conservative commentators complained Sharpton hasn't made such high-profile protests against sexist lyrics by black rappers.

"Sharpton has been out there talking about these lyrics for a long time," says Lee Thornton, a journalism professor at the University of Maryland, College Park, and a former broadcaster.

To some analysts, aggressive language throughout the media is disturbing evidence that popular culture in the United States lacks civility.

"Mainstream media is becoming more like Imus" all the time, says Sheri Parks, associate professor of American studies at the university. "Ridicule and insults are the way we

laugh now. We're moving closer and closer to that culture of meanness being completely mainstream."

As broadcasters, lawmakers and social critics debate the values and dangers of shock media to American culture, here are some of the questions being asked:

Have ethnic jokes and insults become too pervasive in society?

Ethnic putdowns and comedy making light of someone's gender have long been part of American culture. But social critics and other commentators argue that shock jocks, gangsta rappers and other personalities have taken things to the extreme by using slurs to target political opponents or other public figures, increasingly poisoning public discourse. The question is whether practitioners have gone over the line — and where exactly the line is?

Talk radio, at least, "is not getting dirtier, not getting cleaner" although the medium continues to expand, says Michael Harrison, founder and editor of *Talkers* magazine and a longtime observer of the phenomenon. "There's no trend toward nastiness."

In fact, ethnic humor and insults are ancient traditions and have long been a feature of American culture, says Leon Rappoport, professor emeritus of psychology at Kansas State University and author of a recent book on ethnic humor. "Dialect humor" stereotyping groups ranging from "operatic Italians to money-grubbing Jews" was a staple of the music halls and vaudeville stages of the early 20th century, for example, says Rappoport.

Later, when stage performers migrated to radio, joking based on ethnic stereotypes continued, says Rappoport. For example, radio comedian Fred Allen based much of his humor on a cast of invented characters representing stereotyped Irish, Jewish and Southern characters, among others.

Early radio and television talk-show host Joe Pyne regularly ridiculed his guests, sometimes with ethnic insults, through the 1960s, says Douglas Gomery, professor emeritus of journalism at the University of Maryland and resident scholar at the university's Library of American Broadcasting.

In 1968, when blacks rioted in several American inner cities, Pyne was suspended for a week after he pulled a gun out of his drawer while talking with an African-American guest. [10]

But some analysts argue that ethnic and gender slurs, along with other name-calling, have become disturbingly prevalent in media over the past few decades and foster hatred and intolerance.

Imus is "emblematic of our uncivil times," said Charles Haynes, a senior scholar at the First Amendment Center, an education organization in Arlington, Va. "In the Internet age, the impulse to offend apparently knows no bounds. People feel increasingly emboldened to say or write anything — however ugly, vulgar or downright hateful. . . . The anything-goes Web world has raised the bar for what counts as 'offensive speech' in America's public square," and "offensive speech sells," said Haynes. [11]

The open use of ethnic and gender slurs "has gotten worse" in recent years, says E. Faye Williams, a lawyer and businesswoman who chairs the National Congress of Black Women, a group that has long protested the stereotyping of African-American women, including in gangsta rap. Today's American media is rife with comedy, movies and music that negatively stereotype black women, in particular, she says.

Williams says the trend is especially troubling because programming with offensive material is sold to other countries. "It breaks my heart when I go to other countries and see that those negative stereotypes have been exported," Williams says.

Negative stereotypes of African-Americans are evident among Asian and Latin American immigrants to the United States. Many arrive "with anti-black stereotypes in their heads" that they picked up from American media viewed abroad, says Joe R. Feagin, a professor of sociology at Texas A&M University and author of numerous books documenting race-related experiences and attitudes.

In a recent study, for example, rural Taiwanese people who had never seen a black person "had anti-black attitudes" based on viewing American media, he says.

To some, the ethnic and racial putdowns are symptoms of a broader coarsening of American society. Name-calling and stereotyping go "way back in Western culture," says Deborah Tannen, professor of linguistics at Georgetown University and author of the 1999 book *The Argument Culture: Stopping America's War of Words*. But, she adds, "I've found lots and lots of evidence that it got worse in the 1990s," as name-calling and shouting replaced more civil debate in realms ranging from television shows to the courts. For example, several former U.S. senators have declared that they voluntarily left Congress in the 1990s because discourse there became vicious and harshly adversarial. Numerous lawyers say they left their

Media Matters for America

Former conservative journalist David Brock founded the liberal media-watchdog group Media Matters for America, credited with bringing shock jock radio host Don Imus' racially offensive remark to public attention by posting it on the group's Web site the same day he made the comment. The growing prominence of such Internet activism means fewer media gaffes now escape public scrutiny, analysts say.

profession for the same reason, Tannen says.

There's no doubt "we have become a coarse society" over the past few decades, says Maryland's Thornton, whose network television jobs included a seven-year stint booking guests for the Rev. Jesse Jackson's "Both Sides" talk show on CNN.

"I cannot imagine dropping a person from the 1940s into our climate," says Thornton. "Decades ago, although there was racism underneath, people clothed themselves in a mannerly way. There were lines of public behavior. I don't think we know anymore in our culture what the lines are. That's why Imus was as surprised as anyone to find that he had crossed one," she says.

The insult culture "has gone to the point of no return, and we don't know how to rein it in," says Thornton. "The whole shock jock thing has contributed to the coarsening of dialogue," she says. Nevertheless, "The public appetite for this is overrated" by media outlets.

A Who's Who of Shock Jocks

In the beginning was Imus

Don Imus

Don Imus began his career as the first true "shock jock" in 1970 at a Cleveland radio station as a DJ. He quickly developed a popular repertoire of comic and raunchy bits such as asking female callers, "Are you naked?"

In the 1990s, the "Imus in the Morning" show gravitated toward news and political talk, with a growing list of influential guests including members of Congress and journalists from major news organizations such as NBC and *Newsweek*. The show mixed political talk with shock-jock banter. For example, Imus referred to *Washington Post* media reporter Howard Kurtz, a frequent guest, as a "boner-nosed . . . beanie-wearing Jewboy" and described New York Knicks basketball player Patrick Ewing as a "knuckle-dragging moron."

Imus was fired in April by both CBS Radio and MSNBC television, which had simulcast his radio program to rising ratings, after calling the Rutgers University women's basketball team "nappy-headed hos." Fired in the first months of a five-year, $40 million contract, Imus is suing CBS.

Howard Stern

Radio's second iconic shock jock is **Howard Stern**, who got his first radio job in 1976 and transitioned into shock-jock stunts gradually a few years later. Stern's specialty is sex talk, though he's also done parodies like "Hill Street Jews." In 1985 NBC Radio briefly canceled Stern's show over a new segment called "Bestiality Dial-a-Date."

His employer in the early 1990s, Infinity Broadcasting, racked up $1.7 million in Federal Communications Commission (FCC) indecency fines over Stern's show between 1990 and 1993. In 1992, for example, stations carrying Stern earned a $600,000 fine after Stern combined indecency with racial stereotypes when he said "the closest I came to making love to a black woman was I masturbated to a picture of Aunt Jemima on a pancake box."

Despite frequent suspensions, cancellations and station changes, Stern has been employed on radio consistently for more than three decades. Currently he hosts "The Howard Stern Show" on Sirius Satellite Radio.

To some observers, using ethnic stereotypes as veiled or overt insults is an especially egregious form of argument and has gone too far in the media.

The liberal media-monitoring group Media Matters for America was chagrined when conservative radio talk-show host Limbaugh aimed racial stereotypes at both civil rights activist Sharpton and Democratic presidential candidate Sen. Barack Obama by playing a satirical song titled "Barack the Magic Negro," in which a singer impersonating Sharpton urges listeners not to vote for Obama because he's not a "real" black man like rapper Snoop Dogg.

However, others argue that racial stereotyping is no more harmful than strong, argumentative language.

Accuracy in Media's Kincaid says there's no essential difference between denigrating people through racial

stereotypes or denigrating them for their individual actions, as liberal MSNBC host Keith Olbermann does in his nightly feature dubbing several individuals "the worst people in the world" for that day. In either case, it's a matter of "holding people up for public ridicule," says Kincaid.

Should the government do more to restrain hate speech?

The Federal Communications Commission (FCC) has the authority to limit sexually explicit speech and other public discourse it deems "indecent." Some observers believe the agency should adopt a similar approach toward "hate speech" involving demeaning racial or ethnic stereotypes. But such an expansion of regulatory power could collide with First Amendment concerns,

Shock talker **Doug "Greaseman" Tracht** has been an on-air personality since the early 1970s at several East Coast stations. He's most infamous for racist comments he made while working at Washington, D.C.-area stations, where he's spent most of his career.

Douglas Tracht

In 1985, he was widely criticized for saying of the Martin Luther King Day holiday that "they should shoot four more of them and give us a whole week off." Between 1999 and 2002, Tracht was off the air entirely after he was fired over another racist comment. Tracht's broadcast features often-raunchy on-air skits and stories employing a large cast of fictional characters he developed over the years.

After two decades on broadcast radio, **Bubba the Love Sponge** was fired by Clear Channel Communications in 2004 after the FCC fined the company $755,000 based on complaints about Bubba's show, which has featured stunts like butchering a hog on air, shocking guests with electric collars and giving his co-workers

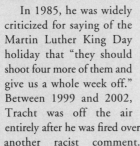

Bubba

a massive dose of laxatives to see who would be the last to move their bowels. Currently the program is carried on Sirius.

Anthony Cumia and Greg Hughes

Jocks Gregg "Opie" Hughes and Anthony Cumia — **Opie and Anthony** — have migrated from broadcast radio to satellite and back again. Among other incidents, they were fired from a Boston station in 1998 for an April Fool's hoax claiming that then-Boston Mayor Thomas Merino had been killed in a car crash.

In May 2007, in an unusual twist, the two were fired by the unregulated subscription-radio service XM Satellite Radio but not by the CBS broadcast network, which also airs their show, after they joked about a homeless man raping Secretary of State Condoleeza Rice.

JV and Elvis — Jeff Vandergrift and Dan Lay — inhabited shock radio's "The Dog House with JV and Elvis" until their show was canceled by CBS in May 2007, in the wake of Imus' firing. Vandergrift and Lay aired a prank phone call in fake accents to a Chinese restaurant, requesting "shrimp flied lice," among other Asian-stereotyping jokes. The call — typical fare for the show — was made before Imus made his "nappy-headed hos" comment, but CBS didn't fire the two until after it fired Imus.

---

particularly the libertarian belief that individuals, not the government, should be responsible for reining in inappropriate speech.

"The FCC needs to take a close look at its policies when it comes to the kind of language people use," says Ohio State University sociologist K. Sue Jewell, author of the book *From Mammy to Miss America and Beyond: Cultural Images and the Shaping of U.S. Social Policy.* Jewell believes name-calling and stereotyping insults by high-profile media figures can strongly influence public opinion, particularly among young people, and "easily escalate to violence."

Williams of the National Congress of Black Women believes the FCC should remove shock jocks for offensive remarks on public airwaves, since they can find new homes on subscription satellite radio stations. She and other experts contend the FCC and Congress could easily justify expanding the agency's mandate, citing historical precedent.

"There are certain words that have historical baggage, and they probably shouldn't be used on the airwaves, which are owned by all of us. Given our national history of racial discrimination, I don't see why the FCC can't make that argument," says Leonard Baynes, a professor at New York's St. John's University School of Law. Baynes says the FCC should even consider levying similar restrictions on cable television content, noting cable operators currently are required to scramble indecent programming and take other steps to police content in order to get franchise licenses.

AP Photo/Richard Drew

Angela Burt-Murray, editor-in-chief of *Essence* magazine, is one of several prominent black journalists — including Gwen Ifill of PBS and Al Roker of NBC — who called for CBS Radio to take a harder stance on Don Imus' April 4 remark about the Rutgers women's basketball team after he was suspended for two weeks. He was eventually fired by CBS on April 12.

But some experts prefer the status quo be maintained, saying they fear government agencies will find it difficult to walk the center line and fight off the temptation to regulate speech that conflicts with an administration's political agenda.

"I support the FCC's ability to regulate obscenity — but I don't want to see their powers expanded" to sanction language that's racist or homophobic, for example, says Accuracy in Media's Kincaid. The answer to speech that offends people is more speech from the side that was offended, he says. "I want to see more speech, not less."

The best response "would be for people [like Imus] to bring onto their shows the people that disagree with them," says Kincaid, who co-hosted CNN's "Crossfire" talk program in the 1980s. Harking back to his on-air experience, Kincaid says, "I liked that show because of the two views" that were part of every program. But ensuring that opposing views are part of every discussion should be left to television and radio networks and hosts, not the government, he adds.

Even the FCC's current powers to regulate for "decency" can be misused to push a political agenda instead, said liberal writer and commentator Ted Rall, who contends the decision to pull shock jock Howard Stern's show from Clear Channel Communications' radio stations in 2004 had less to do with inappropriate remarks than with statements critical of the Bush administration. [12]

"If you don't think me going after Bush got me thrown off those stations, you got another think coming," said Stern. His days on broadcast radio were "numbered because I dared to speak out against the Bush administration and . . . the religious agenda of George W. Bush concerning stem cell research and gay marriage," he said. "What he is doing with the FCC is pushing this religious agenda." [13]

Some legal experts worry that legitimate free speech can be caught up in a dragnet of enforcement actions if the government more stringently polices the airwaves.

"Racist speech is — or should be — always over the line, and Imus' coarse and racist reference to the Rutgers team was all the worse because it seemed so casually uttered," said New York City-based First Amendment lawyer Floyd Abrams. Nevertheless, he said, "I am concerned about policing even errant speech to the point that we risk losing the enlivening and sometimes even acute commentary that accompanies it and of which even offensive speech is sometimes a part." [14]

Radio is by its nature a spontaneous medium, and that means inadvisable words will be uttered from time to time, says *Talkers* magazine's Harrison. "The spontaneity is what keeps people interested," he says. 'The more they regulate radio the more they'll kill it."

Harrison notes that radio has become such a niche medium that there's little reason to apply a new regulatory regime. Broadcast radio today is "just one little street down a much wider avenue" of largely unregulated media, making additional content regulation both unfair and pointless, he says.

Harrison says talk about new regulations smacks of hypocrisy when all types of objectionable discourse and pornography are conveyed on the Internet, which is unregulated.

L. Brent Bozell, founder of the conservative Media Research Center, adamantly opposes increased government regulation of argumentative speech. He argues, however, that a different kind of federal rule would help media consumers squelch such speech on their own, if they chose, at least on cable television. Under a "cable choice" set-up, cable subscribers could order and cancel channels individually, rather than being restricted to a cable company's prepackaged channel tiers.

A rule permitting such "cable choice" would "be a real market solution" to problems like Imus' racist speech, which was carried over MSNBC, says Bozell. "If the customer had the right" to stop paying for individual channels, "NBC and BET [Black Entertainment Television] would be very very careful about who they offended," and "if 2 percent of the people watched a certain network, the other 98 percent wouldn't have to pay for it," as happens today, he says.

Should Don Imus have been fired?

Few people defend the language Imus used to describe the Rutgers players. But while many commentators say his firing was justified, others find it hypocritical, in light of language found elsewhere in the media. And they wonder whether keeping him on the air might have helped spark a more enduring dialogue about racism and misogyny.

Firing Imus "was an appropriate response, and it should have happened sooner," says Ohio State's Jewell, adding that the public airwaves "should not be used to demean a culture."

"Blacks were more likely to want him to be fired," which illustrates the stark "racial divide" in America, says Baynes of St. John's Law School. In the dominant white culture, "there really isn't an appreciation and understanding of this minority point of view," which is the product of a longstanding historical linkage between use of racially demeaning language and racist actions, Baynes says.

"When someone uses that kind of language, it makes the hair on the back of your neck stand up because you don't know what that person would do in terms of firing you without cause or refusing to rent an apartment to you," Baynes says.

In contrast, he continues, "white people know the person who used the language as a friend, an aunt, an uncle, a grandpa, someone who may have loved them and been generous to them." In such a scenario, they are reluctant to speak out against racist language while acknowledging that someone who can be loving to friends and family also is capable of being hurtful.

Imus was fired largely because civil rights activists wielded economic power over advertisers to get him off the air — a positive but not extremely significant outcome, says Marc Lamont Hill, assistant professor of American studies at Temple University. The firing doesn't address any of the real racial problems afflicting African-Americans, such as poor schools or hiring and housing discrimination, says Hill. "I'd take a hundred Imuses if it meant that black people could have access to good health care," he says.

More important than Imus being fired was "the conversation on language that impugns people that's begun" in the wake of the incident, says Karl Frisch, media relations director at the liberal media-criticism organization Media Matters for America, one of the groups that first brought public attention to Imus' slur.

Some who are skeptical about the firing say that a better conversation on race might have ensued had Imus stayed on the job, however.

The firing was understandable but unfortunate, says Tom Taylor, editor of *Inside Radio* magazine. Earlier in Imus' career, after he beat personal problems with drugs and alcohol, "he did a great job of getting other guys alerted to that problem" through public-service work and his radio program. "To me, we've lost the opportunity" to see if "he could have done the same thing with racist language," Taylor says.

Radio is a niche medium where loyal but small audiences are in large part created and sustained by the particular talents of individual on-air personalities. Imus' niche was an unusual one, and his departure will be felt, Taylor says.

The Imus audience "was never large" — 2 and a half to 3 million listeners, says Taylor. "But it was a very interesting audience," made up of "the type of American who watches the Sunday TV talk shows and would like to meet authors." The program "was sort of like an 18th-century Paris salon where you get this volatile mixture of guys" discussing a wide range of topics, he says. In particular, "publishers have been in tears" since the firing because Imus' show "was an almost irreplaceable stop on the book circuit."

C H R O N O L O G Y

1960s-1970s *Supreme Court debates whether government bans on radio shock talk violate the Constitution. In sitcoms and standup comedy, insult humor replaces physical comedy, which is deemed too violent.*

1969 Supreme Court declares that the Federal Communications Commission's (FCC) Fairness Doctrine — requiring on-air controversial discussions to present all sides of the issue — is consistent with the First Amendment guarantee of free speech.

1968 Don Imus takes his first radio job in Cleveland.

1978 In a case involving comedian George Carlin's use of "seven dirty words," Supreme Court upholds FCC's right to bar broadcast of "indecent" material.

1980s *Raucous, risqué "morning zoo" programs become drive-time radio favorites.*

1984 Denver shock host Alan Berg is murdered by right-wing fanatics angered by his outspoken left-wing political and sex talk.

1987 FCC rescinds the Fairness Doctrine.

1990s *Talk radio burgeons after the Fairness Doctrine is scrapped. Political talk hosts pick up shock talk, especially ethnic and gender insults. A new form of hip-hop, gangsta rap, features sexist, violent lyrics.*

1993 St. Louis shock jocks Steve Shannon and D.C. Chymes are fired after telling a caller she is "acting like a nigger." They are soon hired by another local station.

1996 New York radio personality Bob Grant, who has a history of anti-black statements, is fired after a joke about Commerce Secretary Ron Brown, an African-American, who had just died in a plane crash.

1997 Imus is named one of *Time* magazine's 25 most influential Americans.

1999 Washington, D.C., shock jock Doug "Greaseman" Tracht is fired after saying, "Now you understand why they drag them behind trucks," referring to the Texas murder in which James Byrd, an African-American, was dragged behind a truck.

2000s *Shock talkers fired from broadcast radio find new homes on unregulated Internet and satellite radio.*

2003 Conservative radio host Rush Limbaugh is hired then quickly fired by ESPN after he says a biased liberal media pushed black Philadelphia Eagles quarterback Donovan McNabb to star status despite mediocre skills. . . . Rochester, N.Y., shock talker Bob Lonsberry is fired after comparing the city's African-American mayor to a monkey but is soon rehired by the same station.

2004 Rapper Nelly cancels a charity appearance at Spelman College, a historically black school for women in Atlanta, after students protest his sexist videos.

2005 Sportscaster Sid Rosenberg is banned from "Imus in the Morning" after saying singer Kylie Minogue, who has breast cancer, "won't look so good when she's got a bald head with one titty." He later returns to the show as a frequent guest. . . . New York radio host Miss Jones is briefly suspended for a song mocking tsunami victims as "Africans drowning, little Chinamen swept away. You could hear God laughing, 'Swim, you bitches, swim.' "

2006 Shock jock Howard Stern leaves the public airwaves for Sirius Satellite Radio.

2007 On April 4, Imus refers to Rutgers University female basketball players as "nappy-headed hos" and is fired a week later after advertisers pull their spots. Fired three months into a five-year $40 million contract with CBS Radio, Imus is suing the network. . . . CBS Radio fires New York shock jocks Jeff Vandergrift and Dan Lay — J.V. and Elvis — for a prank phone call to workers at a Chinese restaurant. . . . Some in the newly Democrat-controlled Congress mull regulating media violence and reviving the Fairness Doctrine.

Some critics believe firing Imus was hypocritical when one considers the offensive or questionable material that can be found on a daily basis in the media. Kincaid of Accuracy in Media cites MSNBC's decision to air the profanity-laced video made by Seung-Hui Cho, the student who carried out the April 16 Virginia Tech University massacre.

The double standard isn't a particular surprise, however, since both MSNBC and CBS employed Imus because he was an edgy shock jock, then fired him for saying something shocking, says Kincaid. MSNBC, in particular, "helped to make him a star by putting their people on his show" as journalist-guests, he says.

"The policy ought to be that the media is in favor of free speech," says Kincaid. "So if you hire a commentator who's known for saying shocking things, then you accept that he will say shocking things. . . . People can apologize on the air and move on. That's freedom with responsibility."

"I thought CBS overreacted because I think that his intentions weren't derogatory," says Dennis Rome, a professor of criminal justice at the University of Wisconsin, Parkside.

Rome says while the language Imus used was objectionable, it continues to be widely used. He notes that gangsta rappers use words like "hos," saying it's a different thing for African-Americans to demean each other. "I don't agree," he says. "The real problem is that the language is being kept alive, no matter who's using it, and what we need to do is move on from it."

Rome adds, "Rush Limbaugh and others have said a lot worse" than the statement that lost Imus his job, and the damage potentially done by media personalities who use racial and gender stereotyping as part of political discourse "is far stronger, because they intend to be derogatory," Rome says. He predicts nothing will come of the Imus incident because he was quickly fired and the incident was swept under the rug.

"A better approach would have been, 'What do we do to balance this? What else can we put on the air to show more points of view?' " he says.

BACKGROUND

Historical Stereotypes

Imus sought to excuse his use of the phrase "nappy-headed hos" by saying he and his producers had picked up the words from hip-hop music, as well as from the Spike Lee film "School Daze." But historians and linguists say the words have a history stretching back to the days of slavery. [15]

Blacks' "nappy hair" was one of the physical characteristics seized upon by white slave owners to prove that "neither human physiology nor human nature was uniform" as a way of justifying their ownership of other humans, said Zine Magubane, assistant professor of sociology at Boston College. [16]

Slavery in America flourished at the same time many Europeans and American settlers were embracing the ideals of the Enlightenment, including human equality, as the inspiration for the French and American revolutions, Magubane said. To reconcile that apparent contradiction, some focused on physical differences between blacks and whites they said were signs blacks didn't have to be included on equal terms in a social contract.

For example, in his "Notes on the State of Virginia," Thomas Jefferson concluded that blacks couldn't be politically enfranchised members of the new American union because of their "physical and moral" differences from whites, such as not having long, flowing hair, Magubane wrote. [17]

Descriptions like "nappy headed" and "ho" to refer to African-American women are part of "a white, racial frame that we whites invented in the 1600s to explain how we as good Christians could enslave thousands of human beings," says Feagin of Texas A&M. The stereotypes persist, including in some black music like gangsta rap, because "350 of our 400 years of history were years of extreme racial oppression. So in order to see ourselves as good people, we had to come up with" reasons for considering African-Americans lesser people and "hammer it into everybody's head, including black people," Feagin says.

While "ho" itself is a newer coinage, originating in the black community, words stereotyping African-American women as oversexed and as prostitutes — such as "wench" — were common from slavery days, largely to provide a rationale for the growth of a large mulatto class of mixed-race children, says Ohio State sociologist Jewell. "Where were all those mulatto children coming from?" — from "Jezebel — the bad black girl," she says. Words like "wench," "ho" and "Jezebel" convey the message that "these women of African descent are very hyper-sexed, worldly seductresses, and if you aren't careful, they will seduce you," she says.

Societal Conversation on Race Seems Unlikely

Racism experts say they are not surprised

Soon after radio host Don Imus referred to the Rutgers University women's basketball team as "nappy-headed hos," groups like the National Association of Black Journalists and some media commentators began calling for a national "conversation on race." Such a dialogue was needed, some said, to confront the simmering differences that saw many African-Americans calling for the shock jock's firing while many whites saw the comments as no big deal.

But while some dialogue did soon begin about the sexism inherent in the gangsta-rap lyrics from which Imus said he picked up the term "ho," conversation about the radio host's casual use of a racist, sexist insult never really happened. Many racism experts say they're not surprised.

Racism "isn't on the docket as an issue," despite occasional flurries of attention when a celebrity like Imus crosses the line in public comments, says Marc Lamont Hill, an assistant professor of American studies at Temple University.

When whites who use words like "nappy-headed" say, " 'I said that, but I'm not a racist,' I do think that they're being serious," says Hill, who is black. "I believe that Imus could honestly say, 'I don't think I'm better than a black person.' " But "the broader context that makes the whole notion of 'nappy-headed' and 'ho' so painful is that he has the power to put a name on someone," Hill says.

"Being called a nigger isn't just an epithet. It's putting you in a certain position" because a white man has the power to do so, while African-Americans don't, says Hill. "I can call you a cracker, but I can't treat you like a cracker."

In the 1960s, during the civil rights era, "we had a way to talk about race" because discussion centered on laws that could quell overt oppression and segregation, says Shawn J. Parry-Giles, associate professor of communication at the University of Maryland, College Park. Today, with those laws on the books, "There is a sense among the majority group that we've done everything that we need to do." So when a potentially racist incident occurs, "we just individualize it," hoping that firing Imus, for example, ends the problem, Parry-Giles says.

The shock-radio era has "paralleled a societal era of ignoring race, on the grounds that our society should be colorblind," says Lee Anne Bell, director of the education program at Barnard College. "But if you can't talk about it, you can't confront it, and that makes colorblindness very insidious."

Overt racism among whites has drastically receded, but young, white men, especially, "still love to go for a beer with [white] friends and tell racist jokes," says Joe R. Feagin, a professor of sociology at Texas A&M University and co-author of a recent book on racist language and opinions among today's white college students.

And while Imus and the students Feagin surveyed generally excuse their private language, saying it doesn't make them racists, "it does mean something," Feagin says. When comedian and former "Seinfeld" actor Michael Richards railed at some African-American hecklers at a stand-up gig last year, he made "seven uses of the N-word," says Feagin. "That comes from something pretty deep."

If America ever does get serious about having a race conversation, scholars and educators on race and prejudice have some suggestions:

- Everyone must acknowledge, up front, that we routinely act to protect our own individual interests, and that those interests have race, gender and class implications, says Tony N. Brown, assistant professor of sociology at Vanderbilt University. "People say, 'I'm

Today, the stereotypes persist, although Americans generally think that the days of racism are over, says Feagin. "We passed civil rights laws in the 1960s, and now we think all the racial problems are over," he says. But if that had happened, it would mean "hundreds of years of history had been canceled, and that doesn't happen quickly."

In fact, the same racist language, including heavy use of "nigger," continues to be common among white people speaking in all-white groups, says Leslie Houts Picca, a sociologist at the University of Dayton. "We were really quite shocked at just how prevalent casual use of the N-word is," says Picca, who with coauthor Feagin recently published a book detailing race-related incidents that white college students revealed in diaries.

When asked about their objectionable speech, many white students said the words "had lost their racial connotations," says Picca. But in fact they "are centuries-old

not racist or sexist in my language,' "Brown says. "Nevertheless, "in my day-to-day actions, I do reinforce my own racial and gender and class interests, sometimes to the detriment of others' interests. I don't think positive things about the homeless," for example.

Comedian and former "Seinfeld" actor Michael Richards appears on the Rev. Jesse Jackson's radio show on Nov. 26, 2006, to make amends for a Nov. 17 racist outburst at a West Hollywood comedy club. When loud talk from a group of African-American audience members interrupted his act, Richards unleashed a racial tirade, calling the men "niggers" and alluding to lynching.

- Whites, the majority culture, "must be willing to admit there are things we don't know about racism, because people of color have to know when racism is operating just to get along in the world, but white people have our racism detectors set at a very low level," says Tim Wise, a lecturer on race and gender bias and founder of the Nashville-based Association for White Anti-Racist Education. Whites should "start with the assumption that when people of color say, 'Racism is operating,' they probably know what they're talking about, because they've spent a lifetime learning to distinguish between what's racism and what's just everyday insensitivity," Wise says.

- Everyone should hear as many first-person — preferably in-person — stories of Americans of all ethnicities as possible, says Feagin. "The more voices people read or encounter, the more they understand" others' points of view, he says.

- Conversation should "start with objective facts — that women earn 76 cents on the dollar compared to men, for comparable work; that black men are incarcerated at a very high rate," says Brown. "Then we can ask people to give their individual explanations for those facts," he says. "In those explanations, attitudes and beliefs would be revealed" and could then be examined and discussed, he says.

- Everyone should be willing to take responsibility for what they can control, not shift the discussion to what others are doing, says Wise. The nearly immediate shift of the Imus-spurred race discussion from his language to racism and misogyny expressed by hip-hop lyrics shows "how white Americans are so used to shifting the conversation away from things that are our responsibility," he says.

"Why can't we just stop and talk about ourselves for a minute, about our personal responsibility to challenge white people" over racist comments? asks Wise. "Our personal responsibility is to say, 'Cool. The next time something like Imus happens, we whites will deal with our people, just as we expect people of color to hold their group responsible for things like violent rap lyrics,' " he says. Black or white, "own the piece of the problem that's yours, and maybe we can jumpstart the conversation."

Few believe that a true cross-racial conversation on racial matters will begin in America any time soon, Imus or no Imus, however. Says Georgetown University professor of linguistics Deborah Tannen: "Things happen all the time that could spark that conversation, but they don't."

stereotypes, like lazy and criminal. They are not inventing them" but "bringing them down from history."

When used in public, as in Imus' comment, the words call up memories of a painful past for African-Americans, but not for whites, and this deepens the racial divide, says Feagin.

"Mulattos did not come from interracial marriage, and for every time a black man raped a white woman, there were a 1,000 cases the other way" in the days of slavery and legal segregation, a fact that haunts elderly African-American women, in particular, to this day, he says. "One of my grad students has been interviewing elderly African-Americans who lived under legal segregation," Feagin says. In one commonly remembered story, a white man enters a black home and rapes a teenage daughter, says Feagin. "That story has yet to be told" in history books and mainstream media, says Feagin. "Yet these elderly women and men tell these stories routinely. Some 80-year-old black

Ethnic Humor's No Joke for Amateurs

It gets ugly when aggression overwhelms the humor

Why did shock-radio host Don Imus call the Rutgers University women's basketball team "nappy-headed hos?" "I was trying to be funny," Imus explained on his April 9 broadcast, several days after the original comment had blown up into a full-fledged national brouhaha over whether racist and sexist jokes have become a blight on American media.

The debate goes on, in the wake of Imus' firing, with critics arguing that stereotyping jokes have explosive potential and should be used only with caution and, perhaps, not at all. But ethnic humor has a long and robust history, among jokers in public and in private, and few expect to see it abandoned any time soon.

In the 19th and early 20th century, ethnic humor was a staple of stage comedy, but its prevalence receded somewhat as radio brought comedy to the mass media, says Leon Rappoport, professor emeritus of psychology at Kansas State University and author of a recent book on ethnic humor.

The vaudeville stage abounded with "dialect humor," with stereotyped characters like "the operatic Italian" and "the money-grubbing Jew" that audiences easily recognized, Rappoport says. And in the early 20th century, when vaudevillians migrated to radio, the stereotyping humor continued. Fred Allen's radio skits, for example, based their humor on stereotyped characters such as a fast-talking Irishman, a Jewish housewife and numerous others.

Gradually, however, radio comedy "got cleaned up," with ethnic humor mainly expunged, Rappoport says. As a new mass medium, supported by advertisers, radio needed to entice many while offending few, and ethnic jokes — "which can be very aggressive" — risked turning off too many in the unseen listening audience. By the mid-20th century, ethnic humor had become much less prevalent, not only on radio but also on the stage, Rappoport says. By the early 1960s, however, ethnic jokes were being heard again in live comedy, by a new breed of edgy comics whose work was based on irony and social criticism, like Lenny Bruce.

Insult humor was briefly banished from public airwaves, but it returned beginning in the 1970s, says Sheri Parks, associate professor of American studies at the University of Maryland, College Park. Physical comedy and slapstick humor, often fairly violent, once abounded in American mass culture, from Charlie Chaplin to the Three Stooges. But when a 1972 U.S. surgeon general's report declared that violence in media leads to real-life violence, comics once again were forced to find non-physically violent ways to make people laugh, says Parks.

And since a key element in much humor is aggression, comics switched from physical to verbal violence — including stereotyping humor, Parks says. Over the past few decades

women live today with their shades pulled down and no lights on. Their fathers told them to do that to protect themselves against white night riders," he says.

"That's why the black reaction and the white reaction to Imus are so different," says Feagin. "Blacks know that" racially charged language that seems innocuous to whites "can be extremely serious. If it's in a police officer's head, it can get you killed," he says.

Americans' typical reactions to visiting Africans further indicate that language like "nappy headed" and "ho" aren't so much a matter of racial stereotyping but stereotyping of African-Americans who are slave descendants, says Baugh, at Washington University. For example, Baugh says that when he hosted an African Fulbright scholar from Guinea, the man reported that the desk clerk at his American hotel was hostile until he explained that he was visiting from Africa. Then, the clerk's demeanor "changed immediately" to welcome, showing that the issue is not race but history, Baugh says.

Words that negatively stereotype are dangerous for anyone to use, including African-Americans, he says. "It is possible within one's own group to use a derogatory term [for that group] in a positive way," he says. "But when you breach that private world" — which is all too easy to do — "then trouble happens," he says.

For example, "the more you accept these words" for use in your own community, "the more you may be losing your right to claim discrimination" when the words are used against you, says St. John's Law School's Baynes. "If the word loses its currency" as a slur because it's so

"insult has become the dominant mode of comedy."

There may be a serious problem with raising generations of children exposed on a daily basis to insult humor on television, radio and movies, Parks says. Adults believe when children see comedians and sitcom characters insulting each other aggressively "they know that it's unusual behavior that they shouldn't engage in," she says. "But in fact children look to media for normative behaviors, and when they see or hear something, they just go ahead and do it, too."

Adults like Imus may have a similar problem, according to Arthur Asa Berger, professor of broadcast and electronic communication arts at San Francisco State University and author of books on humor and humor writing. "Humor is a very dangerous thing. There's a lot of aggression in it, and when the aggression overwhelms the humor, we don't excuse" the "hostile" joker, he says.

Some professional comedians employ stereotypes "in a mirthful way," using the context of the joke to convince an audience that "they don't actually mean what they're saying" in a stereotyping joke about a drunken Irishman, for example, says Berger.

Lenny Bruce helped bring ethnic humor back to American comedy in the 1950s and 1960s.

AP Photo/John Lindsay

Professional humorists are always aware of their role and develop a sense of how far they can go to get a laugh or make a point without crossing the line into speech that the audience will read as hateful rather than funny or insightful, says Berger. "Comedians work very hard to do that," he says. "But when people who aren't humorists start messing around with humor," most don't even realize what the pitfalls are, he says.

When it comes to ethnic humor, most comedians agree that "anything goes as long as it's funny," says Rappoport. Nevertheless, "context and intent matter, and there has to be a grain of truth to it," he says. Comics like Richard Pryor, Robin Williams and Chris Rock have joked about ethnic groups, their own and other people's, and "the audience finds itself laughing even if they don't want to," Rappoport says.

But ethnic humor can also spell trouble, if the joker leans too heavily on the ethnic and not enough on the humor, he says. "The thing about the Imus statement is simply that it wasn't funny," says Rappoport. In the annals of humor, Imus is "a trivial footnote of somebody who went too far in the wrong context and then got what he deserved."

commonly used by black people, "when somebody uses the word and really means it, then what do you do?"

Shock Value

Risk, danger and excitement all are important components of popular entertainment. Add to that the spontaneity of live radio, and it's easy to see why hosts who "shock" have been a programming staple for decades — and why they sometimes cross the lines of acceptable speech. Nevertheless, media analysts point out that really shocking talk accounts for a small proportion of programming fare.

Shock of various kinds has "always been part of entertainment," so it's no wonder that radio talkers who say shocking things can draw big audiences, says Clarence W. Thomas, associate professor of mass communications

at Virginia Commonwealth University. "A roller coaster, a slasher movie — they carry a shock, and they're beyond the norm of everyday life, and that's what makes them interesting and entertaining."

What puts the shock in shock radio is that "shock jocks pull ideas and images from private spaces and say them out loud," says Parks, at the University of Maryland. Racial and gender insults that most people utter only among friends and family, along with sex talk, are the main types of speech eligible for that treatment.

With radio increasingly segmented to appeal to niche audiences, programmers have determined that shock jocks most appeal to men and younger listeners, says the Library of American Broadcasting's Gomery. That, in turn, draws advertisers seeking to cater to demographically desirable

Getty Images/Bryan Bedder

Many critics of Don Imus' firing contend that a double standard allows black rappers and hip-hop artists — like rapper Snoop Dogg — to use the same kind of offensive comments about women in their lyrics without being held accountable.

niches. So some personalities regularly push the envelope, hoping to touch the hot-button interests of their core audience. Broadcast television networks, in contrast, have always strived to develop programs that appeal to the masses and offend no one, making them a bad fit for shock commentators, Gomery explains.

Shocking talk has existed on radio from its early days.

Father Charles E. Coughlin wielded enormous influence through his on-air commentaries in the 1930s and '40s. But he began to increasingly incense some listeners with anti-Semitic tirades and extreme criticism of President Franklin D. Roosevelt, communism and American involvement in World War II. Both the Roosevelt administration and the National Association

of Broadcasters placed stricter limitations on who could get air time to speak about controversial issues. However, not until Coughlin's bishop ordered him to return to duty as a parish priest was his radio voice finally silenced.

In the 1940s through the '60s, radio host Joe Pyne pushed the envelope on insult speech, calling homeless people "stinky bums" and responding to guests with comments like "Why don't you take your teeth out, put them in backwards, and bite your throat?"

In the 1970s through the '90s, AM radio, in particular, shifted almost entirely away from music to talk formats, while FM became the medium of choice for music because of its better sound quality. The number of commercial news and talk stations swelled from 360 in 1990 to 802 by July 1993, according to Taylor of Inside Radio. Today, of the 10,600 commercial radio stations in the United States, about 1,360 are talk, while many of the 650 non-commercial public radio stations also embrace variants of the news and talk format.

Comedian George Carlin ran into legal troubles more than once over a routine discussing the "seven words you can never say on television," known as the "seven dirty words." In 1973, after a father complained to the FCC that his young son had heard the routine broadcast on a small New York radio station, the station fought the FCC's sanctions on the grounds that they restricted free speech. The legal case went all the way to the Supreme Court, which — in a 5 to 4 decision — upheld the FCC's right to bar broadcast of material the FCC considered "indecent" at times of day when children might hear it. [18]

The rise of talk radio has increased the likelihood of edgy content. This is particularly true during the 6 to 9 a.m. and 4 to 7 p.m. "drive-time" slots, when more males than females are stuck in their cars for long stretches of time, Gomery says. Because radio talk is spontaneous, unedited and generally unplanned, radio is a "hip, edgy, street-y kind of medium," says Harrison of *Talkers* magazine. Nevertheless, Harrison argues that once Imus and Howard Stern "brought radio into the latest chapter of street culture" back in the 1970s, "shock jock" stopped being a very relevant term. Today, "there are bad boys on the radio," he acknowledges. "But how could anything on radio be truly shocking when there's a wild assortment of perversions all over regular television?"

While shock talk is a persistent element in radio, it still doesn't account for much talking time, perhaps only 3 or 4 percent, says Gomery.

Is ethnic and racial humor dangerous?

YES

Arthur Asa Berger
Professor of Broadcast and Electronic Communication Arts San Francisco State University

Written for *CQ Researcher*, May 2007

Ethnic humor divides as it derides. Societies generally contain many ethnic, racial and religious groups, each of which has distinctive cultural traits, beliefs and values. While ethnic humor may seem to be trivial, it corrodes our sense of community and makes it more difficult for us to live together harmoniously. It focuses on our differences and insults, attacks and humiliates its victims. It is based on stereotyping, which suggests that all members of various ethnic or other groups are the same as far as certain traits deemed "undesirable" by those who use ethnic humor are concerned. This humor can lead to feelings of inferiority and even self-hatred by members of groups attacked by it, while it coarsens and desensitizes those who use it.

Humor is an enigmatic matter that has fascinated our greatest philosophers and thinkers from Aristotle's time to the present. Scholars disagree about why we laugh, but two of the dominant theories about humor — Aristotle's view that it is based upon feelings of superiority and Freud's notion that it involves masked hostility and aggression — apply to ethnic humor.

There is an ethnocentric bias reflected in ethnic humor, a feeling held by those who use this humor that they are superior and that their cultural beliefs and values are the only correct ones. While ethnic humor is widespread — it's found in most countries — it varies considerably from mild teasing to terribly insulting and even vicious humor. Every society seems to find some minority "out-group" to ridicule. But sometimes ethnic humor — about Jews and African-Americans, for example — can easily become anti-Semitic and racist.

People who ridicule Jewish-American "princesses" or "dumb Poles" and other ethnic groups think they are just being funny when they tell friends insulting riddles. We might ask "funny to whom?" Such humor isn't amusing to members of the groups that are ridiculed. Those who use ethnic humor feel that they can make fun of ethnic groups with impunity, but in multicultured societies, fortunately, that is no longer the case. The excuse given by people who use ethnic humor, "I was just trying to be funny," isn't acceptable anymore.

Humor can be liberating and has many benefits, but when it is used to ridicule and insult people, it is harmful to members of the ethnic groups that are victimized by this humor and to society at large. Ethnic humor isn't just a laughing matter.

NO

Leon Rappoport
Professor Emeritus of Psychology Kansas State University

Written for *CQ Researcher*, May 2007

It is hard to think of any serious harm associated with ethnic humor if you have ever fallen down laughing at a routine by Whoopi Goldberg, Robin Williams or Chris Rock, or heard Jackie Mason's lines about the differences between Jews and gentiles. Yet controversies over humor based on ethnic, racial or gender stereotypes go all the way back to the plays of Aristophanes (circa 430 B.C.), and subsequent writers and performers, from Shakespeare through Richard Pryor and Mel Brooks, have been catching flak about it ever since.

Modern social-science studies aimed at settling the harm question have not produced any smoking-gun evidence. The cautious conclusion of a 2004 review of experimental research was that exposure to disparagement humor did not reinforce negative images of the targeted group. Relevant field studies have shown that people feel no significant malice when laughing at jokes based on ethnic stereotypes, and common-sense observations support this: Where are all the suffering victims of the Polish jokes, dumb-blonde jokes, Jewish-American mother and princess jokes that have come and gone over recent years, not to mention the Lutherans, Catholics and Unitarians regularly worked over in Garrison Keillor's monologues on "A Prairie Home Companion"?

The prominent ethnic-humor scholar Christie Davies (author of three important books on the subject) maintains that laughter at such jokes has little to do with social attitudes but reflects the powerful surge of pleasure we tend to feel from "playing with aggression." And this includes members of the group being ridiculed, who often are most amused by clever takes on the stereotypes they know best. This was clearly true among the hundreds of diverse college students who took the class on ethnic humor I taught for several years. They would frequently be particularly carried away with laughter when seeing videos of comedians playing with ironic clichés about their own ethnic, racial or gender group. Like most Americans today, these students grew up in our humor-saturated TV culture and are thus well prepared to maintain a healthy sense of critical distance while enjoying satire, parody and ridicule — remember Boris and Natasha on "Bullwinkle"? — in the context of ethnic humor.

Part of what holds our increasingly multiethnic society together is our rich stock of ironic humor. The fact that we can play with our differences, even at the risk of occasionally offending each other, deserves recognition as a matter of pride rather than prejudice.

Getty Images/Alex Wong

Journalist Gwen Ifill — moderator of PBS' "Washington Week" — declined to appear on Don Imus' radio show in 1993 when she was a *New York Times* Washington correspondent. In apparent retaliation, Imus said the *Times* was "wonderful" because "it lets the cleaning lady cover the White House."

Stereotypes Spreading?

Though shock jocks may not be expanding their reach, shocking language, especially racial and gender stereotypes, has been increasingly used in other branches of the media in recent years, including comedy, gangsta-rap lyrics and on some radio shows featuring political talk.

Over the past few decades, for example, stereotyping insults have become a prominent mode of comedy, says Parks of the University of Maryland. Previously, a great deal of comedy in movies and on television was physical comedy, which was usually somewhat violent, she says.

The shift toward insult humor was mainly triggered by a 1972 surgeon general's report citing evidence that violence in media leads to violence in real life, says Parks. When the FCC responded by discouraging violent content, comedians shifted to other forms of humor, mainly opting for insults based on ethnic or racial stereotypes.

The shocking language that's garnered the most attention in the wake of Imus' comment has been racial and, especially, gender stereotypes in gangsta-rap lyrics. As with insult humor, the use of stereotyping in African-American music has greatly expanded in recent years.

"In R&B and soul music, African-American women were respected, and even when hip-hop got started, it didn't focus on misogynistic lyrics," says Ohio State University's Jewell.

Gradually, however, the top-selling, highest-profile hip-hop shifted toward lyrics that celebrate the "bling" and flash of a "gangsta" lifestyle and heavily feature misogynistic language like "bitch" and "ho."

Hip-hop "started as a radical critique of society" and especially of racism, says Feagin of Texas A&M. "When it became clear to the music industry that music with a beat could sell across racial lines," social criticism in lyrics "wasn't sold aggressively. White people — who buy 70 percent of rap records — don't want to hear about it."

Consequently, the most commercially successful hip-hop has been lowest-common-denominator music portraying women, especially African-American women, as wholly sexualized rather than romantic objects, says Jewell. The proliferation of the sexualized stereotypes — and frequent references to women as "hos" and "bitches" — "has some far-reaching consequences" for black women, because they're widely "perceived as having low morals" as well as being powerless, she says.

This has seeped into talk radio and television, says Parry-Giles at the University of Maryland. The racially diverse College Park campus is just outside Washington, where the intersection of media, politics and race is the focus of several academic programs. Stereotyping insults are "pervasive across the right and the left" on talk radio, she says, noting that progressive talk host Stephanie Miller repeatedly uses Asian stereotypes when she discusses North Korea on her program, Parry-Giles says.

Several conservative talk-radio hosts are especially notorious for race and gender stereotypes and insults. Michael Savage, whose San Francisco-based show is nationally syndicated by the independent Talk Radio Network, has frequently labeled countries with non-white populations as "turd world nations" and referred to the May 2000 "Million Mom March" on Washington for gun control as the "Million Dyke March," according to the liberal media-criticism group Fairness & Accuracy In Reporting. [19]

CURRENT SITUATION

New Crackdown

There are comparatively few rules governing broadcast content, and the ones that exist mostly focus on indecent sexual content. While radio stations have occasionally fired or suspended shock jocks for insulting and stereo-typing ethnic and racial comments, sex-related antics have triggered much of the disciplinary action, and most fired jocks have been rehired fairly quickly by their old station or a new one.

Today, however, some liberal media critics such as Media Matters for America are focusing public attention on racist and misogynistic comments and insults. While some commentators applaud, others worry that a crack-down on insult speech could prompt an overreaction by advertisers and regulators.

Advertisers quickly pulled out of sponsorships of Imus' program in the wake of the Rutgers University flap, placing economic pressure on MSNBC and then CBS Radio to fire the veteran host. New York shock jocks JV and Elvis were also recently fired after a racist prank call to a Chinese restaurant, and another New York radio personality, comedian Donnell "Ashy" Rawlings, was fired for anti-Semitic comments. [20]

"The striking thing to me is that this was one of the less offensive quotes from Imus," says Robert Entman, professor of media and public affairs at George Washington University and author of books on media and race and media and political discourse. "He's said many anti-Semitic things and things demeaning to black people that he should have gotten into trouble for decades ago."

This time was different, in part because the target of Imus' remarks was a group of admirable student athletes — as opposed to well-known public figures — which made the "nappy-headed hos" comment seem particularly inap-propriate. The Internet also gave interest groups a 24-hour medium to air their complaints and criticisms.

"Imus lost his job because of the Internet," says Kelly McBride, ethics group leader at the Poynter Institute in St. Petersburg, Fla., a nonpartisan media-education orga-nization. "The Internet provides a new venue where enough people can learn about events, complain to each other and lobby advertisers. Some people describe it as an Internet lynch mob, and I think that can be a danger. But I also think that it's democracy at its finest."

Among those leading the Internet criticism of Imus' comment was Media Matters for America, a group founded in 2004 by conservative-turned-liberal writer and journalism activist David Brock to combat what Brock calls media misinformation that advances a con-servative agenda, including race- and gender-related insults and stereotyping.

Also fueling efforts to get Imus' employers to take action were changing demographics that have given women and African-Americans and other ethnic minori-ties more clout in the workplace and the economy, some analysts say.

NBC weatherman Al Roker, PBS journalist Gwen Ifill and former NAACP President Bruce Gordon, now on the Board of Directors of CBS, were among the African-Americans who called for the networks to cancel Imus after his April comments, and their comments apparently carried weight with the networks and advertisers.

"The more you have diverse voices out there, the less likely incidents like this are to happen," says St. John's Law School's Baynes. "Otherwise, people say, 'Well, it's just words.'"

In addition, "women and African-Americans are major buyers today, both groups much richer than they used to be," and advertisers "want to attract them," as they may not have in the past, says the Library of American Broadcasting's Gomery. "That's a big part of this story."

As for Imus, two days after the controversial remark, he offered an apology: "My characterization [of the team] was thoughtless and stupid. . . . And we're sorry," he said on his April 6 program. Three days later, he added: "Here's what I have learned: that you can't make fun of everybody, because some people don't deserve it. And because the climate on this program has been what it has been for 30 years doesn't mean that it has to be that way for the next five years or whatever, because that has to change . . . and I understand that." [21]

Fairness Revisited?

Much of the media scrutiny of racist and sexist language immediately turned to hip-hop lyrics. However, some conservatives worry that the activists who helped oust Imus also will seek to silence conservative political talk show hosts by pressing the federal government to revive the Fairness Doctrine. Following Imus' remarks, the main public and media debate quickly turned to criticism of hip-hop and to whether the Rev. Sharpton, the Rev.

Jackson and other black leaders who strenuously called for Imus' firing had spoken out against gangsta rappers.

Imus firing "is so hypocritical because big media groups like CBS — which owns BET and MTV — traffic in bad language and racist language like the N-word" every time they show a gangsta-rap video, says the Media Research Center's Bozell. "I think the criticism of Imus is reverse racism." In music, he adds, "it's supposedly OK because black people say it."

The quick backlash against hip-hop happened "because it was a quick and easy scapegoat," says Brown of Vanderbilt. He says the radio comments and gangsta-rap lyrics aren't comparable because gangsta rap is seldom broadcast uncut. "To get these particular lyrics that people are talking about, you have to buy them," he says. In general, "they aren't even played on radio."

Meanwhile, some conservatives argue that Imus' firing was the first shot in a war aimed at getting conservative voices such as Bill O'Reilly, Limbaugh and Neal Boortz off radio and television.

Although Imus wasn't a conservative, he has been a vocal opponent of Sen. Hillary Rodham Clinton, D-N.Y., and that made him a target of the same groups who want to silence conservatives, says Kincaid of Accuracy in Media.

Some Imus opponents have called for FCC regulation of stereotyping, derogatory remarks over the airwaves, Kincaid notes. He fears any group that feels it was denigrated over the public airwaves will be able to seek redress at the FCC, a move he believes could impinge on free speech.

Others believe the FCC should do more to ensure that more views get aired. "Why not bring back the Fairness Doctrine?" asks Baynes of St. John's Law School. The FCC rule was largely scrapped in 1987 because the commission feared it might violate broadcasters' free-speech rights.

The rule may be difficult to police, given the range of views on some subjects, Baynes acknowledges. "But the question is, 'Do you think now is better?' I think it's worse." Baynes says the doctrine should also be applied to cable systems, which now have to comply with some federal regulations, including ones requiring them to scramble sexually explicit content.

Some Democrats in Congress would like to revive the rule. Rep. Dennis Kucinich, D-Ohio, chairman of the House Oversight and Government Reform subcommittee, plans hearings on the Fairness Doctrine. [22] House Energy and Commerce Chairman John D. Dingell of Michigan told a conference of advertisers in May that he, too, wants to explore reviving the doctrine. [23]

But "the Fairness Doctrine is an absolute abomination," according to Bozell. "In simple words, it says, 'There ought to be liberal voices on talk radio to offset conservative voices,' " he says.

"But there's already National Public Radio, and if there were a market for more then there would be more liberal voices," Bozell, adds. When the doctrine was in place, many radio stations simply stopped airing discussion of public issues altogether because it was too difficult to find representatives for all opposing views — clearly not an outcome that anyone is looking for, he says.

OUTLOOK

Business as Usual?

Will Imus' firing mark an end to ethnic and gender insults and stereotyping in American media? Few think that's likely. The main reason: Edginess attracts viewers.

Case in point: When outspoken TV personality Rosie O'Donnell joined the talk show "The View," the ratings went up, says Accuracy in Media editor Kincaid. "Imus' ratings also had been going up before the Rutgers incident," he adds.

"Every couple of years some controversy erupts over race, and generally everybody goes back to their normal activities soon afterward," says George Washington University's media and public affairs professor Entman. Racial tension in America, which did come to the surface briefly following Imus' remark, is "a low-grade infection whose symptoms are always present but are tolerable to the majority," he says.

Advertisers would probably welcome Imus back to radio after the controversy dies down, but it's not clear whether a suitable radio venue exists, industry experts say.

For example, General Motors, a big sponsor that quickly pulled ads from the Imus show when controversy began building, would not rule out advertising on an Imus program in the future. Since Imus has apologized for his remarks and vowed to change his tone in the future, the automaker is "open to revisiting at some point down the road" a stint as an Imus advertiser, should his show return, a company spokesperson told *AdWeek* magazine. [24]

But "media options for Imus appear to be limited," said Mike Kinosian, a columnist for the industry publication *Inside Radio.* [25]

"There are only a handful of major radio networks, and it is hard to imagine one would step forward and take him," and "it would be problematic for him [to be] on a small, low-level, unfunded network," said Cary Pahigian, president and general manager in the Portland, Maine, office of Michigan-based Saga Communications, which owns and operates radio and television stations. Satellite radio also is likely out, for the time being at least, since the two big satellite networks — XM and Sirius — hope to merge, and with FCC scrutiny heavy on them at present, "this isn't something they would want to tackle," Pahigian said. [26]

As for gangsta rap, a newly formed coalition opposing sexist lyrics will increase the pressure for performers and record companies to halt the use of sexist language like "ho" and "bitch," says Williams, of the National Congress of Black Women (NCBW), which has been urging music companies to drop such language for years. This spring, however, other groups including the National Organization for Women and the National Council of Women's Organizations have joined with NCBW to fight the sexist language. "With all of us working together, it's only a matter of time," she says.

When it comes to radio, even more targeted niche programs will develop as audio migrates from the airwaves to satellite and the Internet, analysts predict.

That inevitable shift means that radio "will find room for Imus and his language again," predicts the Media Research Center's Bozell.

Other changes also are in store for radio as audiences inevitably grow restless with the brand of talk radio that's dominated for a decade and a half, says Harrison of *Talkers* magazine. "We've been at the peak of a trend of political talk" that is mainly right-wing, he says. Now "people are tired of it," and public boredom spells the end of phenomena of popular culture. Progressive and liberal talk could burgeon in that climate, he predicts.

More than an opening for progressives, though, Americans currently have an appetite for non-partisan political talk, Harrison says. The talker who likely will flourish next "can be liberal, can be conservative," he says. "They'll express ideas," but not fervently back either political party, he predicts.

As for damping down the culture of insult and argument, "that's basically up to everyone," says Georgetown's Tannen. Many people do object to stereotyping insults, for example, uttered privately or in public. But "it's up to us to say something when we hear that talk," she says.

NOTES

1. Gwen Ifill, "Trash Talk Radio," *The New York Times*, April 10, 2007.

2. "Imus Has Long Record of Incendiary Remarks," National Association of Black Journalists Web site, April 18, 2007; www.nabj.org.

3. Richard Prince, "NABJ Says It Still Wants Radio Host Out by Monday," *Journal-isms* column, Maynard Institute for Journalism Education, April 6, 2007.

4. "NAHJ Condemns Radio Host Don Imus for Racial Remarks," press release, National Association of Hispanic Journalists, April 9, 2007.

5. "Rallying Around Their Racist Friend," media advisory, Fairness & Accuracy in Media, April 11, 2007; www.fair.org.

6. Steve McClellan, "They Bailed for Now, But Advertisers Forgive," *AdWeek*, April 16, 2007; www.adweek.com.

7. Quoted in Alex Koppelman, "Is Rush Limbaugh Next?" *Salon.com*, April 16, 2007; www.salon.com.

8. Quoted in Richard Prince, "After Imus, Sights Set on Rap Music," Journal-isms, Maynard Institute for Journalism Education, April 14, 2007.

9. Quoted in Adam Graham, "Imus Storm Hits Hip-Hop World," *Detroit News*, April 14, 2007; www.detnews.com.

10. Billy Ingram, "Legendary Broadcaster Joe Pyne," TVParty.com; www.tvparty.com/empyne.html.

11. Charles Haynes, "Imus, Coulter, and the Marketplace for Offensive Speech," *Commentary*, First Amendment Center, April 15, 2007; www.firstamentmentcenter.org.

12. Ted Rall, "First They Came for the Shock Jocks," TedRall.com and Common Dreams News Center, March 11, 2004; www.commondreams.org.

13. Quoted in *ibid.*

14. Quoted in Dipayan Gupta and Thomas Rogers, "Safe Speech," *Salon.com*, May 1, 2007; www.salon.com.

15. For background, see John Michael Kittross and Christopher H. Sterling, *Stay Tuned: A History of American Broadcasting* (2002); William Triplett, "Broadcast Indecency," *CQ Researcher*, April 16, 2004, pp. 321-344; Alan Greenblatt, "Race in America," *CQ Researcher*, July 11, 2003, pp. 593-624; Kenneth Jost, "Talk Show Democracy," *CQ Researcher*, April 29, 1994, pp. 361-384; and M. Costello, "Blacks in the News Media," *CQ Researcher*, Aug. 16, 1972; "First Amendment and Mass Media," *CQ Researcher*, Jan. 21, 1970, both available at *CQ Researcher Plus Archive*; www.cqpress.com.

16. Zine Magubane, "Why 'Nappy' Is Offensive," *The Boston Globe*, April 12, 2007.

17. *Ibid.*

18. The case is *Federal Communications Commission v. Pacifica Foundation*, 438 U.S. 726, 98 S. Ct. 3026 (1978). The seven words are: shit, piss, fuck, cunt, cocksucker, motherfucker and tits.

19. "GE, Microsoft Bring Bigotry to Life," Fairness & Accuracy in Reporting, Feb. 12, 2003; www.fair.org.

20. Gil Kaufman, "Is Shock Radio Dead? More Potty-Mouthed DJs Join Don Imus in Doghouse," *MTV News*, May 15, 2007; www.mtv.com.

21. Imus' April 6 apology is quoted in "Cleaning up the I-Mess," transcript, "Paula Zahn Now," *CNN.com*, April 13, 2007, http://transcripts.cnn.com/TRAN-SCRIPTS/0704/13/pzn.01.html; "Imus Puts Remarks Into Context," transcript, "Imus in the Morning," MSNBC.com, April 9, 2007, www.msnbc.msn.com/id/18022596.

22. Nate Anderson, "Dennis Kucinich: Bring Back the Fairness Doctrine," *Ars Technica blog*, Jan. 17, 2007; http://arstechnica.com.

23. Ira Teinowitz, "Dingell Backs Return of Fairness Doctrine," *TV Week.com*, May 2, 2007; www.tvweek.com/news.cms?newsId=11988.

24. Quoted in McClellan, *op. cit.*

25. Mike Kinosian, "Minus Imus," *Inside Radio*, April 19, 2007; www.insideradio.com.

26. Quoted in *ibid.*

BIBLIOGRAPHY

Books

Kittross, John Michael, and Christopher H. Sterling, *Stay Tuned: A History of American Broadcasting,* **Lawrence Erlbaum Associates, 2002.**

The editor of *Media Ethics* magazine and a George Washington University professor of media and public affairs chronicle the growth and development of electronic media and broadcasting in the United States, including the development of shock radio and broadcast-content regulation.

Picca, Leslie Houts, and Joe R. Feagin, *Two-Faced Racism: Whites in the Backstage and Frontstage,* **Routledge, 2007.**

An assistant professor and a professor of sociology from the University of Dayton and Texas A&M University examine the racial attitudes of white college students who chronicled their race-related experiences and thoughts in detailed diaries. They argue that racism has receded from public life in America but that many people still actively engage in racist talk among close friends and family.

Rappoport, Leon, *Punchlines: The Case for Racial, Ethnic, and Gender Humor,* **Praeger, 2005.**

A professor emeritus of psychology at Kansas State University details the history of stereotyping humor and argues that it can serve important social functions, including as a tool to combat prejudice.

Articles

"What Happens When Shock Jocks Go Too Far?" POV: The Fire Next Time, Public Broadcasting Service Web site, www.pbs.org/pov/pov2005/the-firenexttime/special_casestudies.html, 2005.

This Web article by producers of a PBS documentary on how talk radio divided a Montana community relates stories of shock jocks who transgressed community standards for acceptable speech and faced controversy.

Kinosian, Mike, "Don's Gone: Post Imess," *Inside Radio,* **April 26, 2007, www.insideradio.com.**

A columnist for a radio trade publication chronicles Don Imus' career and interviews industry insiders about what his firing may mean to broadcasters.

Koppelman, Alex, "Is Rush Limbaugh Next?" *Salon*, April 16, 2007, www.salon.com.
Panelists at an April meeting of the conservative Free Congress Foundation predicted that congressional Democrats will try to revive the Fairness Doctrine requiring broadcasters to air all sides of controversial issues. They discussed strategies to stop revival of the doctrine, which media analysts argued would endanger conservative political commentators like Rush Limbaugh.

Llorente, Elizabeth, "Hispanics Steamed by Shock Radio Stunt," *The Record* [Bergen, N.J.], March 22, 2007.
Hispanic community leaders in New Jersey protested when shock radio hosts Craig Carton and Ray Rossi, known as "The Jersey Guys," launched a show segment called "La Cuca Gotcha," during which they urged listeners to report suspected illegal immigrants either to the station or to immigration authorities. Critics called for a boycott of the show's advertising, saying that the hosts encouraged racial profiling and vigilante activity.

McBride, Sara, and Brian Steinberg, "Finding a Replacement for Imus Won't Be Easy," *The Wall Street Journal*, April 16, 2007, p. B1.
Controversial radio hosts bring in big audiences and ad revenues, but talented shock talkers who can entertain a national audience aren't plentiful, so stations hire, fire and rehire the same people over and over. Increasing the difficulty for broadcast radio are satellite channels that have lured some top talent to the unregulated medium.

McClellan, Steve, "They Bailed for Now, But Advertisers Forgive," *AdWeek*, April 16, 2007, www.adweek.com.
A journalist who covers the advertising industry argues that advertisers who pulled out of Imus' show didn't want the program canceled.

Steinberg, Jacques, "Talk Radio Tries for Humor and a Political Advantage," *The New York Times*, April 20, 2007.
Shock jocks joked about Virginia Tech mass shooter Seung-Hui Cho while conservative radio hosts speculated about how his Korean background may have played into his becoming a murderer.

Walker, Jesse, "Tuning Out Free Speech," *The American Conservative*, April 23, 2007, www.amconmag.com.
The editor of libertarian *Reason* magazine argues that the history of the Federal Communications Commission's Fairness Doctrine shows that the doctrine stifled speech on the public airwaves.

Reports and Studies

Post-Conference Report: Rethinking the Discourse on Race: A Symposium on How the Lack of Racial Diversity in the Media Affects Social Justice and Policy, The Ronald H. Brown Center for Civil Rights and Economic Development, St. John's University School of Law, October 2006.
Conferees at a 2006 forum provide updates on ethnic diversity in media organizations and how the media shape Americans' views of race.

For More Information

Accuracy in Media, 4455 Connecticut Ave., N.W., Suite 330, Washington, DC 20008; (202) 364-4401; www.aim.org/index. A conservative media-criticism group that tracks and disseminates information about liberal bias it observes in the media.

Ban the N-Word, http://banthenword.com. An activist group that disseminates information about racist language and stereotypes in media, including detailed reviews of movies and new music releases.

Fairness and Accuracy in Reporting, 112 W. 27th St., New York, NY 10001; (212) 633-6700; www.fair.org/index.php. A liberal media-criticism group that disseminates information about and advocates for diverse opinions in media, especially inclusion of minority viewpoints.

Inside Radio, 365 Union St., Littleton, NH 03561; (603) 444-5720; www.insideradio.com. An insider publication for the radio industry that posts up-to-date news and commentary on radio-related events.

Maynard Institute for Journalism Education, 1211 Preservation Park Way, Oakland, CA 94612; (510) 891-9202; www.maynardije.org. A nonprofit education center for minority journalists that chronicles race-related issues in media such as the Imus controversy on its extensive Web site.

Media Matters for America, 1625 Massachusetts Ave., NW, Suite 300, Washington, DC 20036; (202) 756-4100; http://mediamatters.org/index. A liberal media-criticism group that tracks factual errors and misleading statements in the media, focusing on misinformation that may advance a conservative political agenda, and urges journalists to issue corrections of the errors.

Media Research Center, 325 S. Patrick St., Alexandria, VA 22314; (703) 683-9733; www.mediaresearch.org. A conservative media-criticism group that tracks and posts commentary on examples of liberal media bias and on events that threaten conservative media.

Talkers Magazine, 650 Belmont Ave., Springfield, MA 01108; (413) 739-8255; www.talkers.com. A publication covering talk radio that posts news and commentary about the industry on its Web site.

TimWise.org, www.timwise.org. An anti-racism educator who posts essays and reports on historical and current racial dilemmas in America.

12

Mortgage Crisis

Marcia Clemmitt

This house in Pasadena, Calif., is among thousands around the country being sold after the owners defaulted on their mortgages. An estimated 2.2 million borrowers will lose their homes to foreclosure, largely because they had subprime mortgages. Congress and the Bush administration are debating how to help borrowers keep their homes and whether tough, new lending standards are warranted.

From *CQ Researcher*, September 28, 2007.

When retired Chicago office administrator Delores King refinanced her house in 2004, she didn't expect to end up with "a mortgage that's thousands of dollars more than I started with" and payments that "have nearly doubled in two years."

"I have refinanced before, but I've never seen anything like this," King told a Senate Banking panel earlier this year. [1]

King's loan became unaffordable after its initial low interest rate reset to a higher rate and several unexpected, extra fees kicked in. King says her mortgage broker "rushed me through" the loan closing and never explained the mortgage's unusual features. King is one of millions of Americans in mortgage trouble in 2007, and her tale of an apparently "easy" loan that turns catastrophic is all too common, Eric Stein, senior vice president of the Center for Responsible Lending, in Durham, N.C., told a House subcommittee in September.

An estimated 2.2 million families will lose their homes to foreclosure because of a spate of "reckless" mortgage lending in recent years, Stein said. Today's foreclosure levels are the "worst they've been in at least 25 years," said Stein. Moreover, he said, "Millions of other families . . . will be hurt by declines in property values spurred by nearby foreclosures." [2]

The worst problems are concentrated in areas with slow economies, where cheap land encouraged a building frenzy, and in popular places like Phoenix and Florida, where floods of retirees and other new residents heated up the housing market.

Lower-income people are most at risk, but others will also feel pain. "Executives who built second homes out in the Carolinas" with 2- or 3-percent-interest loans that are about to reset to higher

Subprime Foreclosures Affect All Regions

In most of the states, 11-15 percent of the subprime mortgage loans made in 2006 will be foreclosed. In at least a half-dozen states, the failure rate is projected at up to 24 percent. The nation is experiencing the highest foreclosure rate since the Great Depression, according to the Center for Responsible Lending.

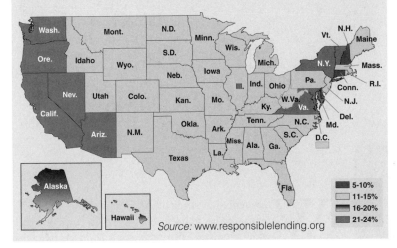

■	5-10%
☐	11-15%
▨	16-20%
▦	21-24%

Source: www.responsiblelending.org

Several large investment funds and banks have already taken billion-dollar hits from losses on defaulting mortgages. Last summer big investment bank Bear Stearns put up over $3 billion to save one of its hedge funds that faced huge losses on mortgage investments. [5] Late last month financial giant Merrill Lynch announced an $8-billion loss on mortgage securities, over $3 billion more than the company had anticipated only weeks earlier. [6]

A combination of easy money, loose lending standards and real-estate bidding wars that sent home prices soaring contributed to today's problems.

The current crisis comes from a "confluence of factors, and if you looked at each individually, it wouldn't be a big problem," says Robert Rainish, a professor of finance at the University of New Haven.

The development in the 1990s of investment instruments known as mortgage-backed securities tempted even cautious investors to buy mortgages, Rainish says.

The so-called securitization of mortgages boosted homeownership by enabling banks and other lenders to sell mortgages, thus raising capital to make additional housing loans. With so much mortgage money available, however, "an incredible ramp-up" of riskier mortgages occurred "in a very short period," says Rainish.

The highest-risk mortgages — known as subprimes — were usually offered to people with poor credit histories at higher interest rates than ordinary mortgages. "Virtually nonexistent before the mid-1990s, subprimes accounted for a fifth of all new mortgages by 2005," said Robert J. Shiller, a Yale University professor of economics and finance. [7]

By 2006, another formerly limited mortgage class was being offered to people with poor credit scores — often without requiring documented proof of income — as lenders sought to write as many mortgages as possible to boost their own bottom lines. Virtually unheard of a decade earlier, subprime and so-called Alt-A loans accounted for $1 trillion of the nation's mortgage debt by 2006, says Rainish.

rates "will have trouble, too," says Robert Schultz, a home-building consultant in Boca Raton, Fla.

Still in question is whether the crunch will spread beyond housing and drag the nation into recession.

"I think the worst is over," wrote Jeremy Siegel, a professor of finance at the Wharton School, in early October. "Everyone is going to say, 'There is going to be a big bomb and . . . a hedge fund . . . is going to go under' " because it invested in mortgage-backed securities that are now defaulting. "Well, we haven't heard anything recently and . . . no news is good news. We are slowly returning to normal here." [3] Others see deeper housing troubles and recession ahead.

"A recession happens every decade, but this is going to be bigger" than usual "because the debt is so extreme," says Peter Cohan, president of a management-consulting and venture-capital firm in Marlborough, Mass. Builders will be hard hit as well as "insurance, furniture, paint and building-supply companies," he says.

Mortgage lenders and insurers are taking big losses, and some — including New Century Financial, the country's second-largest subprime lender — have gone bankrupt as recent loans began defaulting and the housing market slows. [4]

"People who didn't qualify for credit to rent could get credit to buy a house, says real-estate developer Robert Sheridan, of River Forest, Ill.

Many of the new loans had no or very low down payments and were adjustable-rate mortgages (ARMs) with low initial interest rates that would have to be refinanced later, when rates were much higher.

"You couple easy money with the fact that a lot of people were not astute enough to understand" the risks involved in their loans, and "it was a train wreck waiting to happen," says Schultz.

Compounding the problem, the high number of would-be new buyers drove house and condo prices far above what was traditionally thought to be affordable. And the easy mortgage money encouraged hopeful homeowners as well as speculators as they bid up prices to unprecedented levels.

Pre-boom, median home prices typically equaled about 2.5 times the buyer's median income. Today, they're about 4.5 times income, and much higher in some regions, says Rainish. "That's a housing bubble."

Trouble was inevitable when we simultaneously "made home ownership the American dream and then allowed prices to grow way beyond the rate of growth of the rest of the economy," says Corey Stone, CEO of Pay Rent, Build Credit, an Annapolis-Md.-based company that helps consumers repair bad credit histories.

"The average American today can't afford to buy a home at current prices," says Robert Hardaway, a professor of law at the University of Denver. "The average home in California costs $500,000. You can't afford that home." But easy initial mortgage terms made many buyers believe they could, which led to today's record defaults and foreclosures.

Now Congress is contemplating restrictions on risky mortgages.

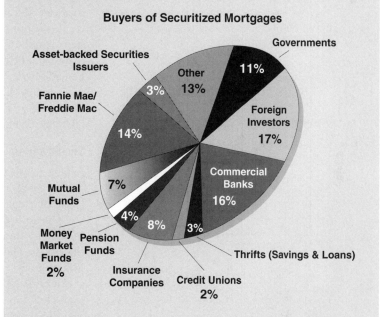

Mortgages Are Widely Purchased

Mortgages held by homeowners are sold to institutional investors in many sectors of the U.S. economy and abroad. The large number of investors, and the fact that many know little about the mortgage market, has led lenders to greatly increase the number and riskiness of mortgages they offer.

Buyers of Securitized Mortgages

- Governments 11%
- Foreign Investors 17%
- Commercial Banks 16%
- Thrifts (Savings & Loans) 3%
- Credit Unions 2%
- Insurance Companies 8%
- Pension Funds 4%
- Money Market Funds 2%
- Mutual Funds 7%
- Fannie Mae/Freddie Mac 14%
- Asset-backed Securities Issuers 3%
- Other 13%

Source: "Mortgage Liquidity du Jour: Underestimated No More," Credit Suisse, March 12, 2007; Federal Reserve

For example, regulators should impose an " 'ability-to-repay' standard" for all loans made to people with poor credit histories, Martin Eakes, CEO of the Center for Responsible Lending, told the Senate Banking Committee in February. ARMs "now make up the vast majority of subprime loans, and they have predictable and devastating consequences for . . . homeowners," who may lose their houses when interest rates change, he said. [8]

The Federal Reserve Board (the Fed) — which governs the nation's banking system and money supply — has cut interest rates on bank-to-bank loans to encourage lenders and investors spooked by rising mortgage-default rates to get back in the financial game.

Lower Fed rates would not directly translate into lower mortgage interest. However, by making it easier for banks to get money, "the Fed is signaling, 'Let's restore confidence and get the economy started again,' "

Housing Costs Swamp Millions of Families

The number of working families paying more than half their income for housing nearly doubled from 1997 to 2005. The increase reflects the rise in housing prices and the larger number of low-income people who obtained mortgages.

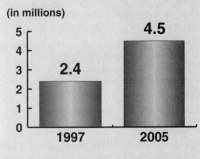

Families Paying More Than Half Their Income for Housing

(in millions)

Source: "The Housing Landscape for America's Working Families," Center for Housing Policy, August 2007

says Philip Ashton, an assistant professor of urban planning and policy at the University of Illinois, Chicago.

The rate cuts get mixed reviews as a strategy to ease the mortgage mess and credit freeze, since many experts partly blame low Fed interest rates in the early 2000s for helping fuel recent excesses.

Meanwhile, states, localities and the federal government — as well as private lenders and the giant Federal National Mortgage Corporation (Fannie Mae) — are making funds and loans available to help struggling homeowners stay put. For example, in hard-hit Cleveland, Cuyahoga County will fund loans to struggling homeowners using $3 million in penalties collected for late payment of property taxes. [9]

And under pressure to stop the bleeding, the nation's biggest mortgage lender, Countrywide Financial Corp., announced in October that it will restructure about 82,000 mortgages to make them more affordable. [10]

But some economists criticize such "bailouts" as unwise tinkering with economic markets.

"Individuals need to be responsible for their own borrowing," says Marvin Goodfriend, a professor of economics at Carnegie Mellon University's Tepper School of Business and a research economist with the Federal Reserve Bank of Richmond. That means much more financial education for everyone, he says. The government, the private sector, and nonprofit groups should step up to the task but haven't yet, he says. "People need to hear another voice besides the voice that's saying, 'No money down.' "

As nervous homeowners and investors wait to see how the mortgage crunch plays out, here are some of the questions that are being asked:

Should certain kinds of risky home loans be banned?

As large numbers of mortgages go into default, Congress debates whether some mortgage-lending practices should be ended altogether.

"At least in the vast majority of situations, and definitely any time federal money is involved," some of the riskiest lending practices should be banned, says Robert Losey, chairman of the Department of Finance at American University in Washington, D.C. For example, "there should be a requirement for significant down payments" for most loans, a tradition that's gotten lost, Losey says. "If someone makes no down payment, they have nothing to risk" and are more likely to walk away from the mortgage if the going gets tough, he says.

Some recent mortgages also have limited requirements for borrowers to document their income and assets — or don't require them at all.

"Oversight should limit or eliminate no-doc [no-documentation] loans," says Sandra Phillips, an assistant professor of finance at Syracuse University. "There should have been a crackdown on these lenders who were originating mortgages based on nonexistent and inflated equity," she says.

It's also become common practice for lenders to certify that borrowers are equipped to pay off adjustable-rate mortgages (ARMs) based on whether they have enough income to pay the loans' initial, low "teaser" rates. Critics call for ARMs to be sold only to borrowers who show they will be able to make payments when interest resets to a higher rate.

The Treasury Department and other federal agencies recommended in October 2006 eliminating ARMs that certify only that borrowers can pay the low, initial rates. According to the agencies, analysis "of borrowers' repayment capacity should include an evaluation of their ability to repay the debt by final maturity at the fully indexed rate." [11]

But many in the mortgage industry protest that strict rules will stifle innovation in lending and keep many people from getting mortgages.

"While it may sound reasonable to require that all borrowers contending for" ARMs "be qualified at the fully indexed rate . . . such an approach will lock some borrowers out of the home of their dreams and deprive them of lower payments," Douglas O. Duncan, senior vice president for research and business development at the Mortgage Bankers Association, told a Senate panel in February. "The magic of today's market is that the widest range of borrowers can get the widest spectrum of loans." [12]

"We cannot agree that underwriting to the fully indexed rate is the correct standard in all situations," said Sandor Samuels, an executive managing director of Countrywide Financial. Many "homeowners who will need to refinance will not be able to qualify under such a standard," and "many first-time homebuyers who can currently purchase a home will no longer . . . qualify . . . under the proposed guidelines," he said. "This will materially reduce housing demand . . . and delay the housing recovery." [13]

The National Association of Mortgage Brokers (NAMB) "believes the problem of rising foreclosures is complex and will not be corrected by simply removing products from the market," said NAMB President Harry Dinham.

Indeed, the availability of subprime mortgages helped push homeownership to an all-time high of about 69 percent of families in the last few years. [14]

Rules can be significantly tightened without banning some kinds of mortgages altogether, many analysts say.

"I would change the way people [in the mortgage industry] get compensated," for example, says Cohan, the management-consultant and venture capitalist.

Instead of paying commissions up front, which gives brokers and some lenders' representatives incentive to push buyers into mortgages whether they can afford them or not, "I'd put half the commission in escrow," Cohan says. If the mortgage "maintained value for 10 years, then brokers would get the money." But if the

Greg Giniel's house in Arizona's Queen Creek housing development in is in foreclosure, but he hopes to buy it back in November. Many borrowers got in trouble because they were saddled with high-risk, high-interest "subprime" mortgages, which are usually offered to people with bad credit histories. However, subprimes were also pushed on many people with good credit.

AP Photo/Ross D. Franklin

mortgage "collapsed, then the money would go to pay the cost of their mistakes."

"Reducing the incentive for volume" by decreeing that commissions can't be based on the number of deals a broker or salesperson arranges would help limit bad mortgages, says Syracuse University's Phillips.

"You need to regulate and supervise the mortgage brokers," says Phillips. To do that, federal laws would have to be reinterpreted or rewritten to allow regulation of brokers, she says. "Right now, they're in the cracks" and unregulated.

Risky loans proliferate partly because current disclosure rules don't require lenders to give borrowers clear, understandable information about exactly what their mortgage provisions mean, says the University of New Haven's Rainish. Today's rules about what lenders must tell borrowers "were made before anybody conceived of the current market," with its proliferation of complex mortgages, he says.

"Borrowers need a one-page summary that explains exactly what their mortgage entails," says Cohan. "Nobody reads these 65-page things" that current disclosure rules require, he says.

Subprime Loans Can Have Abusive Terms

A high percentage of subprime loans carry prepayment penalties and adjustable interest rates that are due to reset in two to three years. More than a third of the loans were issued based on little or no documentation of the borrower's income.

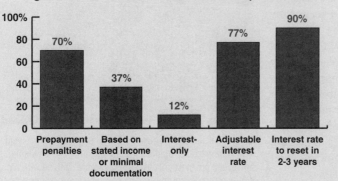

High-Risk Characteristics of Abusive Subprime Loan

Source: Testimony of Michael D. Calhoun, President, Center for Responsible Lending, before the Senate Banking Subcommittee on Housing, Transportation and Community Development, June 26, 2007

Should the government "bail out" borrowers caught in the mortgage meltdown?

Some analysts are encouraging states and the federal government to loosen the rules governing government-guaranteed mortgage programs to include homeowners in default and provide loan funds to help homeowners refinance. The Bush administration, congressional Democrats and several state governments back at least limited bailout plans, but some economists say any bailout encourages "bad behavior" to continue.

"Bailouts are terrible because they create moral hazard" — the tendency of people to make more bad choices in the future because they didn't have to face consequences of earlier choices, says Goodfriend of Carnegie Mellon University and the Richmond Federal Reserve Bank.

Even if bailouts are labeled as being for homeowners, it's lenders — many of whom engaged in risky and even predatory practices — who largely will benefit, some analysts say.

In August, President Bush announced a plan to open up Federal Housing Administration loans to some people struggling in the mortgage crisis. But, while the president

"claims the bailout is for deserving homeowners, the thinly veiled policy changes are obviously meant to ensure that lenders are not defaulted on," commented the investment Web site eFinanceDirectory.com. [15]

Investors who carelessly speculated in high-risk securities would also be winners if fewer mortgages go into default, and the government should not prop them up, some financial analysts say.

"A borrower bailout and an investor bailout are synonymous," said Paul Jackson, a real-estate analyst for the mortgage blog Housing Wire. Furthermore, allowing people who can't afford their mortgages to get new ones for the same properties doesn't fix the fundamental problem — "millions of borrowers who simply can't afford a mortgage on the property they're now in," he said. [16]

Those who hope for a quick and simple bailout will be disappointed, says Illinois real-estate developer Sheridan. Because housing values won't quickly rebound, "federal legislation to help buyers hold on would have to be in place for a long time," he says.

Nevertheless, "there's a natural tendency by Congress and the executive branch to throw money at problems," so bailouts are likely inevitable, says American University's Losey. "But only the people who would qualify for loans anyway should have the opportunity to row their way out," he says.

"People are going to be hurt, but that doesn't mean we should subsidize them for buying a home they couldn't afford," Losey says. "There's no reason to say, 'Now we'll let you stay in that home.' "

Thirty percent or more of buyers in the recent, hot real-estate market "were speculators — non-occupying buyers" who bought homes with easy-to-get mortgages, then tried to "flip" them for a profit as prices rose, says Rainish, at the University of New Haven. Speculators "should not be bailed out," he says. If the government "is going to do a bailout, they need to be sure that only home-occupying buyers get assistance."

"We should not be bailing out people who invested in real estate, but it would be easy enough to separate speculators from owners," says Sheridan. "Just find out who's living in the house. Send them a letter. Show me the bills that come there."

Nevertheless, the sheer size of the foreclosure mess probably requires action, especially since government has stepped into similar crises as rescuer, says Rainish. "The government is trying to come up with a way for credit institutions to refinance these loans, but the question is how far they're willing to go," he says. "They spent $150 billion on the savings & loan crisis" of the late 1980s. [17] "And there's not much reason they can't do something similar to mitigate today's level of foreclosure," he says.

"You will have to say to some people, 'No matter how we restructure the financing, you can't afford the house,'" Rainish says. "But others can handle a restructured loan."

However, he adds, "You can't disentangle helping borrowers and lenders." But he argues that "it's not a bad idea to help the lenders. If lenders are going to come back in the game ever again, you have to help them. Otherwise, you won't have a market."

Left out of the Bush bailout are lower-income people, especially in minority neighborhoods, many of whom were deceived by predatory lenders into taking on more expensive loans than they realized, says Syracuse University's Phillips. "The irony of the proposal is that it only goes to upper-income people with good credit," she says. "I don't think we should leave out the population targeted for predatory loans," she says.

Community-advocacy groups working in neighborhoods hit by predatory lending "are doing a pretty good job helping people find a way to make the payments," says Phillips. A group she works with in Syracuse has helped many people stay in their homes, she says.

Sen. Charles E. Schumer, D-N.Y., has proposed legislation giving $300 million to community groups that specialize in foreclosure prevention. "This seems like a

---

Number of Foreclosures to Double

The failure rate of recent subprime loans is expected to double, affecting 2.2 million borrowers. As housing prices decline, fewer delinquent borrowers have the equity needed to refinance their loan or sell their home to avoid foreclosure.

Chance of foreclosure for loan made in 2005 and 2006:
20 percent (vs. 10% for loans made in 2002)

Cost of foreclosures to borrowers:
Up to $164 billion

Number of foreclosed or soon-to-be-foreclosed loans:
2.2 million

Source: "Losing Ground: Foreclosures in the Subprime market and Their Cost to Homeowners," Center for Responsible Lending, December 2006

---

cost-effective investment to me," said Schumer. "It will save billions in spillover foreclosure costs." [18]

It wouldn't be difficult to provide assistance only to people saddled with predatory loans because the details of those abusive loans are a dead giveaway, says Phillips. "Looking at the loan agreement, in predatory loans you will see substantial charges [not found in other mortgages], and the fees will be high. There will be restrictions on refinancing."

Will the mortgage crisis trigger a larger financial crisis in the United States and elsewhere?

Most everyone agrees that people holding subprime mortgages — mostly low-income borrowers with poor credit — are defaulting and losing their homes. How far subprime fallout will spread in the economy, however, is sharply debated.

"The real bears in this market believe housing will lead the economy into recession," said John Burns, a real-estate consultant in Irvine, Calif. "Thus far, these bears are wrong. The housing market peaked in June 2005 and, two years into the downturn, economic growth is still positive. Unemployment remains very low . . . and consumers have started ramping up their credit-card debt again." [19]

Furthermore, the housing market itself is in good shape, according to Lawrence Yun, senior economist at the National Association of Realtors. "Although sales are off from an unsustainable peak in 2005, there is a histor-

Florida Housing Prices Outraced Income Gains

Reflecting a nationwide trend, the median sales price of a single-family home in Florida increased 77 percent from 2002 to 2005 while incomes remained flat. As the cost of owning a home skyrocketed, more people turned to risky adjustable-rate or interest-only mortgages; many took on second mortgages to pay other bills or renovate.

Source: Florida Association of Realtors

ically high level of home sales . . . this year," he said. "One out of 15 American households is buying a home." [20]

"The speculative excesses have been removed from the market, and home sales are returning to fundamentally healthy levels, while prices remain near record highs, reflecting favorable mortgage rates and positive job gains," Yun said.

"Housing is only about 5 percent of the economy," said columnist Ben Stein at Yahoo! Finance. "If it falls by 15 percent, that would represent a fall-off [in the total economy] of about 0.75 percent. That's not trivial, but it's also not the stuff of which recessions are made." [21]

Eight out of the 10 U.S. recessions since World War II "were preceded by sustained and substantial problems in housing, and there was a more minor problem in housing prior to the 2001 recession," points out Edward E. Leamer, professor of management, economics and statistics at the University of California, Los Angeles. [22]

Nevertheless, "this time troubles in housing will stay in housing," Leamer said. "An official recession cannot occur without job loss, but . . . outside of manufacturing and construction there is little or no job loss. . . . Though this is largely uncharted territory, it doesn't look like manufacturing is positioned to shed enough jobs to generate a recession." [23]

But other analysts are less hopeful.

Some large financial entities, such as hedge funds and institutional investors like pension funds, bought risky packages of subprime mortgages, which are now defaulting at high rates. Worse, some have borrowed a lot of money against these securities, which they can't pay back, spreading the financial pain farther, says financial consultant Cohan. Just how far isn't clear because "we have an unknown amount of money that's been borrowed against these securities, and nobody is willing to mark the [value] truthfully," Cohan says.

The mortgage meltdown is a replay of similar events in the 1970s and '80s, says home-building consultant Schultz, However, "the results are bigger this time because prices were higher."

Adjustable-rate loans will reset to higher interest rates over the next two years, "so during that time people will be wondering, 'How do I move from my home? Can I take such a big loss?' " says the University of New Haven's Rainish. "The resulting uncertainty will freeze up the whole system, and the economy could go into shock."

Retirement funds and other investors who buy mortgage-backed securities "now don't know how to value part of their portfolio," Rainish says. "How do you manage your portfolio if you can't put a value on it? . . . Some of them will go under. If you want to sell these securities, you'll have to sell them at 10 or 15 percent below their real value."

Harvard Professor of Economics Martin Feldstein, a former chairman of the Council of Economic Advisers, said, "If house prices now decline" to traditional levels, "there will be serious losses of household wealth and resulting declines in consumer spending. Since housing wealth is now about $21 trillion, even a 20-percent . . . decline would cut wealth by some $4 trillion and might cut consumer spending by $200 billion or about 1.5 percent of GDP. The multiplier consequences of this could easily push the economy into recession." [24]

BACKGROUND

Losing Homes

The beloved 1946 movie "It's a Wonderful Life," starring Jimmy Stewart and Donna Reed, revolves around the struggle of a small-town banker to help workers hold onto their homes in hard times. The movie provides the traditional image most Americans have of the mortgage business — "there's an S&L [savings & loan] and a borrower, and they know each other," says management consultant and venture-capitalist Cohan.

Today, that picture is way out of date, says Cohan. "There are many, many more players than there used to be," and what happens to mortgages in one U.S. town "has ripples that spread out into the national and even international economy," he says. Moreover, mortgage debt is a much larger piece of each home-owning American's financial picture than in the past. [25]

Before the Great Depression of the 1930s, local savings institutions like banks made mortgage loans, and a mortgage lasted for five to 10 years, after which the outstanding principal had to be paid, or the loan had to be refinanced.

During the Depression, however, as employment and house values plummeted, lenders worried about losing money and refused to refinance mortgages. As a result, lenders repossessed many homes when owners failed to make the big final payment. At the height of the Depression, almost 10 percent of homes were in foreclosure.

The federal government began a series of interventions that gradually changed the way home loans are made. The first such program — the Home Owners' Loan Corporation (HOLC), established in 1933 — bought defaulted mortgages from banks and other lending institutions and returned the houses to owners who'd been foreclosed upon, with new mortgages.

The new HOLC loans lasted 20 years and had fixed interest rates. The new mortgages also were fully amortizing — that is, borrowers paid off both principal and interest for the life of the loan and didn't face a large "balloon" payment of the remaining principal when the 20 years was up.

HOLC was disbanded in 1936. But Congress continued to enact laws to ease access to homeownership over the next several decades.

Because the government didn't want to be in the business of holding the HOLC mortgages, in 1936 Congress created the Federal Housing Administration (FHA) to sell mortgage insurance. To encourage private investors to buy packages of government-originated HOLC loans, borrowers paid premiums into an FHA insurance pool that would protect investors from losses if homeowners defaulted.

Beginning in 1938, Congress created several entities authorized to invest in packages of mortgages in order to free up money at traditional lending institutions, such as banks, so they could offer more mortgages. The Federal National Mortgage Association (known as Fannie Mae) opened in 1938, and the Federal Home Loan Mortgage Corporation (Freddie Mac) was created in 1970 to provide competition for Fannie Mae. Over the years, Fannie's and Freddie's mandate expanded from purchasing government-originated loans to purchasing mortgages from private institutions.

U.S. home ownership — and the mortgage debt that goes with it — has grown over the years. In 1949, total mortgage debt equaled only 20 percent of total household income in the United States. By 2001, mortgage debt equaled 73 percent of income.

Selling Mortgages

While Fannie Mae and other government-initiated programs spurred home ownership, today's commercial mortgage market wasn't created until the 1990s, when more private investors became interested in buying up packages of home mortgages that were sold as financial assets — "securitized." The influx of private money into the housing market helped trigger today's foreclosure problems for subprime loans.

For decades, most private investors were reluctant to invest in packaged mortgages — mortgage-backed securities — "because they would have been bearing the full risk" should homeowners default, as a few inevitably will, says Jay Hartzell, an associate professor of real-estate finance at the University of Texas, Austin.

During the 1990s, however, financial institutions became more adept at "structuring" the securities: slicing up a single mortgage package — totaling hundreds or thousands of loans — into several investment vehicles, or tranches, with a range of risk.

"You take the same loan package, and you say the first 10 percent of the [mortgage] payments go to investors in

CHRONOLOGY

1930s-1970s *After thousands of Americans lose their houses during the Great Depression, the federal government establishes programs to support home ownership.*

1933 Federal Home Owners Loan Corporation (HOLC) repurchases foreclosed homes, reinstates former mortgages.

1936 Federal Housing Administration (FHA) is created to insure HOLC mortgages so that investors will buy them.

1938 Federal National Mortgage Association — Fannie Mae — is founded as a "government-sponsored enterprise" to invest in mortgages, freeing up funds for lenders to make more home loans.

1944 Veterans' Bill of Rights creates a home-loan program for veterans.

1968 Truth in Lending Act passes, requiring lenders to informer borrowers about key terms in their loans. . . . Fannie Mae becomes a private, shareholder-owned company.

1970 Freddie Mac (Federal Home Loan Mortgage Corporation) joins Fannie Mae as a "secondary mortgage market," freeing up lenders' cash to offer more loans.

1974 Congress enacts Equal Credit Opportunity Act to stem lending discrimination against minority borrowers and others. . . . Real Estate Settlement Procedures Act requires lenders to give "good-faith estimates" of mortgage closing costs.

1980s-1990s *Adjustable-rate, interest-only and low down-payment mortgages become popular, spurring private investors to buy mortgage-backed securities. . . . Loans purchased by FHA, Fannie Mae and Freddie Mac decrease as a proportion of housing market.*

1989 First Bush administration and Congress act to bail out the savings and loan industry after S&Ls around the country make bad investments and collapse.

1992 Federal Reserve Bank of Boston concludes that low-income and minority neighborhoods face abusive lending practices and bias from borrowers.

2000s *House prices rise faster than inflation or incomes, and many homeowners take on second mortgages to pay other bills. Investors pour cash into the housing market, leading lenders to offer subprime mortgages, some of which don't document borrowers' incomes. Risky lending and soaring prices create a home-foreclosure crisis.*

2003 New mortgages are written worth $4 trillion.

2004 Federal Reserve Bank raises interest rates, causing a 26 percent drop in new home loans.

2005 Federal Reserve Chairman Alan Greenspan says that "without calling the overall national issue a [housing] bubble, it's pretty clear that it's an unsustainable underlying pattern." . . . Average house price grows more than three times faster than disposable income. . . . Delinquent payments and foreclosures rise. . . . House prices increase 49 percent over 2004 in Las Vegas; 43 percent in Phoenix. . . . Subprime loans make up 20 percent of new mortgages, up from 8 percent in 2003. . . . Forty percent of existing mortgages are refinanced.

2006 New Fed Chairman Ben S. Bernanke says housing market will "cool but not change very sharply." . . . New home construction drops. . . . Mortgage lender Ownit Mortgage Solutions files for bankruptcy. . . . Housing-finance giant Fannie Mae pays $400-million fine on accounting-fraud charges. . . . Risky new mortgages, like interest-only loans and loans that don't require documentation of the borrowers' income account for 13 percent of new mortgages, up from 2 percent in 2003.

2007 Mortgage lenders including New Century Financial, the second-largest subprime lender, file for bankruptcy. . . . Standard & Poor's and other securities-rating agencies downgrade securities backed by subprime mortgages. . . . Mortgage-market problems cause earnings to fall at major investment banks like Bear Stearns and Goldman Sachs; Merrill Lynch posts an $8-billion loss in the third quarter. . . . IDK, a German bank, slashes its earnings targets due to heavy losses on U.S. subprime investments. . . . In May, foreclosure filings are up 90 percent from May 2006.

this security — and it becomes the triple-A-rated, safest security in which the investors will always get paid," regardless of how many borrowers default, explains Rainish of the University of New Haven. That top-level security provides the lowest dollar payouts, but the payment is guaranteed, no matter what the level of default on the loans as a whole.

Then successive layers of security risk are carved out — each with a lesser guarantee of being paid in full but with a higher payout if they do, he says.

"Once people are able to buy the amount of the risk they want, more become willing to invest," says Hartzell.

"Nobody who was risk-averse" would buy mortgage-backed securities before the risk was segmented, explains Rainish. Once selling mortgage packages with different risk levels became widespread practice, however, "we have all this money flowing in" to housing lenders, he says. "We've created a money machine."

But the machine had flaws, says Rainish. Investors didn't really know how risky a buy they were making, a fact that has already led some investment funds to fail and now threatens further instability in financial markets. Bad mortgage loans, which in the past would have affected only a local bank or S&L, now have potential repercussions around the world.

"This is what happened [last summer] with two of [investment bank] Bear Stearns' hedge funds, which placed highly leveraged bets on packages of subprime-mortgage derivative products," says the British financial Web site Market Oracle. "When the value and creditworthiness of these bond packages . . . was cut due to the subprime defaults . . . the effect . . . was to virtually wipe out the total value of the funds that had been rated as low risk." [26]

Security risk was determined based on historical models predicting that between 5 and 10 percent of the mortgages would default, says Rainish. "But fraud and the lack of adequate underwriting" — documenting borrowers' finances and income to be sure they could make the payments — "changed the results," he says. "Investors did not anticipate that the underwriting standards would be changed to the degree they have been."

Determining risk involves seeing how many mortgages have defaulted in the past, then adding any important new factors into your calculation, says Yildiray Yildirim, an associate professor of finance at Syracuse. As the mortgage market heated up, "they didn't use the correct models" to gauge risk, and "some hedge funds and others trading these securities don't even have" a predictive model, he says. "If they see something they think will make money, they go after it."

Among the overlooked factors was how many subprime borrowers — most of whom have poor credit and low incomes — default on their loans after low "teaser" interest rates on their ARMs expired, Yildirim says.

Insecure Securities

Current accounting standards also encouraged non-bank lenders to write unusually risky mortgages, making it harder for investors to discern the true value of the mortgage-backed securities, says John D. Rossi, associate professor of accounting at Moravian College in Bethlehem, Pa.

A mortgage is essentially a liability for a lender until it's paid off in full, and traditionally it would be listed as such on lenders' account books, where auditors and potential creditors could use it to judge organizations' financial health. However, once a non-bank mortgage lender has "sold" mortgages to investors, current rules allow the lender to erase them from its books, even if the securities were sold on the promise that the lender would absorb some losses, should the mortgages default, Rossi explains.

Being able to take loans off their books increased the likelihood that lenders would engage in shoddier underwriting and make riskier loans, says Rossi. "Most likely it made them a lot less diligent," he says.

Securities-ratings agencies, like Standard & Poor's and Moody's Investors Service, rate securities based on risk. But the rating system broke down in the past few years, especially for mortgage-backed securities, many financial analysts say.

Based on the history of mortgage-backed securities, ratings agencies were listing subprime mortgage-backed securities as "A" grade — safe investments — when they were actually "B" grade — high risk, says Rainish. "The ratings agencies have been blindsided as much as others. They were pricing in a different world," he says.

Other analysts say ratings agencies and investors bear much of the blame for their woes.

"Wall Street and rating agencies, rather than state regulators or even lenders, largely decide what types of borrowers obtain subprime loans and how the loan products . . . are designed," Kurt Eggert, a professor at Chapman University School of Law in Orange, Calif., told the

Elderly, Rural and Minority Borrowers Are Easy Targets

Lenders add extra fees, omit key information

Some mortgage lenders have taken advantage of the housing boom to saddle borrowers with loans they can't afford, especially in minority neighborhoods.

It's easy to take advantage of people when it comes to mortgages, says Robert Schultz, a Boca Raton, Fla., home-building consultant. Some lenders have pushed loans that were too good to be true, taking advantage of many borrowers' lack of financial savvy, "much like the credit-card industry trolls through college campuses and preys on kids' taste for instant gratification and the fact that they're not skilled in the ways of finance," says Schultz.

Higher interest "subprime" mortgages are generally offered to borrowers with poor credit. High interest rates on such loans protect lenders against the much higher probability that people with bad credit histories will default. But some lenders not only deceive borrowers about the true nature of the loans they're getting but also add in extra fees. Furthermore, in minority and rural communities, borrowers often are targeted for extremely expensive loans even though their incomes and credit histories would qualify them for lower-cost mortgages.

Some mortgage brokers have steered people into loans they clearly couldn't afford simply "because [the brokers] get the fees up front," says Sandra Phillips, an assistant professor of finance at Syracuse University. "Brokers got credit for volume, so the more you did, the more you got paid by banks."

In today's complex mortgage market, it's easy to slip costly loan provisions past borrowers , says Meghan Burns, co-founder of OfferAngel, a Scottsdale, Ariz., company that reviews and clarifies the terms of a mortgage offer for consumers. Federal rules about what lenders must disclose to borrowers "came out years ago, but meanwhile about 300 mortgage products have come out that weren't dreamed of" when the disclosure rules were written, says Burns.

"A house loan is much more complicated than a car loan, for example," and the disclosure rules make it easy for lenders to simply slip in some hair-raising provisions, she says. For example, lenders aren't required to flatly state in writing whether a mortgage carries a prepayment penalty — which socks the borrower with a substantial fee if they try to sell or refinance a property before a specified number of years have elapsed, says Burns.

Some brokers falsify borrower information on loan applications, sometimes with the borrowers' consent, sometimes without it, says real-estate developer Robert Sheridan, of River Forest, Ill. Lenders reassured borrowers that "we'll help you cook the books" to qualify for a loan, "and if people said they were worried about taking out too big a loan, they said, 'Don't worry! You can refinance!' " says Sheridan. But the reassurance about refinancing often wasn't true, he says. Prepayment penalties prevent borrowers from refinancing, and refinancing doesn't work if home prices don't rise, he says.

"More than ever, I'm seeing junk fees — unnecessary charges that lenders add to borrowers' bills to pad their own profits — and bigger junk fees than ever before," says Carolyn Warren, author of *Mortgage Ripoffs and Money Savers*. "A document-preparation fee! It's ridiculous," Warren says. "As if,

Senate Subcommittee on Securities, Insurance and Investments in April. But "unlike government agencies, ratings agencies work . . . in their own financial self-interest and . . . at the behest of investors and do not have the mandate to ensure consumer protection," he said. [27]

"In the end, Wall Street creates a demand for particular mortgages; underwriting criteria for these mortgages [are] set to meet this demand and [the] underwriting criteria, not the mortgage originator, [dictate] whether a consumer qualifies for this particular loan product," said Harry Dinham, president of the National Association of Mortgage Brokers. [28]

After lenders package mortgages into securities, ratings agencies "put a piece of gold wrapping paper around them," says venture capitalist Cohan. The agencies have a conflict of interest because "the investment banks shop the packages around and give the fee to the [agency] that gives the best rating," he says.

otherwise, they weren't going to prepare documents at the end! It's like a restaurant charging you for a napkin. When I see a $695 processing fee, that's price gouging."

In addition, "a whole group of people inappropriately has been steered to more expensive loans" than they actually qualified for, says Corey Stone, CEO of Pay Rent, Build Credit, an Annapolis, Md., company that helps people rehabilitate bad credit histories.

Most people who've been steered to the worst loans are the nation's most vulnerable people — elderly, rural and minority residents who have less access to traditional financial institutions like banks than other Americans.

"The accumulated home equity and limited incomes of older homeowners have made them a primary target for predatory lending," said Jean Constantine-Davis, senior attorney for the AARP Foundation, a research group operated by the large seniors' lobby AARP. Predatory lenders often target elderly homeowners with pitches to refinance their homes to get extra cash to pay bills, she said. [1]

"One gentlemen, an 86-year-old stroke victim in a wheelchair, had a tax return that described him as a computer programmer who made $30,000 a year," said Constantine-Davis. Brokers and lenders had worked together to fabricate his and other tax returns to make it appear that elderly people "could afford mortgages whose monthly payments, in some cases, exceeded their incomes. Because our clients had owned their homes for decades, they had equity, and that was all the lender cared about."

Rural residents, who have limited access to banks, are among those heavily targeted by predatory lenders, according to the University of New Hampshire's Carsey Institute. In 2002, for example, rural borrowers were 20 percent more likely than urban residents to have mortgages that would sock them with large prepayment penalties if they paid off the loans or tried to refinance them. [2]

Minority borrowers are the most likely to have mortgages with oppressive terms, and many minority borrowers are pushed into expensive, subprime loans even though their incomes and credit histories qualify them for better interest rates.

In a study based on 2005 data, both African-Americans and Hispanics of all income levels were at least twice as likely to have high-cost loans as whites. [3]

In 2005, 52 percent of mortgages to blacks, 40 percent of mortgages to Hispanics, and only 19 percent of loans to whites were high-cost loans, said the Rev. Jesse L. Jackson. [4]

In New York City, 44 percent of mortgages in middle-income, predominantly black neighborhoods were subprime, compared to only 15 percent of the loans in economically comparable white neighborhoods, according to a 2002 study conducted for Sen. Charles E. Schumer, D-N.Y. "In other words, a significant proportion of black residents in New York City are being unnecessarily channeled into more expensive financing," said the report. [5]

This past summer the National Association for the Advancement of Colored People (NAACP) filed a class-action suit against more than a dozen mortgage companies — including Ameriquest, H&R Block's Option One, and Bear Stearns investment bank's Encore Credit — alleging "systematic, institutionalized racism in making home-mortgage loans." [6]

---

[1] Jean Constantine-Davis, testimony before the Senate Committee on Banking, Housing and Urban Affairs, Feb. 7, 2007.

[2] "Subprime and Predatory Lending in Rural America," Policy Brief No. 4, Carsey Institute, University of New Hampshire, fall 2006.

[3] "NAACP Subprime Discrimination Suit," *Mortgage News Daily*, July 16, 2007, www.mortgagenewsdaily.com.

[4] Testimony before Senate Committee on Banking, Housing and Urban Affairs, Feb. 7, 2007.

[5] "Capital Access 2002: Lending Patterns in Black and White Neighborhoods Tell a Tale of Two Cities, www.senate.gov/~schumer/SchumerWebsite/pressroom/special_reports/cap%20access%202002.pdf.

[6] "NAACP Subprime Discrimination Suit," *op. cit.*

"I would be amazed if there weren't massive litigation" by investors against the ratings agencies down the line, says Illinois real-estate developer Sheridan. "They were advising clients how to put lipstick on the pig," and, "at a minimum, they sure didn't ring the fire alarm bell very quickly."

Ratings agencies reject such accusations.

The "issuer-pays business model" does have "potential conflicts of interest," acknowledged Michael Kanef, managing director of Moody's Investors Service Group, to the House Subcommittee on Capital Markets, Insurance, and Government-Sponsored Enterprises on Sept. 27. However, "we believe we have successfully managed" the conflicts by not paying analysts based on revenue earned by companies they rate, posting ratings methodologies on a public Web site, and having a separate analysis team monitor all rated securities on an ongoing basis. [29]

Home Values Always Go Up, Right?

Millions of Americans are discovering otherwise

Between 1890 and 1997, inflation-adjusted house prices in the United States stayed roughly flat. But since around 1998, they've climbed each year, rising about 6 percent annually above inflation, according to Yale University Professor of economics and finance Robert J. Shiller. [1]

This unprecedented housing boom has helped create an urban myth — that home prices always rise, say economists. That idea is in for a severe test, however, as a wave of defaults on home mortgages builds, and the housing market undergoes huge changes.

Over the past several years, many Americans have used novel loan types — such as adjustable-rate mortgages (ARMs) and interest-only mortgages — to buy "more house" than they would have thought they could afford. Such loans have artificially low payments for the first several months or years, and borrowers gamble that, when it comes time for payments to rise, they can refinance into a different loan on the strength of their now much higher home value or sell the house for a profit.

Office manager Chaundra Carnes and her husband Michael, a winery production manager, purchased a $950,000 house just north of San Francisco in 2005 with a $700,000 interest-only mortgage. In the past, the couple's combined $100,000-a-year salary would have been considered far too low to afford the house, but their interest-only loan has low payments and they figured that, before higher payments came due, they'd be able to refinance or sell the house at a profit, as they had with three previous homes. [2]

"The only risk is if housing values go down,"

Chaundra said at the time. "And I guess that's a risk we're willing to take. And I think a lot of other people are too. So we're not alone." [3]

Today, however, the downside of that risk is around the corner, financial analysts say.

U.S. home prices peaked in the first quarter of 2006 and have since fallen 3.4 percent, said Shiller. Although that drop doesn't seem severe, "when there are declines, they may be muted at first" because "home sellers tend to hold out for high prices when prices are falling," Shiller said. "The 17 percent decline in the volume of U.S. existing home sales since the peak in volume of sales in 2005 is evidence that this is happening now."

It should have been clear that the recent, drastic run-up in house prices couldn't continue forever, because people don't have unlimited funds to spend on housing, even though easy mortgage terms made it seem they did, say some real-estate experts.

"The mismatch between income gains and higher real-estate values in some cities is particularly striking," said Jonathan Miller, CEO of the Manhattan-based real-estate appraisal firm Miller Samuel. "How can someone earning $70,000 a year afford a $500,000 home? They can't over the long run." [4]

The price boom began in metropolitan areas of California, the Northeast, and Florida, then spread inland, said Sheila C. Bair, chairman of the Federal Deposit Insurance Corporation. But "while home prices were effectively doubling in . . . boom markets, median incomes grew

Easy Money

More private investors willing to invest in mortgage-backed securities gave lenders an incentive to make more loans. Easy money — and new 1990s technology that allowed financial institutions to automate credit checks and vary interest rates in real time — led lenders to create mortgages that made home ownership seem more affordable.

Investors' interest in mortgage-backed securities increased after the 1990s technology boom went bust, says Ashton, the assistant professor of urban planning and policy at the University of Illinois. With investors

wary of stocks and lenders "figuring out ways to help more and more people afford homes, suddenly the subprime mortgage market looked like a good place to park your capital," he says.

Non-U.S. investment also has flowed into housing. In the developing economies of China and India, "people save a lot of income, they're unsure about their future" and that money needs to be invested, says economist Goodfriend. Oil-producing countries flush with cash from rising oil prices have provided another pot of housing investment, he says.

much more slowly, severely reducing the affordability of home ownership, despite the benefit of historically low interest rates," she said. [5]

But while recent prices may not be strictly "affordable" for the average American, easy mortgage terms blinded many to that reality and led to real-estate bidding wars that drove up prices all over. Good old-fashioned optimism, plus greed, played a role.

For most people who get into trouble, "it's not so much that they shouldn't have bought a house but that they shouldn't have bought such an expensive house," says Seattle-based Carolyn Warren, author of *Mortgage Ripoffs and Money Savers*. "Instead of tailoring their house demands to their budget, they fell in love with a house and then had to take a teaser rate to afford it, and then hope," she says.

Real-estate speculators also helped to drive up prices, says home-building consultant Robert Schultz, of Boca Raton, Fla. In earlier housing booms, flipping — buying a house in order to quickly sell it for a higher price — was relatively rare, says Schultz. But in the 2000s boom, flipping ran rampant. "The loans were so much easier to get this time," says Schultz.

"The number of pure speculators" was much higher than reported: "30 or 40 percent is my gut feeling," says real-estate developer Robert Sheridan, of River Forest, Ill.

With so many bidders in the game, it's no wonder that prices were driven sky-high, Schultz and Sheridan say.

The fact that house and condo prices have soared compared to the rest of the economy has been hidden by the way the government reports statistics, says University of Denver Professor of Law Robert Hardaway. "There was a purposeful 1983 decision to take house prices out" of the Consumer Price Index (CPI), he says.

"The decision was rationalized this way: People don't buy houses every year, so the cost of houses shouldn't be factored into the annual rise of the cost of living," Hardaway says. "But they do buy every six or seven years," he says.

At the same time, with speculators buying up houses they didn't plan to live in, rental properties flooded the market, driving rents down — and rents do get counted in the CPI, Hardaway says. "This makes it seem as if the price of living is rising even more slowly, but this is fraudulent. In fact, the real inflation rate is 15 percent when you put in housing."

Perhaps the most pernicious effect of skyrocketing prices was that it increased the temptation to borrow against homes' value to finance other wants. But if prices fall, a homeowner can end up unable to move without taking a huge loss and paying interest on their original loan many times over.

"Don't use your house as a piggybank for financing inessential things," says Warren. "You need to preserve your precious home equity or you'll end up like the 70-year-old who said to me, 'My bills are killing me! Can I do a debt consolidation?' He had [borrowed so many times on his house that he had] a mortgage of $350,000 even though he'd bought his house 30 years ago for $40,000."

The bottom line on home values is this, says Robert Losey, chairman of the Department of Finance at American University in Washington, D.C., where home prices have skyrocketed: "What goes up doesn't have to come down, but it usually does."

---

[1] Robert J. Shiller, "Understanding Recent Trends in House Prices and Home Ownership," paper presented to Federal Reserve Bank of Kansas City symposium, Jackson Hole, Wyo., September 2007.

[2] Quoted on "NOW," Public Broadcasting Service, Aug. 26, 2005, www.pbs.org/now/transcript/transcriptNOW134_full.html.

[3] *Ibid.*

[4] Jonathan J. Miller, "Unraveling the Pyramid of Bad Practices," Soapbox blog, Dec. 19, 2005, http://soapbox.millersamuel.com/?p=119.

[5] Testimony before House Financial Services Committee, Sept. 5, 2007.

Finally, to keep the overall economy moving, Federal Reserve Bank Chairman Alan Greenspan kept interest rates at historically low levels for three years, until June 2004, when he began raising them again. Although the Fed sets interest rates only for bank-to-bank money transfers, other lenders take their cue from the Fed rate, and mortgage interest also hit historic lows.

In the 1970s and '80s, interest rates in double digits were the norm, soaring to over 20 percent in 1980. In the 1990s, interest on a 30-year, fixed-rate mortgage hovered between 7 percent and 9 percent. Beginning in 2003, however, rates dropped below 6 percent and have hovered at around 6 percent since, according to the mortgage-information Web site Lender 411. [30]

The Federal Reserve "wanted to prevent inflation, but in doing that they made homeownership dirt cheap," says the University of New Haven's Rainish.

Low interest rates created a surge in mortgage demand between 2001 and 2003, especially for refinancings that allowed homeowners to lower their interest payments and tap into extra cash at the same time, said Emory W. Rushton, senior deputy comptroller and chief

How to Avoid Mortgage Troubles

Do's and don'ts for would-be homeowners

Using common sense and being skeptical of hype can help you avoid mortgage trouble, experts say. Among the housing do's and don'ts:

- **Don't be in a hurry to buy.** "If you're going to move in two or three years, you should rent," says Robert Losey, chairman of the Department of Finance at American University in Washington, D.C. Switching houses carries "quite substantial transition costs" — as much as 3 to 4 percent of a home's value, he says.

- **Don't tap into home equity for non-essential purposes.** Second mortgages can mean trouble if home prices fall or you need to move. "You should think of your home as the place you live in, not something you should make money on," says Margaret Mann, head of the restructuring and insolvency practice at Heller Ehrman, a San Francisco law firm.

- **Shop for a house based on what you can afford.** "If buyers would tailor their desires to their budgets," home prices wouldn't rise sky high and lenders wouldn't offer dangerous mortgages like adjustable-rate and interest-only loans, says Carolyn Warren, author of Mortgage Ripoffs and Money Savers. Too often, "a person gets preapproved by a lender for $350,000, but the real-estate agent comes back and asks to get them approved for $399,000," saying "they really want this sunken Jacuzzi," says Warren. That means a riskier loan and a skyward jump in local home prices, she says.

- **Remember that a lender's "good faith estimate" is just that, an estimate**, says Meghan Burns, co-founder of OfferAngel, a Scottsdale, Ariz., company that checks out mortgages for prospective home buyers. "The borrower takes it as gospel, thinking the estimate is a contract, but it's not," she says. "If you have somebody who's trying to lure you in" to a bad loan, "that's the bait in the bait-and-switch."

- **Watch for the signs of predatory lenders**, such as encouraging borrowers to lie about their income or assets to get a bigger loan; charging fees for unnecessary services; pressuring borrowers to accept higher-risk mortgages like interest-only loans; pressuring people in need of cash to refinance their homes; and using high-pressure sales tactics. [1]

---

[1] U.S. Department of Housing and Urban Development, www.hud.gov/offices/hsg/sfh/buying/loanfraud.cfm.

national bank examiner in the U.S. Office of the Comptroller of the Currency.

Surging demand prompted "lenders to expand their operations to boost capacity" and "attracted new market participants, often lenders with little business experience or financial strength," and a flood of new, risky mortgages ensued, Rushton told the Senate Banking Committee in March. [31]

As a result, "Lots of people in the United States who have no money — they are called subprime borrowers — borrowed 100 percent of the value of a house right at the top of a housing market which has since fallen sharply," wrote Paul Tustain, founder of a British investment-information Web site, BullionVault.com. With higher interest and a lower home value, many of these people can't make their new payments or refinance their houses. [32]

"The whole system allowed the frailty of human nature to triumph," says home-building consultant Schultz. "It took away all the restraints."

CURRENT SITUATION

Widespread Pain

Beginning in late 2006 and continuing this year, the wheels came off the mortgage bus. The number of people defaulting — falling behind — on payments, then losing homes to foreclosure, is rising sharply. Some lenders have gone bankrupt, and some recent investors in mortgage-backed securities have seen their investments quickly become worthless.

The financial industry and its regulators "got complacent" as mortgage loans got riskier and riskier, says the

Should the federal government impose stricter rules on the mortgage industry?

YES — Sen. Christopher J. Dodd, D-Conn.
Chairman, Senate Committee on Banking, Housing and Urban Affairs

From a statement to the committee, Oct. 3, 2007

Today we are facing a serious meltdown in the subprime mortgage market. This crisis is the equivalent of a slow-motion, 50-state Katrina, taking people's homes one by one, devastating their lives and destroying their communities. As a result, 2.2 million families are in danger of losing their homes to foreclosures at a cost of over $160 billion in hard-earned home equity that should have been available to finance college educations, pay health-care expenses or [act] as a cushion against uncertainty.

President Bush and his administration need to get fully engaged. They need to press subprime servicers and lenders to modify loans into long-term, affordable mortgages. Where modifications are not possible, the administration must work with Fannie Mae and Freddie Mac to refinance troubled borrowers on fair and affordable terms.

In April, I convened a Homeownership Preservation Summit where a number of the largest subprime lenders and servicers pledged to do these modifications. Unfortunately, a recent report tells us that just 1 percent of subprime adjustable-rate mortgages have been modified. This is wholly inadequate, and the administration must work with us to press the lenders and servicers to live up to their obligation.

While we are focused today on how we can rescue homeowners that have been victimized by predatory practices, we are also mindful that we need to prevent these kinds of abuses in the future.

The federal regulators — the cops on the beat — must be far more aggressive in policing the markets. The Federal Reserve [Board] noted as early as 2003 that problems were developing. Yet, not until it came under intense pressure from the Congress did the Federal Reserve agree to meet its obligation under the Homeownership and Equity Protection Act to prohibit unfair or deceptive mortgage practices. The board has the power to put an end to many of the practices that have gotten us into this mess today. They ought to exercise that power, and they ought to do it comprehensively and quickly.

In addition, a number of us have introduced or outlined anti-predatory-lending legislation. Let me say, the measure of any legislation must be that it creates high lending standards for the subprime market, and it must include remedies and penalties sufficient to ensure those standards are adequately enforced. Today's crisis is a market failure. Legislation must reengineer that market so that it works to create long-term, sustainable and affordable homeownership.

NO — Rep. Tom Price, R-Ga.
Member, House Committee on Financial Services

From a statement to the committee, Sept. 5, 2007

As anyone paying attention can tell you, we're seeing a dramatic increase in the actual number of foreclosures. To put the current "crisis" in perspective, according to the Mortgage Bankers Association in the first quarter of 2007 there are about 44 million mortgages in the U.S. and less than 14 percent of them are subprime. And only about 13 percent of those subprime mortgages are late on payments, with the majority of late payers working through their problems with the banks.

With approximately 561,857 mortgages in foreclosure — up from roughly 517,434 from the fourth quarter of 2006 — the subprime "meltdown" has given us an increase of 44,423 foreclosures. This still represents a small percentage of the number of home mortgages.

One of the main reasons we have seen a rise in foreclosures is that during the housing boom of the last few years, consumers with a higher credit risk qualified for mortgages. Now that those riskier loans are resetting to higher interest rates — a trend that will continue until April of 2008 — a credit crunch is occurring for home buyers. It will take time to determine which of the mortgage-backed securities contain "bad" loans and which don't, partially because the entire securitization process is relatively new and hasn't faced a challenge of this size.

A comprehensive consumer-advocacy-driven predatory-lending bill is not the answer. It is tantamount to fighting the last war and will only make the markets more skittish, as they have to react to new underwriting standards and liability issues, making the situation worse, not better. This would harm all consumers!

By the time a new "anti-predatory-lending" law goes into effect in the marketplace, this problem will already have changed, and we will be left with strict, national underwriting standards that will prohibit various loan products and banish a number of consumers to the rental market forever. This is not a goal that is responsible.

The American economy has more than enough liquidity and is plenty strong enough to weather this bump in the road. Congress should stay out of the way while the market corrects itself or it will only make matters worse. We saw last week just how strong the market is when the Commerce Department reported that the gross domestic product — the broadest measure of economic health — expanded at an annual rate of 4 percent in the April-June quarter, significantly higher than the 3.4-percent rate the government had initially estimated.

AP Photo/Reed Saxon

Auctioneer Travis Toth, right, accepts bids for a foreclosed home on the steps of the Los Angeles County courthouse in Norwalk, Calif., on March 16, 2007. To help struggling homeowners stay put, the nation's biggest mortgage lender, Countrywide Financial Corp., is restructuring about 82,000 mortgages to make them more affordable.

University of New Haven's Rainish. "It wasn't until sometime in 2006 that some of this stuff was starting to smell. Prior to that, nobody really got the gist of the excess that was taking place. But in the latter half of 2006, the most recent securities that were sold defaulted almost immediately," he says.

Midwestern states like Ohio are "national leaders in foreclosures," says the University of Chicago's Ashton. These areas have been in economic hard times for years, as the auto and steel industries waned, says Rainish. "You're seeing an implosion of income" at the same time as cash-flush lenders offered risky loans, he says. "People wanted to fix up, so they refinanced" with ARMs. "Then there was reset [of interest to higher rates], and they lost their equity."

The presence of foreclosed homes in a neighborhood affects everybody there, Rainish says. "Nobody can sell a home, even when they need to. You freeze the whole market. On a personal level, it's tragic."

"Even though we talk about people walking away from homes" and in some cases losing only a little cash since they made small — or no — down payments, "the foreclosure keeps you from buying a home later, and there are legal and moving costs associated with foreclosure, too," says Ashton.

While Chicago is not one of the hardest-hit areas, "there were still a lot of subprime loans for moderate-to-middle-income households in African-American neighborhoods," Ashton says. "It may be years — if ever — before they can get back into a home."

In Florida, Nevada, parts of California and some other sought-after locales, "flippers" — real-estate speculators — are big players in the ongoing crisis, says Ashton. "We've got flippers and speculators simply walking away" from properties, since the loan cost them little in the first place, Ashton says. That leaves lenders holding the bag, he says.

Some banks are ending up as owners of condos whose developers couldn't sell the majority of units before housing sales slowed, says Sheridan.

Banks aren't permitted to permanently manage residential properties, so they must sell them, he says. Meanwhile, "residents who've already bought in are locked into a property that isn't being cared for, whose value is deteriorating and which is likely to become a rental property," which is not what they plunked their money down for, says Sheridan. "The homeowner is not in a happy situation."

The selling and reselling of mortgage-loan packages to ever-more-distant investors may make it harder for some people facing foreclosure to work out a payment plan to keep their homes.

"How do you do a workout when nobody knows who owns what?" says Rainish. In the past, mortgages sold to a secondary market were in a big portfolio with Fannie Mae or Freddie Mac, organizations that are in the business of helping people stay in their houses. "Now the mortgages are owned by investment funds, by foreigners; they've been sold and resold," he says. "How are they going to deal with the workout? We don't know."

Nevertheless, "there still will be in almost every case a local institution that is the servicer" of the loan, says American University's Losey. "They don't have the same vested interest in working it out" as they did when local lenders held onto mortgages. Nevertheless, "I don't know that this means there will be that many more defaults or not," he says. "There should still be pressure from the institutions that own the securities to work out a logical deal."

Interest-Rate Cut

Debate rages over whether the government should bail out homeowners and whether strict new rules for mortgage lending should be created.

The first major action at the national level came from the Federal Reserve Board. [33]

In August and then again in September and late October, new Fed Chairman Ben S. Bernanke dropped key interest rates that make it easier for banks to lend money. [34] The moves came after the world's banks and other financial institutions began tightening credit, spooked by billion-dollar losses suffered by some banks and investment funds that had found their newly purchased mortgage-backed securities to be worthless. Banks became reluctant to loan to anyone, including other banks, because no one knows which institutions are holding the riskiest mortgage-backed securities.

But "the Federal Reserve's solution to the bubble" of rising house prices driven by easy money "is to keep the bubble going as long as possible," says Hardaway of the University of Denver, a critic of the move.

"It's like 17th-century Tulipmania in Holland," when high demand for the showy flowers led hundreds of frenzied speculators into the market, hoping to make a killing, Hardaway says. After prices for single bulbs rose to hundreds of dollars, the mania abruptly stopped as bidders worried that prices could not get any higher. Almost overnight, the price collapsed, bankrupting many middle-class people. [35]

"The Fed's policy is just like Holland: 'Let the mania continue, because if it stops, nobody else will be able to buy tulips,'" says Hardaway. "Better to let the bubble burst now," he argues. "That would flush out all excesses, like the 4-to-5-percent teaser [interest] rate, which is offered to people knowing they won't be able to afford it when it triples."

Others say the rate cut won't solve the problem but could keep it from worsening. "There's sludge in the system" as investors back away from securitized higher-risk mortgages, and "the Fed is reliquifying the system so banks can carry some new debt," says Rainish.

Government Role

Congress, the Bush administration, and several states are contemplating or have already acted to aid struggling homeowners and keep the housing market afloat.

Massachusetts, New York, Ohio, Pennsylvania, New Jersey and Maryland, will build loan funds to help homeowners refinance. Ohio, and Pennsylvania will sell bonds to raise funds, for example. [36]

The federal Office of Federal Housing Enterprise Oversight (OFHEO) gave the green light Sept. 19 for Fannie Mae and Freddie Mac to increase the amount of mortgage loans they invest in by 2 percent annually, as private investors pull back.

The move was a big deal, given recent concerns about financial fraud at the two mortgage giants. In May 2006, OFHEO capped the size of Fannie Mae's portfolio after investigators said some Fannie Mae executives — since departed — had manipulated accounts to show higher earnings to get bonuses. Fannie Mae paid a $400-million fine in 2006. And in September Freddie Mac paid a $50-million fine to settle its own charges of accounting fraud. [37] Nevertheless, the Fannie Mae and Freddie Mac upticks aren't considered large enough to jumpstart the slowing housing market.

Alternative legislation introduced in October by Sen. Schumer and House Financial Services Committee Chairman Rep. Barney Frank, D-Mass., would do more and also would assist current owners trying to hold onto homes. It would raise investment caps for both Fannie Mae and Freddie Mac by 10 percent for six months and direct 85 percent of the money to refinancing subprime mortgages, mostly for low-income borrowers. [38]

Critics of the bill, including the Bush administration, argue that it would be a costly distraction from what they see as a need to reform Fannie and Freddie.

"Frank must know that a temporary increase in the portfolio limits . . . will reduce the pressure for comprehensive reform," said Peter J. Wallison, a resident fellow at the free-market-oriented American Enterprise Institute think tank. [39]

The administration supports another Democratic initiative — eliminating the tax that kicks in for a homeowner when a lender forgives some mortgage debt after a house is sold or a loan is restructured.

"Say you take out a $310,000 mortgage to buy a house and then you find you can't keep up the payments and the house gets sold for $250,000," says developer Sheridan. "The bank may, out of a sense of compassion, and because they can't collect the $60,000 shortfall anyway, simply write it off." That sounds like good news for the strapped consumer, but under current law that money becomes taxable income at tax rates as high as 30 or 40 percent, he says. "That's a $15,000 bill you won't have the money to pay."

Congressional Democrats and the White House have recommended eliminating the tax. Democrats would end the tax permanently and cut tax breaks for sales of some vacation and rental properties to pay it. The White

House wants a temporary elimination and would retain the other tax breaks. [40]

President Bush also has announced a new Federal Housing Administration program, FHASecure, to offer FHA-insured loans to creditworthy borrowers who are delinquent on their mortgages. Delinquent borrowers were ineligible in the past. [41]

Congress also is debating new consumer protections. In September the House Financial Services Committee approved a bill giving several additional federal agencies a watchdog role over mortgage lending. [42] Several states, including Massachusetts, Maine, Minnesota and North Carolina, now require mortgage brokers to scrutinize would-be borrowers more carefully to ensure they can afford their loans. [43]

OUTLOOK

Hitting Bottom

One thing about fallout from the mortgage crisis is not in doubt: Washington will tighten some rules, says American University's Losey. "Congress reacts to crises," he says.

But the changes will come against a backdrop of stark financial pain and an end to giddy times in which people believed that house values would rise forever.

It will be two years or more before all existing ARMs reset, and only then will the extent of home losses be known, says the University of New Haven's Rainish. "For the subprime mortgage holders, the American dream will be crushed," he says. "Even many who have been making full payments won't be able to refinance because of pre-payment penalties" in many subprime mortgages.

He predicts the housing market will be slow for the next two to three years. "The investment community will take a $100-$200 billion haircut, and many people will be hurt. Consumption growth will be slowed."

To emerge from the other side of this crisis, we need house prices to contract 20 percent or even as much as 40 percent, says the University of Chicago's Ashton.

"That's not a painless process," as many homeowners may end up owing more than their houses are worth, Ashton says. Owners with ARMs as their first or second mortgages must either make huge monthly mortgage payments when rates reset or try to refinance. But most won't be able to get a new loan for the full amount of their debt, since falling prices will slash their equity.

"We may hit bottom [on home prices] in early 2009, and maybe 2010 in some markets," says Sheridan. "There'll be a long period of prices staying down."

Most if not all subprime borrowers would have been unable to seek loans except under the conditions of the past few years, "so now that whole demand has gone away," possibly permanently, says Margaret Mann, head of the restructuring and insolvency practice at San Francisco-based law firm Heller Ehrman.

"Builders have almost stopped building," and a glut of housing inventory sits in some markets, says Florida home-building consultant Schultz. In South Florida, for example, three to four years' worth of condo inventory already sits empty, he says. "I doubt that the demand will ever be back to the level of 2007. A lot of regional and national builders will have to scale back."

Commercial real estate could be next to go bust. New, empty office buildings with large construction debts and vacant retail malls are being reported around the country, according to Michael Shedlock, an investment consultant for SitkaPacific Capital Management, in Prairie Grove, Ill.

"Here we are, right near the tip top in commercial real-estate insanity where no price was too high to pay for a building on the silly belief that property values would continually rise," said Shedlock. "Given how rapidly investor psychology is changing in this sector, it won't take much now to send it over the edge." [44]

Furthermore, many analysts say it's only a matter of time before a new boom of risky loans and investments occurs again, followed by inevitable bust.

"People's memories are usually good for five to 10 years, "says Hardaway at the University of Denver. "For that period of time, maybe they'll remember they should look at the collateral."

NOTES

1. Delores King, testimony before Senate Committee on Banking, Housing and Urban Affairs, February 2007.

2. Eric Stein, testimony before House Judiciary Subcommittee on Commercial and Administrative Law, Sept. 25, 2007.

3. "What's Ahead for Financial Markets?" Knowledge @Wharton electronic newsletter, Oct. 3, 2007, http://knowledge.wharton.upenn.edu.

4. David Cho, "Huge Mortgage Lender Files for Bankruptcy," *The Washington Post*, April 3, 2007, p. A1.

5. "Subprime Mess Hits Wall Street Again," *Mortgage News Daily*, www.mortgagenewsdaily.com, June 25, 2007.

6. Doug Noland, "Structured Finance Under Duress," *Asia Times online*, Oct. 30, 2007, www.atimes.com /atimes/Global_Economy/IJ30Dj02.html.

7. Robert J. Shiller, "Understanding Recent Trends in House Prices and Home Ownership," paper presented at the Jackson Hole symposium of the Federal Reserve Bank of Kansas City, September 2007.

8. Martin Eakes, testimony before Senate Committee on Banking, Housing and Urban Affairs, Feb. 7, 2007.

9. For background see J.W. Elphinstone, "Mortgage Bailouts Run Into Opposition," The Associated Press, *The Salt Lake Tribune online*, Sept. 29, 2007, www.sltrib.com/realestate/ci_7038862.

10. Les Christie, "Countrywide Wins Over Critics," CNNMoney.com, Oct. 24, 2007, http://money.cnn .com/2007/10/24/real_estate/Countrywide_plan_wins _support/index.htm?postversion=2007102416.

11. For background, see "Interagency Guidance on Nontraditional Mortgage Product Risks," Office of Thrift Supervision, Department of the Treasury, October 2006, www.ots.treas.gov/docs/2/25244.pdf.

12. Douglas G. Duncan, testimony before Senate Committee on Banking, Housing and Urban Affairs, Feb. 7, 2007.

13. Sandor Samuels, testimony before Senate Committee on Banking, Housing and Urban Affairs, March 22, 2007.

14. "Home Ownership Rates," Danter Co., www.danter.com/statistics/hometown.htm.

15. "Why Bush's Mortgage Bailout Plan Is a Bad Idea," eFinanceDirectory.com, Sept. 4, 2007.

16. "Mortgage Fallout: Interview With Housing Wire," eFinanceDirectory.com, Sept. 6, 2007.

17. For background see "Behind the S&L Crisis," Editorial Research Reports, 1988, Vol. II, *CQ Researcher online*; and "S&L Bailout: Assessing the Impact," *Editorial Research Reports*, 1990, *CQ Researcher online*.

18. "Schumer, Others Propose First Major Legislation to Deal with Subprime Crisis as Weakening Housing Market Threatens Economy," press release, office of Sen. Charles Schumer, May 3, 2007, http://schumer.senate.gov.

19. "The Truly Bearish Case Isn't Playing Out," John Burns Real-Estate Consulting Web site, July 2007, www.realestateconsulting.com.

20. "Improvement in Mortgage Market Bodes Well for Housing in 2008," press release, National Association of Realtors, Oct. 10, 2007.

21. Ben Stein, "How Speculators Exploit Market Fears," Yahoo! Finance, Aug. 2, 2007, http://finance .yahoo.com.

22. Edward E. Leamer, "Housing and the Business Cycle," paper presented at the Jackson Hole symposium of the Federal Reserve Bank of Kansas City, September 2007.

23. *Ibid.*

24. Martin Feldstein, "Housing, Housing Finance, and Monetary Policy," remarks presented at the Jackson Hole symposium of the Federal Reserve Bank of Kansas City, September 2007.

25. For background see Richard K. Green and Susan M. Wachter, "The American Mortgage in Historical and International Context," *Journal of Economic Perspectives*, fall 2005, pp. 92-114.

26. Nadeem Walayat, "Hedge Fund Subprime Credit Crunch to Impact Interest Rates," The Market Oracle: Financial Markets Forecasting and Analysis, July 31, 2007, www.marketoracle.co.uk.

27. Kurt Eggert, testimony before Senate Subcommittee on Securities, Insurance and Investments, April 17, 2007.

28. Quoted in *Ibid.*

29. Michael Kanef, testimony before House Subcommittee on Capital Markets, Insurance, and Government Sponsored Enterprises, Sept. 27, 2007.

30. Mortgage Rates: A Historical Look at Mortgage Interest Rates, Lender 411, www.lender411.com/ mortgage-articles/index_desc.php?art_id=37.

31. Emory W. Rushton, testimony before U.S. Senate Committee on Banking, Housing, and Urban Affairs, March 22, 2007.

32. Paul Tustain, "Bear Stearns and MBS Hedge Funds: What Are the Real Risks Today?" Financial Sense University, June 23, 2007, www.financialsense.com/fsu/editorials/tustain/2007/0623.html.

33. For background see David Masci, "The Federal Reserve," *CQ Researcher*, Sept. 1, 2000, pp. 673-688.

34. For background see Martin Crutsinger, "Fed Approves Cut in Discount Loan Rate," The Associated Press, Yahoo! Finance Web site, Aug. 17, 2007, http://biz.yahoo.com/ap/070817/fed_interest_rates.html.

35. For background see "Tulip Mania," *Encyclopaedia Britannica online*, 2007.

36. For background see "$500 Million-Dollar Bailout Extended to U.S. Mortgage Borrowers," eFinance Directory Web site, July 24, 2007, http://efinancedirectory.com.

37. For background see Kathleen Day, "Study Finds 'Extensive' Fraud at Fannie Mae," *The Washington Post*, May 24, 2006, p. A1.

38. For background see Benton Ives, "Short-Term Foreclosure Fix Could Cloud Long-Term Regulatory Overhaul," *CQ Today*, Oct. 15, 2007, www.cq.com.

39. Quoted in *ibid.*

40. For background see Richard Rubin, "Tax Relief Plan for Struggling Homeowners Would Exclude the Wealthy," *CQ Today*, Oct. 2, 2007, www.cq.com.

41. For background, see "Fact Sheet: New Steps to Help Homeowners Avoid Foreclosure," White House Web site, Aug. 31, 2007, www.whitehouse.gov/news/releases/2007/08/20070831-4.html.

42. For background, see Michael R. Crittenden, "Measure Outlines Expansion of Financial Protections for Consumers," *CQ Today*, Sept. 18, 2007, www.cq.com.

43. Amy Scott, "States Crack Down on Mortgage Market," Marketplace, National Public Radio, Oct. 19, 2007.

44. Michael Shedlock, "Commercial Real Estate Abyss," Mish's Global Economic Trend Analysis blog, Sept. 13, 2007, http://globaleconomicanalysis.blogspot.com.

BIBLIOGRAPHY

Books

Gramlich, Edward M., and Robert D. Reischauer, *Subprime Mortgages: America's Latest Boom and Bust*, Urban Institute Press, 2007.
Two experts recount the history of the subprime-mortgage market and suggest reforms. Gramlich once chaired the Federal Reserve's Consumer and Community Affairs Committee; Reischauer is president of the Urban Institute.

Schwartz, Alex F., *Housing Policy in the United States: An Introduction*, Routledge, 2006.
An associate professor of housing policy at New School University describes the housing-finance system.

Articles

Morgenson, Gretchen, "Can These Mortgages Be Saved?" *The New York Times*, Sept. 30, 2007, Sec. 3, p. 1.
Many borrowers in trouble say mortgage lenders aren't helping them to keep their homes.

Rokakis, Jim, "The Shadow of Debt," *The Washington Post*, Sept. 30, 2007, p. B1.
A once-tranquil Cleveland neighborhood becomes crime-infested after predatory lending leads to massive foreclosures.

Smith, David, "HUD Homes Go Cheap," *Journal & Courier* [Lafayette, Indiana], September 16, 2007, http://m.jconline.com.
The Department of Housing and Urban Development has bought so many foreclosed Indiana properties it is now the state's largest home seller.

Wargo, Brian, "Cancellations of New-Home Purchases Climb," *In Business Las Vegas*, Sept. 21-27, 2007, edition, www.inbusinesslasvegas.com.
Many Nevada homebuyers are canceling sales. Meanwhile, the National Association of Hispanic Real Estate Professionals is trying to protect Latinos from predatory lending.

Reports and Studies

"Ask Yourself Why . . . Mortgage Foreclosure Rates Are So High," *Common Cause*, 2007.
A citizens' group argues that $210 million in campaign funds and lobbying costs spent by the mortgage-lending industry has made Congress unwilling to curb industry practices.

"Mortgage Liquidity Du Jour: Underestimated No More," *Credit Suisse*, March 2007.
A large investment bank concludes dangers lurk in all sectors of the mortgage market, not just subprime loans.

Subprime and Predatory Lending in Rural America, Policy Brief No. 4, **Carsey Institute, University of New Hampshire, fall 2006.**
Affordable housing groups say many rural residents fall prey to predatory lenders, partly because they have little access to mainstream banks.

Essene, Ren S., and William Apgar, "Understanding Mortgage-Market Behavior: Creating Good Mortgage Options for All Americans," Joint Center for Housing Studies, Harvard University, April 2007.
Researchers conclude many consumers can't accurately evaluate the many mortgages that have sprung up.

Larson, Michael D., "How Federal Regulators, Lenders, and Wall Street Created America's Housing Crisis," Weiss Research, July 2007.
A financial analyst describes what house prices, foreclosures and other data reveal about the housing crisis and argues federal regulators underestimated the problems.

Murphy, Edward Vincent, "Alternative Mortgages: Risks to Consumers and Lenders in the Current Housing Cycle," Congressional Research Service, Dec. 27, 2006.
A CRS analyst describes how alternative mortgages have trapped some homeowners.

Schloemer, Ellen, *et al.,* **"Losing Ground: Foreclosures in the Subprime Market and Their Cost to Homeowners," Center for Responsible Lending, December 2006.**
Analysts predict 2.2 million subprime borrowers will lose their houses in the current crisis.

Helpful Web Sites

How to avoid predatory lenders: www.hud.gov/offices/hsg/sfh/buying/loanfraud.cfm.

How to calculate how much house you can afford, whether to buy or rent: www.hud.gov/buying/index.cfm.

What you should know about mortgage brokers: http://homebuying.about.com/od/findingalender/qt/0407LoanOffRep.htm.

Definitions of terms connected with home buying: www.statefarm.com/bank/sr_center/morgloss.asp.

Explanations of mortgage terms and advice about various types of loans: http://michaelbluejay.com/house/loan.html.

For More Information

Carsey Institute, University of New Hampshire, 73 Main St., Huddleston Hall, Durham, NH 03824; (603) 862-2821; http://carseyinstitute.unh.edu. Researches housing and other economic issues in rural America.

Center for Responsible Lending, 302 West Main St., Durham, NC 27701; (919) 313-8500; www.responsible-lending.org. Provides information on predatory lending and other abusive practices.

Fannie Mae, 3900 Wisconsin Ave., N.W., Washington, DC 20016; (202) 752-7000; www.fanniemae.com/index.jhtml. The government-sponsored, shareholder-owned corporation buys mortgages in the secondary market to provide capital for the mortgage industry.

Freddie Mac, 8200 Jones Branch Dr., McLean, VA 22102-3110; (703) 903-2000; www.freddiemac.com/index.html. The government-sponsored company supports the mortgage market.

Joint Center for Housing Studies, Harvard University, 1033 Massachusetts Ave., 5th Floor, Cambridge, MA 02138; (617) 495-7908; www.jchs.harvard.edu/index .htm. Provides information and research on U.S. housing issues.

Mortgage Professor's Web Site, www.mtgprofessor.com/. The University of Pennsylvania's Wharton School of Business provides Financial education and policy analysis written by at.

National Association of Mortgage Brokers, 7900 Westpark Dr., Suite T309, McLean, VA 22102; (703) 342-5900; www.namb.org/namb/Default.asp. Provides information on the mortgage industry, including legislative proposals.

National Association of Realtors, 500 New Jersey Ave., N.W., Washington, DC 20001-2020; (800) 874-6500; www.realtor.org. Provides and analyzes its own data on housing-market trends.

National Mortgage News Online, www.nationalmortgage-news.com/. The independent news outlet covers mortgage-related news.

Office of Federal Housing Enterprise Oversight, 1700 G St., N.W., 4th Floor, Washington, DC 20552; (202) 414-3800; www.ofheo.gov. Oversees Fannie and Freddie and provides data and research on housing.

U.S. Department of Housing and Urban Development, 451 7th St., S.W., Washington, DC 20410; (202) 708-1112; www.hud.gov/. Provides information about mortgages, home buying and related federal programs.

13

Aging Infrastructure

Marcia Clemmitt

Steam explodes from a burst pipe near Manhattan's Grand Central Station on July 18, 2007. One person was killed and several injured. Throughout the country, many facilities and systems are 50-100 years old, and engineers say they have been woefully neglected. Now lawmakers are debating whether aging infrastructure merits higher taxes or other measures, such as turning more highways into privately managed toll roads.

From *CQ Researcher*,
September 28, 2007.

On Aug. 1, 24-year-old Gary Babineau was driving across the I-35 West bridge in Minneapolis when it collapsed, plunging more than 100 vehicles into the Mississippi River and killing 13 people.

After falling about 30 feet, Babineau's pickup truck dangled over the edge of a bridge section as cars hurtled past him into the water. "The whole bridge from one side of the Mississippi to the other just completely gave way," Babineau told CNN. "I stayed in my car until the cars quit falling for a second, then I got out real quick." He and other survivors then helped children in a school bus scramble off the bridge. [1]

The fatal collapse brought to mind other recent infrastructure failures — including the aging underground steam pipe that burst in New York City two weeks earlier, killing a pedestrian and injuring several others. More important, the collapse raised concern about the condition of the nation's dams, water and sewer lines, electric power networks and other vital systems. Many were constructed decades ago, during a 75-year building boom, and are nearing the end of their intended lifespan, engineering groups say.

"The steam pipe that blew up in New York was over 80 years old," says David G. Mongan, president-elect of the American Society of Civil Engineers (ASCE). [2]

Indeed, because of increasing user demand and years of neglected maintenance, the U.S. infrastructure overall rates a near-failing grade of "D" from the ASCE. The group says a $1.6-trillion, five-year investment is needed to bring facilities up to snuff. [3]

Much of the existing U.S infrastructure was built in the 1930s, '40s and '50s and today carries loads that "are magnitudes beyond" what its builders anticipated, he says.

Many Bridges Are 'Structurally Deficient'

Twelve percent of all bridges in the United States — nearly 75,000 structures — are structurally deficient, according to the Department of Transportation. In four states — Oklahoma, Iowa, Pennsylvania and Rhode Island — more than 20 percent of the bridges are deficient.

Percentage of Structurally Deficient Bridges by State, 2006

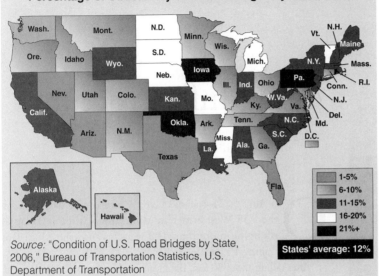

	1-5%
	6-10%
	11-15%
	16-20%
	21%+

States' average: 12%

Source: "Condition of U.S. Road Bridges by State, 2006," Bureau of Transportation Statistics, U.S. Department of Transportation

As the Water Environment Foundation (WEF) puts it: "A hundred years ago, Teddy Roosevelt was president, crossword puzzles hadn't been invented, Las Vegas had a population of 39 people and your sewer system was brand new." The nonprofit advocacy group seeks to focus attention on infrastructure that's mainly out of sight and out of mind until a catastrophic event like a bridge collapse.

Infrastructure consists of the structures and systems that "we can't do without," says Paula R. Worthington, a lecturer in economics at the University of Chicago's Harris School of Public Policy.

While vital, infrastructure is also easy to ignore. In fact, a good definition of infrastructure could be "all the things that we take for granted somebody is taking care of," says Linda Kelly, the WEF's managing director of public communications and the former deputy director of the Portland, Ore., water system.

But Americans have not been taking good care of their infrastructure, many analysts say. For one thing, politicians generally believe they gain more political capital from new projects than from maintaining and

upgrading old systems, even heavily used ones.

Washington "is a classic case," says Heywood Sanders, a professor of public administration at the University of Texas, San Antonio. "There are a great number of older highways" in the nation's capital that need fixing, disastrously deteriorating school buildings and more, Sanders says. "But what you've got is a new convention center and a brand-new ballpark. In a city that needs a great many things, those are the things that happen."

Focusing public attention on the need for maintenance funds "unfortunately takes some kind of major problem," says Rob Villee, executive director of the Plainfield Area Regional Sewerage Authority in Middlesex, N.J. The result is that few infrastructure agencies "do proactive maintenance." In every town, many interests fight for a piece of the public budget, "and until [a sewer] backs up into the house of somebody important," sewer maintenance seldom commands attention and dollars, he says.

Ownership issues also work against proper maintenance and improvements to privately owned infrastructure, such as the electric system, says Richard Little, director of the Keston Institute for Public Finance and Infrastructure Policy at the University of Southern California (USC).

Since government-imposed ownership rules were removed for electrical utilities during the 1990s, "the new owners of transmission capacity" — power lines — "aren't in the electricity-generation business," says Little. Such owners may have little financial incentive to upgrade their systems, he says. "When the system was vertically integrated" — with the same companies owning both power-generation facilities and transmission lines — "there was a stronger business reason for keeping it up." Today, however, "the great national transmission grid is not as integrated as we think" — and potentially more vulnerable to failures such as blackouts.

As the Minneapolis bridge collapse starkly showed, neglect comes with a price.

After the accident, a construction-industry official told the *Minneapolis Star-Tribune* that some workers at the Minnesota Department of Transportation had been "deathly afraid that this kind of tragedy was going to be visited on us." Some "were screaming" to have "fracture-critical" bridges like I-35 West "replaced" sooner than the state had budgeted for. [4]

Bridges aren't the only infrastructure sector that is collapsing. The increasing frequency of sinkholes that swallow people and property is evidence of deteriorating wastewater infrastructure, says Kelly. When an underground sewer pipe springs a leak, soil seeps into the crack and is carried away, and eventually "the soil can't support heavy cars or a building," she explains.

Last December, a 64-year-old Brooklyn, N.Y., woman carrying groceries home was injured when she fell into a five-foot-deep sinkhole that opened under the sidewalk. The same month, a 30-foot-deep sinkhole shut down a stretch of California's famed Pacific Coast Highway near Malibu, while in Portland, Ore., a sinkhole swallowed a 40-foot-long sewer-repair truck. A few months earlier, a 2-year-old boy in Irving, Texas, may have disappeared into a sinkhole while playing in a park; the child was never recovered. [5]

Dams are another growing concern. At least 23 have failed in the past four years, including Ka Loko Dam in Kauai, Hawaii, which collapsed in March 2006 killing seven people and causing at least $50 million in property and environmental damage. [6]

And the spate of air-traffic delays that stranded thousands of vacation travelers just this summer is directly due to a lack of important upgrades to the air-traffic control system, says the ASCE's Mongan. Airports can't land as many planes as they could

Federal Spending Cuts Shift Burden to States

The percentage of federal spending on transportation and water infrastructure has been decreasing since 1981, forcing cash-strapped states to pick up more of the expenses.

Percentage of Public Spending Spent on Infrastructure, 1956-2004

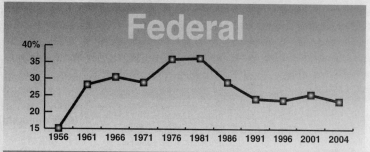

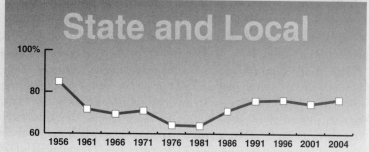

Source: "Trends in Public Spending on Transportation and Water Infrastructure, 1956 to 2004," Congressional Budget Office, August 2007

because outdated radar tracking systems make it unsafe to space planes as closely as modern GPS tracking systems would allow, he says.

Virtually all infrastructure analysts say upgrades and maintenance require more funding, but increasing taxes to raise the money is sparking hot debate in Washington. As early as the 1930s, states introduced fuel taxes to pay for road construction, and the main federal source of highway funds today is an 18.4-cents-per-gallon gasoline tax, last increased in 1993. [7]

"I consider it ludicrous that the United States has the lowest gas taxes in the world," says Lt. Gen. Hank Hatch, a former chief of the U.S. Army Corps of Engineers who chairs the Board on Infrastructure and Environment at the National Research Council. "If we had a higher one, we could do amazing things"

Water from the Ka Loko Reservoir rushes over an earthen dam that gave way on March 14, 2006, killing several people in Lilhue, Hawaii. It is one of 23 U.S. dams that have collapsed in the last four years.

But the Bush administration and some conservatives oppose any tax increases.

"Increasing federal taxes and spending would likely do little, if anything, to address either the quality or performance of our roads," Secretary of Transportation Mary E. Peters told the House Transportation Committee on Sept. 5. The occasion was a hearing on legislation sponsored by Committee Chairman James Oberstar, D-Minn., to raise the federal gas tax to 23.3 cents to create a bridge-maintenance trust fund. [8]

Later, President George W. Bush told Democratic and Republican backers of the increase that the real problem with highway upkeep is funding that lawmakers divert to low-priority pet projects. Bush opposes increasing the gas tax, he said, because it "could affect economic growth" negatively. [9]

With tax funds hard to come by, some highway and water agencies are opting for long-term lease agreements allowing private companies to operate and perhaps build facilities and collect tolls for their upkeep. Such "public-private partnerships" also are hotly debated.

Proponents praise the private sector's ingenuity and efficiency. "We need flexible solutions and, quite often, the most flexible minds are in the private sector," says Eli Lehrer, a senior fellow at the libertarian Competitive Enterprise Institute.

But most citizens feel more confident that their interests will be protected if local government manages infra-

structure, said Wenonah Hauter, executive director of the advocacy group Food and Water Watch, which challenges private takeover of water systems. "They don't want a really important public service like water to be privatized," Hauter said. "They don't want the customer call center to be 1,000 miles away. They don't want their water rates going up." [10]

When it comes down to a choice between taxes and user fees like tolls, the public's first choice is "neither," says Little. "People would rather ride on a nice road for free than pay $6."

As voters, legislators and engineers contemplate solutions to crumbling highways and sewer lines, here are some questions being asked:

Does aging infrastructure endanger Americans?

No one argues the U.S. infrastructure is not deteriorating. But opinions vary about the amount of danger the deterioration poses.

"All materials deteriorate, and fatigue will hit every bridge eventually," says Thomas Baber, an associate professor of engineering at the University of Virginia. "If you put a bridge out there long enough," exposed to traffic stress, water, sulfurous chemicals in the air in industrial areas and road salts, "it will get corrosion," he says. Water alone "is a very effective solvent, eating through paints and through steel," Baber says.

But even engineers are sometimes surprised by structural deterioration, says Ziyad Duron, a professor of engineering at Harvey Mudd College in Claremont, Calif. A few years ago, Duron was "leaning on a bridge in Massachusetts, and all of a sudden I found myself with one of the bolts in my hand."

Life-threatening events like dangerous sinkholes are on the rise, while the risk of other catastrophic events like dam and bridge failures is also increasing, some experts say.

The condition of many U.S. bridges is "quite scary" because many "are approaching the end of their useful life, which is typically 50 to 75 years," and "due to less than adequate maintenance over the years on some of these structures, anything could happen without warning," says Abi Aghayere, a professor of civil engineering at New York's Rochester Institute of Technology.

Dams are likely in worse condition than bridges, some engineers say.

Since 1998, the number of unsafe dams in the United States has increased by 33 percent, according to the

American Society of Civil Engineers. The total number of dams whose failure could cause loss of life has risen from 9,281 to 10,094 over that period, largely because of population growth immediately downstream from dams and underfunding of government dam-safety agencies, according to the advocacy group Dam Safety Coalition. [11]

"Every moment of every day, unsafe dams form a vast reservoir of danger throughout America," warned journalist Gaylord Shaw, who won a 1978 Pulitzer Prize for a *Los Angeles Times* series investigating the nation's dams. "When a dam fails . . . the events usually are viewed as local, transitory incidents rather than a symbol of a national problem," but "the cumulative hazard posed by unsafe dams is huge." [12]

And it's not just dams and bridges. The past year has seen a near-epidemic of sinkholes in most states, and the trend is likely to continue.

When underground sewer pipes break, the soil above falls into the crack and the "broken pipes whisk dirt away like a vacuum cleaner," said Thomas Rooney, CEO of Insituform Technologies, a pipe-repair company in Chesterfield, Mo. "When enough soil disappears above the pipe, but below a road or park or home, a sinkhole forms.

"All over America, engineers are telling city councils, water boards, sewer districts and other public agencies and officials about the dismal conditions of their water and sewer pipes," said Rooney. But "they would rather wait until the next catastrophe." [13]

Nevertheless, most of the infrastructure is basically safe, say many experts.

So-called "truss" bridges, like Minneapolis' I-35 West

Report Card Shows No Improvement

The nation's transportation infrastructure has not significantly improved since 2001, according to the American Society of Civil Engineers (ASCE). Much of the infrastructure has remained either structurally deficient or functionally obsolete, according to the ASCE. Moreover, in most instances, spending for maintenance, repairs and replacements has not met the group's requirements.

Infrastructure Grades, 2001 and 2005

Subject	2001 grade	2005 grade
Bridges	C	C

The percentage of the nation's structurally deficient or functionally obsolete bridges decreased from 28.5 to 27.1 percent from 2000 to 2003. However, it will cost $9.4 billion a year for the next 20 years to eliminate all deficiencies.

Dams	D	D

Since 1998, the number of unsafe dams has risen by 33 percent to over 3,000. Federally owned dams are in good condition. It will cost $10.1 billion over the next 12 years to address all non-federal dams in critical condition.

Drinking Water	D	D-

The United States faces an $11 billion annual shortfall to replace aging water facilities and comply with safe-drinking-water regulations. In 2005, federal funding for drinking water totaled $850 billion, 10 percent less than the total national requirement.

National Power Grid	D+	D

Continual growth in electricity demand and investment in new power plants have not been matched by investments in new transmission facilities. Existing transmission capability leaves consumers vulnerable to blackouts. Maintenance spending has decreased by 1 percent annually since 1992.

Roads	D+	D

Poor road conditions cost motorists $54 billion a year in operating costs and repairs. Americans spend 3.5 billion hours a year stuck in traffic, costing the economy $63.2 billion. Spending on transportation infrastructure currently totals $59.4 billion, well below the necessary $94 billion.

Wastewater	D	D-

Aging wastewater systems discharge billions of gallons of untreated sewage into surface waters each year. The EPA estimates that $390 billion over the next 20 years will be required to replace existing systems, but in 2005 Congress cut funding for wastewater management for the first time in eight years.

Source: American Society of Civil Engineers, www.asce.org/reportcard/2005/page.cfm?id=103

bridge, aren't dangerous in and of themselves, for example, says the University of Virginia's Baber. "We have been building truss structures for about 150 years, and by and large, they're very safe."

Shortfall Projected in Water Spending

The United States will need up to $1.1 trillion to meet future U.S. water infrastructure needs (left). However, Environmental Protection Agency analysts say if present funding trends continue, the U.S. could end up as much as $1.1 trillion short of that goal (right).

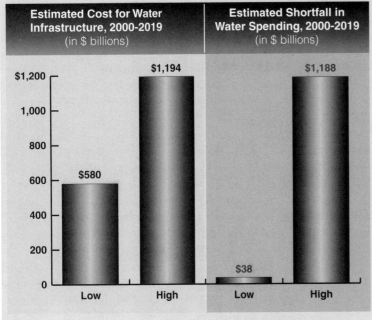

Estimated Cost for Water Infrastructure, 2000-2019 (in $ billions)		Estimated Shortfall in Water Spending, 2000-2019 (in $ billions)	
Low	High	Low	High
$580	$1,194	$38	$1,188

Sources: "Water Infrastructure: Comprehensive Asset Management Has Potential to Help Utilities Better Identify Needs and Plan Future Investments," General Accounting Office, March 2004; Claudia Copeland and Mary Tiemann, "Water Infrastructure Needs and Investment: Review and Analysis of Key Issues," Congressional Research Service, June 13, 2007

Furthermore, "We're much better today at monitoring" structures to catch problems before catastrophic failures, says Donald Vannoy, professor emeritus of civil engineering at the University of Maryland. "This failure in Minnesota is very strange and unusual."

"I don't think we're moving into an era of regular catastrophic failure, like a Minneapolis bridge every three months," says Little at the University of Southern California. In Minneapolis, "a certain bridge didn't get what it needed, and there was a failure."

The main effects of infrastructure aging are low-level, chronic problems, not catastrophes, many analysts say.

For example, if water quality deteriorates because of aging pipes in a region's water-supply system, "there's no

explosion, or 100,000 people" suddenly inundated, as in a dam collapse, says Charles N. Haas, a professor of environmental engineering at Philadelphia's Drexel University. Nevertheless, what does result is "a low-level but continuous exposure" to chemical and biological hazards for hundreds of thousands of people, which may seriously harm the health of some, Haas says.

Some undue alarm about aging infrastructure comes from the way infrastructure deficiencies are categorized and sold to the public and policy makers both by federal agencies and private groups, says Sanders at the University of Texas.

When engineers calculate totals of obsolete structures, the number usually includes both "functionally obsolete" facilities — those that aren't big enough to accommodate today's needs — and "structurally deficient" structures — those that are falling into disrepair, Sanders explains. Furthermore, a "structurally deficient" bridge "may have a bad roadway," which can be fixed by resurfacing and doesn't pose any danger of the bridge falling down, he says. It's important to sort out those categories and not simply assume that all "deficient" structures are actually dangerous, he says.

Should taxes be increased to overhaul the infrastructure?

As both publicly and privately owned infrastructure age, maintenance and replacement costs are inevitable, as are costs for monitoring their safety and reliability. Some analysts argue that current decision-making processes are so flawed that money raised by tax increases would be squandered.

Maintaining aging infrastructure undoubtedly costs more money than we have been spending, most analysts say.

As in many other areas of life, with infrastructure age comes increasing responsibility, says Bernard Wasow, an economist and senior fellow at the liberal Century

Foundation. "It's just like when your kids get older and need a college education. With time, come things you've got to pay for."

Furthermore, "compared to other nations like Japan, we do spend a smaller amount of [the gross domestic product]" on infrastructure, says Texas' Sanders.

In fact, it's the dauntingly high cost of properly maintaining the nation's vast infrastructure that has partly prevented the job from being done, says Little at the University of Southern California (USC). "We need to spend a couple of hundred billion dollars a year forever," and that prospect is too daunting for most policy makers to face, he says.

Many analysts say fuel taxes and other infrastructure-supporting taxes are too low, as are fees for infrastructure use, such as household water fees and highway tolls.

As an anti-tax movement has flourished over the past few decades, distrust of government and the belief that any tax is too high a tax have spread, says Jeffrey Buxbaum, a transportation consultant with Massachusetts-based Cambridge Systematics. Infrastructure maintenance has been stinted by "the legacy of 'No taxes' and 'The government isn't to be trusted,'" he says.

Furthermore, "there's a lack of understanding of how much people actually pay in the form of gas taxes," a common funding source for transportation infrastructure, says Buxbaum. In Massachusetts, for instance, the average person pays about "$150 a year" in state fuel taxes, "and if you wanted to raise it by a few cents" to pay for maintenance, "that would amount to less than $100 a year" per household, he says.

Anti-tax protests over the past couple of decades have all but paralyzed politicians on infrastructure, says Little. "Even if they want to do the progressive thing, they worry because the anti-tax groups are going to get them."

"We've been spoiled in this country. We don't pay market rates for much of anything, and we have allowed the tax rebels to drive the agenda," says Little. "We have people in California in $100-million homes paying only hundreds of dollars in taxes. How silly is that?"

Many infrastructure-related fees also are too low, many analysts say.

"We aren't charging enough" for water to either residential or business users, for example, says Drexel University's Haas.

The federal gasoline tax and many state gasoline taxes are flat, cents-per-gallon taxes that have remained the same for years. Many economists argue that fuel taxes

A sinkhole blocks a road in St. Cloud, Minn., on July 19, 2007. Sinkholes are often caused by deteriorating underground sewer pipes. When they spring a leak, soil seeps into the crack and is carried away, undermining roads and other sites above the pipes.

should be "indexed" to inflation or some other economic marker, simply to prevent them from losing value as all other costs in the nation rise — including the cost of maintaining roads and bridges.

Not only does a non-indexed tax lose its value over time, but the "unit-tax" structure of the current federal gas tax can actually cause tax revenues to drop when the price of gas rises, says Joel B. Slemrod, a professor of business economics and public policy at the University of Michigan. If a higher price leads people to buy less gas, then revenue drops from a cents-on-the-gallon tax, he explains.

Gas taxes "absolutely" should be indexed to rise with other prices, says Robert W. Poole Jr., director of transportation studies at the libertarian Reason Foundation in Los Angeles. "But I've talked myself blue in the face trying to convince" conservative colleagues of that, he says. "Indexing of the fuel tax is not a tax increase; it's just a way of keeping the value of the tax from completely deteriorating over time," says Poole.

New, highly targeted — but relatively painless — taxes also could meet some non-highway infrastructure needs, says Little. To pay for water infrastructure, "you could put a very small 1-cent-per-roll tax on toilet tissue or on soap. That would create a tremendous amount of money," he says. "We would need a responsible agency to dispense it well, however."

Nevertheless, the Bush administration strongly opposes any tax increases, including the gas-tax hike some members of Congress propose to finance a repair fund for aging bridges.

And one federal lawmaker goes so far as to argue that even cutting gas taxes to decrease the cost of driving in this era of high fuel prices would not harm infrastructure maintenance.

Rep. John "Randy" Kuhl, R-N.Y., has introduced legislation to cut the gas tax by 10 cents a gallon if the price of gas rises above $3. The tax cut wouldn't "hurt money that is directed to the Highway Trust Fund . . . as the lower gas prices will send more people to the pumps and generate similar revenue," said Kuhl in a statement. [14]

Even many who support higher taxes say new revenues might accomplish little without better priority-setting.

Maintenance of current infrastructure often loses out in the political process to flashy, perhaps unnecessary, new projects like ballparks or oversized bridges, says Texas' Sanders. "If you pour more money into a system that favors certain kinds of outcomes, you'll just continue to get the same outcomes."

Even when citizens vote for higher taxes to shore up infrastructure, lawmakers often reserve the option to shift the funding to other purposes, says Little.

In 2002, nearly 70 percent of California voters approved legislative Proposition 42 to allocate a portion of the state sales tax to transportation infrastructure. "But there was a kick-out clause," says USC's Little. "The governor could take the money and spend it for a non-transportation budget emergency" if he chose. "So even when you've had a designated [infrastructure] fund, it still gets robbed," he says.

About $2.5 billion of supposedly dedicated transportation funds has been diverted to other purposes under the state's Proposition 42 escape clause since 2002, according to Transportation California, an advocacy group seeking stronger protection for the funds. [15]

But even if infrastructure agencies can hold onto their funds, they should be required to make more thoughtful use of the money, said Robert Puentes, a fellow in the Metropolitan Policy Program at the centrist Brookings Institution.

"Billions of dollars of additional federal investments, without significant reform, will do precious little to fix our rusting bridges, expand our overcrowded transit systems, or unclog our ports," Puentes said. As a condition of approving any new funding, such as a gas-tax hike, "agencies should set annual performance objectives, and consequences should be established for . . . poor implementation," Puentes said. [16]

Should private companies run more of America's infrastructure?

In search of better financing and efficiency, governments around the United States and worldwide are turning roads, bridges and water systems over to private companies under long-term leases and other arrangements. Critics argue that social equity may be threatened, however, when for-profit operators aggressively raise fees to levels that threaten people's access to public facilities.

"Roads run by private companies tend to be kept up a little better because the companies are under contract and have to do certain things or they don't get paid," says Little, at USC's infrastructure institute.

Private groups "really do look at a road as a business," says Poole of the Reason Foundation. For example, while public agencies will immediately build all the on and off ramps they believe a highway will ever need, "a private company is more likely to "just build some, and leave the option of adding more later," speeding the building process and saving upfront dollars, he says.

A major reason for turning over infrastructure operation to a private enterprise that will collect fees for the service is governments' need to find new sources of funding, say privatization supporters.

"Cities, counties and states are maxing out their debt limits," and many can't pay for new infrastructure, says Richard Norment, executive director of the National Council for Public-Private Partnerships, a membership group. That's where the private sector can step in to help, he says.

"Public-private partnerships tap into a much broader and deeper range of funding sources" than are available to governments alone, says the Reason Foundation's Poole. Governments borrow in the municipal bond market, which has inflexible rules and requires money to be repaid on a fixed schedule, says Poole. Guaranteeing such fixed investor returns on an infrastructure project can become impossible "if a project misses its traffic target for five years," for example, he says.

Private companies, on the other hand, can "tap brand-new equity investment funds" whose investors are paid "only when the project is in the black," Poole explains.

But privatized infrastructure projects also have their downsides. In many cases, "governments may lose more than they gain," said Brookings' Puentes. "All that upfront cash looks sweet, but the long-term revenue stream is lost since all the toll receipts flow directly to the private operators. Governments also lose the option to borrow against those future revenues." [17]

Wasow of the Century Foundation questions whether the private sector will maintain its interest in infrastructure over the long haul. "Will private companies necessarily want to keep running infrastructure projects" as roads and structures age and require greater upkeep? he asks. "The first 10 years after something's constructed you've got low maintenance costs. But over time they'll rise," he says.

Furthermore, "what happens to fairness?" Wasow asks. "Everybody — left, right and center — basically believes that maintaining infrastructure is ultimately the province of government," since infrastructure like roads is, by definition, something that all residents need to go about their daily business, he says. "This means that a reasonable question to ask is, If government is not providing these goods that we all agree are public, what happens to fairness? Should everyone be required to pay private tolls" to use public facilities like water and bridges, even those who make very little money?

Experts on all sides of the issue generally agree that the details of a private-management contract can make or break it.

"The key thing" is making sure that private companies "actually take the risk," and not just rake in profits "while the public sector gets screwed" if the private managers fail or bail, says Lehrer of the Competitive Enterprise Institute. There should be "no explicit or implicit guarantee" that the government will bail out a private entity that gets into trouble managing an infrastructure asset, he says. "I believe the profit system is very good for society, but the flip side is that private entities must be exposed to the loss" if they don't manage projects well.

The key to a project that succeeds is "picking your partners carefully," says Norment. In some high-profile private-management failures, contracts have been awarded for political reasons or through cronyism, he says. A Mexican city whose privatized water system collapsed had awarded the contract to a company owned "by a guy who'd never built a water project before, the brother-in-law of the governor," he says.

But while good contracts are crucial, good infrastructure-contracting practices are "probably hard for local governments to understand" today, says Shama Gamkhar, an associate professor of public affairs at the University of Texas, Austin. While the United States did have private toll roads in the 18th and 19th centuries, in recent memory U.S. toll roads have been operated by governments, as are most water systems. Today, however, privatization of toll-based infrastructure like roads and water is a new trend, and "people just learn [about contract design and management] on the job," she says. "There's not much experience to fall back on."

BACKGROUND

Meeting Needs

The late-19th through the mid-20th century was a time of massive infrastructure building in the United States, from interstate highways to sewer lines and water-treatment plants. And in the days when narrow, unpaved roads made travel a nightmare and untreated sewage contaminated rivers and other drinking-water sources, Americans weren't all that reluctant to ante up dollars for improvements. [18]

So vital was municipal infrastructure that water-treatment and power plants often were conceived as "objects of immense civic pride and sometimes monumental beauty," according to the advocacy group Environmental Defense. Buildings like the Boston Water Works were designed by top architects and became models of design for their communities, their styles copied by residential and commercial builders alike. The facilities "served as potent symbols of common purpose and progress in a young and rapidly growing nation," says the group. [19]

The need for clean drinking water to prevent disease spurred heroic infrastructure-building efforts around the country. At the turn of the 20th century, deadly waterborne diseases like cholera and typhoid killed many Americans, as untreated sewage contaminated drinking-water sources. In 1891, for example, 178 out of every 100,000 Chicago residents died of typhoid. [20]

In Chicago, Rudolph Hering, chief engineer for the water-supply system, carried out the massive project of digging a new channel to reroute the Chicago River away from its natural outlet, Lake Michigan, the source of the city's drinking water. Redirecting the Chicago — the dumping ground for the city's raw sewage and industrial waste — into rivers that drain to the Mississippi River immediately gave the city much cleaner drinking water. [21]

In the nation's drier regions, like Southern California, scarce water also led to massive infrastructure efforts. In 1905, Los Angeles voters approved a $1.5-billion bond issue to erect aqueducts to bring drinking water to the

CHRONOLOGY

1900s-1960s *Federal government helps states build national transportation and water infrastructure.*

1908 Jersey City is first water district to chlorinate drinking water.

1916 Congress enacts Federal-Aid Highway Program, giving federal matching funds to states for road building.

1927 New York City and Jersey City are linked beneath the Hudson River by the Holland Tunnel, named for Clifford Holland, who invented the tunnel's fan system — including an 80-foot-diameter fan — that vents deadly car exhaust.

1940 First section opens on Pennsylvania Turnpike, the first U. S. highway with no cross streets, railroad crossings or traffic lights.

1956 President Dwight D. Eisenhower commits $25 billion to the national highway system, raising the federal funding share from 50 percent to 90 percent.

1965 Major power blackout in the Northeast spurs establishment of North American Electric Reliability Council (NAERC), a public-private consortium of power producers to set voluntary infrastructure standards for the electricity industry.

1970s *Federal role in infrastructure building peaks.*

1972 Clean Water Act spurs localities to enlarge water-treatment plants.

1977 President Jimmy Carter becomes an advocate for dam safety after a 78-year-old dam in his home state of Georgia collapses, killing 39 people.

1980s *Concern grows about aging infrastructure.*

1988 "Fragile Foundations" report by the National Council on Public Works Improvement recommends doubling infrastructure spending.

1990s-2000s *Federal funding is cut for highways and wastewater cleanup as engineers complain about neglected maintenance.*

1993 Sewage in Milwaukee's drinking water kills 100 residents.

2000 Milwaukee's Hoan Bridge partially collapses; no one is injured.

2001 Environmental Protection Agency (EPA) says $151 billion is needed over the next 20 years to upgrade drinking-water systems.

2003 Failure of Michigan's Silver Lake Dam causes $100 million in damage. . . . Electrical-transmission grid fails, blacking out 50 million customers in the Eastern U.S. and Canada for up to 24 hours and shutting down air traffic, mass transit and sewer and water systems. . . . EPA says $390 billion is needed to upgrade wastewater systems over 20 years.

2004 Failure of Mississippi's Big Bay Lake Dam destroys 100 homes. . . . NAERC declares "urgent need" for Congress to replace voluntary reliability standards for electric companies with mandates.

2005 Businesses in Taunton, Mass., close for a week after the 173-year-old, 12-foot-tall wooden Whittenton Mills Dam begins to buckle. . . . New Orleans floods when Hurricane Katrina overwhelms the inadequate levee system. . . . Chicago's Skyway toll bridge comes under private management. . . . More than 10 billion gallons of untreated sewage spill into Lake Erie because of broken pipes and overflows from overburdened local sewage systems in northern Ohio.

2006 Ka Loko Dam in Kauai, Hawaii, fails, killing seven people. . . . Three-hour power failure at a Washington, D.C., sewage-treatment plant spills 17 million gallons of raw sewage into Potomac River.

2007 An 80-year-old underground steam pipe bursts in Manhattan, killing one person. . . . A 95-year-old water pipe breaks in Seattle, cutting off residential water service and creating a sinkhole that swallows two cars. . . . I-35 West bridge over the Mississippi River collapses in Minneapolis at rush hour, sending dozens of cars into the water and killing 13 people. In public opinion poll a week later, two-thirds of the respondents oppose raising gas taxes to fix the nation's bridges.

city from the Owens River, more than 230 miles north of the city. [22]

Even financially conservative leaders supported such infrastructure efforts. In 1956, for example, Republican President Dwight D. Eisenhower signed the Federal-Aid Highway Act, calling for states and the federal government to build a vast Interstate Highway System — 41,000 miles of high-quality roads to link the nation. [23] Spurred by his memory of a 1919 cross-country trip that took U.S. Army vehicles 62 days to travel from Washington, D.C., to San Francisco, hindered by rutted roads and sagging bridges, Eisenhower committed the federal government to assume 90 percent of the cost. [24]

Infrastructure-building programs such as the Works Progress Administration and Civilian Conservation Corps, created as part of President Franklin D. Roosevelt's New Deal initiative in the 1930s and '40s, played key roles in "creating fixed assets for the nation," in the form of dams, bridges, post offices, parks and much more, says Michael Pagano, a professor of public administration at the University of Illinois, Chicago.

Not often considered in the budgets and agendas of such programs, however, was the inescapable fact that time brings more costs, Pagano says. "For the first 20 years, upkeep doesn't cost much," but after that the price of maintenance and replacement inevitably rises, often steeply, "and we just haven't ever incorporated those true costs into our thinking," he says.

Additional factors complicate today's infrastructure-upkeep problem. For one thing, infrastructure is owned and operated by many different entities, including the federal government, states, localities and private companies.

Perhaps surprisingly, about 85 percent of U.S. infrastructure is "owned and operated by the private sector," says Daniel Ostergaard, CEO of a homeland-security consultancy, Pelorus Enterprises, and a senior policy fellow at Western Carolina University's Institute for Economy and Future. About 68 percent of U.S. dams are privately owned, for example, according to the U.S. Army Corps of Engineers. [25]

Private ownership of so many public conveniences "poses a unique challenge for the federal government," which has no direct control over infrastructure like the electrical grid and telecommunications networks but nevertheless is ultimately held responsible for keeping Americans safe and productive, Ostergaard says.

Increasingly, though owned and operated separately, aspects of the national infrastructure rely on each other to function, Ostergaard points out. "We can't just look at the water supply on its own but have to look at the electrical grid," too, for example, since water systems need power to function. "You need a great deal of dialogue" to meet such challenges, and cooperative decision-making isn't easy to promote, he says. "If you look from a purely economic viewpoint, each system looks out for its own best interest."

Another threat to proper maintenance grows out of the fact that infrastructure benefits often cross geographic boundaries, and those who pay most to update or maintain infrastructure aren't necessarily those who benefit most. For example, there is a national benefit to having a well-maintained Interstate Highway System, even in sparsely populated areas, but must local residents shoulder costs for big roads that they themselves don't much need?

Water infrastructure is especially prone to such dilemmas. So-called watershed districts in some states — areas that drain into a specific bay, lake or river system — are government-established entities that have responsibility for water quality and flooding throughout the system. But is it fair to make upstream landowners pay for improvements that will only benefit those downriver? Bitter disagreements over this question have stalled many water projects since water-infrastructure efforts began flourishing in the 19th century, and they continue today.

"There's a responsibility for all residents in the watershed . . . to manage the watershed as a whole," even though some will pay for improvements from which they won't directly benefit, said John Hoopingarner, executive director of the Muskingum watershed district in northeastern Ohio, where debate rages over money for dam and reservoir repairs. [26]

But upstream residents often vigorously disagree. "It's unfair. It's unreasonable," said Tony Zadra, who owns a satellite-dish business in New Philadelphia, an upriver town. "People in the upper highlands aren't responsible for [flood] damage downstream." [27]

"You have a property-tax assessment that doesn't increase property value," said Scott Levengood, a farmer in another upriver town, Mineral City. [28]

Rust Never Sleeps

While funding for upkeep is seldom figured into construction budgets, civil engineers think a lot about the

Should America Take the Toll Road?

With roads aging, economists say tolls make sense

The nation's first private toll road opened in 1794, spanning the 62 miles between Philadelphia and Lancaster. Private toll roads flourished in America's early days, as cash-strapped states turned to private investors to fund roads for farmers, merchants and manufacturers to carry goods to market. [1] Today, privately run toll roads may be making a comeback, as states look for ways to expand and maintain aging, overcrowded highway systems.

Over the past decade, states including California, Indiana, South Carolina, Texas and Virginia have entered agreements with private companies to build and/or operate toll roads, with varying degrees of success, and many more are contemplating such arrangements. In 2006, Chicago signed a 99-year lease with private operators to run the existing Chicago Skyway toll road.

In most agreements, the state retains ownership of the road, bridge or other structure, while a company leases it for a specified period — such as 50 years — agreeing to maintain it while collecting toll revenue. [2]

The draw for states is getting upfront cash — typically paid when the lease is signed — without tapping into the government treasury or borrowing on their own.

When private investors built the Southern Connector toll road around Greenville, S.C., "the state was able to get a $200-million federal interstate built without using precious state resources or using the state bond limit," said Pete Poore, communication director for the South Carolina Transportation Department. [3]

While private toll roads exist in many countries, most Americans are familiar only with some publicly run turnpikes and bridges erected during the interstate-highway building boom that began in the 1950s. Most of the tolls were eliminated once the roads were paid for. But with aging highway infrastructure needing critical maintenance as well as expansion, this is a new day, some transportation analysts say.

"In the past, tolling has been there to build a project, and theoretically you take it off when you've paid off the capital debt," says Jeffrey Buxbaum, a transportation consultant with Massachusetts-based Cambridge Systematics. "But the cost of a highway continues when the debt is paid off," and today's tolls would be permanent, not temporary, funding sources.

Economists have long thought a precisely calibrated, distance-based toll would have been the best means of paying for and maintaining interstate highways, "but it was just too difficult to collect," says Michael Pagano, a professor of public administration at the University of Illinois, Chicago. New technologies are making precise toll-collection feasible, however.

Future tolls also will likely feature "congestion pricing," says Pagano. Sensors in the pavement will "fine tune traffic on a highway" by triggering a rise in tolls — which will be posted on overhead signs — when traffic gets heavy, thus discouraging some drivers from entering the road, Pagano says.

future in trying to design infrastructure to last, although the task is ultimately futile.

"All bridges are going to deteriorate," says the University of Virginia's Baber. But "you use the best materials, the best design and the best maintenance you can afford, such as regular painting. And you use as little road salt as you can to make [the structure] last as long as possible."

In the heyday of American highway building — the 1950s through the 1970s — state-of-the-art bridges were expected to last for around 50 years. But even "state of the art" is only as good as the times.

For example, "in the 1960s, [metal] fatigue wasn't as well understood as it is today," a factor that likely played

a role in the I-35 West bridge collapse, says the University of Maryland's Vannoy.

The bridge "probably wouldn't have been built in the exact same way today," says Baber. The design was fine, based on "what we knew in 1967 but not quite right given what we know in 2007. Right now, we aim to design for 75 years," and more structural redundancy is incorporated, he adds. "You don't see many bridges now with only two load-carrying members. You're more likely to see five or six."

Part of improving upkeep involves learning how to build better in the first place, but research funds aren't always adequate for some important but overlooked infrastructure, such as water systems, some engineers say.

California highways developed under public-private franchise agreements in San Diego and Orange County employ such technology today, according to Robert W. Poole Jr., director of transportation studies at the libertarian Reason Foundation in Los Angeles. "At any time during the day when traffic has built to a maximum, they'll up the rate by 25 cents per mile." The high-tech approach permits toll lanes in one congested California freeway to move at 65 mph even at rush hour, Poole says.

Many economists praise tolling as a way of ensuring that those who benefit from a highway are the same people who pay for it. Toll roads are a way to ensure that "people get what they pay for and pay for what they get," says Thomas A. Firey, managing editor of *Regulation* magazine, published by the libertarian Cato Institute. "Americans deep down really do appreciate fair pricing," so if highway tolls are clearly used to maintain a highway, "then they can probably accept that," he says.

Good lease agreements with private road managers can ensure that acceptance, says Poole. Private companies are "more aggressive in toll revenue — increasing the rates annually," for example, he says. "All the recent, highly publicized public-private partnerships like Chicago's Skyway have an annual index for raising tolls" by linking toll hikes to some measure of general economic change, such as the Consumer Price Index, he says.

Such indexing "wouldn't raise tolls much each year, but over 20 or 30 years the increases make a big difference" in the amount of revenue that could be applied to highway upkeep, Poole says. By contrast, the Indiana public toll roads that were handed over to private management in

2006 "had not had an increase in 19 years," even as the roads deteriorated and the cost of maintenance rose, he says.

But critics of private toll roads argue there's too much room in leasing agreements for money to be shifted away from highway needs and that private companies have no reason to care about the general public that uses their roads.

In the past, "public toll roads built in the United States were designed to provide a high-quality ride for the lowest possible toll" to best serve the public, Gregory M. Cohen, president of the American Highway Users Alliance, told the House Highways and Transit Subcommittee in May.

Under private ownership, however, investors would most likely seek "the highest possible returns," shifting the purpose of toll roads from "maximizing the public good to maximizing profits for investors," Cohen said. "Under such a scenario, tolls are raised regularly, and the process is not subject to public or political review." [4]

[1] For background, see Daniel B. Klein and John Majewski, "Turnpikes and Toll Roads in Nineteenth-Century America," *Encyclopedia*, History of Economics Society, http://eh.net/encyclopedia/article/Klein.Majewski.Turnpikes.

[2] For background, see Robert W. Poole, Jr., "For Whom the Road Tolls," Reason Foundation Web site, February 2006, www.reason.org; Sylvia Smith, "U.S. Public-Private Agreements Have Mixed Record," *The Times of Northwest Indiana*, Jan. 23, 2006, www.thetimesonline.com/articles/2006/01/23/news/top_news/73a0efca3665c38b862570fe001a1bee.txt.

[3] Quoted in Smith, *op. cit.*

[4] Gregory M. Cohen, "Highway Users' Perspectives on Public-Private Partnerships," testimony before House Subcommittee on Highways and Transit, May 24, 2007.

The federal Environmental Protection Agency (EPA) devotes under $10 million a year to drinking-water research, and even taking all private and public research funders together, "I'd be surprised if you get close to $100 million" annually, says Drexel University's Haas. By contrast, hundreds of millions of dollars is probably spent every year to research technology related to the nation's electrical grid, he says.

One of the toughest infrastructure-design problems is predicting future usage. For bridges, "it's very difficult to predict traffic trends more than five or six years in advance," says Baber. "Plus, sometimes the bridge attracts traffic," a particularly difficult thing for planners to foresee, he says. "This has happened to a lot of interstate bridges."

"People in the early 1950s did not envision the 21st century," says USC's Little. For example, the inability of planners to accurately see into the future led designers to focus highway and public-transit systems mainly on accommodating transportation between suburbs and central cities, he says. Today, however, the growing prevalence of suburb-to-suburb travel is helping make the transportation system obsolete.

"We also never anticipated the huge growth in imports," which requires not only expanded ports but highway and rail systems to carry a huge proportion of the country's goods inland, Little says.

Also unanticipated in highway design was the new model for stocking large retail stores that freight-hauling companies and retailers like Wal-Mart and Dell Computer have developed over the past few decades, Little says.

Instead of building large warehouses to store goods awaiting shipment, industry now keep much of the nation's freight cargo on trucks traveling the highways at all times. The resulting huge increase in truck traffic wears down roads that were never built for such constant, heavy loads. [29]

"Trucks are responsible for virtually 100 percent of the damage to the roads" because of their high weight per axle, says transportation consultant Buxbaum.

The trucking problem isn't complex to fix, theoretically, but it would involve a major — expensive — overhaul, says the Reason Foundation's Poole. "One idea that has a lot of promise is a truck-only toll lane" equipped with special "high-strength pavement," he says.

Paying It Forward

Between the mid-1950s and today, overall infrastructure spending has risen annually. But funding hasn't kept up with aging and the rapid development of new demands and technologies. Faulty priority-setting processes also cause problems.

So-called pork-barrel spending — inserted into congressional bills as "earmarks" — is a big problem, says the Reason Foundation's Poole. Ostensibly, members of Congress direct funding to specific local projects to please constituents. But "when I talk to [state transportation] directors, they say the projects they get in the federal bills are . . . way, way down the list," Poole says. [30]

The water pipes and roadways we use most are local, giving Congress little obvious role in those major infrastructure sectors. A federal role comes in when "externalities" — benefits and burdens connected to infrastructure — extend to people outside the region, explains Ghamkar of the University of Texas.

The federal role has applied mostly to new construction, she says. Cars and trucks drive across all states, including the less populous ones in the middle of the country, but sparsely populated areas could not be expected to build national-scale highways on their own, so Congress stepped in.

In a similar way, the Clean Water Act of 1972 acknowledged the federal role in assuring that both upstream and downstream communities get clean drinking water. Because upstream communities dump wastewater into rivers that supply drinking water to people downstream, Congress offered federal grants to improve water-treatment plants everywhere to improve water quality regionally.

Some other infrastructure, such as ports, and air-traffic control, for example, is primarily a national responsibility.

Between 1956 and the mid-1970s, federal spending on infrastructure increased by about 7 percent annually, compared to around 1 percent growth in state and local spending, according to the nonpartisan Congressional Budget Office. The federal share of infrastructure spending peaked in 1977, at 38 percent. [31]

Since then, primary responsibility for most government-funded infrastructure has shifted to states and localities. In 2004, the latest year for which complete data are available, the federal government spent $73.5 billion, or about 24 percent, of the total $312 billion in infrastructure spending in the United States. States and localities spent $238.7 billion. Of the total, $143.6 billion went to project construction, while the remaining $168.7 billion funded operation and maintenance, a proportion that's remained relatively stable for the past two decades, despite infrastructure aging.

About 45 percent of federal funds for maintenance and operation go to run the nation's air-traffic control system, and 60 percent of federal construction funds pay for highway projects. Total spending to build capital projects has grown by about 2 percent per year since 1981, while spending on maintenance and operation has risen 2.1 percent. [32]

While states and localities do the bulk of infrastructure funding and planning, Congress periodically modifies federal law to shore up vital systems. For example, the National Dam Safety Act of 2006 offered grants to improve states' dam-safety programs in response to reports that the number of deteriorating dams is increasing, along with the proportion of the population living in the flood path of a shaky dam. [33]

The bill stopped short of offering federal funding for repairs. Dam safety remains primarily a state and private-sector responsibility. The federal government owns only about 4 percent of the nation's dams, and states have primary oversight responsibility for dams, 68 percent of which are privately owned. [34]

Other infrastructure — such as water and sewage systems and the electrical and telecommunications systems, which are privately owned — is funded by user fees. But charging fees high enough to support upgrades is difficult in those sectors as well.

Utilities constantly face the question — Should we patch or replace infrastructure? says New Jersey sewerage Director Villee. "Logically," that decision would be based "on some cost ratio, like, 'If patching exceeds 50 percent we will replace it,' " Villee says "Unfortunately, factors other than logic often take precedence. Money and politics are two of the major players."

It's like having a 10-year-old car with a transmission problem, Villee says. "Logic says get a new car," but "money says we can't afford that. So you roll the dice, fix the transmission and gamble that you can extend the life of the car until you can pay for a new one. That is the game most utilities play. We defer maintenance and capital improvements to keep rates at a politically acceptable level."

Pedestrians crowd New York City's Queensboro Bridge to Queens on Aug. 14, 2003, after a power blackout crippled the city and much of the Northeastern United States and Canada.

CURRENT SITUATION

Bridge Tax?

Since the Minnesota bridge collapse, Congress has been mulling a tax increase for bridge repair, but President Bush opposes it.

House Transportation and Infrastructure Committee Chairman Oberstar is circulating a plan to hike the federal gas tax by five cents per gallon to repair some 6,000 "structurally deficient" bridges, and Congress is expected to discuss the proposal this fall.

But more taxes won't help, said Transportation Secretary Peters at a Sept. 5 hearing. "It is not that we don't have the money," she said, "it's where we're spending" it. [35]

Democratic and some Republican lawmakers say more money is needed and that congressional "earmarking" of funds to specific projects — criticized by many, including the White House — has increased bridge safety.

Ohio Rep. Steven C. LaTourette, a Republican moderate, said that two structurally deficient bridges in his district are being repaired thanks to congressional earmarks. "To say that all things are not on the table," including a tax hike, "cheats the American motoring public, and I would hope that the administration would rethink its position," LaTourette said. [36]

Academic analysts say a more stable long-term funding source and a means to ensure that money is dedicated to the highest-priority problems are also needed.

The gas-tax boost would be "a nice little stopgap solution," says the University of Illinois' Pagano. But as cars' fuel efficiency increases "revenue collections would still fall" under the plan, he points out.

On Aug. 6, President Bush signed a bill sponsored by the Minnesota congressional delegation to waive the $100-million-per-state limit on federal funding for emergency highway reconstruction and allow up to $250 million in funds for the Minnesota bridge.

How the measure will play out is in doubt, however, since actual funds would only be approved as part of highway appropriations legislation, and Bush has already said he'll veto the "irresponsible and excessive" $104.4 billion appropriations measure that's moving through Congress. [37]

Other Proposals

Debate also rages over the Water Resources Development Act of 2007, a bill that in its current form authorizes — but does not actually appropriate — about $21 billion in funding for projects to be undertaken by the U.S. Army Corps of Engineers. [38]

President Bush has threatened to veto the bill, which he and other critics call an expensive mishmash of pork projects. [39]

Some of the bill's earmarks authorize "a series of costly projects that benefit the rich and influential," said Ronald D. Utt, a senior research fellow at the conservative

Funding Programs Discouraged Smart Planning

Upkeep was often ignored

Local economies and home values depend on infrastructure maintenance, but even programs like federal grants for infrastructure building often have ignored the need for continued upkeep.

"We depend vitally on infrastructure services, and ignoring them can cause trouble for communities" down the line, says Richard Little, director of the Keston Institute for Public Finance and Infrastructure Policy at the University of Southern California.

If a community lets its infrastructure — water, sewer and transportation — languish while neighboring communities don't, "pretty soon businesses will say, 'Let's go somewhere else,' " as potholed roads and sewer overflows mount up, says Little. "People will go to a newer place where there don't seem to be the same problems. Housing values drop, so we all have a real vested interest in maintenance," he says.

Federal grants have helped communities build big projects, such as massive water-treatment plants and 10- or 12-lane roads and bridges, for example. But building big may mean ignoring equally important priorities.

The federal Clean Water Act of 1972 offered grants to encourage communities to improve water-treatment plants, says Linda Kelly, managing director of public communications for the Water Environment Foundation (WEF), a nonprofit advocacy group. The law worked, up to a point, she says.

"People got very excited about putting big water plants in. My own utility had 15 little, bitty wastewater plants and consolidated them into four," says Kelly, former deputy general manager of wastewater treatment in Portland, Ore. Meanwhile, localities were left on their own to oversee — and often ignore — thousands of miles of underground pipes, which are the main source of water-system troubles today, she says. "The big plants were new in the 1970s, but the infrastructure in the ground is upwards of 100 years old."

With federal grants available for big projects — and sometimes not available for smaller projects to cover the same needs — many communities over the years have opted to build the biggest ones they could, whether that was the smartest choice or not.

In one classic care of "overbuilding," in 1976 in Pittsburgh, the large Birmingham Bridge replaced the Brady Street Bridge, which, though only a third the size, was nevertheless "adequate" for the site, says Joel A. Tarr, professor of history and policy at Carnegie-Mellon University's Heinz School of Public Policy and Management.

Planned as part of a larger highway system that never materialized, the bridge was reconfigured for local use. The bridge remains too large for the neighborhood traffic it carries and its redesigned on and off ramps twist and turn to link the bridge with local streets it was originally meant to bypass.

"Why is it so big? Because that's the only way they could get funding," says Tarr.

Similar structures abound nationwide, says Michael Pagano, professor of public administration at the University of Illinois, Chicago. Cities and states should have asked, "Do we need 12-lane roads?" Pagano says. Instead, many localities draw up the grandest plans they can to snag federal grants that often favor the biggest projects. Under the Clean Water Act, the federal government would pay 75 percent of the cost, Pagano says. "So the obvious response was, 'Hell, I'll build the biggest plant I can get.' "

Federal grants also sometimes encourage infrastructure neglect, says Heywood Sanders, a professor of public administration at the University of Texas, San Antonio. If a city can get federal funds for a major overhaul, it's easy for local officials to neglect routine maintenance for which they'd have to spend their own money, he says.

"The other big problem with federal funding is the transfer of money among the states," says Robert W. Poole Jr., director of transportation studies at the libertarian Reason Foundation in Los Angeles. The grant formula "was created to get interstate highways built" through sparsely populated regions like Montana that didn't need the highways for their own use. That meant that low-population, low-growth areas get considerably more money than they would if grants were based on population numbers, he says.

But as infrastructure ages, current highway needs run in exactly the opposite direction, Poole says. Today's top transportation need is for upgrades and expansion in the top 25 urban areas, all located in states that get less than the average per-capita share of federal grants, he says.

Within states, a similar problem makes it hard to direct funds to the high-population areas with roads most in need of expansion and heavy-duty maintenance, says Poole. For political reasons, "you have to share the money among all the legislative districts," no matter how little some may need the funds.

Over the years, Congress has made a few attempts to shift more grant money to high-population states but the Senate — where low-density states have equal representation with high-density states — has successfully fought such efforts, Poole says. "There's not much chance" formulas will change in the foreseeable future, he says.

Are toll roads the best way to maintain highways and bridges?

YES
Robert W. Poole Jr.
Director of Transportation Studies, The Reason Foundation

From testimony before House Subcommittee on Highways and Transit, Feb. 13, 2007

To properly maintain of our highways and bridges, we should be spending $6 billion more every year. And to improve the system, to cope with increases in auto and truck travel, we should be spending $51 billion more every year.

The existing state and federal fuel tax and highway trust-fund system seems to be unable to meet these investment needs. Neither the Congress nor most state legislatures have increased fuel taxes to levels that would even offset increases in fuel efficiency and the ravages of inflation, let alone cope with increased travel demand. So increasingly, states are turning to toll finance and public-private partnerships (PPPs). . . .

The newest trend is the long-term concession model, in which an investor-owned company will finance, design, build, operate, modernize and maintain a highway project, financing its expenditures from toll revenues. What this model is all about is extending the investor-owned utility concept from network industries like electricity and telecommunications to the network industry of limited-access highways. This model is what built most of the postwar toll motorway systems in France, Italy, Portugal and Spain, and the trend has more recently spread to Australia, Latin America, Canada, Britain, Germany and other countries.

PPPs offer access to large, new sources of capital; the ability to raise larger sums for toll projects and shift risk from taxpayers to investors.

Long-term concessions are a good vehicle for organizing multi-state projects such as truck-only toll lanes to serve major shipping routes. These projects need to be developed in a unified manner, but individual states are not well-positioned to develop such unified projects; concession companies are.

Comparing the typical U.S. state-run toll agency with the typical European or Australian toll road company, it's clear that the latter are far more customer-oriented, more innovative and generally more commercial. Many state-operated toll agencies are run by short-term political appointees rather than by career toll-road professionals. . . .

One of the most important advantages of investor-owned toll-road companies is their motivation to innovate to solve difficult problems or improve their service, such as by varying tolls to discourage traffic congestion.

None of the transactions that have occurred or are being planned — either for existing toll roads or for new ones — involves the sale of any roads. The government remains the owner at all times, with the private partner carrying out only the tasks spelled out for it.

NO
Bill Graves
President, American Trucking Associations (ATA)

From testimony before House Subcommittee on Highways and Transit, May 24, 2007

We strongly believe that while private financing of highway infrastructure may play a limited role in addressing future transportation needs, certain practices may generate unintended consequences whose costs will vastly exceed their short-term economic benefits. We are very concerned about attempts by some states to carve up the most important segments of the highway system for long-term lease. . . .

Highway user fees should be reasonably uniform in application among classes of highway users and be based chiefly on readily verifiable measures of highway and vehicle use. ATA believes that fuel taxes meet the above criteria, while tolls fail on certain critical points.

Fuel-tax evasion is relatively low compared to other highway user fees. Tolls, on the other hand, are often easily evaded, usually by motorists using alternative, less safe routes that were not built to handle high levels of traffic. There are significant capital and operating costs associated with collecting tolls, while fuel taxes are relatively inexpensive to administer.

Private toll-road operators need not be concerned about the social impacts of toll rates on low-income workers or on the costs to businesses that depend on the highway. Nor do private operators care about the extent of traffic diversion to lesser quality, usually less safe, roads. Their sole concern is to maximize the toll road's profitability. . . .

Privatization boosters point to caps on toll-rate increases that have been a standard part of privatization agreements. However, the two major lease agreements that have been completed in the United States — the Indiana Toll Road and Chicago Skyway — have been accompanied by very large initial rate increases combined with caps on future increases. . . .

It has been suggested that these massive toll-rate escalations are unrealistic because, as has been demonstrated on other facilities, including the Ohio Turnpike, raising the toll rate too high forces significant traffic off the highway. However, the lessee will set a toll rate to a level that maximizes profitability, not traffic.

Indeed, a recent financial report by [Australia-based toll-road developer Macquarie Infrastructure Group] revealed that while traffic on the Indiana Toll Road's barrier system — jointly operated by Macquarie and Spain-based Cintra Concesiones de Infraestructuras de Transport — actually declined by 1.6 percent between July 2006 and March 2007, and increased by just 0.2 percent on the ticket system, revenues shot up by a whopping 46.2 percent due to large toll-rate increases.

A helicopter prepares to drop a sandbag in an attempt to plug the breached London Avenue Canal levee in New Orleans in the wake of flooding caused by Hurricane Katrina in September 2005.

Heritage Foundation. "Notwithstanding continuing concern" over flood protection for cities like New Orleans, "this Congress appears intent on diverting taxpayer dollars . . . to water-sports and other low-priority schemes." [40]

Some congressional Republicans, including self-described fiscal conservatives like Sen. James M. Inhofe of Oklahoma, top-ranking Republican on the Senate Environment and Public Works Committee, strongly oppose Bush's veto threat. [41]

Congress has also held hearings this year on the idea of turning more infrastructure over to private companies for management. "The battle has been joined" over the value of privately operated toll roads, with the Bush administration a strong proponent, says the Reason Foundation's Poole.

Some key Democrats have been highly skeptical, however. In a May 10 letter to state officials, Transportation Committee Chairman Oberstar and

Rep. Peter DeFazio, D-Ore., warned against "rushing" into public-private partnerships (PPPs) and said their committee would undo any such agreements "that do not fully protect the public interest." In June, however, the lawmakers softened their stance, saying that "under the right circumstances and conditions," PPPs can be efficient and effective. [42]

Also in the legislative mix, though receiving little attention, is a proposal by Sens. Christopher J. Dodd, D-Conn., and Chuck Hagel, R-Neb., for an independent federal entity, the National Infrastructure Bank. It would analyze infrastructure projects costing $75 million or more and report to Congress on how to prioritize and pay for them. [43]

The Minnesota bridge collapse spurred quick action by many state and local governments to step up monitoring and repair of aging bridges. On Aug. 29, the Missouri Legislature approved a plan to repair 802 bridges in the next five years, about four times as many as previously contemplated. Tennessee will inspect bridges annually, up from the two-year inspection cycle federal law requires. Wisconsin will install stress sensors to monitor the state of 14 bridges that are more than 50 years old. [44]

In general, states are making better progress than the federal government on improving decision-making processes, says Poole. In California, a state Transportation Commission with members appointed by government bodies with various missions sets priorities. "There is some politics still, but they do a reasonably good job," says the Reason Foundation's Poole.

Some state and local leaders are spotlighting infrastructure needs. Atlanta Mayor Shirley Franklin conducted an aggressive public-awareness campaign on the city's long-neglected water system, "and now the community is funding it," says the Water Environment Foundation's Kelly.

But public support may not be as tough a sell as many believe, says transportation consultant Buxbaum. "Washington state has passed two gas tax increases" in just the past few years, after the state "built more accountability and transparency" into the highway-construction process, he says.

Buxbaum acknowledges that funding may be easier to get in the West, where infrastructure is still being built. Eastern states must mainly fund repairs, and "that's not as sexy," he says.

OUTLOOK

Threats Increase

Infrastructure problems won't get easier to resolve as systems age, population grows and developments like global warming change the very nature of the challenge.

But while problems continue to simmer, most analysts believe the public interest sparked by the Minnesota bridge collapse will be fleeting. "I've learned that the half-life of the public attitude on this issue is very short," says former Corps of Engineers chief Hatch.

Nevertheless, technological developments may make prioritizing maintenance tasks easier, says Harvey Mudd's Duron, who has developed sensors to measure internal threats to a structure's stability that inspectors can't pick up visually.

Such sensors could be attached to structures at all times, at regularly scheduled times throughout the year, or during stressful times — such as during repairs, when the I-35 West bridge collapsed — Duron says. Technology is making it possible to get "a real-time assessment of changing conditions" that can trigger structural failure, and the cost is dropping, he says. Armed with that information, engineers will be better able to explain to policy makers which projects are highest priority, Duron says.

But while technology may help, other changes will increase infrastructure strains.

Climate change will likely trigger more extreme storms and floods, including massive floods in mountainous regions caused by the melting of natural "ice dams" that form glacial lakes today, according to the International Rivers Network. "The world's more than 45,000 existing large dams have not been built to allow for a rapidly intensifying hydrological cycle," says a 2005 article in the group's journal, *World Rivers Review*. [45]

More regions may face drought as climate changes, and that will require attention to water-system deficiencies, says Nancy Connery, an infrastructure consultant in Woolwich, Maine, who chaired the congressionally created National Council on Public Works Improvement in the 1980s. "So much water is lost today, so many leaks and so much flushed down the toilet," she says. "This is a very expensive problem, and one we'll have to face sooner than we imagine."

The future will demand "dramatically new ideas" about infrastructure, perhaps even a new version of the

A car rests against a tree near Purvis, Miss., after a dam holding back Big Bay Lake collapsed, flooding more than 50 homes on March 13, 2004. There are 10,094 dams in the United States whose failure could cause loss of life, according to the American Society of Civil Engineers.

early 20th-century era when infrastructure building was seen as heroic, says Connery.

For example, the myriad small drinking-water systems around the country might be re-envisioned as "regional, networked operations" that share an expert staff, Connery says. But attaining such efficiencies of scale would require new incentives for agencies to inform the public about their operations and to cooperate with each other, she says.

As an example of the innovative thinking she hopes to see more of, Connery cites a small company that tried to run fiber-optic cable carrying broadband Internet house to house alongside existing sewer lines. The plan ultimately stalled after Hurricane Katrina hit their planned roll-out city, New Orleans, in 2005. Nevertheless, the scheme represents "the kind of imaginative idea that could build excitement," she says. "There's so much more that's possible."

Infrastructure "is not about engineering, and it's not about financing," says Little at USC's infrastructure institute. "It's about what we want to leave to our grandchildren, and that's more than blue sky and green trees. It's the infrastructure that allows us to live," he says. "Neglecting it is a failure of imagination."

NOTES

1. For background, see "Driver Who Survived Bridge Collapse: 'I Can't Believe I'm Alive,' " CNN.com, Aug. 3, 2007, www.cnn.com/2007/US/08/02/bridge.survivors/index.html.

2. For background, see James Barron, "Steam Blast Jolts Midtown, Killing One," *The New York Times*, July 19, 2007, p. B4.

3. For background, see "Report Card for America's Infrastructure," American Society of Civil Engineers, www.asce.org/reportcard.

4. Quoted in Laurie Blake, *et al.*, "MnDOT Feared Cracking in Bridge but Opted Against Making Repairs," [Minneapolis] *Star Tribune*, Aug. 3, 2007, p. 1A, www.startribune.com.

5. For background, see William Yardley, "U.S. Faces a Sinkhole Epidemic As Its Century-Old Water and Sewer Infrastructure Leaks and Erodes," *The New York Times*, Feb. 8, 2007, p. A19; Chris Mayer, "The Sinkhole Syndrome," *The Daily Wealth blog*, May 8. 2007, www.dailywealth.com; Thomas Rooney, "The Looming Sinkhole Crisis," March 28, 2007, *Los Angeles Times*, p. A21.

6. "The Need for a National Dam Rehabilitation Program," Dam Safety Coalition, www.damsafetycoalition.org.

7. For background, see Robert Puentes and Ryan Prince, "Fueling Transportation Finance: A Primer on the Gas Tax," Brookings Institution Center on Urban and Metropolitan Policy, March 2003, www.brookings.org.

8. Quoted in Frederic J. Frommer, "Push to Raise Gas Tax for Bridget Repairs," The Associated Press, Sept. 6, 2007, http://ap.google.com.

9. "President Bush Discusses American Competitiveness Initiative During Press Conference," transcript, White House press conference, Aug. 9, 2007, www.whitehouse.gov/news/releases/2007/08/20070809-1.html.

10. Quoted in Megan Tady, "A Win in the Water War," *In These Times* Web site, Aug. 1, 2007, www.inthesetimes.com.

11. Dam Safety Coalition, *op. cit.*

12. Gaylord Shaw, "The Enormous U.S. Dam Problem No One Is Talking About," *The Christian Science Monitor*, Jan. 3, 2006, p. 9.

13. Thomas Rooney, "Fixing Failing Pipes Is a Public Health Issue," *The Chief Engineer* Web site, www.chiefengineer.org.

14. "Kuhl Reintroduces Gas Price Relief Bill," press release, http://kuhl.house.gov/News/DocumentPrint.aspx?DocumentID_65980.

15. For background, see "Transportation California Is Working to Close the Proposition 42 Loophole," Transportation California, www.transportationca.com/displaycommon.cfm?an=1&subarticlenbr=156.

16. Robert Puentes, "Don't Raise that Gas Tax . . . Yet!" position statement, Aug. 22, 2007, www.brookings.edu.

17. Robert Puentes, "Cashing in on the BP Beltway," op-ed originally published in the *Hartford Courant*, March 1, 2007, www.brookings.edu/views/op-ed/puentes/20070301_beltway.htm.

18. For background, see "Trends in Public Spending on Transportation and Water Infrastructure, 1956 to 2004," Congressional Budget Office, August 2007, www.cbo.gov; Kate Asher, The Works: Anatomy of a City (2005); Joel A. Tarr, ed., *Devastation and Renewal: An Environmental History of Pittsburgh and its Region* (2005).

19. Michael Singer, Ramon J. Cruz and Jason Bregman, "Infrastructure and Community," Environmental Defense, 2007.

20. "Reversal of the Chicago River," Of Time and the River Web site, Illinois Department of Natural Resources, www.oftimeandtheriver.org. For background, see Richard L. Worsnop, "Water Resources and National Water Needs," *Editorial Research Reports*, 1965, Vol. II, *CQ Researcher Plus Archives*, www.cqpress.com.

21. "Water Supply and Distribution History II — Early Years," Greatest Engineering Achievements of the 20th Century, National Academy of Engineering, www.greatestachievements.org.

22. "Water Supply and Distribution III — Thirsty Cities," Greatest Engineering Achievements of the 20th Century, National Academy of Engineering, www.greatestachievements.org.

23. For background, see David Hosansky, "Traffic Congestion," *CQ Researcher*, Aug. 27, 1999, pp. 729-752; W. Street, "Interstate Highway System at 25," *Editorial Research Reports 1981*, Vol. II; M. Packman, "New Highways," *Editorial Research Reports 1954*, Vol. II; and B. W. Patch, "Federal Highway Aid and the Depression," *Editorial Research Reports 1932*, Vol. II, all available at *CQ Researcher Plus Archives*, www.cqpress.com.

24. Daniel Schulman and James Ridgeway, "The Highwaymen," *Mother Jones*, January/February 2007, www.motherjones.com.

25. Dam Safety Coalition, *op. cit.*

26. Quoted in Robert Wang, "District Raises Taxes Without a Vote," *The Canton* [Ohio] Repository, Aug. 26, 2007, p. 1A.

27. Quoted in *ibid.*

28. *Ibid.*

29. For background, see Kathy Koch, "Truck Safety," *CQ Researcher*, March 12, 1999, pp. 209-232.

30. For background, see Marcia Clemmitt, "Pork-Barrel Politics," *CQ Researcher*, June 16, 2006, pp. 529-552.

31. "Trends in Public Spending on Transportation and Water Infrastructure, 1956 to 2004," Congressional Budget Office, August 2007, www.cbo.gov.

32. *Ibid.*

33. Dam Safety Coalition, *op. cit.*

34. *Ibid.*

35. Quoted in Kathryn A. Wolfe, "Funding to Repair Bridges Caught in Ideological Gap," *CQ Today*, Sept. 5, 2007.

36. Quoted in *ibid.*

37. *Ibid.*

38. For background, see David Hosansky, "Reforming the Corps," *CQ Researcher*, May 30, 2003, pp. 497-520.

39. For background, see Avery Palmer, "No Conflict Seen in Water Resources Bill, Earmarks and Ethics Measure," *CQ Today*, Sept. 4, 2007.

40. Ronald D. Utt, *The Water Resources Development Act of 2007: A Pork Fest for Wealthy Beach-Front Property Owners*, Heritage Foundation, May 15, 2007, www.heritage.org/Research/Budget/wm1458.cfm.

41. Palmer, *op. cit.*

42. Quoted in Ken Orski, "Committee Chairs Soften Stance Against Public-Private Transportation Deals," *Budget and Tax News*, The Heartland Institute, August 2007, www.heartland.org.

43. "Bill Proposes National Infrastructure Bank," *WaterWeek*, American Water Works Association, Aug. 3, 2007, www.awwa.org.

44. Judy Keen, "States Act Swiftly on Bridge Repairs," *USA Today*, Sept. 3, 2007, p. 1A.

45. Patrick McCully, "And the Walls Came Tumbling Down: Dam Safety Concerns Grow in Wake of Failures, Changing Climate," *World Rivers Review*, June 2005, www.irn.org.

BIBLIOGRAPHY

Books

Ascher, Kate, *The Works: Anatomy of a City*, Penguin Press, 2005.
The executive director of the New York City Economic Development Corporation explains how the city's complex infrastructure works and what maintenance engineers and planners do to keep it running.

Tarr, Joel A., ed., *Devastation and Renewal: An Environmental History of Pittsburgh and Its Region*, University of Pittsburgh Press, 2005.
Essays assembled by a Carnegie Mellon University professor of history and policy detail the conflicting roles of money, politics, industry and the environment in shaping the infrastructure of Pittsburgh and the surrounding region.

Articles

Duke, Kenny, "If the Feds Can't Fix the Bridge, Should We?" *The Cincinnati Post*, Aug. 29, 2007.
A Kentucky state senator proposes a new state finance authority with the power to sell bonds and impose tolls to fund the huge rebuilding projects required by the aging national highway system, such as bridges over the Ohio River.

Hughes, John, and Angela Greiling Keane, "Bridge Disaster Fuels Push to Raise Tax for Repairs," Bloomberg.com, Aug. 20, 2007, www.bloomberg.com/apps/news?pid= 20601103&sid=aUfj43QPplT8&refer=us.
The recent bridge collapse in Minneapolis puts new pressure on federal lawmakers and 2008 presidential candidates to offer plans for future infrastructure funding and priority setting.

Shaw, Gaylord, "The Enormous U.S. Dam Problem No One Is Talking About," *The Christian Science Monitor*, Jan. 3, 2006.
A long-time reporter on dam safety argues that state and federal neglect has led to catastrophic dam failures in the past and threatens to allow more in the future.

Reports and Studies

Hargen, David T., and Ravi K. Karanam, *16th Annual Report on the Performance of State Highway Systems*, The Reason Foundation, June 2007.
A libertarian think tank specializing in transportation issues state-by-state rankings of road performance, capacity and funding.

Drinking Water Distribution Systems: Assessing and Reducing Risks, Committee on Public Water Supply Distribution Systems, National Research Council, 2006.
A national expert panel pinpoints the top priorities in maintaining and upgrading drinking-water systems and describes how new technologies may increase safety.

The Fuel Tax and Alternatives for Transportation Funding, Transportation Research Board, 2006.
A national expert panel examines the history and potential of fuel taxes as the primary funding source for transportation infrastructure and concludes that direct user fees are a better option for the future.

2006 Long-Term Reliability Assessment: The Reliability of the Bulk Power Systems in North America, North American Electric Reliability Council, October 2006.
The industry council that sets voluntary standards for electrical-power delivery finds that in the next decade electricity demands will far outstrip planned maintenance and capacity-building by power-generation and transmission companies.

Privatization of Water Services in the United States: An Assessment of Issues and Experience, Committee on Privatization of Water Services in the United States, National Research Council, 2002.
A national expert panel summarizes the history of U.S. water and wastewater utilities and dissects pros and cons of various privatization schemes.

Report Card for America's Infrastructure 2005, American Society of Civil Engineers, March 2005, www.asce.org/reportcard/2005/page.cfm?id=203.
The most recent in a series of periodic infrastructure assessments by a public-works engineers' group analyzes infrastructure health sector by sector and state by state and references local media coverage of infrastructure issues. The ASCE gives the overall U.S. infrastructure a grade of "D."

Surface Transportation: Strategies Are Available for Making Existing Road Infrastructure Perform Better, Government Accountability Office, July 2007.
Congress' nonpartisan auditing office concludes that greater private-sector involvement, expansion of user tolls and management reforms including the setting of performance measures would improve America's roads.

Trends in Public Spending on Transportation and Water Infrastructure, 1956 to 2004, Congressional Budget Office, August 2007.
Congress' nonpartisan financial-analysis office describes historical patterns in federal and state infrastructure spending for dams, mass transit, railways, air-traffic control and other systems.

For More Information

American Association of State Highway and Transportation Officials, 444 N Capitol St., N.W., Suite 249, Washington, DC 20001; (202) 624-5800; www.transportation.org. Represents state highway departments.

American Public Works Association, 1401 K St., N.W., 11th Floor, Washington, DC 20005; (202) 408-9541; www.apwa.net. Provides information and analysis on infrastructure-related public policy.

American Society of Civil Engineers, 1801 Alexander Bell Dr., Reston, VA 20191-4400; (703) 295-6300; www.asce.org. Issues a periodic report card on U.S. infrastructure needs and updates a list of infrastructure-related news stories.

American Water Works Association, 6666 W. Quincy Ave., Denver, CO 80235; (303) 794-7711; www.awwa.org. Provides information and public-policy analysis.

Federal Highway Administration, U.S. Department of Transportation, 1200 New Jersey Ave., S.E., Washington, DC 20590; www.fhwa.dot.gov. Monitors bridge and highway safety and transportation funding needs.

Greatest Engineering Achievements of the Twentieth Century, National Academy of Engineering; www.greatachievements.org. Web site that details the modern history of infrastructure systems including roads and water systems.

Keston Institute for Public Finance and Infrastructure Policy, School of Policy, Planning, and Development, Marshall School of Business, University of Southern California, Ralph and Goldy Lewis Hall 232, Los Angeles, CA 90089-0626; (213) 740-4120; www.usc.edu/schools/sppd/keston/index.php. Provides research and analysis on California and national infrastructure issues.

National Council for Public-Private Partnerships, 1660 L St., N.W., Suite 510, Washington, DC 20036; (202) 467-6800; http://ncppp.org. Organization of businesses and public officials interested in joint initiatives to provide public services.

Reason Foundation, 3415 S. Sepulveda Blvd. Suite 400, Los Angeles, CA 90034; (310) 391-2245; www.reason.org/index.shtml. Libertarian think tank that analyzes transportation-infrastructure problems and issues reports on highways.

Water Environment Foundation, 601 Wythe St., Alexandria, VA 22314-1994; (800) 666-0206; www.wef.org/Home. Provides information and public-policy advocacy on water-quality issues.

14

Immigration Debate

Alan Greenblatt

A Mexican farmworker harvests broccoli near Yuma, Ariz. With the number of illegal immigrants in the U.S. now over 12 million — including at least half of the nation's 1.6 million farmworkers — tougher enforcement has become a dominant theme in the 2008 presidential campaign. Meanwhile, with Congress unable to act, states and localities have passed hundreds of bills cracking down on employers and illegal immigrants seeking public benefits.

From *CQ Researcher*, February 1, 2008.

John McCain, the senior senator from Arizona and the leading Republican candidate for president, has been hurt politically by the immigration issue.

McCain would allow illegal immigrants to find a way eventually to become citizens. The approach is seen by many Republican politicians and voters (and not a few Democrats) as akin to "amnesty," in effect rewarding those who broke the law to get into this country. Legislation that he helped craft with Sen. Edward M. Kennedy, D-Mass., and the White House went down to defeat in both 2006 and 2007.

McCain rejects the approach taken by House Republicans during a vote in 2005 and favored by several of his rivals in the presidential race — namely, classifying the 12 million illegal immigrants already in this country as felons and seeking to deport them. This wouldn't be realistic, he says, noting not only the economic demands that have brought the foreign-born here in the first place but also the human cost such a widespread crackdown would entail.

On the stump, McCain talks about an 80-year-old woman who has lived illegally in the United States for 70 years and has a son and grandson serving in Iraq. When challenged at Clemson University last November by a student who said he wanted to see all illegal immigrants punished, McCain said, "If you're prepared to send an 80-year-old grandmother who's been here 70 years back to some other country, then frankly you're not quite as compassionate as I am." [1]

As the issue of illegal immigrants reaches the boiling point, however, and as he gains in the polls, even McCain sounds not quite so compassionate as before. In response to political pressures, McCain now shares the point of view of hard-liners who say stronger border security must come before allowing additional work permits or the

California Has Most Foreign-Born Residents

California's nearly 10 million foreign-born residents represented about one-quarter of the national total in 2006 and more than twice as many as New York.

Foreign-Born Individuals by State, 2006 *

Over 1 million	
500,000-999,999	
200,000-499,999	
100,000-199,999	
0-99,999	

* Includes legal and illegal immigrants

Source: Migration Policy Institute

about two suspects in a triple murder in New Jersey who turned out to be illegal immigrants. He argued that President Bush should call Congress into special session to address the matter, calling himself "sickened" by Congress being in recess "while young Americans are being massacred by people who shouldn't be here."

Gingrich said Bush should be more serious about "winning the war here at home, which is more violent and more dangerous to Americans than Iraq or Iran." [4]

Concerns about terrorism have also stoked fears about porous borders and unwanted intruders entering the country.

"Whenever I'm out with a [presidential] candidate at a town hall meeting, it's the exception when they do not get a question about immigration — whether it's a Democratic event or a Republican event," says Dan Balz, a veteran political reporter at *The Washington Post*.

With no resolution in sight to the immigration debate in Congress, the number of immigrant-related bills introduced in state legislatures tripled last year, to more than 1,500. Local communities are also crafting their own immigration policies. (*See sidebar, p. 330.*)

In contrast to the type of policies pursued just a few years ago, when states were extending benefits such as in-state tuition to illegal immigrants, the vast majority of current state and local legislation seeks to limit illegal immigrants' access to public services and to crack down on employers who hire them.

"For a long time, the American public has wanted immigration enforcement," says Ira Mehlman, media director of the Federation for American Immigration Reform (FAIR), which lobbies for stricter immigration limits.

"Is there a rhetorical consensus for the need for immigration control? The answer is clearly yes," Mehlman says. "When even John McCain is saying border security and enforcement have to come first before the amnesty he really wants, then there is really a consensus."

"path to citizenship" that were envisioned by his legislation.

"You've got to do what's right, OK?" McCain told *The New Yorker* magazine recently. "But, if you want to succeed, you have to adjust to the American people's desires and priorities." [2]

Immigration has become a central concern for a significant share of the American public. Immigrants, both legal and illegal, are now 12.6 percent of the population — more than at any time since the 1920s.

Not only is the number of both legal and illegal immigrants — now a record 37.9 million — climbing rapidly but the foreign-born are dispersing well beyond traditional "gatekeeper" states such as California, New York and Texas, creating social tensions in places with fast-growing immigrant populations such as Georgia, Arkansas and Iowa. [3]

Complaints about illegal immigrants breaking the law or draining public resources have become a daily staple of talk radio programs, as well as CNN's "Lou Dobbs Tonight."

In a high-profile speech in August 2007, Newt Gingrich, a former Republican House Speaker, railed

While most of the Republican presidential candidates are talking tougher on immigration today than two or three years ago, Democrats also are espousing the need for border security and stricter enforcement of current laws. But not everyone is convinced a majority of the public supports the "enforcement-only" approach that treats all illegal immigrants — and the people that hire them — as criminals.

"All through the fall, even with the campaign going on, the polls consistently showed that 60 to 70 percent of the public supports a path to citizenship," says Tamar Jacoby, a senior fellow at the Manhattan Institute who has written in favor of immigrant absorption into U.S. society.

There's a core of only about 20 to 25 percent of Americans who favor wholesale deportation, Jacoby says. "What the candidates are doing is playing on the scare 'em territory."

But over the last couple of years, in the congressional and state-level elections where the immigration issue has featured most prominently, the candidates who sought to portray themselves as the toughest mostly lost.

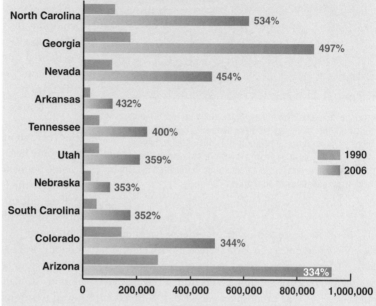

Fastest-Growing Foreign-Born Populations

Foreign populations at least tripled in 10 states since 1990. In North Carolina foreign-born residents increased by a record 534 percent.

Percentage Increases in Foreign-Born Individuals, 1990-2006

State	Percentage
North Carolina	534%
Georgia	497%
Nevada	454%
Arkansas	432%
Tennessee	400%
Utah	359%
Nebraska	353%
South Carolina	352%
Colorado	344%
Arizona	334%

1990
2006

Number of Immigrants in State

* Includes legal and illegal immigrants

Source: Migration Policy Institute

Some analysts believe that, despite the amount of media attention the issue has attracted, anti-immigrant hard-liners may have overplayed their hand, ignoring the importance of immigrant labor to a shifting U.S. economy.

"To be energized we need new workers, younger workers, who are going to be a part of the whole economy. We don't have them here in the United States," Sen. Kennedy told National Public Radio in 2006.

"We need to have the skills of all of these people," he continued. "The fact is, this country, with each new wave of immigrants, has been energized and advanced, quite frankly, in terms of its economic, social, cultural and political life. I don't think we ought to fear it, we ought to welcome it." [5]

Polls have made it clear that the Republican Party, which is seen as generally tougher on the issue, is losing support among Hispanics — the fastest-growing segment of the population.

"The Bush strategy — enlightened on race, smart on immigration — developed in Texas and Florida with Jeb Bush — has been replaced by the Tancredo-Romney strategy, which is demonizing and scapegoating immigrants," said Simon Rosenberg, a Democratic strategist, "and that is a catastrophic event for the Republican Party." [6] Jeb Bush, the president's brother, served two terms as governor of Florida, while Colorado Rep. Tom Tancredo and former Massachusetts Gov. Mitt Romney each sought this year's GOP presidential nomination. *

---

* Tancredo dropped out in December, and Romney has been trailing McCain in the primaries.

A prospective employer in Las Vegas holds up two fingers indicating how many day laborers he needs. One of the few pieces of immigration legislation still considered to have a chance in Congress this year is the SAVE Act, which would require all employers to use an electronic verification system to check the legal status of all workers.

There is a well-known precedent backing up Rosenberg's argument. In 1994, Pete Wilson, California's Republican governor, pushed hard for Proposition 187, designed to block illegal immigrants from receiving most public services. The proposition passed and Wilson won reelection, but it turned Hispanic voters in California against the GOP — a shift widely believed to have turned the state solidly Democratic.

"While there might be some initial appeal to trying to beat up on immigrants in all different ways, it ultimately isn't getting to the question of what you do with 12 million people," says Angela Kelley, director of the Immigration Policy Center at the American Immigration Law Foundation, which advocates for immigrants' legal rights. "It isn't a problem we can enforce our way out of."

But it's not a problem politicians can afford to ignore. There will be enormous pressure on the next president and Congress to come up with a package that imposes practical limits on the flow of illegal immigrants into the United States. Doing so while balancing the economic interests that immigrant labor supports will remain no less of a challenge, however.

That's in part because the immigration debate doesn't fall neatly along partisan lines. Pro-GOP business groups, for example, continue to seek a free flow of labor, while unions and other parts of the Democratic coalition fear just that.

"The Democrats tend to like immigrants, but are suspicious of immigration, while the Republicans tend to like immigration but are suspicious of immigrants," says Frank Sharry, executive director of the National Immigration Forum, a pro-immigration lobby group.

"Republicans want to deport 12 million people while starting a guest worker program," he says. "With Democrats, it's the reverse."

During a Republican debate in Florida last December, presidential candidate and former Massachusetts Gov. Mitt Romney took a less draconian position, moving away from his earlier calls to deport all illegals. "Those who have come illegally, in my view, should be given the opportunity to get in line with everybody else," he said. "But there should be no special pathway for those that have come here illegally to jump ahead of the line or to become permanent residents or citizens." [7]

One of the loudest anti-immigration voices belongs to Republican Oklahoma state Rep. Randy Terrill, author of one of the nation's toughest anti-immigration laws, which went into effect in December 2007. "For too long, our nation and our state have looked the other way and ignored a growing illegal immigration crisis," he said. "Oklahoma's working families should not be forced to subsidize illegal immigration. With passage of House bill 1804, we will end that burden on our citizens." [8] Among other things, the law gives state and local law enforcement officials the power to enforce federal immigration law.

As the immigration debate rages on, here are some of the specific issues that policy makers are arguing about:

Should employers be penalized for hiring illegal immigrants?

For more than 20 years, federal policy has used employers as a checkpoint in determining the legal status of workers. It's against the law for companies to knowingly hire illegal immigrants, but enforcement of this law has been lax, at best.

Partly as a result — but also because of the growing attention paid to illegal immigrants and the opportunities that may attract them to this country — the role of business in enforcing immigration policy has become a major concern.

"I blame 90 percent on employers," says Georgia state Sen. Chip Rogers. "They're the ones that are profiting by breaking the law."

The Immigration and Customs Enforcement agency has pledged to step up its efforts to punish employers who knowingly hire undocumented workers. In response, an Electrolux factory in Springfield, Tenn., fired more than 150 immigrant workers in December after Immigration and Customs Enforcement (ICE) agents arrested a handful of its employees.

Last year, ICE levied $30 million in fines and forfeitures against employers, but arrested fewer than 100 executives or hiring managers, compared with 4,100 unauthorized workers. [9]

One of the few pieces of immigration legislation still considered to have a chance in Congress this year is the SAVE Act (Secure America With Verification Enforcement), which would require all employers to use an electronic verification system to check the legal status of all workers. The House version of the bill boasts more than 130 cosponsors.

Employers are also being heavily targeted by state and local lawmakers. More than 300 employment-related laws addressing illegal immigrants have been recently passed by various levels of government, according to the U.S. Chamber of Commerce.

"There is still this general consensus that although the current employer-sanctions regime hasn't worked, the point of hire is the correct place to ensure that the employee before you is legally here," says Kelley, of the American Immigration Law Foundation.

But for all the efforts to ensure that businesses check the legal status of their workers — and to impose stiffer penalties on those who knowingly hire illegal immigrants — there is still considerable debate about whether such measures will ultimately resolve the problem.

Critics contend there is no easy way for employers to determine legal status. For one thing, documents often are faked. Dan Pilcher, spokesman for the Colorado Association of Commerce and Industry, notes that during a high-profile ICE raid on the Swift meatpacking plant in Greeley in December 2006, many of the arrests were for identity theft, not immigration violations, since so many illegal immigrants were using Social Security numbers that belonged to other people.

"Even when those numbers are run through the system, the computers didn't pick up anything," Pilcher says. "Until that system [of verification] is bulletproof, it

Immigration Is on the Rise

The number of foreign-born people in the United States has nearly quadrupled since 1970, largely because of changes in immigration laws and increasing illegal immigration (top). The increase has pushed the foreign-born percentage of the population to more than 12 percent (bottom).

Number and Percentage of Foreign-Born Individuals in the U.S., 1900-2005

Foreign-Born Population in United States (in millions)

Foreign-Born as Percentage of Total Population (percentage)

Source: Audrey Singer, "Twenty-first Century Gateways: Immigrant Incorporation in Suburban America," Metropolitan Policy Program, Brookings Institution, April 2007

Legal Immigration Has Steadily Increased

The number of legal immigrants has risen steadily since the 1960s, from about 320,000 yearly to nearly 1 million. The largest group was from Latin America and the Caribbean. (In addition to legal entrants, more than a half-million immigrants arrive or remain in the U.S. illegally each year.)

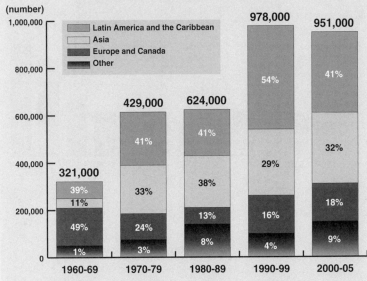

Average Annual Number of Legal U.S. Immigrants by Region of Origin, 1960-2005

(number)

Legend:
- Latin America and the Caribbean
- Asia
- Europe and Canada
- Other

1960-69: **321,000** — 39%, 11%, 49%, 1%
1970-79: **429,000** — 41%, 33%, 24%, 3%
1980-89: **624,000** — 41%, 38%, 13%, 8%
1990-99: **978,000** — 54%, 29%, 16%, 4%
2000-05: **951,000** — 41%, 32%, 18%, 9%

* Percentages may not total 100 due to rounding.

Source: "Economic Mobility of Immigrants in the United States," Economic Mobility Project, Pew Charitable Trusts, 2007

do is give me a program so I can make sure the person is legal for me to hire," says Bryan R. Tolar, director of marketing, education and environmental programs for the Georgia Agribusiness Council.

So far, though, there is no such system. The Department of Homeland Security's E-Verify system, which grew out of a pilot program, is the new checking point of choice. In fact, federal contractors will soon be required to check the residency status of employees using E-Verify. As of Jan. 1, a new state law requires all employers in Arizona to use the E-Verify system.

But such requirements have drawn lawsuits from both business groups and labor unions, who complain that E-Verify is based on unreliable databases. Tom Clark, executive vice president of the Denver Metro Chamber of Commerce, complains that E-Verify is not accurate and worries therefore that the employer sanctions contained in the Arizona law could lead to serious and unfair consequences.

Under the law, companies found guilty of hiring an illegal worker can lose their business licenses for 10 days; for second offenses they are at risk of forfeiting their licenses entirely. "Do you know the [power] that gives you to take out your competitors?" Clark asks.

Supporters of tougher employer sanctions say the databases are getting better all the time. Mark Krikorian, executive director of the Center for Immigration Studies, says E-Verify needs to be made into a requirement for all American employers. Once they are handed a working tool, he says, all businesses need to follow the same rules.

"Legal status is a labor standard that needs to be enforced just like other labor standards," he says. "Holding business accountable to basic labor standards is hardly revolutionary."

The National Immigration Forum's Sharry agrees that employers "need to be held to account for who they

doesn't work to try to mandate that businesses be the front line of enforcement."

Concerns about the verification systems in place are shared across the ideological spectrum. "We're now 21 years after the enactment of employer sanctions, and we still haven't come up with a system that allows for instant verification," says Mehlman, at the Federation for American Immigration Reform. "If Visa and MasterCard can verify literally millions of transactions a day, there's no reason we can't have businesses verify the legal status of their employees."

"When you look to employers to be the ones that are going to have damages imposed for hiring someone who is not properly documented, the first thing you have to

hire." But he warns that imposing stiff penalties against them at a juncture when verification methods remain in doubt could create greater problems.

"Until you create an effective verification system, employer sanctions will drive the problem further underground and advantage the least scrupulous employers," Sherry says.

Can guest worker programs be fixed?

The United States has several different programs allowing foreigners to come into the country for a limited time, usually to work for specific "sponsoring" employers, generally in agriculture. But most of these programs have been criticized for being ineffective — both in filling labor demands and ensuring that temporary workers do not become permanent, illegal residents.

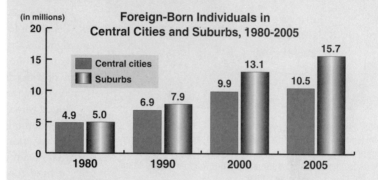

More Immigrants Moving to Suburbs

The gap between the number of immigrants who live in inner cities and suburbs widened significantly from 1980-2005. By 2005 more than 15 million foreign-born people were in suburbs, or three times as many in 1980. The number in cities doubled during the same period. Demographers attribute the popularity of the suburbs to their relative lack of crime, lower cost and better schools.

Foreign-Born Individuals in Central Cities and Suburbs, 1980-2005

(in millions)

Central cities / Suburbs

1980: 4.9 / 5.0
1990: 6.9 / 7.9
2000: 9.9 / 13.1
2005: 10.5 / 15.7

Source: Audrey Singer, "Twenty-first Century Gateways: Immigrant Incorporation in Suburban America," Metropolitan Policy Program, Brookings Institution, April 2007

The best-known guest worker program, the H-2A visa program for visiting agricultural workers, has been derided by farmers as cumbersome and time-consuming, preventing them from timing their hiring of workers to growing and harvesting seasons. Farmers use H-2A visas only to cover an estimated 2 percent of farmworkers.

Instead, growers turn to the black market for undocumented workers. At least half of the nation's 1.6 million farmworkers — and as many as 70 percent by some estimates — are immigrants lacking documentation. [10]

Still, growers' groups have complained about labor shortages as border security and regulation of employers are tightening. Some growers in the Northwest last fall let cherries and apples rot because of a shortage of workers, and some in North Carolina did not plant cucumbers because of a fear they wouldn't find the workers to harvest them. [11]

Three federal agencies — Homeland Security, State and Labor — have been working in recent months to craft regulations to speed the H-2A visa process. But farmworker advocates worry that the sort of changes the administration has been contemplating could weaken labor protections for workers. Some critics of lax immigration policy complain, meanwhile, that the H-2A changes would allow employers to skirt a process designed to limit the flow of immigrant workers.

Changes adopted by or expected from the administration could weaken housing and wage standards that have traditionally been a part of temporary-worker programs, which date back to World War II, according to Bruce Goldstein, executive director of Farmworker Justice, a group that provides legal support to migrant workers.

Those changes would make a bad situation for farmworkers worse, Goldstein contends. "The government has failed to adopt policies that adequately protect workers from abuses and has failed to enforce the labor protections that are on the books," Goldstein says.

The Federation for American Immigration Reform's Mehlman criticizes the proposed changes for "trying to tip the balance in favor of employers.

"There's no evidence that we have a labor shortage in this country," Mehlman says. "You have businesses that have decided they don't want to pay the kind of wages American workers want in order to do these kinds of jobs."

Whether there is an overall labor shortage or not, clearly the numbers don't add up in agriculture. Officials with several immigration-policy groups note that the

After living in Clarion, Iowa, for nine years, undocumented Mexican immigrant Patricia Castillo, right, and her family were deported for entering the country illegally. Townspeople like Doris Holmes and her daughter Kelli threw a fund-raiser to help the Castillos pay their legal bills.

number of people coming to work in this country out-number the visas available to new, full-time workers by hundreds of thousands per year.

"The only way we can provide for the labor needs of a growing and very diverse agriculture industry is to make sure there's an ample workforce to do it," says Tolar, at the Georgia Agribusiness Council. "Americans have proven that they're not willing to provide the work that needs doing at a wage agriculture can support."

Five years ago, a bipartisan group of congressmen, working with farmworkers, growers and church groups, proposed a piece of legislation known as the AgJobs bill. The attempt at a compromise between the most directly interested players has been a part of the guest worker and immigration debates ever since.

The bill would allow some 800,000 undocumented workers who have lived and worked in the U.S. for several years to register, pay a fine and qualify for green cards (proof of legal residency) by working in agriculture for three to five more years. It would also streamline the H-2A visa application process.

Although it won Senate passage as part of a larger immigration bill in 2006, the current version of AgJobs has not gained traction due to complaints that it would reward illegal immigrants and employers with what amounts to "get out of jail free" cards.

In November 2007, Sen. Dianne Feinstein, D-Calif., announced that she would not seek to attach AgJobs as an amendment to a larger farm bill, due to strong opposition to legislation seen as helping illegal immigrants. "We know that we can win this," Feinstein said in a statement. But, she conceded, "When we took a clear-eyed assessment of the politics . . . it became clear that our support could not sustain these competing forces."

Feinstein vows to try again this year. But Krikorian, of the Center for Immigration Studies, which favors reduced immigration, counters that guest worker programs in any form are not the right solution. "They still imagine there's a way of admitting low-wage illegals and not have immigration consequences," he says. "It's a fantasy.

"Guest worker programs don't work anyway," he adds. "There's nothing as permanent as a temporary worker."

The American Immigration Law Foundation's Kelley speaks for many on the other side of the debate who argue that it's not enough to conclude that guest worker programs are problematic. Workers from other countries are going to continue to come into this country, she notes.

"We need somehow to replace what is an illegal flow with a legal flow," Kelley says. "We have a guest worker program now — it's called illegal immigration."

Should illegal immigrants be allowed to attend public colleges and universities?

Miami college students Juan Gomez, 18, and his brother Alex, 20, spent a week in jail in Fort Lauderdale last summer. They were both students at Miami Dade College but faced deportation as illegal immigrants. They had come to the United States from Colombia when they were toddlers.

In handcuffs while riding to the detention center, Juan managed to type out a text message to a friend on his cell phone. The friend set up a Facebook group that in turn led 3,000 people to sign petitions lobbying Congress on the brothers' behalf.

In response, Rep. Lincoln Diaz-Balart, R-Fla., and Sen. Christopher Dodd, D-Conn., introduced legislation to prevent their deportation. As a courtesy to Congress, immigration officials delayed their deportation for two more years. [12]

But the brothers may still face deportation, because Congress failed to pass the DREAM (Development, Relief and Education for Alien Minors) Act. The bill would protect students from deportation and allow young adults (up to age 30) to qualify for permanent legal status if they completed high school and at least two years of college or military service.

On Oct. 24, 2007, the Senate voted 52-48 to end debate and move to a vote on final passage — eight votes short of the 60 needed under Senate rules to end a filibuster. Opponents of the measure claimed it was an unfair plan to grant amnesty to illegal immigrants.

The debate over illegal immigration has regularly and heatedly intersected with questions about education for illegal immigrants: Do young people deserve a break even if their parents skirted the law in bringing them to this country? Should illegal immigrants be barred from publicly supported colleges?

The courts have made it clear that states must provide elementary and secondary educations to all comers, including illegal immigrants. But higher education is another matter entirely.

Ten states have passed legislation in recent years granting in-state tuition to children of illegal immigrants. Most passed their laws during the early years of this decade, before immigration had become such a heated political topic.

Similar proposals in other states have died recently, with critics charging that it would be wrong to reward people who are in the country illegally with one of American society's dearest prizes.

"It is totally unfair if you're going to grant in-state tuition to illegal aliens in Georgia and charge out-of-state tuition to someone from Pennsylvania," says Phil Kent, national spokesman for Americans for Immigration Control.

Katherine "Kay" Albiani, president of the California Community Colleges board, stepped down last month along with two other board members in response to criticism from Republican legislators. The board had voted unanimously last year to support legislation that would have allowed illegal immigrants to qualify for student financial aid and community-college fee waivers.

"We have the best benefit package of any state for illegal immigrants, so they come here," complained California Senate GOP leader Dick Ackerman. [13]

Some argue that illegal immigrants should be barred not only from receiving tuition breaks but also from attending public colleges and universities altogether. Public institutions of higher education, after all, are subsidized by taxpayers, and therefore all students — including illegal immigrants — receive an indirect form of aid from state or local governments.

"Every college student is subsidized to the tune of thousands of dollars a year," says Krikorian, of the Center for Immigration Studies. "They are taking slots and huge amounts of public subsidies that would otherwise go to Americans or legal immigrants."

"Our view is that they shouldn't be there in the first place, and they certainly shouldn't be subsidized by taxpayers," says Mehlman of FAIR. "The typical illegal immigrant isn't coming to the U.S. for higher education. But once you're here, if the state says we'll subsidize your college education, that's a pretty good incentive to stay here."

Others argue that banning students because their parents chose to break the law would be a mistake. "We are a better country than to punish children for what their parents did," former Arkansas Gov. Mike Huckabee said during the Nov. [28] CNN/YouTube GOP presidential debate. Huckabee says he opposes the congressional DREAM Act, but his opponents in the primary campaign have pointed out his former support as governor for in-state tuition for longtime illegal residents.

Beyond the question of whether it's fair to punish students for decisions their parents made, some argue it would be a mistake to deprive illegal immigrants of educational opportunities. A college education may be an extra inducement for them to stay in this country, but the vast majority are likely to remain in this country anyway.

"If these are people who are going to live here for the rest of their lives, we want them to be as educated as possible," says the Manhattan Institute's Jacoby.

The American Immigration Law Foundation's Kelley agrees. She describes the DREAM Act as a reasonable compromise, saying it would protect students but wouldn't give illegal immigrants access to scholarships or grants. She argues that states that do offer in-state tuition rates to illegal immigrant students have not seen "a huge influx" of them.

"Saying to students who have been raised here and by all accounts are American and are graduating in high numbers and are doing well — 'You can't advance and go any further' — doesn't make sense," Kelley says. "It would be helpful to our economy to have these kids get college degrees."

BACKGROUND

Earlier Waves

The United States was created as a nation of immigrants who left Europe for political, religious and economic rea-

CHRONOLOGY

1920s *Hard economic times and public concern about the nation's changing ethnic makeup prompt Congress to limit immigration.*

1921-1929 Congress establishes immigration quota system, excluding Asians and Southern and Eastern Europeans.

1924 U.S. Border Patrol is created to block illegal immigrants, primarily Mexicans.

1940s-1950s *Expansion of U.S. economy during World War II attracts Mexican laborers. U.S. overhauls immigration laws, accepts war survivors and refugees from communist countries.*

1942 Controversial Bracero guest worker program allows Mexicans to work on American farms.

1952 Landmark Immigration and Nationality Act codifies existing quota system favoring Northern Europeans but permitting Mexican farmworkers in Texas.

1960s-1970s *Civil Rights Movement spurs U.S. to admit more Asians and Latin Americans.*

1965 Congress scraps national quotas, gives preference to relatives of immigrants.

1980s *Rising illegal immigration sparks crackdown.*

1986 Apprehension of a record 1.7 million illegal Mexican immigrants prompts lawmakers to legalize undocumented workers and for the first time impose sanctions on employers.

1990s-2000s *Congress again overhauls immigration laws amid national-security concerns.*

1993 Middle Eastern terrorists bomb World Trade Center; two had green cards.

1994 California voters pass Proposition 187, blocking illegal immigrants from receiving most public services; three years later it is largely declared unconstitutional.

1996 Number of illegal immigrants in U.S. reaches 5 million.

Sept. 11, 2001 Attacks on World Trade Center and Pentagon focus new attention on porous U.S. borders.

2004 The 9/11 Commission points to "systemic weaknesses" in border-control and immigration systems.

2005 Congress passes Real ID Act, requiring proof of identity for driver's licenses. . . . President Bush calls for a "temporary worker" program excluding "amnesty" for illegal immigrants. . . . House passes bill to classify illegal immigrants as felons and deport them.

2006 On April 20, Homeland Security Secretary Michael Chertoff announces a federal crackdown on employers who hire illegal aliens. . . . On May 1, hundreds of thousands of immigrants demonstrate across the country to call for legal status. . . . On Nov. 7, 69 percent of Hispanic voters support Democrats in congressional races, according to exit polls.

2007 On May 9, churches in coastal cities provide "sanctuaries" for undocumented families. . . . On May 17, President Bush and a bipartisan group of senators announce agreement on a comprehensive bill to strengthen border protection and allow illegal immigrants eventual access to citizenship. . . . On Aug. 10, the administration calls for more aggressive law enforcement, screening of new employees by federal contractors and firing of workers whose Social Security numbers don't match government databases. . . . On Oct. 24, the Senate fails to end debate on a proposal to protect illegal immigrants who are attending college from deportation. . . . On Dec. 26, Bush signs spending bill calling for 700 miles of "reinforced fencing" along U.S.-Mexico border.

Jan. 1, 2008 Arizona law holding employers responsible for checking legal status of workers is the most recent of hundreds of punitive, new state immigration laws. . . . On Jan. 22, Michigan stops issuing driver's licenses to illegal immigrants. . . . Implementation of Real ID Act, slated to go into effect in May, is postponed.

sons. After independence, the new nation maintained an open-door immigration policy for 100 years. Two great waves of immigrants — in the mid-1800s and the late-19th and early-20th centuries — drove the nation's westward expansion and built its cities and industrial base. [14]

But while the inscription on the Statue of Liberty says America accepts the world's "tired . . . poor . . . huddled masses," Americans themselves vacillate between welcoming immigrants and resenting them — even those who arrive legally. For both legal and illegal immigrants, America's actions have been inconsistent and often racist.

In the 19th century, thousands of Chinese laborers were brought here to build the railroads and then were excluded — via the Chinese Exclusion Act of 1882 — in a wave of anti-Chinese hysteria. Other Asian groups were restricted when legislation in 1917 created "barred zones" for Asian immigrants. [15]

The racist undertones of U.S. immigration policy were by no means reserved for Asians. Describing Italian and Irish immigrants as "wretched beings," *The New York Times* on May 15, 1880, editorialized: "There is a limit to our powers of assimilation, and when it is exceeded the country suffers from something very like indigestion."

Nevertheless, from 1880 to 1920, the country admitted more than 23 million immigrants — first from Northern and then from Southern and Eastern Europe. In 1890, Census Bureau Director Francis Walker said the country was being overrun by "less desirable" newcomers from Southern and Eastern Europe, whom he called "beaten men from beaten races."

In the 1920s, public concern about the nation's changing ethnic makeup prompted Congress to establish a national-origins quota system. Laws in 1921, 1924 and 1929 capped overall immigration and limited influxes from certain areas based on the share of the U.S. population with similar ancestry, effectively excluding Asians and Southern and Eastern Europeans, such as Greeks, Poles and Russians. [16]

But the quotas only swelled the ranks of illegal immigrants — particularly Mexicans, who needed only to wade across the Rio Grande River. To stem the flow, the United States in 1924 created the U.S. Border Patrol to guard the 6,000 miles of U.S. land bordering Canada and Mexico.

After World War II, Congress decided to codify the scores of immigration laws that had evolved over the years. The landmark Immigration and Nationality Act of 1952 retained a basic quota system that favored immigrants from Northern Europe — especially the skilled workers and relatives of U.S. citizens among them. At the same time, it exempted immigrants from the Western Hemisphere from the quota system — except for the black residents of European colonies in the Caribbean.

Mass Deportation

The 1952 law also attempted to address — in the era's racist terms — the newly acknowledged reality of Mexican workers who crossed the border illegally. Border Patrol agents were given more power to search for illegal immigrants and a bigger territory in which to operate.

"Before 1944, the illegal traffic on the Mexican border . . . was never overwhelming," the President's Commission on Migratory Labor noted in 1951, but in the past seven years, "the wetback traffic has reached entirely new levels. . . . [I]t is virtually an invasion." [17]

In a desperate attempt to reverse the tide, the Border Patrol in 1954 launched "Operation Wetback," transferring nearly 500 Immigration and Naturalization Service (INS) officers from the Canadian perimeter and U.S. cities to join the 250 agents policing the U.S.-Mexican border and adjacent factories and farms. More than 1 million undocumented Mexican migrants were deported.

Although the action enjoyed popular support and bolstered the prestige — and budget — of the INS, it exposed an inherent contradiction in U.S. immigration policy. The 1952 law contained a gaping loophole — the Texas Proviso — a blatant concession to Texas agricultural interests that relied on cheap labor from Mexico.

"The Texas Proviso said companies or farms could knowingly hire illegal immigrants, but they couldn't harbor them," said Lawrence Fuchs, former executive director of the U.S. Select Commission on Immigration and Refugee Policy. "It was a duplicitous policy. We never really intended to prevent illegals from coming."

Immigration Reform

The foundation of today's immigration system dates back to 1965, when Congress overhauled the immigration rules, scrapping national-origin quotas in favor of immigration limits for major regions of the world and giving preference to immigrants with close relatives living in the United States. By giving priority to family reunification as a basis for admission, the amendments repaired "a deep and painful flaw in the fabric of American justice," President Lyndon B. Johnson declared at the time.

States Racing to Pass Restrictive Immigration Laws

Arizona, Georgia and Oklahoma seek to outdo Colorado

Andrew Romanoff, the speaker of the Colorado House, offers a simple explanation for why his state enacted a sweeping immigration law in 2006.

"The immigration system is, by all accounts, broken," he says, "and the federal government has shown very little appetite for either enforcing the law or reforming the law."

In the absence of federal action on immigration, in 2007 every state in the nation considered legislation to address the issue, according to the National Conference of State Legislatures (NCSL). It released a study in November showing that states considered "no fewer than 1,562 pieces of legislation related to immigrants and immigration," with 244 passed into law in 46 states. [1] Both the number of bills and the number of new laws were three times higher than the totals in 2006.

When Colorado's law was enacted in 2006, it was considered perhaps the toughest in the country. It requires anyone older than 18 who is seeking state benefits to show identification proving legal status and requires employers to verify the legal status of workers. But it provides exemptions for certain types of medical care and was designed to hold harmless the children of illegal immigrants.

Colorado's approach has since been superseded by states such as Arizona, Georgia and Oklahoma, which have taken an even harder line. In fact, if there's one clear trend in state and local legislation, it's toward a stricter approach.

In Hazelton, Pa., a controversial set of laws has been held up by the courts. The ordinances would require businesses to turn employee information over to the city, which would then verify documents with the federal government.

Prospective tenants would have to acquire a permit to rent by proving their legal right to be in the country.

"It used to be that state and local activity was all over the map," says Mark Krikorian, executive director of the Center for immigration Studies, which advocates reduced immigration. "Those that are loosening the rules now are the exception."

Georgia's law touches on every facet of state policy that relates to illegal immigrants. Under its provisions, state and local government agencies have to verify the legal residency of benefit recipients. Many employers will have to do the same whenever they make a hiring decision. And law enforcement agencies are given authority to crack down on human trafficking and fake documents.

Thousands of immigrants, both legal and illegal, have left Oklahoma following the November enactment of a law (HB 1804) that makes it a felony to knowingly transport illegal immigrants and requires employers to verify the immigration status of workers. It also limits some government benefits to those who can produce proof of citizenship.

Employers in numerous sectors, including hotels, restaurants and agriculture, have complained about labor shortages. But Republican state Rep. Randy Terrill, who wrote the law, says it will save the state money due to the abolition of public subsidies for illegal immigrants. "There's significant evidence that HB 1804 is achieving its intended purpose," he said. [2]

States just a few years ago were debating the expansion of benefits for illegal immigrants, such as in-state tuition

However, the law also dramatically changed the immigration landscape. Most newcomers now hailed from the developing world — about half from Latin America. While nearly 70 percent of immigrants had come from Europe or Canada in the 1950s, by the 1980s that figure had dropped to about 14 percent. Meanwhile, the percentage coming from Asia, Central America and the Caribbean jumped from about 30 percent in the 1950s to 75 percent during the '70s.

In 1978, the select commission concluded that illegal immigration was the most pressing problem facing

immigration authorities, a perception shared by the general public. [18] The number of border apprehensions peaked in 1986 at 1.7 million, driven in part by a deepening economic crisis in Mexico. Some felt the decade-long increase in illegal immigration was particularly unfair to the tens of thousands of legal petitioners waiting for years to obtain entry visas.

"The simple truth is that we've lost control of our own borders," declared President Ronald Reagan, "and no nation can do that and survive." [19]

rates for college. But now politicians in most locales who appear to be aiding illegal immigrants in any way are widely castigated.

New York Gov. Eliot Spitzer, a Democrat, proposed in fall 2007 that illegal immigrants should be eligible for driver's licenses, arguing that would make them more likely to buy insurance. But the idea touched off a political firestorm not only in his state but also within the Democratic presidential campaign and he quickly backed down.

Early this year, Maryland Democratic Gov. Martin O'Malley called for his state to stop issuing driver's licenses to undocumented immigrants. (It's one of seven that currently do so.) "When you've got a New York governor getting clubbed over the head for trying to institute what Maryland has . . . you realize we are out of sync with the rest of the nation," said state House Republican leader Anthony J. O'Connell. [3]

Legislatures in at least a dozen states are already considering bills modeled on the get-tough approaches taken elsewhere. Legislators in states neighboring Oklahoma,

A demonstrator in Tucson supports Proposition 200 on Dec. 22, 2004. The voter-approved Arizona law denies some public benefits to illegal immigrants.

AP Photo/John Miller

for instance, say that they feel pressure to introduce restrictive legislation, particularly from constituents in areas where immigrants who had lived in Oklahoma have relocated.

The fact that there's a sort of legislative arms race going on, with states trying to outdo each other on the immigration issue, has many people worried. A patchwork approach, with tough laws in scattered places driving some immigrants toward more lenient jurisdictions, is clearly not the way to resolve a national or even international issue such as immigration.

"Obviously, 50 different state immigration policies is ultimately unworkable," says Romanoff. "All of us much prefer a federal solution.

"The question is, how long should we wait? In Colorado we decided we could wait no longer."

[1] "2007 Enacted State Legislation Related to Immigrants and Immigration," National Conference of State Legislatures, Nov. 29, 2007, www.ncsl.org/print/immig/2007Immigrationfinal.pdf.

[2] Emily Bazar, "Strict Immigration Law Rattles Okla. Businesses," *USA Today*, Jan. 10, 2008, p. 1A.

[3] Lisa Rein, "Immigrant Driver ID Rejected by O'Malley," *The Washington Post*, Jan. 16, 2008, p. B1.

In the mid-1980s, a movement emerged to fix the illegal-immigration problem. Interestingly, the debate on Capitol Hill was marked by bipartisan alliances described by Sen. Alan K. Simpson, R-Wyo., as "the goofiest ideological-bedfellow activity I've ever seen." [20] Conservative, anti-immigration think tanks teamed up with liberal labor unions and environmentalists favoring tighter restrictions on immigration. Pro-growth and business groups joined forces with longtime adversaries in the Hispanic and civil rights communities to oppose the legislation.

After several false starts, Congress passed the Immigration Reform and Control Act (IRCA) in October 1986 — the most sweeping revision of U.S. immigration policy in more than two decades. Using a carrot-and-stick approach, IRCA granted a general amnesty to all undocumented aliens who were in the United States before 1982 and imposed monetary sanctions — or even prison — against employers who knowingly hired undocumented workers for the first time.

Are Voters Ignoring Immigration?

Iraq War, other issues, may resonate more

Immigration has emerged as a pervasive political issue, a part of seemingly every state and local campaign and presidential debate. "No issue has dominated the Republican presidential nomination fight the way illegal immigration has," *The Washington Post* reported in January. [1]

A poll conducted by the *Post* and ABC News in December found that more Republican voters in Iowa picked immigration as the first or second most important issue to them — 30 percent — than any other issue. Only 6 percent of Iowa Democrats rated the issue so highly. [2]

Yet illegal immigration has also emerged as a key concern in the Democratic contest. After Sen. Hillary Rodham Clinton, D-N.Y., gave conflicting answers during an October debate about her opinion of Democratic New York Gov. Eliot Spitzer's abortive plan to issue driver's licenses to illegal immigrants, her opponents attacked her. That moment has been widely characterized as opening up the first crack in the façade of her "inevitability" as the Democratic nominee.

"This is a real wedge issue that Democrats need to get right," wrote Stan Greenberg and James Carville, two prominent Democratic Party strategists. [3]

Despite the attention that the issue gets from both candidates and the media, however, there's as yet scant evidence that illegal immigration resonates as strongly with voters as other issues such as the economy, health care or the war in Iraq. "The bottom line is, to most people it's not a pocketbook issue," says Arizona pollster Jim Haynes, "and the pocketbook tends to be seminal in determining how somebody's going to end up voting."

In 2006, several House incumbents and candidates who made tough stances against illegal immigration the centerpiece of their campaigns went down to defeat, including Reps. J.D. Hayworth, R-Ariz., and Jim Ryun, R-Kan.

The track record for gubernatorial candidates who focused their campaigns on immigration was no better that year. Len Munsil in Arizona, Ernest Istook in Oklahoma and Jim Barnett in Kansas all ran against Democratic incumbents and tried to take advantage of their opponents' seeming vulnerability on the immigration issue. None won more than 41 percent of the vote.

Rep. Tom Tancredo, R-Colo., based his presidential campaign on his strong support for tougher immigration measures, but never broke out of the low single digits in polls before dropping out of the race in December.

It was also difficult for candidates to make immigration decisive at the ballot box during the off-year elections of 2007. Even in contests where the issue played a prominent role, it didn't have the influence many observers had predicted. In local contests in New York, for example, Democrats did not pay the predicted price for Spitzer's idea of issuing driver's licenses to illegal immigrants. Instead, they fared better.

In Virginia, Republicans made tough talk on immigration central to their plans for holding on to their threatened majority in the state Senate this past November. They ended up losing control of that body after a decade in power. Local Virginia elections told much the same story.

In Loudoun County, where arguments about illegal newcomers have been intense for several years, Sheriff Stephen Simpson lost a primary bid for renomination but came back to win as an independent against an opponent who had accused him of being soft on immigration. "I think it was hyped up quite a bit in the election, not just in my race but in the area," Simpson says.

In numerous other local contests in Virginia, the injection of immigration as a central concern not only failed to change

Changes in 1996

In the 1990s nearly 10 million newcomers — the largest influx ever — arrived on U.S. shores, with most still coming from Latin America and Asia.

Bill Clinton realized early in his presidency that the so-called amnesty program enacted in 1986 had not solved the illegal-immigration problem. And in the Border States,

concern was growing that undocumented immigrants were costing U.S. taxpayers too much in social, health and educational services. On Nov. 8, 1994, California voters approved Proposition 187, denying illegal immigrants public education or non-essential public-health services. Immigrants'-rights organizations immediately challenged the law, which a court later ruled was mostly unconstitu-

the outcome but barely shifted the winner's share of the vote from previous elections.

There were some races where opposition to illegal immigration was an effective political tactic. Tom Selders, the mayor of Greeley, Colo., lost after expressing sympathy for illegal immigrants snared in a federal raid on a local meatpacking plant. By showcasing immigration concerns, Republican Jim Ogonowski ran a surprisingly close race in an October special election in a Massachusetts congressional district that has long favored Democrats, although ultimately he lost.

"This issue has real implications for the country. It captures all the American people's anger and frustration not only with immigration but with the economy," said Rep. Rahm Emanuel of Illinois, chairman of the House Democratic Caucus and chief strategist for his party's congressional candidates in 2006. "It's self-evident. This is a big problem." 4

But it has become surprisingly hard to outflank most candidates on this contentious subject. Last November's challenger to Charles Colgan, a Democratic state senator in Virginia, tried to paint him as soft, going so far as to distribute cartoons depicting Colgan helping people over the wall at the border. But Colgan countered by pointing out his votes in opposition to extending various benefits to illegal immigrants. "The first thing this nation must do is seal the border," he says. "We cannot let

Rep. Tom Tancredo, R-Colo., based his presidential campaign on his strong support for tougher immigration measures but got little traction and dropped out of the race in December 2007.

this influx continue." Colgan won reelection easily.

Why hasn't immigration, which is getting so much attention, proved to be a central concern when voters cast their ballots? For one thing, not everyone agrees on every proposal to make life tougher for illegal immigrants. And the GOP's hard line on immigration threatens to push Hispanic voters over to the Democratic Party.

But illegal immigration may be failing to take off as a voting issue not because of opposition to the hard-line proposals but because something like a consensus in favor of them has already emerged. It's a simple matter for any candidate to communicate a belief that border security should be tightened and that current laws should be more strictly enforced.

The emergence of that kind of consensus suggests that hardliners have in fact won a good portion of their argument. In his statement announcing he was leaving the presidential race, Tancredo said, "Just last week *Newsweek* declared that 'anti-immigrant zealot' [Tancredo] had already won. 'Now even Dems dance to his no mas salsa tune.' "

1 Jonathan Weisman, "For Republicans, Contest's Hallmark Is Immigration," *The Washington Post*, Jan. 2, 2008, p. A1.

2 "What Iowans Care About," *The Washington Post*, Jan. 3, 2008, p. A11.

3 Perry Bacon Jr. and Anne E. Kornblut, "Issue of Illegal Immigration Is Quandary for Democrats," *The Washington Post*, Nov. 2, 2007, p. A2.

4 Jonathan Weisman, "GOP Finds Hot Button in Illegal Immigration," *The Washington Post*, Oct. 23, 2007, p. A7.

tional. But the proposition's passage had alerted politicians to the intensity of anti-illegal immigrant sentiment. 21

House Republicans immediately included a proposal to bar welfare benefits for legal immigrants in their "Contract with America," and in 1995, after the GOP had won control of the House, Congress took another stab at reforming the rules for both legal and illegal

immigration. But business groups blocked efforts to reduce legal immigration, so the new law primarily focused on curbing illegal immigration.

The final legislation, which cleared Congress on Sept. 30, 1996, nearly doubled the size of the Border Patrol and provided 600 new INS investigators. It appropriated $12 million for new border-control

A pro-immigrant rally in Atlanta draws a crowd on May 1, 2006. The nation's rapidly rising foreign-born population is dispersing well beyond "gatekeeper" states such as California and Texas to non-traditional destinations like Georgia, Arkansas and Iowa.

devices, including motion sensors, set tougher standards for applying for political asylum and made it easier to expel foreigners with fake documents or none at all. [22] The law also severely limited — and in many cases completely eliminated — non-citizens' ability to challenge INS decisions in court. [23]

But the new law did not force authorities to crack down on businesses that employed illegal immigrants, even though there was wide agreement that such a crackdown was vital. As the Commission on Immigration Reform had said in 1994, the centerpiece of any effort to stop illegal entrants should be to "turn off the jobs magnet that attracts them."

By 1999, however, amid an economic boom and low unemployment, the INS had stopped raiding work sites

to round up illegal immigrant workers and was focusing on foreign criminals, immigrant-smugglers and document fraud. As for cracking down on employers, an agency district director told *The Washington Post*, "We're out of that business." The idea that employers could be persuaded not to hire illegal workers "is a fairy tale." [24]

Legal immigration, however, has been diminished by the government response to the terrorist attacks of Sept. 11, 2001. In fiscal 2002-2003, the number of people granted legal permanent residence (green cards) fell by 34 percent; 28,000 people were granted political asylum, 59 percent fewer than were granted asylum in fiscal 2000-2001. [25] But the growth of illegal immigration under way before 9/11 continued, with 57 percent of the illegal immigrants coming from Mexico. [26]

Due to the family-reunification provision in immigration law, Mexico is also the leading country of origin for legal immigrants — with 116,000 of the 705,827 legal immigrants in fiscal 2002-2003 coming from Mexico. [27] No Middle Eastern or predominantly Muslim countries have high numbers of legal immigrants, although Pakistan was 13th among the top 15 countries of origin for legal immigrants in 1998. [28]

Public Opinion

The combination of concerns about terrorism and the growing number of illegal immigrants — and their movement into parts of the country unused to dealing with foreign newcomers — made illegal immigration a top-tier issue.

In 2005, Congress passed the Real ID Act, which grew out of the 9/11 Commission investigations into how Arab terrorists burrowed into American society to carry out the Sept. 11, 2001. Of the 19 hijackers, 13 had obtained legitimate driver's licenses, said Rep. F. James Sensenbrenner Jr., R-Wis., author of the legislation. The commission called for national standards for the basic American identification documents: birth certificates, Social Security cards and driver's licenses. In states that adopt the strict requirements of the law — which begins to go into effect in May 2008 — license applicants will have to present ironclad proof of identity, which will be checked against federal and state databases. [29]

After the House in 2005 passed a punitive bill that would have classified illegal immigrants as felons, demonstrations in cities across the country drew hundreds of thousands of marchers during the spring of 2006. On May 1, hundreds of thousands more participated in what

Would tighter border security curb illegal immigration?

YES   Mark Krikorian
Executive Director, Center for Immigration Studies

Written for *CQ Researcher*, Jan. 23, 2008

Border security is one piece of the very large controlling-immigration puzzle. But policing borders, including the use of physical barriers where necessary, has been integral to the preservation of national sovereignty for centuries. In our country, some two-thirds of the illegal population has snuck across the border with Mexico; the rest entered legally — as tourists, students, etc. — and never left.

As part of the development of a modern, national immigration system, Congress in 1924 created the U.S. Border Patrol. As illegal immigration grew to massive proportions in the late 1970s, the Border Patrol's work became something of a charade, with a handful of officers returning whatever Mexican border-jumpers they could nab and then watching them immediately turn around and try again.

The first step in closing that revolving door came in 1993 and 1994, when new strategies were implemented in San Diego and El Paso, where most illegal immigration occurred, to deter crossings altogether rather than simply chase after people through streets and alleys after they'd already crossed.

Over the past decade-and-a-half, the enforcement infrastructure at the border has grown immensely, but it is still laughably inadequate. Although the number of agents at the Southern border has tripled, to some 12,000, that still represents an average of no more than two agents per mile per shift.

Expanded fencing has also been part of this build-up. In the past, when the region on both sides of our Southern border was essentially empty, the limited fencing in place was intended simply to keep cattle from wandering off. Now, with huge metropolises on the Mexican side, serious fencing is being built — first in San Diego, where illegal crossings have plummeted as a result, and now along more than 800 additional miles of the border, though this is still a work in progress. In addition to these physical barriers, we have had for years additional security measures (deceptively labeled "virtual fencing"), such as motion sensors, stadium lighting and remote-controlled cameras.

But while border enforcement is a necessary element of immigration control, it is not sufficient. There are three layers of immigration security — our visa-issuing consulates abroad, the border (including legal entry points) and the interior of the country. Improvements at the border are essential, and many are already under way. The weakest link today is the interior, where efforts to deny illegal immigrants jobs, driver's licenses, bank accounts, etc., are being fought at every turn by the business and ethnic lobbyists who benefit from open borders.

NO   Douglas S. Massey
Professor of Sociology, Princeton University

From testimony before House Judiciary Subcommittee on Immigration, April 20, 2007

As envisioned under [the North American Free Trade Agreement], the economies of the U.S. and Mexico are integrating, and the rising cross-border movement of goods and services has been accompanied by migration of all sorts of people. Since 1986, the number of exchange visitors from Mexico has tripled, the number of business visitors has quadrupled and the number of intra-company transferees has grown 5.5 times.

Within this rapidly integrating economy, however, U.S. policy makers have somehow sought to prevent the cross-border movement of workers. We have adopted an increasingly restrictive set of immigration and border-enforcement policies. First, the Immigration Reform and Control Act of 1986 granted $400 million to expand the size of the Border Patrol. Then the 1990 Immigration Act authorized hiring another 1,000 officers. In 1993, these new personnel were deployed as part of an all-out effort to stop unauthorized border crossing in El Paso, a strategy that was extended to San Diego in 1994. Finally, the 1996 Illegal Immigration Reform and Immigrant Responsibility Act provided funds to hire an additional 1,000 Border Patrol officers per year through 2001.

In essence, the U.S. militarized the border with its closest neighbor, a nation to which it was committed by treaty to an ongoing process of economic integration. Rather than slowing the flow of immigrants into the U.S., however, this policy yielded an array of unintended and very negative consequences.

The most immediate effect was to transform the geography of border crossing. Whereas undocumented border crossing during the 1980s focused on San Diego and El Paso, the selective hardening of these sectors after 1993 diverted the flows to new and remote crossings. Undocumented Mexican migration was thus nationalized. The migrants got wise and simply went around built-up sectors. As a result, the probability of apprehension plummeted to record low levels. American taxpayers were spending billions more to catch fewer migrants.

And, rather than returning home possibly to face the gauntlet at the border again, Mexicans without documents remained longer in the U.S. The ultimate effect of restrictive border policies was to double the net rate of undocumented population growth, making Hispanics the nation's largest minority years before Census Bureau demographers had projected.

At this point, pouring more money into border enforcement will not help the situation, and in my opinion constitutes a waste of taxpayer money. We must realize that the solution to the current crisis does not lie in further militarizing the border with a friendly trading nation that poses no conceivable threat.

President George W. Bush announces the bipartisan compromise immigration deal he struck with Congress on May 17, 2007. The agreement would have granted temporary legal status to virtually all illegal immigrants. Despite the backing of most Democrats and several conservative Republicans, the package was defeated. Bush is flanked by Homeland Security Secretary Michael Chertoff, left, and Commerce Secretary Carlos Gutierrez.

some billed as "the Great American Boycott of 2006." The idea was for immigrants, legal and illegal, to demonstrate their economic contribution to the country by staying away from their jobs on May Day.

In terms of numbers alone, the demonstrations of April and May were impressive. But they may also have spurred a backlash among some sectors of the public. "The size and magnitude of the demonstrations had some kind of backfire effect," John McLaughlin, a Republican pollster, told reporters after the first round of marches. "The Republicans that are tough on immigration are doing well right now." [30]

That turned out not to be the case come election-time, however. Some prominent critics of current immigration policy, including Republican Reps. Jim Ryun of Kansas and J.D. Hayworth of Arizona, went down to defeat in November 2006. Republicans in general paid a clear price among Hispanics for their tough stand. Exit polling in 2006 suggested that 30 percent of Hispanics voted for Republicans in congressional races that year, while Democrats garnered 69 percent. President Bush had taken 40 percent of the Hispanic vote in his reelection race two years earlier. [31] "I don't think we did ourselves any favors when we engaged the public in a major topic and didn't pass the legislation to deal with it," said Sen. Sam Brownback, R-Kan., who dropped out of the GOP presidential primary in October 2007. [32]

Perhaps partly in response, Republicans just after the 2006 elections selected as their new national chairman Florida Sen. Mel Martinez, a prominent Cuban-American who had served in the Bush Cabinet. The Federation for American Immigration Reform's Mehlman, then the outgoing party chairman, told reporters that he was concerned about where the party stood with Hispanics. "Hispanics are not single-issue voters, but GOP officials said the tone of the immigration debate hurt the party's standing with the fastest-growing minority group," *The Washington Post* reported. [33]

CURRENT SITUATION

Difficult Fix

Currently, immigration is the subject of countless legislative proposals at all levels of government. Congress under the new Democratic majority ushered in with the 2006 elections has generally considered more lenient legislation, but any proposal that seems to offer any sort of aid to illegal immigrants has failed to gain traction. In states and in many localities, meanwhile, hundreds of punitive bills have passed into law.

Amid much fanfare, President Bush and a bipartisan group of 10 senators announced an agreement on May 17, 2007, on a comprehensive compromise plan to tighten border security and address the fate of the nation's 12 million illegal immigrants. "The agreement reached today is one that will help enforce our borders," Bush said. "But equally importantly, it will treat people with respect. This is a bill where people who live here in our country will be treated without amnesty, but without animosity." [34]

The 380-page plan was worked out just in time to meet a deadline for the beginning of Senate debate on the issue. "The plan isn't perfect, but only a bipartisan bill will become law," said Sen. Kennedy. [35]

But immigration is the rare issue that cuts across partisan lines. Despite the backing of most Democrats, the Bush administration and conservative Republicans such as Kennedy's negotiating partner, Sen. Jon Kyl, R-Ariz., the package went down to defeat. Supporters were unable to muster the support of 60 senators necessary even to bring it to a vote in the face of determined opposition.

The agreement would have granted temporary legal status to virtually all illegal immigrants, allowing them to apply for residence visas and citizenship through a lengthy process. They would have to wait for eight years before applying for permanent resident status and pay fines of up to $5,000; in addition, heads of households would be forced to leave the country and reenter legally.

But the process could not begin for any illegal aliens — and a new guest worker program would also be put on hold — until after a tough border crackdown had gone into effect. The deal called for the deployment of 18,000 new Border Patrol agents and extensive new physical barriers, including 200 miles of vehicle barriers, 370 miles of fencing and 70 ground-based camera and radar towers. In addition, funding would be provided for the detention of 27,500 illegal immigrants, and new identification tools would be developed to help screen out illegal job applicants.

Conservative opponents of the package in the Senate — as well as most of the 2008 GOP presidential hopefuls — derided it as an "amnesty" bill, giving an unfair citizenship advantage to people who had come into the country illegally.

But liberals and immigration advocacy groups also questioned the terms of the Senate proposal, particularly a change in visa applications. In contrast to the current system, which stresses family ties, a new, complex, point system would favor skilled, educated workers. About 50 percent of the points would be based on employment criteria, with just 10 percent based on family connections.

Even if the Senate had passed the bill, its prospects in the House would have been dim. Despite the change in partisan control of Congress, there was still less sentiment in the House than in the Senate for any bill that was perceived as giving a break to illegal aliens. "Unless the White House produces 60 or 70 Republican votes in the House, it will be difficult to pass an immigration bill similar to the Senate proposal," Rep. Rahm Emanuel, D-Ill., chairman of the House Democratic Caucus, said in May 2007. [36]

Those votes would have been tough to get. Some staunch critics of immigration policy were defeated in the 2006 elections, but for the most part they were replaced by newcomers who also took a hard line against illegal immigration. "This proposal would do lasting damage to the country, American workers and the rule of law," said Lamar Smith of Texas, ranking Republican on the House Judiciary Committee, in response to the deal between senators and the White House. "Just because somebody is in the country illegally doesn't mean we have to give them citizenship." [37] The House did not vote at all on comprehensive immigration legislation in 2007.

Federal Inaction

Not long after the Senate's comprehensive bill failed, the attempt to extend legal status to immigrants attending college also failed. The DREAM Act would have protected students from deportation and allowed young adults (up to age 30) to qualify for permanent legal status if they completed high school and at least two years of college or military service.

On Oct. 24, Senate supporters fell eight votes short of the 60 needed to end debate on the bill and bring it to a final vote. The following month, supporters of legislation to address the issue of temporary guest workers — the AgJobs bill — announced that the political climate had turned against them, and they would drop their efforts at least until 2008.

"Amnesty for illegal immigrants is dead for this Congress," says Krikorian of the Center for Immigration Studies. "When the pro-amnesty side couldn't even pass small measures like the DREAM Act and the AgJobs bill, there's little doubt that legalizing illegal immigrants is dead in the water at least until 2009."

Given the pressure on Congress to do something to address the topic, those lobbying for tougher restrictions remain optimistic that this year could see passage of the Secure America With Verification Enforcement Act. The SAVE Act would require all employers to use an electronic verification system to check the legal status of all workers.

In the absence of successful congressional action thus far, the Bush administration last August unveiled a package designed to break the stalemate. The strategy includes stepped-up work-site raids and arrests of fugitive illegal immigrants. The administration also created a new requirement for federal contractors to use the E-Verify system for screening the legal status of new employees.

In October, a federal judge issued a temporary injunction blocking a part of the Homeland Security package that would have required employers to fire workers whose Social Security numbers do not match information in government databases.

The Immigrations and Customs Enforcement agency in January announced a plan to speed the deportation of foreign-born criminals. Under current law, immigrants convicted of crimes are only deported after serving their sentences. ICE intends to work with states to create parole programs that would allow for the early release of non-violent offenders if they agreed to immediate deportation. The program would place a strain on federal detention centers but provide fiscal relief and bed space to state and local governments housing such prisoners. Last year, ICE sent 276,912 people back to their home countries, including many who were not arrested for crimes but had violated civil immigration statutes. [38]

OUTLOOK

Tough Talk

Immigration will clearly remain an important part of the political conversation in this country. The factors that have made it so prominent — the record number of immigrants, both legal and illegal, and their dispersal into parts of the country that had not seen large influxes of immigrants in living memory — show little sign of abating.

The course that any policy changes will take will depend on who wins the presidency. Attempts at addressing the issue in a comprehensive way in Congress failed, due to concerted opposition to the compromise package brokered between the Bush White House and a bipartisan group of senators. Since that time, more modest bills have not been able to advance.

That means the issue will not be resolved as a policy matter until 2009, at the earliest. Instead, it will remain a major theme of the presidential campaign. Immigration has become, perhaps, the dominant issue among the Republican candidates, as well as one that Democrats have had to address in several particulars.

In a December interview with The Boston Globe, Illinois Sen. Barack Obama, one of the Democratic front-runners, predicted that any Republican candidate, save for McCain, would center his race on two things — fear of terrorism and fear of immigration. [39]

But the immigration issue has not broken along strictly partisan lines. Krikorian of the Center for Immigration Studies predicts that even if the election results in a Democratic president and Congress, the broad policy trajectory will be toward further tightening of immigration policy.

"I don't care whether it's a new Democratic or a new Republican president, they're going to have to address it," says Kent, of Americans for Immigration Control. "The new president will have to toughen up the border."

Politicians of all stripes indeed now pay homage to the idea that border security must be tightened and that current laws need more rigorous enforcement. But debate is still hot over questions of how much to penalize illegal immigrants and employers — and whether efforts to do just that may ultimately prove counterproductive.

Mehlman of the Federation for American Immigration Reform says "the forces that have been trying to promote amnesty and lots of guest workers are not going to go away." Mehlman says that even if current campaign rhetoric generally supports the tough approach his organization favors, the dynamic of actually changing policies in 2009 and after may not change that much.

"It wouldn't be the first time a politician said one thing during the campaign and acted differently once in office," he says.

He notes that the business groups that encourage immigration have deep pockets, but he believes that "this is an issue that the American public is making a stand on."

The National Immigration Forum's Sharry counters that the policy debate has been hijacked by heated political rhetoric and that it's become difficult to discuss what would be the best solutions without accusations being hurled if a proposal sounds at all "soft" on illegal immigrants.

Nevertheless, he notes, most people do not support the toughest proposals that would treat illegal immigrants as felons and seek their mass deportation. "I suspect it's going to take one or perhaps two election cycles to figure out who does it help and who does it hurt," Sharry says. "My prediction is that the Republican embrace of the extreme anti-immigrant groups will be seen in retrospect as an act of slow-motion suicide."

Douglas S. Massey, a Princeton University sociologist, agrees that the politics of this issue may play out poorly over the long term for those proposing a serious crackdown. He notes that there have been many occasions in American history when "beating on immigrants" has been an expedient strategy, but he argues it's never played well successfully as a sustained national issue.

"It's not a long-term strategy for political success, if you look at the future composition of America," Massey says, alluding in particular to the growth in foreign-born populations.

The political debate clearly will have a profound influence on the policy decisions made on immigration in the coming years. But the underlying demographic trends are likely to continue regardless. "With the baby boomers retiring, we will need barely skilled workers more than ever," says Jacoby, of the Manhattan Institute, referring in part to health-care aides.

She argues that growth in immigration is simply an aspect of globalization. Although people are uncomfortable with change and tend to see its downsides first, she believes that people will eventually realize large-scale migration is an inevitable part of the American future.

"We're in a bad time, and our politics are close to broken," she says, "but eventually American pragmatism will come to the surface."

NOTES

1. Quoted in Ryan Lizza, "Return of the Nativist," *The New Yorker*, Dec. 17, 2007, p. 46. For more on immigrant families that face being split up, see Pamela Constable, "Divided by Deportation: Unexpected Orders to Return to Countries Leave Families in Anguish During Holidays," *The Washington Post*, Dec. 24, 2007, p. B1.

2. Quoted in Lizza, *op. cit.*

3. Ellis Cose, "The Rise of a New American Underclass," *Newsweek*, Jan. 7, 2008, p. 74.

4. William Neikirk, "Gingrich Rips Bush on Immigration," *Chicago Tribune*, Aug. 15, 2007, p. 3.

5. Jennifer Ludden, "Q&A: Sen. Kennedy on Immigration, Then & Now," May 9, 2006, NPR.org, www.npr.org/templates/story/story.php?storyId=5393857.

6. Lizza, *op. cit.*

7. "GOP Hopefuls Debate Immigration on Univision," www.msnbc.msn.com/id/22173520/.

8. David Harper, "Terrill Leads Way on Issue," *Tulsa World*, Oct. 30, 2007, www.TulsaWorld.com.

9. Julia Preston, "U.S. to Speed Deportation of Criminals Behind Bars," *The New York Times*, Jan. 15, 2008, p. A12.

10. "Rot in the Fields," *The Washington Post*, Dec. 3, 2007, p. A16.

11. Steven Greenhouse, "U.S. Seeks Rules to Allow Increase in Guest Workers," *The New York Times*, Oct. 10, 2007, p. A16.

12. Kathy Kiely, "Children Caught in the Immigration Crossfire," *USA Today*, Oct. 8, 2007, p. 1A.

13. Patrick McGreevy, "Gov's Party Blocks His College Board Choice," *Los Angeles Times*, Jan. 15, 2008, p. B3.

14. Unless otherwise noted, material in the background section comes from Rodman D. Griffin, "Illegal Immigration," April 24, 1992, pp. 361-384; Kenneth Jost, "Cracking Down on Immigration," Feb. 3, 1995, pp. 97-120; David Masci, "Debate Over Immigration," July 14, 2000, pp. 569-592; and Peter Katel, "Illegal Immigration," May 6, 2005, pp. 393-420, all in *CQ Researcher*.

15. For background, see Richard L. Worsnop, "Asian Americans," *CQ Researcher*, Dec. 13, 1991, pp. 945-968.

16. For background, see "Quota Control and the National-Origin System," Nov. 1, 1926; "The National-Origin Immigration Plan," March 12, 1929; and "Immigration and Deportation," April 18, 1939, all in *Editorial Research Reports*, available from *CQ Researcher Plus Archive*, http://cqpress.com.

17. Quoted in Ellis Cose, *A Nation of Strangers: Prejudice, Politics and the Populating of America* (1992), p. 191.

18. Cited in Michael Fix, ed., *The Paper Curtain: Employer Sanctions' Implementation, Impact, and Reform* (1991), p. 2.

19. Quoted in Tom Morganthau, *et al.*, "Closing the Door," *Newsweek*, June 25, 1984.

20. Quoted in Dick Kirschten, "Come In! Keep Out!" *National Journal*, May 19, 1990, p. 1206.

21. Ann Chih Lin, ed., *Immigration*, CQ Press (2002), pp. 60-61.

22. William Branigin, "Congress Finishes Major Legislation; Immigration; Focus is Borders, Not Benefits," *The Washington Post*, Oct. 1, 1996, p. A1.

23. David Johnston, "Government is Quickly Using Power of New Immigration Law," *The New York Times*, Oct. 22, 1996, p. A20.

24. William Branigin, "INS Shifts 'Interior' Strategy to Target Criminal Aliens," *The Washington Post*, March 15, 1999, p. A3.

25. Deborah Meyers and Jennifer Yau, "US Immigration Statistics in 2003," Migration Policy Institute, Nov. 1, 2004, www.migrationinformation.org/USfocus/display.cfm?id=263; and Homeland Security Department, "2003 Yearbook of Immigration Statistics," http://uscis.gov/graphics/shared/statistics/yearbook/index.htm.

26. Jeffrey S. Passel, "Estimates of the Size and Characteristics of the Undocumented Population," Pew Hispanic Center, March 21, 2005, p. 8.

27. Meyers and Yau, *op. cit.*

28. Lin, *op. cit.*, p. 20.

29. For background, see Peter Katel, "Real ID," *CQ Researcher*, May 4, 2007, pp. 385-408.

30. David D. Kirkpatrick, "Demonstrations on Immigration are Hardening a Divide," *The New York Times*, April 17, 2006, p. 16.

31. Arian Campo-Flores, "A Latino 'Spanking,' " *Newsweek*, Dec. 4, 2006, p. 40.

32. Rick Montgomery and Scott Cannon, "Party Shift Won't End Immigration Debate," *The Washington Post*, Dec. 17, 2006, p. A11.

33. Jim VandeHei, "Florida Senator Will Be a Top RNC Officer," *The Washington Post*, Nov. 14, 2006, p. A4.

34. Karoun Demirjian, "Bipartisan Immigration Deal Reached," *Chicago Tribune*, May 18, 2007, p. 1.

35. *Ibid.*

36. Robert Pear and Jim Rutenberg, "Senators in Bipartisan Deal on Broad Immigration Bill," *The New York Times*, May 18, 2007, p. A1.

37. Demirjian, *op. cit.*

38. Julia Preston, "U.S. to Speed Deportation of Criminals Behind Bars," *The New York Times*, Jan. 15, 2008, p. A12.

39. Foon Rhee, "Obama Says He Wants a Mandate for Change," www.boston.com/news/politics/political-intelligence/2007/12/obama_says_he_w.html.

BIBLIOGRAPHY

Books

Massey, Douglas S., ed., *New Faces in New Places: The Changing Geography of American Immigration*, Russell Sage Foundation, 2008.
A collection of academic pieces shows how the waves of recent immigrants have been dispersed across America by shifts in various economic sectors and how their presence in areas outside traditional "gateways" has led to social tension.

Myers, Dowell, *Immigrants and Boomers: Forging a New Social Contract for the Future of America*, Russell Sage Foundation, 2007.
A demographer suggests that rates of immigration already may have peaked and argues that rather than being stigmatized immigrants need to be embraced as a replacement workforce for an aging Anglo population.

Portes, Alejandro, and Ruben G. Rumbaut, *Immigrant America: A Portrait*, 3rd ed., University of California Press, 2006.
This updated survey by two sociologists offers a broad look at where immigrants settle, what sort of work they do and how well they assimilate.

Articles

Bacon, Perry Jr., and Anne E. Kornblut, "Issue of Illegal Immigration Is Quandary for Democrats," *The Washington Post*, Nov. 2, 2007, p. A4.
Immigration is a wedge issue that can work against Democratic presidential candidates and is perhaps the strongest card in the GOP's deck.

Bazar, Emily, "Strict Immigration Law Rattles Okla. Businesses," *USA Today*, Jan. 10, 2008, p. 1A.
Numerous business sectors in Oklahoma are complaining about worker shortages in the wake of a new state law that makes transporting or sheltering illegal immigrants a felony.

Goodman, Josh, "Crackdown," *Governing*, July 2007, p. 28.
States are reacting to immigration pressures largely by enacting new restrictions on illegal immigrants and the employers who hire them.

Greenhouse, Steven, "U.S. Seeks Rules to Allow Increase in Guest Workers," *The New York Times*, Oct. 10, 2007, p. A16.
Bush administration officials say they will allow farmers to bring in more foreign labor.

Kiely, Kathy, "Children Caught in the Immigration Crossfire," *USA Today*, Oct. 8, 2007, p. 1A.
A million young, illegal immigrants in the United States face potential deportation since the failure of a bill designed to grant permanent legal status to those who finish high school and at least two years of higher education.

Lizza, Ryan, "Return of the Nativist," *The New Yorker*, Dec. 17, 2007, p. 46.
How a hard line on immigration became central to the

GOP Republican debate, taken even by candidates who had previously favored a more conciliatory approach.

Preston, Julia, "U.S. to Speed Deportation of Criminals Behind Bars," *The New York Times*, Jan. 15, 2008, p. A12.
A federal agency pledges to step up arrests of employers who knowingly hire illegal immigrants, while speeding deportation of immigrants who have committed crimes.

Sandler, Michael, "Immigration: From the Capitol to the Courts," *CQ Weekly*, Dec. 10, 2007, p. 3644.
The lack of action on Capitol Hill has encouraged scores of state and local jurisdictions to step in with immigrant-related legislation.

Weisman, Jonathan, "For Republicans, Contest's Hallmark Is Immigration," *The Washington Post*, Jan. 2, 2008, p. A1.
Illegal immigration has been a dominant issue in the GOP presidential primary contests.

Reports and Studies

"2006 Yearbook of Immigration Statistics," Department of Homeland Security, Sept. 2007, www.dhs.gov/xli-brary/assets/statistics/yearbook/2006/OIS_2006_Yearbook.pdf.
A wealth of statistical information about immigrant populations is presented, as well as enforcement actions.

"2007 Enacted State Legislation Related to Immigrants and Immigration," National Conference of State Legislatures, Nov. 29, 2007, www.ncsl.org/print/immig/2007Immigrationfinal.pdf.
Last year, every state considered legislation related to immigration, with more than 1,500 bills introduced and 244 enacted into law. The amount of activity "in the continued absence of a comprehensive federal reform" was unprecedented and represented a threefold increase in legislation introduced and enacted since 2006.

"2007 National Survey of Latinos: As Illegal Immigration Issue Heats Up, Latinos Feel a Chill," Pew Hispanic Center, Dec. 19, 2007; available at http://pewhispanic.org/files/reports/84.pdf.
The poll finds that the prominence of the illegal-immigration issue has Hispanics more concerned about deportation and discrimination but generally content with their place in U.S. society.

For More Information

American Immigration Law Foundation, 918 F St., N.W., 6th Floor, Washington, DC 20004; (202) 742-5600; www.ailf.org. Seeks to increase public understanding of immigration law and policy, emphasizing the value of immigration to American society.

Center for Comparative Immigration Studies, University of California, San Diego, La Jolla, CA 92093-0548; (858) 822-4447; www.ccis-ucsd.org. Compares U.S. immigration trends with patterns in Europe and Asia.

Center for Immigration Studies, 1522 K St., N.W., Suite 820, Washington, DC 20005-1202; (202) 466-8185; www.cis.org. The nation's only think tank exclusively devoted to immigration-related issues advocates reduced immigration.

Federation for American Immigration Reform, 25 Massachusetts Ave., NW, Suite 330; Washington, DC 20001; (202) 328-7004; http://fairus.org. A leading advocate for cracking down on illegal immigration and reducing legal immigration.

Metropolitan Policy Program, The Brookings Institution, 1775 Massachusetts Ave., N.W., Washington, DC 20036; (202) 797-6000; www.brookings.edu/metro.aspx. The think tank produces numerous reports on both immigration and broader demographics, including geographical mobility.

Migration Dialogue, University of California, Davis, 1 Shields Ave., Davis, CA 95616; (530) 752-1011; http://migration.ucdavis.edu/index.php. A research center that focuses on immigration from rural Mexico and publishes two Web bulletins.

Migration Policy Institute, 1400 16th St., N.W., Suite 300, Washington, DC 20036; (202) 266-1940; www.migrationpolicy.org. Analyzes global immigration trends and advocates fairer, more humane conditions for immigrants.

National Immigration Forum; 50 F St., N.W., Suite 300, Washington, DC 20001; (202) 347-0040; www.immigrationforum.org. A leading advocacy group in support of immigrants' rights.

15

U.S. Policy on Iran

Peter Katel

Whide U.S. troops fight in Iraq, the Bush administration is waging a war of words with neighboring Iran.

Bad blood has existed between Washington and Tehran for nearly three decades. But the verbal conflict is getting so intense that even Middle East experts — long accustomed to pugnacious rhetoric — say bullets could start flying.

At issue are Iran's nuclear development efforts and its perceived military support of Iraqi insurgents. Washington says Iran is seeking to develop nuclear weapons, but Iranian President Mahmoud Ahmadinejad says the program is for peaceful uses.

In October, President George W. Bush said he had "told people that if you're interested in avoiding World War III, it seems like you ought to be interested in preventing [Iran] from having the knowledge necessary to make a nuclear weapon." [1]

For his part, Ahmadinejad calls the United States an international bully intent on keeping Iraq violent to justify continued occupation.

"No day passes without people [in Iraq] being killed, wounded or displaced," Ahmadinejad said during an address to the U.N. General Assembly in September. "And the occupiers not only refuse to be accountable and ashamed of their adventure, but speak in a report of a new market for their armaments as a result of their military adventure."

"We're in a serious and dangerous situation," says Bruce Riedel, a senior fellow at the Brookings Institution's Saban Center for Middle East Policy, a centrist think tank. "We'd be better served by lowering the rhetoric."

Meanwhile, hundreds of U.S. troops in Iraq have been killed by sophisticated roadside bombs that Bush and his top military com-

From *CQ Researcher*,
November 16, 2007.

A Major Presence in the Middle East

Heartland of the ancient Persian Empire, Iran is the biggest non-Arab country in the Middle East. It has the biggest Shiite population of any nation and the only officially Shiite constitution in the world. It also maintains the region's biggest military force and is among the world's top petroleum producers.

Iran at a Glance

Population: 65.4 million (July 2007 est.)

Population below poverty line: 40% (2002 est.); Per capita GDP: $8,700

Religion: Muslim 98% (Shiite 89%, Sunni 9%); Other 2% (includes Zoroastrian, Jewish, Christian and Baha'i)

Gross domestic product: $222.9 billion (2006)

Military expenditures: 4.5% of GDP (2005)

Percentage of world's total proven oil reserves: 10%

Ranking among OPEC crude oil producers: No. 2 at 3.8 million barrels per day (Saudi Arabia is No. 1, at 9.2 million)

Natural gas reserves: 974 trillion cubic ft., second-highest in world after Russia (1,680 trillion cubic ft.)

Total military manpower: 545,000 (next highest in the region: Saudi Arabia, 199,500)

Sources: CIA *World Factbook*, updated Nov. 1, 2007; Anthony Cordesman and Martin Kleiber, "Iran's Military Forces and Warfighting Capabilities: The Threat in the Northern Gulf," Center for Strategic and International Studies, 2007; Energy Information Administration, Department of Energy; *Political Handbook of the World, 2007*

manders say are coming from Iran, which denies supplying them.

Amid the fighting and the fighting words, a glimmer of hope appeared in November. Lt. Gen. Raymond T. Odierno, second in command in Iraq behind Gen. David Petraeus, told reporters on Nov. 1 the number of attacks involving deadly EFPs (explosively formed penetrators) had dropped from 177 in July and August to 105 in September and October.

Defense Secretary Robert M. Gates said Iran had promised to clamp down on shipment of EFPs. "I don't know whether to believe them," Gates said. "I'll wait and see." [2]

Some of the skepticism grows out of Iran's reported role in a 33-day war last year between Israel — America's key Middle East ally — and Lebanon's Hezbollah militia, which was created and armed by Iran. Ahmadinejad has expressed the hope that Israel would be wiped off the map, much as the Soviet Union disappeared. "Was it done through war?" he asked at a September news conference at the United Nations. "No. It was through the voice of the people." [3]

Three weeks later, Bush made his "World War III" remark. And four days after that Vice President Dick Cheney called Iran "the world's most active state sponsor of terror," adding: "The Iranian regime needs to know that if it stays on its present course, the international community is prepared to impose serious consequences. The United States joins other nations in sending a clear message: We will not allow Iran to have a nuclear weapon." [4]

Iran Ranks Among World Leaders in Energy

Iran ranks third in proven oil reserves, with nearly 140 billion barrels; world leader Saudi Arabia has almost twice as much (left). Iran has nearly a quadrillion cubic feet of natural gas reserves, second only to Russia (right).

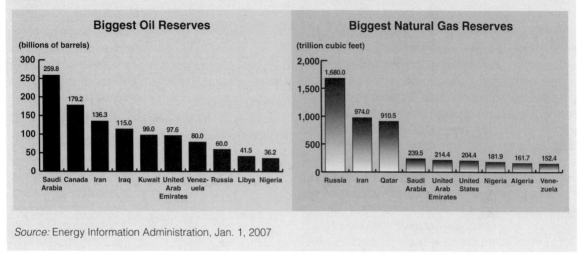

Biggest Oil Reserves

(billions of barrels)

Saudi Arabia	259.8
Canada	179.2
Iran	136.3
Iraq	115.0
Kuwait	99.0
United Arab Emirates	97.6
Venezuela	80.0
Russia	60.0
Libya	41.5
Nigeria	36.2

Biggest Natural Gas Reserves

(trillion cubic feet)

Russia	1,680.0
Iran	974.0
Qatar	910.5
Saudi Arabia	239.5
United Arab Emirates	214.4
United States	204.4
Nigeria	181.9
Algeria	161.7
Venezuela	152.4

Source: Energy Information Administration, Jan. 1, 2007

The White House followed the tough talk with new economic sanctions designed to halt or slow down business transactions for anyone doing business with banks or other companies linked to the Iranian Revolutionary Guard, a military and covert-action agency long accused of supporting and aiding terrorism in the region.

What will the future bring? If past relations between the two countries are a guide, it will be a bumpy ride. In 1953 the United States orchestrated a coup against a nationalist Iranian prime minister, throwing its weight behind the country's pro-Western monarch, Shah Mohammed Reza Pahlavi. The United States, like the then-new state of Israel, saw Iran — successor to the ancient Persian Empire — as a key ally in a dangerous neighborhood. Iran, like other Middle Eastern nations, was Muslim. But Iranians are not Arabs and were seen as distant from the Israeli-Arab confrontation. In 1979 a revolution toppled the shah and installed the anti-American, anti-Israel theocracy that now rules Iran. Since then, U.S.-Iranian relations have been schizophrenic — marked by the 1979-81 hostage crisis involving 52 U.S. Embassy personnel in Tehran but also by quiet cooperation during the U.S.-led invasion of Afghanistan.

Tension has been climbing since Ahmadinejad launched himself globally as a challenger to American power following his election as president in 2005. Yet his real power largely is limited to economic policy. Under Iran's constitution, a clergyman, elected by a clerical Assembly of Experts, has the last word in all major affairs of state. Only the supreme leader, for instance, can declare war. [5]

Despite the confusing division of power, hawks argue that one thing is clear about the Iranian government: It wants to destroy the United States and Israel. "We're under attack; they're at war with us," says Michael A. Ledeen, who holds the title of "freedom scholar" at the conservative American Enterprise Institute and is the author of a new book on Iran. [6] "They're killing Americans [in Iraq] and intend to kill as many as they can. They want to destroy us." [7]

Other foreign-policy watchers deride such arguments as war-mongering fantasy. "Iran has an economy the size of Finland's and an annual defense budget of around $4.8 billion," wrote Fareed Zakaria, editor of *Newsweek International,* in a widely discussed column. "It has not invaded a country since the late 18th century. The United States has a GDP that is 68 times larger and defense expenditures that are 110 times greater." [8]

Hawks and doves alike place great importance on the survival of Iran's pro-democracy/human rights community, or "civil society." Its members have always risked prison and torture, but increased repression this year is

AP Photo/Vahid Salemi

A police patrol boat guards the Neka oil terminal on the Caspian Sea on Iran's northern coast. Despite its huge petroleum reserves, Iran has a faltering economy and an 11 percent unemployment rate.

causing renewed alarm. Among other moves, the government imprisoned several visiting Iranian-American professionals on suspicion of trying to help the Bush administration topple the government. Iran acted after the administration created a $75 million fund to promote civil society in Iran, in part by supporting pro-democracy organizations.

The unintended consequence of that support, some exiled dissidents and their American allies say, is to validate the Iranian government's contention that opposition members are American stooges. "Any Iranian who seeks American dollars will not be recognized as a democrat by his or her fellow citizens," Akbar Ganji, one of Iran's leading democracy activists, wrote in an op-ed in October. "Iran's democratic movement does not need foreign handouts." [9]

U.S. hawks argue that blaming the Bush administration for the latest crackdown ignores history. Iran's government, they point out, was jailing and torturing dissidents long before Bush took office. And, Ledeen says, the dissidents represent Iran's future, so helping them makes more sense than bombing a nuclear site.

In fact, few experts advocate military action. "There's a remarkable consensus across Washington about what the consequences would be," says Michael Rubin, a hawkish American Enterprise Institute scholar who lived in Iran in 1999 and speaks Farsi. "I don't know anyone who thinks a strike is a good idea." Military action, he says, likely would rally Iranians to the government's side. Systematic attacks against U.S. forces in Iraq could also be expected, as could sabotage of oil export facilities in the Persian Gulf, further driving up petroleum prices. [10]

But prominent neoconservative * Norman Podhoretz does advocate air strikes against Iran's nuclear research sites. The United States has "only one terrible choice, which is either to bomb those facilities and retard their program or even cut it off altogether or allow them to go nuclear," said Podhoretz, editor-at-large of *Commentary* magazine." [11]

Podhoretz insisted that Ahmadinejad is today's version of Adolf Hitler. "If we allow Iran to get the bomb," he argued, "people 50 years from now will look back at us the way we look back at the men who made the Munich Pact with Hitler in 1938 and say, 'How could they have let this happen?' "

Most experts scoff at such analogies, despite Iran's hostility to Israel. "The idea that Iran presents to the region and world a threat as big as Hitler's is absurd," says Iranian-born historian Shaul Bakhash of George Mason University, who is Jewish. "Iran is very unlikely to get involved in military adventures abroad."

Israel's reported bombing on Sept. 6 of a possible nuclear site in Syria — an Iranian ally — has fueled fears of U.S. designs on Iran. But even experts concerned about a U.S. attack worry more about the impact of the Iraq War. "I think the president is telling the truth when he says he doesn't intend to bomb," says Riedel, a former Middle East policy director at the National Security Council. "But the war by proxy we're fighting with Iran

---

* "Neoconservative," or neocon, originally referred to a small band of left-wing writers and academics who jumped to the Republican Party in the 1970s and '80s. It now is applied broadly, usually pejoratively, to strongly pro-Israel supporters of the Bush administration.

in Iraq could escalate unpredictably because of events on the ground."

As tension mounts, here are some of the issues being debated:

Would a nuclear-armed Iran endanger the United States?

Concern about Iran's nuclear development program had been simmering for several years. Worries heated up after Ahmadinejad's election in 2005. But the country's nuclear ambitions actually predate the 1979 revolution that led to the Islamic Republic.

Shortly before his overthrow, the shah had been hoping to obtain reactors and other nuclear technology from the United States, his closest ally. Nuclear-generated power would allow Iran to sell more of its oil abroad, bringing in more much-needed revenue. Today, the Islamic Republic — created by the same men who toppled the shah — justifies its nuclear program on the same grounds. [12]

Iranian officials have declared repeatedly their nuclear program excludes plans for any weapons. "We consider the acquiring, development and use of nuclear weapons inhuman, immoral, illegal and against our basic principles," Deputy Foreign Minister G. Ali Khoshroo said in 2003. [13]

To be sure, Khoshroo served in the administration of reformist President Mohammed Khatami. But his successor, Ahmadinejad, sounded the same note. "We are not after an atomic bomb because it is not useful, and our religion does not allow us to have it," he says on his Web site. [14]

In addition, Iran's alternately compliant and defiant dealings with the international nuclear regulatory system — even before Ahmadinejad's rise — have led experts with connections to the Bush administration to be deeply skeptical of Iran's objectives. "Iran has too often dictated the pace of diplomatic progress, giving the impression that it is playing for time," David Albright, president of the Institute for Science and International Security, wrote in 2004. The apparent aim was to stall the regulatory process until its nuclear facilities were up and running, Albright and a colleague wrote. [15]

So widespread are suspicions, in fact, that even critics of the Bush administration's war talk assume Iran's nuclear program is designed to produce weapons. Retired Gen. John Abizaid, former U.S. commander in the Middle East, faced the issue head-on during a talk in Washington last September. "There are ways to live with a nuclear Iran," he said. "Let's face it, we lived with a nuclear Soviet Union; we've lived with a nuclear China; we're living with other nuclear powers as well." [16]

The American Enterprise Institute's Rubin, among the most prominent advocates of a tough policy on Iran, bluntly rejects Abizaid's thesis: "I think he's wrong."

But Rubin isn't worried about nuclear war. Instead, he argued, nuclear weapons will block any attempts to force Iran to play by international rules. He cited a bombing raid by Turkish warplanes on Iranian territory in 1999, apparently aimed at punishing Iran for sheltering a Kurdish guerrilla organization that had been attacking Turkish troops for years. "After that, Iran stopped sheltering them," Rubin says. "But if Iran has a nuclear deterrent, no one is going to risk correcting its behavior." [17]

Brookings' Riedel, the former Middle East policy director at the National Security Council, says the United States has numerous options for pressuring Iran. "I do not see evidence from Iranian behavior over the last 30 years that this is a crazy state," he says. "Iran's behavior shows an understanding of the limits of its capability." He cites fighting between the United States and Iran during the 1980-88 Iran-Iraq War, when U.S. forces were protecting shipping in the Persian Gulf from Iranian attacks. "In the end, they chose to stop the conflict and to de-escalate," he says.

The question of whether Iran is a fundamentally rational power is crucial to the debate over nuclear intentions. True, deterrence worked against America's adversary in the Cold War, says the American Enterprise Institute's Ledeen, a former National Security Council consultant during the Reagan administration. But, he adds, "The Soviet Union was not governed by insane millenarian fanatics. The [Iranian government] wants to rule the world."

"Millenarian" signifies a belief in an approaching end of days, or change on a cataclysmic scale. For many Shiites, including Ahmadinejad, the return of the holy, historic figure known as the Mahdi, or the "Hidden Imam," would herald such a period. "With his 'second coming' there will be a reign of justice until the return of Jesus" — a revered figure to all Muslims — "at which time the world will end," writes Vali Nasr, a political scientist at Tufts University who specializes in the Shiite world. [18]

But Nasr also argues that the key to the future of the Middle East is the evolution of the historic Shiite-Sunni rivalry. And *Newsweek*'s Zakaria, in a television debate with Podhoretz, noted that past communist dictators had their own version of millenarianism that was just as terrifying, on paper — but not in reality — as

Ahmadinejad Takes Aim at the United States

Tough talk is the president's specialty

Mahmoud Ahmadinejad may be only 5'2" tall, but he looms large as the embodiment of U.S., Israeli and European fears about Iran and its state ideology of religion-laced nationalism.

Seemingly on any given day, if the Iranian president isn't questioning whether the Holocaust occurred, he's accusing the United States of deliberately keeping Iraq unstable to justify the war or defying international nuclear watchdogs.

"Nations and countries don't have to obey the injustice of certain powers," Ahmadinejad told the U.N. General Assembly on Sept. 26, unmistakably referring above all to the United States. "These powers . . . have lost the competence to lead the world because of their hideous acts." And, he went on: "I officially declare that the age of relations arising from the Second World War, as well as materialistic thoughts based on arrogance and domination, is well over now. Humanity has passed a perilous precipice, and the age of monotheism, purity, affinity, respecting others, justice and true peace loving has commenced." [1]

Ahmadinejad's bill of particulars against the United States and its Western allies includes the creation of Israel, their responsibility for poverty and disease in poor countries and the global arms race.

To be sure, any number of developing-nation leaders — including other Iranian presidents — have leveled similar accusations. But Ahmadinejad's talent for provocative oratory, coupled with his position — albeit largely symbolic — as head of a major oil power, has amplified his voice.

Yet, by all accounts, the former mayor of Tehran owes his 2005 election to the presidency less to his international stands than to the political identity he carved out as the voice of the little man hammered by economic problems. Born in 1956, Ahmadinejad is the son of a blacksmith and a veteran of the horrific eight-year war with Iraq. Afterwards, overcoming many hardships, he earned a doctorate in civil engineering. [2]

"Most people voted for Ahmadinejad because he promised they would never have to feel sad again on New Year's Eve in front of their children," Farshid Bakhtieri, a young computer salesman, said in February. [3]

But those promises haven't been fulfilled, Bakhtieri added. Iranians complain they aren't getting the benefits of Iran's status as a major oil power, as the 11.5 percent official jobless rate indicates. And in June, government-imposed gasoline rationing ignited rioting in Tehran and other cities. Although it has the world's third-largest reserves of oil, Iran has built an insufficient number of refineries to produce enough gasoline — which it provides at low, subsidized rates — to meet growing domestic demand. Thus, the country depends heavily on imports,

---

Ahmadinejad's. Zakaria quoted the late Chinese ruler, Mao Zedong: "If the worst came to worst and half of mankind died, the other half would remain, while imperialism would be razed from the ground." [19]

Trita Parsi, president of the National Iranian American Council, which advocates a diplomatic resolution of U.S.-Iran tensions, argues that Iran's claim of a peaceful purpose for its nuclear development program is accurate — though weapon construction may be on the agenda as well. If the latter succeeded, he says, the existence of the U.S. and Israeli nuclear deterrent will prevent nuclear war. "Coexistence is possible," he says. The Iranians are deterrable." Parsi is also author of a new book chronicling the post-revolutionary relationship between Iran, the United States and Israel. [20]

Does U.S. support help pro-democracy dissidents influence Iran's policies?

President Ahmadinejad's frequently bellicose speeches may suggest Iran is ruled, and populated, by religious, revolutionary fanatics. But the country's cadre of human-rights campaigners, labor-union organizers, student activists and investigative journalists is bigger than one might think. "Iranian society has refused to be coerced into silence," wrote Shirin Ebadi, a human-rights lawyer who won the Nobel Peace Prize in 2003. "Human-rights discourse is alive and well at the grass-roots level; civil-society activists consider it to be the most potent framework for achieving sustainable democratic reforms and political pluralism." [21]

Ebadi received the Nobel Prize at the moment when expectations of change reached their highest point in

which require cash outlays. Rationing was designed to reduce Iran's gasoline import payments if international sanctions over the country's disputed nuclear-development activities restrict access to cash. [4]

But average Iranians had little sympathy for the government's rationing strategy. "We live on an ocean of oil," said Kambiz Rahmati, 25, an electronics engineer. "Why should we pay a high price for gasoline or suffer rationing?" [5]

Some Iranian pro-democracy activists tie Ahmadinejad's economic failures to his aggressiveness in the international arena. Indeed, says an exiled dissident, the president might see it in his interest to bait the United States into military action over Iran's insistence on building nuclear facilities. "Limited war would give a good excuse to accuse the foreign states — 'it's their fault that the Iranian economy has problems,' " says Ali Afshari, an exiled student leader who spent nearly three years in prison. "Second, he would use this for a complete militarization of the country, and suppress all dissident activities."

But Iran's supreme leader, Ayatollah Ali Khamenei, doubts even a limited U.S. strike against Iran's nuclear facilities would be strategically advantageous, Afshari theorizes. And Khamenei's opinion counts: Only he can declare war or command the military. [6]

But Khamenei makes few public comments these days. Ahmadinejad has come to be seen as the man in charge because he issues a steady stream of commentary on hot-button issues. About the Holocaust, for instance, he shocked listeners when he said last year: "I will only accept something as truth if I am actually convinced of it." In 2001, Khamenei got only sparse attention when he said Zionists had been "fabricating figures related to the Holocaust." [7]

Such statements don't surprise Shaul Bakhash, an Iranian-born historian at George Mason University in Fairfax, Va. "These statements are not as new as people seem to imagine," he says.

In fact, points out Michael Rubin, a resident scholar at the American Enterprise Institute, Iran's nuclear program has been around much longer than Ahmadinejad. "The presidency in Iran is about style, not substance."

[1] Address to 62nd U.N. General Assembly, Sept. 26, 2007, www.president.ir/en/.

[2] See Nazila Fathi, "Blacksmith's Son Emphasized His Modest Roots," *The New York Times*, June 26, 2005, p. A11. See also "Iran-Iraq War (1980-1988)," globalsecurity.org, undated, www.globalsecurity.org/military/world/war/iran-iraq.htm.

[3] Quoted in Kim Murphy, "Iran reformists want U.S. to tone it down," *Los Angeles Times*, Feb. 11, 2007, p. A1.

[4] See Ramin Mostaghim and Borzou Daragahi, "Gas rationing in Iran ignites anger, unrest," *Los Angeles Times*, June 28, 2007, p. A5; Najmeh Bozorgmehr, "Iran pushes on with fuel rationing in face of riots," *Financial Times* (London), June 28, 2007, p. A7. Also see Peter Behr, "Energy Nationalism," *CQ Global Researcher*, July 2007, pp. 151-180.

[5] Quoted in *Los Angeles Times*, ibid.

[6] See Ray Takeyh, *Hidden Iran: Paradox and Power in the Islamic Republic* (2006), pp. 24-25.

[7] Quoted in Christopher De Bellaigue, "Hanging of 'CIA Spy' Dents Iran's Overtures to U.S.," *The Independent* (London), May 24, 2001, p. A19. Ahmadinejad quoted in Michael Slackman, "Deep Roots of Denial for Iran's True Believer," *The New York Times*, Dec. 14, 2006, p. A3.

recent years, during the term of reformist President Khatami. Under Ahmadinejad, those hopes have dimmed.

A crackdown that intensified this year included enforcement of the religious code against revealing clothing, including scanty head scarves on women and tight shirts on men. "Those who damage the system under any guise will be punished," Intelligence Minister Gholamhossein Mohseni Ejei warned in April. He accused the civil-society movement of conspiring to topple the government. [22]

Controversy over direct American aid for Iranian dissidents leapt to the top of the agenda in 2006, when Secretary of State Condoleezza Rice asked Congress for $75 million to fund activities that included expanding Farsi-language news broadcasts into Iran — and support for Iranian civil-society groups. "The United States will actively confront the policies of this Iranian regime, and at the same time we are going to work to support the aspirations of the Iranian people for freedom in their own country," Rice told the Senate Foreign Relations Committee. Congress granted the request. The administration is now asking for the same amount in 2008. [23]

Debate over the usefulness of the money has been raging since the first request, with most supporters of Iranian civil-society groups opposed to the funding. Human Rights Watch is among several groups lobbying against the program as the House and Senate Appropriations committees negotiate the funding. "Iranian activists don't want it and can't get it," Saman Zarifi, Washington advocate for Human Rights Watch,

Haleh Esfandiari, left, appears on Iranian television after her arrest early last year in Tehran. The Middle East Program director of the Woodrow Wilson International Center for Scholars in Washington spent eight months in jail along with several other U.S. pro-democracy activists. She was released in September 2007. Ali Afshari, a former student human-rights activist, spent most of 2000-2003 in prison, where he endured torture and 400 days of solitary confinement.

said in October. "Second, it supports Iranian government efforts to cast activists as foreign agents." [24]

Earlier in the year, Iran added fuel to the conflict by arresting four visiting American human-rights supporters: Haleh Esfandiari, Middle East Program director of the Woodrow Wilson International Center for Scholars in Washington; Kian Tajbakhsh, an urban planner who had been a consultant to the Open Society Institute of the New York-based Soros Foundation; Parnaz Azima, a reporter for Radio Farda, the Persian-language arm of Radio Free Europe/ Radio Liberty; and Ali Shakeri, 59, a mortgage broker and a founding board member of the Center for Citizen Peacebuilding at the University of California, Irvine. After solitary confinement and frequent interrogation, the four were freed. [25]

Iranian citizens, however, have spent years in prison. Ali Afshari, a former student human-rights activist, spent most of 2000-2003 in prison, where he told CQ Researcher, he endured 400 days of solitary confinement. He now lives in the United States and is a doctoral student in engineering.

Afshari says U.S. support for the Iranian human-rights movement should be limited to programs that remain within U.S. borders. "In Iranian political culture, it's taboo for any organization to get money from any foreign state," he says. "It harms civil society because the government uses it as an excuse to repress."

Some advocates of tough U.S. action against the Iranian government cite the crackdown as evidence of an urgent necessity for financing as many Iranian pro-democracy organizations as possible. The American Enterprise Institute's Rubin says the arrest of Esfandiari and the other Iranian-Americans shows a government feeling weak. "Governments with self-confidence about their peoples' attitudes don't arrest 67-year-old grandmothers," he says, referring to Esfandiari.

The apparent insecurity begs to be exploited, Rubin argues. As for Afshari's view — which is widely echoed — that U.S. funding would provide a rationale for more repression — Rubin notes that repression is a longstanding tradition in the Islamic Republic. "It's safe to say that crackdowns happened long before democracy funding was an issue," he says.

Bakhash, the Iranian-born historian, disputes the notion that American funding would help those for whom it's intended. "Given the way Iran is now, I don't think it's at all helpful for the American government to be involved directly in such activities," he says. "The sensitivity to foreign funding in the Middle East is huge, enormous. The idea that foreign-funded political groups in-country can cooperate freely with political groups out of the country is a rather difficult concept; it can lead to a charge of treason."

Bakhash has a personal stake in the matter. Esfandiari is his wife, and after her release from eight months of imprisonment she coauthored a piece opposing U.S. government aid to Iranian pro-democracy groups. "Governments should talk to governments," she wrote with Robert Litwak, director of international-security studies at the Wilson Center, "while Iranian and American [non-governmental organizations] should be permitted to interact in a transparent fashion without the intrusion of governments." [26]

But some Iranian exiles argue in favor of American funding. "It's very helpful," says Akbar Atri, a former student activist who was also imprisoned. He dismisses as a well-worn accusation, long predating the Bush administration, that all dissidents are tools of American subversion. "The regime said the American government is helping these Iranians, but before these funds they all the time accused the opposition of being the puppet of U.S. intelligence agencies."

Atri, a longtime student democracy activist who fled Iran in late 2004 while under investigation for his political work, is a member of the Washington-based

Committee on the Present Danger, co-chaired by R. James Woolsey, former CIA director in the Clinton administration, and George P. Shultz, who was secretary of State in the Reagan administration. The organization favors "regime change" in Iran. [27]

Is Iran fomenting instability in Iraq?

The U.S. overthrow of Saddam Hussein did an enormous favor for Iran, which had good reason to consider Iraq's dictator an enormous threat. As the instigator of the 1980-1988 Iran-Iraq War, Saddam was responsible for at least 300,000 Iranians killed and an estimated 700,000 wounded. [28]

U.S. destruction of Iran's enemy would seem to make Iran and the United States de facto allies. But the U.S. military accuses Iran of supplying weapons to anti-American Shiite militias in Iraq. "There is absolutely no question," said Gen. Petraeus, the top U.S. commander in Iraq, "that Iranians are funding, arming, training and even in some cases, directing the activities of extremists and militia elements." [29]

Specifically, Petraeus and Lt. Gen. Odierno say the Iranian Revolutionary Guard Corps is supplying "explosively formed penetrators" (EFPs), roadside bombs that can penetrate vehicle armor. [30]

Iranian officials have consistently denied all such accusations. And U.S. military brass have backed away from disclosing what they call definitive evidence. [31]

But even without conclusive proof, some administration critics call the U.S. allegations plausible. "I think the administration is telling the truth when it says Iran is targeting American soldiers in Iraq and Afghanistan," says Riedel, the ex-CIA and National Security Council official. "What that says to me is that the Iranians are demonstrating that we're vulnerable. I have no doubt the U.S. Air Force and U.S. Navy can inflict enormous pain on Iran, but I also know that Iran can inflict enormous pain on the U.S. in Iraq, the Persian Gulf and diplomatic installations. They're prepared to play hardball with us."

Nonetheless, for some Iran-watchers, the question looming over the war in Iraq is whether Iran could be persuaded to help U.S. forces disengage.

Iran hawks say that hope is futile. Rubin of the American Enterprise Institute argues that Iran has settled on a policy of keeping U.S. forces tied down in Iraq. In testimony last July before the House Foreign Affairs Committee, Rubin cited a July 13 sermon by former

Iranian President Hashemi Rafsanjani in which he ridiculed American weakness. "What a superpower is the United States when it can be easily trapped in a small country like Iraq?" he said. [32]

Based on the sermon and other evidence, Rubin testified: "The assumption that Iraq's neighbors seek a peaceful, stable Iraq is false. . . . Iranian strategists believe limited instability [in Iraq] and free rein of pro-Iranian militias to be in their best interest." [33]

Parsi of the National Iranian American Council shares Rubin's analysis, up to a point. "If a larger accommodation doesn't take place, my thinking is that the Iranians will not help stabilize Iraq," he says. "The fear in Iran is that the ultimate goal of the United States is to attack Iran and remove its government." Based on that perception, he says, Iran sees a benefit in American forces facing continued threat in Iraq.

But unlike the Iran hawks, Parsi argues that Iran could become a force for peace in Iraq. "They want something in return — better relations with the United States in which the U.S. recognizes Iranian security interests and doesn't attack Iran.

Hardliners ridicule the notion that any deal can be reached with a government that sees itself as an implacable enemy.

"They're just trying to kill us in Iraq," says Ledeen of the American Enterprise Institute. "We have been looking for a modus vivendi with Iran since 1979." The only conclusion to be drawn, he argues, is that there is no Iranian interest in cooperating with the United States.

Riedel argues that view closes off any possibility of peaceful resolution. "If Iranians believe we are only interested in regime change, we're killing any chance of a serious dialogue," he says. "The Iranians need to know when they enter into any kind of dialogue with us that it is not a subterfuge for overthrowing the Islamic Republic."

In any event, he adds, "If an overthrow is anyone's goal, it's a fantasy." The present Iranian government will not disappear "any time in the near future."

BACKGROUND

Mossadegh Overthrown

Modern U.S.-Iranian relations began with the CIA-engineered overthrow of Prime Minister Mohammed Mossadegh in 1953. Mossadegh, an ardent nationalist,

CHRONOLOGY

1950s-1978 *CIA ousts nationalist prime minister, ushering in an era of close ties to Iran's monarch.*

April 28, 1951 Iran's parliament nationalizes country's oil industry.

Aug. 19, 1953 CIA directs coup that ousts Prime Minister Mohammed Mossadegh, who spearheaded oil nationalization.

1963 Shah Mohammed Reza Pahlavi's U.S.-originated "white revolution" on socioeconomic issues receives 99 percent approval in an obviously rigged referendum that prompts a wave of protests.

1964 More protests greet a new law granting immunity to thousands of Americans working in Iran if they are accused of crimes. . . . Ayatollah Ruhollah Khomeini, a cleric leading the protests, is forced into exile.

1977 President Jimmy Carter toasts the shah in Tehran as a beloved promoter of stability.

Jan. 1978 Officially sponsored publication of an article defaming Khomeini sparks demonstrations.

1979-1989 *Incapable of quelling the protests, the shah flees, and Khomeini returns from exile to become the country's dominant leader under a quasi-parliamentary system dominated by religious leaders.*

Jan. 1979 Shah goes into exile.

Nov. 4, 1979 Shah's arrival in United States for cancer treatment prompts students to storm the U.S. Embassy in Tehran and take 52 hostages.

1980 Iraqi dictator Saddam Hussein, a Sunni, launches a war against Iran's Shiite government — which he perceives as a threat to his regime.

1981 Iran frees the hostages the day Carter leaves office. . . . Crash of a plane carrying Israeli arms for Iran signals Israel's tilt in Iran-Iraq war.

1983 Hezbollah terrorists allied with Iran attack U.S. Embassy and Marine barracks in Beirut, Lebanon, killing 304 Americans.

1986 President Ronald Reagan admits his administration illegally sold weapons to Iran and funneled profits to the "contra" guerrillas fighting Nicaragua's left-wing Sandinista government. . . . U.S. confirms providing intelligence to Iraq to help its bombing campaign against Iran.

1989 Ayatollah Khomeini dies.

1990-2007 *Conservative cleric appointed to Iran's most important post. Relations with the U.S. deteriorate.*

1990 Conservative Ayatollah Ali Khamenei named supreme leader.

1997 Reformist cleric Mohammed Khatami elected president in a landslide.

1998 Khatami seems interested in reopening relations with the U.S.

2000 Dissident journalist Akbar Ganji and other democracy activists imprisoned.

2001 Khatami wins second term. . . . Iranian security forces help U.S. military during invasion of Afghanistan.

2002 Bush calls Iran a member of the "axis of evil," along with North Korea and Iraq.

2005 Populist hard-liner Mahmoud Ahmadinejad elected president following failure of Khatami's reforms.

Dec. 23, 2006 U.S. military says Iran is arming Iraqi militias. . . . U.N. Security Council imposes financial sanctions on Iran for failing to halt uranium enrichment. . . . Iran holds conference on Holocaust, with Holocaust deniers invited.

2007 Security Council orders new sanctions against Iran for its refusal to quit uranium enrichment. . . . Senate resolution demands that the U.S. "combat" Iranian activities in Iraq. . . . President Bush says Iran's nuclear program raises specter of "World War III." . . . Israeli bombing in Syria raises fear of Israeli or U.S. strike on Iran. . . . Ahmadinejad vows no retreat from nuclear program. . . . October talks between Iran and nuclear-watchdog agency produce no agreement.

had been at the center of a crisis that had been building since the late 1940s over the future of Britain's long-standing oil concession, which effectively controlled Iran's major natural resource. [34]

Mossadegh had accepted the post of prime minister from the shah on condition that parliament end the concession, which it did on April 28, 1951. "The anniversary of the passing of the oil nationalization bill," writes historian Ali M. Ansari of the University of St. Andrews in Scotland, "is perhaps the closest thing to an Iranian independence day." [35]

But for the CIA — which worked closely with the British — Mossadegh's nationalization of Britain's Anglo-Iranian Oil. Co. showed him to be a threat to Western interests, and politically unreliable, in a region where the Soviet Union was a looming presence. President Dwight D. Eisenhower approved a coup plan. One attempt failed, leading the shah to take a sudden vacation in Rome. Then, on Aug. 19, 1953, a CIA officer directed a move against Mossadegh, who eventually surrendered. "The shah became the centerpiece of American foreign policy in the Islamic world," writes *New York Times* correspondent Tim Weiner in a recent history of the CIA. But, "A generation of Iranians grew up known that the CIA had installed the shah." [36]

Although the United States poured money into Iran after the coup, it didn't buy all Iranians' friendship. Abolhasan Ebtehaj, a government official who lost his post after disputes with American officials, faulted the free-spending U.S. approach. "Not so many years ago in Iran, the United States was loved and respected as no other country, and without having given a penny of aid," he said in a 1961 speech in San Francisco. "Now, after more than $1 billion of loans and grants, America is neither loved nor respected; she is distrusted by most people and hated by many." [37]

The John F. Kennedy administration, which came to power in 1961, pushed the shah even harder to shake up his country's social structure. Arguing that Iran's land-tenure system amounted to "feudalism," creating conditions that made Iran ripe for a communist revolution, the Americans demanded private land ownership for peasants.

But when the shah's so-called "white revolution" occurred, it brought repercussions that the Americans hadn't foreseen. Rural, land-owning aristocrats and members of the clergy, who had been instrumental in pushing out Mossadegh, opposed the change, in some cases more

because it was American-imposed than because of its objectives. The shah, with U.S. encouragement, also proposed the political emancipation of women, which angered conservatives, especially religious leaders.

When a national referendum showed 99 percent approval for the "revolution," riots broke out because the election clearly had been rigged. Ruhollah Khomeini, a previously obscure clergyman, became one of the strongest voices against the shah.

For Iranians, what the shah and his American advisers called reform was something quite different. "The shah's modernization program — which created less an authentic development than a consumer society for privileged elites — quickly enriched the members of the royal family and the court, the entrepreneurs (almost all subcontractors for large Western firms), the powerful merchants, the importers of spare parts and consumer goods, the speculators," wrote French journalist Eric Rouleau in 1980. [38]

Then the United States prompted the shah to introduce legislation granting immunity from the Iranian legal system for any American citizen accused of a crime. On the same day the bill was approved — after the shah fixed the parliamentary vote — Iranian lawmakers also approved a $200 million loan from the United States.

"The dignity of Iran has been destroyed," Khomeini declared. "They wanted a loan, and America demanded this in return." In 1964 Khomeini was sent into exile. [39]

Shah Overthrown

The United States and the shah deepened their relationship in the 1970s. Israel, too, enjoyed close ties to the shah, whose quiet acceptance of the Jewish state enraged Arab governments — and many Iranians. By 1977, there were some 30,000 American government personnel and businesspeople in Iran, President Jimmy Carter noted during a toast to the shah on New Year's Eve in Tehran. [40]

"Iran, because of the great leadership of the shah, is an island of stability in one of the more troubled areas of the world," said Carter, in words that would later embarrass him. "This is a great tribute to you, your majesty, and to your leadership and to the respect and the admiration and love which your people give to you." [41]

Only weeks later, however, the monarchy's collapse began. In January, after the shah-approved publication of a defamatory newspaper article about Khomeini, well-organized street protests broke out in several cities, creating a crisis atmosphere.

Presidential Hopefuls Targeting Iran

Democrats and Republicans disagree on military action

U.S. military action against Iran may or may not occur, but candidates for the 2008 presidential nomination are fighting about whether it would be a good idea.

For now, the big Iran knockdown is taking place among Democratic candidates. Debate centers on a Sept. 26 Senate resolution urging the United States to "combat, contain and roll back the violent activities and destabilizing influence" of Iran's government inside Iraq and declare the Iranian Revolutionary Guard Corps a terrorist organization. The resolution passed, 76-22. [1]

Former Sen. John Edwards, D-N.C.

Antiwar Democrats called the amendment a barely veiled authorization to scramble warplanes over Iran. "It's an enormous mistake to give George Bush the first step in the authority to move militarily on Iran," said former North Carolina **Sen. John Edwards**. "The resolution on the Iranian Revolutionary Guard did that." [2]

Edwards' comment was aimed not only at the Bush administration but at frontrunner **Sen. Hillary Rodham Clinton**, D-N.Y., who drew fire from antiwar Democrats for supporting the resolution.

Sen. Hillary Rodham Clinton, D-N.Y.

Clinton responded that she hadn't been voting for war. "I oppose any rush to war but also believe doing nothing is not acceptable — diplomacy is the right path," she said in a mailing to prospective primary voters in Iowa. [3]

Perhaps in response to criticism of her vote, Clinton on Oct. 1 signed up as a cosponsor of a bill introduced last March by Sen. Jim Webb, D-Va., that would bar military action against Iran without congressional authorization. [4]

Webb, a Marine combat veteran of Vietnam, was among the critics of the resolution, which had been sponsored by Sen. Joseph Lieberman, I-Conn., whose hawkish views on Iraq cost him the Democratic Senate nomination in his state in 2006, and Sen. Jon Kyl of Arizona, a conservative Republican. "Those who regret their vote five years ago to authorize military action in Iraq should think hard before supporting this approach," he said, "because, in my view, it has the same potential to do harm where many are seeking to do good." [5]

While Clinton's support for Webb's bill might have seemed an opportunistic response to recent attacks, last February she had demanded that Bush make no move against Iran without congressional authorization. [6]

In any case, Clinton's opponents didn't drop the Iran issue. By late October, another front-runner nipping at her heels advocated a sharp break with the Iran policy espoused by the administration — notably going further than Clinton in marking a distance from Bush.

Sen. Barack Obama, D-Ill.

"I would meet directly with Iranian leaders," **Sen. Barack Obama**, D-Ill., told *The New York Times*. "We would engage in a level of aggressive, personal diplomacy. . . . Iran and Syria would start changing their behavior if they started seeing that they had some incentives to do so, but right now the only incentive that exists is our president suggesting that if you do what we tell you, we may not blow you up." Obama didn't vote on the resolution that brought Clinton so much heat.

Among Republican presidential hopefuls, Iran has served mostly as a contest over who can advocate the toughest mea-

Sen. John McCain, R-Ariz.

sures. Arizona **Sen. John McCain** seemed momentarily to have won that contest. In April, sitting in his tour bus, he sang a few bars of the chorus of "Bomb Iran," by Vince Vance and the Valiants, an AM radio favorite of the 1979-1981 hostage-crisis period (based on the Beach Boys' "Barbara Ann").[7] But after cries of indignation, McCain protested that he'd only been kidding. "People got to lighten up, get a life," McCain said.[8]

Nevertheless, in a more serious setting McCain answered affirmatively when asked at an October debate whether he would take action against Iran — without con-

Former Gov. Mitt Romney, R-Mass.

sulting Congress — to stop it from acquiring nuclear weapons. But he added a proviso — "if the situation . . . requires immediate action to ensure the security of the United States of America."[9]

Former Massachusetts **Gov. Mitt Romney** was widely judged to have stumbled when he answered the same question: "We're going to let the lawyers sort out what he needed to do and what he didn't need to do," Romney said, seemingly referring to whichever president might be facing the issue, "but certainly what you want to

Former Mayor Rudolph Giuliani, R-N.Y.

do is to have the agreement of all the people in leadership of our government, as well as our friends around the world where those circumstances are available."[10]

Of all the Republican contenders, former New York City Mayor **Rudolph W. Giuliani** has made the most of the Iran issue. His senior foreign policy adviser

on Iran is Michael Rubin of the American Enterprise Institute, who advocates stepping up aid to Iranian democracy activists. Also advising is *Commentary* magazine Editor-at-large Norman Podhoretz, a prominent neocon who calls for bombing Iranian nuclear facilities.

During a September visit to London, Giuliani said that if Iran got close to building a nuclear weapon, "We will prevent them or we'll set them back five or 10 years." He added, "That is not said as a threat. That should be said as a promise."[11]

But even if he won the nomination and the election, Giuliani wouldn't be deciding Iran policy until early 2009. For now, the constant stream of events, speculation, declarations and rumors about Iran is fueling the political process to such an extent that liberal *New York Times* columnist Frank Rich theorized that the Bush administration is keeping the tension high mainly to torment Democratic candidates.

"Whatever happens in or to Iran," Rich wrote, "the American public will be carpet-bombed by apocalyptic propaganda for the 12 months to come."

[1] See Senate Amendment 3017 to HR1585: "To express the sense of the Senate regarding Iran," Sept. 20, 2007, www.govtrack.us/congress/amendment.xpd?session=110&amdt=s3017.

[2] Quoted in Dan Balz, "Iran Becomes an Issue in Democratic Contest," *The Washington Post*, Oct. 25, 2007, p. A7.

[3] *Ibid.*

[4] See "Senator Clinton Announces Co-Sponsorship of Webb Legislation Prohibiting the Use of Funds for Military Operations In Iran," press release, Oct. 1, 2007, www.senate.gov/~clinton/news/statements/details.cfm?id=284618.

[5] Quoted in Shailagh Murray, "Webb Seen as a Potential 2008 Running Mate," *The Washington Post*, Oct. 28, 2007, p. A4.

[6] "Clinton: No Military Action on Iran Without Congressional Authority," press release, Feb. 14, 2007, www.senate.gov/~clinton/news/statements/record.cfm?id=269287.

[7] See "Vince Vance and the Valiants," neworleansbands.net, undated, www.neworleansbands.net/music/bands/161/.

[8] Quoted in Mark Leibovich, "Falling From the Top Lands McCain in a Scaled-Back Comfort Zone," *The Washington Post*, Oct. 7, 2007, p. A1.

[9] Quoted in Adam Nagourney and Marc Santora, "Romney and Giuliani Spar as New Guy Looks On," *The New York Times*, Oct. 10, 2007, p. A1.

[10] *Ibid.*

[11] Quoted in Michael Finnegan, "Giuliani warns Iranians against nuclear ambitions," *Los Angeles Times*, Sept. 20, 2007, p. A15.

To the surprise of observers, the shah and his notorious secret police, SAVAK, proved incapable of coping. In the past SAVAK had arrested, tortured or killed hundreds of thousands of genuine or alleged oppositionists. Israel had a close working relationship with SAVAK, growing out of antagonism between the shah and the Arab states. That relationship fueled popular antagonism toward the Jewish state.

A year later, on Jan. 16, 1979, the shah fled Iran. Two weeks later, Khomeini returned home from exile in Paris, turning the revolutionary process definitively toward his brand of socially conservative, politically aggressive and theocratic Shiite politics. Some secular democrats who were involved in an early provisional government were pushed aside. "At every step of the way, [Khomeini] and his supporters proved more ardent in their faith, more manipulative in their conduct and more merciless in their retaliations," writes Ray Takeyh, a historian and senior fellow at the centrist Council on Foreign Relations. [42]

Khomeini's strategy bore fruit on Dec. 3, 1979, when Iranian voters approved a constitution that created today's Islamic Republic of Iran, directed by a religious leader who would not be accountable to the public or to elected officials. A Guardian Council, mainly clerics, would have the final word on all legislation.

The referendum passed amidst a frenzy of enthusiasm generated by a crisis that still reverberates. A month earlier, on Nov. 4, a band of student militants overran the U.S. Embassy in Tehran, taking 52 hostages, to punish the Carter administration for allowing the shah into the United States for cancer treatment.

Khomeini applauded the takeover, and the United States cut relations with Iran — which haven't been restored to this day. Khomeini's forces, meanwhile, used CIA and other U.S. documents the students found to discredit domestic enemies shown to have connections to the United States. The hostage crisis ended 444 days after it began, with the inauguration of Ronald Reagan on Jan. 20, 1981.

Besides broken diplomatic relations, U.S. sanctions against Iran imposed during the hostage crisis also have survived. The United States first imposed financial penalties on Iran during the crisis, when the Carter administration banned Iranian oil imports and froze Iranian assets in the United States. In 1987, Reagan banned imports of all Iranian goods and services, citing Iranian support for international terrorism. In 1995, Clinton banned U.S. participation in petroleum develop-ment in Iran, also citing Iranian support for terrorism as well as efforts to acquire weapons of mass destruction. In 1997 Clinton extended the previous order by explicitly barring Americans from virtually all trade and investments involving Iran — a ban that was eased in 2000 to allow imports of Iranian dried fruits, nuts and caviar. [43]

Israel's Tilt

During the hostage crisis, in September 1980, Saddam Hussein launched a war against Iran over its alleged violation of a bilateral treaty. But, pretext aside, Saddam wanted to crush the new republic. As a Sunni ruling a majority-Shiite populace, Saddam viewed Iran's Shiite government as a powerful threat to his predominantly Sunni regime.

Saddam also posed a serious threat to Israel, given his nuclear ambitions. Iran seemed a lesser danger, despite its anti-Israel rhetoric. But for the United States, still reeling from the hostage crisis, Iran was the main enemy. The Iran-Iraq war would see the United States helping Iraq, while Israel secretly shipped arms to Iran. These alignments later shifted — with the United States toppling Saddam and Israel coming to fear Iran. But even during the 1980s, U.S. officials at one point joined in a scheme with Israel to sell arms to Iran.

During the eight-year war, Israeli leaders occasionally acknowledged their tilt toward Iran. "For 28 of 37 years, Iran was a friend of Israel. If it could work for 28 years . . . why couldn't it [again], once this crazy idea of Shiite fundamentalism is gone?" asked Yitzhak Rabin, Israel's defense minister, in 1987. [44]

But in addition to talking, the Jewish state was supplying arms to Iran. Both countries had reasons to keep the supply line secret, but in July 1981 an Argentine airplane carrying Israeli weapons to Iran crashed, leading to reports of a $200 million arms deal between the two countries. [45]

A few years later, Israeli — and American — arms sales to Iran became front-page news during the so-called "Iran-Contra" scandal. In November 1986, a Beirut newspaper revealed a secret visit to Iran by President Reagan's national security adviser, Robert McFarlane. Weeks later, Reagan admitted his administration had sold weapons to Iran — violating a U.S. arms embargo — and funneled the profits to the "contra" guerrillas fighting Nicaragua's left-wing Sandinista government.

Further complicating an already tangled tale, the Reagan administration also acknowledged it had fed secret intelligence to Iraq from U.S. satellite photos, allowing it to assess damage from bombing strikes on Iranian targets. "Because we could see the fact that Iran at various times clearly had the upper hand, and had the manpower to continue much further than Iraq could," the American assistance was necessary, an unnamed White House official said. [46]

By that time, the United States had another reason to help Iran's enemy. Following the 1982 Israeli invasion of Lebanon, Iran — eager for a base in the Arab countries — helped create the terrorist organization and political movement Hezbollah (Party of God). Its base was Lebanon's marginalized Shiite population, which had turned against Israel.

The following year, Hezbollah was implicated in a deadly bombing that destroyed the U.S. Embassy in Lebanon's capital, Beirut, killing 63 people. Six months later, a Hezbollah truck bomb hit the U.S. Marine barracks in Beirut, killing 241 Marines serving as peacekeepers.

Opinions are divided about whether Iran played a role in a terrorist attack that killed 19 airmen in 1996 at Khobar Towers, an apartment building serving as Air Force quarters near Dhahran, Saudi Arabia. In December 2006, U.S. District Judge Royce C. Lamberth of Washington ruled Iran responsible in connection with a lawsuit by victims' families against the Islamic Republic. [47]

Lamberth's decision echoed Attorney General John Ashcroft's conclusion in June 2001 that "elements of the Iranian government inspired, supported and supervised" the attack. Some experts challenge that conclusion. "There was a paucity of credible evidence," writes historian Ansari. [48]

Rise of Repression

After Khomeini's death in 1989, Iran's clerical overseers chose conservative Ayatollah Ali Khameini as the next supreme leader. "He believes that the mission of the Islamic Republic is to uphold religious norms and resist popular attempts to alter the regime along democratic lines," writes a critic, historian Takeyh. [49]

By the late 1990s, however, the popular call for more democracy was picking up strength. In 1997, by a landslide of nearly 70 percent, voters elected Mohammed Khatami as president. Khatami, a mid-ranking cleric who had emerged as a foe of repression, had studied Western philosophy, from which he quoted freely. And he knew Western social and political norms up close, having lived in Germany. That broader outlook and

experience showed. "State authority cannot be attained through coercion and dictatorship," he had written. [50]

In 1998, Khatami indicated a willingness not only to loosen controls on Iranians but also to enter into negotiations aimed at renewing relations with the United States. Using a 1998 interview with CNN to broadcast his views to the West, Khatami condemned terrorism "in all its forms." And speaking of the hostage crisis — still looming over U.S.-Iranian affairs — Khatami said it grew out of Iranian grievances such as the 1953 coup but also reflected the chaos of a revolutionary period — a condition that no longer applied. "Today, our new society has been institutionalized," he said, "and there is no need for unconventional methods of expression." [51]

In his first year in office, more than 200 new newspapers and magazines and 95 political parties and organizations were permitted. The new freedom sparked public debates on topics that had been out of bounds, including Israel and the Palestinians.

In 2001 Khatami swept into office a second time, with a 77 percent victory. But even supporters admitted that political liberalization had advanced, despite continued repression, while the economy had fallen off a cliff. One-quarter of the workforce was unemployed, and 40 percent of the population lived below the poverty line. [52]

Not surprisingly, the high hopes Khatami had inspired turned into disillusion. Economic disaster aside, Iranians who had hoped for reopening relations with the United States had experienced only disappointment. Iranian-U.S. cooperation early in the invasion of Afghanistan hadn't led to closer ties. "Before and during the war in Afghanistan, the Iranians were quite helpful to the United States," writes Kenneth Pollack, director of Persian Gulf Affairs at the National Security Council in the Clinton administration "They shared our hatred of al Qaeda and the Taliban, and they provided us with extensive assistance on intelligence, logistics, diplomacy and Afghan internal politics." [53]

And yet, the year after the Afghanistan campaign began, Bush in his first State of the Union address called Iran a member of the "axis of evil," along with North Korea and Iraq. "Iran aggressively pursues these weapons [of mass destruction] and exports terror," Bush said, "while an unelected few repress the Iranian people's hope for freedom." [54]

In 2005, Ahmadinejad, then Tehran's mayor, won a presidential-election runoff with 62 percent of the vote. A veteran of the bloody Iran-Iraq War and an engineer of working-class origins, he combined Khomeini-era rhetoric against the United States with denunciations of economic injustice.

Where reformists in Iran had hoped for eventual restoration of relations with the West, the new president and his circle looked to China, India and Russia for capital and trade links. "Our nation is continuing the path of progress and on this path has no significant need for the United States," Ahmadinejad said shortly before his election. [55]

CURRENT SITUATION

New Sanctions

The Bush administration is gearing up to start enforcing a new set of financial sanctions against an Iranian military force that the administration charges with terrorism. The sanctions also are designed to stymie what the administration regards as Iran's nuclear-weapons development program.

On Oct. 25, 2007, the State Department barred U.S. citizens and businesses from dealing with banks, businesses and individuals linked to the Revolutionary Guard, Iran's military logistics agency, or the Aerospsace Industries Organization, both of which the administration says are helping in developing ballistic missiles or nuclear weapons. [56]

The State Department also listed a unit of the Revolutionary Guard — the Qods [Jerusalem] Force — as a terrorist agency. The administration says the force, which has been described as a 5,000-man "unconventional warfare" wing of the Guard, provides "material support" to Lebanon's Hezbollah; three Palestinian organizations, including the militant Palestinian Islamic group Hamas; Afghanistan's Taliban and Shiite militias in Iraq "who target and kill coalition and Iraqi forces and innocent Iraqi civilians." [57]

Administration officials suggested that the sanctions represented a commitment to cracking down on Iran short of war. "We do not believe that conflict is inevitable," said Under Secretary of State for Political Affairs R. Nicholas Burns after the measures were announced. "This decision today supports the diplomacy and in no way, shape or form does it anticipate the use of force." [58]

Whether the sanctions will bite into Iran's nuclear development project is another question. "It is unlikely that these sanctions are going to impede the Iranian pursuit of nuclear capabilities," says Jon Wolfstahl, a senior fellow at the Center for Strategic and International Studies. "It is not going to seriously affect their financial situation because oil prices have risen so high." [59]

But a former National Security Council (NSC) official, Lee Wolosky, sees the sanctions as capable of slowing down Iran's use of the international financial system. European governments may ignore the sanctions, he acknowledges, but European banks could cooperate, if only to avoid complicating their own dealings with the United States. "Already, a great deal of of informal pressure is being applied to European banks to re-analyze relationships with Iran," he says.

"This has had a certain measure of success," he continues. "You're going to see non-U.S. banks cease to do business with [Iranian entities]." [60]

Days after his remarks, according to *The New York Times*, Western diplomats said most major European banks had quit dealing with the Iranian banks named in the sanction orders, or were getting ready to do so. [61]

The new sanctions have reverberated at the World Bank, where officials said in November they were holding up $5.4 million for four projects in Iran — earthquake relief, water and sanitation, environment management and urban housing. The bank acted because the sanctions left it without an Iranian bank through which to funnel funds. [62]

An Iranian official, meanwhile, scoffed at the new measures. "Sanctions have been imposed on us for the past 28 years," said Saeed Jalili, who recently replaced Ali Larijani as Iran's representative before the International Atomic Energy Agency (IAEA). "The new sanctions, like those before, will have no effect on Iran's policies." [63]

Whatever effects the past sanctions may have had, they clearly haven't stopped Iran's nuclear development efforts, according to Paul Pillar, the CIA's former national intelligence officer for the Near East and South Asia. He worries the latest sanctions raise tensions between Iran and the United States. "They strengthen the positions of the relative hard-liners," Pillar says. "I think we played into the Iranian president's hands." [64]

Iran in the U.N.

Amid the new sanctions, and the stepped-up war of words between Washington and Tehran, the U.N. Security Council is jockeying with Iran over its nuclear program.

Are President Bush's recent statements on Iran dangerously provocative?

YES Sen. Robert C. Byrd, D-W. Va.
Chairman, Senate Appropriations Committee

Written for *CQ Researcher*, November 2007

Yes. Every day now, it seems that the confrontational rhetoric between the United States and Iran continues to escalate. The main point of contention is Iran's pursuit of nuclear weapons. While few doubt Iran's desire to attain a nuclear bomb, there is little evidence that they are close to acquiring such a capability.

Yet, the White House has been busy unleashing almost daily claims of an imminent nuclear threat in Iran, as it did with Iraq. Fear, panic and chest-pounding do not work well in the conduct of foreign policy. This is a time to put diplomacy to work. There is ample opportunity to coordinate with our allies to constrain Iran's ambitions. But instead of working with our partners, the Bush administration has unveiled new unilateral sanctions against Iran. Instead of direct diplomatic negotiations with Iran, the administration continues to issue ultimatums and threats.

We have been down that path already. We know where it leads. Vice President Cheney recently threatened "serious consequences" — the exact phrase that he used in the run-up to the invasion of Iraq — if Tehran does not acquiesce to U.S. demands. The parallels are all-too-chilling. President Bush warned that those who wish to "avoid World War III" should seek to keep Iran from attaining nuclear weapons. Secretary of Defense Robert Gates has admitted in the press that the Pentagon has drafted plans for a military option in Iran. The president's $196 billion request for emergency war funding included a request for "bunker-buster" bombs that have no immediate use in Iraq.

Taking all of it together — the bellicose rhetoric, the needlessly confrontational unilateral sanctions, the provocative stationing of U.S. warships in the region, the operational war planning and the request for munitions that seem designed for use in Iran — there are reasons for deep concern that this administration is once again rushing headlong into another disastrous war in the Middle East.

The Bush administration apparently believes that it has the authority to wage preemptive war — and can do so without prior congressional approval. That is why I am cosponsoring a resolution with Sen. Richard Durbin, D-Ill., which affirms that any military action taken against Iran must be explicitly approved by Congress before any such action be initiated. The White House must be reminded of the constitutional powers entrusted to the people's branch. Let us halt this rush to another war. Let us not make the same disastrous mistake as we did with Iraq.

NO Michael Rubin
Resident Scholar, American Enterprise Institute

Written for *CQ Researcher*, November 2007

On Oct. 17, President Bush raised the specter of war with Iran. "If you're interested in avoiding World War III," he said, it's necessary to deny the Islamic Republic "the knowledge necessary to make a nuclear weapon." Condemnation of his comments was swift. Sen. Robert Byrd, D-W. Va., accused the president of using "rhetorical ghosts and goblins to scare the American people, with claims of an imminent nuclear threat in Iran."

Navel-gazing is a Capitol Hill pastime, but such criticism is misplaced. Since the disclosure of Iran's covert enrichment program, International Atomic Energy Agency (IAEA) inspectors — not the CIA or Iranian exiles — report a litany of lies. IAEA inspectors discovered traces of uranium metal used to build bombs, not fuel reactors. IAEA inspectors also found that Iran had experimented with chemical separation of polonium, a material used to initiate nuclear detonation. Iran still has not revealed what rogue Pakistani scientist A.Q. Khan sold on his trip to Tehran.

Diplomacy should always be the strategy of first resort, but its track record with Tehran does not encourage. While it is fashionable to blame Iran's nuclear desire upon U.S. presence in Iraq and Afghanistan, Tehran's program predates such interventions by 15 years. In the name of engagement, the European Union nearly tripled trade with Iran between 2000 and 2005. But rather than invest that windfall in schools and hospitals, the Iranian government — then under reformist control — poured money into its military and centrifuge programs. Tehran has yet to provide the West a single, confidence-building measure.

Iranian diplomats say their program is peaceful, but officials close to Supreme Leader Ali Khamenei suggest otherwise. On Feb. 14, 2005, Ayatollah Mohammad Baqer Kharrazi, secretary-general of Iranian Hezbollah, said, "We are able to produce atomic bombs, and we will do that." Three months later, Gholam Reza Hasani, Khamenei's representative to West Azerbaijan province said, "An atomic bomb . . . must be produced." And, on Sept. 3, 2007, Khamenei himself said, "Iran will outwit the West on the nuclear issue."

Iran's centrifuge cascade, Syria's surprise nuclear plant and North Korea's role in its construction suggest time is limited. To avert escalation, the White House must demonstrate diplomacy to be Tehran's best option. Bush's rhetoric dampens Iran's overconfidence and underscores U.S. seriousness, both in Tehran and at the United Nations. Bashing Bush may make good politics, but it is irresponsible and may hasten the result which Bush's domestic critics most fear.

Mohammed ElBaradei, director of the IAEA, has been trying to negotiate a program of tough inspections to ensure Iran's uranium-enrichment program stops short of producing weapons-quality fuel. While he has argued against trying to stop enrichment altogether, he has also warned that Iran may have to "come clean" about possible past work on weapons development. [65]

"We cannot give Iran a pass right now, because there's still a lot of question marks," ElBaradei said on CNN in late October. He added that the agency hasn't seen any definitive evidence Iran is pursuing an "active weaponization program." [66]

ElBaradei's remarks came about six weeks before he is scheduled to tell diplomats from the United States, Britain, France, Germany, Russia and China whether doubts over Iran's nuclear intentions have been resolved. If not, at least some of those countries favor new U.N. sanctions designed to force Iran's compliance with IAEA regulations.

In early November, the British Foreign Office announced that all six countries had agreed to approve such sanctions, but China and Russia hadn't confirmed Britain's statement. Days earlier, President Vladimir V. Putin asked, "Why make the situation worse, bring it to a dead end, threaten sanctions or even military action?" [67]

The climate surrounding Putin's statement — already made tense by the Foreign Office's announcement and the earlier statements by Bush and Cheney — was further supercharged by military action by Israel. On Sept. 6, Israeli warplanes bombed a building in Syria that American officials said housed a nuclear project aided by North Korea. Israel has maintained official silence and imposed military censorship on its aggressive press. And Syria has denied doing any nuclear work — with North Korea or without it. "The rumors have been deliberately fabricated by Israel to justify its recent act of aggression against Syria," Syrian Prime Minister Mohammed Naji al-Otri said. [68]

Whatever effect the bombing may have had on Syria, Iran was also indirectly a target, some Washington strategists said. "If you are Israel and you are looking at this, the value of striking Syria is that it sends a signal, including to the Iranians," said Michael Green, a former director of Asian affairs at the National Security Council and now an associate professor at Georgetown University's School of Foreign Service. "This follows the Chinese proverb that sometimes you have to kill the chicken to scare the monkey." [69]

Iranian officials gave no sign of being scared, nor of willingness to bend to international pressure to suspend their efforts to enrich uranium. "Suspension is the crucial issue if the Iranians want to get off the hook of more sanctions," said a participant in talks in Rome in October between Iranian negotiators and Javier Solana, foreign policy director of the European Union. "They seem to think they are doing enough." [70]

Last March, and also in December 2006, the Security Council approved sanctions aimed at forcing Iran to stop its enrichment efforts. [71]

The first of those two sets of sanctions banned the import and export by Iran of materials and technology used in uranium enrichment and ballistic missiles. In addition, the assets of 12 Iranian individuals and 10 companies allegedly involved in nuclear and missile work were frozen. [72]

Then, in March, after Iran still hadn't satisfied objections to its nuclear program, the Security Council approved tougher sanctions, including a ban on all weapons sales to Iran and on any grants or loans to Iran not involving humanitarian and development aid. [73]

In the weeks leading up to the scheduled November meeting, the outlook for Iran to back away from enrichment seemed dim, judging by President Ahmadinejad's blunt remarks just before the Rome talks were to start. "Iran will not retreat one iota," he said. "We are in favor of talks, but we will not negotiate with anyone about our right to nuclear technology."

Ahmadinejad's declaration represents one face that Iranian officials have presented to international bodies who try to control the proliferation of nuclear technology.

The other face showed in statements made after Iranian officials met in Rome with E.U. representatives. "We are after no adventure, and we are after no trouble-making," Larijani told reporters. [74]

But, in a further complication for those trying to decode Iran's strategy, Larijani — seen by some as a voice of moderation — was replaced as Iran's chief negotiator on the nuclear issue. Larijani denied that his removal signaled a hardening of Iran's position. Some Iranian politicians didn't buy the denial. "It is very disappointing that the government does not tolerate even views of a person like Mr. Larijani and would eliminate him in such a manner," said Mohammed Hashemi, a former vice president and the brother of former President Ali Akbar Hashemi Rafsanjani. [75]

Larijani's replacement, in fact, was among the latest in a long sequence of events that have prompted suspicion of

Iran's intentions. In 2005, for example, the IAEA reported that Iran had acquired engineering drawings on how to cast uranium into the exact shape of a nuclear bomb core. Equally important, the source of the drawings was the infamous A. Q. Khan of Pakistan, who had made a mission and a business out of selling nuclear plans to developing countries, especially Muslim-majority nations. [76]

Hovering over the entire issue of Iran and nuclear development is the question of when Iran could be ready to produce a nuclear weapon. Defense Secretary Gates has reported that intelligence agencies estimate 2010 at the earliest, or 2015 at the latest. But Israel's military intelligence research chief, Brig. Gen. Yossi Baidatz, told the Israeli parliament in early November that the date could come as early as 2009. Some Israeli officials have suggested that Israel would never let Iran get that far. Sallai Meridor, ambassador to the United States, said in late October that Israel should always be prepared "to preempt, to deter, to defeat if we can." [77]

But Israel's political-military elite isn't of one mind on the subject. Efraim Halevy, Israel's retired chief spymaster, disputes the notion that Iran poses a threat to Israel's existence. "I believe that Israel is indestructible," Halevy told *The Washington Post.* And if Iran does produce an atomic weapon, he said, Israel has "a whole arsenal of capabilities" to deter nuclear aggression from Iran, whose leaders would consider it a religious violation to put their country's survival at risk. [78]

OUTLOOK

Popular Uprising?

What will Iran be like 10 years from now? George Mason University historian Bakhash refuses to hazard a prediction. "There are too many variables," he says.

Indeed, from the 1953 coup to the flight of the shah to the embassy hostage crisis to the horrific war with Iraq — and more — Iran has experienced enough volatility for 10 countries.

"Iran is a very emotional and changeable society; it's better to forecast the next six months," says human-rights activist Afshari, sounding a similar note of caution. But he does sketch out a possible near-term future.

"In the next 10 years, Iranian society will be in a much better situation in the field of democracy and human rights and justice," he says. "A basic change will

have happened. The government can't continue like this. They have to give in to the Iranian people's demands."

Afshari sees the present government as incapable of maintaining its current nuclear development efforts. "It cannot continue outside the control of the international community," he says.

Moreover, he predicts, citing the collapse of the Soviet Union, sweeping changes will be brought about, but not by popular elections. "There will be big social changes — civil disobedience like in Poland, and also like the Islamic Revolution," he says.

Such a scenario could come about, says Iran hawk Rubin of the American Enterprise Institute. But a far bleaker one is equally possible, he says: "Either you're going to have a Romania-style change, or else the regime will have crushed all dissent." [79]

Rubin agrees with Afshari that working within legal channels won't produce the kind of deep change that democracy activists and their supporters abroad support. "If you believe that your legitimacy comes from God, you don't care what 90 percent of the people think." Hence, any hopes are futile that the government would respond even to a massive negative vote, he says.

Rubin's American Enterprise Institute colleague Ledeen depicts the government's position even more starkly. "The problem is not the fanaticism of the people, it's the fanaticism of the regime — a thin veneer on top of a civilized and cultured country. They're pro-Western and pro-American, they understand a lot about self-government, they're well-educated, and they've had constitutions. Why aren't we working for their freedom?"

Parsi, the Iranian-American advocate of a negotiated reduction in tension in Tehran, argues that lowering the level of hostility between the governments will make democratic change more possible in Iran. "If we manage to avoid conflict, if there is significant reduction of tension between the two countries and if Iran is included in the regional political and security structure — in return for significant changes — then Iran can be a constructive player in the region," he says. Indeed, he adds, "Then pro-democracy forces will have greater maneuverability to move Iran in a more democratic direction."

Riedel of the Brookings Institution's Saban Center says the failure of reformist President Khatami to produce fundamental changes shows the obstacles the democracy movement faces. "It is a pretty dramatic demonstration that it's not going to move as fast as its own supporters — or outsiders — would like.

"I'm not an optimist about civil-society movements in the Middle East — not on a 10-year cycle. Maybe 50 years."

For the moment, though, Riedel and other Iran-watchers are paying much closer attention to the immediate future, and the prospects for peace.

"The possibilities of avoiding war — if we can get through the end of the Bush administration, they're reasonably good," he says.

NOTES

1. Quoted in Sheryl Gay Stolberg, "Nuclear-Armed Iran Risks 'World War III,' Bush Says," *The New York Times*, Oct. 18, 2007, p. A6.

2. Quoted in Thom Shanker, "Gates Says Iran Gave Assurances on Explosives," *The New York Times*, Nov. 2, 2007, p. A10.

3. Quoted in Warren Hoge, "Iran's President Vows to Ignore U.N. Measures," *The New York Times*, Sept. 26, 2007, p. A1, www.nytimes.com/2007/09/26/world/26nations.html.

4. See "Vice President's Remarks to the Washington Institute for Near East Policy," The White House, Sept. 21, 2007, www.whitehouse.gov/news/releases/2007/10/print/20071021.html.

5. See Ray Takeyh, *Hidden Iran: Paradox and Power in the Islamic Republic* (2006), pp. 24-25.

6. Other institute scholars include John R. Bolton, former U.S. ambassador to the United Nations, who now criticizes the administration for being soft on North Korea. See John R. Bolton, "Bush's North Korea Meltdown," *The Wall Street Journal*, Oct. 31, 2007, p. A21.

7. See Michael A. Ledeen, *The Iranian Time Bomb: The Mullah Zealots' Quest for Destruction* (2007).

8. See Fareed Zakaria, "Stalin, Mao and . . . Ahmadinejad?" *Newsweek.com*, Oct. 29, 2007, www.newsweek.com/id/57346.

9. See Akbar Ganji, "Why Iran's Democrats Shun Aid," *The Washington Post*, Oct. 27, 2007, p. A21.

10. For analysis of oil market effects, see Steven Mufson, "Strike on Iran Would Roil Oil Markets, Experts Say," *The Washington Post*, Oct. 26, 2007, p. A1.

11. See "Debate Stirs Over Possible U.S. Military Action Against Iran," transcript, Online News Hour, Oct. 29, 2007, www.pbs.org/newshour/bb/middle_east/july-dec07/iran_10-29.html.

12. See Sharon Squassoni, "Iran's Nuclear Program: Recent Developments," Congressional Research Service, updated Dec. 26, 2006, pp. 1-2, http://fpc.state.gov/documents/organization/78477.pdf; Jonathan C. Randal, "Shah's Economic Projects Hit Snags, Periling His Regime," *The Washington Post*, April 2, 1978, p. A22; Susanna McBee, "Shah Reportedly Pledges Neutrality on Oil Prices," *The Washington Post*, Nov. 16, 1977, p. A1.

13. Quoted in Squassoni, *ibid.*, p. 2.

14. Quoted in Thom Shanker and William J. Broad, "Iran to Limit Cooperation With Nuclear Inspectors," *The New York Times*, March 26, 2007, p. A6.

15. David Albright and Corey Hinderstein, "Countdown to Showdown," *Bulletin of the Atomic Scientists*, November/December 2004, p. 67, http://thebulletin.metapress.com/content/y718r48304663rg9/fulltext.pdf.

16. "Smart Power Speakers Series, Gen. John Abizaid (Ret.)," Sept. 17, 2007 www.csis.org/media/csis/events/070917_smartpower_abizaid.pdf.

17. For brief background on the 1999 bombing raid, see "Iran wants compensation for Turkish air raids," Deutsche Presse-Agentur, Aug. 1, 1999.

18. See Vali Nasr, *The Shia Revival: How Conflicts within Islam Will Shape the Future* (2006), p. 67.

19. See "Debate Stirs. . . .," *op. cit.*; see also Andrew Higgins, "The bomb-makers of Asia," *The Independent* (London), Nov. 21, 1991, p. A29.

20. Trita Parsi, *Treacherous Alliance: The Secret Dealings of Israel, Iran, and the United States* (2007).

21. See Shirin Ebadi and Hadi Ghaemi, "The Human Rights Case Against Attacking Iran," *The New York Times*, Feb. 8, 2005, p. A25. For background on Ebadi see "Shirin Ebadi, The Nobel Peace Prize 2003, Autobiography," http://nobelprize.org/nobel_prizes/peace/laureates/2003/ebadi-autobio.html.

22. Quoted in Bourzou Daragahi, "Iran tightens the screws on internal dissent," *Los Angeles Times*, June 10, 2007, p. A1.

23. Quoted in Glenn Kessler, "Rice Asks for $75 Million to Increase Pressure on Iran," *The Washington Post*, Feb.

16, 2006, p. A1. See also Adam Graham-Silverman, "Family Planning Programs and Policy Fuel Senate Debate on Spending Bill," *CQ Today*, Sept. 26, 2007.

24. Quoted in Robin Wright, "Cut Iran Democracy Funding, Groups Tell U.S.," *The Washington Post*, Oct. 11, 2007, p. A15.

25. See Neil McFarquhar, "Iran Frees One Detainee as Another Family Waits in Hope," *The New York Times*, Sept. 20, 2007, p. A12; Tony Barboza, "Diplomacy in New York: Divestment; OC man freed from Iran prison," *Los Angeles Times*, Sept. 25, p. A10.

26. See Haleh Esfandiari and Robert S. Litwak, "When Promoting Democracy is Counterproductive," *Chronicle of Higher Education*, Oct. 19, 2007, http://chronicle.com/free/v54/i08/08b00701.htm.

27. See Eli Lake, "An Iranian Student Makes His Escape In face of Charges," *The New York Sun*, Jan. 3, 2005, www.nysun.com/article/7065. See also, "Iran — An Update," Committee on the Present Danger, Jan. 23, 2006, www.committeeonthepresentdanger.org/portals/4/iranpaperjan23.pdf.

28. See "Iran-Iraq War (1980-1988)," undated, globalsecurity.org, www.globalsecurity.org/military/world/war/iran-iraq.htm.

29. Quoted in Cesar G. Soriano, "General discusses Iran's, al-Sadr's influence in Iraq," *USA Today*, June 14, 2007, p. A13.

30. See Michael R. Gordon, "U.S. Says Iran-Supplied Bomb Is Killing More Troops in Iraq," *The New York Times*, Aug. 8, 2007, p. A1.

31. Quoted in Sam Enriquez, "Conflict in Iraq: Guarding the Border; Officer Sentenced," *Los Angeles Times*, Oct. 20, 2007, p. A1.

32. For the full report on Rafsanjani's sermon see "Rafsanjani: World should admire Iran's nuclear achievements," IRNA — Islamic Republic News Agency, July 13, 2007, republished at Globalsecurity.org, www.globalsecurity.org/wmd/library/news/iran/2007/iran-070713-irna02.htm.

33. See "Policy Options in Iraq," House Foreign Affairs Committee, Committee Testimony, July 17, 2007.

34. Except where otherwise indicated, this subsection is drawn from Ali M. Ansari, *Hidden Iran* (2006); and (for details of the CIA's role) Tim Weiner, *Legacy of Ashes: The History of the CIA* (2007), pp. 81-92.

35. See Ansari, *op. cit.*, pp 36-37.

36. See Weiner, *op. cit.*, p. 92.

37. Quoted in *ibid.*, p. 46. See also, Frances Bostock and Geoffrey Jones, *Planning and Power in Iran: Ebtehaj and Economic Development Under the Shah* (1989), pp. 160-161.

38. See Eric Rouleau, "Khomeini's Iran," *Foreign Affairs*, fall 1980.

39. Quoted in Ansari, *op. cit.*, p. 53.

40. Unless otherwise indicated, material in this subsection and the one that follows is drawn from Ansari, *op. cit.*; Takeyh, *op. cit.*; Trita Parsi, *Treacherous Alliances: The Secret Dealings of Israel, Iran, and the U.S.* (2007), p. 62; and Rouleau, *op. cit.*

41. See "Tehran, Iran, Toasts of the President and the Shah at a State Dinner," Dec. 31, 1977, The American Presidency Project, www.presidency.ucsb.edu/ws/index.php?pid=7080&st=&st1=.

42. See Takeyh, *op. cit.*, p. 23. Also see Shaul Bakhash, *The Reign of the Ayatollahs: Iran and the Islamic Revolution* (1990).

43. See Bernard Gwertzman, "Iraq Gets Reports From U.S. for Use in War With Iran," *The New York Times*, Dec. 16, 1986, p. A1. U.S. Department of the Treasury, *op. cit.*

44. Quoted in Glenn Frankel, "Israeli Critical of U.S. Policy in Gulf War," *The Washington Post*, Oct. 29, 1987, p. A33.

45. See Benjamin Weiser, "Behind Israel-Iran Sales, 'Amber' Light from U.S.," *The Washington Post*, Aug. 16, 1987, p. A1.

46. Quoted in Gwertzman, *op. cit.*; See also Bob Woodward, "CIA Aiding Iraq in Gulf War," *The Washington Post*, Dec. 15, 1986, p. A1.

47. See Carol D. Leonnig, "Iran Held Liable in Khobar Attack," *The Washington Post*, Dec. 23, 2006, p. A2.

48. See Ansari, *op. cit.*, p. 180; Ashcroft quoted in Barbara Slavin, "14 indicted in barracks bombing," *USA Today*, June 22, 2001, p. A6.

49. See Takeyh, *op. cit.*, pp. 33-34. For background, see Katel, *op. cit.*

50. Quoted in Takeyh, *op. cit.*, p. 44.

51. See "Iranian President Favors People to People Dialogue," CNN "Worldview," Jan. 7, 1998.

52. See John Ward Anderson, "With Stalemate Ended, Khatami Takes Oath in Iran," *The Washington Post*, Aug. 9, 2001, p. A12.

53. See Kenneth M. Pollack, "Don't Count on Iran to Pick Up the Pieces," *The New York Times*, Dec. 8, 2006, p. A35.

54. See "The President's State of the Union Address," The White House, Jan. 29, 2002, www.whitehouse.gov/news/releases/2002/01/20020129-11.html.

55. Quoted in Takeyh, *op. cit.*, p. 133.

56. See "Fact Sheet: Designation of Iranian Entities and Individuals for Proliferation Activities and Support for Terrorism," Treasury Department, Oct. 25, 2007, www.treasury.gov/press/releases/hp644.htm.

57. See Anthony H. Cordesman and Martin Kleiber, "Iran's Military Forces and Warfighting Capabilities," Center for Strategic and International Studies, 2007, pp. 78-79.

58. Quoted in Helene Cooper, "In Sanctioning Iran, U.S. Plays Its 'Unilateralism' Card," *The New York Times*, Oct. 26, 2007, p. A12.

59. Wolfstahl spoke during a conference call on Oct. 25, 2007, with journalists arranged by the National Security Network, an organization of former Democratic officials. He served as special policy adviser on non-proliferation at the Department of Energy in the Clinton administration.

60. Wolosky, now a Washington attorney, served as transnational threats director at the National Security Council under Clinton and, briefly, President George W. Bush. He spoke during the National Security Council conference call on Oct. 25, 2007.

61. See Steven R. Weisman, "U.S. Sanctions Force World Bank to Halt Some Iran Aid," *The New York Times*, Nov. 3, 2007, p. A14.

62. *Ibid.*

63. Quoted in Nazila Fathi, "Iranians Dismiss Sanctions From U.S.," *The New York Times*, Oct. 27, 2007, p. A7.

64. Pillar spoke during the National Security Council conference call on Oct. 25, 2007.

65. Quoted in Elaine Sciolino and William J. Broad, "To Iran and its Foes, an Indispensable Irritant," *The New York Times*, Sept. 17, 2007, p. A1. Also see

Kenneth Katzman, "Iran: U.S. Concerns and Policy Responses," Congressional Research Service, updated Aug. 6, 2007, p. 20, http://fpc.state.gov/documents/organization/91002.pdf.

66. Quoted in Maggie Farley, "U.N. still probing Iran nuclear case," *Los Angeles Times*, Oct. 30, 2007, p. A4.

67. Quoted in "Britain Reports Plan for New Sanctions on Iran," *The New York Times* [Reuters], Nov. 30, 2007, p. A7.

68. Quoted in Joby Warrick and Robin Wright, "Suspected Location of Syria's Reactor Cleared," *The Washington Post*, Oct. 26, 2007, p. A17. See also, Mark Mazzetti and Helene Cooper, "Israeli Nuclear Suspicions Linked to Raid," *The New York Times*, Sept. 18, 2007, p. A11; Glenn Kessler and Robin Wright, "Israel, U.S. Shared Data on Suspected Nuclear Site," *The Washington Post*, Sept. 21, 2007, p. A1.

69. Quoted in David E. Sanger, "Pre-emptive Caution: The Case of Syria," *The New York Times*, Oct. 14, 2007, p. A8.

70. Quoted in Elaine Sciolino and Peter Kiefer, "Iran Has New Nuclear Negotiator, But Similar Stance," *The New York Times*, Oct. 24, 2007, p. A6.

71. See "Uranium Enrichment," U.S. Nuclear Regulatory Commission, Sept. 20, 2007, www.nrc.gov/materials/fuel-cycle-fac/ur-enrichment.html.

72. See Helene Cooper, "Diplomats to Begin Drafting New U.N. Sanctions on Iran," *The New York Times*, Feb. 27, 2007, p. A9.

73. See "Security Council tightens sanctions against Iran over uranium enrichment," UN News Centre, March 24, 2007, www.un.org/apps/news/story.asp?NewsID=21997&Cr=Iran&Cr1#.

74. *Ibid.*

75. *Ibid.*

76. See David E. Sanger and William J. Broad, "Bush and Putin Want Iran to Treat Uranium in Russia," *The New York Times*, Nov. 18, 2005, p. A1. See also Douglas Frantz, "From Patriot to Proliferator," *Los Angeles Times*, Sept. 23, 2005, p. A1, and Roland Flamini, "Nuclear Proliferation," *CQ Global Researcher*, January 2007, pp. 1-26; and Mary H. Cooper, "Nuclear Proliferation and Terrorism," *CQ Researcher*, April 2, 2004, pp. 297-320.

77. Meridor quoted in Hilary Leila Krieger, *Jerusalem Post*, online edition, Oct. 23, 2007, www.jpost .com/servlet/Satellite?pagename=JPost%2FJPArticle %2FShowFull&cid=1192380626865; Baidatz quoted in Mark Weiss and Sheera Claire Frenkel, "Mofaz: 2008 is decisive for stopping Iran's nuclear drive," *Jerusalem Post*, online edition, www.jpost .com/servlet/Satellite?cid=1192380749027&page-name=JPost%2FJPArticle%2FShowFull.

78. Quoted in David Ignatius, "The Spy Who Wants Israel to Talk," *The Washington Post*, Nov. 11, 2007, p. B7.

79. The 1989 Romanian revolution, one of the last nails in the coffin of Eastern and Central European commu-nism, toppled dictator Nicolae Ceausescu, who was shot by firing squad on national television, along with his wife, Elena. See William Horsley, "Romania's bloody revolution," BBC News, Dec. 12, 1999, http://news.bbc.co.uk/2/hi/europe/574200.stm.

BIBLIOGRAPHY

Books

Ansari, Ali M., *Confronting Iran: The Failure of American Foreign Policy and the Next Great Crisis in the Middle East*, Basic Books, 2006.
A historian at the University of St. Andrews in Scotland chronicles and analyzes the complexities of the U.S.-Iran relationship.

Ledeen, Michael A., *The Iranian Time Bomb: The Mullah Zealots' Quest for Destruction*, St. Martin's Press, 2007.
The Iranian leadership is far more dangerous than most Westerners realize, argues a longtime Iran hawk.

Parsi, Trita, *Treacherous Alliance: The Secret Dealings of Israel, Iran, and the U.S.*, Yale University Press, 2007.
An adjunct professor at Johns Hopkins University's School of Advanced International Studies traces the shifting alliances that have marked the crucial three-way relationship.

Takeyh, Ray, *Hidden Iran: Paradox and Power in the Islamic Republic*, Times Books, 2006.
A Middle East expert at the Council on Foreign Relations explores the twists and turns of Iranian politics.

Articles

Barboza, Tony, "Iranians in U.S. weigh the price of activism," *Los Angeles Times*, Sept. 16, 2007, p. B1.
The imprisonment of liberal Iranian-Americans visiting their homeland sends a chill through the Iranian exile community.

Daragahi, Borzou, "Iran tightens the screws on inter-nal dissent," *Los Angeles Times*, June 10, 2007, p. A1.
The Iranian regime is intensifying its repression of pro-democracy Iranians and those who break dress codes.

Daragahi, Borzou, "U.S.-Iran rivalry has a familiar look," *Los Angeles Times*, July 5, 2007, p. A6.
The complicated, tense standoff between the United States and Iran has parallels to the Cold War.

Hersh, Seymour M., "Shifting targets: The administra-tion's plan for Iran," *The New Yorker*, Oct. 8, 2007, www.newyorker.com/reporting/2007/10/08/071008fa_ fact_hersh.
A leading investigative journalist reports that adminis-tration strategy on Iran has met some detours and com-plications.

Montagne, Renee, (host), "The Evolution of Iran's Revolutionary Guard," National Public Radio, (tran-script), www.npr.org/templates/transcript/transcript .php?story Id=9371072.
Iran experts discuss the Iranian force at the center of the U.S.-Iran standoff.

Sciolino, Elaine, "To Iran, Iraq May Be the Greater Satan," *The New York Times*, Nov. 3, 2002, Sect. 4 (*News of the Week in Review*), p. 14.
In the run-up to the Iraq War, a veteran correspondent examines the complicated world of Middle Eastern alliances.

Wright, Robin, "Free Thinker; Iranian Dissident Akbar Ganji at Libert to Speak His Mind, at Least Until he Goes Back Home," *The Washington Post*, Aug. 14, 2007, p. C1.
A celebrated dissident assesses the grim state of civil liberties and democracy in Iran, but plans on returning.

Reports

Clawson, Patrick, and Michael Eisenstadt, "Deterring the Ayatollahs: Complications in Applying Cold War Strategy to Iran," Washington Institute for Near East Policy, July 2007, www.washingtoninstitute.org/templateC04.php?CID=280.
Washington think tank scholars compiled essays on how Iran might be persuaded not to develop nuclear weapons.

Cordesman, Anthony H., "Iran's Revolutionary Guards, the Al Quds Force, and Other Intelligence and Paramilitary Forces," Center for Strategic and International Studies, Aug. 16, 2007, (draft), www.csis.org/media/csis/pubs/070816_cordesman_report.pdf.
A veteran military analyst describes what is known about the key Iranian military and unconventional-warfare units.

Katzman, Kenneth, "Iran: U.S. Concerns and Policy Responses," Congressional Research Service, Aug. 6, 2007, http://fpc.state.gov/documents/organization/91002.pdf.
A dispassionate run-down of the issues at stake in the faceoff between the United States and Iran.

Sadjadpour, Karim, "Iran: Reality, Options, and Consequences — Iranian People and Attitudes," testimony to House Committee on Oversight and Government Reform, Subcommittee on National Security and Foreign Affairs, Oct., 30, 2007, www.carnegieendowment.org/files/2007-10-30_ks_testimony.pdf.
An associate at the Carnegie Institute for International Peace with extensive experience in Iran reports that public alienation from the government is unlikely to lead to popular revolt in the near future.

Yaphe, Judith S., and Charles D. Lutes, "Reassessing the Implications of a Nuclear-Armed Iran," Institute for National Strategic Studies, National Defense University, 2005, www.ndu.edu/inss/mcnair/mcnair69/McNairPDF.pdf.
A book-length study examines Iran's nuclear ambitions, including their effects on Israel.

For More Information

American Enterprise Institute, 1150 17th St., N.W., Washington, DC 20036; (202) 862-5800; http://aei.org. Conservative think tank advocates hawkish policies on Iran.

Committee on the Present Danger, P.O. Box 33249, Washington, DC 20033; (202) 207-0190; www.committeeonthepresentdanger.org. Conservative organization favors regime change in Iran.

National Iranian American Council, 1411 K St., N.W., Suite 600, Washington, DC 20005; (202) 386-6325; www.niacouncil.org/index.php. Favors negotiations to establish a new U.S. relationship with Iran.

Saban Center for Middle East Policy, Brookings Institution, 1775 Massachusetts Ave., N.W., Washington, DC 20036; (202) 797-6000; www.brookings.edu/saban.aspx. Studies U.S. policy options in the region.

U.S. Department of State, 2201 C St., N.W., Washington, DC 20520; (202) 647-4000; www.state.gov/p/nea/ci/c2404.htm. Web site provides information on events and policy matters regarding Iran.

Washington Institute for Near East Policy, 1828 L St., N.W., Suite 1050, Washington, DC 20036; (202) 452-0650; www.washingtoninstitute.org. Think tank that devotes much attention to Iran.

16

Cost of the Iraq War

Peter Katel

AP Photo/Columbus Dispatch/Chris Russell

Combat boots at the Ohio Statehouse in Columbus in June 2006 memorialize U.S. soldiers killed in Iraq as part of the exhibit "Eyes Wide Open: The Human Cost of War in Iraq." More than 4,000 U.S. troops have been killed so far, and some 30,000 wounded. Experts differ on the eventual cost of the fighting in Iraq and Afghanistan, but several projections — including care for wounded veterans, reconstruction of Iraqi cities and towns and interest on foreign debt — approach or exceed $2 trillion.

From *CQ Researcher*,
April 25, 2008.

Two major events in American life intersected in March 2008. A major Wall Street investment bank collapsed. And the country marked the five-year anniversary of the U.S.-led invasion of Iraq.

The demise of Bear Stearns came amid a national mortgage crisis that has helped precipitate an economic slowdown and rising joblessness. And the war's anniversary prompted a grim accounting: more than 4,000 Americans killed, tens of thousands wounded (plus millions of Iraqis killed or forced to flee their homes) and some $700 billion in taxpayer money spent so far. [1]

Experts differ on the eventual total cost of the conflict, but several projections approach or exceed $2 trillion.

As both parties gear up for the November presidential election, foes of the George W. Bush administration are insisting on a direct linkage between the big issues of the political season. "There are not two concerns in this coming election. There is one," says economist Joseph E. Stiglitz of Columbia University in a conference call with reporters. "The war is very much related to the weakness of the economy."

In a best-selling new book, Stiglitz, winner of the 2001 Nobel Prize in economics, lays out the most detailed and sustained economic case against the Iraq intervention, which he and co-author Linda J. Bilmes calculate will cost the United States upwards of $3 trillion. [2]

President Bush summarily rejects the war-economy link. "I think the economy is down because we've built too many houses," he told the NBC "Today Show." [3]

Even some Bush administration critics share that opinion. The war "didn't have much effect on the housing market or on the willingness or unwillingness of banks or others to provide credit," says

War Cost Could Exceed $3 Trillion

The total budgetary cost of the Iraq and Afghanistan wars could exceed $3 trillion, according to a best-selling new book by Nobel Prize-winning economist Joseph E. Stiglitz and federal budget expert Linda J. Bilmes, former chief financial officer of the U.S. Department of Commerce. Under a "best-case" scenario, they say the costs still would exceed $2 trillion.

Budgetary Costs of the Iraq and Afghanistan Wars

Cost factors	COST SCENARIOS (in $ billions)	
	Best-Case*	Realistic-Moderate**
Total Operations to Date	$646	$646
Future Operations	521	913
Future Veterans Costs	422	717
Other Military Costs	132	404
Total (without interest payments)	**$1,721**	**$2,680**
Plus interest		
Interest costs	$613	$816
On past, present and future debt		
TOTAL (with interest)	**$2,334**	**$3,496**

Assumes most optimistic speed of U.S. withdrawal, casualty levels and veterans' needs. Troops decline to 180,000 in 2008, then fall to 75,000 by 2010 and by 2012 to a non-combat force of 55,000. Overall, the number of unique troops deployed to the conflict by 2017 will total 1.8 million, which is "critical in determining future veterans' medical and disability costs."

Assumes longer deployment timeframe for active-duty troops, higher demand for medical needs and more comprehensive tally of costs to the government and country. Assumes troop levels decline more slowly as number approaches 75,000 in 2012; these troops continue in primarily military function, including offensive operations against al Qaeda. The number of troops needed will total 2.1 million by 2017.

Source: Joseph E. Stiglitz and Linda J. Bilmes, *The Three Trillion Dollar War: The True Cost of the Iraq Conflict*, 2008

"Isn't it time for the Iraqis to start bearing more of those expenses, particularly in light of the windfall in revenues due to the high price of oil?" Sen. Susan Collins, R-Maine, asked Ambassador Ryan Crocker, the U.S. envoy to Iraq, during an April 8 hearing of the Senate Armed Services Committee. [4]

"Senator, it is," Crocker replied. He and Gen. David H. Petraeus, the top military commander in Iraq, said the Iraqi government has agreed to channel $300 million to U.S. authorities for reconstruction projects. [5]

The presumptive Republican presidential nominee, Sen. John McCain, R-Ariz., a vocal supporter of the Iraq intervention, endorses that approach. "The Iraqis . . . need to move a portion of their growing budget surpluses into job-creation programs," he said at the same hearing, "and look for other ways to take on more of the financial burdens currently borne by American taxpayers. [6]

President Bush had already signaled a shift toward insisting that the Iraqi government lessen financial dependence on the United States.

"The Iraqi government is stepping up on reconstruction projects," Bush said in a March 27 speech at the National Museum of the United States Air Force in Dayton, Ohio. "Soon we expect the Iraqis will cover 100 percent of those expenses. The same is true when it comes to security spending. Initially, the United States paid for most of the costs of training and equipping the Iraqi security forces. Now Iraq's budget covers three-quarters of the cost of its security forces, which is a total of more than $9 billion in 2008." [7]

But Stiglitz and Bilmes calculate that the United States spends more than that — $12 billion — in just one month on Iraq operations. Their overall estimate of $3 trillion includes interest payments on the entirely borrowed funds for the war, and takes in the cost of Iraq

Robert D. Hormats, vice chairman of Goldman, Sachs (International), a Wall Street firm.

Still, the Democratic contenders for the presidential nomination, New York Sen. Hillary Rodham Clinton and Illinois Sen. Barack Obama, are starting to echo some of the Stiglitz-Bilmes critique. And some of their fellow lawmakers, Republicans included, are taking up the simpler argument that the United States is spending money that the Iraqi government — a major oil producer — ought to be paying for defense and rebuilding.

(and Afghanistan) operations since 2001 — when the Global War on Terrorism was launched, the Afghanistan intervention began and pre-invasion planning for the Iraq conflict started up — through 2017. [8] The Democratic staff of the Congressional Joint Economic Committee produced a nearly identical estimate of $2.8 trillion. And the nonpartisan Congressional Budget Office (CBO) came up with an estimate of $1.2 trillion to $1.7 trillion. The CBO's total could rise to as much as $2.4 trillion if future interest payments on borrowed money are added. [9] Scott Wallsten, a former economist at the World Bank and the American Enterprise Institute who has been tracking Iraq costs for years, told the congressional Joint Economic Committee that Iraq expenses would reach close to $2 trillion. [10]

None of these estimates are easily compared with one another because the underlying calculations were based on different methodologies and time horizons; some also do not account for oil-price fluctuations, debt interest payments and the effects of inflation. Some of these contrasts are apparent in projections on the costs of veterans' care. (*See sidebar, p. 378.*)

In any event, however much the United States spends in the future, there's no question that it already has spent far more than the administration ever projected. The closest thing to an official cost estimate ran to $60 billion tops, by Mitchell E. Daniels, then the head of the Office of Management and Budget, in December 2002. And a White House adviser, Lawrence B. Lindsey, then director of the administration's National Economic Council, who in 2002 gave an unofficial projection of up to $200 billion, was fired shortly after that.

The administration's projections "presupposed a relatively short conflict that would have had us out of there in a matter of months," says Dov Zakheim, who was

Cost Reductions Hinge on Troop Reductions

The United States has spent more than $600 billion on the Bush administration's "War on Terrorism" in the six years following the Sept. 11, 2001, terrorist attacks, according to the Congressional Budget Office. The CBO calculates the cost at $1.7 trillion if current troop levels in Iraq and Afghanistan — about 200,000 — are reduced to 75,000 by 2013. The total cost could be as much as $2.4 trillion if interest on foreign debt is added to the CBO numbers.

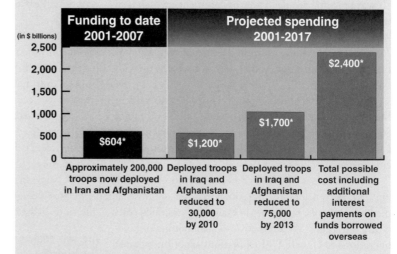

U.S. Costs for War on Terrorism

* Includes funding for U.S. and Iraqi military operations, diplomatic operations and reconstruction and veterans' benefits and services

Sources: "Estimated Costs of U.S. Operations in Iraq and Afghanistan and of Other Activities Related to the War on Terrorism," Congressional Budget Office, Oct. 24, 2007; Senate Budget Committee

assistant secretary of Defense and the Pentagon's budget chief in 2001-2004. Instead, "The war became a lot more intense than people anticipated, and the thing has gone on a lot longer than people anticipated." Zakheim is now a vice president of Booz Allen Hamilton, a McLean, Va.-based consulting firm.

Cost figures and economic theories notwithstanding, the Iraq-costs debate ultimately turns on issues of national security policy.

"We're supporting a vital national interest, which is a stable Middle East," says James Jay Carafano, a retired U.S. Army lieutenant-colonel and a military affairs and foreign policy specialist at the conservative Heritage Foundation. Of the Stiglitz-Bilmes thesis, he says,

"These are political arguments, not economic arguments. It's not even saying 'I've done this economic analysis and it has political implications.' That's prostitution, as far as I'm concerned. [It amounts to] 'I'm going to prostitute my craft for politics.'"

In an interview later, Stiglitz says, "We've obviously hit a raw nerve." He adds that he and Bilmes make clear they oppose the war. But they began laying out their thesis in a 2006 paper published by the National Bureau of Economic Research, a nonpartisan, nonprofit forum. [11] "It was open for people to give us comments, which is in the nature of an academic process. We were very careful in responding to issues that were raised in open debate. The remarkable thing, from the Heritage Foundation or from the administration, is that they won't come up with their own numbers."

White House press secretary Dana Perino said in March, when asked about Stiglitz's calculations: "I'm not going to dispute his estimates. . . . But it's very hard to anticipate, depending on conditions on the ground and circumstances, how much the war is going to cost." [12]

In any case, war critics aren't the only economists studying Iraq. Even before the invasion, a trio of economists at the University of Chicago began examining projected costs of the war against the alternative — maintaining military operations to enforce United Nations sanctions against Iraq (referred to as "containment"). The analysts calculated that containment would have cost $297 billion while military action would cost $414 billion. [13]

"The cost of the war is certainly far in excess of the baseline cost that we estimated for containment," the study's leader, Steven J. Davis, concedes. But Davis, a professor at the University of Chicago's Graduate School of Business, disputes the idea that the underestimate by him and his colleagues strengthens the Stiglitz-Bilmes argument. "Their whole premise is that, in the absence of war, things would have been fine and dandy in the Middle East," something he calls a "questionable assumption."

A military-spending specialist agrees decisions on going to war can't be reduced entirely to dollars and cents. "It's not like investing in real estate," says Steven M. Kosiak, vice president for budget studies at the Center for Strategic and Budgetary Assessments, a nonpartisan think tank. "You have to take into account all kinds of things that are not budgetary or economic; there may be times when it is worth going to war even if there is a high budgetary cost."

Still, President Bush has not been relying on that argument alone in recent comments about the costs and economic effects of the war. "I think, actually, the spending on the war might help with jobs, because we're buying equipment and people are working," he told the NBC "Today Show." [14]

But the classic World War II argument that military spending benefits the entire economy is finding little resonance among lawmakers managing a $239 billion federal budget deficit, whose constituents fear recent economic developments and hear that no plans exist to end the war.

As Hormats points out, "War spending is a highly inefficient way of boosting U.S. jobs and growth; spending on roads, bridges, energy research and education at home would have a far more beneficial and enduring effect on the economy than artillery and tanks."

"We must ask ourselves," said Sen. Charles Schumer, D-N.Y., said at a February hearing of the Joint Economic Committee, "is it worth spending trillions of dollars on such an uncertain and unpredictable outcome?" [15]

As Congress, the presidential candidates and the public debate the cost of the Iraq War, here are some of the questions being asked:

Are war costs contributing to the current economic downturn?

Shortly before the April 9 anniversary of the fall of Baghdad, the federal Bureau of Labor Statistics announced that the economy had shed 232,000 jobs since the beginning of the year — 80,000 in March alone. With that, the national jobless rate rose to 5.1 percent, the highest since the post-Hurricane Katrina month of September 2005. But the latest losses aren't confined to any one region or industry. [16]

And the statistics all but ended debate on whether the country has entered a recession. Ian C. Shepherdson, chief domestic economist for High Frequency Economics, an analytical firm for institutional investors, told *The New York Times*: "We are in for a much longer recession than Wall Street thinks. This particular downturn is driven by a rare contraction in consumer spending, and that is starting to hurt a broader range of people than those hurt by the mortgage crisis." [17]

In general, economists say an oversupply of houses started the dominoes falling. Previously, a construction boom had enabled a big uptick in homeownership, particularily among first-time buyers whose incomes had been too low to qualify for mortgages. These customers were steered into high-interest "subprime" house loans. When property values dropped, subprime mortgage-holders couldn't borrow against their houses to keep making payments, which had risen when their variable-interest-rate loans "reset" to higher rates. The result: foreclosure proceedings against 1.5 million homeowners last year alone. [18]

Foreclosures rocked Wall Street investment banks that had invested heavily in packages of home loans that included subprime mortgages. One major firm, Bear Stearns, went broke and was rescued only by a competitor's acquisition, made possible by a $29 billion line of credit from the Federal Reserve. Other banks slowed their lending. [19]

In this climate, it's not surprising that politicians are reciting lists of government services that could have been funded with money being spent in Iraq. The Democratic staff of the Joint Economic Committee, for instance, picked a few examples of what the Iraq spending could have paid for: enrollment of 57,500 more children in the Head Start preschool program, 153,000 Pell Grant higher-education scholarships and 9,000 more police officers nationwide. [20]

Stiglitz and Bilmes argue that such investments in domestic health, education and infrastructure would have provided more benefits to the country at large than the money spent in Iraq. For instance, they say, a Nepalese employee of a military contractor in Iraq doesn't use his paycheck to buy goods and services in the United States (unless he happens to buy a U.S.-made product).

Going a step further, Stiglitz and Bilmes claim that the combined effect of Iraq War investments was to suppress demand in the United States — because of the goods and services not bought here.

The Federal Reserve, whose mission includes helping keep the economy running, responded by increasing liquidity, Stiglitz explains, in order to ensure an easy supply

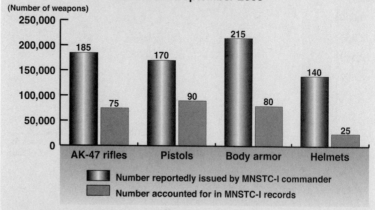

Many Weapons Given to Iraq Are Missing

U.S. military officials cannot account for hundreds of thousands of rifles, pistols and other equipment issued to Iraqi security forces by the Multinational Security Transition Command-Iraq (MNSTC-I). Some analysts say the unaccounted-for weapons fell into the hands of insurgents or were sold on the black market. MNSTC-I officials blame a lack of adequate staffing for the inconsistencies.

Missing Equipment Issued to Iraqi Security Forces, June 2004-September 2005

(Number of weapons)

	AK-47 rifles	Pistols	Body armor	Helmets
Number reportedly issued by MNSTC-I commander	185	170	215	140
Number accounted for in MNSTC-I records	75	90	80	25

Source: "Stabilizing and Rebuilding Iraq: Actions Needed to Address Inadequate Accountability Over U.S. Efforts and Investments," Government Accountability Office, March 2008

of money to lenders. "They kept interest rates lower than they otherwise would have been. The more they had to do that, the more they encouraged people to take out mortgages. If the economy were going gangbusters, they would have raised interest rates, and at higher interest rates there's less refinancing of mortgages."

But other economists including Hormats of Goldman, Sachs — while emphasizing that funds spent in Iraq would been much more beneficial to the U.S. economy if spent on infrastructure, worker training, medical research and homeland security in this country — discount the role of war spending in the foreclosure-sparked financial emergency that helped slow the entire economy. "This downturn was the result of two major factors that converged — overbuilding of homes and disruption in the credit markets," Hormats says. "People lent too much money in the housing sector, and the assets that backed up those loans deteriorated. It's hard to see that war spending itself played much of a role."

Iraq War Cost Ranks Near the Top

If Congress approves a pending request for additional 2008 funds, the wars in Iraq and Afghanistan will have cost $756 billion by the end of this fiscal year (not including costs for veterans' care) — second only to World War II. A recent best-selling book contends that when veterans' costs and other factors are added, the war will end up costing $3 trillion, about the same as World War II.

Costs of Major U.S. Wars
(in $ billions, in 2007 dollars)

($ billions)

* Total for fiscal years 2001-2008. Another $102.9 billion supplemental request is expected to be approved for this fiscal year.

** Total Union and Confederate costs

Sources: Congressional Research Service and Office of Management and Budget data, available on Web site of the Center for Arms Control and Non-Proliferation, www.armscontrolcenter.org/policy/securityspending/articles/historical_war_costs/.

Bilmes and Stiglitz also point to the war as a force pushing up world oil prices. Crude oil in late April was fetching about $116 a barrel, creating higher costs for producers, retailers and — ultimately — consumers, throughout the economy. In their book, Stiglitz and Bilmes said the war contributed, conservatively, $10 to $15 of that price increase.

In the week that the war started, the average world oil price was about $27 a barrel. "The futures markets expected that the price would remain for the next decade at that kind of price," Bilmes says during a March 18 conference call with reporters. "They anticipated that demand was rising considerably from India and China but that supply would rise to meet the demand. So the question is what changed that equation; certainly the main thing that changed was the invasion of Iraq." [21]

Still, many economists reject their view of the war's effect on the oil market. "If you press me and ask, 'Did the war cause less Iraqi oil in the market than would otherwise be the case?' I'd say 'yes,' " Hormats says. "But you can't make the case that that's the main factor in pushing oil prices to $116 a barrel."

Some other economists echo that view. But they add that war costs are now playing a major role in how the economic drama unfolds. "You can absolutely blame the war for restricting our ability to take countermeasures," says Jared Bernstein, living standards program director at the Economic Policy Institute, a liberal think tank. "We've added so much to our national debt. If you believe, and many people do, that we'll ultimately need another stimulus package, it's going to be tougher to add to the debt because of the war. Those $600 billion you wouldn't have spent otherwise limit your future options."

But Davis, the University of Chicago economist, says that thesis amounts to "picking on the Iraq War to make a political argument." In an environment in which the government is already borrowing money to finance its activities, anything and everything on which the government spends money drives up the debt, Davis argues.

Did the Bush administration low-ball projections of war costs?

The costs of fighting wars have challenged American leaders as far back as the American Revolution, before the United States had even been founded. During the Vietnam War, the most recent lengthy conflict before Iraq and Afghanistan, President Lyndon B. Johnson's struggle to finance escalating costs without sacrificing domestic social programs led to political standoffs that prompted him to abandon politics.

Today's war-spending conflict centers on the administration's prewar cost projections. The disparity between those estimates and actual spending lead some to argue that the administration deliberately kept projections low.

These numbers ranged no higher than White House economic adviser Lindsey's high-end estimate of $200 billion. In a newly published memoir, he wrote that his Iraq estimate surely contributed to his ouster, though the administration never said that. "Putting out only a best-cases scenario without preparing the public for some worse eventuality was the wrong strategy," Lindsey wrote this year. "It is too bad for the country that his [Bush's] credibility was squandered by the White House for not being upfront about what the war might cost." [22]

The first non-governmental expert to question the validity of official estimates was William D. Nordhaus, a professor of economics at Yale University. In a paper published six months before the war began, he wrote: "The Bush administration has made no serious public estimate of the costs of the coming war. . . . Perhaps, the administration is fearful that a candid discussion of wartime economics will give ammunition to skeptics of the war." [23]

Shortly after the conflict began, skepticism about administration numbers emerged in the mass media. Stiglitz and Bilmes quote an exchange between Ted Koppel, then-host of ABC News' "Nightline," and Andrew Natsios, then the administrator of the U.S. Agency for International Development (USAID). Clearly in a state of disbelief, Koppel challenged his guest's claim that U.S. expenses for rebuilding Iraq would total $1.7 billion.

"I want to be sure that I understood you correctly," Koppel said at one point, before asking Natsios to spell out his estimate all over again. The USAID official said that Iraq's projected $20 billion a year in oil revenues would pay for the bulk of the rebuilding. [24]

Lawrence J. Korb, a former assistant Defense secretary in the Reagan administration and a U.S. Navy veteran, points to the Natsios episode as evidence that the administration was deliberately keeping estimates low. "They had to be," he says. "I can't imagine anybody who knew anything saying it was going to cost $1.7 billion, or that Iraqi oil would pay for it. They would have known that the oil infrastructure was not in very good shape and that the people who did not want us to come there were not going to allow the oil to be used."

Bush administration officials had plenty of reason to downplay costs, Korb says. If the American people had been given an idea of the real price they'd be paying to topple a tyrant and sponsor elections in his country, the administration would have been "laughed out of the ballpark." Korb, a frequent critic of the administration's foreign policy, is now a fellow at the Center for American Policy, a liberal think tank directed by former staff members in Democratic administrations and congressional offices.

From the other side of the political divide, former Pentagon financial officer Zakheim rebutted the low-balling claim. Administration estimates might have proved accurate, Zakheim argues, if top U.S. administrator in Iraq L. Paul Bremer III had not dissolved the Iraqi armed forces. That May 23, 2003, order effectively turned 350,000 trained fighters onto the street in a state of rage at the United States.

"If anything drove the cost of the war up, it was the decision to demobilize the Iraqi army," Zakheim says, adding that he opposed the move at the time (as did Colin L. Powell, then the secretary of State, and others). "If they had stuck to the original plan, I think it would have been a very different situation." [25]

Zakheim's argument echoes the impression at the time of Army Col. Alan King, then a civil affairs officer in Iraq. "When Bremer did that, the insurgency went crazy," he told *Washington Post* correspondent Thomas Ricks. [26]

Still, some longtime government-watchers remain skeptical of the intentions behind the prewar estimates. "If you had sat down and tried to realistically tally expected costs, you would have come up with a number well above $50 billion," says Bernstein at the Economic Policy Institute. "You would have been low-balling, but you wouldn't have known that at the time."

All in all, Bernstein says, the prewar estimates were an exercise in "fuzzy math." He defined the term as production of "a number intentionally biased to achieve support for something instead of a more realistic, higher, number that might cost you that support. It's easier to sell something if it's cheaper."

But Davis, the University of Chicago economist, argues that intentional underestimating wouldn't explain the gap between prewar projections and actual costs. Officials under-projected, he argues, out of belief in U.S. power to speedily alter the reality on the ground in Iraq.

"There was active resistance in the administration, by [Defense Secretary] Donald Rumsfeld, and I don't know how deeply in the Defense Department itself, to costing out the longer-term consequences of the war, to careful planning for the post-major combat phase," he says.

"That meant that the American electorate wasn't sufficiently prepared for what would come after."

Is the Iraq war worth the expense?

Debates over Iraq War costs and their consequences are only partly economic. The question of what the United States has obtained for the billions of dollars it spent underlies the entire subject. Even before the war began, some of the debates over whether to support what was clearly a looming invasion touched on the issue of costs vs. benefits.

Three days before Bush ordered the invasion, a reporter for *The Washington Post* summed up the dollars-and-cents side of the debate this way: "In the longer term, many experts expect that the cost of reconstructing Iraq, including care of refugees, troops to keep the peace and repairs to bombed infrastructure, would add scores — even hundreds — of billions to a federal deficit already spiraling out of control," David Von Drehle wrote. [27]

Five years later, President Bush focused on the other side of the argument during one of a trio of speeches timed to the war anniversary season. The costs of withdrawing at this point — "retreating," as he put it, "would be a propaganda victory of colossal proportions for the global terrorist movement, which would gain new funds, and find new recruits, and conclude that the way to defeat America is to bleed us into submission." [28]

Critics of that view include foreign-policy veterans. Rand Beers, who resigned from the State Department in 2003 in disagreement over the imminent Iraq War, argues that it is distracting the United States from growing dangers in Afghanistan and Pakistan. Osama bin Laden and his network have "reconstituted their capabilities to operate in Afghanistan and around the world, to be able to become much more of a threat to the United States," Beers says, speaking on a conference call with reporters in February. "They now represent a danger to the homeland of the United States."

Given the scale of U.S. operations in Iraq, "all the other challenges we face are being unattended or are only modestly dealt with," Beers says. When he quit the State Department, he was assistant secretary for international narcotics and law enforcement affairs. Earlier, he had served Republican and Democratic administrations on the National Security Council.

But Zakheim, the former Pentagon finance chief, argues that some benefits of the U.S. invasion and its aftermath are already evident. "Having an Iraq that doesn't attack its neighbors and whose neighbors don't attack it is already a factor in the region," he says. "If the outcome of this exercise is not just that we got rid of Saddam Hussein but got a country that's no longer busily attacking others and being attacked, you've made a fundamental change in the region, in a situation that's gone on for 60 years."

By contrast, Bernstein, a liberal critic of the war, makes an effort to distinguish between his "gut reaction" that the war clearly isn't worth the cost and a more objective view. "I can imagine making an argument that in the absence of this action we'd be faced with a whole set of difficult and deadly situations that we're not facing," he says. "At this point it's awfully hard to make a positive cost-benefit analysis. But it's probably also too soon to do that in any believable way."

Carafano at the Heritage Foundation argues against any suggestion that the costs overwhelm benefits. "We've already turned the corner," he says, arguing that U.S. forces are stabilizing the country. "I can spin numbers that show that the American Revolution was a mistake. To argue that the United States, with a $13 trillion economy, is even remotely near spending so much on security that it's undermining the ability to be a viable state is laughable. You can hate the war and think all the money has been squandered, and even if that's true, in terms of the long-term competitiveness of the nation, it's irrelevant."

At the same time, Carafano argues against withdrawing U.S. forces too quickly. "What has to happen is that there has to be trust and confidence among the Shia, the Sunni and the Kurds such that nobody can steal a march on anyone else," he says. "Now, the guarantor that they can't do that is the U.S. government. You don't want to whittle that military presence below the point at which people don't think it's influential any more."

Korb of the Center for American Progress holds that the five-year results of the Iraq war make clear that the American investment yielded negative results. "Say this was early 2003 and we did a cost-benefit analysis of getting rid of Saddam Hussein — you would not have gone in," he argues. "Are you more secure than you were five years ago? No."

Other pro-war arguments vanished soon after Saddam was toppled, Korb says, referring to the administration's claims that Saddam's regime was storing weapons of mass destruction and developing new ones. In addition, he argues, speaking as if to an administration official, "The costs you projected were way too low. That's where you are now."

President Bush, in an April 10 speech, responded to cost-benefit criticism by noting that today's military budget amounts to about 4 percent of the nation's gross domestic product (GDP). "During other major conflicts in our history, the relative cost has been even higher," he said from the White House. At the height of the Cold War, during the Truman and Eisenhower administrations, the defense budget ran to 13 percent of GDP, Bush said. [29]

"We should be able to agree that this is a burden worth bearing," he said, predicting that "violent extremists" would be encouraged if America were to "fail" in Iraq. "This would . . . increase the threat of another terrorist attack on our homeland." [30]

But Wallsten, formerly of the World Bank and now vice president for research at the Technology Policy Institute, a think tank (formerly iGrowthGlobal), responds that that benefit is far from clear. "Nobody has shown that there's a link between Iraq and discouraging another 9/11," he says.

Stiglitz and other economists note that pointing to the relative size of the defense budget leaves out the Bush administration's reliance on borrowing to pay for the war — hence adding billions in interest payments ($800 billion alone for Iraq and Afghanistan by 2017, Stiglitz and Bilmes calculate). [31] "This war was financed, for the first time for any major war in American history, entirely by borrowing — entirely," Goldman, Sachs' Hormats says. "The next generation of taxpayers will have to foot the entire bill." The lenders are the same buyers of U.S. bonds who finance all of the federal government's deficit spending. Forty percent of that money, Hormats says, comes from abroad.

BACKGROUND

Paying for War

How the United States should pay for war is an issue that goes back to the founding of the nation. When the Continental Congress couldn't come up with all the money George Washington needed to feed and supply his troops, independence movement leaders assigned Benjamin Franklin and John Adams to negotiate loans from France and from backers in the Netherlands. [32]

Those loans precipitated one of the first political crises in U.S. history. After independence, several states separately owed a total of $25 million in war debts.

Alexander Hamilton, the first Treasury secretary, wanted the federal government to assume the loans. Otherwise, he argued, any state stalling on repayments would affect the entire country's creditworthiness.

Southern politicians led by James Madison of Virginia, then a member of the House of Representatives, feared "assumption" as an erosion of states' rights. The standoff was resolved when Hamilton and his allies gave way on the Southerners' proposal to establish the national capital in the South, further from the Northern financial and commercial interests that Madison and his allies distrusted.

From then until the present conflicts in Iraq and Afghanistan, the federal government never had to borrow money from abroad to finance wars. But from the War of 1812 onward, war spending did force the central government to go into debt to domestic creditors.

Washington and Thomas Jefferson, among other early members of the U.S. political class, discouraged long-term indebtedness. The first president, in his celebrated farewell address, urged future lawmakers and presidents to "discharge the debts which unavoidable wars may have occasioned, not ungenerously throwing upon posterity the burdens we ourselves ought to bear." [33]

His successors maintained that doctrine during the nation's first 150 years. Military spending caused major budget deficits during the Civil War and both world wars. But postwar spending limits, as well as prosperity that raised tax revenues, brought down indebtedness following all those conflicts.

Of all U.S. military conflicts, World War II involved by far the biggest U.S. commitment of troops, industrial production and money. With all males ages 20-45 eligible for the draft, 5.4 million men were serving in the U.S. Army alone by the end of 1942. [34]

Hormats, in his history of war financing, emphasizes that the military mobilization was accompanied by rationing and wage controls in the civilian sector. President Franklin D. Roosevelt also fought for tax policies that didn't unfairly benefit the well-to-do. The Roosevelt administration also raised millions by selling war bonds to ordinary citizens, a policy that Hormats credits with "binding Americans together in a commitment to the success of the war effort."

But the end of World War II in 1945 saw the opening of a new kind of conflict, the Cold War, which lasted until 1991. The rivalry between the United States and the Soviet Union, both nuclear powers (from 1949 on,

CHRONOLOGY

1790-1941 *From the American Revolution until World War II, presidents and lawmakers avoided long-term indebtedness to pay for military conflict.*

1790 Alexander Hamilton and James Madison forge a compromise in which the federal government assumes the states' Revolutionary War debt.

1796 George Washington warns against saddling "future generations" with war debts.

1866 Federal government's interest obligations on its Civil War borrowing amount to twice the size of the entire budget before the war started.

1919 Major increase on personal and business income taxes covers about one-third of U.S. costs for World War I.

1941-1968 *An era of massive, long-term military spending begins with the biggest military conflict in U.S. history and continues into the long Cold War.*

1942 A year after the United States enters World War II, 5.4 million men are serving in the U.S. Army.

1945 The fifth of a series of war bond drives among the public raises $20.6 billion - for an overall total of $87.3 billion. . . . Wage and price controls and rationing hold down civilian spending. . . . Wartime tax-code changes dramatically boost the number of taxpayers to 42 million, from 4 million before the war.

1951 With the Korean War under way, President Harry S Truman proposes a $10 billion tax increase, settles for $7.2 billion.

1968 Tet Offensive by North Vietnamese military fails but shocks U.S. public and politicians with its sweep and intensity. . . . President Lyndon B. Johnson proposes 10 percent tax surcharge to help finance war, accepting $6 billion in cuts to social programs. . . . U.S. forces in Vietnam expand to 536,000.

1990-2002 *Iraq becomes a major U.S. military adversary under dictator Saddam Hussein.*

1990 Saddam orders his military to seize neighboring Kuwait. . . . President George H. W. Bush begins assembling an international military coalition to free Kuwait.

1991 After weeks of air bombardment, U.S.-led land forces expel Iraq in 100 hours of fighting. . . . The United States provides the majority of troops and thus pays only $13 billion of the cost, while allies pay $48 billion.

2000 U.S. contingent enforcing United Nations sanctions against Iraq includes 30 Navy vessels, 175 airplanes and as many as 25,000 soldiers at a total cost of $16.4 billion.

2002 Following the Sept. 11, 2001, terrorist attacks, President George W. Bush begins laying the groundwork for "regime change" in Iraq. . . . President's chief economic adviser estimates war costs at $100-$200 billion and is replaced. . . . Office of Management and Budget director estimates cost at up to $60 billion.

2003-2008 *U.S. intervention in Iraq is far longer, more complicated and expensive than the administration projected.*

2003 Assistant Defense Secretary Paul D. Wolfowitz predicts Iraq's oil revenues will finance reconstruction. . . . Bush administration proposes $20.3 billion for Iraq reconstruction. . . . Senate proposes money be lent instead of granted but backs down.

2006 Iraq spends only 23 percent of its annual reconstruction budget.

2007 Iraq's oil revenues rise to $41 billion, up from $31 billion in 2006.

2008 War costs rise to an expected $160 billion for the year, following year-by-year increases from $53 billion in 2003. . . . Increase in foreclosures, collapse of Bear, Stearns and rise in unemployment prompt growing concerns over economy. . . . Number of American military personnel killed exceeds 4,000. . . . Economist Joseph E. Stiglitz and budget expert Linda J. Bilmes intensify war-cost debate by calculating total eventual cost at $3 trillion.

in the case of the Soviets), saw the establishment of a large standing military during peacetime for the first time in U.S. history. Conscription — the draft — for all males above the age of 18 made that possible, though a system of deferments for college enrollment, disabilities and hardship made avoiding military service relatively simple for many potential draftees.

Military preparedness during the Cold War also saw active development and manufacture of weapons of all kinds, including nuclear arms. As military spending grew, along with new social programs, massive government borrowing became commonplace.

Korea and Vietnam

The Cold War was punctuated by the wars in Korea and in Vietnam. Both involved fierce combat by draftees. But neither war measured up to World War II in scale, and neither conflict was fought under a congressional declaration of war.

Even so, the 1950-53 Korean conflict provoked a major debate on how to pay its costs. "During World War II, taxes were not high enough, and the government was forced to borrow too much," President Harry S Truman told Congress in 1951, arguing for a $10 billion tax increase.[35] Congressional Republicans fought the proposal. But they didn't scrap it, instead cutting it to $7.2 billion.

During the next two decades, fights over funding the Vietnam War far exceeded the Korea debates in intensity. (*See graph, p. 372.*) These debates also spanned a greater period of time, as did the conflict itself. It began in 1964 (though U.S. military aid began earlier), when Congress passed a resolution authorizing the president to take whatever action he saw fit to defend Southeast Asia, and ended in 1973, when the United States formally ended its combat role. In 1975, communist North Vietnam conquered U.S. ally South Vietnam, finally concluding the war.

The scale of U.S. military participation can be measured by the size of the American contingent — from 22,000 at the end of 1964, to 184,000 at the end of 1965, to 536,000 by the end of 1968.

President Lyndon B. Johnson, who escalated the war during his time in office (1963-1969), was determined not to let military spending erode the "Great Society" social programs he had created. But reality dictated otherwise. As the war intensified, its costs pushed defense spending from $50 billion in 1965 to $78 billion in 1968. As a result, economists projected that the budget

deficit would quadruple from $4.5 billion in 1967 to $19 billion in 1968. Top presidential advisers pressed Johnson to propose a tax hike to meet skyrocketing revenue demands.

But Johnson resisted, fearing that conservatives would counter by threatening to slash Great Society programs. Finally, in 1967, Johnson proposed a temporary 6 percent surcharge on income taxes for individuals and corporations. As he had feared, Congress' leading tax legislator demanded some spending cuts as the price for supporting a tax hike.

With the financial picture worsening, Johnson upped his proposal to a 10 percent tax surcharge. But he made no headway in Congress. Then, in January 1968 the North Vietnamese mounted a major offensive to coincide with the lunar New Year, known as Tet. American and South Vietnamese forces came under intense and sudden attacks that reached into the U.S. Embassy itself.

The Tet Offensive failed militarily but put a major dent in public support for the war. Stalemated on the financing and political sides, Johnson made a surprise announcement that he was pulling out of the 1968 presidential nomination race, in effect, retiring from public office.

Following that move, congressional leaders pushed through the president's 10 percent surcharge, at the cost of $6 billion in cuts from Great Society programs. In the end, Vietnam turned into an American defeat, and little of the Great Society package survived the decades that followed.

Desert Storm

After Vietnam, U.S. military actions in Grenada, Panama, Somalia, Haiti and the Balkans were all of relatively short duration and low cost. The next major military theater would be the Middle East, specifically, the region bordering the Persian Gulf. The United States had long maintained a political presence there through an alliance with Shah Mohammad Reza Pahlavi. He was overthrown in 1979 and replaced by a Shiite Muslim and fiercely anti-American government. The U.S. government cut relations with Tehran after radical students stormed the American Embassy there and took 52 embassy personnel hostage for more than 14 months.

In 1980, Saddam launched a war against the new government in neighboring Iran. During that eight-year conflict, in which Iraq openly used chemical weapons, the Reagan administration tilted toward Iraq — the

Veterans' Care Cost Estimates May Be Too Low

Authors of new book challenge government calculations

The authors of the *Three Trillion War: The True Cost of the Iraq Conflict* say the future costs of caring for wounded Iraq War veterans may be vastly more than government estimates. [1]

"Some of the issues in Iraq and in the Middle East are not entirely under our control," says co-author Linda J. Bilmes. "But the way we take care of the veterans is entirely under our control. It's a matter of national attention and priorities."

Bilmes, a lecturer in public policy at Harvard University's Kennedy School of Government, did the research underlying veterans'-care cost projections in the new book, co-authored with Columbia University economist Joseph E. Stiglitz, winner of the 2001 Nobel Prize in economics.

Stiglitz and Bilmes base their projections on lifetime costs for all care and government compensation for veterans who served in Iraq from 2003 to 2017, including Social Security payments. The projections range from a minimum of $371 billion under a reduced combat scenario to a more "realistic" sum of $630 billion. [2]

The Congressional Budget Office (CBO), using the same military scenarios utilized by Stiglitz and Bilmes, calculated its own projections, which differ enormously from the Stiglitz-Bilmes estimates, in part because the CBO didn't try to project lifetime care costs. As a result, the CBO estimates that veterans' benefits and services in 2001-2017 would cost $12 billion under a more favorable reduced-combat, scenario, or $13 billion under a scenario that envisions more fighting.

The "best-case" scenario (the Stiglitz-Bilmes term) involves a gradual drawdown of U.S. forces in Iraq and Afghanistan by 2012 to 55,000 stationed there long-term (or 30,000 by 2010, in one of the CBO scenarios) and assigned to non-combat duty. A more realistic scenario, according to Stiglitz and Bilmes, would involve continued combat and drawing troops down to about 75,000 by 2013.

"The funding needs for veterans' benefits comprise an additional major entitlement program along with Medicare and Social Security," they write. [3]

Numerous other assumptions about federally funded care for vets are built into the Stiglitz-Bilmes projections, including:

- Forty-eight percent of Iraq-Afghanistan veterans will seek treatment from the Department of Veterans Affairs (VA). That projection is based on an average of five disabling conditions claimed by Iraq-Afghanistan veterans, compared to the average of three disabling conditions claimed by Persian Gulf War veterans and on the 45 percent claim rate by Gulf War veterans and the 37 percent rate by Iraq-Afghanistan veterans thus far, of which 88 percent have been granted, or partially granted.

- The number of post-traumatic stress disorder (PTSD) claims will "rapidly" pass the 19,000 filed when Stiglitz and Bilmes did their research in 2005-2007; the average payment per PTSD claim will remain at $7,109, the 2007 amount. They base that projection in part on a Government Accountability Office (GAO) finding last year that processing a PTSD claim can take up to a year. An earlier GAO report notes that the "intense and prolonged combat" that characterizes service in Iraq and Afghanistan puts veterans of those conflicts at high risk for PTSD. [4]

Bilmes and Stiglitz based their calculations on official data. But they were charting new territory. Neither the executive branch, nor the GAO nor the Congressional Research Service has made public any long-range projections of the costs of Iraq War veterans' care, says Bilmes, who has made a specialty of calculating the cost of veterans' care. She adds that a VA economist's request for a professional conference last year on her methodology was canceled by the agency but that she then met with then Veterans Affairs Secretary R. James Nicholson, at his request, to discuss her calculations.

The longest-range projections of the costs of caring for veterans are those by the CBO. CBO Director Peter Orszag wrote a detailed blog posting laying out his agency's differences with the Stiglitz-Bilmes numbers. The differences go beyond the lifetime versus year-to-year costs.

---

enemy of America's new Iranian enemy. Reagan ordered his top diplomatic, military and intelligence officials in 1984 to plan on how to "avert an Iraqi collapse." Paradoxically, during the Iran-Iraq War members of the Reagan administration set up a scheme — later known as "Iran-Contra" — to illegally sell weapons to Iran, using the proceeds to fund the "contra" guerrillas fighting the left-wing government of Nicaragua. [36]

"It may appear surprising to some readers, but veterans of the recent conflicts, on average, require less medical care from VA than veterans of other conflicts," Orszag wrote, noting also that he is a friend of Stiglitz, with whom he has co-authored papers. For instance, he wrote, the VA in 2006 actually spent only an average of $2,610 per veteran — an average that reflects a relatively low incidence, so far, of more expensive PTSD treatment. [5]

And Stiglitz and Bilmes seem to have failed to account for disability claims by veterans who didn't serve in Iraq or Afghanistan, Orszag said. Those projected costs should be subtracted from war-related projections, he wrote. [6]

And he concludes that because of the differing spending estimates, and related disagreements, Stiglitz and Bilmes over-estimated VA medical costs by at least $100 billion. [7]

Stiglitz notes, for his part, that CBO didn't take into account data showing that PTSD claims escalate with repeated deployments. "We have not yet gotten back those who've been deployed, two, three, four times. Our number is an underestimate." CBO may have relied too heavily, he says, on initial health-care costs for Iraq veterans, which arise more from diagnosis than from treatment, which is more expensive.

Paul Sullivan, executive director of Veterans for Common Sense, a Washington-based nonprofit that advocates more efficient treatment, says of the Stiglitz-Bilmes calculations: "I know with absolute certainty that their estimates are low." For instance, he points out, veterans with other options — such as private insurance or a free county clinic — may avoid the VA after hearing of long waits for treatment.

Sullivan, a veteran of the 1991 Gulf War and a former VA project manager, adds, "The VA is the best place to go for mental health care, traumatic brain injury and prosthetics, because they have real combat injury experience of 60-plus years."

But veterans' needs are going unmet because the agency is underfunded, say advocates. Veterans for Common Sense and a California-based organization, Veterans for Truth, have filed a class-action lawsuit against the VA claiming its system for processing PTSD claims has essentially collapsed under the weight of growing demand. "Delays have become an insurmountable barrier preventing many veterans from obtaining health care and benefits," the organizations said in the 2007 complaint launching the suit. [8]

The Bush administration takes the position that "wounded warriors" — the term now in favor — are getting all the service they require. "I believe that we are getting adequate funding," Michael J. Kussman, the VA's undersecretary for health, told the Senate Veterans Affairs Committee last year. "And with your support and the administration's support, we've been very appreciative of the very significant increases in the budget over the last couple years." [9]

Appropriations to the VA for all operations have risen from $47.95 billion in fiscal 2001 to $87.6 billion in the present fiscal year. The latter amount includes about $3 billion in emergency supplemental funding. [10]

For Stiglitz and Bilmes, the VA's reliance on supplementals shows that the agency is pushed past its limits. "The pattern of underfundng . . . has repeated itself every year of the war," they write about the stream of supplemental funds. "The VA has told Congress that it can cope with the surge in demand, despite overwhelming evidence to the contrary." [11]

---

[1] For background, see Peter Katel, "Wounded Veterans," *CQ Researcher*, Aug. 31, 2007, pp. 697-720.

[2] See Joseph E. Stiglitz and Linda J. Bilmes, *The Three Trillion Dollar War: The True Cost of the Iraq Conflict* (2008), pp. 81-90.

[3] *Ibid.*, p. 89.

[4] See "Post Traumatic Stress Disorder: DOD Needs to Identify the Factors Its Providers Use to Make Mental Health Evaluation Referrals for Servicemembers," General Accountability Office, May 2006, p. 20, www.gao.gov/new.items/d06397.pdf. See also "GAO Findings and Recommendations Regarding DOD and VA Disability Systems," Government Accountability Office, May 25, 2007, p. 3, www.gao.gov/new.items/d07906r.pdf.

[5] See Peter Orszag, "Director's Blog," April 8, 2008, http://cboblog.cbo.gov/.

[6] *Ibid.*

[7] *Ibid.*

[8] See Veterans for Common Sense and Veterans United for Truth, Inc., v. R. James Nicholson, *et al.*, July 23, 2007, www.veteransptsdclassaction.org/pdf/ courtfiled/veteranscomplaint.pdf. Other documents in the case are available at www.veteransptsdclassaction.org.

[9] See "Senate Veterans' Affairs Committee Holds Hearing on Veterans' Affairs Health Care Funding," *Congressional Transcripts*, July 25, 2007.

[10] See Daniel H. Else, "Military Construction, Veterans Affairs, and Related Agencies: FY 2008 Appropriations," Congressional Research Service, June 12, 2007, p. 7, www.fas.org/sgp/crs/natsec/RL34038.pdf.

[11] Stiglitz and Bilmes, *op. cit.*, p. 85.

U.S. policy shifted in 1990, when Saddam ordered his forces to invade tiny Kuwait, declaring the oil-producing nation a province of Iraq. The favorable U.S. attitude to Iraq during the war with Iran may have persuaded Saddam that he could count on President George H. W. Bush to turn a blind eye to the invasion. But Kuwait's long and close alliance with the United States weighed far more heavily. And neigh-

Soldier's Death Reveals Spending Abuses, Corruption

Billions of reconstruction dollars may have been lost

Staff Sgt. Ryan Maseth died in Iraq, but not by enemy fire. "When Staff Sergeant Maseth stepped into the shower and turned on the water," House Oversight and Government Reform Committee Chairman Henry A. Waxman, D-Calif., wrote in a March 19 letter to Defense Secretary Robert M. Gates, "an electrical short in the pump sent an electrical current through the water pipes to the metal shower hose, and then through Staff Sergeant Maseth's arm to his heart." [1] Contractor KBR was responsible for maintenance on the living quarters at the Radwaniyah Palace Complex in Baghdad, where Maseth died.

In looking into Maseth's death, Waxman's committee staff found reports of the electrocution deaths of at least 12 military personnel since 2003. Waxman's letter prompted a Pentagon investigation, which is still under way. Whether contractor construction or maintenance may have played a part in the other deaths isn't clear, a committee staff member says.

A lawyer for Maseth's family found documents showing that KBR had spotted the hazard that killed him, The New York Times reported. But the company's contract may not have required repair. KBR said in a statement that "safety and security . . . remains KBR's priority, and we remain committed to pledging our full cooperation with the agencies involved in investigating this matter." [2]

News of Maseth's death surfaced amid renewed attention to Iraq War spending and concern that billions of dollars in U.S. funds may have been stolen, wasted or otherwise misspent. "The United States is entering its fifth year of efforts to rebuild and stabilize Iraq, but these efforts have neither consistently achieved their desired outcomes nor done so in an economic and efficient manner," U.S. Comptroller General David M. Walker told the Senate Appropriations Committee on March 11. [3]

Walker said waste is the biggest problem for U.S. agencies working in Iraq.

On the Iraqi side, the issue is criminal conduct, Walker said. "With regard to fraud and corruption, that is a major problem with regard to the Iraqi government and Iraqi funds," Walker said. Those funds include, he said, the $45 billion that the United States has spent on Iraq reconstruction. [4]

A subsequent witness spoke in graphic terms about the predominant outcome of that rebuilding work. "Sir, the infrastructure in Iraq is equal to zero," said Radhi Hamza al-Radhi, an Iraqi judge who headed Iraq's Commission on Public Integrity in 2004-2007, which was established to root out corruption in government contracting. "If you visited Baghdad, you would see for yourself that there is no water, no electricity, no sewer systems, no streets. Everything is destroyed." [5]

Al-Radhi resigned his post after death threats and what he termed political pressure from the Iraqi government. Thirty-one of his former staff members and 12 of their family members have been assassinated, he told the committee. *Portfolio* magazine reported a total of 28 of al-Radhi's former colleagues have been killed. [6]

boring Saudi Arabia, America's most important Arab friend in the region — and at the time the world's single biggest oil exporter — feared it might be next on Saddam's list.

President Bush assembled a military coalition that would drive Iraq out of Kuwait in 1991 in a massive military operation dubbed Operation Desert Storm. Victory came after about 100 hours of ground fighting.

The American military contingent comprised more than 540,000 troops; coalition members contributed another 270,000 personnel. When it came to paying for the conflict, though, the roles were reversed. In cash terms, the allies paid most of the money — $48 billion paid by coalition members, in addition to $6 billion in fuel and other material. The U.S. share was $13 billion.

The war seemed to end Saddam's territorial ambitions. But it opened a new chapter in efforts by the United States and other nations to limit Saddam's attempts to repress rebellious sectors of the Iraqi population — members of the Shiite majority in southern Iraq, and Kurds, a Muslim but non-Arab people in the north. The United States and other U.N. members were also involved in trying to pressure Hussein into ending what was believed to be his development and production of weapons of mass destruction (WMD).

The former anti-corruption boss fled to the United States, where he is seeking asylum. Some officials who worked with him praise his past efforts. Stuart Bowen Jr., the special inspector general for Iraq reconstruction who had frequently praised al-Radhi, told the Appropriations Committee that he stood by a past statement that the Iraqi is "an honorable man and an effective crime fighter in Iraq." [7]

Bowen and Walker also generally agreed with al-Radhi's explosive allegation that about one-third of U.S. grants and contracts to the Iraqi government wind up in the hands of Shiite and Sunni militias. "I can't attest to that percentage, but it is a significant problem," Bowen said. [8]

Lack of accountability has plagued U.S.-controlled projects as well — apart from heavily reported past episodes such as the disappearance of some of the 363 tons of cash — $12 billion worth — flown into Iraq in 2003-2004. [9]

Defense Department Inspector General Claude Kicklighter told the Senate Appropriations Committee that his agency's investigations of fraud and corruption have yielded $840 million in questionable spending and 34 federal criminal charges, 25 felony convictions and recovery or forfeiture of $11.1 million.

Republicans on the committee challenged none of the expert testimony. "Over the past five years, U.S. programs to bolster anti-corruption institutions in Iraq have been inconsistent, suffering from poor coordination, weak planning and limited resources," Bowen said. [10]

Other U.S. officials have used even stronger language. "Challenges to the rule of law, especially corruption, are enormous," Ryan Crocker, U.S. ambassador to Iraq, told the Senate Armed Services and Foreign Relations committees on April 8. The next day he told the House Foreign

Affairs Committee, "We're engaged in doing everything we can to assist on this. We've recently reorganized our own anti-corruption effort within the embassy." [11]

---

[1] See letter, Rep. Henry A. Waxman, chairman, House Oversight and Government Reform Committee, to Secretary of Defense Robert M. Gates, March, 19, 2008, http://oversight.house.gov/documents/2008 0319091300.pdf. Also, see James Risen, "G.I.'s Death Prompts 2 Investigations of Iraq Electrocutions," *The New York Times*, March 20, 2008, p. A15.

[2] Quoted in Risen, *ibid.*

[3] See David M. Walker, "Stabilizing and Rebuilding Iraq: Actions Needed to Address Inadequate Accountability over U.S. Efforts and Investments," Government Accountability Office, March 11, 2008, www.gao.gov/new.items/d08568t.pdf.

[4] "Senate Appropriations Committee Holds Hearing on Iraq Funding Waste, Fraud, and Abuse," *Congressional Transcripts*, March 11, 2008.

[5] *Ibid.*

[6] See Christopher S. Stewart, "The Betrayal of Judge Radhi," Portfolio.com, April, 2008, www.portfolio.com/news-markets/international-news/portfolio/2008/03/17/Iraq-Top-Fraud-Cop-Judge-Radhi.

[7] *Ibid.* Quoted in Alissa J. Rubin, "Blaming Politics, Iraqi Antigraft Official Vows to Quit," *The New York Times*, Sept. 7, 2007, p. A12. Also, see Matt Kelley, "Iraqi's resignation hurts fight against corruption," *USA Today*, Sept. 10, 2007, p. A4.

[8] *Ibid.*

[9] For background, see Peter Katel, "New Strategy in Iraq," *CQ Researcher*, Feb. 23, 2007, pp. 169-192.

[10] See "Senate Appropriations Committee Holds Hearing on Iraq Funding Waste, Fraud and Abuse," *op. cit.*

[11] See "Senate Armed Services Committee Holds Hearing on Iraq," April 8, 2008; "Senate Foreign Relations Committee Holds Hearing on Iraq," *Congressional Transcripts*, April 8, 2008; "House Foreign Affairs Committee Holds Hearing on the Crocker/Petraeus Iraq Report," *Congressional Transcripts*, April 9, 2008.

U.S. forces protected what became a Kurdish enclave in the northern mountains. And U.S. warplanes patrolled over both southern and northern Iraq, enforcing U.N. Security Council resolutions prohibiting Saddam from using his air power to bomb and strafe the Kurds and Shiites (though the latter did suffer Saddam's retaliation before the protective measures took effect). Naval vessels from the United States and seven other countries also enforced economic sanctions designed to force Iraqi compliance with U.N. weapons inspections. [37]

The forces used in these operations reached nowhere near the strength of current U.S. military contingents in

Iraq and Afghanistan, but they were sizable. Davis and his trio of economists from the University of Chicago calculated that about 28,000 troops, 30 ships, and 300 aircraft participated in the various "containment" efforts. The economists estimated the total cost at about $14.5 billion a year. [38]

Estimates and Reality

Only about seven months after President George W. Bush was sworn into office, suicide terrorists from al Qaeda — the Afghanistan-based terrorist network headed by Osama bin Laden — carried out the attacks of Sept. 11, 2001.

In their wake, the Bush administration launched an intensive search for possible connections between al Qaeda and Saddam's dictatorship. Meanwhile, U.S. forces spearheaded the invasion of Afghanistan in October, 2001, an operation that toppled the fundamentalist Taliban, who had allowed bin Laden to set up his headquarters in their country.

And on a third track, the Bush administration ratcheted up the pressure on Saddam to dismantle the WMD development and manufacturing operations that — according to U.S. intelligence agencies — Iraq still maintained.

By 2002, Bush was signaling that he planned to topple Saddam by military means. Indications were strong enough that Sen. Kent Conrad, D-N.D., chairman of the Senate Budget Committee, and Rep. John M. Spratt Jr., D-S.C., top Democratic member of the House Budget Committee, asked the Congressional Budget Office (CBO) to project the costs of war in Iraq.

In September of that year, the CBO estimated the war would cost $6 billion to $9 billion a month and that the monthly cost of an occupation would run from $1 billion to $4 billion. The budget specialists said they couldn't estimate the costs of reconstruction. [39]

That same month, Lindsey, then the president's chief economic adviser, estimated war costs at $100 billion to $200 billion. (That projection led to Lindsey's replacement three months later.) [40]

In October, Congress authorized "the use of armed forces against Iraq." By the end of 2002, the director of the Office of Management and Budget (a White House position), put war costs at $50 billion to $60 billion. [41]

By 2003, a combination of supposed intelligence reports and Saddam's on-again, off-again handling of U.N. weapons-inspection demands persuaded the administration that the Iraqi dictator (and his two sons, who held top Iraqi government posts) represented a global menace that could not be contained by peaceful means.

On March 17, 2003, Bush delivered a public ultimatum. In a televised speech, he warned Saddam and his sons to leave Iraq "within 48 hours" or face "military conflict." [42]

Two days later, Bush launched the invasion with a bomb and missile strike on a complex of buildings where Saddam had been reported to be hiding (he was in the same compound, its owner said, but not in a targeted building). A fast-moving ground assault followed. By April 9, 2003, U.S. troops had started taking over Baghdad, even as looting broke out there and in other cities where Iraqi soldiers fled or surrendered. [43]

In Baghdad, the looting — carried out in full view of U.S. troops as well as numerous journalists — dominated news coverage and raised a barrage of questions about the near-term stability of a country over which the United States was assuming control. Defense Secretary Rumsfeld responded furiously at a Pentagon news conference. "Stuff happens," he said. "Freedom's untidy. And free people are free to make mistakes and commit crimes and do bad things. They're also free to live their lives and do wonderful things. And that's what's going to happen here." [44]

Rumsfeld's optimism was shared by his colleagues. "We're dealing with a country that can really finance its own reconstruction, and relatively soon," Deputy Defense Secretary Paul D. Wolfowitz had told the House Appropriations Subcommittee on Defense five days after the war began, citing Iraq's potential oil revenues. [45]

But by October of that year, the administration proposed spending $20.3 billion on Iraq reconstruction projects. The Senate trimmed that figure to $18.4 billion and also voted to lend rather than grant the money. But key senators backed down on the loan proposal after Bush threatened a veto. [46]

As for combined military and reconstruction costs, these soon outstripped administration projections. Costs for the first two fiscal years of Iraq operations alone (not including Afghanistan spending) totaled nearly $129 billion. By early 2008, spending had risen to almost $526 billion. [47]

In the intervening years, Iraq costs rose from $53 billion in fiscal 2003 to $76.4 billion so far in fiscal 2008, with $82.3 billion more expected to be requested. [48]

CURRENT SITUATION

Iraq in Politics

Vying for the Democratic presidential nomination, Sens. Clinton and Obama are trying to tie the United States' economic slide to the war in Iraq. In doing so, they're trying to reawaken an apparently fading public interest in the conflict.

"When you're spending over $50 to fill up your car because the price of oil is four times what it was before Iraq, you're paying a price for this war," Obama, an Illinois Democrat, told a rally at the University of Charleston, in West Virginia. "When Iraq is costing each household about $100 a month, you're paying a price for this war." [49]

Are the Iraq War's results worth the price paid?

YES James J. Carafano
Senior Research Fellow, Heritage Foundation

Written for *CQ Researcher*, April 2007

Critics of the Iraq War repeatedly focus on its financial costs, as if dollar signs alone explain why the United States should leave precipitously, whether or not the Iraqi government can provide security and services for its people.

Unfortunately, most attempts to estimate the actual costs of the war are driven by political considerations and ultimately end up as convenient overestimations. The recent book by Joseph Stiglitz and Linda Bilmes, *The Three Trillion Dollar War*, is one such example.

The reality is that the overall U.S. defense budget for both Iraq and Afghanistan still makes up only a modest proportion of the federal budget. Indeed, spending on Social Security, Medicare and Medicaid far exceeds what taxpayers spend to provide for defense.

As a percentage of the U.S. economy, defense spending remains historically low. Over the last 40 years, America has spent an average of 5.7 percent of gross domestic product (GDP) annually on defense. Yet Iraq War costs have ranged from 0.5 percent of GDP in fiscal 2003 to 1.3 percent in 2008.

By comparison, it cost almost 9 percent of GDP to pay for the Vietnam War and 14 percent for the Korean War. Also, the U.S. economy is significantly larger than during any previous conflict and can more easily absorb the costs today.

Moreover, our resources are not just being invested in bullets and bombs. We're also rebuilding schools, courthouses and other infrastructure, as well as Iraq's security forces, so the country can thrive long after American forces depart.

There's no denying the Iraq War is costing more than anticipated. However, spending alone doesn't tell the whole story. We must also consider what the war means to the wider war on terror and America's security.

Iraq, unlike Afghanistan, is a potentially wealthy country at the heart of the Middle East. Currently both al Qaeda (through its subsidiary al Qaeda in Iraq) and Iran (using its Qods Force unit) have committed their resources to America's defeat.

An early pullout would cede the battlefield to al Qaeda and Iran and allow Iraq to fall into chaos. Eventually, Americans could well be required to intervene again.

Meanwhile, America's enemies would interpret our retreat as a testament to their strength and our weakness. American credibility among Islamic moderates, our true allies in the region, would suffer. We must prevent this outcome by spending the reasonable amount needed to defeat al Qaeda and Iranian proxy forces while upholding our moral commitment to Iraqis. That's a wise investment in a more secure future.

NO Brian Katulis
Senior Fellow, Center for American Progress

Written for *CQ Researcher*, April 2007

Five years into the Iraq War, the results do not justify the substantial costs to date; nor do the potential results from maintaining the current policy of strategic confusion justify staying in Iraq with no end in sight for decades to come — the policy that most conservatives propose today.

More than 4,000 families have lost loved ones serving in the military in Iraq. All too often forgotten — particularly in the Bush administration's mishandling of veterans' affairs — are the tens of thousands, scarred both physically and mentally by the war. Beyond the human costs, U.S. taxpayers are now spending about $12 billion a month for the war — all for a policy that still has no clear and realistic end.

In addition, overall military readiness has suffered as a result of the extended troop deployments. Now the vast majority of active-duty units are suffering from critical shortages in personnel and equipment, resulting in low readiness levels.

Beyond these immediate costs, the Iraq War has resulted in broader strategic failures. When historians look back on 2003 to 2008, they will see a period when America's ability to shape and influence events around the world became severely constrained. Preventing advances in nuclear weapons programs in North Korea and Iran, completing the mission left unaccomplished in Afghanistan and eradicating the threat posed by the global al Qaeda movement have all fallen in the list of national security priorities because of the fixation on Iraq.

For what benefit? Saddam Hussein was a brutal dictator, but he was contained, and his regional and global influence was weakening. It is good that he is no longer in power, but the sad truth is that the living situation and human-rights conditions for most Iraqis is not much better — and for some groups like Christians and women — conditions have deteriorated.

America's leaders must recognize that it is past time to begin drawing down the troops — that the strategic costs outweigh the benefits of staying with some open-ended commitment, whether it is wrapped up in a banner of "strategic patience" or "conditional engagement."

Until America's leaders demonstrate the courage to take back control of U.S. national security by setting a course of redeployment of U.S. forces, the United States will remain trapped in this quagmire, paying rising costs for a policy with no end in sight.

Obama was broadcasting the thesis developed by Stiglitz and Bilmes — and taking advantage of the fact that he opposed the war from the beginning. Clinton, too, though she voted for the 2002 "war powers" resolution that authorized Bush to order the invasion, is linking the economy to the war.

"We spend $12 billion a month in Iraq, and that does affect the economy," New York Democrat Clinton said, also echoing Stiglitz and Bilmes. "That's one of the reasons we've gone into more and more debt. We've got to begin not only to withdraw our troops but bring that money back home."

No data have emerged publicly on whether the candidates, along with antiwar critics in general, have persuaded citizens that Iraq spending helped create today's economic climate. But in late February and early March, a survey by the nonpartisan Pew Research Center for the People and the Press found that only 28 percent of adults questioned knew that about 4,000 U.S. military personnel had died in Iraq. Less than a year earlier, more than half of respondents accurately estimated the number of deaths. The survey correlated the drop in awareness to a decline in media coverage of the war. [50]

On the Republican side, Sen. McCain hasn't shown any inclination to get drawn into the dollars-and-cents debate on war costs. But he isn't shying away entirely. "We must increase levels of reconstruction assistance so that Iraq's political and economic development can proceed in the security that our forces and Iraqi security forces provide," he said in a speech to the Veterans of Foreign Wars in Kansas City, Mo., on April 7. McCain didn't mention amounts. And a statement he gave at a Senate Armed Services Committee hearing swung more towards Iraqi government funding. In that statement, McCain called on the Iraqi government to contribute to the Commander's Emergency Relief Program, a U.S. fund that pays for reconstruction and jobs programs. Other rebuilding projects should be entirely Iraqi-funded, he said. [51]

But two of his key supporters have responded to the war-costs criticism from the Democratic contenders and other war critics. "Today's antiwar politicians have effectively turned John F. Kennedy's inaugural address on its head, urging Americans to refuse to pay any price, or bear any burden, to assure the survival of liberty," Sens. Joseph I. Lieberman, I-Conn., and Lindsey Graham, R-S.C., wrote in *The Wall Street Journal* in early April.

"There is no question the war in Iraq — like the Cold War, World War II and every other conflict we have fought in our history — costs money. But as great as the costs of this struggle have been, so too are the dividends to our national security from a successful outcome, with a functioning, representative Iraqi government and a stabilized Middle East." [52]

Lieberman and Graham published their op-ed on the eve of congressional testimony by Gen. Petraeus and U.S. Ambassador to Iraq Crocker. Arguably, their appearance, along with a continuation of recent combat between the U.S.-backed Iraqi government and a militia commanded by Moqtada al-Sadr, a nationalist, anti-American Iraqi Shiite leader, would help return the war to public awareness. Thirty-four Americans were killed in March, the month that the Iraq government launched an offensive against Sadr, though not all those deaths could be attributed to those clashes. During the first week of April, however, five of 11 U.S. military deaths did result from combat with Sadr's militia. [53]

In the days leading up to the Petraeus-Crocker appearance, attempts to link Iraq and the economy weren't noticeable in campaigns for congressional seats — all 435 House seats and 33 Senate posts are up for election in November. "They do talk all the time about spending for the war — that those dollars haven't been used for other things, like health care," says Stuart Rothenberg, a specialist in congressional elections and publisher of the nonpartisan *Rothenberg Political Report*. "I haven't heard anyone say there's a causal relationship between [Iraq] spending and the recession." He adds, "I could see how they could."

Funding Fight

Even as presidential candidates, economists, administration officials and others joust over the big picture of war spending, lawmakers and administration officials have started skirmishing over the newest appropriation proposals for military and reconstruction operations in Iraq.

Democratic critics demand to know why Iraq, flush with oil revenue, isn't spending more of its own money on reconstruction. The Bush administration insists that Iraq's contribution is growing.

The fight is coming to a head over the Bush administration's latest "emergency supplemental" request for funds to maintain operations in Iraq. The administration is expected to seek $82.3 billion to cover operations for the remainder of the current fiscal year, which will end Sept. 30. [54] Supplementals — money requests that aren't part of the regular budget — have been the major source of Iraq funds since the beginning of the conflict. Reliance on supplementals is controversial in itself. But whether to wean the Iraqi government from its reliance on U.S. reconstruction funds presents a more immediate issue — and one with potential to arouse taxpayer interest in a time of economic insecurity marked by higher gasoline prices.

Iraq saw its petroleum revenues increase from $31 billion in 2006 to $41 billion in 2007, the Government Accountability Office (GAO) reported. Sen. Ben Nelson, D-Neb., told *USA Today* that he expected Iraq to earn $60 billion from oil this year. [55]

Opening a Senate Armed Services Committee hearing where Petraeus and Crocker would testify, panel Chairman Carl Levin, D-Mich., said he heard the following story from an unnamed senior U.S. military officer: "He asked an Iraqi official, 'Why is it that we're using our U.S. dollars to pay your people to clean up your towns instead of you using your funds?' The Iraqi replied, 'As long as you are willing to pay for the cleanup, why should we do it?' " [56]

To illustrate the point, Levin cited a January 2008 report by the Special Inspector General for Iraq Reconstruction showing the Iraqi government spent only 23 percent of its $6.2 billion capital budget for 2006. [57]

Matters apparently didn't improve in 2007. Levin noted that the GAO reported it could not confirm an administration claim that the Iraqi government had spent 24 percent of its capital budget as of July 15, 2007. The GAO said Iraqi government data showed that only 4.4 percent of the budget had been spent as of August 2007. [58]

McCain, the senior Republican on Armed Services, showed some sensitivity to the issue of the Iraqi government's use of U.S. funds. Acknowledging that the Iraqi government "continues to take in revenues it finds difficult to disburse," McCain proposed that Iraq put some of its money in the main U.S. fund that pays for reconstruction projects — the Commanders Emergency Response Program. [59]

The administration is expected to ask for $500 million for that program. How much an Iraqi contribution — if it's made — might reduce that request, wasn't immediately clear.

As for major rebuilding — of power stations, oil production facilities and the like — Ambassador Crocker told Armed Services that the Bush administration has turned a page. "The era of U.S.-funded major infrastructure projects is over," the envoy said. "We are seeking to ensure that our assistance, in partnership with the Iraqis, leverages Iraq's own resources." [60]

However the fight over the next big Iraq appropriation is resolved, the conflict over reliance on supplementals remains. "That is unusual," says Kosiak of the Center for Strategic and Budgetary Assessments. "In the case of Vietnam and Korea, the last wars of any significant duration, in the first years they did use supplementals but then attached war funding to regular budget requests."

Supplementals are taken up on a faster track and come with less in the way of supporting material, Kosiak says. The administration did use the conventional process for the 2008 fiscal year (which will end on Sept. 30), but returned to the supplemental route in the present budget cycle for fiscal 2009.

"I haven't met one person who believes this is a good way to do business," says Bernstein of the Economic Policy Institute, saying that attitude crosses party lines. "It's obviously a tactic to keep these expenditures off-budget."

But Zakheim, on whose watch the first supplementals went to Capitol Hill, says the rapidly changing nature of the conflict left no other option. "When you put together a budget, you're putting it together roughly 18 months before the money is actually to be available on the ground," he says. "The nature of this kind of war is so highly unpredictable that to risk through the normal budget process defies logic. You can't have the resources in the field immediately."

OUTLOOK

Continued Presence

Critics and supporters alike of the decision to invade Iraq tend to agree that the United States will stay in Iraq or its neighborhood for the foreseeable future — a presence that will keep costing billions of dollars.

Davis of the University of Chicago says that whatever happens to the military presence in Iraq there's no question that troops will be stationed nearby. "It's a politically and militarily unstable part of the world that sits on most of the world's low-cost oil reserves. Whether we have forces in Iraq or not is going to be influenced by elections and political decision-making. But I have no doubt that there will be a major U.S. military presence in the region; we have had one for 50 years or so."

To the extent that conditions today set the stage for conditions 10 years from now, the official short-range forecast from the top U.S. military commander in Iraq offers little in the way of conclusive judgments. During two days of hearings before Senate and House committees Petraeus refused to be pinned down even concerning the pace at which the U.S. would keep drawing down forces in the wake of last year's "surge" of troops.

Explaining his recommendation to Bush for a 45-day halt in withdrawals now under way, Petraeus said that his proposal "does not allow establishment of a set withdrawal timetable." He added, "It does provide the flexibility those of us on the ground need to preserve the still-fragile security gains our troopers have fought so hard and sacrificed so much to achieve." By July, the total U.S. military contingent in Iraq is expected to number about 140,000 personnel. [61]

In a recent interview, former Assistant Defense Secretary Zakheim says he's advocated for some time that the United States keep 70,000 troops stationed on Iraq's borders. That move could put troops facing Iran, Syria, Saudi Arabia, and Kuwait. "If the goal is to protect stability in the region, that is what it's going to take."

And Zakheim says he's optimistic that "at a minimum" the U.S. intervention will have brought that stability. "Petraeus seems to have turned the corner," Zakheim adds. "I'm reasonably optimistic. He's had a huge impact."

It would be hard to find a more opposite view than that of Paul Sullivan, executive director of Veterans for Common Sense. "The war is lost — irretrievably," says Sullivan, a veteran of the 1991 Persian Gulf War and a former Veterans Administration data project manager. "We can temporarily hold violence down, but until the Iraqis have a legitimate, functioning government and the electricity, water, schools and economic infrastructure are rebuilt, Iraq will remain in a state of violent anarchy."

On the home front, Sullivan says only major funding increases for the Department of Veterans Affairs will head off catastrophe in veteran care. "On the current course we see disaster on the horizon — an increase in the number of broken families, divorce, increased unemployment, drug and alcohol [abuse], homelessness, preventable suicides," he warns.

Hormats of Goldman, Sachs agrees with Sullivan — and with *Three Trillion Dollar War* authors Stiglitz and

Bilmes — that the demand for veterans health care will be far higher than the Bush administration projected. And that demand will have to be met. "Our nation has a moral obligation to provide the best care possible," Hormats says.

And he points to another expense category often overlooked outside of specialist circles. It's called "reset" in Pentagon jargon — the reconditioning of military equipment worn down by the grind of performing in a combat zone. "A lot of weapons have been destroyed or deteriorated to the point that they're unusable," Hormats says. "The Defense Department has to repair or replace them. That's expensive."

Bilmes sees little chance of Iraq intervention costs coming down in the next two years. The big question, she says, centers on what the next president does to start paying the bills for the operation — "whether we continue to borrow all this money or ask people to tighten their belts or raise taxes or buy war bonds."

How those decisions turn out, she says, "will determine not just the cost of the war, but how much of the war we're asking our children to shoulder and how much interest we have to pay on all the money we're borrowing."

NOTES

1. See Peter Orszag, "Estimated Costs of U.S. Operations in Iraq and Afghanistan and of Other Activities Related to the War on Terrorism," Congressional Budget Office, Oct. 24, 2007, p. 3, www.cbo.gov/ftpdocs/86xx/doc8690/10-24-CostOf War_Testimony.pdf.

2. Joseph E. Stiglitz and Linda J. Bilmes, *The Three Trillion Dollar War: The True Cost of the Iraq Conflict* (2008).

3. "Bush Dismisses Iraq Recession," "The Today Show," NBC, March 18, 2008, http://youtube.com/watch?v=lIbdnM8Ts88&feature=related.

4. See "Senate Armed Services Committee Holds Hearing on Iraq," *Congressional Transcripts*, April 8, 2008.

5. *Ibid.*

6. *Ibid.*

7. "President Bush Visits Dayton, Ohio, Discusses Global War on Terror," The White House, March 27, 2008, www.whitehouse.gov/news/releases/2008/03/2008032 7-2.html.

8. *Ibid.* See also Stiglitz and Bilmes, *op. cit.*, pp. 32-60, 114-131.

9. See Orszag, *op. cit.*; "House Budget Committee Holds Hearing on the Costs of the Iraq War," House Budget Committee, Oct. 24, 2007, *Congressional Transcripts*; Ken Dilanian, "Wars may cost $2.4T," *USA Today*, Oct. 24, 2007, p. A1; "War At Any Price?: The Total economic Costs of the War Beyond the Federal Budget," Joint Economic Committee majority staff, November 2007, http://jec.senate.gov/Documents/Reports/11.13.07IraqEconomicCostsReport.pdf.

10. See Orszag, *op. cit.*; and "House Budget Committee Holds Hearing on the Costs of the Iraq War," *op. cit.*; Dilanian, *op. cit.*; Joint Economic Committee majority staff, *op. cit.*

11. See Linda Bilmes and Joseph E. Stiglitz, "The Economic Costs of the Iraq War: An Appraisal Three Years After the Beginning of the Conflict," February 2006, National Bureau of Economic Research, www2.gsb.columbia.edu/faculty/jstiglitz/download/2006_Cost_of_War_in_Iraq_NBER.pdf.

12. "Press Briefing by Dana Perino," The White House, March 10, 2008, www.whitehouse.gov/news/releases/2008/03/20080310-4.html.

13. Steven J. Davis, *et al.*, "War in Iraq versus Containment," National Bureau of Economic Research, March 2006, www.nber.org/papers/w12092.pdf.

14. "Bush Dismisses Iraq Recession," Feb. 18, 2008, http://video.google.com/videoplay?docid=-7744258843658177585.

15. See Joint Economic Committee, *op. cit.* For monthly Iraq operations cost, see Orszag, *op. cit.*, p. 2.

16. For statistics, see Louis Uchitelle, "80,000 Jobs Lost; Democrats Urge New Aid Package," *The New York Times*, April 5, 2008.

17. Quoted in *ibid.*

18. For foreclosure proceedings statistic, see "Chairman Ben S. Bernanke at the Independent Bankers of America Annual Convention," Federal Reserve, March 4, 2008, www.federalreserve.gov/newsevents/speech/bernanke20080304a.htm. Extensive coverage of the ongoing events includes Julie Creswell, "A Nervous Wall St. Seems Unsure What's Next," *The New York Times*, March 31, 2008, p.

C1; David Leonhardt, "Can't Grasp the Credit Crisis? Join the Club," *The New York Times*, March 19, 2008, p. A1; Carrick Mollenkamp and Mark Whitehouse, "Banks Fear a Deepening of Turmoil," *The Wall Street Journal*, March 17, 2007, p. A1, and Marcia Clemmitt, "Mortgage Crisis," *CQ Researcher*, Nov. 2, 2007, pp. 913-936.

19. *Ibid.*

20. Joint Economic Committee, *op. cit.*, p. 22.

21. For 2003 oil prices see, "All Countries Spot Price FOB Weighted by Estimated Export Volume (Dollars per Barrel)," Energy Information Administration, http://tonto.eia.doe.gov/dnav/pet/hist/wtotworldw.htm.

22. See Lawrence B. Lindsey, "What the Iraq war will cost the U.S.," *Fortune*, Jan. 11, 2008, http://money.cnn.com/2008/01/10/news/economy/costofwar.fortune/index.htm?postversion=2008011112.

23. See William D. Nordhaus, "The Economic Consequences of a War With Iraq," Yale University, Oct. 29, 2002, p. 41, www.econ.yale.edu/~nordhaus/iraq.pdf. A shorter version was published in the *New York Review of Books*, Dec. 5, 2002, www.nybooks.com/articles/15850.

24. Quoted in Stiglitz and Bilmes, *op. cit.*, pp. 7-8.

25. Concerning Powell, see Michael Gordon, "Fateful Choice on Iraq Army Bypassed Debate," *The New York Times*, March 17, 2008, p. A1.

26. Quoted in Thomas E. Ricks, *Fiasco* (2006), p. 164.

27. See David Von Drehle, "Economic Costs Could Weaken Bush Politically," *The Washington Post*, March 16, 2003, p. A13.

28. See "President Bush Visits Dayton, Ohio, Discusses Global War on Terror," The White House, March 27, 2008, www.whitehouse.gov/news/releases/2008/03/20080327-2.html.

29. See "President Bush Discusses Iraq," The White house, April 10, 2008, www.whitehouse.gov/news/releases/2008/04/print/20080410-2.html.

30. *Ibid.*

31. Stiglitz and Bilmes, *op. cit.*, pp. 54-55.

32. Unless otherwise indicated, material in this subsection is drawn from Robert D. Hormats, *The Price of Liberty: Paying for America's Wars* (2007).

33. Quoted in *ibid.*, p. 26.

34. See "Mobilization: The U.S. Army in World War II," undated, U.S. Army, www.history.army.mil/documents/mobpam.htm.

35. Quoted in *ibid.*

36. See "National Security Decision Directive 139," April 5, 1984, www.gwu.edu/~nsarchiv/NSAEBB/NSAEBB82/iraq53.pdf. The document is part of a collection, "Shaking Hands With Saddam Hussein: The U.S. Tilts Toward Iraq, 1980-1984," The National Security Archive, www.gwu.edu/~nsarchiv/NSAEBB/NSAEBB82/.

37. See Davis, *et al.*, *op. cit.*

38. *Ibid.*, pp. 8-18.

39. See "Estimated Costs of a Potential Conflict With Iraq," Congressional Budget Office, September 2002, p. 4, www.cbo.gov/ftpdoc.cfm?index=3822&type=0.

40. See Elizabeth Bumiller, "White House Cuts Estimate of Cost of War With Iraq," *The New York Times*, Dec. 31, 2002, p. A1; and Lindsey, *op. cit.*

41. *Ibid.*

42. See "Bush: 'Leave Iraq within 48 hours," CNN, March 17, 2003, www.cnn.com/2003/WORLD/meast/03/17/sprj.irq.bush.transcript.

43. For Saddam's whereabouts during raid, see Robert F. Worth, "Advice of Iraqi, Now in Beirut Cell, Finally Heeded," *The New York Times*, April 2, 2008.

44. See "DOD News Briefing — Secretary Rumsfeld and Gen. [Richard B.] Myers," U.S. Department of Defense, April 11, 2003, www.defenselink.mil/transcripts/transcript.aspx?transcriptid=2367.

45. See "House Appropriations Subcommittee on Defense Holds Hearing on FY2004 Appropriations," *Congressional Transcripts*, March 27, 2003.

46. See Juliet Eilperin, "Senators Overturn Vote on Aid to Iraq," *The Washington Post*, Oct. 30, 2003, p. A6; "Splitting Hairs Over Iraq's Reconstruction," *The New York Times*, Nov. 9, 2003, Sect. 4, p. 2.

47. See Amy Belasco, "The Costs of Iraq, Afghanistan, and Other Global War on Terror Operations Since 9/11," Congressional Research Service, updated Feb. 8, 2008, pp. 11-12, www.fas.org/sgp/crs/natsec/RL33110.pdf.

48. *Ibid.*, p. 8.

49. Quoted in Jeff Zeleny and Michael Cooper, "Obama Links Effects of War Costs to Fragility in the Economy," *The New York Times*, March 21, 2008, p. A19.

50. For survey data see "Awareness of Iraq War Fatalities Plummets," Pew Research Center for the People and the Press, March 12, 2008, http://people-press.org/reports/display.php3?ReportID=401.

51. "Remarks by John McCain To The Members of the Veterans of Foreign Wars," McCain campaign Web site, April 7, 2008, http://johnmccain.com/Informing/News/Speeches/3d837545-5ac8-4124-929c-33c3f0ee9fe5.htm. See also "Text of Sen. John McCain's Opening Statement at Senate Armed Services Committee," *USA Today*, April 8, 2008, www.usatoday.com/news/mmemmottpdf/McCain-Iraq-Hearing-4-8-2008.pdf.

52. Joe Lieberman and Lindsey Graham, "Iraq and Its Costs," *The Wall Street Journal*, April 7, 2008, p. A13, http://online.wsj.com/article_print/SB120752308688293493.html.

53. See "Iraq Index," Brookings Institution, updated March 31, 2008, p. 18, www.bropokings.edu/saban/~/media/Files/Centers/Saban/Iraq%20Index/index.pdf. Also see Leila Fadel, "Sadr cancels million-man march; 11 U.S. dead since Sunday," McClatchy Newspapers, April 8, 2008, www.mcclatchydc.com/homepage/story/32986.html.

54. See Belasco, *op. cit.*

55. See Matt Kelley, "Dems take aim at Iraq reconstruction," *USA Today*, April 8, 2008, p. A8. For past oil revenues, see "Stabilizing and Rebuilding Iraq: Actions Needed to Address Inadequate Accountability over U.S. Efforts and Investments," Government Accountability Office, March 11, 2008, p. 22, www.gao.gov/new.items/d08568t.pdf.

56. "Opening Statement of Sen. Carl Levin, Senate Armed Services Committee Hearing on the Situation in Iraq with Ambassador Crocker and Gen. Petraeus," press release, April 8, 2008, http://levin.senate.gov/newsroom/release.cfm?id=295684.

57. See "Update on Iraq Reconstruction — Section 2," Special Inspector General for Iraq Reconstruction, Jan. 30, 2008, p. 123, www.sigir.mil/reports/QuarterlyReports/Jan08/pdf/Section2_-_January_2008.pdf.

58. "Iraq Reconstruction: Better Data Needed to Assess Iraq's Budget Execution," Government Accountability Office, January 2008, p. 1, www.gao.gov/new.items/d08153.pdf.

59. McCain opening statement, *op. cit.*, http://tpm-muckraker.talkingpointsmemo.com/2008/04/mccain_on_iraq_we_should_choos.php.

60. "Testimony of Ambassador Ryan C. Crocker Before the Senate Armed Services Committee," April 8, 2008, http://armed-services.senate.gov/statemnt/2008/April/Crocker%2004-08-08.pdf.

61. Quoted in Thom Shanker and Steven Lee Myers, "General Resists Timetable for Withdrawal of Troops in Iraq," *The New York Times*, April 8, 2008, www.nytimes.com/2008/04/09/world/middleeast/08cnd-petraeus.html?hp.

BIBLIOGRAPHY

Books

Feith, Douglas J., *War and Decision: Inside the Pentagon at the Dawn of the War on Terrorism*, Harper, 2008.
The undersecretary of Defense for policy when the war was planned and begun explains how errors were made and defends himself against charges that pitfalls weren't foreseen.

Hormats, Robert D., *The Price of Liberty: Paying for America's Wars*, Times Books, 2007.
A Wall Street banker with lengthy government experience examines the financing of major U.S. military conflicts and the political and economic issues involved.

Ricks, Thomas E., *Fiasco: The American Military Adventure in Iraq*, Penguin, 2006.
A Pulitzer Prize-winning reporter provides one of the best accounts of the war on the ground and how little it corresponded to pre-invasion plans.

Stiglitz, Joseph E., and Linda J. Bilmes, *The Three Trillion Dollar War: The True Cost of the Iraq Conflict*, W.W. Norton, 2008.
A Nobel Prize-winning economist (Stiglitz) and a federal budget expert make a detailed case that the Iraq war is damaging the U.S. economy.

Articles

Kaplan, Fred, "This Is Not an Emergency: Supplemental war funds are a backdoor way to boost the defense budget," *Slate*, Feb. 20, 2008, www.slate.com/id/2184804.
The online magazine's military-affairs correspondent argues against funding war via "supplemental" budget requests.

Krueger, Alan B., "The Cost of Invading Iraq: Imponderables Meet Uncertainties," *The New York Times*, March 30, 2006, p. C1.
The Times' then-economics columnist, a Princeton professor, examines the complexities of running a cost-benefit analysis of a war.

Shapiro, Robert, "The Cost of Toppling Saddam: Will an Iraq war hurt the economy?," *Slate*, Oct. 2, 2002, www.slate.com/id/2071811.
Before the Iraq War, a Clinton administration economist predicts it will not hurt the economy.

Stevenson, Richard W., "War Budget Request More Realistic But Still Uncertain," *The New York Times*, Sept. 10, 2003, p. A1.
The Bush administration acknowledges for the first time that Iraq War costs will be far higher than projected.

Weisman, Jonathan, and Juliet Eilperin, "In GOP, Concern Over Iraq Price Tag," *The Washington Post*, Sept. 26, 2003, p. A1.
Some early uneasiness over Iraq War costs came from President George W. Bush's own party.

White, Josh, " 'Hidden Costs' Double Price of Two Wars, Democrats Say," *The Washington Post*, Nov. 13, 2007, p. A14.
Democratic congressional staffers come up with Capitol Hill's first trillion-dollar-plus forecast of war costs.

Zorpette, Glenn, "Keeping Iraq in the Dark," *The New York Times*, **March 11, 2008, p. A23.**
The executive editor of *IEEE Spectrum*, the magazine of the Institute of Electrical and Electronics Engineers, examines Iraq's continuing electricity crisis.

Reports and Studies

"Integrated Strategic Plan Needed to Help Restore Iraq's Oil and Electricity Sectors," Government Accountability Office, May 2007, www.gao.gov/new.items/d07677.pdf.
Congress' auditors examine the extent of damage to the two most critical elements of Iraq's infrastructure, concluding that billions of dollars more are required for rebuilding — even after the U.S.' expenditure of $8.9 billion.

Davis, Steven J., *et al.*, **"War in Iraq versus Containment," National Bureau of Economic Research, March 2006, www.nber.org/papers/w12092.pdf.**
A trio of economists from the University of Chicago analyzes the projected costs of the Iraq intervention against the costs of the pre-invasion "containment" operations.

Grasso, Valerie Bailey, "Defense Contracting in Iraq: Issues and Options for Congress," Congressional Research Service, updated Jan. 29, 2008, www.fas.org /sgp/crs/natsec/RL33834.pdf.
The nonpartisan agency lays out the extent of military contracting and the choices lawmakers face.

Walker, David M., "Stabilizing and Rebuilding Iraq: Actions Needed to Address Inadequate Accountability over U.S. Efforts and Investments," Government Accountability Office, March 11, 2008, www.gao.gov/ new.items/d08568t.pdf.
In one of his last projects before resigning to head a new foundation, the GAO director examines the state of spending controls on U.S.-funded projects and concludes the Defense Department still lags in overseeing contractors' work.

For More Information

American Enterprise Institute, 1150 17th St., N.W., Washington, DC 20036; (202) 862-5800; www.aei.org. Conservative think tank has strong links to the Bush administration and the "surge" strategy.

Brookings Institution, 1775 Massachusetts Ave., N.W., Washington, DC 20036; (202)-797-6000; www.brookings.edu. The liberal-leaning think tank's Iraq research projects include a regularly updated statistical summary of conditions in Iraq.

Center for American Progress, 1333 H St., N.W., 10th Floor, Washington, DC 20005; (202) 682-1611; www.americanprogress.org. Liberal think tank Web-publishes analyses of the Iraq conflict and U.S. options.

Heritage Foundation, 214 Massachusetts Ave., N.E., Washington, DC 20002; (202) 546-4400; www.heritage.org. Conservative think tank maintains a program of military and political analyses of the Iraq conflict.

Special Inspector General for Iraq Reconstruction, 400 Army Navy Dr., Arlington, VA 22202; (703) 428-1100; www.sigir.mil. The congressionally created agency investigates and audits rebuilding projects in Iraq.

Veterans for Common Sense, P.O. Box 15514, Washington, DC 20003; www.veteransforcommonsense.org. Publicizes deficiencies in veterans' care.